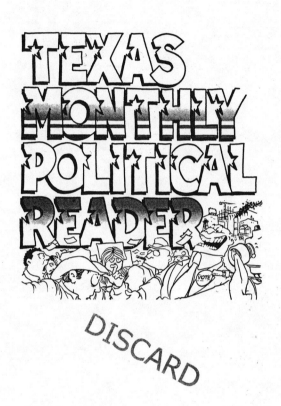

DISCARD

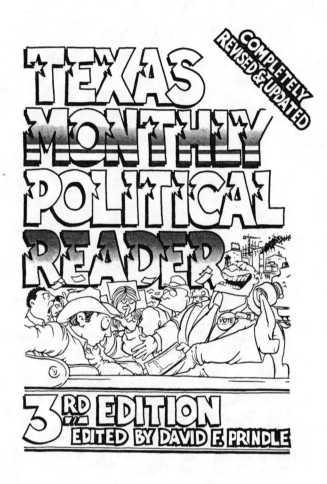

TEXAS MONTHLY POLITICAL READER

COMPLETELY REVISED & UPDATED

3RD EDITION
EDITED BY DAVID F. PRINDLE

Illustrations by Ben Sargent

★

TexasMonthlyPress

Texas Monthly Press, Inc.
P.O. Box 1569
Austin, Texas 78767

A B C D E F G H

Library of Congress Cataloging in Publication Data
Main entry under title:

Texas monthly's political reader.

    Bibliography: p.
    Includes index.
    1. Texas—Politics and government—1951-   —Addresses, essays, lectures.
I. Prindle, David F. (David Forrest), 1948-   . II. Texas monthly (Austin,
Tex.). III. Title: Political reader.
F391.2.T485   1985   320.9764   84-24067
ISBN 0-87719-003-8

Cover design and illustration by Ben Sargent
Text illustrated by Ben Sargent

★ CONTENTS ★

Introduction 1
  I. Citizens
    The Second Battle of the Alamo by Paul Burka (December 1977) 5
    The Seeds of Discontent by Michael Ennis (February 1981) 16
    Offensive Weapons by Susan Duffy (June 1981) 17
    One Woman's Tiny Problem Confronts Dallas City Hall
      by John Bloom (September 1981) 19
    The Unkindest Cut by Peter Applebome (January 1983) 27
    I Beat Ben Barnes and John Connally in a Fair Fight
      by Kaye Northcott (March 1984) 28
  II. Influentials
    The Kingmaker by Paul Burka (February 1980) 33
    I Have a Scheme by Harry Hurt III (October 1981) 35
    The Bishop Drops a Bomb by Joseph Nocera (June 1982) 45
    The Guardians Who Slumbereth Not by William Martin (November 1982) 49
    Come On Walter . . . Smile! by Paul Burka (February 1984) 56
  III. Interests
    Inside the Lobby by Richard West (July 1973) 63
    The Highway Establishment and How it Grew and Grew and Grew
      by Griffin Smith (April 1974) 69
    Paper Tigers by Mitch Green (January 1977) 81
    Squeaky Wheels by Stephen Chapman (September 1983) 84
  IV. Parties
    Getting the Bugs Out by Paul Burka (August 1981) 87
    The Party's Over by Douglas Harlan (January 1982) 89
    Behind the Lines by Gregory Curtis (December 1982) 92
  V. Politicians
    A. Legislators
    The Star-Crossed Palm of Billy Clayton by Paul Burka (May 1980) 95
    The Deal That Didn't Work by Victoria Loe (August 1981) 97
    The Making of a Congressman by Victoria Loe (January 1983) 102
    A Monumental Man by Paul Burka (January 1983) 111
    The Ten Best and Ten Worst Legislators by Staff (July 1983) 114
    B. Executives
    The Governor's New Clothes by Stephen Harrigan (May 1981) 125
    James A. Baker, III, Politician by Taylor Branch (May 1982) 132
    Mark White's Coming-Out Party by Paul Burka (May 1983) 144
    George Bush, Plucky Lad by Harry Hurt III (June 1983) 148
    Cosmic Plowboy by Peter Elkind (December 1983) 158
    C. Jurists
    The Real Governor of Texas by Paul Burka (June 1978) 167
    Long Row to Hoe by Gene Lyons (August 1980) 175
    The Strong Arm of the Law by Peter Elkind (October 1983) 177
  VI. Cities
    A. Mayors
    The Last Patrón by Susan Duffy (July 1981) 181
    Mr. Rogers, Tough Guy by Peter Applebome (July 1982) 183
    Whitmired by Peter Applebome (June 1983) 184
    Mayor of the Unfinished City by Jim Atkinson (October 1983) 186

B. Episodes
Cable Madness by John Bloom (December 1980) 195
Bad Water by Suzanne Winckler (April 1982) 197
Fantasy Island by Joseph Nocera (November 1983) 200
Dog Day in Dogwood City by Jim Atkinson (November 1983) 206
VII. Issues
Behind the Lines by William Broyles (January 1980) 209
Double-Talk by Gene Lyons (July 1980) 211
Behind the Lines by William Broyles (January 1981) 213
Case Closed by Susan Duffy (August 1981) 215
God's Happy Hour by Dick Reavis (January 1983) 216
Behind the Lines by Gregory Curtis (April 1983) 222
The Beaten Paths by Suzanne Winckler (September 1983) 224

★INTRODUCTION★

I. Citizens

In Texas, as elsewhere, the stuff of politics is human conflict. Struggles between individual people and government, fights between groups, or arguments between an individual and an organization, when they are waged in the public arena, make up the political process. And in Texas, as elsewhere, publicity often focuses on the conflicts of extraordinary people. So much attention falls on special individuals that it is easy to forget that much of politics is about ordinary citizens.

Yet people with no special claim to uniqueness also have their political battles. If their conflicts usually attract less notice than the clashes of the rich and famous, they are no less productive of injustice, folly, pathos, and courage. Although common citizens are small as heroes go, their stories are worth telling.

The following section contains six articles about the political experiences of more or less ordinary people. It will come as no surprise that most of these stories have the flavor of a David and Goliath conflict, with the small and anonymous confronting the celebrated and great. And as is often the case in a democratic society like Texas, the little people's chief resource is organization. Elected officials respond best to the needs of people who represent large blocs of potential votes. The best tactic for ordinary citizens faced with a collective problem is therefore to unite and to attempt to achieve in numbers what they cannot do as individuals.

Some of the people depicted in the following six articles have succeeded in their purpose; some have failed; for some the outcome is still in doubt.

Paul Burka's 1977 investigation of COPS, San Antonio's largely Mexican American citizens' organization, begins the parade. Then Michael Ennis reports the efforts of some Dallas residents to gain control over their neighborhoods by joining an organization named ACORN. Citizen organization is easier in the cities, but it also occurs in the country, as Susan Duffy shows in her article on the efforts of West Texas farmers to keep the M-X missile out of their vicinity.

Not all citizens feel the need to organize. In the next article John Bloom chronicles one woman's determined and apparently endless struggle to get the City of Dallas to enforce its own noise control regulations.

The next article makes clear that it is not just city hall that ordinary people fight—they also squabble with each other. Peter Applebome discusses one cleavage between blacks and Hispanics in Corpus Christi.

Last, Kaye Northcott fulfills a fantasy for all of us by recounting how her neighborhood organization took on a development corporation owned by rich and famous Texans and fought it to a draw.

II. Influentials

Between the millions of Texans who participate in governing occasionally and indirectly or not at all and the elite who actually hold the reins of power, there stands a group of citizens who possess extraordinary influence despite their lack of official title. Although the position of these people in the web of power is informal, they are often at least as important to the state's future as many designated officials are; either they may control some resource that politicians want, or they can affect their fellow citizens to support or oppose the plans and careers of the formal decision-makers. Seven of these unusual members of the body politic are profiled in the following five articles.

Since money is, in Texas, the most important political resource, anyone who can marshal and direct large amounts of it will be of consequence. The subject of the first article, Walter Mischer, is as powerful as any elected politician in the state because he is the most important fundraiser in Houston. Paul Burka describes his power and how it grew.

Votes are just as vital to power as money is—and more directly so. In the next article Harry Hurt discusses two black residents of Houston, one an activist and one a judge, who became important by virtue of their apparent leadership of that city's black voters. This article makes it clear that influence, so difficult to attain, is easy to lose.

It is not so much his influence over the explicitly political behavior of Catholic residents of Amarillo that makes Bishop Leroy Matthiesen politically important; it is more his possible effect on their consciences and thereby on their work. The Pantex Corporation, the area's largest single employer, is the one institution in the country that assembles nuclear warheads. The bishop proclaimed that nuclear weapons are immoral and thus strongly implied that those who make them are in danger of losing their souls. Joseph Nocera describes the aftermath of this pronouncement on Matthiesen's community.

The influence of Mel and Norma Gabler, like the political importance of Bishop Matthiesen, is no less powerful for being hard to measure. The Gablers, like many other Texans, are fundamentalist Christians. Unlike many others, they have devoted their lives to eradicating doctrines they consider blasphemous, including that of biological evolution, from the state's educational system. Their vigorous and persistent efforts to eliminate teachings they believe to be un-Christian and unpatriotic from school textbooks have had a major impact on what the state's children are taught. William Martin reports their tactics and evaluates their characters.

Finally, since so many people want to be elected to office, anyone who can credibly claim to be able to tell candidates how to run successfully is bound to find that his advice is respected. Paul Burka examines media consultant Roy Spence and reveals that knowledge can sometimes be the most influential resource of all.

III. Interests

Where money is involved, organization follows, and organization is power. This section deals with the efforts of some of Texas' wealthy interests to use money and organization to influence national and state politics to favor themselves.

For a variety of reasons examined in the following articles, these efforts are often successful. Campaign contributions purchase access to politicians, if not their outright loyalty. Propaganda affects public opinion, which in turn helps determine policy. Threats by sizable groups to punish elected officials at the polls are taken very seriously. Moreover, groups seeking special favors from government are intensely devoted to their own welfare, whereas the mass of ordinary citizens, who will pay for the privileges the groups desire, are frequently uninformed and uninvolved. As a consequence, special interests speak with a loud and unambiguous voice, while the voice of the public is muffled and confused. The result is familiar—the rich get richer, and the rest of us get taxes.

Three of the articles in this section are classics, having appeared in two previous editions of the reader. In 1973 Richard West described the efforts of numerous lobbies to influence the Texas Legislature. Although the context of state politics has altered considerably since that year and although some of the individuals he discusses have died or have been replaced, his insights remain as true and relevant as when the article first appeared.

The next two pieces deal with powerful private interests and their relationship to state administrative bodies. In one important respect, circumstances have changed since they were written: there is now a Texas "Sunset" process that forces agencies to justify their existence to the Legislature every six years and thereby to be somewhat more accountable to the public. The basic marriage of wealthy interest to sympathetic state agency has not, however, been changed significantly. These articles, written in the seventies, are consequently still pertinent to Texas politics of the eighties.

The final article deals with what is by most accounts the most powerful interest in the state: the independent oil producers. This group lives in the best of all political worlds—it is extraordinarily wealthy, yet able to present an image of itself as composed of the small and weak. Stephen Chapman discusses the manner in which the independents have parlayed such advantages into lobbying clout in Washington.

IV. Parties

Political parties are by definition organizations that work, through discipline and cooperation, to mobilize masses of ordinary citizens to gain power and then to govern. If the definition is correct, however, Texas parties are scarcely worthy of the name. The following three articles paint a portrait of the Texas Democratic and Republican parties in which the common state of affairs seems to be internal feuding and external ineffectiveness. Indeed, to judge by the evidence in this reportage, Texas and the United States are governed in spite of, not because of, their political parties.

In the first article Paul Burka examines the phenomenon of the "Boll Weevils"—the conservative Democrats, many of them Texans, who despite their official party allegiance consistently vote in the U.S. Congress to support the programs of Ronald Reagan, a Republican president. Burka's account illustrates the truth that in American politics local circumstances are far more important than party labels. Because Texas has a Confederate history, most of its citizens are traditional Democrats. Yet because those citizens also share a conservative Southern outlook, their political preferences are often more in line with Republican policies. The result is confused maneuvering in both Washington and Austin, and a national and state Democratic party that defies rational explanation.

If the Democrats are chaotic, however, the Republicans are contentious. As long as Texas Republicans were out of power at the state and national levels, they managed to suppress personal antipathies and present a united public front. As Douglas Harlan explains, however, Bill Clements's victory in 1978 and Ronald Reagan's in 1980 removed the inhibitions to animosity, and the leaders of the party were soon quarreling. Harlan's article is a reminder that, for all the high principles and broad interests involved in political conflict, personal rivalry is still an important ingredient.

Perhaps Texas Republicans were so busy fighting among themselves in 1982 that they forgot to fight the opposition. At any rate, Democrats swept every statewide office in that year's general election. In a discussion of the voters in one precinct in Tarrant County, Gregory Curtis speculates on the causes of the Republican debacle. His conclusions illustrate that, for all its recent success in Texas, the GOP still enjoys only minority support here and cannot afford to relax in its contests with the Democrats.

V. Politicians

At the center of the political process are the people who actually do the governing: legislators, executives, and jurists. Holding office, they make the decisions that determine the rules of the political game, what will be considered right and wrong, and who gets what. In accordance with the importance of such professional politicians, this section is a long one, comprising thirteen articles.

Money is the single most important force in Texas politics, so it is appropriate that the section on legislators begins with Paul Burka's account of House Speaker Billy Clayton's legal difficulties with an unorthodox campaign contribution. Victoria Loe then details the failed efforts of the 1981 Legislature to satisfy the demands of interests, parties, individuals, and federal courts in creating three new U.S. House districts. Next the scene shifts to one of the new districts that was eventually created, as Loe recounts the saga of Mike Andrews's successful run at Texas 25th District seat in Houston in 1982. The power of money is once again highlighted in this article, but that emphasis is complemented by the author's recognition of another potent force in electoral politics: media.

From the present time, Paul Burka then takes us back to a former era in the state's history, as he reviews Robert Caro's celebrated biography of Lyndon Johnson's early years as a legislator. This section ends with one of *Texas Monthly's* most popular continuing features, a discussion of the ten best and the ten worst state legislators, as they distinguished themselves in the 1983 session.

Legislators are a group, but an executive is a single individual. For that reason, accounts of the lawmaking process are usually discussions of social forces, but articles about executives are profiles of personality. The five articles making up the next section are consequently heavy on character analysis. Stephen Harrigan offers his observations on blunt, abrasive, truthful Bill Clements, Texas's only Republican governor in the twentieth century. Taylor Branch sketches a portrait of James Baker, the consummate organizer who runs Ronald Reagan's White House. In a switch of parties, Paul Burka chronicles the amazing transformation of Democratic governor Mark White, elected in 1982, from conservative stalwart to populist rabble-rouser.

Next, Harry Hurt tells a story that is becoming very familiar—that of the Yankee who came to Texas and made good—as he describes George Bush's journey from Connecticut to Odessa to Houston to Washington, D.C. Finally, Peter Elkind describes the manner in which Jim Hightower has parlayed a sensitivity to injustice and a knack for generating publicity into the job of Texas agriculture commissioner and a bright political future.

The least-publicized politicians are those who labor in the courts. Indeed, jurists are often not even considered to be part of the political process. The next three articles, however, demonstrate just how political the courts in Texas can be. Paul Burka profiles federal judge William Wayne Justice, a man who has so disturbed and directed state government that he can be termed "the real governor of Texas." Moving to the other side of the bench, Gene Lyons describes how the young lawyers of Texas Rural Legal Aid have changed the relationship between farmers and migrant workers in the Panhandle. Last, Peter Elkind describes how judicial power and hunger for publicity have come together to make San Antonio district attorney Sam Millsap the most visible city prosecutor in the state.

VI. Cities

The image Texans have of themselves often seems to be that of a rural people. They dress in cowboy hats and boots, ride mechanical bulls in bars, and listen to country-and-western music. The reality for 80 per cent of the population, however, is a life spent in a city, or a suburb, with perhaps occasional holidays in the country. A people of ranches and the frontier in their imagination, in their daily existence Texans are firmly rooted in the urban America of the late twentieth century.

Because four-fifths of the state's population lives in cities, most of the political process takes place there. Although governments in Austin and Washington have more glamour, the bulk of the decisions that affect how people must live—where they may build a house, how often their trash will be collected, whether their neighborhoods will be patrolled by police officers, how much they must pay for electricity, the quality of their schools—are made in governments much closer to home. The following eight articles explore the Texas political process at a local level, in communities ranging in size from among the largest in the nation to mere hamlets.

Mayors are vitally important to the politics of cities, and the first section deals with them. Susan Duffy describes the harsh political style of McAllen mayor Othal Brand, whose patronizing attitude toward Mexican Americans and seeming indifference to their treatment by local police officers touched off a revolt in 1981 that nearly toppled him from power.

The next two mayors, quite different from Brand, are similar to each other in that they attempt to project themselves as nonpolitical "managers." Needless to say, to be accepted as a nonpolitical mayor in Texas' conflict-ridden cities takes great political skill. One who seemed to be succeeding in 1982 was Jonathan Rogers of El Paso. As depicted by Peter Applebome, Rogers was trying to avoid the pitfalls of McAllen-style ethnic confrontations by proclaiming that his only goal was to run the city "like a business." Whether he will succeed in this unlikely attempt is a question that will require further reporting to answer. Another mayor who yearns to be accepted as a neutral manager is Kathy Whitmire of Houston. But in an era of tightening city budgets, it is desperately difficult for city leaders to maintain the fiction of nonpolitical efficiency. Applebome discusses Whitmire's problems as she wrestles with the fact of diminishing revenue.

Dallas has a somewhat different problem: should it retain its traditional no-holds-barred, pro-growth policies, or attempt to make itself a more livable city? Jim Atkinson describes Mayor Starke Taylor's efforts to mediate between developers and neighborhood preservationists in an article that confirms that whatever else city government is, it is political.

The second section consists of four provocative glimpses of city politics in action. In a reassuring article, John Bloom details the method that Dallas used to pick the—surprise!—best cable television company to service city residents. On a less optimistic note, Suzanne Winckler updates the continuing degradation of Austin's famed Barton Springs as greed and growth overcome the efforts of the partisans of urban amenities to shield this natural wonder from pollution. Then Joseph Nocera traces the intricate relationship of public and private power in Houston, as developers and politicians attempt to finance a building project near downtown. Finally, lest anyone think that hardball politics is a monopoly of the metropolis, Jim Atkinson recounts a furious but futile struggle to incorporate a tiny East Texas community known as Dogwood.

VII. Issues

Those of us who enjoy politics as a spectator sport sometimes are distracted by its "game" aspect—the stratagems and ballyhoo, the oratory and personality, the thrill of victory and the agony of defeat—and forget that governments make decisions that determine the way we live. But politics is not, of course, just an entertaining contest; it is about things that matter to real people. Behind most political conflicts are serious issues about which the antagonists are in dead earnest. The final section includes seven articles that explore some of the issues that divide Texans.

Political issues, like most things, fall into several categories. In Texas, one of the most contentious is ethnicity. As a society more or less permanently divided into Anglos, Hispanics, and blacks, Texas perennially faces the major problem of juggling the competing demands of these groups. One of the hottest of these conflicts is that of school desegregation. In the first selection, William Broyles considers the pros and cons of busing to achieve racial balance in the schools. Then Gene Lyons reports on the equally difficult and nearly as emotional issue of bilingual education.

A second frequently encountered issue in the state's politics is the management of natural resources. Texans have of course been struggling for most of the twentieth century for control of the state's number one resource, petroleum. But another liquid that threatens to generate as much conflict in the future as oil has in the past is water. A saying that is common in Wyoming—"Water is like sex: everybody thinks there's more of it around than there really is and that somebody else is getting more than his fair share"—will be applicable to Texas in the near future. William Broyles sketches the outlines of the problem in an article from 1981. Look for more words on the topic in coming years.

A third issue deals with different views of right and wrong. Questions of morality are not particularly numerous, but when they appear they generate more emotion than all the others Three articles examine the intense struggle in Texas over moral problems. Susan Duffy recounts the reasons for the closing of Houston's publicly funded abortion clinic. Dick Reavis observes the tenacity of rural prohibition. And Gregory Curtis discusses the determination of many citizens to keep pari-mutuel horserace betting out of the state. Together, the three articles suggest that the usual political virtues of compromise and conciliation are not particularly welcome in conflicts over ultimate good and bad. In these articles, more than elsewhere in this book, there is less a sense of politics as a game and more a sense of it as warfare.

A fourth issue is probably the most common and the most complex. It involves the determination of who gets what—in most cases, who gets how much of the public treasury. Suzanne Winckler discusses the ongoing argument over the disbursement of the state highway fund. The principal lesson to be learned from the article seems to be that when it comes to slicing up the public pie, a good argument can be made against any conceivable distribution. This suggests that the battle will go on endlessly—but that's politics in Texas.

★ CITIZENS ★

THE SECOND BATTLE OF THE ALAMO

by Paul Burka

When a group of Mexican Americans learned how to fight city hall, they touched off a revolution that may engulf all of San Antonio— themselves included.

The rain began late Wednesday afternoon, a slow soaking that lasted through the night. When he awoke on Thursday morning and saw that the rain was still falling, Andres Sarabia knew that it would be a bad day for San Antonio's heavily Mexican American West Side. Soon families on Inez Avenue, a few blocks south of Saint Mary's University, would be packing up their belongings and seeking refuge on higher ground; every time there was a big rain, the giant Mayberry drainage ditch behind their houses would turn into an immense thrashing lake. Muddy water lines on the houses ominously marked the extent of the most recent floods: two feet, sometimes three feet, high on the white frame exteriors.

Closer to town, Elmendorf Lake couldn't hold the water that was streaming into it, and neither could Apache Creek, which wound east and south from the lake toward the stockyards and packing houses southwest of downtown. Apache Creek was a killer; few rainstorms hit the city that the creek didn't claim a life or two, usually kids trapped on the side away from home by the sudden overflow.

Sarabia shook his head and allowed himself a short, bitter smile. People said this was an act of God; well, he knew better. There was just too much water with no place to go. Aside from a major thoroughfare or two, no street on the West Side had any drainage. You could drive for miles on curbless streets without seeing a storm drain. Even the huge ditches, some as wide as a river, that were supposed to carry off the water were choked by high grass, trees, and everything from grocery carts to old washing machines. None had even been cleared, much less channelized. Instead the water just seeped into

the ground until the ground couldn't hold any more, then it flowed down the streets toward the drainage ditches until *they* couldn't hold any more, then it just stayed where it was, sometimes for days. Sarabia got into his car and began to pick his way through the flooded streets toward Kelly Air Force Base, where, like thousands of West Siders, he was employed as a civil service worker. Something had to be done. But what?

South of the stockyards Beatrice Gallego watched the river flow in front of her home and asked herself the same question. Actually that wasn't a river; it was Winnipeg Street, but heavy rains turned it into a muddy torrent. She thought about her oldest child, Terry, whose trophies for beauty contests and softball tournaments were all over the house, walking to school barefoot, ankle-deep in mud. Perhaps she should ask one of her women's clubs to send another petition to the city; maybe the city would do something this time.

The city would do something, all right, though not this time. On that rainy September day four years ago, Sarabia and Gallego couldn't have foreseen—they didn't even know each other —that they would help change the face of the city, not only physically but also politically; that they would become the leaders of the most unlikely political organization any Texas city has ever seen; or that they and their followers, most of whom earn less than $10,000 a year, would decide how the nation's tenth-largest city spends hundreds of millions of dollars.

Today their organization, known as COPS (Communities Organized for Public Service), is firmly established in San Antonio as a major political force —some would say *the* major political force. It has won victory after victory, everything from large drainage projects and neighborhood parks to single-member city council districts, and yet its importance transcends any or all of these. For COPS has proved that you *can* fight city hall; it has challenged the basic assumption that pervades municipal government in every major American city: that ordinary citizens should leave things to experts, interest groups, and politicians. And, perhaps most important, it has unleashed San Antonio's majority (and politically long dormant) Mexican American population, a fact that has in turn panicked the Anglo North Side, where people speak openly of a city divided into two camps and a Second Battle of the Alamo for political control of the city.

For most of the last quarter century, the quest for power in San Antonio was a triangular struggle among the staid Anglo business and social establishment, an increasingly large and vocal group of fast-money Anglo land developers and other outsiders who wanted action and lots of it, and an ambitious Mexican political clique trying to shoulder its way into the game. (Local folks of both ethnic groups use Mexican as shorthand for Mexican American, just as Bostonians talk about the Irish, rather than Irish Americans.) Most of the time the old-money gentry held the upper hand, and the standard interpretation of San Antonio politics has been that this ruling class sought and exercised power out of a sense of noblesse oblige, while the fast-money boys sought power mainly to further their own interests. It didn't really matter why the Mexicans sought power because they never got any.

All that has changed now. The political arm of the ruling establishment, the Good Government League (GGL) is in ruins; the developers' hegemony, after four stormy years, has been shattered, and the Mexicans can no longer be ignored. It is anybody's ball game—literally anybody's; the rise of Andy Sarabia and Beatrice Gallego is proof enough of that. What a strange place for all of this to be happening: stuffy old San Antonio, the only city in the U.S. outside of New Orleans where social status is determined by men; a city where what club you belong to really *matters*, not just socially but politically and economically; a city that somehow missed out on the economic miracles that transformed Houston and Dallas—something its self-conscious citizens have never accepted and can't understand. And here it is, the first city in Texas to experience the ethnic political upheavals that will someday surely come to Houston, Dallas, and the rest: from noblesse oblige to the Second Battle of the Alamo in five years.

White Man's Burden

Asked if San Antonio is in fact headed for a Second Battle of the Alamo, a local Mexican activist snapped, "Yes—and this time we're going to win." They won the first time, of course, but no one, Anglo or Mexican, thinks of it that way. The Alamo is where it all started, this century and a half of ethnic tension that has gripped and shaped and at times even blessed San Antonio, giving it a unique character and depth no other Texas city can approach. Seldom has that tension been pushed far into the background: not in the years immediately following Texas independence (Mexican national troops intermittently occupied the town between 1836 and 1848); not by the time the railroad arrived in the 1870s (Germans began to control the town's banking and commerce and had replaced Mexicans as the town's dominant ethnic group); and certainly not in the first half of the twentieth century, when San Antonio neighborhoods were segregated by deed restrictions, San Antonio schools were segregated by tradition, and even downtown was tacitly segregated by Flores Street.

But seldom has the city been as divided as it is today. With the 1970 Census, Mexicans are again a majority of the population—a fact that by itself would be enough to make Anglos uneasy. Enrollment in the San Antonio Independent School District is 70 per cent Mexican and only 14 per cent Anglo; the school board is in Mexican hands and the eleven-member city council is headed that way. It has five Mexicans and one black, giving ethnic minorities a majority, and crucial votes often split right down the ethnic line—a development that delights some of the Mexican councilmen and dismays others. For the first time the central fact of San Antonio's existence—its ethnic diversity—is reflected in its politics, and though there is an almost universal sense that this is healthy, no one seems to know where to go from here. Like Europe before 1914, San Antonio appears headed for a war nobody wants and nobody thinks can be avoided. There is no ground swell for bridge builders, though one of the Mexican councilmen, University of Texas at San Antonio professor Henry Cisneros, is ideally suited for the role. For a time he seemed destined to be the city's first Mexican American mayor in over a century, but events may have overtaken him.

Even Anglos of goodwill—and there are many in San Antonio—are starting to be afflicted by the same kind of doubts that plagued sympathetic white Southerners during the civil rights movement. What is wrong with these aliens in our midst? Why can't they become "Americans?" Why can't Mexicans do what the Germans and the Irish and the Italians and the Jews did when they came to this country?

There is no one answer to such questions. Some say the discrimination has been greater; some point to the psychological burden of being a conquered people (going back long before the Alamo, all the way to Cortés); others talk of vast cultural differences, theorizing that the Protestant ethic so basic to the Texas character is missing from the Mexican's heritage. But at least part of the reason rests on something so basic as geography. When the Germans, the Italians, the Jews, came to America, they came in great waves—and they stopped. There was an ocean between them and the Old Country. They had to assimilate; there was nothing else to do.

The difference between the European and the Mexican is the difference between an ocean and a river. There was no single wave of Mexican immigration; rather it was a steady trickle that began in the early years of the twentieth century, when South Texas was cleared for agriculture and revolution broke out in Mexico. There were always more Mexicans arriving, more family to be cared for, and though the front end of the community disappeared into the melting pot, the back end never seemed to diminish. The constant tension between front and back tugged on the middle and never allowed it to break loose from its past.

Meanwhile most Mexicans had little to do with the political or economic life of San Antonio, mainly because they were too busy trying to survive; tens of thousands got through the Great Depression by shelling pecans for a few pennies a pound. Who had the money to throw away for a poll tax?

A few Mexicans, though, were very much involved in politics. From the twenties through the forties San Antonio was run by a strong and corrupt political machine that stayed in power by handing out municipal contracts and city jobs. During the height of the Depression opponents charged that there were 3000 mattress inspectors on the city payroll; the machine hired city employees for their political connections and expected them to deliver their friends and relatives on election day. To this core the machine added the small ethnic vote on the Mexican West Side and the black East Side. No racial ideology was involved; the machine simply bought the loyalties of a few key organizers with favors, and these henchmen in turn bought poll taxes for their minions. Usually the favors involved protection for vice: West Side political meetings took place above the brothels on El Paso Street, and every prostitute had a poll tax.

The machine gave way to the Good Government League in the fifties, and politics began to open up a little for the West Side. A Spanish-language newspaper editor's son named Henry B. Gonzalez ran for city council and won; he survived a turbulent term when the city went through 48 councilmen in two years to win again. For the West Side Gonzalez was the right man at the right time. As basic as drainage was to be in the seventies, the issue in the fifties was more basic still: it was philosophical and political acceptance of the Mexican American as a part of San Antonio. Gonzalez symbolized that acceptance, but just as important, he was worthy of it. He took no money, he cut no deals, he spoke out for what was right, and his people revered him for it. He shattered his constituents' own stereotypes about corrupt Mexican politicians and eradicated the memory of the whores with their poll taxes. That is why even today there are hundreds of people on the West Side like the old man who runs a gas station on Zarzamora Street, proudly showing visitors a frayed, yellowed letter Henry B. wrote him twenty years ago.

The GGL began as a reform movement, bent on bringing professional city government to San Antonio ("a copy of the American corporate structure applied to politics," Walter McAllister called it; he would become mayor in 1961, at the age of 72, and serve into his eighties). For a century, ever since the early Germans had been too busy making money to pay much attention to politics, San Antonio's leading citizens had shunned city hall, but now they invaded it to run the town as it had never been run before: everything from paving long-neglected streets to bringing the city a world's fair and a branch of the University of Texas.

And yet, underneath the smoothly running exterior, all was not well. From the start the GGL made no effort to cultivate new Mexican political talent and develop a critical mass of West Side support. Instead, like the old machine, it chose to deal with the West Side through a few handpicked intermediaries—although in keeping with the changing times, its contacts were Mexican American businessmen, not vice peddlers. As a result there was no political outlet for ambitious young Mexicans: no spots on the city council, not even appointments to city boards and commissions. As for other electoral races, that didn't sit well with Gonzalez, who by the time McAllister became mayor in 1961 had gone off to Congress—but not before spreading the word around the West Side that "there is only one politician here and that is me." The only refuge left for Mexican political hopefuls was whatever liberal

Democratic organization happened to be functioning at the time: Viva Kennedy, PASO, Mexican American Democrats. The names changed but the clique didn't. They sat around, drinking and complaining and talking of the days when they would have power and cutting each other up, as liberals will. Some went on to become lackluster state legislators; others, even now, are waiting their turn, laying plans to reap the spoils of the Second Battle of the Alamo.

Ambitious Mexicans weren't the only ones who felt excluded by the GGL. San Antonio's council-manager system had gone to great lengths to keep politicians from making money out of government. (Two crucial city departments, water and electric utilities, were governed by self-perpetuating boards completely free of council control.) But no system could erase the fact that money was there to be made. Fortunes depended on where the city built water mains, how it enforced subdivision regulations, and what it decided about zoning. Builders and land developers yearned for city policies that stimulated growth, but the GGL was composed primarily of Chamber of Commerce types—downtown businessmen and merchants, many from old families, who had little incentive to tilt city policies in favor of suburban growth. These natural economic tensions were heightened by the social conflicts between the GGL's old families and developers with nothing but contempt for bloodlines.

After McAllister finally stepped down in 1971, no one could hold the GGL together. The telling blow was delivered by a maverick GGL councilman named Charles Becker, son of the founder of the Handy-Andy grocery chain and a member of an old San Antonio family. Despite his GGL ties, Becker had far more affinity with the fast-money boys than with the stodgy old downtown crowd who, said Becker, spent their time "lollygagging" around the San Antonio Country Club and the Argyle Club, pruning their family trees. When the GGL needed the West Side votes, they weren't there, and suddenly the GGL was O-U-T. Familiar names on city boards and commissions were replaced by Becker allies; before long, the president of the Greater San Antonio Builders was in charge of the planning commission and a major developer was chairman of the powerful water board.

Becker loved to talk about his feud with the GGL; his favorite saying was, "I'm gonna kill me some snakes." But, it turned out, that was all he did; he destroyed the old order but built nothing new to take its place. When he quit in 1975, his legacy was a power vacuum.

Old Story, New Ending

In the fall of 1973, about the time Charles Becker was busily killing snakes, Father Edmundo Rodriguez was listening to yet another plan for organizing San Antonio's Mexican American community. A pudgy, gentle Jesuit priest in his late thirties, Rodriguez looked more like the ideal person for the part of Santa Claus in a secular Christmas pageant than a crusading reformer. But his visitor, himself a bulky 200-pounder, knew he had come to the right place. Working out of the fading red brick Our Lady of Guadalupe Church on the near West Side, not far from the old Missouri Pacific Railroad Station, Rodriguez had been active in numerous causes: U.S. Civil Rights Commission hearings in San Antonio, bilingual and bicultural committees, and a drive to get the Bexar County Hospital Board to respond to patient grievances. Equally important, Rodriguez was active in interfaith organizations and knew who might be willing to back their sympathy for the poor with cash.

Rodriguez wasn't optimistic. There always seemed to be another social activist with a plan for organizing the West Side. He had watched them talk to people in the barrio about the obvious issues—racial discrimination, bilingual education, police brutality, unemployment—and had seen lots of heads nod in agreement, but somehow the organizers never made any progress. People didn't seem to care, at least not enough to act.

Nevertheless, Rodriguez sensed that this one was different. His name was Ernie Cortes, he was a native of the West Side, and he had a solid grasp of how power worked in San Antonio. Furthermore, his bulk gave him an air of authority that made him hard to ignore. Cortes, thirty, had gotten his formal education at UT in economics, his political training on the Bexar County Hospital Board as an appointee of County Commissioner Albert Peña, and his practical experience as an economic development specialist for the Mexican American Unity Council. (It was as a member of the hospital board that he had first met Rodriguez.) Moreover, Cortes had received training earlier that year as a community organizer at the late Saul Alinsky's Industrial Areas Foundation in Chicago. Alinsky, a self-described radical whose goal was to bring power to the powerless, first came to national prominence in the thirties as a friend of labor boss John L. Lewis; he later organized Chicago's Back of the Yards area (Upton Sinclair's *Jungle*) and led the fight against Eastman Kodak on behalf of Rochester's ghetto blacks. Alinsky was no idealist or social dreamer; he was a hard-core realist who wrote extensively about how to overcome the weaknesses of the poor by exploiting those of the rich and powerful.

All this Rodriguez knew. But what most impressed him was that Cortes didn't seem to be just another hustler looking for no-strings-attached dollars from the church. He wanted money, to be sure, but Cortes agreed that it should come from an ecumenical sponsoring committee that would closely monitor the project and hold the staff accountable for the money. (Several San Antonio churches had already been stung by self-appointed organizers who had little to show for their efforts—including financial statements.)

Rodriguez agreed to try to raise the money. It wasn't easy, but he was able to pry loose some contributions from Church of Christ, Methodist, and Episcopal sources, and to win the essential support of San Antonio Archbishop Francis Furey. The money would be doled out in stages and could be cut off at any time. Only Rodriguez could sign the checks. The sponsoring committee, made up of churchmen from the donating denominations, was formalized in January 1974 and hired Cortes as the organizer at a salary of $16,000 a year. The movement was uninspirationally labeled the Committee for Mexican American Action, and Cortes went to work.

He started at the churches, asking pastors for the names of parishioners who were leaders, whether churchgoers or not. Cortes wasn't interested in people who were active in politics; he was looking for those who organized church socials, ran PTAs, or perhaps were union stewards. *Natural* leaders, he called them: not people who were showy, but those who got others to show. He found a woman in a public-housing project who spent Saturdays cooking food for shut-in senior citizens; later, when the neighborhood organization tried to get a bridge across a creek for schoolchildren, she had no trouble getting people to turn out in support—they trusted her. He found Andy Sarabia, the chairman of the community life committee of Holy Family Church, who was already spending much of his time finding out what the parish could do about problems in the area. And he found Beatrice Gallego, a PTA leader and Head Start volunteer who was also involved with senior citizens and Catholic women's groups. Cortes looked for anyone who had a following, and he found them in every Mexican neighborhood, people with no history of political involvement.

After identifying who to organize, Cortes' next problem was to find what

to organize them around. Instead of picking the obvious civil rights issues that had mesmerized previous organizers, Cortes took the simple but crucial step of asking his new contacts what mattered to them. The answers were startling: drainage, high utility bills, chugholes in the streets, sidewalks for their children. There was not a single mention of any of the more glamorous causes traditionally embraced by minority politicians.

Rodriguez was elated. It was, he said later, like one of those light bulbs that suddenly appears in cartoons. No wonder previous efforts had failed. They had been on the wrong track. The myth that Mexicans could never be organized, that they didn't really care about social issues, had been repeated so many times he had almost begun to believe it himself. Many of his parishioners did believe it. But the problem had been with the technique, not with the people. It was so obvious; why hadn't he seen it earlier? For the first time he allowed himself to think that this thing might actually work.

Cortes went from parish to parish during the winter and spring of 1974, recruiting leaders, weeding out the weak from the strong, researching issues, and setting up independent neighborhood groups organized around parish churches. It took him seventeen phone calls before Beatrice Gallego would even agree to a meeting. By the summer he was ready to take the crucial step: bringing the area groups together under one umbrella organization. Cortes and Rodriguez knew that this was where previous organizing attempts had been undercut by jealousies and personality conflicts. Certainly the potential was present for that to happen again. Neighborhood leaders would be vying for power in the central organization, and only a few could succeed. People who had spent their whole lives fighting for their own neighborhoods were suddenly going to have to shift their efforts on behalf of other areas. Yet without a strong umbrella, the local groups would have no clout. Projects like drainage were too big and too costly for one parish to attack.

Cortes and Rodriguez did the groundwork for the changeover. They taught their inexperienced troops that in politics, size is power. They explained about trade-offs: you help this parish get a park and they'll help you get drainage. They promoted a merit system for leaders: those who produced rose higher; those who didn't were limited. They talked to people about their fears and learned that most didn't worry about losing jobs, or what their neighbors would think, but that they would be made fools of in public

by people who knew more than they did. So Cortes helped them learn how to do research: where to look for answers and what to ask for when they went to city hall. The area leaders met in midsummer at a parish social hall to form their new union. There was a tense moment or two while the group debated what issues to focus on—a sizable contingent, incensed over spiraling utility bills, wanted to go to war with the city's natural gas supplier, Lo-Vaca Gathering Company—but Cortes channeled the discussion toward whether anything could be done. Gradually, the group perceived, unhappily, that the utility crisis was in the hands of the courts, the Texas Railroad Commission, the Arabs, the energy companies, and, locally, the independent CPS (City Public Service) Board—none of which could be affected much by what some angry citizens in West Side San Antonio had to say. But drainage was different; it was localized, focusable, in the hands of a city manager, a city council, and, ultimately, voters, who had to approve bond issues.

The leaders settled on drainage ("*We couldn't tell them,*" says Rodriguez. "It had to be understood and agreed on by the people themselves"), and Rodriguez breathed a sigh of relief. The center had held. Now it was time for a meeting with City Manager Sam Granata. But first, there was one more thing to do. That insipid name, the Committee for Mexican American Action, had to go. In a strategy session for the confrontation with city hall, someone jokingly suggested the name COPS: "You know, they're the robbers and we're the cops." Someone else, still bitter about those utility bills, pointed out that "PS could stand for public service, just like CPS, only we really mean it." And the group that would fill Charles Becker's power vacuum had its name.

Ask and Ye Shall Receive

When Ernie Cortes called, Beatrice Gallego knew what he wanted—word passed quickly on the West Side, even though nothing had appeared in the news media about Cortes' organizing efforts—but she didn't want to talk to him. She had heard it all before, young radicals talking about confronting the system, full of socialism and kill the gringo, trying to convince her that she should get involved. Get involved! What about Head Start, the PTA, the church, substitute teaching? Those were the things that really mattered; who cared about another march to protest police brutality? There wasn't any time left for politics, even if she'd been inclined that way. Besides, like most of the women she knew, even the most active, she considered home her first priority—her three children and her husband Gilbert, a hardware salesman who had built their house in a modest middle-class neighborhood called Palm Heights.

There was another reason she didn't want to talk to Cortes. The whole idea of radicalism appalled her. The youngest of seven children, she had wanted to be a nun until she met her future husband. Like many Mexican Americans, she had been raised in a strict family atmosphere and been instilled with a respect for authority (though occasionally her father shocked her with bitter complaints about the city's Anglo leadership and their neglect of the West Side). Long after her name had become a household word in San Antonio political circles, she recounted to him a small victory she had won at a public hearing New Braunfels Congressman Bob Krueger had arranged to hold in San Antonio. As she described Krueger's reactions, her father interrupted his youngest child, "Baby, did you call him Krueger? You shouldn't say that. He's *Congressman* Krueger."

At the urging of a priest, Gallego finally met with Cortes. He asked her about problems in her neighborhood. "I had to laugh," she recalls. "What wasn't a problem? We had no drainage, no sidewalks, no curbs, no parks, we were cut in half by an expressway, we didn't have enough water pressure to water the yard and draw bath water at the same time."

She was still skeptical, though, as the fledgling organization prepared for its showdown with the city over drainage. COPS tried to arrange a West Side assembly with Granata: he refused to come. So they took their plea for a meeting to city hall, jamming into the small council chambers in such numbers that one councilman was reminded of Travis' famous message from the Alamo: "I am besieged with a thousand or more of the Mexicans." The council took one look at the crowd and ordered Granata to meet with the West Siders. The session was set for August 13, 1974, at a West Side high school.

Cortes and Rodriguez were worried about the upcoming confrontation. They knew that turnout was critical; COPS had to make a good showing. More important, they wondered whether their people were psychologically prepared for what lay ahead. Most, like Gallego, had been brought up to respect authority. The Alinsky approach did not require breaking the law, but it did not shirk from bending it a little. Its guiding principle was to encourage and focus the latent anger of the poor by showing how the sys-

tem worked against them. But everything was predicated on that anger; it had to come naturally. Just how angry were these homeowners and churchgoers? Angry enough to forget their upbringing? Angry enough to implement the Alinsky tactic that "ridicule is man's most potent weapon"? Angry enough to overcome the lack of confidence and fear of ignorance they all were sure to feel? Another of Alinsky's cardinal rules was "Never go outside the experience of your own people." Was militance itself a violation of that rule?

Cortes did the best he could to prepare his people. At training sessions they rehearsed the confrontation, anticipated the double-talk bureaucrats excel at, and drilled on pinning the city manager down to yes or no answers.

Poor Sam Granata. Not only was COPS laying for him, but also the sky was about to fall on him. On August 7, just five days before the meeting and practically a year after the destructive 1973 rainstorm, the heavens opened again. Forty families were forced out of their homes, and on Inez Street floodwaters drove an old woman with a 105-degree fever out into the mud. A bridge across the Mayberry ditch caved in, and streets all over the West Side were impassable. COPS didn't have to worry about the turnout anymore: 500 angry people showed up. "That bolstered our faith in God," said Sarabia of the rain.

Granata was greeted with slides showing typical West Side scenes after a storm. The city manager was on the defensive from the start. COPS researchers had uncovered histories of drainage projects that had been authorized by the council but never funded—the Mayberry project had been part of the city's master plan since 1945—and others that had been funded in bond elections but never implemented. COPS wanted to know why, and the only answer the beleaguered Granata could come up with was "We dropped the ball." In the audience, Beatrice Gallego could hardly believe what she had heard; her last doubts about COPS' tactics melted away. The authorities weren't so smart after all. Why, COPS knew more about drainage than the city manager! These people weren't worthy of her respect. Now she *was* angry. Granata made matters worse by lamely defending the city's inaction with an explanation that would come back to haunt the city: "If you want something, you have to ask for it." Beatrice Gallego vowed to herself that no one would ever have to say that again. She went home that night and started drawing up lists.

Granata's ill-advised admission that

San Antonio government operated by the squeaky-wheel-gets-the-grease method did more to politicize COPS' membership than all their careful training. It exploded the myth most of them had accepted for years—that the city in its wisdom would take care of them in good time. The battle lines were drawn for keeps.

The aftermath of the Granata confrontation was immediate victory. When he refused to promise any action on drainage, the meeting ended in a shouting match, and COPS returned to the council chambers. Becker, who eventually would turn against COPS when the organization began sniping at developers, professed astonishment that the Mayberry project had been neglected for thirty years and told the city staff to come up with a plan for financing it. That fall the council drew up a $46 million bond issue that passed in November—the same month that COPS held its first annual convention, formalized its structure, and elected Sarabia president.

Perhaps more than any other person in COPS, Sarabia epitomizes the idea of a natural leader. When he talks about city politics, his eyes bore into you like lasers, with the fierce intensity of focused anger. He is outwardly calm, with none of the gestures of the polished speaker, but the listener is transfixed by the eyes. It is only later that you realize he is quiet and soft spoken. He seems to shout without raising his voice.

"We got into COPS because we cared about our neighborhoods," he recalled recently. "We weren't looking for any handouts—we're taxpayers, and we found out our tax money wasn't working for us. They'd promise us projects and then they'd use the money for something on the North Side. We found case after case of it. It made us angry. Then we found that they were incompetent. When you learn something emotionally, I guarantee you, you never forget it.

"You're educated to become one of *them*. If you want to make it, you have to leave your neighborhood, move to the North Side, forget what you left behind. It doesn't just happen; the city's policies are planned that way. Ignore the old, subsidize the new. But what if you don't want to move to the North Side? What if you'd like your children to stay in your neighborhoods?"

COPS invited the city council to its first annual convention so they could learn about the needs of the neighborhoods. None showed up, so COPS decided to go over their heads to the symbolic leaders of the business community. They tried to arrange a meeting with the head of Joske's ("We had lots of charge accounts with him, so we assumed he'd help us," said Sarabia, who is no longer so naive as to assume anything of the sort). The counteroffer came back: would Sarabia meet him alone? No deal. Sarabia took 200 people to Joske's, and they spent hours examining fine dresses, trying on expensive coats, asking sales personnel about jewelry—and buying nothing. With 200 Mexicans and a half-dozen TV cameras clogging the store, Joske's didn't do much business that day. The next day Sarabia led the group to the Frost Bank, the city's largest. Again they broke no laws but merely lined up at tellers' windows to exchange dollars for pennies, then moved to the adjacent window to trade pennies for dollars. Upstairs, Tom Frost, Jr., agreed to meet with a COPS delegation, admitted they had legitimate complaints about the way the city had neglected their neighborhoods, but declined to say it publicly. The next day, however, the head of the Greater San Antonio Chamber of Commerce appeared at COPS' shabby West Side headquarters. All he learned was that next time he'd better make an appointment first. Cortes refused to see his unannounced visitor.

Not surprisingly, the tie-ups caused a storm of protest in the city about COPS. Bewildered North Siders couldn't understand what these people wanted; hadn't the city responded to their requests with a bond issue? They didn't understand that COPS was interested not just in projects but also in power—a permanent share of the decision-making process. But not all the protests came from the North Side. One Mexican on the West Side recalled her reaction to the tie-ups: "I couldn't believe the church was involved. They're always saying, 'Mind your manners.' How could they support such things? It was just horrible, walking over people like that. I can't figure out to this day what made me change my mind and join COPS." But she did.

Who Are Those Guys?

Occasionally there are moments that capture perfectly in one insignificant incident the unending historical tension between past and future. Such a moment came to San Antonio in early 1975 at, of all places, a hearing on how the council should spend $16 million in federal funds. COPS was there in force, with more than 200 supporters, presenting its case for putting the money into old neighborhoods for parks, drainage, and streets. But Mrs. Edith McAllister was there too, the daughter-in-law of the ex-mayor, soliciting $300,000 for the San Antonio Museum Association to renovate the

old Lone Star Brewery. It was clear that COPS didn't think much of her request when there was water standing in the streets, and it was equally clear that she didn't really comprehend why all these people were up in arms. How could she make them understand? She summed up her plea to the room: "Man does not live by sewers alone. He also needs museums."

From the beginning Anglo San Antonians have had a difficult time understanding just what COPS is. Their perplexity is understandable, because COPS is an organization built on paradoxes and contradictions. It is a radical organization made up of people whose personal style is intensely conservative. It is a political organization made up of people who have no use for politicians. It is an organization made up mostly of Mexican Americans, but it has nothing to do with traditional ethnic issues.

Yet someone with as long and proud a record of public service as former Mayor McAllister can say, in all seriousness, that "I haven't got any use for a communist organization." And lest that be interpreted as just the bitterness of an 88-year-old man, John Schaefer, one of the city's leading developers and the chairman of the City Water Board, says, "To be kind to them, I'd say they're socialist. Their philosophy is straight out of the communist manifesto: from each according to his means, to each according to his needs." A local oilman has a somewhat more charitable view: "They're just looking for a handout. I bet most of them are on welfare."

In fact, most of them detest welfare. Carmen Badillo, COPS vice president, tells how her father bought cheap land near a creek rather than go into a housing project. The home cost $2500 and consisted of four walls—he had to build the inside walls himself—no sewers, no running water; it took him twenty years to pay for it. But it was better than public housing. "There are a lot of people on welfare who shouldn't be," she says. "It's gotten to be the thing to do. But it's wrong. It robs you of your dignity. Welfare people don't participate. They don't get angry." So antagonistic is COPS toward handouts that its charter bars the organization from accepting federal funds. (Although in its early years COPS relied heavily on religious foundations, it is now entirely self-sufficient, financing its $100,-000 annual budget through dues and an advertising booklet that brought in $47,000 in four weeks.)

As for economic philosophy, the COPS ranks are not exactly crawling with Marxists. A case can be made— as one area leader said—that "we're more conservative than Tom Frost."

(Frost, who actually has considerable respect and admiration for COPS— "They're good people and they're good for the city," he says—seems to be the organization's favorite symbol for the Anglo power structure, even though he cannot accurately be called a power broker.) "Let me tell you what kind of free enterprise system they believe in," says Andy Sarabia. "It's only free for themselves. *Our* taxes pay for *their* free enterprise."

Most Anglos have been unable to make the distinction between radical *tactics*, which COPS enthusiastically embraces—shouting, intimidation through numbers, rudeness, threats of mass action against politicians and financial institutions—and radical *people*, which it should be obvious by now are few and far between in COPS. Some might say there is no difference, but that is a terribly shortsighted view with terrible consequences for San Antonio. For there are Mexicans in town who do not share COPS values, who, though they do not use radical tactics, do aspire to control the city in a way COPS does not.

One of the things least understood about this organization is its contempt for politicians—all politicians, Mexicans included. Before major elections COPS holds "candidates' accountability nights," when office seekers are asked to give their views on issues COPS regards as crucial. COPS permits only yes or no answers—a tactic not so admirable when practiced by, say, the AFL-CIO, but the difference is that both COPS' issues and its membership are broader based than the usual pressure group's. And while there is much disagreement in town over COPS' tactics, there is no dispute over its power at the polls. COPS will not endorse particular candidates, but it will raise unholy hell about those who openly oppose their goals. One unfortunate Mexican politician came to accountability night a little too full of booze and macho; he said no to their questions and they walked the streets to beat him at the polls. On two important citywide referendums—one over halting development on the Edwards Aquifer northwest of town, the other on single-member city council districts—COPS showed its muscle when both propositions passed. During the single-member districting election, word got out at midafternoon that the West Side turnout was too light and in three hours of working door-to-door, COPS boosted the turnout high enough to help districting squeak through by 2000 votes.

The only people in town who seem to have figured out that COPS has no political ambitions beyond its issues are the politicians themselves. Several councilmen complain privately (they wouldn't dream of saying so publicly) that COPS never gives any credit to politicians who help with their projects.

As an organization, COPS views all politicians as the same. "A politician is a politician," Gallego is fond of saying; they would all rather make a speech than a commitment. Undoubtedly there are COPS members who emotionally would like to see the city elect a Mexican American mayor, but once the votes were counted, ethnic ties would make no difference. Earlier this year COPS attacked the Anglo majority on the school board for voting to spend $1.6 million on a new administration building instead of refurbishing rundown schools; the April elections produced a Mexican majority and COPS promptly attacked them on another issue. That produced a phone call to COPS the next day: "What's the matter with you people? Don't you realize we have to stick together?"

Of all the things about COPS, this disinterest in personal or ethnic political power is the hardest for other San Antonians to believe. Many people thought that when Sarabia voluntarily gave up the presidency last year (to be succeeded by Gallego), he was preparing to run for county commissioner. He didn't, he says, "because then I'd have to face all these crazy people." Sarabia talked about why he could never have switched over to politics:

"If anyone really thought that, it proves they didn't understand COPS. Politicians don't matter—people matter. The whole basis of this organization is a tremendous faith in people.

"Can you imagine what it was like in the beginning? *Nothing* was easy. We got calls in the middle of the night: 'Why don't you go back to Mexico?' We were awed when we went to city hall. We didn't know anything about a single issue. All we had was our own anger—and trust. COPS started as a blind trust; it was *built* on trust. Now no one wants to violate it."

"Let San Antonio Grow"

High up in one of San Antonio's tallest bank buildings, The Lawyer made it perfectly clear *he* didn't trust COPS. He had tried to understand them, tried to deal with them, but it was useless. He had even suggested that his clients, some of San Antonio's biggest land developers, read Alinsky's manual *Rules for Radicals*, but demand was so high local bookstores couldn't keep it in stock. Meanwhile, COPS kept attacking his clients even more fiercely.

"I can't understand it," The Lawyer said. "There's only one answer to the West Side's problems, and that's better jobs. Who else in this town besides

the developer pays double the minimum wage? If we don't build houses, what's left here economically except the military."

The Lawyer proceeded to reel off a dismal litany of statistics. Houston's building permits are up 40 per cent; San Antonio's down 2 per cent. San Antonio's unemployment rate is twice that of Dallas. Houston has 122 home-based companies listed on the New York and American stock exchanges; industry-poor San Antonio by comparison has only 11. Manufacturing accounts for only 13 per cent of the labor force, compared to 27 per cent nationally; almost all of that is concentrated in products for local use, or in the needle trade—businesses that pay minimum wage: $2.30 an hour, $92 a week, less than $5000 a year. More than one job in four is on a government payroll; only Washington, D.C., has a higher percentage. The federal government alone accounts for a third of San Antonio's total wages. The picture is not a good one, nor, says The Lawyer, is it an accident: "Before we got involved in politics, there was *nothing* here. The dumb bastards that ran this town did everything they could to keep industry out and build a wall around this town. They didn't want outsiders here."

One outsider they particularly didn't want was Henry Ford. Long before World War II he wanted to build an automobile assembly plant in the city, but the local gentry didn't exactly greet him with open arms. It is said that they tried to snooker him on the land deal and otherwise made it known he could take his factory and his labor unions elsewhere without being terribly missed. When Ford finally realized he wasn't wanted, the story goes, his parting shot was "You people are crazy."

But the business leaders of that era didn't care. After all, the banks were full of cattle money and oil money—but no one stopped to consider that little of it ever seemed to be plowed back into San Antonio. Instead it was invested in the oil patches and grasslands of South Texas. Its owners had no stake in the city's economic vitality. The economy came to rely increasingly on the military—another group, like cattlemen and oilmen, without a permanent stake in the community. No one paid much attention in 1933 when a small company named Frito picked up and moved to Dallas; no San Antonio bank would advance it the capital for expansion, so it had to look elsewhere. But the loss of that company, which now employs 17,000, typified the complacent attitude of the business leadership. True, the city made some nominal efforts to attract industry—the council even voted tax dollars to help support the local Chamber of

Commerce—but the Chamber was dominated by merchants who benefited from the abundant supply of cheap Mexican labor. When a new plant was lured to the city, it usually turned out to be something like Levi Strauss, another nonunion minimum-wage shop. And despite the city's gloomy economic statistics, some of the city's leading figures, like former Mayor McAllister, still maintain that San Antonio shouldn't go after heavy industry.

"We broke that up," The Lawyer says. "*Anything's* possible here now. Where do you think COPS would be if we hadn't opened things up? I can't figure out why they hate us."

The Lawyer leaned back in his chair, locked his fingers behind his head, and inspected the ceiling through fashionably large glasses. "The trouble with this town," he summed up, "is that it's got too many old rich and too many new poor. They're just alike. They're la-zy and i-dle"—he drew out the first syllables contemptuously—"and contribute nothing. Give me the nouveau riche every time."

There was a time, when the GGL was falling apart in the early seventies, that astute San Antonians involved in politics thought the alliance of the future would unite the Hungries (Anglo developers and Mexican West Siders) against the Satisfieds (old families and downtown interests). Similar coalitions have sprung up in other cities—Austin, for one, where ethnic minorities broke with the no-growth policies favored by students and other liberals. But such predictions reckoned without COPS.

Once COPS realized that money had been diverted from projects planned for older parts of town, they looked to see where it went. They found, for example, that the widening of Pleasanton Road, a major South Side artery, had been approved in a 1970 bond issue—but when the road builders went to work, it was San Pedro Avenue on the North Side that got their attention. More often than not, that was the pattern: the diverted funds went to build a water main extension to a new subdivision, to pave streets or build drainage systems in the newer parts of town. Issue after issue came down to who would get the money, new or old, and it became clear that city policies, intentionally or not, usually favored the new. The consequences were obvious: people wanted to live where the roads were, where the drainage was, where the money was spent.

Other city policies benefitted not just suburban areas generally, but their developers. COPS was particularly outraged at City Water Board procedures, instituted after developer John Schaeffer became chairman, that called for the city to provide auxiliary water main materials free to subdividers. The materials may have been free to developers, COPS protested, but not to inner-city taxpayers who continued to cope with substandard mains and low water pressure while their tax dollars were handed out to developers in the form of subsidies. Furthermore, COPS noted, developers were supposed to reimburse the city for the much larger suburban mains the city built out to their subdivisions—but in practice both the developers and the city generally ignored the debt. That, of course, amounted to another subsidy. Now COPS had the ammunition to challenge the most basic of assumptions about the modern city: that the decline of the core and the sprawl of the fringe are inevitable.

So the developers became the enemy. They were in power; they were the ones shuffling money around to encourage growth outside of town. Nothing underscored their attitude—and their power—more clearly than their reactions to a study by an upper-level city planner suggesting that all growth in San Antonio for the next 25 years could take place within Loop 410. During a public hearing, a developer on the city council threw a copy in the trash can, proclaiming vehemently, "That's where it belongs." Soon the author was canned too.

The feud between COPS and the developers broke into the open in July 1975 when 250 shouting, boisterous COPS supporters jammed a small room at the City Water Board to protest a proposed rate increase. But COPS wasn't there just to protest; its style is always to have an alternative. Stop subsidizing developers—make them pay for their own water mains—COPS said, and you won't need a rate increase; and they hauled out facts and figures to back it up. Eventually the board agreed to change its subsidy policies and consented to a compromise on the rate increase. COPS had proved that it was not just a powerful neighborhood organization, but a force to be reckoned with citywide.

A few months later COPS successfully challenged the developer crowd again. The city council narrowly voted to buy a suburban golf course from a developer for a price considerably above appraised value; for added controversy, the council planned to finance the deal with federal funds earmarked for the inner city. Beatrice Gallego vowed publicly that if the purchase went through, she would make a national scandal of it. The city was spared when COPS was instrumental in getting federal officials to veto any diversion of the funds.

But even more important than the individual victories COPS was winning was the political change that was taking place in the city as a whole. People were getting fed up with the developers. Subsidies, sweetheart deals, insider transactions, stacked boards and commissions—COPS had helped put San Antonio city government under the microscope and people didn't like what they saw. The developers suffered an overwhelming defeat when COPS and Anglo environmentalists forced a referendum on a council decision to allow construction of a shopping mall over a thin slice of the Edwards Aquifer northwest of town. Environmentalists managed to portray the fight as a clean water issue, but COPS *knew* the real issues were growth and power. Voter turnout trebled expectations, and the developers—who had run newspaper ads warning that COPS was trying to take over the city—were routed by a 4–1 margin. The developers' brief rule was in serious trouble, and suddenly they began showing up at council meetings wearing buttons pleading "Let San Antonio Grow." But they were finished. A year later, in March 1977, another referendum ushered in single-member council districts and in the April election, developers were routed all over town: their candidates were beaten not just on the West Side and South Side, but North and Southeast as well.

Curiously, despite the fact that COPS has publicly insulted them and contributed greatly to their loss of political power, some developers hold a grudging admiration for COPS—much more than for the old guard that once ran the town. Perhaps it is because, despite Anglo fears of an ethnically divided city, there is still a large reservoir of goodwill in San Antonio. John Schaeffer—though he considers Sarabia "definitely radical," thinks that COPS is "out to take over the city," and says COPS members have threatened him personally—nevertheless bought a $1000 spread in COPS' fund-raising ad booklet this summer. Jim Dement, who helped finance Charles Becker's 1973 mayoral campaign and this year made an unsuccessful council bid himself, is similarly ambivalent. He accuses COPS of "fostering hatred and real problems," but he concedes, "They had to do something drastic to get the attention of the public." And he adds, "I see dedication to San Antonio that wasn't here three years ago. There's more hope and conversation in this town than in a hundred years. And I love it. This is a town where you can have nothing and be somebody. Now don't tell me COPS is bad."

A Call to Arms

On a warm October night Henry Cisneros interrupted dinner with an old friend to speak to one of several Anglo citizens' organizations that have sprung up in San Antonio with hopes of emulating COPS' success. It had not been a good week for bridge building—the council had split twice along ethnic lines amid much controversy—and Cisneros was a little nervous.

It was a Friday, so a lot of parents and most of the students were at high school football games. Nevertheless, about forty members of the CDL (Citizens for Decency through Law) showed up at a small church to hear Cisneros talk about the spreading menace of pornography in the city. It is an issue that truly outrages Cisneros—a few days earlier he had walked into a West Side convenience store with his two young daughters to discover a tabloid on the counter featuring the story How TO RAPE A WOMAN—but despite this affinity between speaker and audience, something didn't click. Cisneros can call on a pretty rousing speaking style, but on this night he was subdued, content to rely mainly on homilies that are the ultimate refuge of every politician. He closed with a rhetorical question—"What can a small group of people do?"—but it soon became apparent that this small group of people was unlikely to do very much.

Someone asked Cisneros, "What can be done by the city council?" and he quickly flipped the ball back: "You people who have studied and worked on the problem need to come up with a plan to present to the city." Hah! COPS would never have let him get away with that. They would already have had a plan. Then someone complained that the Witte Museum was displaying pictures of naked women. Cisneros bravely tried to point out that political organizations are more effective when they stick to things a large number of people can agree on, but the zealots persisted. It was another mistake COPS would never have made, another trap they would have avoided. It is inconceivable, for example, that COPS would embrace a cause currently popular among Hispanics in the U.S. Northeast: bilingual law courts. COPS stays sighted in on targets that are carefully chosen—so carefully chosen that in a recent poll, 70 per cent of San Antonians said they agreed with COPS *goals,* despite the general unpopularity of COPS *tactics.*

Finally a white-haired lady at the back of the room caught on. "I don't approve of COPS," she told Cisneros, "but they certainly know what they're doing, don't they?"

They do indeed. The truth is that the CDL felt the same anger about pornography as COPS felt about drainage. It is a fair guess that everyone at the church that night was more affluent and better educated than 99.9 per cent of COPS' members. Yet, if that meeting is any indication, CDL is unlikely to approach COPS' success. COPS has managed to do the one thing that is essential to success in politics—or in business, athletics, or just about anything else. It has discovered the elusive formula of how to build an organization that works.

Not that anyone would want to use COPS' organization chart for a model. It looks like a map of the New York subway system. Technically COPS is an organization of organizations—the only time individuals are counted is when attendance is added up at the annual November convention—but no one can say for sure how many groups are part of COPS at any one time. It depends on the issue and who's paid dues recently. Right now there are 33 primary organizations, known as locals, with another three or four on the periphery. Most are Catholic parishes (which on the West Side is the same thing as a neighborhood organization, since neighborhoods there are defined by parish boundaries), but there are also block clubs and churches from other denominations: a small Anglo COPS chapter in the northeast, which joined because the area couldn't get city help for their drainage problems, and a growing black East Side COPS group.

Each local is virtually autonomous in choosing its own neighborhood issues. If, for example, Andy Sarabia's Holy Family local wants a park, a footbridge for schoolchildren, or some vacant lots cleared of weeds, it plans its own research and strategy—though obviously its chances will not be hurt by operating under the COPS banner.

There has to be a central organization, however, to set policy, raise money, and hammer out compromises on citywide issues like drainage priorities. COPS has managed to come up with a structure that allows everyone to take part without hampering the ability of a few skilled leaders. How this works is too complicated to be explained in detail, but it involves an executive committee (composed mostly of citywide leaders), a steering committee (composed mostly of neighborhood leaders), and a delegates' congress (composed of any member of a COPS local who shows up to vote). In theory the committees recommend and the delegates ratify, but in practice the power lies with the committees. If this sounds too labyrinthine, try substituting *management, directors, shareholders,* and *General Motors* for executive committee, steering committee, delegates' congress, and COPS.

One important omission from this bureaucracy is the Alinsky-trained organizer. This is no oversight. The organizer's primary job is to spot new natural leaders in the community—to provide the group with a continuing supply of new blood. In the beginning, of course, Ernie Cortes did that and far more: he plotted strategy, helped lead actions, trained the Sarabias and Gallegos and other emerging leaders. It was too much, and to his credit Cortes had the wisdom to see it; to last more than a year or two, COPS had to be run by the people themselves. So Cortes left for Los Angeles in August 1976, to be replaced by someone who is as different in temperament and background from Cortes as Cortes is from Tom Frost. Cortes is from San Antonio, Mexican, and Catholic; Arnie Graf, his successor, is from upstate New York, Anglo, and Jewish, and for that matter doesn't speak a word of Spanish. Nor was Graf well versed on COPS' central issue. When he was interviewed by Beatrice Gallego, she inquired what he knew about the 39 Series; all he could think of was, "Didn't Cleveland win?"* She was asking about drainage, not baseball, but Graf's record as organizer of a white working-class Milwaukee neighborhood eventually carried the day and got him the job.

The Alinsky connection is probably the least understood, and most feared, aspect of COPS among San Antonio's Anglo community. Many see it as the cause of the trouble. They pointedly mention that Father Rodriguez, Sarabia, Gallego, and other COPS leaders have gone to the Industrial Areas Foundation for training, and former Mayor McAllister bluntly calls the IAF "Saul Alinsky's communist school in Chicago."

Arnie Graf chuckles at the unlikely sight of Beatrice Gallego, mother of Miss Teenage San Antonio, earnestly watching a demonstration of how to make Molotov cocktails, or studying the Bolshevik Revolution. "Most businessmen could go to Chicago and get something out of it," Graf says. "You learn how to read a city budget, how to deal with the news media." Rodriguez says the most important subject is how to run a meeting, for that is where most organizations fail—either by having the same people make all the decisions, or by falling into endless unresolved debate. So the IAF teaches such mundane skills as how to plan and stick to an agenda, and how to resolve an issue.

No, the Alinsky connection was not the secret. At most it provided a useful frame of reference. Far more important were factors unique to San Antonio. There were breakdowns in city services that even the most sheltered Anglo could agree were inexcusable. There was a power vacuum in the city's leadership, so no one could mobilize to stop COPS when it was still vulnerable. Many COPS leaders like Andy Sarabia held civil service jobs and were immune to Anglo threats of economic retribution. San Antonio's ethnic minority had just become a numerical majority, so the old argument that Mexicans were powerless no longer had any validity. And most important, COPS had the Church.

It was as much a marriage of convenience as love at first sight. The Church has traditionally maintained a paternalistic attitude toward its Mexican American subjects. Only seven local Mexican American priests have been ordained in the San Antonio archdiocese in 250 years. Many priests never mastered Spanish, still the lingua franca on the West Side. Then, after Mao booted Belgian missionaries out of China, many came to the West Side in search of other downtrodden subjects. But by the seventies things were changing. Protestant denominations had been the great force for social reform during the civil rights fights of the sixties, but the Catholic Church was catching up. In San Antonio, as the West Side continued to deteriorate and young people moved to the North Side, it became obvious that the economic self-interest of the parish church lay in keeping the neighborhood up. San Antonio is not a rich archdiocese; there would be no help from the hierarchy. So COPS became not only good politics but also good religion.

The support of the Church was the crucial factor that got COPS started and kept it going. The Church was the only institution in the community that had the widespread allegiance of the people. It provided a financial base and a sense of permanence. It was a reservoir of leadership talent, and a way for people to keep in touch. But most of all, it gave COPS something no previous movement had had: a stamp of legitimacy. That is why even today the average COPS member would rather be led into battle by Father Albert Benavides, a fiery, immensely popular West Side priest, than any other COPS leader, even Gallego or Sarabia.

The role of the Church points the way to another of the reasons for COPS' success. The organization draws on the inherent strengths of the Mexican American community—qualities like loyalty, belief in basic values, and a love for family. COPS *is* a family, an extended family in the Mexican tradition. This pays off in unexpected ways: when COPS speakers approached the podium during early confrontations, the audience, without coaching, crowded around them to give moral support. *They* knew how awed their leaders were by symbols of power, but of course the council or the water board didn't; to them these tactics smacked of intimidation. That was fine with COPS —these moves became part of the game plan.

---

* No, the Yankees.

For all of its strengths and successes, COPS is approaching a critical phase in its history, one that may well test the ability of the organization to endure as a political force. Its leaders have chosen to tackle the most basic—and most elusive—of all issues in San Antonio: economic development. They have had enough of the traditional San Antonio wage scale, skewed toward the minimum wage and ranking far below the other big cities in the state. They want to bring high-paying industries to the city and they want them located near their neighborhoods, not far out on the North Side.

This will prove to be a very different fight than anything COPS has undertaken before. In the past the battle was in the political arena; COPS was dealing with people who at least nominally answered to them. There was always the ultimate weapon of the ballot box, as more than one candidate found out to his sorrow last spring. But in economic development the enemy is better insulated. At an October training session, COPS area leaders stood beneath a wall chart eight feet high listing the names and positions of the members of the elite Economic Development Foundation that is practically a roster of the San Antonio establishment. It includes bankers, downtown businessmen, and developers, who together have personally chipped in $1.5 million in the last three years to bring industry to San Antonio—mostly without success.

COPS leaders are convinced that the EDF, like the businessmen who ran off Henry Ford, prefers smaller industries that are harder to unionize and won't upset the wage scale. Cheap labor is also a useful selling point to counter fears of runaway utility bills. The EDF vigorously denies pushing cheap labor ("Who says that?" asks Tom Frost. "We don't. I've been there. That's the worst thing you can say. Plants want skilled labor"), but someone neglected to tell the EDF's consultant to soft-peddle the cheap labor issue. In a secret report COPS somehow managed to sneak a look at, the consultant warned the EDF "not to attract industries that would upset the existing wage ladder." All the evidence indicates that the EDF is following this advice to the letter. For example, the report carefully identifies the high-wage and low-wage sectors of the metal industry; one of the EDF's proudest acquisitions, Bakerline oil tool supplier, matches the description of a cheap-labor operation.

But the issue may be moot, says Frost. "Asking me if I want heavy industry is like asking a man dying of thirst in the desert if he'd like a beer when there isn't one for a thousand miles. Sure I'd like it, but we can't get it. That kind of industry locates near markets, transportation, and water, and we haven't got any of them."

COPS, of course, disagrees (and so, for that matter, do some of the hustlers on the EDF itself, like developer Jim Dement). But what galls COPS above all else is that the EDF, which is the primary group trying to attract business to the city, conducts all its business in secret. No one in the city outside of the membership has a voice in anything the EDF does. "It is our future they're determining," Gallego told the COPS training session, "and they should be determining it out in the open." So COPS is committed to bringing the EDF out of the closet.

That almost happened a year ago—or more precisely, COPS was invited into the closet. A well-intentioned EDF member offered to put up $20,000—then the price of two memberships—"so that underprivileged groups on the Mexican American West Side and the black East Side can become part of the economic efforts for progress." But the affair was bungled from the start. The offer was made in the press rather than in person; its tone was insulting; and it smacked of tokenism. Sarabia rejected the offer, also in the press, by announcing that "COPS is not for sale," and added scathingly, "By the way, we don't consider ourselves underprivileged, because we have the will to fight for our dignity. We think *they're* underprivileged."

Everything about the coming battle with the EDF points to a tough struggle. The issue is a hard one to grasp; it is hardly as easy to understand as, say, water in the streets. The first COPS training session did not go well; the area leaders were slow to respond to Gallego's attempts to draw out their feelings. Finally Sarabia, exasperated, stood up in the corner of the room. He scolded them for their lack of anger—some were even making jokes—and asked, "Don't you know what cheap labor means? They're talking about *you.* Our kids can't find a decent job here. All they talk about is going to Houston or Dallas." That subdued things for awhile, but the feeling still filled the room that this was going to be a long, long fight. One important stratagem of an organization like COPS is to keep morale up by pointing to a continuing series of successes. That is possible with drainage, but how do you show results in economic development? Even if COPS can remove EDF's cloak of secrecy, that still doesn't produce one plant or one job. The economic cards, as Frost suggests, may be stacked against the city—and even if they aren't, even if COPS succeeds as it has before, the rewards may not trickle down to the neighborhoods for a dozen years.

For once COPS may also have the wrong side of the timing. The organization is entering a transitional phase, with the original leaders gradually turning over the reins to new recruits. Perhaps it is too early to say, but the second generation doesn't appear to have the intensity or the ability of the first. Gallego and especially Sarabia are remarkable people who have an almost mystical empathy with their constituency. No one coming up seems to have that. The theory of organizations like COPS is that people grow with their responsibilities, so perhaps someone will develop. But some of the newer COPS people seem to lack that most basic of ingredients—anger. Maybe that anger is only possible for those who remember the beginning; maybe COPS has grown fat with too many successes.

The most serious threat to the future of COPS, though, is the one least within its control. It is the pace with which San Antonio is rushing toward ethnic politics. The Mexican political clique, shut off from power all these years, finally got a base when they took over the San Antonio School Board last April; their first action was to fire the district's longtime Anglo lawyers and replace them with Mexicans from their own crowd—who took exactly one month to raise the district's legal fees astronomically. The targets for 1978 include the district attorney's office and a northwest San Antonio state senatorial district. Then there are the true Mexican radicals, a small but disproportionately vocal segment of the community, who also have a power base in the form of a couple of council seats. To both groups, ethnic political control of the city is the primary issue, and the more noise they make about it, the more the North Side is coming to view that as the sole issue too. And even though that is the one thing COPS does *not* care about, it may be COPS that suffers most.

The first shots in the Second Battle of the Alamo could be fired in January, when the city votes on a bond issue that contains many of COPS' pet projects—too many, some North Side critics are already saying. The numbers aren't encouraging: despite the fact that San Antonio has become a majority Mexican American city, the bulk of the voter turnout is still concentrated on the North Side. That could be fatal to the bond program's chances, and developer Jim Dement, for one, doesn't think it has a hope of passage.

No matter how the vote turns out, ethnic tensions are sure to be exacerbated. What if COPS loses? Make that loses *again*, for a COPS-backed school bond proposal went down to defeat by less than a thousand votes last spring. When the crunch comes, will COPS vote issues or race—and if it sticks to issues, will anyone listen? San Antonio in all likelihood is in for some rough years ahead, and the direction it is moving does not augur well for COPS. In the ethnic politics of the late seventies and early eighties, the "radicals" of today may well become the conservatives of tomorrow.

But even if COPS never accomplishes another thing, its legacy is indelible. Long after time has dulled the recently laid concrete on the storm drains and sidewalks of the West Side, long after San Antonio has had its first Mexican American mayor, the repercussions of COPS will still be felt. For the real significance of COPS is not that it has changed streets but that it has changed people—its own people. There are for the first time ordinary folks on the West Side of San Antonio who do not see themselves as strangers in a strange land. Andy Sarabia, Beatrice Gallego, and a thousand others were awed the first time they set foot in city hall; now they are no longer prisoners of the myths and stereotypes that bound them up, and neither are their children.

One family active in COPS lives beside a drainage ditch on the South Side; even a moderate rain threatens their home and leaves water standing in the street. Late one evening this fall a politician and a friend stopped in front of the house to look at the tall grass that clogged the ditch and caused the flooding. The politician was pointing animatedly when a six-year-old boy emerged from the house, walked up to the strangers, and asked, "Are you COPS?"

Five years ago he would have meant something else. ♦

The Seeds of Discontent

ACORN's activists have a long row to hoe.

In August, a savings and loan company, Dallas Federal, received permission from the Federal Home Loan Bank Board to open a branch office in Longview. In November, an attorney then at Dallas Legal Services filed suit in U.S. District Court to force the board to reverse its ruling. The suit, still under litigation, accuses Dallas Federal of "red-lining," deliberately avoiding mortgage loans in predominantly minority, low-income neighborhoods. It was filed on behalf of Dallas ACORN, the Association of Community Organizations for Reform Now.

It was the kind of thing that happens every now and then in Dallas, the rearguard action that can occasionally be heard firing away against the heavy artillery of the Dallas success story. In a city distinguished by a remarkable absence of political activism among low-income or minority groups, Dallas ACORN, a nonpolitical defender of "the rights of low- to moderate-income consumers," has become a symbol of opposition to Dallas's enthusiastic embrace of headlong economic expansion.

Now a nationwide organization, ACORN emerged in Little Rock, Arkansas, in 1970, right on the cusp of the quixotic sixties and the pragmatic seventies. This may explain why ACORN sometimes seems tactically schizophrenic, contrasting tight organization and careful research of local issues with periodic outbursts of attention-getting stunts. But the formula has been sufficiently successful to attract 35,000 member families in 22 states (about 4500 of them in Texas). The organization has a full-time staff of two hundred, of whom all but a handful are in-the-field neighborhood organizers.

In 1975 Dallas ACORN organized and immediately began to grab headlines. Its members showed a flair for the dramatic—if not necessarily effective—gesture, such as paying their electric bills in pennies or presenting a "lie, cheat, and steal" game to the president of Dallas Power & Light at a rate hearing. But they also did their homework, and the issues they've addressed have evolved from banning peep shows in East Dallas and protecting trees to promoting mass transit and generic drugs and opposing freeway construction and the red-lining of low-income neighborhoods.

Dallas ACORN has 1600 member families in 22 neighborhood chapters concentrated in East Dallas and Oak Cliff, two youthful full-time staffers who get paid about $4500 a year, and headquarters in a white frame house just south of Ross Avenue. Despite the young staff and spirited tactics, it is not a youth-oriented organization. Most members are either senior citizens, middle-aged, or rapidly approaching middle age, and the issues they choose reflect the anxieties of low-income people in a city where, they feel, they are voices crying in the wilderness. At monthly meetings they devise strategies that range from demonstrations to canvassing to serving on civic boards.

ACORN paints a vivid and not entirely inaccurate picture of its opponents, who are perceived as an affluent few who dominate the body politic for their own gain. Particular targets include Mayor Bob Folsom, whose suburban real estate developments have made him wealthy, and homebuilder David Fox of Fox & Jacobs, a firm that is displacing inner-city residents to build Bryan Place, a batch of plush $120,000 town houses in the shadow of downtown. Then there are the city council, which ACORN says opposes it on most issues, the utilities that charge higher rates for smaller users, and the proposed freeways that would displace low-income neighborhoods. Faced with this panoply of power, ACORN is soberly realistic. "They're going to do what they want to do," said Eddie Jimmerson, Jr., a warehouse manager who lives near Bryan Place. "We know we're not going to change the whole world. We just want to stay in the arena."

Most of ACORN's local successes have been modest, like persuading the gas company not to discontinue service on Fridays. More sweeping victories have come on issues of concern to middle-income residents, like a $90 million bond package defeated in 1978 (which was trimmed considerably and passed a year later over ACORN's opposition) and the thwarted Roseland Parkway, a thoroughfare that would have cut through East Dallas neighborhoods that are being increasingly infiltrated by new, upwardly mobile homeowners. It seems clear that in a city where the delivery of basic services is good—relative to many Texas cities—and where neglect of lower-income neighborhoods has yet to become an embarrassment, a wider, politically unified base is necessary for substantial clout. But ACORN isn't moving in that direction. It does not endorse local political candidates, although the national organization did submit a "people's platform" to the Democratic party's national convention last summer —a gesture that, in light of Reagan's victory, appears doubly futile.

For now, the legal system seems to be Dallas ACORN's most effective forum. Current legal actions include a formal protest that blocked a six-lane thoroughfare that would have divided a Mexican American neighborhood near Harry Hines Boulevard; a complaint against allegedly discriminatory bus fare increases; attempts to force Parkland Hospital to spend capital improvement funds on neighborhood clinics for indigent patients; and the suit designed to halt Dallas Federal's Longview expansion.

The Dallas Federal suit shows what ACORN probably can—and can't—accomplish. When Dallas Federal applied for a Longview office in 1979, ACORN's attorneys made a study of the company's lending patterns. On the basis of those statistics, they concluded that Dallas Federal, after saturating the white, affluent North Dallas market, was bypassing minority neighborhoods in South Dallas and southeast Oak Cliff to seek more attractive markets in other cities. Citing the 1977 Community Reinvestment Act, which charges "regulated financial institutions" with the "affirmative obligation to meet the continuing credit needs of the local communities in which they are chartered," the lawyers filed a protest with the bank board on behalf of Dallas ACORN. The board rejected that protest, and ACORN filed suit.

Here history seems to be repeating itself. In 1977 attorneys representing ACORN filed suit against Texas Federal Savings and Loan (formerly First Federal) for discriminatory red-lining. The U.S. Justice Department entered the case on behalf of ACORN, and after a secret settlement the suit was finally dismissed in June 1979. Because of legal niceties no one at ACORN will claim that they had anything to do with the settlement, but the following spring Texas Federal opened a new home loan counseling office in West Dallas with ACORN members acting as advisers. Similarly, Dallas Federal recently applied for a branch in South Dallas.

Whether such isolated changes can save Dallas's low- to moderate-income neighborhoods from decay or the encroachment of more affluent homeowners remains to be seen. But for most ACORN members, any sign of victory is important. "What we are doing right now is saying, 'Look, fellows, you've at least got to give us some window dressing,' " says one ACORN attorney. "But I think if you can move these institutions even a very small amount, there can be a snowball effect when the people realize that they do have power."

In the long run, however, the real key to ACORN's power may be the extent to which its concerns are adopted by the middle-income families who are coming back to economically marginal neighborhoods as the congestion and remoteness of the suburbs makes the inner city desirable once again. And until these middle-class people decide that unequal utility rates, poor community health services, predatory freeways, and expensive, inadequate mass transit are their problems too, Dallas ACORN will remain an idea ahead of its time.

Offensive Weapon

Panhandle farmers gird up to fight the M-X missile.

One blustery April day, just over a hundred farmers and ranchers and environmentalists—some in business suits and others in gimme caps and work-worn denim—shuffled into the Amarillo Civic Center's cinder-block meeting room, where five bleary-eyed men in Air Force blues were waiting for them. This was one of the Air Force's early stops on a whirlwind public relations tour to sell the M-X missile system: a $33.8 billion plan to plow up 147,000 acres of the Staked Plains and plant a crop of two hundred mobile intercontinental ballistic missiles (ICBMs). Don Fortenberry, a burly Friona farmer, stood vigil at the auditorium's entrance, passing out leaflets hurriedly composed by farmers and ranchers who oppose tearing up the Golden Spread, which produces 25 per cent of this country's food and fiber. Fortenberry's home and farm lie smack in the middle of the proposed "nukeplex." "I've planted one thousand trees. My life's work has gone into it," he said plaintively. "Can those be moved?"

When word first got out last year that the Air Force was casting its eye on the Panhandle as a site for the M-X, farmers and ranchers organized, some of them for the first time in their lives, to oppose what they see as no less than the destruction of a way of life. The Air Force actually prefers to put the M-X machine in the desolate Great Basin of Nevada and Utah, where the federal government already owns the land. But hundreds of residents from that area stormed preliminary hearings with their protests, forcing the Air Force to turn to Texas–New Mexico as a serious alternative.

The Texas Wheat Producers and Corn Growers associations testified alongside environmental activists and students. This is not to say that the farmers were comfortable about being there. In fact, "associating with them peaceniks" at the Lubbock hearing left Carl King of the Corn Growers with such a bitter taste in his mouth that he asked another farmer to pinch-hit for him in Amarillo. But despite the discomfort it's causing, the M-X issue is one that environmentalists and rock-ribbed conservatives can see eye to eye on.

To sow the M-X in Texas and New Mexico, 30,000 construction workers would have to cut a giant swath through precious farmland and ranchland in a 33-county area bounded by Amarillo, Dalhart, and Clovis, New Mexico. Cranes and bulldozers would prepare the way for two hundred missile clusters, each with 23 shelters spaced about a mile apart along a six- to ten-mile roadway. Once the system was completed (it would take ten years and 3000 cubic yards of concrete to construct), a 180-foot long, five-hundred-ton Transporter truck would trundle along each roadway, carrying a launcher and a missile armed with ten independently targetable warheads. The Transporter would stop at each shelter on the loop, secretly depositing the missile in one of them. This is the Air Force's version of the hydrogen fusion shell game, a massive subterfuge to prevent Soviet intelligence from knowing exactly where among the 4600 shelters to aim their missiles in a surprise first strike. If it is played out in Texas, the M-X will supplant wheat and barley and milo as the Panhandle's major crop.

So scores of skeptical citizens showed up in Amarillo to catch the M-X road show. The Air Force brass kicked off the session—held to get reactions to its third in a $23 million series of environmental impact studies—with a slide show and a candy-coated spiel designed to bring disbelievers into the fold. "To maintain the balance of power," a fresh-faced officer said urgently, "we must move swiftly." (Of course, it will take ten years to build the M-X, but that's beside the point.) A list of "impacts" flashed onto the screen, among them depletion of water from the already wanting Ogallala Aquifer, the unavoidable uprooting of 1400 families and removal of thousands of acres of farmland from production, and the boom and bust caused by bringing in an army of construction workers and their families who will leave once the job is finished. The narrator dismissed these problems with the vague assurance that "the long-term benefits [jobs and an initial economic boom] could override the short-term impact." His audience was not convinced.

Torn between their deeply felt patriotism and their fierce commitment to the countryside, local speakers bent over backward to make the Air Force boys feel welcome despite their dubious mission. "We're proud of the fine job y'all are doing for us" was often the preface to the residents' expressions of concern about living in a nuclear bull's-eye. Many of their remarks were good-humored, if pointed: "I'm not too crazy about becoming part of a nuclear sponge," grumbled one crusty farmer, "but with our cheap-food policy I'm too poor to move."

What bothered the local people most was that the Air Force would even consider desecrating prime farmland. M. C. Osborn, a towering farmer-rancher dressed in business suit, Stetson, and fancy cowboy boots, patiently informed the military men that he represented an array of organizations, including the Texas Wheat Producers, Grain Sorghum Producers, numerous soil and water conservation districts, and cattle associations—about two or three million people. "This is one of the greatest food-producing areas in the world," Osborn argued. "Parmer and Deaf Smith counties are the two leading cattle-feeding areas in the entire United States. They are also the two leading agricultural production areas, having the highest corn, cotton, grain sorghum, wheat, and barley production per acre. That's why this area is called the Golden Spread. What you're proposing is an absolute nightmare."

One by one, people stepped up to the microphone to tell the Air Force to dump the project elsewhere. House Speaker Billy Clayton, who farms in Lamb County and represents the region, sent a message via State Representative Chip Staniswalis: put it in Nevada. But as one young man whispered audibly to his friend, "We all know who's going to determine where it goes—Senator Laxalt." Paul Laxalt, a senator from Nevada and one of Reagan's closest advisers, opposes having the M-X in his home state. But if the M-X comes to Texas, the men in blue will have to haggle over land and water rights.

Colonel Bill Sims, an articulate spokesman for the Air Force, stressed that if the M-X does wind up in Texas the government will pay full compensation to farmers who lose all or part of their land. Sims also tried to allay fears about the parched High Plains' declining water table—which is falling in some parts by two feet per year—with assurances that the military would pay for water rights. The M-X will sap 78,000 acre-feet of water over ten years of construction (enough to cover 78,000 acres with a foot of water) from the Ogallala Aquifer. Sims's words were small comfort to farmers who dread the fast-approaching day when the well runs dry.

Almost the only speakers ready to welcome the M-X unreservedly were one American Legion stalwart and a representative of the local pipe fitters' union, who heaved a sigh and scolded, "Everybody wants a strong national defense, but they just don't want it here. I represent about six thousand construction workers," he continued, directing his speech to the Air Force and away from the glares of the audience. "There *are* some people who will support the Air Force." The pipe fitter's sentiments were echoed at later hearings in Clovis, New Mexico, where a group of businessmen and the city council wholly embraced the M-X, not seeing the bust for the boom. But Amarillo residents still remember what happened when the Strategic Air Command closed its base and abandoned the community in 1968; city fathers had to scramble to lure industry in and salvage their economy.

Toward the end of the hearing a woman asked, "What kind of attack would you expect?" She wore blue jeans and had a child strapped to her back. The child's presence wasn't lost on the audience or on the military men.

"Why," said Lieutenant Colonel Tom Holycross solemnly, "the purpose of M-X is to deter attack. I tell you with the fullest integrity I have that the M-X isn't to have war but to deter nuclear war."

People shifted in their seats, and there were some snickers. One gray-haired man jumped up and, as former CIA director Stansfield Turner did recently, shot holes in the idea that the M-X shell game would stop the Soviets from knocking out our missiles. He echoed Turner's suggestion to keep the missiles moving—by sea or air. "There's no sense destroying pristine prairie farmland," said H. T. Brooks, "for a system that will be archaic before it's finished."

The outcome will, of course, depend on President Reagan and Secretary of Defense Caspar Weinberger and, ultimately, Congress. By late summer they will decide just where to put this hot potato: Nevada and Utah, Texas and New Mexico, all four states, or nowhere. A soft-spoken history teacher hit upon yet another alternative: "If Washington wants this thing so badly, put it in the Potomac Valley."

ONE WOMAN'S TINY PROBLEM CONFRONTS DALLAS CITY HALL

by John Bloom

Everybody knows Dallas is the city that works. So why did it have so much trouble with a noisy air conditioner?

The adjustors meet every other Tuesday in a place I have come to regard as a kind of civic cathedral. First-time visitors to the Dallas City Council chambers, which the adjustors usurp twice a month for their meetings, are sometimes so bewildered and intimidated upon beholding the room that they ask permission of the receptionist before entering. The chamber was not constructed for the timid: it reaches some fifty feet from floor to ceiling, with a bank of corporate-green opera chairs descending amphitheatrically toward the adjustors' swivel chairs, which are ranged in a half-moon around a speaker's lectern. To the person who stands at the lectern, only the heads of the adjustors are visible. The rest of them is concealed behind a high gray panel, the better for the adjustors to keep the glare away from their closed-circuit TV screens. Above them, perhaps twelve feet in diameter and dominating the scene like an extraterrestrial icon, is a five-pointed star of purest white, part of the seal of the City of Dallas.

On May 26, 1981, the aforementioned adjustors, more commonly known as the Board of Adjustment, gathered in regular session at 1:56 p.m. The time could be verified by reference to any of the dozen or so digital-readout clocks in the room, from the one at the lectern to the over-sized one just below the slide projectionist's peephole at the rear. Waiting in the opera chairs were perhaps thirty people, one of whom called across the room to a friend, breaking the hush and drawing stares. Clearly something Very Important was about to occur. At two o'clock the chairman of the Board of Adjustment, Jay Hauteman by name, began the meeting by quietly reading a statement of principles into the microphone (with so much technology, gavels are passé), among which the most important was this: "No decision of this board shall establish a precedent."

Though few people in the room were aware of it, one of the most ancient forms of civil procedure had just been convened. If this had been the tenth century, the petitioners would have brought their families, and the ones with the most illustrious reputations would undoubtedly have prevailed. In the fifteenth, those who thought the law too harsh would have appealed to one man, probably a baron who doubled as a justice of the peace, for a special dispensation. Even today, if this had been, say, Chicago or New Orleans instead of Dallas, the proper avenue of appeal would have been through the ward committeeman. For the people gathered today in the council chambers all had one thing in common: they believed, for one reason or another, that the law should not apply to them. In the eyes of the city, these were favor seekers.

It has been recognized in almost all nations and times that the granting of favors and exceptions is a necessary part of government, that justice strictly applied will eventually result in injustice, and that the letter of the law and its spirit are rarely the same. Even the most cynical machine politicians of the past probably believed there was some higher good—like peace and harmony—to be gained by rewarding the few, even at the expense of the many. In Dallas, however, as in many other Texas cities, the leaders have taken the process of granting favors out of the hands of politicians and vested it in a group of citizens: the ubiquitous civic board. For matters dealing with taxation, that group takes the form of the Equalization Board. In this case, for matters dealing with the Comprehensive Zoning Ordinance, which is virtually the Ten Commandments of Dallas government, the operative body is the Board of Adjustment. Those who feel wronged come here, and here their grievances are settled with a final yes or no. The board may or may not decide to give a reason for its decision; nothing the board has done before need affect what it does today; no one—not even the city council that appointed the board—can overrule it. Unless one goes to the formal courts, this is where the buck absolutely stops.

The Board of Adjustment is quaintly known as "an autonomous body"—a group of five people who do whatever they please. It has been established that way for a purpose, of course. Dallas is the largest city in the nation to use a city manager form of government, and the purpose of letting a manager run the city is to insulate the system from politics. The Board of Adjustment carries that concept even further. By appointing a group of leading citizens who are answerable to no one, the city hopes to achieve an impartiality beyond the reach of both politicians and bureaucrats. Since these board members aren't paid salaries, who could possibly question their motives?

Prelude:
The Parade of Petitioners

Having established the ground rules, Hauteman—who is a real estate broker when he's not chairing the board—called for the first case. A gray-suited, bespectacled man rose on behalf of Cadillac Fairview, a huge Canadian development company. The chairman referred to the man as "Bob," and Bob referred to the chairman as "Jay," and they seemed to know each other well.

"Bob," said Jay, "did you talk to anyone with the city about the problems we had last week?"

"Yes, Jay," said Bob, "I interfaced with several of the city departments, and I discussed this with both Don and Doug in Urban Planning. I want to emphasize that this particular project is in joint-use development between ourselves and the city."

"I understand," said Jay. "By the way, what kind of trees are those on your diagram there? Live oaks or what?"

"Let me see," said Bob, referring to a huge architectural drawing he had brought along to set in front of the lectern. "Yes, those are live oaks."

Another adjustor asked to be recognized. "I hope you realize that we can't approve a site plan that doesn't have an adequate legend," she said. "We didn't know whether those trees were four feet or eight feet or live oaks or bushes or what."

Still another adjustor chimed in. "There seems to be some discrepancy between our staff briefing this morning and what we're seeing here."

"A lot of these problems," said Bob, "are caused simply by our unfamiliarity with procedure. We're sort of the new kids in town at this point."

"We understand that," said Jay. After a few more minutes of banter, the Cadillac Fairview request—whatever it was, since the audience could only guess at its substance—was approved unanimously.

Once Bob's request was dispensed with, the parade of petitioners began in earnest. The first was a well-groomed, boyish attorney named Rick Addison, appearing for a man who wanted to convert the garage of his Oak Lawn residence into a hobby shop. The board was not kindly disposed to the idea. Adjustor W. A. Bonds, a balding man in a light yellow suit, a builder by profession, started the questioning: "We're a hardship board, Mr. Addison. What's your hardship?" The attorney pointed out that the garage was very old and had been built before the more stringent building regulations of the mid-sixties were passed; since it was right up against the property line, he couldn't rebuild it there without obtaining a variance on its placement. Adjustor Michael W. Brown wouldn't accept that argument. Brown, an architect with aquiline features and a bushy moustache who wears his hair in a modified pompadour, is considered the toughest questioner on the board. "That is called a nonconforming use," said Brown. "We're trying to eliminate those." Finally the attorney, apparently surprised by Brown's vehemence, offered to modify his building plan and return in two weeks. The board agreed.

Next came James Turney, bearded and bespectacled, wearing a light jacket with open collar. If ever a man seemed to have a hardship, it was Turney. He patiently explained to the board that his family had operated General Trading Post, a kind of ghetto flea market frequented by blacks and Mexican Americans, at the same location, a decaying industrial area just east of downtown, ever since 1963. There about a hundred merchants regularly sold merchandise like used sewing machines, velvet paintings, old records, and the like, but unless the board found in his favor, he would have to close. The building inspector had ruled that he was in violation of zoning laws that forbid open-air stalls.

A disinterested observer might conclude, as Turney had, that a zoning regulation ignored by the city for eighteen years could not possibly result in the clos-

ing of one hundred small businesses simply because a building inspector had at last recognized the error or, more likely, ceased to look the other way. Turney was wrong.

"Just because you get away with something for eighteen years," said Hauteman, "doesn't mean it's legal."

"And even if it was legal eighteen years ago," said Brown, repeating his theme, "we're still trying to eliminate nonconforming uses."

And at that point Brown made a motion to deny the application. There was no debate whatsoever. A vote was taken, and the motion passed four to one. The dissenter was the only woman on the board that day, an interior decorator named Diana Cobb. No reason for the vote was given, except what could be surmised from the questions. James Turney had just learned what "autonomous" really means.

Next came Michael Green of 10239 Deermont Trail, and the basis of his request and the details of its resolution will forever be lost to history. Before he could even open his mouth, an adjustor moved to approve his petition. The motion passed unanimously by voice vote, and Green sat down.

Then came Pedro Aguirre, accompanied by his wife, Carmen. He explained that he needed approval to build an "outdoor living room" onto his house. Since several of the adjustors apparently didn't know exactly what an outdoor living room was, Aguirre launched into a baroque explanation of "our long-range plan for our home," which had begun in 1965 with the purchase of a lot in East Dallas and had continued for sixteen years. Unfortunately, Aguirre had ended up with two buildings instead of one—he had never built the connecting rooms—and now the building inspector said he couldn't build his outdoor living room to connect the two parts of his residence. "If any of you have seen the Spanish-style homes in Mexico," said Aguirre, "then you know that this is traditional."

Brown, Bonds, and Hauteman didn't immediately respond to this presentation but huddled among themselves behind the high gray panel until finally Bonds asked Aguirre if he would agree to a few minor modifications. He said he would, the matter was put to a vote, and the first outdoor living room in the history of the Dallas building code was approved.

There were several other petitioners that day, but the most intriguing by far was a woman named Vesta Cawley. Mrs. John Cawley, as she was listed in the formal petition, was an attractive woman in her early thirties dressed in a stylish white silk dress. Unlike most of the others, she spoke from prepared remarks. Her voice trembled at first, as though she feared she wouldn't be understood, but then she settled into a clear, understated recitation of her grievances and her hopes for relief.

As the adjustors listened, they seemed, for once, wholly perplexed.

April Fools' Day: But the Noise Is No Joke

Vesta Cawley's story is being told here because she, like most people, is neither a politician nor a bureaucrat nor a professional complainer of the sort that frequent city council meetings. I could have chosen a thousand other people to write about; I picked her more or less at random. She had, in the great scheme of things, a very small problem, a problem so small that it mattered to almost no one except her. But since it involved the ancient, universally recognized right to peace and quiet, it should not have been small to the City of Dallas. Vesta Cawley's search for a solution led her directly to the city hall that touts itself and is sometimes touted by others (most recently *Time* magazine) as the last urban bureaucracy that really works. For Vesta Cawley, as for most people, this probably would be the one and only time that she would need to call on that bureaucracy. I wanted to see whether that bureaucracy worked.

Vesta Cawley would later recall, with only mild amusement, that the problem began on April Fools' Day, 1980. Everything else in her life seemed to be in order. She was recently, and very happily, married. Her husband had just left Burgess Industries to form his own computer software company. She was making a nice salary as a project administrator at Frito-Lay. Her seven-year-old son by a previous marriage was doing wonderfully at a neighborhood elementary school. And best of all, they had just moved into the house of their dreams.

It had been a compromise—she preferred the northern suburbs, while her husband was more used to the pace of the inner city—but now both of them were sold on the big cream-colored house with muted gold trim in East Dallas. It was an example of what is known as Prairie School architecture, and it was located in the up-and-coming Munger Place Historic District. At first the Cawleys had been hesitant. The area was growing in respectability, but the crime rate was still higher than average, the result of jamming expensive restoration jobs right next to slums. Swiss Avenue, the most opulent of the restored Dallas neighborhoods, was only two blocks away, but in between were the stolid brick apartment buildings of Gaston Avenue. Once the grandest residential street in the city, Gaston was now a mixture of old apartments, down-at-the-heels duplexes, and convenience stores. The Cawleys' house was seventy years old and situated on Junius Street, halfway between the apartments and the low-income areas, and, well, it was a gamble.

The house was too beautiful to pass up,

though. For twenty years it had stood vacant (the neighborhood kids thought it was haunted), and then in 1979 someone had realized its value and fully restored it. Once used to house four families, it was returned to its original design and painted its original colors, as historical district codes require. With its pillared porch, the extra bedroom over the garage, the larger-than-average back yard, and the park and tiny shopping area directly across the street, it was one of the best houses around. John and Vesta already had great plans, including the redecoration of the bedroom over the garage and the addition of a swimming pool with deck, where they hoped to do some entertaining, as well as enjoy the use of their back yard during the summer months.

But those plans came to an abrupt halt on April 1, 1980, a Saturday. John had left for the office to put in a few hours overtime and Vesta was working in the back yard, when suddenly a great metallic rumbling noise—she later described it as a kind of miniature explosion—pierced the silence of the spring afternoon. "It startled me so that you could have picked me off the ground," she said.

She went to the gate at the back of the yard and opened it, and there she saw the culprit: a two-story industrial air conditioner behind one of the apartment buildings on Gaston, directly across the alley from her house. Flustered, she went into the house and quickly dialed John at the office. When he came on the line, she said simply, "Listen to this," and held the receiver up to the window.

"What is that?" he said.

"That," she answered, "is the air conditioner across the alley. I guess they just turned it on for the season."

"I don't even have to come home," he said, "to tell that that's too noisy. It's at least ten or twenty decibels too loud."

This was one of those rare occasions when an ordinary citizen knew what he was talking about. John's previous employer, Burgess Industries, had occasionally done work in the area of noise control, so he was familiar with the federal standards. When he returned home that day, his first impression was confirmed. The racket was too loud for sleeping with the windows open—the air conditioner fan was, by chance, at the exact height of the Cawleys' upstairs windows. It wasn't so much the volume of the machine that bothered them—although it was every bit as loud as a very noisy restaurant in which conversation becomes difficult—but the fact that the noise was not continuous. As any noise expert will tell you, continuous noise is always more tolerable than discontinuous noise, which is what makes airports and noisy mufflers so exasperating. The air conditioner cycled on and off about every five minutes —just long enough for the Cawley family to get accustomed to the quiet before the rumble started again.

On the following Monday, Vesta wasted no time. The first thing she wanted to do was find out what rights she had under the law. So she called the Environmental Protection Agency, which referred her to the City of Dallas Action Center, which referred her to Air Pollution Control, which referred her to something called the Environmental Assessment Program, which referred her, finally, to a person named Fred Barnes.

Fred Barnes is a jovial man with a bushy moustache and square-rimmed glasses who wears mint-green pants and paisley ties to the office. He likes his work, often staying well past the four-thirty closing time, and ingratiates himself with the cleaning women by sometimes giving them presents like giant cellophane bags of popcorn. To the confusion of some people who know who he is, Barnes works not at the stylish new city hall, designed by I. M. Pei and featured in all the slick tourist brochures, but in one of the buildings where the real work of the bureaucracy goes on: 1500 West Mockingbird. The Mockingbird Annex, a low-slung brown and white converted warehouse across the street from Sigels Liquor Store, is the home of a small army of city employees. It is full of long, cavernous, squeaky-clean corridors distinguished only by their little square, white signs with black letters, which point the way to warrens and cubbyholes deep in the bowels of the building. Somewhere within that maze is a tile-floored room full of drafting tables and metal cabinets, and beyond that room is a cubicle with a window, and through that window, on most days, you can see Fred Barnes. Over his right shoulder hangs a map of the world.

Fred Barnes is an important enough man to have three titles. He is not only the environmental health officer of the City of Dallas but also the acting assistant director of the Environmental Health and Conservation Department and the manager of the Environmental Assessment Program, the Air Pollution Program, and the Environmental Health Laboratory. It was in his role as manager of the Environmental Assessment Program that he took a phone call on April 3, 1980, from one Vesta Cawley, of 5301 Junius, pertaining to a complaint of excessive noise.

Fred Barnes loves to talk noise. It is, he will tell you, one of his favorite fields of study. He is convinced that urban noise causes stress and heart problems to an extent not generally recognized by the public, and one of his earnest desires is to make people realize just how noisy the world is. Still, when Vesta Cawley called he was able to be sympathetic to her problem without really being encouraging. It was not uncommon, he warned her, to find that people "turned a deaf ear to noise." He told her that even if she was absolutely right about the noise level of the air conditioner, she would probably have a long fight ahead of her. And then he explained that all he could do was measure the noise and tell her whether it was indeed excessive. Then the matter would be out of his hands.

Vesta agreed that that was a good start, and so Barnes dispatched J. W. Fowler, an inspector for the Environmental Assessment Program, to determine the noise level of the air conditioner. Fowler got out to the Cawley house within three days (usually Barnes can promise a 24-hour response time), and his measurements showed a clear violation: the air conditioner registered at about 75 decibels, whereas the city's standards were 56 decibels in the daytime and 49 at night.

Barnes called Vesta to give her the good news—she was right about the excessive noise—and the bad—his agency had no powers of enforcement. If she wanted anything done about the problem, she would have to call a man named Sam Harting, in the Building Inspection Department; Barnes would send Harting a letter.

It was some measure of Sam Harting's position in life that he occupied an office a mere twenty feet from the front entrance of the Mockingbird Annex, an office large enough to contain a dozen or so wall decorations, including a calendar from the Ridge Tool Company, several joke posters, a yellowed map of the United States, and a picture of his family. Harting has only one title, but it's a good one: assistant building official of the Building Inspection Division of the Housing and Urban Rehabilitation Department. A 23-year city employee, Harting has thinning hair and a moustache and favors white highlight stitching on his shirts. He received Vesta Cawley's phone call and Fred Barnes's noise report at almost precisely the same time.

At this point there is some discrepancy as to exactly what transpired. According to Vesta Cawley, Harting responded as follows: "Yeah, I've got the report, but I've got *important* things to do here. I don't have the time or the staff for noise."

Sam Harting remembers it differently: "I don't remember exactly what I said. I talked to her several times. I don't regard noise complaints as any different from any other complaint."

The result was the same: nothing happened. Harting did send a man to the apartments, but he gave him instructions to try "voluntary compliance" first. That meant the owner would suggest solutions to the problem, allowing Harting to go back to the more pressing matters of building inspection. For a week or so, Vesta awaited a call and expected a quick solution. Then, growing impatient, she called Fred Barnes again and asked him what to do. He suggested that they try another noise reading and again sent an inspector to determine the decibel level. Again the inspector detected a clear violation. Again Barnes sent a report to Harting. Again nothing happened.

Six Months Later: There Goes the Back Yard

In the meantime the Cawleys had begun to alter their lifestyle. For one thing, they scrapped all plans for building the swimming pool or refurbishing the garage apartment, at least until this was resolved. It would be impossible to converse around the pool, and it would be almost impossible to sleep over the garage, since that room was much closer to the air conditioner than was the main house. Then, when it became apparent that no quick and easy solution was in sight, they closed the windows of the house for the summer and—reluctantly—installed a window air conditioner in their bedroom. "We finally had to use noise to fight noise," said John Cawley. "The window unit gave off a continuous noise that drowned out the intermittent noise of the apartment air conditioner."

It occurred to Vesta that perhaps a sympathetic politician could prod the bureaucracy into action. So the next person she called was her city councilman, a young Princeton-educated attorney named Lee Simpson who had just been elected on a platform that included neighborhood revitalization issues. It hadn't taken Simpson long to learn the limitations of his job. He told Vesta frankly that he could do very little to help her; a councilman wasn't allowed even to *speak* to a city employee below the assistant city manager level—which limits his contact to the top five employees—and about all he could do was write a letter like any other citizen and hope his name carried extra weight. Vesta later talked to a mayor's aide who had indeed received a letter from Simpson; apparently the mayor can't do anything more than a councilman can, because the aide had passed the letter along to the city attorney's office.

Vesta was beginning to think of the city bureaucracy as an aimless organism without any clear idea of its own powers. Having dealt now with two city departments, a councilman, and the mayor's office, she turned with unflagging persistence down another avenue: before winding further through the city bureaucracy, she decided to see what the owner of the apartments intended to do in the now unlikely event that he or she was given a citation.

The apartments in question represented one of the nicer units on Gaston, a two-story white brick building with wooden portcullises on the balconies and attractive landscaping along the street. The sign out front read "The Mandalay," and beneath this name was a phone number. Vesta picked up the phone and dialed.

When Betty Hibbler answered that number, Vesta thought for a moment that all her worries were at an end. It was positively one of the kindest voices she

had ever heard, and after Vesta explained the problem the woman became most cooperative. Betty Hibbler was not the owner—in fact, Vesta didn't even know who the owner was, but Hibbler did have some authority. In fact, one of her workmen had already told her that a city building inspector had visited the Mandalay apartments, so she was not altogether unprepared. She promised to have workmen take a look at the air conditioner and see what could be done.

Shortly thereafter, the workmen did do a few things—washed out the unit and greased the fan belts—and the result was a small lessening of the noise. Then, after three or four weeks, even that improvement disappeared, and the unit returned to its former cantankerous self. Still frustrated, and wondering whether anything else was being done, Vesta called Betty Hibbler again. Again she was sympathetic and agreed to draw up plans to either move or redirect the air conditioner in such a way as to draw the noise away from the Cawley property.

For a while Vesta had some hope of a change. Then Hibbler confessed that the job was bigger than she had originally thought, and that in order to do *anything* to the unit, it would have to be shut down for two weeks. Since summer was imminent—the summer of the great heat wave—it would be economic suicide to shut off the air conditioner for that long. The tenants would never stand for it. Could the Cawleys possibly wait until fall for the changes to be made? Of course, said Vesta—and all the home improvement plans were put off until the following year.

There is a point at which mere practical complaints take on moral and philosophical overtones. Vesta wanted the air conditioner fixed, but she also wanted the city to listen to her. She had a very mundane complaint on one level—it's too noisy around here—but on another level she was talking about a fundamental right, long established in the common law, of "peace."

Vesta first started thinking about rights and wrongs sometime around September 30, 1980, one day before the six-month anniversary of the problem. She didn't want to be pushy, but she did want to know whether the owners of the Mandalay apartments intended to go through with their promise to shut down the unit and move it so that the noise went elsewhere. And she wondered, coincidentally, what Sam Harting had done with her request for enforcement of the city's noise ordinance.

To find out, she called her old friend Fred Barnes. Discreetly, he told her that the matter had grown a little more complex. A letter had arrived at city hall from one Betty Hibbler, who was—surprise!—petitioning the city to revise its noise standards. And soon Vesta found out why. When she called Betty Hibbler she was told that the workmen had finally told her that they could just *possibly* get the noise level at her property line down to 56 decibels, the daytime limit, but there was no way they could get it down to the nighttime limit of 49. If the city would change its standards to correspond to Environmental Protection Agency guidelines—55 decibels day *and* night—then the Mandalay unit might be in the ball park. Otherwise, there was no chance.

There was no way Vesta could have known it at the time, but Betty Hibbler had taken it upon herself to let Mayor Folsom know what was going on. It so happened that the owner of the Mandalay Apartments and Hibbler's boss, Arnold Ablon, had done business in the past with Folsom, and Folsom himself was an apartment owner. "It wasn't such a big thing if we just had to fix this one air conditioner," said Hibbler later, "but for an owner who has apartments throughout the city, the implications could be a little scary. I was right, too. Mayor Folsom had no idea this ordinance was even on the books."

Meanwhile Vesta decided to check up on that long-ago letter from Lee Simpson that was passed through the system, so she turned her attention to the city attorney's office. The attorneys would have to decide whether the city's noise standards were reasonable or not in the event of any legal challenge, and they would also be able to rule on whether Vesta's plea for enforcement of the ordinance was valid. Miraculously, after explaining her problem to several people in that office, Vesta got the city attorney himself, Lee Holt, on the phone. And Holt not only took an interest in her problem but promised to inspect the air conditioner personally and have another noise reading done. "Now, I don't know how effective this is going to be," he finally said, "and it might take some time."

"How much time?" asked Vesta.

"Would you mind waiting four or five days?"

"Heavens, no!" she shrieked. That night when she got home from work she exclaimed to John, "I've found my dream man at last!"

Lee Holt did take the time to inspect the air conditioner, but shortly thereafter he left for a governmental conference in San Antonio and turned the entire case over to a young attorney named Barry Knight.

Two weeks after the epochal conversation with Holt, Knight called to tell her that nothing could be done about her problem. The reason: he had researched the records and discovered that the apartment building in question had been constructed in 1962, whereas the noise ordinance had been passed in 1965. Hence the building and its air conditioner were "grandfathered," and the noise ordinance didn't apply in this case.

"But Betty Hibbler told me the air conditioner was moved in 1971," said Vesta.

"We would have no way of knowing that," he said, "because you are not required to file a building permit to replace or move an air conditioner."

Later I asked Harting why he hadn't simply asked Betty Hibbler whether the unit had been moved. He said that her admission, even if true, would not be acceptable proof. He needed a city document. "As far as we're concerned," said Harting, echoing Knight, "we never should have even taken this case, because those apartment people have rights that existed *before* that ordinance."

Even after all this time, Vesta and Hibbler were still conversing more or less regularly, although the tone of their calls had changed somewhat. At one point Hibbler said that, frankly, she thought it was unfair for the apartment owner to have to spend any large amount of money—she mentioned the figure $10,000—just to satisfy one homeowner. Another time she said she simply didn't believe the noise-level readings made by the city, since it didn't sound noisy to her. But eventually the two women decided that a compromise would be in order; that way no one would have to deal with the city anymore.

Actually Vesta was more than happy to accept the 56-decibel level, which the air conditioner experts said was possible, and she told Hibbler as much. In fact, the two women seemed on the verge of reaching a totally satisfactory resolution of the entire problem. All Vesta asked for was a reasonable decrease in the noise. All Hibbler asked for was a reasonable assurance that if she did spend the money to reduce the noise level to 56, there would be no more complaints.

In order to get that assurance, Vesta called both Barry Knight and Sam Harting to tell them that a compromise had been reached. You can imagine her shock, then, when Harting said, "Don't touch that unit. If you do the slightest thing to it, you'll have to bring it into full compliance with the ordinance."

Twelve Months Later: Off to See the Wizards

On March 27, 1981, Vesta Cawley finally decided to go for broke. She had tried other things. She had written more letters. She had spoken to the president of the Munger Place Homeowners Association, but he told her that the association could sponsor only causes that affected more than one family. She had even called the *Dallas Times Herald* "Action Line" in the hope it could do something for her. (Little did she know that "Action Line" sent her complaint directly to the City of Dallas Action Center, which routed copies to three people: Fred Barnes, Sam Harting, and Barry Knight.) And then one night, just a few days before the first anniversary of that day when she heard the air conditioner rumble into action, she said to

John, "I'm going down to pay my hundred dollars."

Everyone had told her to do this. Fred Barnes suggested it. Barry Knight echoed his suggestion. Even Sam Harting thought it was an excellent idea. "Go to the Board of Adjustment," they all said, as though pointing Dorothy and Toto toward the Emerald City. There was only one thing: it would cost $100 if she wanted the five wizards on the board to listen to her problem.

Vesta squawked about the money. "Why should *I* pay," she asked, "to get the city to enforce its own ordinance?"

Because, she was told, the board is doing people a favor by letting them present reasons for getting special treatment under the law. At this point the system had gone far beyond questions of right and wrong. What we were talking about was a special favor for Vesta Cawley.

So Vesta swallowed her pride and drove over to the Mockingbird Annex to pay her $100. There she was told that she would also need to prepare five copies of the site plan of her house and the apartment building, complete with property lines and parking spaces, and a clear transparency for the projectionist at the hearing. This she dutifully did, copying out the site plan by hand and paying a friend to do the transparency for her.

Then she was told to wait two months because the Board of Adjustment was busy.

Fourteen Months Later: "Don't Call Us..."

After sitting through the hearings for Bob from Cadillac Fairview, the hobby shop attorney, the proprietor of the ghetto flea market, the mysterious Mr. Green, and Pedro Aguirre of the outdoor living room, John and Vesta were highly encouraged. From their seats in the third row they had studied carefully the arguments of each adjustor, looking for the prejudices that might give a clue as to how their case would be handled. The encouraging thing was this: all of the adjustors, and especially Michael Brown the architect, seemed to be very hard on so-called nonconforming uses (or grandfathered properties). "Whenever possible," said Brown at one point, "our policy is to eliminate such uses." A nonconforming use was precisely what the Mandalay apartments had.

When the Cawleys' case was finally called, Vesta glanced around to see if Betty Hibbler or perhaps the apartment owner was present (she had never seen either of them in the flesh). But John and Vesta were the only two people who rose to be sworn in.

After Vesta's brief summary of the case—in which she appealed to the board to apply the strict letter of the law to the Mandalay apartments and to order the building inspector to issue a citation for every day the air conditioner exceeded noise standards—several of the members had questions. One asked whether the noise the day it was measured was representative of the usual volume of the unit. She said it was slightly quieter than normal that day. Another asked the board's executive coordinator, Jim Self, whether the apartment owner had been notified. Self replied that the owners of every property within two hundred feet of the Cawley home had indeed been notified by regular mail.

But Hauteman, the chairman, persisted. "Do we know for sure that they got the letter?" he asked.

Self shook his head.

"Then what I suggest is that we postpone a ruling until we can call the man and see whether he wants to appear here. Sometimes those letters get lost in the mail."

Before the motion was put to a vote, Hauteman turned back to Vesta. "But let me assure you, Mrs. Cawley," he said, "that whether the owner is here or not at our next meeting, we *will* give you a decision on this. And we'll put you first on the docket for next time."

Fourteen and a Half Months Later: "The Fixer" Weighs In

Jay Hauteman was not as good as his word. Two weeks later, when Vesta returned for what she thought would be the final hearing (alone this time; John couldn't leave his job), she was not first on the docket. That distinction went to the hobby shop attorney. And when Vesta's case was called, the board did everything except make a decision.

Anyone who had visited the Board of Adjustment that morning at its less formal but more important meeting—the "staff briefing"—would have quickly realized that the case of Vesta Cawley had taken a new course in the intervening two weeks. Normally the adjustors assemble in the early morning, then ride around the city in a small bus looking at the property they are going to rule on. Often a vague consensus emerges then, a consensus that usually prevails that afternoon at the regular session. Now, instead of a matter to be disposed of with a simple vote, Vesta Cawley's problem had become a case with political implications. The reason: Joe Geary. As the adjustors gathered at eight-thirty that morning, Jim Self made a point of telling each one, "Joe Geary told me he's representing the apartment owner."

And Jim Self was not the only person who had gotten a call from Geary. Just four days before the meeting, Fred Barnes had taken a call from Geary that he later described as "angry."

Who was Joe Geary and why did he matter? He was known to bureaucrats at city hall as "the fixer" for his skill in getting controversial measures approved. He mattered because he was a former city councilman and ex-mayor Bob Folsom's personal attorney, and he had become a most familiar face at city council meetings and board hearings. Scarcely a week goes by that Geary or someone in his firm doesn't represent a developer or builder or other problem-beset company in need of a favorable vote. All Geary had to do to create a commotion was tell Jim Self that he was sending a colleague to represent the Mandalay apartments on behalf of Arnold Ablon.

"Mrs. Cowley?" said Hauteman, mispronouncing her name.

Vesta Cawley rose and gave a briefer version of her speech of the previous week. There was no nervousness in her voice this time, and there was a little more passion. She even threw in a line about "our very high property tax rates" in the Munger Place Historical District. After she finished, she answered a single question from Hauteman: "Is this a continuous noise or something that starts and stops?"

"The unit recycles once every six minutes," she replied.

Next witness: Kirk Williams, an attorney in the law firm of Geary, Stahl, and Spencer. Williams, continuing the mispronunciation of Cawley, rose to argue that "we are exempt and grandfathered" from the noise ordinance because the apartments were constructed before the enactment of the law. Then, to bolster his assertion that the board had no choice but to throw this complaint out, Williams produced a second witness, a "noise expert" named John Joiner, who proceeded to testify that *traffic* noise near the Cawley home was measured at 71 decibels, approximately the same level as the air conditioner. Joiner went on to say that the air conditioner in question was no louder than any other comparable air conditioner in the city of Dallas.

Little did Vesta Cawley know, as she sat in her front-row seat feeling a little intimidated by this two-on-one attack by the experts, that the Board of Adjustment staff was on her side. In a report on the Cawley problem handed to each of the adjustors that very morning, they had recommended approval of her request for enforcement of the ordinance and even added an additional provision: "It is recommended that only a short period of time for compliance be given." Had Vesta known about that report, or been present at the morning meeting (members of the public are entitled to be there but never attend), she might have had some idea of what was happening. She didn't.

Questions from the adjustors rambled wildly in several directions at once. One person asked whether the noise ordinance was even reasonable. Another called on Fred Barnes, who was sitting in the audience, to report his own noise readings. Michael Brown frankly asserted that he didn't consider the air conditioner very loud. "I was able to carry on a normal conversation right next to it," he said. Jim Self said he had been to the site and was "taken" by the noise. Given such disorder, it is in the nature of large groups to seek obvious solutions away from the main issue—so gradually the suspicion grew that it was *technologically* impossible to cool the Mandalay apartments with an air conditioner that would conform to the 1965 noise standards.

"Mr. Joiner," asked Diana Cobb, "are you saying it's impossible to air-condition these apartments within the noise levels?"

"It *is* possible, yes," said Joiner, "but no air conditioner in Dallas does, and you're talking about a lot of money to do that."

Vesta, growing frustrated, asked again to be recognized. "You *cannot* speak in a normal tone of voice when that unit is running," she said. "And the expense of purchasing a new air conditioning unit can be depreciated on a very favorable schedule."

"Well, our first position," said Williams, in an attempt to sum up, "is that we are not subject to these performance standards. And frankly, we're a little surprised that we even have to come before you today. We have been trying to do something about this problem since at least June of 1980. We've looked at putting a muffler on it. We've looked at relocating it. We've looked at turning the blower so it's parallel with the Cowley house instead of perpendicular to it, but that doesn't help because noise is omnidirectional. We've looked at using a deflecting wall along the alley, but there's not enough room. It would take several thousand dollars to turn the unit around and put a two-wall screen around it, but it would be physically impossible to meet your forty-nine-decibel level even then."

At that point adjustor W. A. Bonds made a tentative motion to hold the case over yet again, so that the Mandalay apartments could bring an air conditioner expert to the hearing to testify what noise level could reasonably be expected if any of those changes were made. Oddly, Williams didn't even encourage the delay. "We already know what the air conditioning man is going to say," he said. "He's not going to say anything new."

But the motion passed anyway. Vesta Cawley, much to her chagrin, had been held over a second time, and Michael Brown's last remark didn't do much to cheer her up.

"I think we need to remember," he said, "that our decision in this case could result in an entire apartment building's being closed down during the summer. At our next meeting we really need to bite the bullet on this one and make a tough decision. We can't keep putting it off and putting it off."

Vesta didn't want the matter to be cast as a choice between her minor complaint and the comfort and well-being of 75 or so apartment dwellers. If it was, she knew who would win and who would lose.

Fifteen Months Later: A Familiar Compromise

Vesta Cawley arrived at her third hearing thoroughly prepared to lose. She had perceived the questioning at the second hearing as slightly hostile to her position, with an undertone that suggested no one really took her problem seriously. When she took her seat in the council chambers, she noted with some surprise that one of the five adjustors was a new face—Mary Stoddard, a housewife and one of the regular adjustors, who had returned to her position, replacing alternate Manuel Cervantes, owner of Supreme Engraving Company. (Self explained that the board is made up of five regular members and four alternates. Since business cannot be conducted without five people present at all times, the four alternates are frequently used to replace members who cannot make it to a meeting.) Vesta wondered to herself how Stoddard could possibly understand all that had gone before.

Again Vesta had to wait for her case to be called. First the board dealt with a parking-space variance requested by the owners of a North Dallas shopping center. (The case was held over when one of the board members pointed out that the building permit for the property called for high-rise hotels and office buildings, not the one-story mall that had been built there. This caused a flurry of stammers and quizzical expressions, followed by a pained request for a delay. The board agreed.)

At last the "Cowley" case was recalled. Vesta deferred to Kirk Williams, who produced, as promised, an air conditioning engineer as well as another noise expert.

"Let me just repeat," said Williams, "that our position remains the same. We don't believe we should be subject to these regulations. But we do have two experts here today who will testify that by turning the air conditioner ninety degrees and constructing a baffling wall on two sides, we *can* reach the fifty-six-decibel rating. There is no possible way to reach the forty-nine level."

Vesta asked to be recognized. "If you can promise me that the level will be no higher than fifty-six at all times," she said, "then I can live with that."

But Bonds was still concerned about the effects of making such a change to the air conditioner during the summer. "Is the apartment owner here today?" he asked.

"Mrs. Hibbler is the general property manager for Mr. Ablon," said Williams.

Betty Hibbler, who turned out to be a tall, immaculately groomed woman of middle age, rose and tentatively ap-

proached the lectern.

"How many people," asked Bonds, "live in these apartments?"

"We have fifty-three units there," she said, "with both single and double occupancy."

"And what length of time would it take to do this work?" asked Bonds.

Hibbler stepped aside for Morris Steinberg, the air conditioning engineer. "It could conceivably be done in a day or two days," he said, "but there's no guarantee of what's gonna happen. We have to coordinate plumbers, electricians, boom operators all at the same time, and in the event that we damaged that unit trying to move it, it could take a lot longer. But a day at the least."

It was apparent that, once again, the discussion was moving away from the theoretical—is this lady's request reasonable?—toward the technological—can this be done? Hibbler stepped forward again.

"I would just like to point out," she said, "that in all our discussions of noise levels, we shouldn't forget that we're still going to have the cycling on and off. We can't do away with that. We're still going to have that."

But the implications of that statement seemed to be lost on the board—which was fine with Vesta, since that line of reasoning would only weaken the emerging consensus. "At what point," asked Michael Brown, speaking for the first time, "do you think you would be able to have this work scheduled?"

Williams turned to his experts, and they conferred among themselves for a moment. "We would need at least forty-five days," he answered.

"Are there any other questions for either Mrs. Cowley or any of the others?" asked Hauteman. ". . . Then, if there are none, the chair is ready for a motion."

Nothing happened. All five adjustors sat contentedly behind the high gray panel, waiting for someone to say something. The silence seemed to last minutes, though it couldn't actually have been more than fifteen or twenty seconds.

Finally Bonds asked to be recognized. "Mr. Chairman," he said, "I move that the Board of Adjustment deny the special exception requested, with the provision that the air conditioner in question be maintained at fifty-six decibels, and that . . .

"If I might pause here for just a moment, I would like to say that I have great concern for these seventy-five people who are going to be without air conditioning for at least one day, and I'm thinking that maybe we'll want to put a sixty-day time limit on this instead of forty-five. That way the apartment owner would have the option of waiting for a relatively cool day to do the work."

"I don't want to second that motion quite yet," said Brown, "because I think that anything we do here today could be

almost superfluous if we wait until the summer is over with and they're ready to turn the air conditioner off anyway. Personally I prefer to limit it to a little bit shorter time, no more than forty-five days."

But another adjustor seconded the motion by Bonds, and after this complicated exchange—procedurally defective but clear to everyone in the room—Hauteman called for a vote. The ayes were unanimous. The noise level was to be set at 56 decibels, and the Mandalay apartments would have sixty days to come into compliance.

The saga of Vesta Cawley took place within the government of the city that works. I mention that only because politicians and the public alike hold the sacrosanct belief that other urban areas may be going to hell in a handbasket, but Dallas will always continue to hum with military precision. In large part I still believe this is true, but with an important exception. When called on to satisfy public needs on a massive scale—revitalizing downtown, building a new city hall or library, securing a sixty-year water supply, maintaining an extensive sewage system—Dallas's network of business, political, and philanthropic leaders does get the job done. (A notable exception is the recent collapse of plans for the downtown arts district, caused by the Dallas Symphony's inability to purchase land. I'm amazed by this and am confident that some miracle will rescue the idea.)

But Vesta Cawley was not part of that business-political complex, and she had no bearing on the larger problems of the day. She may even have been dead wrong. But her case was presented here as a way of looking at Dallas city government—not from the macrocosmic viewpoint of the daily newspapers and the insulated city council but from that of the single person with a problem in the public domain who is up against the machinery of government.

The theoretical justification for having a city manager, as opposed to mayoral, form of government, is that the latter concentrates excessive power in the hands of one man, which leads to patronage, corruption, machine politics, favor seeking, and unequal applications of the law. But it is also true that those governments have a unique virtue: the *individual* usually gets his problems attended to, especially when the public is not inclined to notice. It has to work that way; otherwise the ward committeeman or councilman will begin to lose his political base.

But observe what happens when an individual comes to the city manager form of government with an individual problem that can be solved only by government intervention. In this case, at least, no one seems willing to deal with it. They don't have to; they're protected by civil service. The politicians can't; the city charter insulates them from the bureaucracy. That leaves people like Vesta Cawley fighting a system of memoranda, buck passing, fine legalistic points, and, above all, procedure.

Even so, you could reasonably argue that after all was said and done, Vesta Cawley received a just decision, and that the system indeed worked after all. Quite aside from the fact that a victory won after a full sixteen months of battling is not the most solid testimony for the efficiency of the process, that argument would be misleading. The reason Vesta Cawley won her case was that she was more persistent and tenacious than most people. She was intelligent and well educated. Her husband was knowledgeable about noise standards. She was in a high enough position at Frito-Lay to be able to take off work to appear at public hearings held during the workday. She was not intimidated by people who held important titles or law degrees. She was well dressed, attractive, and spoke well in public. If she had been timid, poorly educated, tied to a low-paying job in, say, a secretarial pool, and ignorant of noise standards, she would still have a two-story air conditioner pointed at her bedroom window.

But there are more fundamental flaws as well. For this story illustrates a system where the *appearance* of justice is almost more important than justice itself. When Betty Hibbler and Vesta Cawley tried to compromise—by jointly agreeing on the 56-decibel level—it was the city bureaucracy that told them not to do it. Nine months later, the Board of Adjustment arrived at exactly the same compromise. The difference: instead of spending $1500 to move and repair the air conditioner, the apartment owner will end up spending more than $6000. (The additional expense covered attorney's fees and the professional services of the noise expert and the engineer.) The sole purpose, then, of the past nine months had been to legitimate what had already been proposed as a just solution.

Then there is the matter of the Board of Adjustment itself. As Vesta Cawley learned, this board was established to make exceptions in hardship cases, but in fact it is used by the bureaucracy to make tough decisions that city employees cannot or will not make. This wouldn't be so troubling if the board abided by any form of procedure recognized by Anglo-Saxon law or tradition. But the board does anything it pleases. It listens to experts who have presented no credentials. (In this case, John Joiner, of the consultant firm Joiner, Pelton and Rose, *was* a bona fide expert, but his testimony included references to traffic noise—which was beside the point and had no legal bearing on the case—that went unchallenged by the board.) It allows attorneys to appear against people who have no legal representation (unlike, say, a small claims court, where attorneys are barred to ensure fair play). It precludes effective cross-examination. It doesn't even use the one democratic safeguard that legislative and judicial bodies almost always adhere to—free and open debate. To this day it's a mystery just why the board decided for Vesta Cawley. No board member ever publicly expressed an opinion on the case. There were questions but no arguments. Most damning of all, the board never really addressed the central point of Vesta Cawley's complaint: does one woman, or one family, having freely chosen to live in a dense urban environment, have the right to force a neighboring property owner to spend thousands of dollars merely to make her environment tolerable? Even among noise law experts, there would be disagreements on this issue. Some would hold that the protection against noise extends only to the indoor portion of her dwelling; others would argue that it applies to her yard and swimming pool as well. We don't know what the Board of Adjustment thought because it never did address the real conflict between the legal rights of the apartment owner and the perceived injustice to Vesta Cawley. Instead, the adjustors' attention was focused firmly on the practical, technological side of the problem: Is it feasible to alter the air conditioner? If so, when can it be done? Who else will be affected? It was very easy to lose sight of what was at issue.

Seventeen Months Later: And Still Counting

One weekend shortly before this article went to press, I called Vesta Cawley to find out what had finally happened. She said a crew of workmen had turned the unit ninety degrees, with little or no effect on the noise level. She hoped the men would be back to do more. I asked her if she felt she had beaten city hall.

"I still don't know," she said. "I won't feel I've accomplished anything until the work is complete."

And what happens if the noise level remains above 56 decibels even after the prescribed changes?

"Fred Barnes says he will come out here and take a reading," she said, "and then he will pass it along to Sam Harting."✦

The Unkindest Cut

Corpus Christi's blacks and browns are fighting for power—fighting each other.

It's called the Cut, a fittingly hard-edged term for some of the bleakest turf in Corpus Christi. Bordered by a sewage treatment plant, a rail yard, a housing project, and a highway, the Cut is the decaying remnant of what used to be the social center for blacks in the days of segregation. On almost any afternoon it is filled with unemployed men sitting in front of places like the Cotton Club, the Charles Game Room, and the Ebony Recreation Spot. The Cut is no longer central to Corpus Christi's black community the way it once was, but it's an appropriate backdrop for a story whose outlines are only beginning to become clear: the relationship between blacks and Hispanics in Texas and the nation.

There's something particularly sobering about the plight of blacks in a town like Corpus Christi. Anglos, who make up 42 per cent of the town's 232,000 people, still overwhelmingly dominate its economic and political life. Hispanics, who make up nearly half the total but only 41 per cent of the voting age population, are the biggest and most vocal minority, a political force that can't be ignored. Tucked away in obscure neighborhoods, accounting for perhaps 7 per cent of the population, blacks in Corpus are all but invisible.

Corpus has one black city councilman, Herbert Hawkins, who became the town's first black attorney since the fifties when he arrived in 1977. There is one black school board member, the Reverend Elliott Grant, who is the only black ever to serve on the board. They owe their positions to two things. First, Corpus Christi, like many of Texas' mid-sized cities, elects all councilmen and most school board members at large rather than from single-member districts. Second, the blacks have allied themselves not with the Hispanics but with the conservative Anglos. Hawkins was elected as a member of an otherwise all-white slate. Grant was appointed by a white-dominated board and then reelected.

This status quo doesn't sit too well with the Hispanic leaders; in 1981 they filed suit to force the city to adopt single-member council districts. If they succeed, perhaps a third of those districts will elect Hispanics. The suit has drawn vocal opposition from several black leaders on the grounds that it would cost them the one seat they now hold. "We ourselves raised the umbrella of equal opportunity, equal employment, equal education, all those things," complains Grant, who is probably the most influential black in town. "Our people have died for those things, been beaten, had dogs set on them. And now that the laws are on the books, your Mexican American lawyers and your Mexican Americans with clout do all the screaming. They want to stand under our umbrella while we stand out in the rain."

For their part, Hispanics, realizing that the blacks need them more than they need the blacks, haven't made any great efforts to forge coalitions. Ruben Bonilla, former president of the League of United Latin American Citizens, says blacks and browns have always been rivals in Corpus, a situation that was solidified politically in the late sixties. That was when conservative Anglos, worried about black unrest, began to court allies among black leaders. Their alliance has continued since then, and blacks have come to expect one spot on conservative Anglo council slates. "There's been such a long history of blacks' competing with Hispanics that it's going to take years for us to form any kind of uneasy truce," Bonilla says. "As long as blacks are playing politics with the traditional enemies of Hispanics, things aren't going to change."

Rhetoric like that smacks of playing to the peanut gallery, but there's more at stake here than the egos of Ruben Bonilla and Elliott Grant. You wouldn't know it driving along Corpus Christi Bay on Ocean Drive or viewing the new construction downtown, but Corpus remains an extremely poor town. Its per capita income is $8754, nearly $1000 below the state average, and that disparity is directly related to the city's high percentage of minorities. The black unemployment rate is estimated at 14.2 per cent, almost double the rate for the city as a whole, and older blacks worry that young blacks with good educations tend to go elsewhere for jobs. "We're losing our young leaders," says Lena Coleman, executive director of the HIALCO-OIC neighborhood center, a black community center not far from the Cut. "When they graduate from CCSU [Corpus Christi State University] or Texas A&I, they leave for cities like Dallas and Houston. At some point we have to find a way to keep them here."

One way, of course, is to promise them greater influence over the life of the community. Political mechanisms often do work: when it's time to spray for mosquitoes or get substandard buildings demolished in the neighborhood around the Cut, Grant is able to get things done because of his clout at city hall. Logically, a coalition could accomplish even more. In the U.S., poverty has never been as potent a unifying force as race, but it's undeniably the central issue for both blacks and browns. When it comes to funding for education, or incentives to businesses that build in depressed areas, or jobs programs, or any number of other concerns, being the have-nots should count for more than skin color. But common needs can also lead to competition for the means to meet those needs, and that's been the usual result in Corpus and elsewhere.

Some politicians *are* trying to bridge the gulf. Herbert Hawkins, who has raised eyebrows in the Anglo establishment by pushing for affirmative-action hiring at city hall, has also disappointed some blacks by stressing the hiring of browns as well as blacks—even though Hispanics can't be expected to do much for his political future. "I don't consider myself a councilman just for blacks," he says. "People who resent it are politically naive. If a person really ran just on the basis of representing blacks, he could never be elected in Corpus."

The city's lopsided racial mix does make it atypical, but Hispanics are expected to make up a much greater share of the state's population in the future, so blacks will increasingly find themselves in the role of the second minority. For those at the bottom of the economic heap, the people of the Cut and their counterparts on Corpus Christi's Hispanic West Side, political clout was supposed to be the way to a better life. But if Corpus is any indication, growing political power and even common problems may prove to be less a bond than a barrier in the years to come.

"I beat Ben Barnes and John Connally in a fair fight"

The two politicians-turned-developers wanted to build apartments in a quiet Austin neighborhood. Here's how they got stopped, sort of.

— by Kaye Northcott

Of all the developers in the world, it would have to be Ben Barnes and John Connally who decided to build in my neighborhood. I had not

> **"I was innocent of traffic-impact analyses, special permits, and all the ins and outs of urban planning. For self-defense, I had to learn the rules of the real-life Monopoly game that is being played for high stakes all across the state."**

seen much of Barnes, the former lieutenant governor, since he lost a bid for the governorship in 1972. But as editor of the liberal *Texas Observer*, I had written a jubilant account of his defeat, beginning with a verse of "Ding, dong, the witch is dead." Over the years I'd penned some fairly tacky things about former governor Connally too. So when the two politicians-turned-developers announced their plans to build apartments just two blocks from my home in South Austin, I enlisted in the neighborhood army. This is the story of our first struggle. It began one long year ago, when I didn't know the ABC's of zoning law, when I was innocent of traffic-impact analyses, site plans, special permits, signalization criteria, and all the ins and outs of urban planning. For self-defense, I had to learn the rules of the real-life Monopoly game that is being played for high stakes all over the state.

Across Texas, people like me are battling rapid and inappropriate urban growth. The frontier credo that a Texan should be able to do anything he damn well pleases with his property is being challenged—although by no means vanquished—by homeowners who think that their local government is not protecting their interests. Austin, with more than 175 registered neighborhood associations, tops other Texas cities. In San Antonio the River Road neighborhood raised the first red flag in opposition to Clinton Manges' plan to use Alamo Stadium for pro football. In unzoned, sinking Houston, a recent poll indicated that 66 per cent of the registered voters want a comprehensive zoning ordinance. The Williamsburg neighborhood in North Dallas, already

Kaye Northcott lives in Austin and writes a regular neighborhood column for Third Coast *magazine.*

plagued with well-nigh interminable traffic jams, has hired its own traffic engineer, as well as a zoning lawyer to fight further commercial development.

The oldest homes in my neighborhood were built in the early fifties, and many of the original inhabitants are being replaced by a second generation of owners. The residents are an amalgam of Anglos and Mexican Americans, blue collars and white collars. Lots of us are remodeling, and the neighborhood is looking better than ever before. Unfortunately, we are close to the central city, and builders are snapping up undeveloped tracts for apartment complexes, office buildings, and medical condos. Traffic is getting worse, and crime is on the rise.

Still, we'd never been inspired to protest until we found out about Barnes-Connally Investments' scheme to build 344 apartments on a fifteen-acre rectangular plot that cut deep into the neighborhood. The property stretched west from the congested four-lane South First Street to South Fifth, a street used almost exclusively by the neighborhood. The apartments would be built across the street from an elementary school and would rub up against homes on three sides.

We got our first clue to Barnes and Connally's plans when one of my neighbors stumbled upon a notice of a zoning hearing hidden behind a clump of weeds. He and all the other property owners within two hundred feet of the site subsequently received letters announcing Barnes-Connally's request for a zoning change. The letters arrived on a Friday; the hearing before the planning commission was the following Tuesday. From the city we learned that about 10 of the 15 acres were zoned O, for offices and apartments. (We never learned how this acreage got its O zoning. Perhaps it had been obtained by the nursing home that once occupied the old stone building on the site.) The rest of the land, 4.29 acres, was zoned A, for single-family houses and duplexes. Barnes-Connally wanted the planning commission and the city council (it's a two-step process) to change the zoning of that smaller section to B, which would allow apartments. We knew we had to fight the zoning change, but we didn't know how to go about it.

A helpful soul in the city planning department explained to us that the most effective way to stop rezoning is to get the owners of 20 per cent of the property within two hundred feet of the site to sign a petition opposing it. When a group presents a valid petition, the zoning change must be approved by three fourths of the city council instead of the usual simple majority. That meant that two of the seven council members could keep Barnes and Connally from putting apartments on the A acreage. And we figured that we could count on at least two of the more liberal members to vote with us.

That weekend a number of people, in-

cluding four who live on my street, canvassed the neighborhood, gathering signatures and urging residents to attend the planning commission meeting. Some people signed because they opposed all apartment construction; others didn't want fifteen acres of green space to be bulldozed. Parents with young children were worried that the apartments would make the traffic congestion around the Molly Dawson Elementary School across the street even more dangerous. Another developer on South First had built some three-story apartments on a hillside, blocking the neighbors' view of the city. This time the residents wanted to look carefully at the developers' plans. Most alarming was the possibility that the city would want the project to extend Havana Street along one side of the planned apartments to South Fourth, which ends in a wooded cul-de-sac. Indeed, that turned out to be what the traffic planners had in mind.

Our debut at the planning commission was a lesson in city politics. If there had been no angry neighbors present that night, Barnes and Connally would have gotten their zoning change. Instead, the commissioners agreed to postpone the vote until the developers told us exactly what they intended to build.

I was out of town the first time Barnes and Connally's representatives presented their plans to the group. At the second meeting, held in a law-firm conference room high in the big gold American Bank Tower downtown, the neighborhood was ready with some questions. Besides myself, our group included three students, two full-time housewives, a mid-level state bureaucrat, an architect, and a carpenter-contractor. Barnes and Connally were represented by Gary Davis, who was to oversee the construction of the apartments, and Jack Morton, a young at-

> **"Our debut before the planning commission was a lesson in city politics. If no angry neighbors had been present that night, Barnes-Connally would have gotten the zoning change. Instead, the commissioners agreed to postpone the vote."**

torney with Brown, Maroney, the firm hired to guide the project through the city-permit process. We had no sooner arranged ourselves around the polished conference table than Morton lit into Jack Howard, one of our neighborhood leaders who had attended the first meeting. "Jack," he said, "I thought we were friends, and now I hear you have been circulating a petition behind my back. I'm really disappointed in you."

From the guilt-trip gambit, Morton moved to a threaten-the-neighborhood-with-something-worse ploy. He maintained that Barnes-Connally Investments could build as many as 400 apartments on the ten acres zoned O. But since the developers wanted an especially nice project, they planned to buy the four-plus A-zoned acres, giving them room for "garden apartments" on all fifteen acres. They would build about 24 apartments per acre, fewer than the ordinance allowed, and they prepared to roll the O zoning back to B, Morton explained with an air of magnanimity. Since there was no benefit to us in changing O zoning to B—both permit 46 units per acre—and we would lose the A zoning, their offer was unacceptable.

I wish I could report that my team showed more class than Morton did, but this was our maiden negotiation. I have a vague but painful memory of angry wisecracks, detours into issues that turned out to be red herrings, and wistful proposals such as "Why can't this be a park?" Somewhere in our rumbles and grumbles, however, was the germ of a coherent response. To wit, the city planning department had recommended BB zoning for this project, which allows no more than 24 units to the acre. After all, the land was close to an elementary school in an area that already had serious traffic problems; the city planners estimated that at B density the apartments would increase traffic by 14 per cent. We might accept 24 units an acre on the O land, but using our petition as a bargaining tool, we tried to hold Barnes-Connally to 12 units per acre (the maximum density allowed by A zoning) on the rest of the land.

Gary Davis' angry retort was that 344 garden apartments were going up on fifteen acres whether we liked it or not. We told him that we were not about to give up A zoning so Barnes-Connally could build more apartments.

"But our bond funding is specifically for apartments," Davis answered.

"What bonds?" I asked. He refused to say another word about them, implying that the financial details were none of our business and too complicated for us to understand anyway.

Then we offered some suggestions concerning the placement of driveways out of the complex. We made a pitch for saving as many live oaks as possible. We suggested that they build fewer efficiency apartments for single people and more two-bedroom units to accommodate families. We asked for a greenbelt and fencing around the property. We asked that the

three-story apartment buildings be in low-lying areas and away from neighboring homes. Both sides opposed the extension of Havana Street. But the negotiations promptly bogged down when Davis asked us to withdraw our opposition in exchange for the improvements. When we balked, he threatened to proceed without a nod in our direction. I wanted to see if he was bluffing, so I grabbed my purse and prepared to leave. Morton jumped to his feet and said, "Well, perhaps Gary was being a bit hasty here." I put my bag down, but the session soon ended in an uneasy standoff.

The next day, I started investigating the bonds that Davis had mentioned. It turned out that Barnes-Connally was taking advantage of a government program allowing local governments to lend their tax-exempt bond status to apartment builders. In theory, this tax break enables developers to build housing that the poor and the middle class can afford. It seemed to me, however, that the program primarily benefited Barnes-Connally. Travis County had authorized the firm to sell $10 million worth of tax-exempt housing bonds—enough to finance the entire project—at an interest rate of 9.98 per cent, lower than the prevailing commercial rate. In exchange for these goodies, rents had to be affordable to families earning less than $35,000 a year, and one fifth of the apartments had to be set aside for low-income tenants. (Under government guidelines, a family of four earning up to $18,000 a year qualified as poor. These folks would not get a reduction in rent, mind you, just an opportunity to rent at rates ranging from $355 to $525 a month.) The most interesting tidbit I picked up was that Barnes and Connally had already sold their bonds, which locked them into building at least 344 garden apartments, even though they didn't have city approval to build them yet. No wonder Davis and Morton had become so agitated when we tried to discuss alternatives with them.

Most Austin neighborhood leaders believe that the city's nine-member planning commission is tilted toward developers, but even the pro-developer members are committed to a rational planning process. The planning commissioners I called were at first incredulous, then angry when I explained that Barnes-Connally had sold bonds before getting the proper zoning. It dawned on me that I wasn't the only greenhorn in this skirmish; Barnes and Connally were neophytes too. Suddenly the match seemed to be a little more even.

I called Jack Morton to ask why he hadn't explained the nature of the funding to us the night before. He explained that many groups opposed subsidized housing in their neighborhoods. I pointed out that we were not well-to-do and that we had no quarrel with low-cost housing. What we objected to was apartments being built on land that we thought should be used for houses or duplexes. Morton ignored my point but said that he liked my "style" and was sure that our negotiations would go

better in the future.

At the next planning commission meeting, the newly christened Dawson Area Neighborhood Group (our motto: Give a DANG) turned out fifty strong, wearing orange Day-Glo name tags. I immediately spotted Barnes' big blond Hereford head towering above the crowd. He was standing in the back of the city council chamber, next to Jack Morton and David Armbrust, the senior city lobbyist for Brown, Maroney. Barnes and I greeted each other in the best Texas political tradition—*abrazos,* effusive compliments and endearments—while Morton looked on uncomfortably. Barnes squeezed my hand and said he was proud of me for turning out such a whopping herd of neighbors. (He gave not a hint of our past differences. A master politician never stops trying to seduce his adversaries.) "Kaye," he said, "can't we go somewhere and talk this out—just you and me?" I was not about to go anywhere alone with Ben Barnes. He's too persuasive. Besides, my neighbors might think I was selling them out.

I asked a few members of DANG to join us in the conference room behind the city council chambers. Soon the room was packed with people telling Barnes that more traffic on South Fifth would make it almost impossible for them to get out of their driveways safely. The PTA president said that a single, aged crossing guard guided grade-school children through the heavy traffic on South First and that the city refused to put a signal at the school because it wasn't at a four-way intersection. Barnes, as personable as ever, listened carefully and responded with disarming candor. "I know how terrible traffic around schools can be," he said. "In Brownwood, my hometown, a school guard was killed." By the time our case was called, however, we had found no way to reconcile our differences.

After hearing us out, the planning commission put off its vote again, instructing the developers to meet with the neighborhood once more to search for a compromise. We were satisfied with the commission's decision. It rarely rejects anything outright, but sometimes a project is postponed to death.

Our reception was significantly more cordial the next time we ascended to the conference room in the big gold bank building. Barnes was there, and before we could sit down, he asked, "Who wants coffee? I'll send the girl—uh, Kaye, why don't you and I get the coffee?" Off we went, alone at last, pouring coffees with and without sugar. Barnes explained to me that he had rushed to sell his tax-exempt bonds before the bond market changed. He said he earnestly hoped we could work something out, because he wanted to build a first-rate complex that would be a credit to the neighborhood.

Back at the conference table, I laid out our position. We had a valid petition on the 4.29 acres of A-zoned property, and we saw no reason to drop our opposition to the project unless Barnes-Connally built houses, duplexes, or townhouses at A density on that land. David Armbrust, scrupulously unemotional, presented a counteroffer: they would put duplexes on two acres, and we could choose where to place them. The units "lost" in that area would be built on the property zoned O, keeping the total at 344 apartments. We agreed to consider the proposal, but it wasn't very attractive.

At the next DANG meeting, we voted to hold our ground. For two weeks yards went unmowed and children were ignored as we recontacted the planning commissioners, appeared on a radio talk show, and got our side of the story in the newspaper and on the TV news. We also introduced ourselves to city council members on the assumption that win or lose, the case would eventually go to the council. Since city elections were only a month away, no fewer than four campaigning council members visited our meetings.

Our last session before the planning commission was a rerun of the first, except that the neighborhood's worst traffic scenario was confirmed by the analysis ordered by the commission. The study indicated that the northbound morning traffic from the apartments would use South Fifth and that congestion would reach a dangerous level in front of the elementary school. The only assistance the city could offer was a signal a few blocks south of the school, which, with luck, would provide some gaps in the traffic flow.

Armbrust told the commissioners that Barnes-Connally Investments had bent over backwards to accommodate the neighborhood. He argued that 344 units was a reasonable number to put on the site. We argued that the four-plus A acres would provide a buffer between the apartments and the rest of the neighborhood. We showed slides of rush-hour traffic around the school and tried to convince

the commissioners that the only way to address the traffic problem was to reduce the density of the project, but Barnes had said he couldn't do that because he had already sold his bonds.

It was almost midnight when the hearing ended. "This is one of the worst cases we've ever had," groaned a weary commissioner. The commission debated an outright denial of Barnes' zoning request, then reconsidered and asked us to try one more round of negotiations. Commissioner Larry Jackson, a former Black Panther and now a force to be reckoned with in East Austin, seemed to take pleasure in lecturing Barnes, who was slumped in a chair in the back of the chamber. "There are no votes on this planning commission for your project at your proposed level of density," Jackson said. "I suggest you look for an alternate site."

Barnes took Jackson's advice. A few weeks later he called me to say that he was moving his apartments to another location and was giving up his option to buy the 4.29 acres. It has since been optioned by an Austin architect who says he doesn't yet know what he will build. The neighborhood will have to do battle over it again if he asks for a zoning change.

Barnes went on to say that he had found a developer in San Antonio to buy the ten O acres and wanted to know if we would go along with 24 apartments to the acre on that section. Our eventual answer was yes. Our leverage had been the petition on the A land, which was essential to the Barnes-Connally project. Now our only recourse was to convince the city to block the special permits necessary for the new project. Since we had seen such permits approved routinely in the recent past, we decided it would be futile to object.

In retrospect, I wish we had gone through the motions of a fight. But we were simultaneously battling three other

zoning bids and a plan to build a road through the floodplain, and we just didn't have the energy to take on what seemed a lost cause. So we gave the new developer our tacit approval in exchange for every live oak he could possibly save and stringent runoff control to alleviate the serious flooding problems we had discovered nearby. The project will still penetrate all the way to South Fifth and cause traffic problems, but at least there will be 104 fewer units than Barnes intended to build, and no apartments will be built on the land closest to the school.

Barnes also has had some regrets concerning the apartment project. He recently said that he was politically naive in his dealings with DANG. He was quoted as saying, "I told them the truth. I should have told the neighborhood people I wanted thirty-two units to an acre and scaled it down to twenty-six. Then they could have won a great victory." Still, he said, he had the last laugh: he made $350,000 on the sale of the property.

DANG has turned out to be about six consistently active people. I resent spending so much time in the neighborhood wars, but I don't believe I have much choice. Even in the most neighborhood-oriented city in Texas, momentum is on the side of the developer. The good news is that DANG is now allied with other active groups in Austin. People who had never voted before were interested enough to do volunteer work in last year's city elections. Best of all, we've actually become a neighborhood. We gossip on the phone, give each other rides to the grocery store, have potluck dinners, share Weed Eaters and pruning shears. We may be whittled down to a mere splinter of a neighborhood surrounded by offices, apartments, and traffic jams, but at least we'll be in this thing together.

Ben Barnes should be proud.♦

★INFLUENTIALS★

The Kingmaker

Walter Mischer develops land and politicians.

The most powerful man in Texas politics holds no public office. You will not find his name in *Who's Who,* not even in the Southwest edition. His headquarters is one of downtown Houston's least prestigious office suites. Wearing a typical uniform of brown suit, brown shirt, brown tie, brown socks, and brown shoes—all plain—he would not look out of place sitting on a park bench feeding pigeons. But make no mistake: Walter Mischer, whose name is unknown outside his circle, has become the embodiment of the Houston establishment, heir to the mantle of George R. Brown and James Elkins and, before them, Jesse Jones.

The last three mayors of Houston could not have been elected without Mischer's support. The same goes for Attorney General Mark White. Mischer is John Connally's chief fundraiser and the principal reason Connally has the largest war chest of any presidential aspirant. He is the only person to be named to state boards by the last four governors. He is the architect of a money machine that pumps impressive sums into legislative races statewide. Newspaper articles have described him as a friend of *all* Houston city councilmen. The president of his bank holding company sits on the State Finance Commission, close to the process of distributing the most coveted pieces of paper in Austin—state bank charters.

What really sets Mischer apart, however, is not his power but his style. He is unassuming to an extreme, just an ol' country boy turned kingmaker. It is impossible to think of him as a fat cat. He stutters. He lisps. For someone who is big-rich, he lives conservatively, a throwback to the German heritage of his early years in Gillett, a South Texas hamlet near Karnes City. His name rarely appears in the gossip columns. Unlike, say, John Connally, who radiates pomp at all times, Mischer lulls his company to ease. He has a way of saying things—he leans forward slightly and his eyes light up as if he's already enjoying the line he's about to deliver—that for the moment obscures the fact that this is the pronouncement of a man of strong ideas who will go to great lengths to see them carried out. Once, an avid supporter of an office seeker whose name is lost to history tried to stampede Mischer into a campaign contribution. Give early, Mischer was told, if you expect to be remembered favorably. Mischer's reply—"There's always time to buy a ticket on the late train"—has entered the political lexicon, and it says a great deal not only about Mischer's understanding of the eternal verities of politics, but also about Mischer himself. He is shrewd, tough, intuitive, and disarming—and not easily moved.

Though he now has a downtown financial base—as chairman of Allied Bancshares, the largest state bank holding company in Texas—Mischer got his formative experience in the construction industry. That separates him from most corporate magnates: oilmen and insurance company presidents can go for years without being touched by city hall, but a builder has to worry every day about housing codes and inspectors and land-use decisions. As a developer Mischer had to work with politicians, and he learned the secret most businessmen never discover: a common skill—an instinct about people—unites the two professions.

Mischer came to Houston during World War II. He got into development just as Houston began thirty years of explosive growth. It did not take him long to figure out that money manipulation was the key to success, and he seized on a way to speed up the process of realizing his profits from development. He bought up undeveloped suburban land and got some friendly politicians to designate the area a water district. Some friends moved into the unpopulated district temporarily and voted in an election authorizing the district to issue bonds. Since Houston was growing and would annex the district eventually, there was a ready market for the securities. Mischer's friends were elected directors of the district. His construction company put in streets and drainage and sewers, and proceeds from the bond sale paid for that work. Thus Mischer didn't have to wait for the houses to sell to start getting his money out of that project and into the next one.

As Houston grew, so did Mischer. Eventually he covered just about every way to make a dollar out of growth. He bought land and sold it. He acquired banks and lent money to other developers. His contracting firm hired itself out to homebuilders, turning their raw land into streets and finished lots. He built sewer systems using pipe supplied by a Mischer subsidiary. Sometimes he put up houses himself, and even when he didn't, whoever did used Mischer-supplied kitchen cabinets and air conditioning equipment. When the new homes were ready for occupancy, a Mischer savings and loan could finance the mortgage. And if housing prices were a little steep, he had a solution: both parents could work while a nearby Mischer child care center looked after the kids.

Mischer's political influence was keeping pace with his economic success. In the late sixties he became part of Houston's fabled "8-F crowd"—Brown, Elkins, Gus Wortham, and other potentates who met in that room of the Lamar Hotel on Wednesday afternoons to play cards and drink whiskey and talk about politics. In 1963 he was instrumental in raising money to elect Louie Welch mayor, and by 1970 he was the Houstonian closest to the two most powerful politicians in Austin: Speaker Gus Mutscher and Lieutenant Governor Ben Barnes. When the Sharpstown banking scandal laid them both low in 1972, Mischer remarked ruefully that while his own banks were unscathed, "I lost a hell of an interest in good government." But by the time Dolph Briscoe was elected governor that fall, Mischer had his ticket on the late train.

Though his banking empire is the city's most profitable, Mischer's real power base remains the construction industry. His cohorts in the business regard him as a father figure rather than a competitor. He's advanced many of them credit—not as a banker but as a contractor and supplier—and has carried them through rough times. He's entered joint ventures with them, bought savings and loans with them, hunted quail with them. Despite his weighty influence, on issues like more state money for highway construction he'll let the trade association do his talking. The industry, in turn, follows his lead in politics, particularly when it comes to opening their wallets. "The homebuilders and contractors won't give you a dime until Mischer moves," says new Houston councilman Lance Lalor. "The first question out of almost everybody's mouth is 'What's Walter doing?'" In the recent Houston mayoral campaign, word got out that Mischer was looking for a possible opponent for incumbent Jim McConn, and McConn's contributions dried up. Then Mischer came out for McConn and raised over $100,000 in one afternoon.

The question that always arises about kingmakers is what's in it for them, and certainly Mischer has gotten his share of the goodies. A developer profits from growth, and so he has thrown his influence and money behind a huge bond program for the Port of Houston and a mass-transit authority for the metropolitan area. Back in Welch's heyday, Mischer and another close mayoral associate emerged with Houston's first cable TV franchise. It was revoked amid controversy, but when five new franchises were awarded in 1979, six years and two mayors later, Mischer got one of the prizes.

But it would be a mistake to think of Walter Mischer as just another self-serving businessman dabbling in politics. In an era when politics is dominated more and more by special interests, Mischer is one of the few remaining generalists. The organization he uses to funnel money to business-oriented legislative candidates does not lobby and never asks for a vote. Most legislators, including those from Houston, rarely hear from him, not even on an issue as vital to his politicking as moving up the date of the Texas presidential primary to help John Connally. A few of the newer generation of hustlers sneer at his aloofness from the day-to-day wars ("Walter believes that preserving a sound business climate was left out of the Ten Commandments by mistake," says one Austin lobbyist), but they overlook the fact that in politics not having to ask for favors is itself a form of power.

Mischer is partial to conservatives, but he is more partial to winners. He is not about to let ideology stand in the way of influence. He supported Charlie Wilson, now a congressman, when he was a liberal East Texas legislator running for the state senate. Some Connally people would like to punish liberal Houston state senator Gene Jones for participating in the Killer Bee walkout that ended hopes for a separate presidential primary, but Mischer has been quietly working to protect Jones, whose Capitol office is Austin headquarters for Houston's lawyer-lobbyist crowd. So pragmatic is Mischer that in 1974 the Friday Club, a group of Houston political insiders that meets weekly for lunch at (where else?) the Lamar Hotel, gave their mentor their annual Flexibility Award for "the ability to rise above principle when demanded by the exigencies of the situation."

There are a few issues, however, on which Mischer will give no quarter. He is for the right-to-work law, against a corporate income tax, and against a new state constitution. He bankrolled the 1975 fight against revision and is content that executive power currently rests in the hands of independent boards, mostly composed of businessmen. When revision supporter Joe Christie ran for the U.S. Senate in 1978, Mischer wouldn't give him a dime, even though Christie's treasurer was a close friend of his.

And that is the final dimension of Walter Mischer. He doesn't talk tough and he doesn't threaten, but he is so hardnosed that even now, at 57, he gets into fistfights with his own construction foremen. "He's a coldhearted Houston banker," said a coldhearted Austin lawyer. "I ain't afraid of Jesus, but don't you tell Walter Mischer I talked to you."
Paul Burka

I Have A Scheme

by Harry Hurt III

How two civil rights leaders learned to love money and power.

Andrew Jefferson rose to answer the telephone with the deliberate dignity of a man born to be on the United States Supreme Court. Six feet three inches tall and a broad-shouldered but portly 250 pounds, Jefferson was wearing a blue shirt with French cuffs and gold links, a conservative striped tie, and the trousers of a brown business suit. His coat hung on the wall as if waiting to be exchanged for judicial robes. With his large, handsome, balding head, his bushy gray sideburns and thin black moustache, the 47-year-old Jefferson looked like a figure out of a nineteenth-century painting, a portrait of old-fashioned wisdom made all the more powerful by the dark mahogany color of his skin. But because he wasn't wearing his black gown, he also seemed a little naked as he went to the telephone.

"Hello," he said into the receiver. "This is Andrew Jefferson. May I help you?"

There was a brief pause.

"Oh, hello, Smitty," Jefferson said heartily.

Jefferson listened for a few moments, then he interrupted.

"Do you have a report on the well?" he asked.

There was another pause, this one a little longer than the first two.

"Do I love you?" Jefferson suddenly interjected histrionically. "You know I love you. I just don't love your geologist.

I love *my* geologist. So send me what you've got and I'll have him look at it right away."

Jefferson smiled and nodded, anticipating the effect his words would have on his caller.

"Okay, fine," Jefferson said after another short pause. "I'll get back to you in a day or two."

He hung up and returned to an armchair in front of his imposing wooden desk. He sat down and propped his big brown brogans in the seat of another armchair, stretching his legs so that his belly bulged like that of a Buddha. A smile broke across his face as he looked at the visitor sitting on the couch.

"I was showing off a little bit for you," Jefferson confessed.

Friends Through Thick and Thicker

During his years as a state district court judge, Andrew Jefferson acquired an exalted public image. A 1975 survey of 1300 Harris County lawyers ranked Jefferson first among all local state district judges both overall and in the specific categories of knowing and applying the law, judicial temperament, impartiality, and fairness.

Upon his return to private practice, Jefferson became known as one of the most

influential leaders in Houston's black community as well as the man with the best chance to become his city's first black mayor. Thus it was hardly surprising that in the fall of 1979, acting on the recommendation of his merit selection committee, President Carter nominated Andrew Jefferson for a seat on the U.S. Fifth Circuit Court of Appeals. What did come as a surprise to many was that by the time President Reagan took office early this year, Jefferson was still not confirmed to the Fifth Circuit, and his nomination, a logical stepping-stone on the path to the Supreme Court, was dead.

The demise of Jefferson's nomination may be traced to various causes, but perhaps the most important was his association with Larry C. Cager, a man Jefferson has described as "my best friend." Cager does not radiate the authority of a great public servant. He is lean and of medium build with a well-trimmed Afro that is counterpointed by a small tuft of blondish hair, a birthmark, on the back of his head. He likes to wear stylish clothes and heavily aromatic cologne. But like Jefferson, Larry Cager exudes a charisma that once made him a powerful force in Houston's black community.

Until the end of July, Cager was the executive director of the Houston Area Urban League. He resigned that post in the wake of one of the most controversial and destructive scandals in the history of Houston black politics. The scandal centered on allegations that Cager, with the help of Jefferson and other Urban League board members, manipulated the non-profit, federally funded social service agency for his own financial and political gain. Cager, who has an interest in a cable television franchise, was indicted last year on charges of forcing Urban League employees to work on former mayor Fred Hofheinz's 1975 reelection campaign and on a 1978 cable TV referendum petition. In April 1981 a federal jury acquitted Cager of the Hofheinz campaign charges, and the cable charges were subsequently dropped. But during the time between Cager's indictment and acquittal, Jefferson's Fifth Circuit nomination foundered.

The Urban League scandal is a civil rights parable of our times. Both Andrew Jefferson and Larry Cager owe their personal success to the achievements of the civil rights movement of the fifties and sixties. The changes advocated by black leaders before and after Martin Luther King, Jr., made it possible for Jefferson and Cager to get their professional educations and ultimately their jobs. At the same time, the drives to register black voters enfranchised a bloc with the potential of duplicating or even surpassing the political machines created a century ago in the Northern cities by Irish and Italian minorities. In the seventies, the federal government further reacted to the civil rights movement by deluging organizations like the Urban League with federal funds. This, in turn, created a new power base in the black community. While WASPs based their power on business success and ethnic minorities relied on urban political patronage, the avenue to affluence and political clout for blacks was the local administration of federal programs.

Because of the moral righteousness of the civil rights movement, black leaders of the sixties and seventies were assumed to be interested in the advancement of their race rather than in the success of particular individuals. But the reality of the situation was far more complicated. Like the leaders of the feminist movement and other modern social causes, black leaders faced seemingly unresolvable conflicts about the goals of their political cause. Was the point of the movement and the federal programs to help all blacks at all socioeconomic levels or merely to permit the talented and gifted few to achieve their potential? Was it possible to pursue both goals at the same time? And if so, was it proper for the local supervisors of federal programs to use those programs to advance their personal goals and political interests? In Houston, where the movement was relatively weak and politics has traditionally been a sideshow to a three-ring circus of economic development, these questions were especially

difficult to answer.

Despite the murkiness of the Urban League scandal, the game plan Jefferson and Cager have been following is clear. Both men candidly admit that they have been using politics to carve out a bigger piece of the economic pie—for both blacks in general and themselves in particular. They have tried to emulate the wheeling and dealing of the white establishment, attempting to become black counterparts of John Connally, Leon Jaworski, and Walter Mischer. Jefferson and Cager even formed their own semi-secret power circle of businessmen and politicians. Known simply as "the Group," this all-male political fraternity is much like a black version of the famous 8-F Crowd of white power brokers that used to meet in suite 8-F of the Lamar Hotel under the aegis of the late Jesse Jones and the still-powerful George Brown. The troubles that have recently befallen Jefferson, Cager, and the Houston Area Urban League vividly dramatize the dilemmas confronting gifted and ambitious young middle-class blacks in the seventies and early eighties.

Looking Out For Number One

Andrew Leon Jefferson, Jr., learned two important lessons at an early age: the value of a dollar and the necessity of playing the game. Born in Dallas in the Depression year of 1934, he grew up the son of a carpenter in the black ghettos of Houston's east side. One day when Andrew was seven years old, his father gave him a nickel to buy rice for the family's supper. But instead of getting the rice, Andrew spent the nickel on a movie, *God Is My Co-pilot*. That night the Jeffersons ate grits for dinner.

As he grew older, Jefferson began earning his own movie money by doing odd jobs, painting houses, mowing lawns, clerking at a local grocery. He took up photography and found he could make a decent income processing film. While attending high school at all-black Jack Yates, Jefferson dreamed of studying architecture at the Tuskegee Institute. But when graduation rolled around, he discovered he could not afford to go to college out of state. He enrolled at Texas Southern University in Houston and eventually set his sights on law school.

In 1956 Jefferson won a scholarship to the University of Texas at Austin. His first year in law school was also the first year of undergraduate desegregation at UT; the landmark cases of *Brown* v. *Board of Education* and *Sweatt* v. *Painter* were already history. Four other blacks besides Jefferson were enrolled in the first-year law class at UT, along with such white scions as Joe Jaworski, son of Leon. Even if a great deal remained to be done on the civil rights front, Jefferson was content to

leave political activism to others while he studied and worked part-time in a photo lab and at the post office. "I wasn't trying to make the world better," he says. "I was looking out for number one."

After gaining admittance to the bar, Jefferson was determined to get ahead in the white man's world. He practiced law briefly in Houston, then served five years as an assistant U.S. attorney in San Antonio. In July 1968 he got a job as trial and labor relations counsel for Humble Oil and Refining Company (now Exxon USA) in Houston. Suddenly he was known as *the* successful young black lawyer in Houston. In December 1970 he was appointed judge of Harris County Domestic Relations Court No. 2. Although the salary of $28,000 a year was considerably less than he could make at Exxon, the appointment was an honor the 36-year-old Jefferson could not refuse.

During his rapid rise to the bench, Jefferson participated in a few civil rights marches in San Antonio and in the liberal-reform-oriented Citizens for Good Schools in Houston, but he was never a movement leader. Most of his community involvement consisted of service on boards and committees for various charities, such as the YMCA and the United Fund. He was very much a moderate, considering himself somewhat to the right of Martin Luther King, Jr., and slightly to the left of National Urban League director Whitney Young.

One day in 1969, while Jefferson was serving as chairman of the United Fund admissions committee, he received a proposal from an organization called the Houston Area Urban League. Founded in the summer of 1968, the Houston Area Urban League was an affiliate of the National Urban League. The stated purpose of the national league, established in 1910 and present in many major American cities since the thirties, was "to eliminate racial discrimination and segregation in the United States, increase the economic and political empowerment of blacks and other minorities, and, in short, help them share equally in the responsibilities and rewards of full citizenship." The fledgling Houston affiliate, which had started as an offshoot of the YMCA, was anxious to carry on that mission by offering antipoverty programs financed by the United Fund.

The United Fund admissions committee originally turned down the Urban League's proposal, but Jefferson persuaded the committee to give the agency $15,000 as a special limited-term grant. This relationship proved successful, and the Urban League eventually became a regular recipient of United Fund money (at the rate of more than $100,000 a year). In the meantime, the grateful league elected Jefferson to its local board of directors and later to the national board of trustees.

Although his efforts with the United

Fund gave Jefferson considerable clout at the Houston Area Urban League, he did not run the organization. That full-time job belonged to the executive director. In 1971 the national league recommended that a new executive director join the Houston affiliate. His name was Larry C. Cager.

All Roads Lead To Politics

Larry Cager could not match Andrew Jefferson in playing the get-ahead game, but he did know a thing or two about playing politics. Born in 1940, the son of a New Orleans laborer, Cager grew up in Chalmette, Louisiana, the site of the Battle of New Orleans and a part of the famous political domain of the Leander Perez family. In Perez country as well as in Louisiana as a whole, politics was everything. It was the means to just about all major forms of wealth and power, and to even an average citizen it meant not only voting in elections but getting jobs, houses, food, medical care. Larry Cager could not have helped but have his impressions of politics formed by the proudly obvious corruption and racial discrimination that were a way of life in southern Louisiana. He saw all things in politics and politics in all things.

Unlike the career-conscious Andrew Jefferson, who is six years his senior, Cager did have an urge to change the world. After attending high school in New Orleans, he enrolled at the city's predominantly black Dillard University, where he studied psychology, then did graduate work at Trinity University in San Antonio. Following a brief stint in the Army as a psychology technician, Cager returned to New Orleans and found work as a counselor with the Institute of Human Relations at Loyola University. Then in 1967, at the age of 26, Cager got a job on the staff of the Greater New Orleans Urban League.

Founded in 1930, the Greater New Orleans Urban League was much better established than its Houston counterpart. But for all its good intentions, the chapter was hardly making a dent in the massive poverty and unemployment afflicting the city's blacks. Cager saw a serious lack of effective black leadership in New Orleans. Though the Voting Rights Act had passed in 1965 and though the city's close historical connection to the slave economy helped stoke the fires of civil rights activism, the black ministers, who held most of the political clout in black New Orleans, had failed to push for voter registration efforts or much of anything else. Cager took a dim view of the older men's general inability to "deal with the system."

Cager hoped to influence the Greater New Orleans Urban League to play a major role in organizing the black communi-

ty. His chance came when the National Urban League awarded New Orleans a $35,000 grant for a voter registration project in 1967. The local league selected a predominantly black section of the city and not only registered blacks to vote but also educated them about politics, notably the white politicians' ploy to split the black vote by paying black candidates to run against them. Encouraged by the results of the project, Cager and his colleagues later organized a black primary to select candidates for the upcoming tax assessor and city council races. One of the winners went on to be elected to a council seat.

"After the black primary we were bombarded with young people," Cager recalls. "In the sixties black was beautiful. Young people enjoyed participating in the political process. If there was an opportunity to participate in something in the sixties, you'd be insulted if you were left out."

In 1969 Cager provided just such an opportunity by starting a group called Black Organization for Leadership Development (BOLD). Although the group had no official connection with the Urban League, Cager later credited the league with helping to organize it and confirmed that at least some league staffers were also members of BOLD. Like the Urban League, Cager's new group worked on voter registration and getting jobs for blacks. But unlike the league, it endorsed political candidates. Even though Cager founded it, he never became an official member. He soon organized yet another political endorsement group called Community Organization for Unified Progress (COUP). Once again, there was no official connection with the Urban League, but the new group had league staffers for members and benefited from the advice and counsel of founder (but nonmember) Larry Cager. The major achievement of BOLD and COUP was to join with another black political group, the Southern Organization for Unified Leadership, to get out the black vote that contributed to the upset victory of white liberal Moon Landrieu in the 1969 mayor's race.

Throughout this period, Cager slipped easily back and forth between his duties at the avowedly nonpartisan Urban League and his activities in the political arena. According to Cager, his fellow Urban Leaguers did not object. "I never had any problems, nor did the National Urban League express problems, with political involvement," he recalls. "We knew politics was a natural part of the system. If you're going to get involved in changing things, you're going to get involved in politics."

In fact, instead of reproving Cager for his political activities, in 1971 National Urban League director Whitney Young offered him the job of executive director of the Houston league. Young told Cager

he wanted new blood in Houston because the affiliate was "having trouble getting off the ground." Cager accepted the challenge.

Going to the Mountaintop

When Larry Cager arrived in Texas, most of the city's blacks were no better off in boom town than they would have been in New Orleans. Although Houston boasted an overall unemployment rate far below the national average, black unemployment was still around 7.5 per cent and underemployment (low wages, poor working conditions) was even higher. Houston blacks lived mainly in four neighborhoods: Acres Home, the Fifth Ward, the Fourth Ward, and the Third Ward. All these areas had poor housing, inadequate or nonexistent city services, rampant crime, and heavy drug trafficking. Only the Third Ward, part of which had once been an affluent white neighborhood, included even a few well-kept middle-class homes and attractive landscaping.

The causes of these conditions were as deep-seated and complex as in any other metropolis, but in Houston most of the white powers weren't trying even half-heartedly to improve the situation. Although blacks accounted for at least 25 per cent of the city's population, Mayor Louie Welch had appointed only one black to an executive post in his administration, and that job involved honorary duties like presenting dignitaries with keys to the city at black banquets. While proudly refusing to accept federal funds for law enforcement, antipoverty, or any other programs, Welch gave an almost free hand to police chief Herman Short, a man whose alleged use of police brutality against minorities made him feared and hated throughout the black and brown communities.

Houston's black leadership did not seem to be willing or able to improve things in the city's minority neighborhoods. Unlike New Orleans, Houston was never much of a center for the civil rights movement; it *was* the center of a revitalized American capitalism. Political power in the black community rested mainly with a coalition of churches, civic groups, and social clubs called the Harris County Council of Organizations and with a confederation of black preachers called the Baptist Ministers Alliance. But by the early seventies both of these organizations were led by older men increasingly out of touch with a citizenry whose median age was 27, and at any rate their endorsements had always been rumored to be buyable.

The Houston Area Urban League office that Cager moved into was a two-story concrete and glass building on the corner of Dowling and Blodgett streets. Decorated with the Equal Opportunity logo (two bars surrounded by a circle), the building served as the administrative headquarters for three types of projects. The first was an On the Job Training (OJT) program funded by the Department of Labor; its purpose was to place hardcore unemployed people in jobs where they could learn a skill. The second was a tutoring program funded by the Department of Health, Education, and Welfare; its aim was to find jobs for potential high school dropouts so that they could stay in school and at the same time earn money for their families. In addition to these federal programs, which accounted for about $400,000 a year in federal funds, the Urban League also had a $50,000 grant from the United Way to run a program that included monitoring school desegregation, finding jobs for temporarily unemployed workers, and helping senior citizens.

Cager found that the tutoring program was doing well enough, but the OJT program was in a serious bind. Most big companies wouldn't touch it. Many already had their own training programs that they could run without the detailed paperwork that went with receiving federal funds. Cager decided to take a shotgun approach to saving OJT. Instead of turning to big corporations, the league would encourage small businesses, like machine and welding shops, to take on OJT workers. Though some small businesses did sign on, Cager's plan proved sounder in theory than in practice. Many small companies simply couldn't afford to hire additional workers and match the federal portion of their paychecks. For a long time, OJT remained a frustration for Cager.

Meanwhile, the league became involved in an issue of growing political importance in Houston—cable television. The first chapter in the Byzantine cable saga was written not long after Cager arrived, when Mayor Welch made a deal to award the franchise for the entire city to his crony Lester Kamin. But in early 1973, as news of the mayor's cable deal became public, white liberal activist Kathy Whitmire organized a petition for a citywide referendum on the issue. About this time, the National Urban League gave the Houston league a $3000 grant to conduct a community education project on cable. According to Cager, the money was used to hire some young attorneys and "to bring in some speakers from Washington, D.C.," for a workshop on cable. It so happened that Houston voters subsequently rejected the cable TV deal the mayor had made, thus denying a cable franchise to anyone for the time being. Though Cager never pretended that the modest league-sponsored workshop mobilized the black community, he noted that the black vote had been instrumental in defeating Welch's deal.

On a national level, the politicization of the league was becoming a source of internal dispute. Because of certain foundation law changes in 1969, the national office was concerned about maintaining its status as a tax-exempt nonprofit organization. Staying out of partisan politics was one of the requirements. In March 1972 the National Urban League issued an internal policy statement that prohibited the "participation, intervention, or involvement, either direct or indirect, in support of or in opposition to any candidate for elective office" by the league and its affiliates. It also prohibited employees from running for office without obtaining the league's permission and then resigning.

Though Larry Cager believed that the Urban League was a political animal, he kept a low profile and stayed out of major campaigns during his first few years in Houston. But he did have strong feelings about the lack of black leadership. "What disturbed me wasn't the age of the individual leaders, it was their attitudes," he says. "I got the distinct feeling that blacks who negotiated on behalf of the black community didn't negotiate at all. The white politicians used the black organizations, but the blacks did not raise questions like 'What influence can I have in determining who's going to be police chief? Are you going to give us some department heads? How many?'"

Cager started raising such questions, but to no avail. He was new in town and didn't know the players or their histories. He had not found the pressure points in the system. In an effort to gain a sound political education, he began to gravitate to a man who had impressed him at his first Urban League board meeting in Houston: Judge Andrew Jefferson.

"I admired the man," Cager says of Jefferson. "I admired his ability and guts on the bench. I began to call on him to get advice and information. He knew the people, he knew the system. We began to talk frequently. Sometimes we'd talk in his office. Sometimes in the evenings we'd stop and have a drink." Jefferson, for his part, admired Cager's political savvy and his pragmatic approach to black problems.

The Empire Strikes It Rich

The beginning of that friendship coincided with two events that would have a significant effect on the future of Houston's blacks as well as the future of Jefferson and Cager. One was the December 1973 runoff victory of Fred Hofheinz in the mayor's race. The son of a former mayor and Astrodome promoter, Hofheinz, a white liberal, beat Dick Gottlieb, a conservative former city councilman and television announcer. Hofheinz won because of a large black voter turnout, more than 90 per cent of which went to him. Although neither Jefferson nor Cager worked in the 1973 Hofheinz campaign, they, like most other Houston blacks, welcomed Hofheinz's victory and confidently expected that some long-awaited changes in city govern-

ment would be forthcoming.

They were disappointed. Although police chief Herman Short resigned after the election, the Hofheinz administration made no immediate sweeping changes. There were no major black appointments.

But Houston blacks did receive a windfall from the unlikely hand of President Richard Nixon. In 1973, acting on a Republican states' rights impulse, Nixon directed that the task of contracting federal antipoverty grants be transferred from Washington to the individual cities that were getting the money under the Comprehensive Employment and Training Act (CETA). In the case of funds that went to groups like the Houston Area Urban League, the Department of Labor would transfer the money to the City of Houston; the city would then choose the local social service agencies that would apply the money to various programs. Since Mayor Hofheinz, unlike his predecessor, had no qualms about accepting federal money, the Nixon plan, along with a Democrat-controlled Congress, rapidly increased the flow of federal dollars to Houston agencies. The Urban League's budget quickly grew from $400,000 per year to roughly $1 million.

The new money immediately created a bigger agency. With a new CETA-funded Manpower program the staff expanded from twenty to nearly fifty. Like the OJT program, the aim of the Manpower project was to find jobs for black people, but it offered training in the classroom rather than on the job. The addition of the program required the leasing of a nearby church building; other new leases followed, and soon the Urban League was spread out among four buildings.

Another immediate effect of the new federal money was an increase in wealth and power for executive director Larry Cager. Records later disclosed by the *Houston Post* showed that in 1974–75 Cager collected a salary of $35,000, paid through the general fund for 100 per cent of his time, and $5000 in federal funds for an additional 23.8 per cent of his time in connection with the Manpower project. In the months that followed, Cager invested in a variety of enterprises, including a liquor store and real estate. He also tried unsuccessfully to put together a Popeye's Fried Chicken franchise group.

One of Cager's new ventures involved renting space to the Urban League. A building next door to the league headquarters had been rented to the league before Cager bought it. Cager claimed that he and Dr. Clarence Higgins, the husband of board member Edwina Higgins, bought the property when the previous owner went bankrupt to ensure that the Urban League could keep renting its space. Cager also claimed that he and Higgins, who owned the property under the name CAHIG, asked the Urban League to pay the same rent it had in the past. For that reason, Cager said, he saw no conflict of interest in renting the building to his own employer. Unfortunately for Cager, others would one day disagree.

Several board members had struck business deals with the league: H. J. Susberry provided group insurance. Marcellas Day provided general insurance. Edwina Higgins rented property to the league through CAHIG. Later, still another board member, Robert Combre, rented property to the league. Cager insisted that all these arrangements were legitimate, favors the board members did for the league, rather than favors the director gave them. And if anyone on the board worried that an outsider might not see such dealings the same way, no mention of it was made at the time.

Though not directly affected by the federal money, Jefferson was also enjoying success in the get-ahead game. In 1974 Governor Dolph Briscoe appointed Jefferson judge of the 208th Criminal District Court in Harris County. The appointment meant a modest decrease in salary to $25,000 but a major increase in prestige. Only Congresswoman Barbara Jordan could vie with Jefferson for the title of the city's most respected black. People began to say that Andrew Jefferson was bound for the Supreme Court. Apart from Jefferson himself, probably no one wanted that prediction to come true more than Larry Cager.

"Larry, Is This The Group?"

Besides enlarging his bank account, the new federal money apparently boosted Cager's political confidence. The Urban League was a secular congregation, one he could use to build a political base. As he became disillusioned with the Hofheinz administration, Cager began to feel that the time had come for him to take decisive political action. One night in early 1975, after a church-affiliated gathering at the Hyatt Regency in downtown Houston, Cager and some friends were having drinks and bemoaning the situation at city hall. Someone asked who was negotiating with Hofheinz on behalf of the black community; everyone assumed the black ministers were, but no one knew for sure. That startling realization seemed indicative of how factionalized Houston's black leadership had become.

Cager decided to remedy the situation by calling a private council of the black community's most prominent leaders. With the help of a politically active dentist named Art Higgs, he drew up a list of seventeen names. It included such disparate personalities as Mickey Leland, a former radical and a state representative at the time; John B. Coleman, a relatively conservative physician and businessman; John Chase, an architect and a board member at the Walter Mischer–dominated Allied Bank; city councilman Judson Robinson; State Representative Anthony Hall; Otis King, TSU law school dean;

Vince Rachal, a Foley's executive; Al Hopkins, a pharmacist; Clarence Higgins, league landlord; A. M. Wickliff, a lawyer and board member; A. W. Parker, a Teamsters local president; Granville Sawyer and J. Don Boney, educators; Earl Lloyd, a physician; H. L. Garner, a retired labor leader; the Reverend Bill Lawson, a former civil rights activist; and, of course, Judge Jefferson.

Cager's list was not a complete who's who of black power in Houston. Those summoned represented a cross section of the kind of men Cager believed could provide Houston blacks with some aggressive new leadership. Missing (with the exception of the iconoclastic Lawson) were the traditional black leaders, the ministers. Also missing was the most powerful person in the black community, Congresswoman Barbara Jordan.

Cager and Higgs convened the men for a weekend meeting in Freeport to discuss the problems and potential positions available in their areas of expertise. After listening to each other's presentations, they decided to set up meetings with public officials to make demands for change.

The first official to meet with them was Mayor Hofheinz. Cager and his colleagues told Hofheinz that they wanted to have a say in who was to become police chief. They also demanded the appointment of blacks to top posts in the branches of city government most affecting blacks: the Parks and Recreation Department (on the theory that blacks were the greatest users of such facilities) and the CETA program (on the claim that blacks were also the poorest group in the city).

Well aware of the importance of the black vote to his 1973 victory and to his upcoming bid for reelection, Hofheinz proceeded to grant almost everything Cager's group asked and more. According to Cager, the Group met with and approved Pappy Bonds before he was named police chief. Hofheinz made the appointments they wanted in Parks and Recreation and the CETA program. The mayor also named Hortense Dixon an executive assistant and made Otis King city attorney. Cager credited these developments to the influence of the black leaders he had convened.

At first, Cager's group did not even have a name. When they originally met with Hofheinz, the mayor simply referred to them as "the group," as in "Larry, is this the group?" Thereafter, Hofheinz's appointments secretary noted the mayor's meetings with the Group. Lacking any better name, Cager and the others eventually began referring to themselves as the Group, too. Unlike the 8-F Crowd, the Group didn't, as Cager put it, "have the money or the stroke." They also came at power from a different angle. The 8-F Crowd's wheeling and dealing in politics rested on the power of their pocketbooks; Cager and his group based their influence

on the power of their people, on the assumption that together they represented major segments of the black electorate. Their ability to deliver those votes had never been put to the test, but that did not work against them as long as those they were dealing with believed they could.

The Group met at least once a month, in the office of one of the members or at the Urban League building, where the league would pick up the tab for liquor and refreshments. Although they did not make official endorsements, the members did interview candidates for local races and decide informally which ones merited their individual support. The unspoken rule was to keep a low profile. Though the Group's influence may have been based on the voting strength of the black community, its various constituents, such as they were, did not know their leaders were meeting. As Cager later admitted, the Group was much better known among members of the white establishment downtown than it was out in the Fifth Ward. But the Group preferred to keep it that way.

New, Improved BOLD

While Cager's Urban League domain expanded, Andrew Jefferson grew restless on the bench. Honors and distinctions were pouring in, but while Jefferson enjoyed his prestige, it did not pay the bills. His state district judge's salary was far less than he could have been making in private practice. Having spent ten of the previous fifteen years in public service jobs, Jefferson, who was now approaching his 41st birthday, began to feel that the time had come to think again about number one. In October 1975 Jefferson announced that he was resigning from the bench. The reason he gives now is simple and to the point. "I wanted to make some money."

But Jefferson did not go immediately into making money. Instead, at the time of his resignation he announced that he was going to become the cochairman of Fred Hofheinz's reelection campaign. The election was only a few weeks away, and Hofheinz was being stoutly challenged by his old nemesis, Gottlieb, and by former Harris County district attorney Frank Briscoe, a conservative law-and-order man despised by the city's minorities. A runoff seemed inevitable, and Hofheinz would again need strong black support to carry him through. Presumably, having a prominent black like Jefferson as campaign cochairman, a first in Houston politics, would give black voters a strong signal that Hofheinz was still their man.

Conveniently, just about the time Jefferson was preparing to leave the bench for the Hofheinz campaign, his friend Larry Cager was starting yet another political organization. This time the project was a Houston version of BOLD. Like its New Orleans predecessor, this BOLD purported to be dedicated not to a particular candidate but to raising political issues and to helping young blacks get some of the gravy. Its main business, however, was endorsing politicians. The first candidate BOLD endorsed was Urban League worker Billie Smith, who was on leave to run for the school board. The second endorsement was for Mayor Hofheinz. It came after Hofheinz's new campaign cochairman, Andrew Jefferson, had addressed the organization.

Cager, once again, did not join the organization. BOLD's first president and vice president were young lawyers Robert Jones and Alexander Green. But Cager wasted no time in introducing BOLD to the staff of the Houston Area Urban League. Exactly how he went about doing this was later hotly disputed. Cager claims he simply explained the concept of BOLD to his staff, mentioned that the Urban League was to some extent responsible for BOLD's creation, and "encouraged them to get involved." He was talking about getting involved in the Hofheinz campaign, BOLD's main project. Cager says he tried to "make it clear to the staff that their participation was voluntary, that their participation was to take place after five or on their own time."

At least half a dozen Urban League staffers later alleged that Cager did not make the voluntary aspect of participating in BOLD clear at all. They charged that he implied they must work for BOLD or lose their jobs. Manpower worker Lois Shorten, for example, claimed that Cager simply told her she had to work for BOLD, but the message was clear to her. She believed from what he said that if she did not work on the Hofheinz campaign, she "wouldn't be around there much longer."

Though Cager denied the charges, there is no dispute that his staff followed his cue. On a BOLD membership list submitted as evidence in federal court, 21 of the 60 members listed were league employees, but former league staffers have said that at least 20 other Urban League employees also did work for BOLD. Since most of the league staff was female, most of BOLD's membership was female, too. The leadership, however, remained all male, a fact not lost on some of the new recruits. "BOLD was basically a group of young, inexperienced women led by a group of men," one former league staffer recalls. "All the guys who joined were given some sort of title or responsibility. The women were not."

The $25 membership dues for BOLD were paid for most Urban League staffers with Urban League checks signed by Larry Cager and other agency officials. Cager later stated that these dues came from the league's general fund, not from federal funds, and that supporting BOLD and paying dues were appropriate Urban League projects. Whether the league board was ever aware of these expenditures is not clear, but at least one board member—Andrew Jefferson—says he first heard about it from a reporter in the summer of 1981, six years after the fact.

The workers who claimed they were forced to join BOLD also claimed Cager directed them to do campaign work on federal time, a violation of the Hatch Act, which forbids federal employees above the policymaking level to participate in politics. According to Shorten, former acting director Charlene Priester, and several other former staffers, league staffers did campaign work on federal time before both the November 1975 general election and the December 1975 runoff election. While considerable BOLD work went on after office hours and on weekends, those who did campaign work could take off a corresponding number of hours from their Urban League jobs during the week. But quite a bit of campaign work allegedly went on during regular office hours, too, with some staffers handling routine campaign responsibilities on a day-to-day basis rather than attending to their jobs.

The peak of the political activity came on the days of the general and the runoff elections; a skeleton crew answered the telephones at the Urban League offices while the rest of the employees drove sound trucks, circulated literature, and got voters to the polls for Hofheinz. Former Manpower program worker Marie Rudison charged that Cager instructed her to falsify the time sheets of league workers who were doing campaign work for Hofheinz. These allegations suggested that Cager used the Urban League to build his own illegal campaign army, his own political rent-a-crowd, on federal time and at taxpayers' expense.

While conceding that some league employees may have campaigned on federal time without his authorization, Cager denied instructing any staffers to do political work during regular business hours or to falsify federal time sheets. Cager maintains he was merely encouraging community involvement and that he kept BOLD and the Urban League officially separate.

Whichever version of the story is closer to the truth, soon after BOLD was formed it confronted the question of money. Although BOLD did not want to "sell" its endorsement for collection plate contributions as the black preachers allegedly did, the organization was not opposed to being paid for campaign work. That opportunity came when Hofheinz campaign cochairman Andrew Jefferson put Cager in touch with a political public relations firm called Parmer Marketing. The Hofheinz campaign had hired Parmer to get out the vote in the black community, and Parmer needed paid workers to canvass the TSU campus and other locations. A representative of Parmer Marketing, Wanda Ybarra, met with Cager and a group of potential canvassers shortly before the 1975 runoff election. Ybarra later testified that while she was explaining that each worker must sign daily time sheets in order to receive payment, Cager asked to speak with her in private. Ybarra said Cager then instructed her not to discuss money with the campaign workers but to allow him to keep the time sheets; Cager also allegedly suggested that he and BOLD should receive payment from Parmer. Although Cager later denied taking Ybarra aside and asking to be paid the money for the canvassing, Parmer Marketing quickly terminated its relationship with BOLD.

On December 2, 1975, Fred Hofheinz won reelection over Briscoe by a vote of 137,456 to 104,650. Once again, the black vote proved the key. Some 97.5 per cent of it went to Hofheinz.

BOLD's impact on the election remains unclear. One former member claimed that the organization distributed 10,000 posters and 100,000 leaflets in the black community. That was a worthy contribution, but it could hardly have been decisive. Blacks had voted overwhelmingly for Hofheinz in 1973, and with a law-and-order archconservative running against him this time, the repetition of the 1973 turnout was no great surprise. Nevertheless, a faction in BOLD that included Urban League staffers Billie Smith and Marie Rudison requested some $18,000 from the Hofheinz campaign for supplying canvassers. Parmer Marketing, which saw no way BOLD could have earned such a sum, advised Jefferson not to pay the bill. Cager concurred. Then, according to Cager, "vicious rumors" circulated in BOLD headquarters that he and Jefferson were pocketing campaign money. In order to set those rumors to rest, Cager said, the Hofheinz campaign paid BOLD $5500.

Not surprisingly, Cager and BOLD soon parted company. BOLD remained intact under the leadership of Al Green and others, but its active membership dwindled. In the absence of a campaign to work on, the organization could maintain neither its enthusiasm for political work nor the presence of the Urban League staffers.

"Evil People Have To Work Someplace."

Though estranged from BOLD, Cager continued to participate in the Group, the most enduring of his creations. He also presided over an ever-expanding Urban League. In four years, the league budget grew from $1 million per year to $4 million. This increase in funding naturally meant an increase in power for Cager. Besides his salary from the general budget and the CETA program, Cager carried a credit card paid for by the Urban League. Copies of some of the credit card receipts show that Cager sometimes spent as much as $1000 per month on dining and entertainment he claimed were related to Urban League business. Among his favorite haunts were Courtlandts Restaurant in the

Montrose area and the Rivoli in Southwest Houston. Cager also frequented the Foxtrappe, a club on the south side of town owned by his friend and league board member Robert Combre.

But bigger trouble was brewing. Several of the small businesses that had agreed to take on OJT employees when Cager tried to revive that program happened to be owned by members of the Urban League board. One was Andrew Jefferson. Another was Robert Combre. One man, Charles Brawley, originally came to the Urban League as a client—that is, a hardcore unemployed person seeking a job—and subsequently won an OJT contract to *hire* workers for a security company he started; Brawley also wound up on the Urban League's board. Still other contracts went to influential blacks like city councilman and Group member Judson Robinson.

Cager's detractors later alleged that at least some OJT workers were not really hard-core unemployed but ordinary workers whom board members and other employers friendly with Cager merely sent to the Urban League to be qualified for federal wage supplements. Cager and Jefferson vigorously rebutted these allegations by pointing out the small sums of money involved and by claiming that board members who took on OJT workers were merely trying to set an example for other employers.

Besides the program problems, the Urban League offices were rife with sexual intrigue and rumors that just about everyone was sleeping with just about everyone else. Marie Rudison claimed that Cager had been forcing her to have sex with him since early 1972. According to Rudison, Cager would call her at home early in the morning before her children had left for school "and say he wanted to come by and use me." Cager, a married man, later denied ever sleeping with Rudison and accused her of being "evil." Asked why he kept her on the Urban League staff, he replied, "All over the world, evil people have to work someplace. And she knew the [CETA] program."

When the Urban League dropped the Manpower program in the summer of 1976, the agency's internal problems threatened to erupt. Three former Manpower workers complained to the United Fund that they had been forced to do political campaign work on federal time. The Urban League board appointed an ad hoc committee chaired by board president Dale Fridley, a white Exxon executive, to investigate. But before the committee could make much headway, the board voted in a special session to replace Fridley's group with a new committee chaired by Jefferson. Three of the four members on the first committee resigned in protest. Fridley himself stayed on until March 1977 to complete his term as president, but he never received a report from the Jefferson committee, which claimed

that the complaining workers refused to make a formal statement.

In Bed With Briscoe

While Cager managed the Urban League, Andrew Jefferson plunged into private practice. He formed the firm of Jefferson, Maness, Valdez, and Mimms, a law partnership that included two blacks, a white, and a brown, making it, according to Jefferson, the only multiracial law firm in the city. Soon he began doing exactly what he had left the bench to do—make money. Though still in demand for speaking engagements and United Fund committees, he had time to play golf regularly at the Hermann Park course, and he took up tennis. He lived like any successful lawyer except that instead of having a house in River Oaks or Tanglewood, he and his wife, Mary, and their two sons lived in a house on Palm Street in the Third Ward.

In the summer of 1977, Fred Hofheinz surprised the city by announcing that he would not run for reelection. Jefferson seriously considered making the race. He had visions of a candidacy that would appeal to blacks, liberals, and the downtown power structure. To test the waters, he went to Walter Mischer and other white power brokers and made a pitch for his candidacy. Though cordial, their reception was distinctly lukewarm. Jefferson decided not to run, leaving the field to whites Frank Briscoe and Jim McConn.

Cager also eyed the 1977 mayor's race, but from a different angle. With Jefferson not in the running, blacks could only vote against the hated Briscoe rather than for any of the other contenders. The candidate most likely to defeat Briscoe was McConn, the man BOLD was endorsing. But early polls showed Briscoe with a commanding lead over McConn, so Cager reached the unpleasant conclusion that Briscoe was going to win. And if he did, Briscoe would have no obligation to black people because no blacks were supporting him in the campaign. Cager decided to remedy that situation by forming GAPPS —the Greater Association for Political Power in the South. GAPPS did not pretend to be anything other than a one-candidate group. It was, as Cager's attorney Dick DeGuerin puts it, "sort of like 'Niggers for Briscoe.'"

Like Cager's other recent political creations, GAPPS was staffed with Urban League employees. The cofounder and first president of the organization was league controller Stephen Mouton. GAPPS became controversial because of a press conference it held in October 1977 to announce its support for Briscoe. Acting under Mouton's direction, an estimated 23 Urban League staffers spent from 10 a.m. to 2 p.m. setting up the press conference and impressing the attending reporters with GAPPS's popular support. This activity took place on federal time,

and Mouton was later convicted of directing that a time sheet of one of the Urban League workers attending the press conference be falsified. Though such illegal goings-on might well have damaged Briscoe's candidacy, they did not become public knowledge at the time.

Supporting a man with an anti-minority reputation as strong as Frank Briscoe's seemed like a classic sellout, even though there was no evidence that the Briscoe campaign paid GAPPS for its support. The endorsement was based on what Cager, disregarding the moral issues involved, considered the pragmatic thing to do. The irony of Cager's move is that he bet on the wrong horse. When Briscoe and McConn wound up in a runoff, Hofheinz dramatically announced his endorsement of McConn. That boost was enough to push McConn past Briscoe on election day. Once again, the black vote, which rolled for McConn without Cager's help, proved decisive.

A Piece of the Cable Action

By the time McConn took office in early 1978, Jefferson and Cager were dealing with him as if he had been their man all along. Like his predecessor, McConn knew the importance of the black vote. He could hardly snub a delegation of the black community's most prominent leaders, so he began meeting regularly with the Group.

McConn responded to the Group even more strongly than had his predecessor. In addition to reappointing Al Hopkins to the Metropolitan Transit Authority board, McConn saw to it that the MTA met and surpassed its goal of hiring 20 per cent minority contractors. McConn also ensured that minorities got a shot at city architectural and engineering jobs. The changes most noticeable to the average black citizen were street repairs: McConn fixed potholes in black neighborhoods, widened one main thoroughfare (Scott Street), and made improvements on another (Bellfort Avenue). Such road maintenance might seem routine to an outsider, but it had never before been done in the black community.

Jefferson and Cager got even bigger plums from McConn. Just as the new mayor was taking office, the cable TV issue came up again. As usual, the leading contenders for franchises were white companies with close ties to establishment figures like George Brown and Walter Mischer. Black leaders inside and outside the Group hoped to see one of the franchises awarded to a black group, both on general principles of equity and on the theory that cable TV programming by black people could be a powerful communications and educational force in the community. The only black group that applied for a franchise was Houston Community Cablevision (HCC), a company of eleven investors represented by attorney John Sherman. Though Sherman happened to be a young partner in Jefferson's new law firm, Jefferson was not one of the original investors. However, when Sherman began writing to city hall on Jefferson, Sherman & Mimms stationery, rumors circulated that Jefferson was behind the HCC bid.

About this time, Larry Cager began circulating a petition calling for another referendum on cable. The move gave him a powerful bargaining tool. If a black franchisee was in line for a franchise, the petition drive could be halted. On the other hand, if the petition drive succeeded, there could easily be a repeat of the 1973 experience when no one got a franchise.

Once again, Cager recruited his signature collectors from the Urban League staff, thereby sowing the seeds of still another controversy. As in the BOLD and GAPPS episodes, there were charges that the work was done on federal time. And as in the other cases, Cager staunchly denied telling anyone to work on the cable petition on federal time, maintaining that he asked them to gather signatures only after 5 p.m. or during their lunch breaks.

Subsequent events made the referendum petition unnecessary. HCC's proposal had been rejected by the city's cable expert, Bob Sadowski—not because it was black but because it wasn't black enough. The proposal contained no mention of black programming and evinced no intention of even building a studio. But Sadowski's objections were overridden by the mayor's office (see "Invasion of the Cable Snatchers," TM, March 1980). When word came back from city hall that HCC would be joining the four other franchise winners in the rich Houston market, the petition suddenly died. HCC later sold its franchise to Stoner Broadcasting under a curious arrangement that included a buy-back provision.

A federal grand jury is still trying to determine exactly how Houston's cable franchises were awarded. One of the more interesting sidelights to the story is that shortly after the franchisees were announced but before they were finally approved by the city council, Andrew Jefferson and Larry Cager became members of the HCC group. What, if anything, Jefferson and Cager did to be included remains a mystery. Jefferson claims the HCC invited him because of the prestige he would give the company, and he suggests that the last-minute addition of his name struck some as odd only because he was black. "If Walter Mischer or someone else in the white community had done it, no questions would have been asked," Jefferson maintains. "I am a pretty important figure, too. Or at least I'm perceived as being important."

Jefferson states that he and Cager are among the company's four biggest shareholders, and there have been reports that

Cager made $46,000 on the sale of HCC. There have also been reports that other black investors made many times that. Regardless of specific profits, no one denies that the HCC group has made a bundle and might make even more.

Living by the Sword

By the time the Houston City Council finally approved the cable franchises in January 1979, Jefferson and Cager appeared to have their larger shares of the pie—at least for themselves and for certain other black people. At a National Urban League conference in Wisconsin just a few weeks before the final cable awards, Cager bragged about the league's success in organizing BOLD in New Orleans and about his own association with the Group, which he referred to as a group that endorsed candidates. He went on to urge league executives to take an active political role by doing such things as influencing at least one congressman per city.

To his chagrin, Cager found that his views did not sit well with national league director Vernon Jordan. At the conference, Jordan said he was "frightfully disturbed" by Cager's membership in the Group and observed that "this kind of information in the hands of a Bill Clements or a John Tower could do irreparable damage to the agency." Reminding the Urban Leaguers not to confuse "the art of politics with what this agency is about," Jordan warned that "if you live by the sword, you die by the sword."

Back in Houston, Cager ignored Jordan's warning—at least at first. Things at the Houston Area Urban League went the same as before, only better. Cager's familiarity with city hall paid off in 1979 when the city awarded a new CETA program to the league. Cager in effect exchanged the troublesome OJT program for part of a program called Public Service Employment (PSE), which placed blacks in jobs with public service institutions like schools, hospitals, and churches. Since these institutions were more amenable to hiring unemployed workers than big corporations or small businesses were, the Urban League's task would presumably be simpler. And the PSE program meant more money for the league—$3 million.

Cager also continued to do business with the Urban League. One of his new deals involved a building that housed a nightclub called the Point After, located on Blodgett Street not far from the main office. In January 1979, Cager sold the property to Robert Combre, who then rented the upstairs and part of the downstairs to the league. The rest of the building remained a club, which was renamed Studio III. The partners in the nightclub included Cager, several members of the Urban League staff, and later Andrew Jefferson. Cager saw no problems with these insider deals.

That spring, some embittered former

Urban League employees, including one man recently fired from the agency, complained to the Houston Post of irregularities at the league. Post reporter Bill Inman then broke a series of stories revealing Cager's business deals, the alleged political activity on federal time, and other questionable operations. Cager was quoted as denying any wrongdoing, but the stories prompted investigations by the Department of Labor and the Justice Department. Jordan's warning was prophetic, after all.

A Snag in the Judge's Robes

As things got hot for Larry Cager, life was nothing but cool, clear sailing for Andrew Jefferson. In October 1979, President Carter nominated him for a seat on the U.S. Fifth Circuit Court of Appeals. Jefferson's name had been selected not in the old-fashioned, purely political way popular under Lyndon Johnson, but by a merit selection committee. His nomination was also formally supported by U.S. Senator Lloyd Bentsen and by Congressman Mickey Leland. Leland told the Senate Judiciary Committee that Jefferson "is the best we can send from our community."

Back in Houston, news of Jefferson's nomination was greeted warmly by both the black community and the white media. Jefferson's confirmation appeared to be only a formality. In fact, he was already complaining that he would have to take a substantial cut in salary.

Then some snags developed. At the confirmation hearings in November, representatives of the Houston Police Patrolmen's Union testified that Jefferson had shown "an unreasonable disdain for law enforcement agencies and a corresponding unjustified sympathy for criminal defendants resulting in the release of dangerous and violent persons contrary to the best interests of society" during his years as a criminal district court judge. They also accused Jefferson of favoritism toward some criminal defense attorneys whom he later joined in private practice. Jefferson defended himself ably, but the charges slowed his confirmation. The process was slowed even further when, shortly after the November hearings, Senate Judiciary Committee chairman Edward M. Kennedy decided to run for president.

Persecution or Prosecution?

Jefferson's problems did not appear to be too serious, especially compared to Cager's plight. The Houston Post was continuing its series on irregularities at the Urban League, and the U.S. attorney's office in Houston had opened a federal grand jury investigation. Subpoenas went out for records, and several Urban League employees were called to testify, among them Larry Cager. The lawyer who first represented Cager in connection with his grand jury appearance was Fifth Circuit Court nominee Andrew Jefferson. But the U.S. attorney's office advised Cager to get a new lawyer on the grounds that Jefferson himself would be called to testify before the grand jury. In the midst of all this, an enraged Jefferson reportedly told then U.S. attorney J. A. "Tony" Canales that it would be racist to indict Cager. Canales, a Mexican American, supposedly replied, "No, we're equal opportunity indicters. We'll indict blacks, whites, Mexicans, anybody." Jefferson denies having such a run-in with Canales, but he does not deny accepting an estimated $5000 in legal fees from the Urban League for representing employees called before the grand jury.

On May 30, 1980, the federal grand jury handed down indictments against Cager and controller Stephen Mouton. Cager was charged with falsifying the time sheets of federal employees and threatening to fire them if they did not work on the 1975 Hofheinz campaign. Later, Cager was indicted on separate but similar charges in connection with the 1978 cable television petition. The grand jury charged Mouton with falsifying a federal employee's time sheet in connection with the GAPPS press conference in 1977, threatening to fire a federal employee if she did not do campaign work, and using a league computer to conduct private business.

The indictments caused a major shakeup at the Houston league. Cager went on a leave of absence as executive director, though he arranged to receive his regular salary as a consultant's fee. He was replaced by veteran Urban Leaguer Charlene Priester. Board president Alice Bonner, a former state district judge, resigned and was replaced by J. C. Helms, a white real estate developer with Republican connections. Helms's first official act was to accept a subpoena for Urban League documents needed in the Cager and Mouton cases.

Mouton went to trial in July. He was convicted in short order of falsifying the time sheet but was acquitted of threatening to fire an employee. The conviction carried a maximum penalty of five years in jail and a $5000 fine, but the judge sentenced Mouton to four hundred hours of supervised community service work over the next two years.

In the meantime, the Senate Judiciary Committee stepped up its investigation of Andrew Jefferson. Although he was not indicted or accused of any wrongdoing by the federal grand jury, the scandal at the Urban League and his well-known closeness to Cager tainted his reputation. Details of the cable TV scandal were also surfacing, which did not help. Senate investigator Carmine Bellino, a veteran of the Mafia probes conducted by Robert Kennedy, was not impressed with Jefferson and his friends.

Jefferson's nomination remained tech-nically alive for the rest of 1980, but for all practical purposes it died that fall after the Senate committee staff reviewed Bellino's findings. The judiciary committee never issued an official recommendation against Jefferson; it simply never acted on his nomination. Since seventeen of Carter's eighteen nominees to the federal bench suffered the same fate, Jefferson claims that his nomination failed because of Kennedy's run for the presidency and the lame duck president's failure to push through his nominees.

Jefferson did not abandon his friend Cager. In early 1981 he defended Cager at a series of Urban League board meetings. The board was divided into a pro-Cager group and an anti-Cager group. The latter, which considered itself more pro-Urban League than anti-anything, was led by board president Helms and interim director Priester. A stickler for procedures, Helms was appalled by the sloppy record keeping at the agency, the lack of rudimentary financial controls, the apparent conflicts of interest in business deals, and the failure of the board to rotate its membership as called for in the Urban League charter. Helms's fears were substantiated by a Department of Labor audit released in early 1981 that showed more than $100,000 in questionable expenditures in connection with the OJT and PSE programs during the eighteen-month period between October 1977 and March 1979. An audit sponsored by the league disclosed another $165,000 in exceptions and inadequately documented expenditures for the 1979–80 period. These disclosures caused problems with the United Way, the league's other main source of money, which insisted on an unqualified audit before committing to continued funding.

On top of all this, the Houston league's relations with the National Urban League had grown more strained than ever. Part of the problem stemmed from Houston's debt of $22,000 in back dues to the national office. But most of the difficulty involved the unfolding Cager scandal. After an attempt on his life, Vernon Jordan had cancelled a visit to Houston in the summer of 1980; when Priester wanted him to attend the annual dinner in June 1981, Jordan kept putting her off, saying, "The problem down there is the board—they're all in cahoots together."

Priester and Helms had to agree. Through the end of 1980 and the beginning of 1981, matters involving Larry Cager kept coming before the board. There were disputes about the inadequacy of the two-page report Cager submitted to document his work as a consultant, about Priester's contention that Cager was showing up at the agency less and less frequently, and about whether to keep paying Cager after the first six-month term of his leave expired. Helms and Priester saw the pro-Cager faction of the board, led by Jefferson, take up for Cager all the way. Finally, at a March 1981 board meeting,

the strife came to a head. At issue was whether to renew Cager's consultant's contract or to reinstate him as executive director. Several board members, including Jefferson, spoke up for Cager. Then Helms asked who wanted to speak for the league. There was silence. A short time later, the board gave Cager a vote of confidence. Helms resigned, citing the board's insistence on deciding things on the basis of "what was good for Larry Cager and not what was good for the Urban League." Priester also resigned as acting director, saying she could no longer work for an agency that "violates its own bylaws."

That same month, Cager went to trial on federal charges that he threatened to fire Urban League employees unless they did political campaign work and falsified federal time sheets. Cager's defense attorney, Dick DeGuerin, attacked the credibility of the prosecution's star witness, Marie Rudison, the Urban League worker who claimed that Cager forced her to have sex with him, by disclosing that Rudison had received electric shock treatments and repeated psychiatric care. In one of the uglier incidents surrounding the trial, another federal witness who testified against Cager, former Urban League worker Lois Shorten, went home one day to find her kitchen vandalized and the words "You're next, rat fink" written on the wall.

The final jury arguments aptly summarized the conflicting public images of Larry Cager. Assistant U.S. attorney Michol O'Connor alleged that Cager was not "just stealing a little money—he was taking away from you people the right to decide who was going to be the mayor of the City of Houston." DeGuerin claimed that "Larry Cager is not a criminal, ladies and gentlemen. He is a hero, a true American folk hero. . . . He was helping the black community and by this prosecution the black community and the Urban League are shattered."

At the end of the six-week trial, which often seemed more like a personal conflict between prosecution and defense, it took the jury only one hour to acquit Cager of all eighteen counts against him. Judge Carl Bue used a recently adopted judicial rule to prevent anyone from questioning the jurors about how they reached their rapid decision, but DeGuerin has a few ideas of his own. "I think it was clear to the jurors after the trial got under way what was going on," DeGuerin says. "It was a persecution, not a prosecution."

A short time later, the government dropped the cable-TV-related charges against Cager.

A New Game Plan

Less than a month after Larry Cager's acquittal, the Urban League board voted to reinstate him as executive director. But Cager requested as part of his reinstatement that he serve as executive director for no more than sixty days, presumably to aid the league in the transition to a new director. True to his word, Cager left the agency at the end of July to take a still-undisclosed job in private business.

"It's in the best interest of the league for me to leave," Cager told the press. "If I stayed, everyone would wonder 'Is he taking advantage of the Urban League?' I don't think people will ever understand some of what happened."

While the Urban League board searches for a new executive director, the agency's problems continue. Auditors are still trying to account for $125,000 of apparently improper expenditures uncovered by the Department of Labor audit. The Office of the Inspector General is studying conflict-of-interest charges involving Cager and CAHIG. Big Brothers and Big Sisters of Houston, another charitable agency, has threatened to file suit against the league for $3300 in unpaid CETA wages due its workers under the PSE program.

One of the few encouraging developments so far is that relations with the national office have improved. After Cager's acquittal, Jordan addressed the Houston league's annual dinner this past June. National officials later worked out a plan for the payment of Houston's $22,000 in back dues. But as interim board president Priscilla Hill Ardoin admits, the coming months promise to be critical ones for attracting money and developing programs.

Unfortunately for the Urban League, that is a formidable task. Reminded of Jordan's warning that agencies that become involved in politics "live by the sword" and "die by the sword," Larry Cager shrugged his shoulders, smiled wanly, and said, "He may have been right."

Jefferson's future is not nearly as uncertain as the league's or Cager's, but there are certainly some clouds on his horizon. In recent years, Jefferson's name has added weight to two major political campaigns—the 1975 Hofheinz campaign and Mickey Leland's 1978 congressional race. It is doubtful, though, that his name will soon reappear atop a major candidate's campaign committee list. And given the present Republican dominance, it is equally doubtful that he will soon be nominated for a federal judgeship.

Jefferson is clearly bitter over the prosecution of Cager. "When John Connally gets acquitted, it's okay, because he's 'Big John,' " says Jefferson. "But when Larry Cager gets acquitted, it's 'F— Larry Cager.' " Jefferson is also bitter over the rotation of Urban League board members, a condition of continued funding from the United Way that will move him from an active to an honorary role, and over what he sees as a retrenchment by the league in the face of outside pressure. It seems hypocritical of the government to fund a branch of the civil rights movement and then to insist that it stay out of politics, if only to keep its tax-exempt status. "The Cager style, the Cager practicality of leadership has to continue," Jefferson asserts. "The Urban League has to realize what it means to operate in a system controlled by politics and politicians."

For now, the Jefferson-Cager leadership team is lying low. Neither man is actively supporting a candidate in the 1981 mayor's race, which must be particularly frustrating since Mayor McConn was instrumental in the cable TV franchise awards and challenger Al Green was an officer of BOLD. Speculation in Houston political circles is that Green's candidacy is merely a bargaining ploy by a Jefferson-Cager faction to get more concessions from a scandal-tarred, vote-hungry mayor and that Green will eventually drop out of the race and support McConn. But all the principals deny this rumor, and Jefferson still fumes over a *Houston Chronicle* story that took his statement "Al Green is my friend and I plan to vote for him" as an indication that he is supporting Green, which he says he is not. The Group, still meeting regularly, has not issued a formal endorsement, but sources close to it say the members are leaning toward McConn.

Jefferson insists that this period of political quiescence is only temporary. "If people think Cager and Jefferson have been brought to their knees and we need not fear their speaking out in the future," he says, "they are wrong."

It is fairly certain that when Jefferson and Cager next speak out, it will not be from the federal bench or the executive office of the Houston Area Urban League. By successfully obtaining a cable television franchise, they have cut a bigger piece of the economic pie for themselves. By forming the Group, they have won a bigger piece of the pie for many other blacks as well. But in the process, they have lost the very things that helped them reach their goals: the righteousness of the civil rights movement and prestige in the black community. Instead of resolving the "do good" *and* "do well" dilemma facing gifted middle-class blacks, they have become its victims. But the real victim of the story is the black community, which still faces the same frustrating problem that it confronted before Jefferson and Cager arrived on the scene: a lack of effective leadership.♣

THE BISHOP DROPS A BOMB

When an Amarillo bishop spoke out against the nuke, he made his parishioners feel guilty—and he made himself a star.

Late last summer, when Ronald Reagan announced his decision to go ahead with the production of the neutron bomb, Leroy T. Matthiesen, the Catholic bishop of Amarillo, immediately issued a statement in opposition. Actually, "issued" is not the most precise word for what he did. Upon hearing the news, Matthiesen sat down at his desk, wrote out his statement, and, figuring someone from the press would solicit his opinion, "waited for the telephone to ring."

At the time, Matthiesen had been Amarillo's bishop for little more than a year, but he had come to the position determined to do a few things differently from his predecessor. "The previous bishop, Lawrence DeFalco, kept a very low profile," Matthiesen recalls. "I don't think he gave an interview the whole time he was bishop. Since I came out of a journalism background"—Matthiesen edited the diocesan newspaper for most of his 36 years as a priest in the Panhandle—"I was more willing to open myself up to the media. When this announcement came out about the neutron bomb, well, that seemed to me like just the kind of thing I should be commenting on." The local press, however, was not yet wise to the ways of the new bishop, so the phone stayed silent.

L. T. Matthiesen didn't need a media adviser to tell him what he'd done wrong. About a week later, he took his statement from the drawer and gave it to the editor of the diocesan newspaper. He also had a press release drawn up, which he distributed to various organs of journalism in Amarillo. The next day, the bishop's action bore its intended fruit: his statement was on the front page of the *Amarillo Globe-News* (BISHOP DECRIES NEUTRON BOMB) and on all the local television stations. That was ten months ago. His phone hasn't stopped ringing since.

Mattiesen is hardly the first Catholic bishop to come out against nuclear weapons. At last count, 136 of America's 285 active bishops had endorsed a bilateral nuclear weapons freeze. Yet to judge from the national press, Matthiesen is the Catholic leader who has most come to symbolize the large, and growing, number of bishops-in-opposition. His statement was the one to be singled out by the *Time* and *Newsweek* in their respective cover stories on the nuclear freeze movement. ABC and NBC have both done stories about Matthiesen, as have the *New York Times*, the *Washington Post*, the *Boston Globe*, and *People* magazine.

Why all the attention on Matthiesen? At first glance it's a little surprising, since other bishops have made more eloquent statements and taken more dramatic action. But the Amarillo bishop has one thing his fellow bishops lack, and it is this element the press finds irresistible: he is the bishop with the local angle. They build the Bomb in his back yard.

"They," of course, is the federal government. Since 1952, the government has been making nuclear weapons on a site seventeen miles northeast of Amarillo, at a 10,000-acre complex called Pantex (see "Ten, Nine, Eight, Seven . . . ," TM, January 1980). Today it is the only place in America where such work is done.

In the more specific and personal sense, "they" also means the 2400 people who assemble the nuclear bombs made at Pantex. And because Bishop Matthiesen believes that everyone who plays a role in the making of nuclear weapons—even the person whose job it is to paint the bombs—shares a degree of complicity in the "inherent evil" of such weapons, he felt he could not avoid mentioning those Pantex workers when he made his statement last August. So he made a special point of singling them out. The bulk of his condemnation, to be sure, was directed at Washington, where the neutron bomb decision had been made. But to those of his fellow Amarilloans whose labor would build those bombs, he had this to say: "The matter is of immediate concern to us who live next door to Pantex. . . . We urge individuals involved in the production and stockpiling of neutron bombs to consider what they are doing, to resign from such activities and to seek employment in peaceful pursuits." This is the part of his statement that made it a thing of controversy—and made Matthiesen the most quoted bishop in America.

During the next few months, Matthiesen continued to say controversial things about Pantex, although what he said seemed to depend upon whom he was talking to. When Amarillo was the intended audience, Matthiesen's remarks were often conciliatory in tone; outside the city, however, his statements became increasingly shrill. The Reagan administration, he told one such gathering, was "spoiling for a war"; living in the shadow of Pantex, he liked to say, was like "living in the shadow of death"; Pantex workers were in a "sinful situation." Implicit in such comments, as Matthiesen admits when asked, is this basic belief: "The bottom line," he says, "is that there is something morally wrong in working at Pantex."

Because of Matthiesen's outspokenness about Pantex, he has been portrayed in the press as a man of courage who, in speaking out as he he did, was simply following the dictates of his conscience. Without intending to impugn either the bishop's courage or his conscience, I have to admit that I find this glorification of Matthiesen's stance troubling. I find it troubling because, first of all, it turns out that casting the bishop in this light requires a good bit of journalistic myth-making—myth-making that is not necessarily justified by the facts. It is also troubling because, despite all the praise that has been heaped on the bishop, I'm not convinced that he was right to say some of the things he has said. The underlying thesis of all the press coverage, of course, is that he was. But after interviewing the bishop, even though I came away with no doubts at all about his sincerity and his own deep conviction that he is doing "the right thing," I also came away with none of my doubts quelled. So I'm still left wondering: is it fair of him to lay so much of the burden and responsibility for the nuclear arms race at the feet of those people who work at Pantex? Is he really in a position to judge the morality of their work? Is that the sort of thing religious leaders should be doing in any case? And as to the larger issue, are Matthiesen and the other antinuclear bishops justified in believing that a nuclear freeze is the only moral course in the nuclear age? Courageous Matthiesen certainly is, but does that, in and of itself, make him *right*?

To understand the Matthiesen affair you must first understand this: Pantex is by far the most important industrial facility in Amarillo. It is the second-largest employer in the area, with an annual payroll of about $55 million. Practically from the day it opened, the Pantex plant has been the one unshakable anchor in the local economy. As a result, today Pantex is the kind of factory where people will wait for years for a position to open up because the work is steady and the wages good.

Naturally, the citizens of Amarillo are not unaware of the plant's importance to the city; just as naturally, this awareness acts as a prism through which the city views most questions surrounding the building of nuclear weapons. For one thing, Amarillo has a rather obvious vested interest in seeing

such weapons built. More money appropriated in Washington for bombs means more jobs for Amarillo; the link is clear and direct. There is thus a tendency for the city to look at, say, a debate in Congress over whether or not to build a particular nuclear weapon from a pork-barrel perspective.

Second, most people in Amarillo feel that the nation needs to continue manufacturing nuclear weapons in order to stay secure. Rather than being defensive about the Pantex plant, Amarilloans feel an element of pride in having it nearby. There is a sense that the government, by deciding to make its bombs at Pantex, has put a great deal of faith in Amarillo. After all, over the years the government has shut down every other facility that did similar work; only Pantex is still going strong. Most people think that this says something fundamentally good about Amarillo.

There is another, more subtle way in which the plant's location affects the way the people in Amarillo think about what is done there. Because Pantex is such a large facility and employs so many people, just about everybody who lives in Amarillo knows at least one Pantex worker and probably more. If you're a citizen of Amarillo and have neighbors who work at Pantex, you instinctively know, first of all, that there is an important unwritten rule you must abide by: never, under any circumstances, ask them about their jobs, which are highly classified. To break that rule is to risk the possibility that those neighbors will spurn your company forever after. Assuming, however, that you stay within bounds and become better acquainted with your neighbors, you soon come to realize that they are good, solid citizens, not unlike yourself, with the same basic set of concerns and interests that you have—in other words, they're perfectly normal, perfectly nice people who just happen to make nuclear bombs for a living. This daily exposure to Pantex workers—this firsthand knowledge that they are not, at bottom, bad people—makes it that much more difficult for the populace of Amarillo to believe that what they do is inherently wrong. It is always easier to perceive villainy from afar. In Amarillo, people see that their Pantex friends hardly count as villains, so they wonder: how can they be doing evil at work every day?

It should be no surprise, then, that Amarillo was not at all pleased by Matthiesen's blast last summer. In the immediate aftermath, Amarillo officials put out counterstatements taking issue with the bishop. Rick Klein, the mayor, declared himself "shocked and surprised" and suggested that the bishop had no business sticking his nose into politics. At the plant, administrators hewed to a strict no-comment policy, but the workers themselves, Catholics included, had plenty to say. "He's got it all wrong, in my opinion," said one Pantex employee. Another called the bishop "idealistic" but naive. It was difficult, in fact, to find anyone in Amarillo, other than the dozen or so local antinuclear activists, who thought the bishop was correct in saying what he did—and

again, this includes most of Matthiesen's own flock. Many people quickly added, though, that the bishop had the right to express himself publicly, "just like everyone else."

Unlike most man-versus-community controversies, this one just wouldn't go away. Long after the initial outcry, it kept finding new ways to bubble to the surface. In September, the other Texas bishops signed a statement expressing their support for their colleague. In November, Matthiesen's appearance on the Phil Donahue show—where he debated the nuclear weapons issue with the Reverend J. Alan Ford, Amarillo's Moral Majority spokesman—was the subject of extensive local coverage and discussion. In December, the *Globe-News* printed a full page of letters devoted to "The Bishop, Bombs, Peace and Pantex." By the beginning of this year, the nuclear freeze movement was getting its first binge of publicity, which kept the Matthiesen controversy in the foreground. And for most of this time, Matthiesen's various speeches before antinuclear groups were reported as news in the *Globe-News*. If part of what the bishop was trying to accomplish was to get people in the region to start talking about Pantex and nuclear bombs—and he says that it was—then he succeeded.

In February the Matthiesen affair hit its peak when the bishop issued a press release announcing that he had accepted a $10,000 gift from a Catholic order so that the diocese could establish a job counseling service and financial aid program for Pantex workers who wanted to quit for reasons of conscience. He said the money would be turned over to Catholic Family Services (CFS), the social service arm of the diocese, which would run the program. Pantex workers were outraged by this, and they retaliated: they began withholding their United Way contributions on the grounds that United Way gave an annual $61,000 grant to CFS. Soon thereafter, United Way, because it feared losing as much as $500,000 in contributions from Pantex employees and other angry citizens, announced that it would have to "reconsider" its CFS grant unless the Catholic agency repudiated the job counseling program. This CFS refused to do, so in mid-March United Way officials decided to withdraw the grant. As of April 1, the money was cut off.

The Catholic Family Services–United Way feud is what really drew the attention of the national press to Amarillo. For reporters, the Matthiesen controversy appeared to be one of the great stock stories in journalism: the saga of the lonely Voice of Enlightenment struggling valiantly to tell hard truths to the Town That Wouldn't Listen. Here, for example, is how the *Washington Post* set the scene in its Matthiesen story: "It is part of the psychology of this town that no one ever 'sees' the incoming trucks, even though the semis carry Amarillo's most important product [nuclear weapons parts]. This is a place where folks don't see what they don't want to see and sometimes get angry when others force them to look." A given in this kind of story is that the Voice of Enlightenment is forcing the townspeople to face a painful reality; thus the *Post* called the bishop's original statement a "moral manifesto" and added, "If it is the job of a priest to touch souls . . . Matthiesen has laid the soul of Amarillo bare." The final element of the story is the town's reaction. Stung by the words of its local conscience, it lashes back, perhaps irrationally. Again from the *Post:* "The counterattack was swift and, what they might call in the trade, massive retaliation."

This last part of the clichéd version of the Matthiesen affair is right. Catholic Family Services does useful and important work in Amarillo, as most Amarilloans admit. The $61,000—about 7 per cent of the CFS budget—was used to fund maternity and adoption programs, home and family intervention programs, and youth programs. The United Way decision, in other words, did nothing at all to stop the proposed Pantex job counseling service, but it did hurt several programs of proven merit. Any way you look at it, that was a small, mean-spirited act.

But in every other respect the newspaper slant to this story has been out of kilter. For example, the generally accepted thesis that

> "When Bishop Matthiesen says that making nuclear bombs is immoral, what he really means is that Pantex workers are sinners, potential candidates for the fires of hell."

no one in Amarillo knew nuclear bombs were being manufactured there until the bishop blew the whistle is just plain wrong. For the last five years, the *Globe-News* has been scrupulous about identifying Pantex as "the final assembly point in America's nuclear arsenal." But even before that—even in the days when the Amarillo paper rarely used the words "Pantex" and "nuclear" in the same story—most longtime residents knew, in a general way, what went on behind those gates. "For as long as I can remember, I knew they made nuclear bombs out there," says José Rael, an Amarillo school board member (and a Catholic). "There was no great awakening. It was just something you always knew."

More troublesome is the question of whether the bishop was right to say the things he did. My own belief is that he was not. I think it was a mistake for the bishop to use his position as a platform from which to make statements about the "immorality" of Pantex work. That word packs an awesome punch; after all, when Matthiesen says that what is done at Pantex is immoral, what he really means is that Pantex employees are *sinners,* potential candidates for the fires of hell. That's not easy to shrug off. And in the case at hand, the bishop's fixation on Pantex has the added effect of laying an enormous burden of guilt on the individual workers while letting the decision makers at the Pentagon off lightly. It looks like he's picking on the little guy.

What's more, I'm not so sure that this kind of grass-roots finger-pointing makes much sense as a general course of action for local religious leaders. By this, I don't mean that bishops have no business talking about social issues; of course they do. But religious leaders are usually at their most effective and influential on social issues when they confine themselves to setting a moral tone—to establishing certain parameters of right and wrong, and then letting the populace at large decide how to stay within those parameters. Bishops who publicly opposed segregation on moral grounds were surely right to do so. Today, they do us all a service when they raise nagging questions about poverty or racism or even the use of nuclear weapons. But having made those simple and direct moral statements, should they then spend their time making additional moral judgments on all the details of and disagreements over how best to achieve the basic goal? If a bishop has spoken out publicly against segregation, does that mean he must then pass moral judgment on every proposed amendment to the Voting Rights Act? Or if he is against poverty, do we need to go back to him for a decision as to whether expanding the welfare state is more moral than supply-side economics?

What Matthiesen has done in Amarillo is not much different. From a basic belief that dropping a nuclear bomb would be an abhorrently immoral act, the bishop has taken the next step: he has tried to make a case that there is only one right way and one wrong way to avoid nuclear catastrophe. On one hand, the nation can stop building bombs, on the theory that enough is enough, and Pantex workers could find jobs in "peaceful pursuits." On the other hand, America can continue making nuclear weapons, in the belief that only by keeping pace with the Russians can the country remain safe from a nuclear attack, though this would mean that Pantex would stay open. You may have a personal preference for one of these choices, but I don't see how you can extrapolate from either that one course is moral and the other is not.

Another problem with getting bogged down in the details is that once you start doing it, you are then compelled to start making fine moral distinctions and splitting moral hairs in order to cover every contingency that may arise. Inevitably, that's going to take its toll in credibility. Two examples from my interview with Matthiesen illustrate the problem.

One of the distinctions Matthiesen makes is between the people who build conventional bombs and those who make nuclear bombs. It is not just that nuclear weapons are so much more destructive than conventional bombs. It is also, in the words of the bishop, that "nuclear bombs are the only weapons in the history of man whose sole purpose is to kill civilians." Even more than their destructiveness, it is this aspect that the bishop—and his church—finds immoral. Although conventional weapons "can be abused," he says that they are at least built with the intention that they will be used to attack soldiers. Because the conventional-bomb builder doesn't know for sure how *his* bomb is going to be used, he is, in a sense, off the hook. Yet this view of conventional bombs strikes me as extremely unrealistic. Since World War II, it has been a basic defense stratagem to use conventional bombs on civilian centers as a way of destroying the enemy's morale. These are hardly isolated cases of abuse.

Another fine distinction Matthiesen makes is between "repairing" nuclear weapons and making new ones. Repair work, he says, can be moral: "I can justify in my own mind the military's possessing the nuclear weapons it already has. I can certainly justify keeping those weapons in tip-top shape. What I have real problems justifying is new bombs." The dilemma this poses is that bombs don't always need to be repaired, but they do need to be replaced. The Navy is replacing all its Poseidon missiles with new Trident missiles. Is it moral to repair such a missile but immoral to replace it? Matthiesen's answer to this is yes. It is difficult to see, however, how this wouldn't lead to a kind of unilateral disarmament by attrition, something the bishop also says he is against.

There is a larger, more fundamental misconception involved here, and it is important to point it out because Matthiesen has built his entire case around this idea. The misconception is that the strategy of nuclear deterrence, which has been the basis of American defense policy for the past 35 years, is immoral. When the antinuclear Catholic bishops rally around the freeze movement, and when Bishop Matthiesen points his finger at Pantex, it is this larger point they are trying to make.

Why do the bishops oppose deterrence? I think it's fair to say that at least part of the reason is that they are terribly naive about the Russians. Matthiesen's views on the subject are fairly typical. "The Russians do have an antinuclear movement," he told me. "There are people like Sakharov. Admittedly they're getting clobbered, but they are going to have some effect on their government." In any case, he said, "we have to clarify our perception of who the enemy is. We need to study the Russian people and their anxiety. If we better understood them we would know that they don't want nuclear war any more than we do." He added that part of the problem between America and Russia lies "in our stress on sovereign nationhood. As a religious person, I would like to see the human family as one. That ideal is tremendously far off, I know, but if nationhood can be preserved only through the use of nuclear weapons, what kind of world will it be to live in?"

But another reason the bishops don't like deterrence is that they believe it is immoral even to threaten to use nuclear weapons. Deterrence, obviously, is little more than a threat to use the bomb. It means you always have to keep your enemy worried enough about your retaliatory capability to prevent him from ever launching a nuclear attack. On the other hand, nuclear deterrence has the key advantage of having worked. It has kept the Russians from attacking us, and it has kept us from attacking them. What's more, it also can serve as a basis for real

arms reduction, through mechanisms like SALT. SALT, of course, is stalled right now, but it has always offered a more realistic way to reduce arms than other, more emotional, more simplistic ideas like the nuclear freeze. I don't necessarily expect the bishops to line up behind SALT, but I do wish they could look past the theory of deterrence to its reality: it has kept the two greatest enemies the world has ever known from coming even remotely close to war. How can that be immoral? How can that even be bad?

As for Amarillo, as yet no Pantex worker has resigned for reasons of conscience. The national press has come and gone, but Mayor Klein says he is glad the reporters showed up. "I think we showed them that we don't look upon Pantex as being any different from any other industry in Amarillo," he said. The local civil defense planner, a

fellow named Don Goforth, still gives interviews claiming that Amarilloans would probably survive a nuclear attack—Amarillo is one of the five most likely places to be hit should nuclear bombs ever rain on Texas—but no one really believes him. In late March, Bishop Matthiesen gave another interview to the *Globe-News* in which he said he thought there had been too much publicity over his stance, and that it was now time to stop talking and to "reflect." But later he was in Santa Fe to give a speech marking the opening of Ground Zero Week. And at the end of April, the diocese put out an announcement: in order to make up the $61,000 lost in the United Way fight, Catholic Family Services began soliciting donations; it has now recouped the sum. One place CFS turned was to Vietnamese families, nearly all of whom were originally resettled in the area by CFS. At last count, the Vietnamese had given about $7000. ❧

THE GUARDIANS WHO SLUMBERETH NOT

by William Martin

Nothing about the pinkish brick home on the oak-shaded street in Longview distinguished it from its neighbors or suggested that it housed one of the most controversial educational organizations in America. No marker, not even a doorbell plaque, indicated that this was the home of Mel and Norma Gabler and their nonprofit textbook-screening organization, Educational Research Analysts—though a construction-paper stop sign in the window, perhaps placed there by a grandchild, served as an apt symbol of the activities within. A neat young woman met me at the door, led me past a bookshelf crammed with copies of *Reader's Digest* and *National Geographic* into a kitchen–family room, and introduced me to Norma Gabler, who was dressed in the weekday uniform of middle-aged Texas church ladies: a vested pantsuit with a polka-dot blouse. In a few moments Mel Gabler came in from another room, looking less like a celebrated educational gadfly than the retired Exxon clerk he is. I had seen their pictures and read about them for years, but it was still disarming to realize that this quiet man padding about in house slippers and this cheery woman carrying on about a device that makes one cup of brewed coffee—"It is *the* most amazing thing we have come up with"—are the same folk who cause textbook publishers to quake with anxiety, liberal educators to fume with indigna-

tion, and indignant conservative parents to regard them as heroes in the struggle against humanism, communism, evolution, and moral relativity.

"We don't censor anything," Norma said, raising the issue I had planned to get into only after covering some less sensitive matters. "We don't care what the publishers put out. We just don't have to buy everything they put out. I don't think that's wrong. If you have a choice between books, why not get the best?" Critics of the Gablers dismiss that defense as sophistry, insisting that censorship is not defined by the point at which it occurs in the communication process. But whatever one calls their attempts to control or heavily influence the selection and content of textbooks that our children will use in school, the Gablers go about their work with such dedication, thoroughness, and persistence as to make plausible the claim by one censorship expert that they are "the two most powerful people in education today."

Norma and Mel Gabler entered the field of textbook reform twenty years ago, after their son Jim came home from school disturbed at discrepancies between the 1954 American history text his eleventh-grade class was using and what his parents had taught him. The Gablers compared his text to history books printed in 1885 and 1921 and discovered differences. "Where can you go to get the truth?" Jim asked. "Well," Norma told me, "I'm Irish, and that got my Irish up." When the Gablers

"Nearly every part of their home is crammed with files, books, and desks. What was once a living room is filled with bookshelves. 'Our kids have to stay in a motel when they come to see us,' says Norma Gabler."

approached the superintendent, he explained that the school was permitted to purchase only those textbooks that had been screened and placed on an approved list by the State Board of Education. Then, in one of those casual comments that change history, he suggested, "Why don't you go to Austin? That's where you can have some impact." Norma did indeed go to Austin, and for the past two decades few people have had greater impact on what American schoolchildren read than Mel and Norma Gabler.

Although 21 other states also use a

statewide textbook adoption system, Texas is the nation's largest single purchaser of textbooks, and that gives the Gablers enormous influence. Making the Texas list is practically a guarantee of profit for a publisher; failure to make it may doom a book, or a whole series of books, to extinction. Thus most publishers are understandably sensitive to pressures to make their books acceptable for use in this state's 1100 public school districts.

Under the Texas system, the State Board of Education issues a textbook proclamation each spring, announcing the subjects and grade levels for which new books will be selected that year and inviting publishers to submit any books they wish to have considered. The board also appoints a fifteen-member committee, at least eight of whom must be classroom teachers in the pertinent subjects, to evaluate the books that are submitted. A list of these books can be obtained by anyone who requests it, and the books themselves are available at regional centers throughout the state. Citizens having objections to any books are invited to file written "bills of particulars" containing their specific complaints. Positive comments or general statements of disapproval are neither sought nor accepted. Near the end of the summer, the textbook committee meets to hear objections from citizens who have filed such bills and the publishers' replies, then sends its recommendations, which may include as many as five books per subject, to the state commissioner of education. The commissioner considers the textbook committee's list and may strike books from it (but not add to it) before submitting it to the board. Meanwhile, the Texas Education Agency scrutinizes the recommended books, the committee's reviews, and the citizens' objections and decides whether to request that publishers make changes in their texts. After a last round of hearings, the board makes its final decision. Then, following a similar set of procedures, local school boards decide which of the approved books they will select for use in their schools.

Norma Gabler went to the hearings for the first time in 1962—and she went without Mel. "I had never traveled anywhere in my life by myself," she explains, "but Mel said, 'Honey, you've got to go, because I can't.' I said, 'What will I do when I get there?' and he said, 'I don't know, but you can do something.' I was just going to do it that one year, but it was just something that went on and on."

Mrs. Gabler recalls that in the early years she was sometimes treated badly by both publishers and textbook committee members. But she took her lumps, protested vociferously when the committee violated its own rules to give her opponents an advantage, and in 1970 won her first real victories. Beginning that year, publishers of science books containing material on evolution were required to include an introductory statement saying that evolution is a theory, not a fact. Publishers were also put on notice that no book would be adopted if it contained offensive language that would cause embarrassing situations in the classroom. Finally, the board agreed that all books up for adoption would be made available at twenty regional educational centers well in advance of the deadline for filing bills of particulars. "Those were the three biggest gains we ever had," Norma says, "and it has been different from then on."

During the seventies, the Gablers' successes were more than procedural. Though they admit they can never be sure the textbook committee would not have reached the same decisions on its own, their objections clearly had an impact on the process. Today, publishers' responses to their bills of particulars are often longer than the bills themselves.

As the Gablers gained credibility in Austin, they achieved hero status in the eyes of thousands of concerned parents, fundamentalist religious leaders, and conservatives of the sort now identified with the New Right. They began using hired assistants and volunteers to review textbooks and made copies of those reviews available to anyone who requested them. In 1973, after Mel took early retirement from Exxon Pipeline, thereby sacrificing some of the pension he would have received in seven more years, the Gablers formed Educational Research Analysts and have given full time to their mission ever since.

At last summer's hearings Norma Gabler and the two young women who accompanied her dominated the first day of the proceedings. For six hours, with a break in the morning and one for lunch, they repeated and elaborated on the objections contained in their bills of particulars, which filled six bound volumes and were available at a special table reserved for the press. An official with an overhead projector kept everyone informed of elapsed time—a citizen is allowed ten minutes for each publisher whose books he opposes, though he can use his total allotment as he sees fit—but one sensed the Gabler women knew precisely where they stood every moment, as if they had carefully rehearsed and timed their performance. Members of the textbook committee, facing the Gabler team across an enormous conference table, occasionally showed wry amusement at some of their complaints, and textbook authors and publishers seated in a gallery of folding chairs at one end of the smoky room sometimes muttered in irritation or disbelief as they heard their books attacked, but it was clear they all took this East Texas grandmother quite seriously.

In addition to inundating the textbook committee, the Gablers produce a continuous stream of textbook-related materials and distribute them to conservative parents and groups in every state in the union and over two dozen foreign countries. They also maintain a hectic schedule of travel to meetings, consultations, and speaking engagements that takes them away from Longview more than two hundred days a year. They have been featured on *60 Minutes*, *Today*, *Nightline*, *Good Morning America*, *Donahue*, *Freeman Reports*, *The David Frost Show*, syndicated religious broadcasts, and numerous local radio and television talk shows. A book describing their work, James Hefley's *Textbooks on Trial*, went through four printings and is available in an updated paperback edition titled *Are Textbooks Harming Your Children?*

More important, they have become an integral institution of the New Right, whose agenda they share almost point for point. Their work is commended by Moral Majority leader Jerry Falwell, anti-ERA activist and Eagle Forum founder Phyllis Schlafly, and New Right direct-mail expert Richard Viguerie. They participate in gatherings sponsored by such New Right organizations as the Committee for the Survival of a Free Congress and the Texas-based Pro-Family Forum.

The Gablers receive no compensation from Educational Research Analysts; they live on Mel's retirement and "a little Social Security." They take an exceedingly modest honorarium ($300 plus expenses for the two of them) for their speaking engagements, and they put this money into the organization to cover salaries for assistants, printing and mailing costs, and travel to Austin. They charge a small fee for various publications but have to depend on contributions from supporters to cover much of their $120,000 annual budget. Critics sometimes speculate that they must be receiving secret payments from some conservative cabal, but a visit to

"In one of those casual comments that change history, the school superintendent suggested to the Gablers, 'Why don't you go to Austin? That's where you can have some impact.'"

their home makes it clear that they are what they profess to be: a totally dedicated couple who have surrendered their money, their time, and their space to a cause they judge to be of overwhelming importance.

Nearly every part of their four-bedroom home is crammed with files, books, office equipment, and desks where young people pore over textbooks, answer letters, and assemble packets of material for parents' groups and individuals who request their aid. What was once a living room is filled with bookshelves that jut out into the room, library style. A peninsula of files covers most of the floor space in another room. "There used to be a bed under here," Norma said, "but we had to move it out. Our kids have to stay in a motel when they come to see us. We only have two hundred and twenty file cabinet drawers in our house." Their own bedroom and the kitchen–family room are somewhat less densely packed, but the walls attest to their efforts with awards and plaques such as that from the Pro-Family Forum and the Eagle Forum of Southern Nevada, which declares them to be "Valiant Warriors of God who have devoted their lives to combat the evil forces that would destroy the virtue, nobility, and lofty potential of the youth of this nation."

That textbooks should be regarded as dangerous weapons in an effort to destroy the minds and moral fiber of our nation's children may strike some as surprising, but the Gablers certainly see them as such. "What we're fighting," Mel likes to say, "is mental child abuse." *Are Textbooks Harming Your Children?* quotes McGraw-Hill president Alexander J. Burke, Jr., as observing that "textbooks both mirror and create our values" and cites publisher D. C. Heath's dictum "Let me publish the textbooks of a nation and I care not who writes its songs or makes its laws." The Gablers evince no doubt that inferior, improper, and blatantly destructive textbooks are responsible for leaving young people unprepared to face the challenges of adulthood, for destroying confidence and pride in America, for undermining Judeo-Christian values, and for creating a society in which crime, violence, drugs, pornography, venereal disease, abortion, homosexuality, and broken families have become facts of everyday existence. "UNTIL TEXTBOOKS ARE CHANGED," one of their information sheets declares, "there is no possibility that crime, violence, VD and abortion rates will decrease. . . . TEXTBOOKS mold NATIONS because they largely determine HOW a nation votes, WHAT it becomes, and WHERE it goes!"

In their efforts "to rescue the hearts and minds of children" who are "a captive audience" to what is presented to them in their textbooks, the Gablers and their helpers subject every book under consideration to a painstaking page-by-page, paragraph-by-paragraph, line-by-line, word-by-word examination, ferreting out what they regard as unsound or harmful material and preparing bills of particulars and reviews that sometimes run to well over a hundred pages per subject. It is this uncompromising thoroughness that makes them such formidable opponents, since they often know the books far better than do the members of the textbook committee, and sometimes better than even the publishers who try to answer their objections.

The Gablers' views are straightforward and comprehensive. They believe that the purpose of education is "the imparting of factual knowledge, basic skills and cultural heritage" and that education is best accomplished in schools that emphasize a traditional curriculum of reading, math, and grammar, as well as patriotism, high moral standards, dress codes, and strict discipline, with respect and courtesy demanded from all students. They feel the kind of education they value has all but disappeared, and they lay the blame at the feet of that all-purpose New Right whipping boy, secular humanism, which they believe has infiltrated the school at every level but can be recognized most easily in textbooks.

Though they have gained most of their notoriety for protests that reflected ultraconservative political and religious views, the Gablers have consistently—and rightly, in my view—stressed basic academic skills, with particular attention to the use of intensive phonics to teach reading. Their handbook on phonics is a helpful collection of articles and references that thoroughly documents the superiority of the phonetic over the "look-say" method of reading instruction, a method whose wide use in American schools seems to me not only to negate the chief advantage of an alphabet over pictographs but also to deserve much of the blame for the depressingly high rate of functional illiteracy in this country.

But the Gablers also feel that even those students who learn to read through intensive phonics, memorize their "times tables," diagram sentences perfectly, and win spelling bees and math contests must still cope with an educational system that is geared to undermining their morals, their individuality, their pride in America, and their faith in God and the free enterprise system. Much of this corrosive work is accomplished through textbooks in history, social sciences, health, and homemaking.

The Gablers seem to believe not only that the proper subject of history is facts rather than concepts but also that all the essential pertinent facts are well known and should be taught as they were in older textbooks, in a clear chronological arrangement with a tone that is "fair, objective, and patriotic." They object to texts that omit reference to classic patriotic speeches such as Patrick Henry's "Give me liberty or give me death" or that slight traditionally major figures in favor of lesser-known characters, particularly women and minorities. They think it absurd for Crispus Attucks or Abigail Adams to get as much attention as Paul Revere or Benjamin Franklin and are deeply offended that George Washington Carver and Booker T. Washington have been de-emphasized in or dropped from some history books because they are perceived as having exemplified an Uncle Tom attitude that is no longer fashionable. "They dropped Carver along about 1960," Mel observes, "because his philosophy was wrong. He thought every man ought to earn respect for himself. That's not the philosophy of welfare." Of a book that cited both Martin Luther and Martin Luther King, Jr., as reformers, the Gablers issued this criticism: "These two men should not be put in the same category. Martin Luther was a religiously-dedicated, non-violent man." In another particularly ethnocentric objection, they charged a textbook that described America as a nation of immigrants with presenting a derogatory view that did not foster patriotism.

As for contemporary events and issues, the Gablers object to texts that seem to manifest a bias—often documented by a meticulous counting of lines and pages given to a topic—not in keeping with familiar New Right positions on defense, capital punishment, gun control, civil rights, Taiwan, the Panama Canal, the labor movement, or women's liberation. They dislike civics books that emphasize the flexibility rather than the stability of the U.S. Constitution, and they criticize any material that seems to encourage or condone change, dissatisfaction, rebellion, or protest, even though the major part of their lives is spent protesting and encouraging others to protest against the standing order in education and much of their own success stems from their having been able to get rules changed by bringing pressure to bear at critical points.

On matters of economics, the Gablers stand foursquare on the side of free enterprise and regard as inept any text that points out its shortcomings or that fails to take a hard line against socialism or communism. They are offended by books that depict the economic advances of the People's Republic of China, and they quarrel with a text that lists America as third in per capita income, after Sweden and Switzerland, because it might lead children to believe that socialism, as practiced in Sweden, is something other than a radical system that always fails.

They are similarly protective of Christianity. When a world geography book suggests that primitive peoples may have developed religion and conceptions of gods in response to the uncertainties associated with harvests—a commonplace speculation among students of religion—they charge it with undermining traditional Judeo-Christian beliefs and ask, "How many parents are going to want their children to be taught that religion was developed merely to explain a natural phenomenon?" They object to books containing myths and legends that are reminiscent of Bible stories, though such stories abound in human culture, and to a suggestion that students check to see how many Asian religions have a concept like the golden rule at their core. Rather than regard such an assignment as an opportunity to amass evidence of the essential oneness of humanity—evidence that could easily be cited in defense of theism—they assert that "the significance of religions is their differences, not their similarities."

The Gablers' resistance to cultural variation and social change is seen nowhere more clearly than in their attitude toward sex roles. Predictably, their view of the family falls into the Father-Mother-Dick-Jane-Spot-and-Puff mold, with no doubt as to who does what. When texts note the desire of women to earn pay equal to that of men, the Gablers complain that such equality could come only if women "abandon their highest profession—as mothers molding young lives." They oppose any suggestion that divorce may have positive outcomes on the grounds that "divorce violates the religious opinions of many." Books showing parents as flawed—not wicked, just imperfect and uncertain—are criticized for "emphasizing that parents, not teens, have problems." And a text that observes that the environment in some homes may not be pleasant is criticized for weakening family relationships and justifying discontent.

Another prominent weapon in the humanists' alleged attack on the family is sex education, which, the Gablers charge, offers young people an abundance of sexual information but no moral framework. As examples of books to which they have objected in past years, they showed me texts sporting pictures of vaginas and penises, describing homosexual acts, and repeatedly using the word "masturbation." They also showed me, with some glee, a book that described the average penis as 38 millimeters in circumference. "An inch and a half around," Norma chortled. "That's less than a half-inch in diameter. That's less than your little finger. I had Mel cut me a little dowel the size they said a penis was. That got quite a laugh down at Austin." More seriously, they regard sex education as a parental right that should not be usurped by the school even if the parent is failing to provide it. "Silence," they observe, "is a most underrated virtue. Talk in the classroom is no substitute for a quiet example at home."

The Gablers feel that drug education is appropriate for schools, but they have presented a battery of objections to the way health textbooks deal with it. At the August hearings, they were consistently critical of books that gave more attention to alcohol, tobacco, coffee, and various over-the-counter drugs than to heroin, cocaine, or marijuana. Citing reports from *Reader's Digest* and *Ladies' Home Journal,* they attack books for saying that not all the dangers of marijuana are known, since many *are* known, and they ask for the removal of references to positive medical uses of marijuana, such as treat-

ing glaucoma and relieving nausea associated with chemotherapy, because "no such documentation has been offered." On the contrary, they allege, "many scientists consider marijuana the world's most dangerous drug." Norma also criticized as unwise one text's revelation that marijuana could be mixed into foods, noting, "This was tried here in Austin last month."

In the scientific realm, the Gablers direct most of their fire at textbooks that espouse evolution, which they regard as a cornerstone of secular humanism (see box on page 148). They are, of course, well versed in the materials cited in support of a creationist, "young earth" viewpoint and claim they would not object to evolution's being taught (as a theory, not a fact) if evidence for "sudden creation" were presented at the same time. It seems clear, however, that they would greatly prefer that textbooks give children no reason to think the universe might have been here for more than a few thousand years or that various forms of life have undergone significant evolutionary changes. They often introduce their criticisms of texts by describing them as being "blatantly evolutionary" or containing an excess of "evolutionary speculation" or "notable references to evolution," and their publications speak approvingly of books in which most or all references to evolution have been eliminated. In response to a text that says, "As more knowledge is gained, and as new theories are tested against observed fact, ideas about the origin and structure of the universe and of our own world will no doubt continue to be changed and modified," they complain, "This shows bias in favor of evolution." Of another text that states, "No one knows exactly how people began raising plants for food instead of searching out wild plants," they say, "The text states theory as fact, leaving no room for other theories, such as the Biblical account of Cain as a farmer."

The Gablers' attention to content is far-reaching and thoroughgoing, but they express almost equal dissatisfaction over the tone, values, emotions, and techniques they believe to be characteristic of modern education. They repeatedly object to what they call negative thinking. They have, I think, a valid point. There is a tendency in our culture to give more attention to bad news than to good and to offer handsome rewards to those who exploit our vulnerability to terror and our propensity to violence. Still, life even at the junior high level is not all Beaver and the Bobbseys, and I can't help but think the Gablers are overreacting when, for example, they dismiss Poe's classic tale "The Cask of Amontillado" as "gruesome, murderous, bizarre content. Not suitable for a literature class. The murderer shows no sign of regret!"

Closely related to the Gablers' concern over negative content is their fear that public schools are undermining "absolute values." Lest anyone misunderstand what

they mean by this term, a pamphlet they distribute clears up most ambiguities. "To the vast majority of Americans," it asserts, "the terms 'values' and 'morals' mean one thing, and one thing only; and that is the Christian-Judeo morals, values, and standards as given to us by God through His Word written in the Ten Commandments and the Bible. . . . After all, according to history these ethics have prescribed the only code by which civilizations can effectively remain in existence!"

Any textbook that casts this viewpoint into the slightest doubt is targeted for opposition. Predictably, they object strenuously to books or teachers' guides that describe in morally neutral terms such primitive customs as exchanging wives or abandoning old people to die or that ask students if they can think of situations in which it might be permissible to tell a lie. Such texts, they claim, endorse situation ethics and subtly chip away at character and trustworthiness, making it difficult for children to stand firm in the traditional values they have learned at home. The best protection against this erosive process, they seem to believe, is to avoid any suggestion that people may legitimately differ on questions of value. Mel Gabler even feels that the new math contains the seeds of cultural disintegration. "When a student reads in a math book that there are no absolutes," he has said, "every value he's been taught is destroyed. And the next thing you know, the student turns to crime and drugs."

One of the key defenses the Gablers use against what they regard as an attack on home-taught values is to charge texts and teachers with engaging in an invasion of privacy. Some of their fears are understandable, whether or not one happens to share them. I find it difficult, however, to understand what harm could come from asking children to take an inventory of the resources they use each day or to write about one way their lives have been influenced by their environment. Yet the Gablers view these exercises as unacceptable invasions of privacy. Indeed, in the name of privacy and protection of values, the Gablers object virtually anytime a text asks, "What do you think?" or "What is your opinion of . . . ?" In testimony before the committee, a member of the Gabler team even objected to a home-making book because "it continually encourages students to be more introspective and not only to analyze themselves but also their parents, friends, and family."

It is not a simple matter to discern just how successful the Gablers have been at influencing the decisions of the textbook committee. Norma readily acknowledges that "there is no way we can claim credit or success, because we don't know what puts a book on or off a list. It could be the committee rejected a book for a different reason. They never tell us how they judge. But what is encouraging to us is that back in 1973, six out of eight books we objected to in sociology and psychology were kicked out. In one year, seventeen out of twenty-seven were eliminated. In 1980, eleven out of twenty-one were eliminated. We hope some of that was because of what we did, but we can't say for sure that it was."

Some longtime observers and participants in the process feel the Gablers' power is overrated. One such skeptic notes that in a recent year they objected to all twelve books in a given category. Since only five were selected, they could claim that seven out of twelve were eliminated without explaining that this would have been true had they not objected and that they had found fault with all of the books that eventually made the approved list as well. Allan O. Kownslar, a Trinity University historian, also doubts that the Gablers are as powerful as some believe. "I have written six textbooks for Texas," he says. "They objected to almost all of them, and all of them were accepted."

The publishers themselves walk something of a diplomatic tightrope. On the one hand, they voice concern over First Amendment rights, express a preference for leaving the preparation of textbooks to experts rather than to conservative ideologues who wish to force their views on all members of society, and manifest confidence that the textbook committee will make a wise decision. On the other hand, they acknowledge that the Gablers are a force to be reckoned with, prepare careful, detailed responses to the bills of particulars, and avoid direct confrontations with Norma and her assistants at the hearings.

Where the Gablers' impact is more tangible, however, is in the content of the textbooks themselves. Without question, textbooks are changing along lines favored by the Gablers and the conservative parents' groups that use their materials and tactics. The word "evolution," for example, does not appear in a new biology text published by Laidlaw Brothers, a division of Doubleday. "We deleted the term," Laidlaw executive Eugene Frank explained, "because we wanted teachers to be permitted to teach biology without being forced to face controversy from pressure groups." The volume in question is Doubleday's only high school biology text. Another text, *Land and People: A World Geography,* put out by Scott, Foresman, was dropped from the Texas list because of its emphasis on evolution.

If we assume, as seems justified, that Mel and Norma Gabler do indeed wield sizable influence over American education, what are we to make of them and that circumstance? I found them to be courteous, pleasant, good-natured people who are earnestly, honestly, and unselfishly committed to helping the young obtain what they regard as the best possible

education. I found myself applauding their concern, admiring their dedication, and agreeing with a number of their objections to specific texts. Yet I believe their crusade, if successful, will have a devastatingly negative effect on American education and culture.

To begin with, their attack on humanism as an evil spell that has been cast over Western civilization—an attack in which they are joined by most of their New Right colleagues—is dangerously misleading. There are a few people who fit the New Right image of a humanist, who are indeed antireligious atheists and who blaspheme on the side. But for most people whom the New Right lumps into the secular humanist category, humanism is not a religion but an approach to the world. It is not, I think, an inherently reprehensible approach. It conceives of humans as having capacities of reason, mind, and will that far exceed those of other creatures and endow them with a singular dignity. It values diversity of opinion and rejects imposed or authoritarian approaches to knowledge, such as appeals to tradition or Scripture or other ostensibly revealed truth, in favor of free and critical inquiry, scientific methods, and individual and collective reflection. It maintains that to deserve our allegiance, beliefs about the world, society, and humanity should be based on—and not contradict—available evidence. It is skeptical of all claims to ultimate truth, because it has learned that not all the evidence is in.

In education, this humanistic approach does not seek to ply children with pot, pills, pornography, and polymorphous perversity. Rather, it strives to instill in them habits of mind and qualities of spirit that will include a love for knowledge, a depth and breadth of understanding, an ability to think well and critically for themselves, a belief in their essential worthiness and in that of others, and a desire and ability to work for the common good. It is not only part of the heritage of Western civilization, it is one of its best parts, and those who lump humanists into the same category as robbers, murderers, perverts, and "other treacherous individuals," as prominent New Right leaders have done, are guilty at best of serious ignorance and at worst of slander and immorality of a contemptible sort in which Jews and Christians and other men and women of goodwill and integrity should have no part.

A major result of the Gablers' misunderstanding of a humanistic approach to learning is a stunted and barren philosophy of education. In a manner typical of those distrustful of the intellectual enterprise, they take pleasure in scoring points against the professionals; Norma says she has read so many textbooks that "I figure I know enough to be a Ph.D." It is clear, however, that they have little appreciation or understanding of the life of the mind as it is encouraged and practiced in many in-

stitutions of learning. They tend to cite the *Reader's Digest* as if it were the *New England Journal of Medicine* and to regard a single conversation with a police chief or a former drug user as an incontrovertible refutation of some point they oppose.

In general, they know precisely where they stand but have difficulty dealing with a question that originates from different premises. Norma showed me a ninth-grade history book that observed that the route most likely taken by the Israelites in their exodus from Egypt would have been across a swamp known as the Sea of Reeds. The books adds: "It may be that the Sea of Reeds was later called the Red Sea by mistake." Norma found this highly amusing: "Can you just imagine pharaoh's army, with all his horses and all his men, completely disappearing into a swamp? Now, that's a miracle!" I pointed out to her that many scholars feel the biblical story may be an embellished, rather than strictly accurate, account of Israel's escape from slavery. I noted that there is no record in Egyptian history of such a catastrophic event, and that the Hebrew Bible does indeed say "Reed Sea," not "Red Sea." She faltered, then said, "But still . . . okay . . . what happened to pharaoh's army?"

In similar fashion, questions posed by members of the textbook committee at the August hearings characteristically received oblique answers or a puzzled "I don't think I understand the question." That, of course, is the point: when one regards education as simply the ingestion of facts and not also the investigation and analysis of ironies, ambiguities, uncertainties, and contradictions, one will be far less likely either to understand the question or to provide a useful answer. And that kind of trained incapacity will endanger the vitality and ultimately the survival of treasured forms of religious, political, social, and economic life.

Norma Gabler's difficulty with unanticipated questions is a communicable disease, and she is working to spread it. "What some textbooks are doing," she has complained, "is giving students ideas, and ideas will never do them as much good as facts." Further, in her view students should apparently not show any interest in facts not found in their textbooks. Norma objected to a fourth-grade book that urged students to verify facts by consulting other sources, on the grounds that "it could lead to some very dangerous information." When committee members pressed her to elaborate, she said, "I just don't think questions should be asked unless the information has already been covered in the text."

The shortcomings of the Gablers' view of education—as a process by which young people are indoctrinated with facts certified to be danger-free, while being protected from exposure to information that might challenge orthodox interpretations—can be seen by looking at three areas: history, science, and the social sciences. One may or may not agree with the particular objections the Gablers make to various history books, but it is clear that they are oblivious to the idea that the writing of history has never been, nor can it ever be, factual in any pure sense. Those who provided eyewitness accounts and other records with which historians work were engaged in interpretation, not only in adjusting the light under which they chose to display the materials they assembled but even in their selection of events, dates, and people from the infinite possibilities open to them. And to imagine that they or anyone else engaging in the historical enterprise does so free of the influence of his or her values, perceptions, and ideological biases is to believe something no reputable historian has believed for generations.

The Gablers seem incapable of considering the possibility that a textbook might meet their criteria of fairness, objectivity, and patriotism and still be critical of any aspect of American life. To bend a metaphor, it is as if they hoped that by refusing to acknowledge the existence of new materials, techniques, social conditions, and fashions, they might somehow persuade the emperor to keep wearing his comfortable, if somewhat threadbare, old clothes. To be sure, new versions of history may be inferior to earlier ones. But with free inquiry, each new construction can be examined for accuracy, adequacy, method, logic, and insight. When orthodoxy is the only criterion, there can be no search for the broader, deeper, more lasting truths that make men and women and children free.

Efforts by the Gablers and other fundamentalist Christians to negate the teaching of evolution are probably even more detrimental to the educational process and the long-term welfare of the country. Fundamentalists typically belittle evolution as "just a theory, not a fact," as if theories are mere speculations or guesses dreamed up by scientists in idle moments. As scientists use the term, however, a theory is a description of natural phenomena, based on long observation and, if possible, experimentation. To obtain the status of theory—as in cell theory, quantum theory, and the theories of gravitation and relativity—these descriptions must be supported by an abundance of evidence that has been critically examined, argued over, and organized into what is regarded as the best explanation for the phenomena in question, or one of a very small number of competitors. Evolution is such a theory. Creationism is not.

Millions of fundamentalist Christians believe in sudden creation and a young earth because that appears to be required by a literal reading of Genesis. Other millions of Christians regard the Genesis account of creation not as a scientific description of the origins of the earth and humankind but as a religious story—a myth, if you insist—whose purpose is to affirm the belief that behind the universe is God. Other cultures have comparable stories. This one is ours. It is a fine story, perhaps "true" in some ultimate sense, but it should not be asked to bear the weight of a scientific theory, because it cannot. Creationists can mount a case that sounds impressive to a layperson and can sometimes score points against scientists unaccustomed to defending their views in public debates or on radio and television talk shows. But when they tackle true scientists who are onto their game, as in the 1981 Arkansas creationist trial, they lose, and they lose because creationism is neither demonstrable fact nor theory but a religious belief that runs counter to available evidence. The case for creationism is not made by people who have had any noticeable impact as scientists. As the Arkansas trial revealed, no reputable scientific journal has published an article espousing scientific creationism. Moreover, several leading spokesmen of creationism claim doctoral degrees from institutions that, if they exist at all, are unaccredited.

Just because the tenets of creationism are scientifically insupportable, however, does not mean creationists will lose—witness the changes, already noted, in biology books used in this state. If the earth is indeed several billion years old and if evolution is the best explanation for life on this planet, as experts in anthropology, archeology, astronomy, biology, biochemistry, ethology, geology, and physics insist is the case, then to deny young people access to the best available theory is to leave them incapable of continuing the astonishing scientific advances that have been a hallmark of this nation.

The Gablers' attack on moral and cultural relativism is aimed primarily at the social sciences. Without question, the loss of certainty engendered by opening windows on a wider world can be distressing. It is probably true, as many social commentators have observed, that civilizations work better when there is consensus on basic values, and that some of our most pressing social problems—crime, for example—are closely related to a breakdown of such consensus. We have, since at least the sixties, experienced a crisis of values that has led to a crisis of legitimation in which we have withdrawn from basic institutions—family, schools, business, government, religion—the confidence and trust we once granted them, replacing those attitudes with skepticism, cynicism, and hostility. This is not a benign development, and the upsurge of evangelical religion, the Moral Majority, the Coalition for Better Television, Educational Research Analysts, and other manifestations of conservative ideology is a reaction to it.

One of the great challenges facing our society—and there is no guarantee that we will meet it successfully—is to reestablish a balance between adherence to a set of basic values and acceptance of individual and cultural variation. I appreciate the Gablers' desire to participate in that effort. I do not, however, think we will be well served by believing that either Longview or Houston is the center of the universe, that all flags should be red, white, and blue, or that "Jesus Saves" should be adopted as the international anthem. We live in a multicultural world—something children learn very early, mainly from television but also from newspapers, from movies, and, particularly in large cities, from their neighbors and schoolmates. If we cannot learn to accept that fact and its profound implications, which social scientists are committed to explore and explain, we may not be able to keep our world.

A final quarrel I have with the Gablers is their contribution to a growing climate of censorship. In the two years since the New Right's impressive show of muscle in November 1980, complaints to the American Library Association about attempts to remove or restrict access to materials in classrooms and libraries have risen by more than 300 per cent. As one consequence, some teachers admit that they avoid introducing anything controversial into their classes, or they tape class discussions that might conceivably be misconstrued, or they teach material that is no longer relevant or in which they do not believe, simply to keep from losing their jobs or being hassled by unhappy parents.

As noted earlier, the Gablers claim they are not censors because they do not try to say what can be published. They also object to being judged by a double standard. "When we try to get changes made," Norma said, "it's called censorship. When minorities and feminists do the same thing, nobody complains." But whether regarding them as censors or as honest competitors in the marketplace of ideas, their critics have become increasingly vocal.

One group of critics is People for the American Way, founded in 1980 by TV producer Norman Lear and led in Texas by Michael Hudson, a graduate of West Point and the University of Texas law school. Though he did not open an Austin office until mid-July, Hudson managed a quick and impressive victory when the State Board of Education let him respond in writing to the Gablers' bills of particulars. He still feels, however, that citizens should be permitted not only to register objections but also to speak in favor of textbooks they find especially meritorious. A number of educators and publishers agree, although most regard the Texas system, with its openness, as the finest in the country. Aside from some procedural fine-tuning, it would appear that what is needed is not less input from the Gablers but more from those with a different view and experience of education.

I have three children. Two are now grown men; my daughter entered the eleventh grade this fall. My wife and I have attempted for over two decades to expose them to a kind of education and cultural experience that is radically different from that endorsed by the Gablers. And yet they have mastered basic skills, they have good values, they work hard, they know a great deal, they think exceptionally well, and they have made solid contributions to the varied groups in which they have participated. They are not perfect, but they please me enormously. What is more, I have taught thousands of young people who have experienced a similar kind of education and who seem to me to be, well, almost as promising as my own offspring.

It may not be possible to prove that an open mind is better than a closed one, or that the proper antidote to a bad idea is not censorship but a good idea, or that a society in which some questions are never answered may be preferable to one in which some answers are never questioned, but I believe these things to be true. I not only believe them; I have bet my life on them. ☙

COME ON, WALTER

...Smile!

The toughest job of the presidential campaign has gone to a young Texas media pro with no national political experience. If Roy Spence succeeds, he could make stuffy Walter Mondale the next president of the United States.

BY PAUL BURKA

A CHILLING JANUARY WIND IS BLOWING OFF THE POTOMAC as the fortieth president of the United States finishes his inaugural address. Behind Walter Mondale on the platform, dignitaries hunch into their overcoats, but here and there enough of a face remains visible for a television commentator to identify it. The man applauding politely is Lloyd Bentsen, the new vice president, falling into the subservient role he must play for the next four years. The tall man staring through small circular glasses, looking like the consummate Washington pro, is Jim Johnson, Mondale's campaign chairman, who will succeed James Baker as White House chief of staff. And the young, athletic-looking one with the thick blond hair? The commentator searches his memory. Ah, yes. That is Roy Spence, the 36-year-old adman who came out of Texas to mastermind the TV blitz that carried Mondale past Ronald Reagan in the campaign's final days.

So much for fancy; now for fact. With Inauguration Day a year away, Walter Mondale is not the betting favorite to be the next president of the United States. He is merely the Democratic front-runner, a perilous position that makes him a prime candidate for a New England Life advertisement. Even if he wins the nomination, he will be a decided underdog against a popular president. Lloyd Bentsen's chances are even more problematic. But Roy Spence's future is secure—win or lose. When he won the job as Walter Mondale's media adviser last spring, he automatically joined the Democratic establishment, state and national. He is positioned to become a power in Texas politics for years, even decades. That's no small feat for someone who has yet to handle even one successful statewide campaign from start to finish.

How did Roy Spence catch Mondale's eye? Why did he get the job? What does he plan to do with it? The answers to those questions explain a lot not only about the Mondale campaign but also about Texas politics. A dozen years ago Spence, just out of UT and still wearing his hair in a ponytail, ventured into politics for the first time. His client: Ralph Yarborough, beloved of the old-line liberals, bane of the John Connally conservatives, who was making a futile bid to return to the U.S. Senate. The effort that earned Spence his national reputation, though, was his work for Mark White in the closing weeks of the 1982 governor's race. The journey from Yarborough's race to White's—from ideological division to relative unity—was the same path taken by the Texas Democratic party as Texas became a two-party state. And nothing so clearly explains the imperatives of modern politics as the fact that the person who most symbolizes this transformation is Roy Spence, not a politician but a consultant.

● ● ●

Roy Spence's chosen profession does not rank high among America's most admired occupations. The books critical of political consultants would fill a shelf. The first was *The Selling of the President 1968*, Joe McGinniss' detailed account of how Richard Nixon's admen sold the notion that there was a "new" Nixon. The most recent work in this lineage is *The Permanent Campaign*, by Sidney Blumenthal, who states his thesis in the first sentence: "Political consultants are the new power within the American political system."

Reading these books is a lot like reading about genetic experimentation. As much as the authors admire the technique, they never let you forget how dangerous to society they believe it to be. Out of this literature emerges a gospel: television has replaced the political machine; the consultants are the new bosses; they are hired guns who have technical skills, but unlike the old bosses, they respect no loyalties, deliver no votes, provide no public services, and enforce no discipline; they deal in images rather than realities; they have permanently transformed American politics—for the worse.

Just how important are these guys, really? Talk to enough pols and pros and you will find that three theories emerge:

(1) The Bum Phillips theory of media omnipotence. Remember when Phillips coached the Houston Oilers? The Oilers were good, and the New Orleans Saints were hopeless. Now Phillips coaches the Saints, and it is the Saints who are good, the Oilers who are hopeless. The lesson is that the coach is more important than the players or, to return to politics, that the consultant is more important than the candidate. Under the Bum Phillips theory, anybody can be elected to high public office—provided he can afford the right media man. Example: the 1978 Florida governor's race, when Bob Squier started the campaign with zero per cent of the vote and zero name identification and won the race. By the way, the candidate's name was Bob Graham; Squier, based in Washington, is one of the leading Democratic media consultants. Squier will have another opportunity to test the Bum Phillips theory in Texas this spring. He is handling Kent Hance's campaign for the U.S. Senate, and Hance is starting out about where Graham did.

(2) The arms race theory of media escalation. Modern campaigns are like the nuclear buildup: candidates deploy more and more weapons (there are specialists not only for advertising but also for polling, mailing, and telephoning), technological superiority is fleeting, and the cost keeps going up all the time. Consultants are important, but only to neutralize the other side's consultants. Example: the 1982 Texas governor's race. Back in the seventies a candidate could get the jump on an opponent, just as Bill Clements used polls and phone banks to sneak up on an

overconfident John Hill in 1978. By 1982, however, Mark White knew enough to match Clements consultant for consultant.

(3) The sow's ear theory, as in, you can't make a silk purse out of the wrong candidate or the wrong year. Example: Jim Collins against Lloyd Bentsen. Or the 1981 San Antonio mayor's race between rising star Henry Cisneros and the old guard's John Steen. Steen hired John Deardourff, one of Washington's glamour consultants, but to no avail: the election was the crest of a 250-year tide, in which Deardourff was no more than a droplet, leading to the election of the city's first Mexican American mayor.

Which theory is right? They all are; it depends on the race. Free of constraints, a consultant can work miracles—but there are always constraints. Money is one: TV, an expensive buy, favors the rich. Exposure is another: television is a superb tool for gaining name recognition and establishing an image, as Bill Clements did in 1978. It is less useful when a candidate already has name recognition and an established image, as Bill Clements did in 1982. There are so many variables that a consultant's judgment and instinct are as important as technological mastery. Political consulting is really three professions in one—film, sales, and politics, possibly the three most fickle professions on earth —and the best media campaigns work on all three levels. Just as with movie directors, there are enormous differences in quality, not only between consultants but also within each consultant's work. That is why, despite the hullabaloo about the power of media men, the essence of politics will always be more art than science.

● ● ●

Walter Mondale is not a product of the media age. A preacher's son, he has a style that on camera ranges from pious to stuffy. Mondale was first elected to the U.S. Senate in 1966, before the era of modern media politics. Mondale doesn't like TV campaigning—it was one of the reasons he balked at the starting gate of the 1976 presidential race—and he particularly doesn't like media consultants.

One afternoon in January 1983 his dislike was showing. He was in his suite at the Adolphus Hotel in Dallas and had just found out that his next visitor, someone named Roy Spence, was a media man. The trouble was, a few days earlier Mondale had had a miserable meeting with a consultant from California, who had been full of jargon and ways for Mondale to change his image. Afterward, Mondale gave orders that he didn't want to meet with any more media consultants for a while. When he found out about Spence, he was furious, but he agreed to go ahead with the meeting. Spence walked into the room and said, "I understand that you don't like media people worth a damn."

Spence and Mondale went on to talk for 45 minutes. They talked substance—how the defense issue might be turned against Reagan by showing how unbusinesslike defense spending has become. And they talked philosophy—Spence's philosophy of running campaigns. Spence is not a disciple of the Bum Phillips theory that the consultant is more important than the candidate. "That's bullshit," he told me during the Christmas campaign lull this winter. "I really try to tap into the truth about a candidate. The truth *sells*. It has an aura around it that people can *see*. It *pops*." Spence talks in cadences that are almost Germanic—his sentences end in verbs, reserving the punch for last. "Voters don't have to believe everything a candidate believes, but they have to believe that he *believes*."

Spence had been well briefed for the Mondale visit. The appointment had been set up by Bob Beckel, Mondale's campaign manager. Beckel and Spence had become friends in 1980, when Beckel came to Texas with the hapless assignment of running Jimmy Carter's reelection campaign. Later, Beckel stayed in Austin to do some consulting; he handled the reelection of Austin mayor Carole McClellan in 1981, turning often to Spence for counsel. Beckel, whose role in the Mondale campaign is not as grandiose as his title, was a little reluctant to push a national novice, but under prodding from mutual friends in Austin, he arranged the meeting. Spence, a salesman first and a consultant second, did the rest.

● ● ●

Roy Spence has always been a salesman. He was a high school quarterback, a salesman's position if ever there was one, on a state championship team in Brownwood. At UT in the late sixties, he was an antiwar activist but not a dropout or a flower child. In his spare time he and some friends picked up money by putting on mixed-media events, like light shows for fraternity parties and slide shows for trade associations gathering in Austin. Upon graduation they decided to stay in Austin and start an advertising agency. Spence became the one who made the sales pitch to prospective clients.

The company, now known as Gurasich, Spence, Darilek & McClure, or GSD&M, began life with the accounts of

ROY SPENCE'S GREATEST HITS

His campaign ads combine folksy candidates with tough rhetoric.

The Disappearing-Signature Spot

KRUEGER VERSUS TOWER, 1978

In early campaign ads Spence softened Krueger's image as a stuffy academic by showing him in casual attire. When the campaign heated up, Spence found a way to turn Tower's use of his own signature as a campaign logo against him. The scene is a senator's office. The senator, shown from the neck down, walks into the room while a voice recalls the accomplishments of other Texas senators—the GI bill, NASA. A hand drops a piece of legislation on the desk. As the senator signs Tower's name to the bill, the voice continues, "After seventeen long years, there is not one single piece of major legislation called the John Tower bill." The signature disappears.

The Caviar Spot

WHITE VERSUS CLEMENTS, 1982

The scene is a lavish party. Men and women in formal dress approach a buffet table laden with rich food, silver, and crystal. A woman in a pink chiffon dress smoothes caviar onto a cracker, her pearl necklace hanging down, as a voice says, "Up here the Texas economy looks rosy. That's why Bill Clements says unemployment is insignificant, supports an increase in the gasoline tax, and sides with the big utility companies." Then the camera switches to Mark White, wearing jeans and a work shirt. "Bill Clements listens to big shots on Wall Street," White says. "As governor I'll work for the people on Main Street."

The Headliners Spot

AUSTIN MAYOR'S RACE, 1983

Spence's client, a prim, colorless city councilman named Ron Mullen, took on Lowell Lebermann, scion of the downtown establishment. The opening shot of men in three-piece suits sipping drinks and shaking hands around an hors d'oeuvres table is accompanied by a voice: "Years ago, a small, elite group of men tried to run our city behind closed doors. Fortunately, that's changed. And yet Lowell Lebermann has come back to run for mayor, saying, and I quote, 'If you can't get it done at the Headliners Club, you can't get it done.'" Then a prim, colorless Ron Mullen pledges to make his decisions in the public arena. Spence even gets Mullen to strike a casual pose—he takes off his glasses.

two local retailers. Today GSD&M has branch offices in Dallas, Houston, and San Antonio and a subsidiary for developing real estate. Its annual billings exceed $50 million. Its clients include Southwest Airlines, Coors, and a pizza chain that was the agency's first big success story. Asked by a client to distinguish his shops from the Pizza Inns and the Pizza Huts, GSD&M ran combinations of Italian-sounding syllables through a computer and came up with Mr. Gatti's.

Because the founders flouted the established guidelines for reaching the big leagues of Texas advertising—they chose youth over experience, Austin over Dallas, the political left over the right—they were often an object of derision in advertising circles. What the initials GSD&M really represented, competitors said, was Greed, Sex, Drugs, and Money. Roy Spence used the line himself. "They say that's what we stand for," the salesman would tell potential clients. "Now let me tell you what we really stand for."

Politics has never been a big money-maker for GSD&M. But politics has helped the firm prosper in less direct ways. In 1974, for example, Spence handled the advertising in Bob Krueger's first congressional campaign. The leading fundraiser, previously unknown to Spence, was L. D. Brinkman, the world's largest floor-covering dealer. Years later Brinkman bought Mr. Gatti's in a deal GSD&M helped swing; he remains a major commercial client today. One can safely assume that it would not hurt GSD&M's commercial business to help elect the next president.

The agency's first venture into politics, the 1972 Yarborough race, was a disaster. Spence got the contract mainly because the established firms wanted no part of Yarborough and other possible competitors were scared away by the former senator's inability to raise money. Spence ended up borrowing money personally to pay for media spots, but he was left holding the bag when Yarborough lost the primary to Barefoot Sanders. For several years afterward Spence helped organize fundraising dinners for Yarborough until he and other creditors were paid.

In 1973 his luck changed. The state Senate seat from Austin opened up with the resignation of the incumbent. Spence handled Lloyd Doggett's advertising in a successful campaign that turned out to be a minor technological watershed. Texas media politics still wasn't very sophisticated in 1973. The only two memorable campaigns had been aimed at Ralph Yarborough, by Lloyd Bentsen in 1970 and by Allan Shivers in the bitter 1954 governor's race. Shivers ran a devastating anti-union TV spot displaying the deserted, trashed-out streets of downtown Port Arthur as evidence of what would happen if Yarborough were elected governor. (What the spot did not say was that the scene had been shot at dawn on a Sunday

morning.) In the Doggett race Spence did something that was less dramatic but totally new. He prepared different radio spots for each local station, targeting the message to the particular audience, instead of the usual single spot distributed to all stations. The technique is common today, but Spence is credited with being the first to use targeting in Texas.

That same year Bob Krueger, an English professor at Duke University, decided to come back to Texas and run for Congress from his family's hometown of New Braunfels. He called a political science professor at UT for advice; his friend recommended that he talk to a smart young fellow named Roy Spence. Krueger hardly seemed suited to the huge district, larger than Pennsylvania, that sprawled from northwest San Antonio to the Trans-Pecos, and Spence spent much of their first meeting trying to persuade the candidate to move to Austin, a district more likely to elect a university professor. Krueger resisted, staying home to enter a six-man race in which two of his opponents were better-known political veterans. But 1974 was the height of the Watergate furor, and the voters were receptive to outsiders.

Just before the election, Spence produced a coup. A San Antonio newspaper picked the ten most powerful men in town. All ten supported one of Krueger's opponents, a San Antonio state senator. Spence, displaying for the first time a trait that one day would intrigue Walter Mondale and Jim Johnson, turned the news to his advantage. He swiftly put out a tabloid that trumpeted, "If you believe that ten politically powerful men in San Antonio should have the power to handpick your next congressman, don't read the following pages." Spence had discerned what few Texans understood in 1974: the real division in Texas politics was no longer liberal-conservative but urban-rural. The sheep and goat ranchers voted against the city power brokers and for the scholar with the curly hair. So did the anti-establishment sector of the San Antonio electorate. Krueger won.

By the mid-seventies, GSD&M's commercial business was booming and Spence had less time for politics. His next big campaign, Krueger's 1978 race against John Tower, was one that belied the power of media consultants: Krueger started close, stayed close, and finished close, and nothing Spence came up with, including a dramatic TV spot of Tower's signature vanishing, altered the numbers. In 1980, a Republican year, Spence handled Jim Wright's reelection to Congress from Fort Worth. That race later impressed the Mondale people, because the House majority leader, too heavy of eyebrow and oratory, comes across even worse on TV than Mondale does.

The big one, though, was the 1982 governor's race. Spence came in late, taking over Mark White's radio with three

months to go and his TV a month later. The Republicans outspent the Democrats two to one, but the Democrats generated a huge turnout of new voters. The Democratic candidate used television to get across his message that the Republican incumbent didn't care about ordinary people. The Democrat won a race that the experts said couldn't be won. When Jim Johnson examined the Mark White–Bill Clements race the following spring, he saw something familiar. It was very much the scenario he envisioned for Walter Mondale against Ronald Reagan.

●●●

Among the books and papers on Jim Johnson's desk is an unusual fixture—a large bottle of aspirin. As the boss of the Mondale campaign, he has had many headaches in the past year. One of the biggest was choosing a media consultant.

Johnson had barely heard of Roy Spence when Mondale himself called after the Dallas meeting. "I met a guy you're really going to like," Mondale said. Johnson knew what that meant: Mondale had met a guy *he* really liked. Still, given Mondale's opinion of media men, that was saying something.

Johnson had in his mind a picture of the ideal consultant for Mondale. Most of all, he had to get along with the candidate; that hurdle was already cleared. As Johnson began checking out Spence with Texans friendly to Mondale, like Jack Martin, Lloyd Bentsen's 1982 campaign manager, and Buddy Temple, erstwhile candidate for governor and an early Mondale backer, Johnson began to think he might have found his man.

He wanted someone who emphasized, in his words, "real issues." Johnson learned how Spence had used utilities against Bill Clements. (Never mind that the utility issue was more phony than real.) Johnson wanted a consultant who could react quickly to events. He learned that Spence had stayed up all night after a Clements-White debate to produce spots blasting Clements for supporting a gasoline tax increase. Johnson wanted one major campaign post to go to an outsider—the Mondale organization was top-heavy with old Washington hands, from Johnson himself to Beckel and pollster Peter Hart. Thus Spence's lack of national experience was no barrier. Finally, Johnson wanted someone who would be an asset in an important state. Texas is essential for Mondale; no Democrat has ever been elected president without carrying it. Spence had roots into the entire Democratic field; he transcended the old days when the party was deeply divided. His clients ranged from state treasurer Ann Richards on the left to Bob Krueger in the center to Mark White on the Dolph Briscoe right.

One thing remained to be done: the Mondale team had to review the reel of Roy Spence's work. To a political pro,

TV spots might as well carry the consultant's signature; his fingerprints are all over the screen. The Mondale pros were looking for Roy Spence's signature. They saw Bob Krueger, normally a starched and formal man, wandering past a gazebo wearing an outdoor jacket and a blue shirt open at the neck. They saw Mark White in jeans and a work shirt, lambasting Bill Clements for listening to Wall Street instead of Main Street. They saw Jim Wright standing before a classroom of schoolchildren, leaning forward and saying, "Yes, Lisa, I believe in school prayer." They saw Garry Mauro, more a backroom operator than a media candidate, walking coatless over sand dunes by the Gulf of Mexico.

Three things about Spence's work stood out. First, it was casual. He had taken a bunch of TV corpses and made them seem like just plain folks. Maybe he could do the same for Walter Mondale. Second, it was tough. Spence's negative spots against Tower and Clements are regional classics, such that they have even acquired titles in Texas political circles—"The Disappearing-Signature Spot," "The Caviar Spot." They exploit the fatal weakness of an opponent in the mind of the viewer; George Shipley, Texas' leading pollster, calls them "ice picks to the brain." Third, it was good film. In his best spots Spence used props to create drama before the viewer knew he was watching a political ad: an opulent cocktail party to portray the type of people who support Bill Clements; a quill pen and a green eyeshade to indicate the backwardness of the state treasurer's office. The Mondale people liked what they saw. By June the deal was struck. Roy Spence's job description with the Mondale campaign? Reduced to a single phrase, it was to get Walter Mondale to loosen up on television.

Walter Mondale's media consultant is not the all-powerful political boss of *The Permanent Campaign.* That says less about Spence than it does about Jim Johnson. The inner circle of the Mondale campaign is more like a dot: Johnson is both strategist and boss. The success of Johnson's 1983 strategy—circle the bases of the Democratic pressure groups, scoring endorsements from labor, teachers, women, and blacks—has vindicated his one-man rule. So has the deterioration of Mondale's leading opponent, John Glenn, whose campaign has been plagued by infighting at the top. Between September and December Mondale stretched his lead over Glenn in *Time*'s poll fourteen points, from 26–24 to 34–18. Unless Glenn reverses his fortunes in the initial skirmishing—the Iowa caucuses and the New Hampshire primary in late February and the Southern primaries on Super Tuesday, March 13—he could be knocked out in round one.

That would suit Roy Spence just fine. He confesses to being "behind the learning curve" for a presidential race. Austin friends describe him as uncomfortable with the serial nature of the nominating process, where climactic battles are fought, then forgotten, as new fronts are opened up. A head-to-head confrontation between Mondale and Reagan is much more Spence's style.

The media strategy for the nomination, Spence says, is to move gradually from personality to issues. "First a voter has to know the person," he says. "Then he has to know his values. Then he has to know where his values will take the country." Spence does not intend to let Mondale repeat Jimmy Carter's mistake in 1976, when Carter almost lost big leads for both the nomination and the election: Carter never got into specifics, and as the campaign dragged on, voters began to have second thoughts—for good reason.

The strategy has already started. Ads currently running in Iowa and Boston show Mondale talking about trade, rebuilding America, and the economy. Other spots in that series, already shot but not yet aired, deal with jobs, defense, and—a Spence hardy perennial—utilities. The spots reflect Spence's uneasiness about the nomination campaign; they are not his best work. They use head shots of Mondale—no props, no drama—and the militant rhetoric doesn't quite ring true: "I am not a sucker." . . . "We want to get tough again. We want to be first again." . . . "They must know we're not going to be pushed around." . . . "Agreements with the Soviet Union are not based on trust." . . . "When we stand up for arms control, we're not weaker, we're stronger." Only the utility spot, inspired by the AT&T breakup, rises above the prosaic. Mondale's criticism of high bills is interrupted after each sentence by cutaways to just plain folks complaining about burdens on the middle class.

In getting Walter Mondale to loosen up, though, Roy Spence has had more success. On December 10, 1983, Walter Mondale's presidential campaign went public in a five-minute program that was shown nationwide. It opens with a shot of a cork bobbing on a fishing line, then switches to a hand on a casting reel. The viewer, hooked, hears Mondale's voice before he sees his face. "I'm sort of a farm kid. I worked on a farm. I love the out-of-doors"—now Mondale is walking by a white fence in a sylvan setting—"I love to fish, and I get a lot of strength out of it." Mondale is wearing a brown checkered sport shirt with a brown pullover sweater. At the neck, his T-shirt is showing. He looks like a Roy Spence candidate, folksy and loose. Really loose: Mondale moves onto a tennis court, whacks at a ball, and starts chasing the return. He misses. "Yes, that shot was in," he shouts to an unseen opponent, "and you're fired."❧

★INTERESTS★

INSIDE THE LOBBY

by Richard West

On a fine spring Saturday morning in mid-May, nine days before the end of the legislative session, Bill Abington sat in the Senate gallery and nervously puffed on his cigar, awaiting the final vote on a bill that was as important to him as any he could remember.

His intelligent, pale-blue eyes moved from the list of 31 Senators in his hand to the men themselves, 30 feet below him, as he tried to predict the outcome for the one-hundredth time.

The measure in question was the compulsory oil and gas unitization bill, and as director of the 3000-member Texas Mid-Continent Oil and Gas Association, he personally felt responsible for its passage or defeat.

As he gazed around the gallery, Abington spotted the Exxon boys, Gaylord Armstrong and Wade Spilman. Armstrong is a strapping 6′ 3″ Austin attorney with reddish-blond hair who used to travel with Ben Barnes and looks enough like him to be kin; Spilman is a former House member, attorney, and the acknowledged expert in oil and gas, insurance, and alcoholic beverage law among the lobbyists. Their company had worked so hard for the bill's passage that during the recent committee hearings it was referred to as "the Exxon Bill."

As Abington continued to gaze at his list, he couldn't figure out why he felt something was wrong. On paper everything looked good.

The bill had easily passed the House earlier in the year by a vote of 103-36. Thirteen Senators, three short of a majority, had co-signed the bill when it was originally introduced. Senator Jack Hightower, a teetotalling, hard-shelled Baptist from Vernon who was the bill's sponsor on the floor, was regarded as an expert and able leader.

Abington was growing impatient as the Senate plodded through regular business. Part of the trouble was that you couldn't depend on anything this session. It was *so* different. His great friend Ben Barnes, who *knew* how to run the Senate, was gone. Gus Mutscher, a little slow but always reliable,

was a convicted man now living in Brenham. Even ole Preston looked good at this point. You don't miss your water till your well runs dry.

Abington had worked long hours for months on this bill. Now, what was done was done. It was up to those 31 politicians milling around below him who, within the hour, would pass or kill the bill for two more years. Abington settled back in his gallery seat to wait.

Bill Abington is a prominent member of a group of a hundred or so men and a few women who make up the "Third House" of the legislature. Highly paid, thoroughly acquainted with legislators and legislative procedure, they are known, for better or for worse, as The Lobby.

Basically, a lobbyist is a person with no official government position who attempts to influence government decisions and policy. Lobbyists traditionally try to influence legislatures, but may work with the executive branch as well. The name originated during Andrew Jackson's first presidential term, but the popular use derived from persons who, since they were not allowed on the floor, literally hung around in lobbies of legislatures, collaring members for lunch after adjournment.

To lobby successfully requires a great deal of energy from a man who must wear many different hats. Lawyer. Educator. Entertainer. Friend and companion. And if the occasion arises, procurer.

A good lobbyist does five fundamental things: 1. Makes clear who he represents; 2. Makes clear what his interest is; 3. Makes clear what he wants to do and why; 4. Answers questions; 5. Provides enough back-up material and information so politicians can make a judgment.

He also never asks a legislator to vote for or against a bill; this is considered bad form. He explains his position on the bill, answers questions, and, if he is smart, warns how it might hurt back home in the next election.

A good lobbyist has a well developed system of seeing that people in home districts who are interested in legislation are contacted and, in turn, ask politicians to vote for the bill in question.

The Texas State Teacher's Association (TSTA), Texas Trial Lawyers, and the Texas Medical Association are the recognized experts at this "grass roots lobbying." In a town of 50,000, the TSTA will have 300 lobbyists and husbands (or wives) who, upon command from lobbyist L. P. Sturgeon, can flood the legislature with letters or themselves.

The smart lobbyist has this man-power working for him and remains above the nitty gritty of pressure tactics. He is just the good guy who offers information, buys lunches ever so often and, when the vote is near, puts his arm around shoulder after shoulder and says, "This bill is coming up and we need the vote. I sure hope we can count on you."

Many lobbyists are former members of the legislature, and are hired not for their knowledge of the client's business, but because they know legislative procedure and the legislators themselves. Of course, being a lawyer helps, but is not essential.

This past session, six freshmen lobbyists were members two years ago: Ralph Wayne, Texas Mid-Continent Oil and Gas; Ace Pickens, Texas Medical Association; Gerhardt Schulle, Texas Association of Realtors; James Slider, Lone Star Steel; Joe Golman, Dallas Chamber of Commerce, Dallas Community College, and the National Association of Theatre Owners; J. P. Word, Texas Association of Taxpayers.

A few lobbyists learned the ropes as administrative assistants to governors or other Capitol officials. Howard Rose (Padre Island Investment Corporation) was Gov. John Connally's first administrative assistant. Weldon Hart (Texas Good Roads Association) was the top assistant under Gov. Shivers. Dan Petty, (the University of Texas System's Director of Public Affairs) served under Gov. Preston Smith. Buck Wood was the Secretary of State's Director of Elections before taking his present job as lobbyist for Common Cause.

To become chief legal counsel for the Texas Railroad Association was almost inevitable for Walter Caven. He grew up in Marshall, which at that time was the shop town for the Texas and Pacific Railroad. His father was an attorney who represented the railroads, so it wasn't surprising that after serving one term in the House in 1949, Caven went to work for the Railroad Association.

Former members who have secured profitable niches representing their clients before the Legislature are many. A few prominent ones are: Reuben Senterfitt, former speaker of the house (utilities); Terry Townsend (trucks); Bill Abington (oil and gas); Johnnie B. Rogers (insurance); George Cowden (insurance); Searcy Bracewell (Houston Natural Gas, Gulf States Utilities, etc.); Dick Cory, Jep Fuller, Buck Buchanan (Beer); Robert Hughes (independent auto dealers); Gene Fondren (Texas Auto Dealers Association).

The way lobbyists work is as varied as the clients they represent. Where they work most effectively is long before the session begins, in campaigns a full year before the legislature convenes. For instance, there are 414 wholesale beer distributors in Texas who are members of the Wholesale Beer Distributors of Texas. When a man becomes a candidate for the House or Senate, these men find out one thing: Does he drink an occasional beer or is he high tenor in the Baptist Church choir who denounces demon rum every Sunday?

It doesn't matter if he is a Commie-Red-Pinko-Symp or worships the spirit of Joseph Goebbels. Will he vote wet or dry? A study on the candidate's background is sent to their chief, Turner Keith, who studies each candidate's profile carefully before deciding yea, nay, or who cares.

A major change in lobby techniques has occurred in this area in recent years. Previously, the lobby looked at the field of announced candidates and picked out one to support. Today, a strong grass roots organization such as the TSTA will actually recruit a young man or woman to run, particularly if the incumbent has proven an irritant.

With the crack of the gavel convening the new session, the lobbyist begins the endless round of gratuities. They drop by member's offices daily, offering to buy lunch, drinks, or just to chat. Those legislators who respond to flattery are shamelessly backslapped. Those who are fiercely independent are treated at arm's length. Lobbyists know how busy most legislators are and they are always there to hold hands, lift spirits, run messages—being everything from page to lawyer.

One of the bright, new lobbyists explains why this daily contact is important: "Even when nothing is happening that affects my client, I have to keep circulating because inevitably the time will come when it is critical that I know this or that particular member.

"It's like being a fireman. You spend a lot of time polishing the brass and revving up the engine because it has got to work when the bell rings." But this same lobbyist is critical of how some industries play the game. "The railroads have eight to ten men down here all session and they are all assigned certain people to take to lunch every day. John Eck of Southern Pacific has asked Hawkins Menefee every day for lunch, and here it is the last day of the session, and Hawkins ain't been yet. It's not a personal thing but the Hawk just doesn't want to spend his noon hour with a railroad lobbyist."

It is doubtful if any member has ever changed a vote because of two or three meals. Days and nights of constant dinners, parties, attention, favors, and celebrations *do*, however, create bonds of friendship and companionship in what for many legislators is a lonely town. It is terribly hard to vote against a friend, and to some extent, everyone is influenced by that personal touch. The sole reason for all this effort on the lobbyist's part is indeed to make a friend of the legislator, to gain access to his office, and once there, to make his pitch.

Lobbying is much more sophisticated today than it was in the 1950's. Bourbon, beefsteaks, and blondes were three formidable weapons in the lobbyist's arsenal then. Not far out South Congress Avenue were two of the better whorehouses in Texas; many of the girls were working their way through UT and were not your average hookers. Hattie's and Peggy's were lively on a Sunday night, and lobbyists gladly followed along to pick up the members' tabs.

Today, the few hookers are free lancers whose business is going down. One young lady interviewed said, "Yeah, I get an occasional legislator or businessman but they're older and just get drunk and pass out. I still get the hundred bucks though, don't you worry about that."

Because it's expensive and, more importantly, because of the Sharpstown scandal's effect on such ostentation, junketeering has been throttled the past few years. Gone are the days of lobby-paid trips to Keeneland Race Track in Lexington, Ky., and mass migrations to Matamoros or Juarez under the auspices of inspecting the state's coastal lands or Texas Western College. This year, unless you wanted to view the Houston Ship Channel courtesy of the Chamber of Commerce, it was stay in Austin and gut it out.

Gifts to legislators have also dropped off sharply. No longer is there a flood of turkeys, transistor radios, packages of imported cheeses, whiskey, etc.

For the legislators and for most of the lobby, the 1973 session was just unpleasant and exhausting. As a lobbyist from Houston put it: "It was an isometric session. You pulled and strained as hard as you could and got nowhere. There was never a game plan, but you kept going back everyday hoping you could catch hold of what was going on." Reuben Senterfitt, the powerful lobbyist for the utility industry, was overheard saying, "I did okay this time, but I dreaded every day going to the Capitol and doing business."

What was going on was an attempt by 77 new House members and 14 new Senators to deal with confusion, distrust, and two presiding officers who chose to preside rather than lead; and to try in the process to pass some legislation.

In the spirit of ree-form, Speaker Price Daniel, Jr. announced he would be speaker only one term. The immediate and continuing result of that pronouncement was that an immediate speaker's race was created, and from the first day forward, trust among House members was minimal at best. This, in turn, meant no floor leadership. If the speaker doesn't provide strong direction, it must come from experienced, respected members on the House floor. Those who tried were suspected of cutting deals and furthering their own cause.

In the Senate, things weren't so bad. A slightly smaller percentage of freshmen, a lighter work load, and experienced men chairing crucial committees helped. Lt. Governor Bill Hobby didn't. To campaign and be elected lieutenant governor in a state whose Constitution makes him the most powerful presiding Senate officer in any of the 50 states, and then to disavow and turn away from this authority, is a waste.

No one, however, accused either chamber of laziness. House and Senate members began with a mole-like diligence, burrowing through Saturday meetings as early as March and attending non-controversial committee meetings that often lasted until the early morning. By the session's end, the unfortunate result was a totally exhausted legislative membership. So many House members were vowing not to run again that the turnover in 1975 may be 25 or 30 more than the normal average of 47.

Despite problems, changes, and realignments of old political alliances, work was accomplished, bills passed and defeated, and in the end, there were definite winners and losers among the lobby.

The reason many thousands of dollars are spent lobbying the legislature is because the stakes are enormous. Almost without exception, every industry and business is affected by decisions made every two years in Austin. The basic rule for the lobbyist is that money is the root of all lobbying: Keep the client from paying it out; pave the way to bring it in.

For the men representing the major industries—oil and gas, beer and liquor, utilities, chemicals, railroads, trucks, sulphur—the overriding task is to avoid taxation. This they did and, therefore, were winners.

Other associations had specific battles to fight: Kill this bill, pass this one, amend this one. Some did and some didn't.

One spectacular fight, one in which there were definite losers and winners, involved Bill Abington, the lobbyist for Texas Mid-Continent Oil and Gas Association, whom we left waiting in the Senate gallery for a key vote. Abington's battle contained all the elements of a good novel: forceful characters, strong developing plot, a large purse at stake, and a smashing dramatic climax.

In one corner: Texas Mid-Continent Oil and Gas Association, made up of 3000 members of almost all the independent and major oil companies in Texas, and considered the strongest industrial lobby in Texas; the Texas Manufacturing Association; 12 major Chamber of Commerce groups; four environmental groups; 32 Texas newspaper editorial endorsements.

In the other corner: Senator Peyton McKnight, Tyler; several independent oil men, notably Wesley West of Houston and Robert Payne of Dallas; the Permian Basin Petroleum Association, a small association of independent oil men headquartered in Midland.

At issue was the passage of the oil field unitization bill (HB 311). Unitization is a complicated concept, but basically the bill would have allowed 75 per cent of the operators in a given oil field to require all operators in that field to pay for, and share proportionately the benefits of, secondary recovery methods in fields where normal drilling could no longer efficiently recover oil.

Senator McKnight's opposition to the bill was well known. His view was that the voluntary unitization law in Texas was already working in over 400 fields and that this new bill would force smaller oil operators with good producing wells into unitization with a larger field of less productive units. The energy crisis (used by supporters to gather votes for the bill) is a phony issue, McKnight claimed, because, 1) the only way to solve the crisis is to

find more oil reserves and increase the capacity of existing refineries and, 2) the secondary recovery method is not guaranteed to work and may not contribute a thing.

The Mid-Continent Oil and Gas boys made their first mistake early in the session. McKnight felt his position was hopeless, so he offered to work out some amendments to the bill which would help protect the small operators. Mid-Continent refused to discuss compromise with McKnight (as it later turned out, a big mistake).

The lobby had no trouble in the House. Opposition was fragmented; the bill's sponsors, Dave Finney of Ft. Worth and DeWitt Hale of Corpus Christi, were both veteran, respected leaders. One seemingly innocuous amendment was tacked on involving a relatively inexpensive severance compensation program for laid-off oil workers. This was done because of the successful work of the president of the Texas Oil and Chemical Union, Morris Aikins, and resulted in shifting 15 to 20 labor votes in the House. More importantly, Senator D. Roy Harrington of Port Arthur, a labor man, then changed sides and supported the measure. The bill passed the House 103-36, thus strengthening the confidence of the lobby.

McKnight dug in for an all-out battle. His strategy was to delay consideration of the bill as long as possible, giving him time to explain the bill point-by-point to other Senators. As the only oil man in the upper house, his words carried much weight.

He insisted on a full presentation of testimony before the Natural Resources Committee and those hearings lasted over a month. When the bill arrived from the House, he insisted on hearings on the House amendments, then presented a series of unsuccessful committee amendments that took two more weeks. When the bill's sponsors tried to get it out of committee, McKnight surprised the committee with a rule requiring a transcript of all hearings prior to final action, delaying passage for another week.

McKnight had another opponent, one that really curled his socks. Lt. Gov. Bill Hobby broke his trance, and for the first and only time during the session, actively worked the floor for a major bill, urging his colleagues to vote "aye." Hobby needlessly tweaked McKnight's nose by refusing to re-refer a minor bill from an unfriendly to a more favorable committee, a common Senatorial courtesy usually granted from the floor.

McKnight fought back, refusing to back down to the presiding officer. He announced that "Billy Hobby may well have an East Texas opponent next year."

The climax came on that spring Saturday morning with the vote Bill Abington had been awaiting a long time. Greg Hooser, Sen. McKnight's aide, noticed that all 31 members were present, very rare for a Saturday. As he looked around the gallery, he also noticed that the oil and gas lobby was all there, including Mr. Abington himself. Then it struck him that this must be the day, the final try to shake McKnight's hold on the bill and to bring it out of committee for a vote. But Hooser remembered one of the recently adopted joint rules. It stated that no House bill could be brought up except on regular House bill days (Wednesday and Thursday) without a two-thirds vote of both Houses. It seemed unlikely to Hooser that such votes could occur in both Houses this morning.

Senator Jack Hightower stood up and moved to take up House Bill 311, the unitization bill. McKnight objected, citing the new joint rule. To Hooser's amazement, Lt. Gov. Hobby overruled McKnight. Then followed a series of personal privilege speeches by fellow senators. Senators Bill Patman and Max Sherman objected to the ruling, but the dean of the Senate, A. M. Aikin, spoke in support of Hobby.

Once again, Sen. Hightower moved to suspend the regular Senate rules and take up H.B. 311 for a vote. This required a two-thirds vote, 21 members out of the full 31 present. Secretary of the Senate Charles Schnabel began calling the role in his steady baritone: "Adams?" "Aye."; "Aiken?" "Aye."; "Andujar?" "Aye."; "Blanchard?" "No."; "Braecklein?" "Present."

Braecklein was the first surprise, and the first hint that McKnight might win. A wealthy man from Dallas, Braecklein had many friends in the oil business, but he thought McKnight's arguments rang true.

The vote continued down the list. The final vote: 17 for, 13 against, one present. The lobby had needed 21 votes. The bill was dead, short by four votes. McKnight had won. Knowing the personal battle he had waged against the measure since January, his fellow Senators mobbed McKnight and congratulated him on his victory.

Upstairs, Bill Abington, defeated, tucked away his pen and quickly made his way out of the gallery and toward the elevators. He suddenly felt tired; the only bright thought that occured to him was that the session's end was only nine days away. Despite all the money, pressures, and manpower, this time the lobby had lost. What happened?

They were overconfident. The early success in the House helped many lobbyists forget that the legislature had repeatedly defeated the bill since 1949.

Overconfidence led them to refuse to compromise, the biggest mistake of all. They also put too much reliance on their early legislative commitments. Getting 13 Senators to co-sponsor the bill in January did not necessarily mean the rest would follow. Because of the complexity of the bill, some Senators couldn't cast a vote on its merits and had to rely on the judgment of McKnight.

The oil and gas lobby did not move quickly enough. They were caught off guard time and time again by McKnight's tactics. Each day that passed was a small victory for him because, as the session drew to a close, his colleagues did not want their own bills stymied by a potential McKnight filibuster.

McKnight proved that one Senator who had enough skill, and would fight hard enough, could defeat, for better or for worse, the largest industrial lobby in the State.

Although Abington was a loser, the lobbyist who was the biggest winner was probably Buck Wood, a first-term lobbyist for Common Cause, a citizens' group which was focusing its attentions on the legislature for the first time. Wood pushed his programs through against the opposition of practically every other lobbyist and many of the legislators themselves, although the strong support of Speaker Daniel and his team helped immensely.

Legislative reform was top priority for the 5500 members of Common Cause. With a new governor, lieutenant governor, attorney general, and speaker of the house, and with a legislature pledged to reform, Wood knew that it was now or never to put an end to the practices that had allowed the Shapstown scandals and which in his eyes subverted the democratic process.

Wood was hired in September, 1972. By late November he had drafted five bills that focused on ethics of legislators and state officials; lobby registration and reporting of expenditures; campaign finance reporting; expansion of the open meetings law; enlarging the public's access to government information. On December 5, a full month before the session, copies of the bills were mailed to House and Senate members as part of Speaker Daniel's reform package.

The first bill passed the House on February 8, and the rest followed in rapid succession. The Senate received them with less than total enthusiasm, and Lt. Gov. Hobby announced that no action would be taken until his own citizens conference convened in mid-March.

When it became clear that passing the bills would require the same grinding drudgery that must accompany the typical lobbyist's bill, Wood settled down to it, ushering the bills from subcommittee to full committee.

After countless hours of work and untold committee meetings, the key reform bills came right down to the wire on the last day of the session. Only one key aspect, a proposed Ethics Commission, bogged down hopelessly in a House-Senate conference committee and had to be abandoned for the sake of passing the whole ethics bill.

Besides the ethics bill, Common Cause secured its other goals: an improved open meetings law; tightened controls over campaign contributions and expenditures; easier public access to government records; and, most importantly for the lobby, tightened control over lobbyists and their spending.

Almost all lobbyists hated this part of the reform package (HB 2). It will require them to report expenditures while the legislature is not in session. Lobbying expenses can no longer be reported under a lump sum but must be categorized. Also, individual members of organizations must now report their expenditures on lobbying. These new requirements rankle some of the lobby, but by and large they still leave the lobby with plenty of room.

One should not get the impression, however, that the old guard is completely moribund. Against Harry Whitworth of the Texas Chemical Council, the environmentalists and their legislative package didn't have a chance. If bringing up the nine reform bills didn't start a lobbyist spluttering with indignation, certainly the mention of the major environmental measures would. Virtually all the business and industrial lobby stood in ranks solidly against these bills, making their passage next to impossible.

Harry Whitworth entered the starting gate at the session's beginning riding a mule instead of his customary thoroughbred. In 1963, he had spotted a tall, red-haired, rough-edged House member named Ben Barnes and decided he was unique. As head of the powerful Texas Chemical Council, Whitworth had entreés, money, and information, all of which he gladly shared with young Ben.

Barnes' capacity to learn astounded even his most ardent admirers, and in 1965 he was suddenly elected Speaker and was on his way. Whitworth had displayed his most valuable talent: choosing an unknown out of the gaggle and staying hitched to him.

In January, 1973, Barnes was building shopping centers in Brownwood and Whitworth was awaiting the beginning of a new session as he had done for many years. He had always performed well. The chemical industry flourished, and because of his efforts, they paid no special state taxes.

There were two bills that Whitworth had to kill this session: 1) H.B. 205 by Hawkins Menefee of Houston, which would have allowed any Texan to file suit to stop pollution of the air or water—a privilege now belonging only to the state and to those who suffer specific provable damages from the hands of the polluter. It also would have allowed suits against state agencies by persons who believed their clean air and water standards were not set high enough or were not well enough enforced. 2) H.B. 646 by Carl Parker of Port Arthur, which would have set state policy on the environment and would have created an umbrella environmental protection agency to which all state agencies would have to submit environmental impact statements on planned projects. The new office would have authority to veto projects that would harm the environment.

Whitworth's work was cut out for him. The first thing was to decide who would also find this bill disastrous. That impact statement had to be a nuisance for lots of folks. He began by calling John Terrell, lobbyist for the Texas Association of Builders. Old John didn't like it at all. Certainly cities would be affected, so Whitworth forewarned the executive director of the Texas Municipal League (TML), Richard Brown. Almost every mayor and city official in Texas belongs to the TML, and it has *clout*.

The next step was to find a freshman House member, unknown, conservative, unscarred, to work the floor. To Whitworth, Pete Laney from Plainview seemed ideal. Pete put out a farm and ranch journal and was a farmer up in the Panhandle. Whitworth was interested in farming, and soon the two were old friends. Whitworth never asked him for anything regarding the bill, but only to study it carefully and assay how much it might hurt the farm and ranch business.

Joining Whitworth, the homebuilders, and the Texas Municipal League in opposition were the Texas Water Quality Board, Texas Mid-Continent Oil and Gas, Texas Independent Producers and Royalty Owners, and West Central Texas Oil and Gas Association.

On May 2, after two crippling amendments were added, Rep. Parker angrily pronounced his bill dead. Pointing to the lobbyists in the gallery he said, "I see the vultures up there waiting to pick the bones. They have done their work well in representing their clients."

The Houston Chronicle reported that the noise of the lobby leaving the gallery was so great after Parker admitted defeat that Speaker Daniel told the House to stand at ease until quiet was restored. Watching the phoning and commotion was Mr. Whitworth, as serene and secure as a moo-cow.

A similar fate killed Rep. Menefee's bill almost exactly a month earlier. A crippling amendment won passage and the bill never saw the light of day.

Sadly enough, the 63rd Session passed only a few environmental reform measures, one the endangered species act. Mrs. Char White, chairwoman of Environmental Action for Texas, no doubt wishes Harry Whitworth was one of those critters included on the list under her new law. But Whitworth's still very much around and, although not in the cat bird seat, still a winner.

Another winner this session, as at every session he participates in, was Frank C. Erwin, Jr., a man few people have ambivalent feelings about. Depending on your point of view he has either single-handedly ruined the University of Texas or he has pulled it up into the 20th Century.

He is a complex man: emotional, mean as a rattlesnake in a sleeping bag, defiantly loyal, shy but unfailingly polite with women. He is what used to be known as a gentleman of parts, a man who is as much at home with Puccini's *Turandot* as he is passing statehouse gossip with the coarsest representatives.

Since 1965, Frank Erwin has presented the huge UT System's budget before the House Appropriations Committee and the Senate Finance Committee, as well as testified for or against bills affecting the UT System.

He has a brain as sharp as an awl, and as the Appropriations Committee chairman makes his way through the several-inches-thick budget, it's very clear that Erwin has done his homework. Erwin's participation began in 1965 when one of Governor John Connally's aides recommended vetoing funds for UT's Memorial Museum. Erwin was appalled that such a thing could occur to his beloved UT.

That year the appropriation for the UT System was $77 million. Erwin has lobbied for UT every session since, and, for the 1974-75 biennial, the UT System will receive $427 million, a 453 per cent increase over 1965. Even with new institutions added in, it is an impressive figure and a credit to Erwin's skill.

"There was a considerable difference in the House Appropriations Committee this time. Many committee members were new and were unfamiliar with the institutions and their backgrounds," said Erwin.

"However, I think the appropriations bill is exceptionally good, considering the no-new-tax constraint and flexible welfare situation the committee had to work under."

He concluded: "Gov. Briscoe gave us no leadership or help whatsoever. He has expressed interest in vocational education, which is fine, but he has made no pitch for higher education, either general or academic instruction, medical or dental units."

The Coordinating Board of Colleges and Universities introduced five bills to denude UT's power. None was enacted. There were 35 or so unfriendly bills introduced, mainly by freshmen members. All failed.

Erwin and UT are used to being number one. Railroads, on the other hand, are not. If his friend and fellow power-lobbyist Bill Abington was left holding the bag, Walter Caven had the other half. Chief legal counsel for the Texas Railroad Association since 1959, the tall, patrician-looking, blue-eyed Caven had the dubious pleasure of having a much sought-after bill become Gov. Briscoe's first veto.

Caven's bill would have authorized special railroad agents to be peace officers, carry weapons, and move from one county to another with no legal hassles. There was no indication of trouble and Caven was confident. When Sgt. Julius Knigge of the Houston police department, lobbyist for the Texas Municipal Police Association, found out about these about-to-be 150 new peace officers, however, he fired off a letter to Gov. Briscoe protesting that for the first time private industry would have its own police force.

That's all it took. In a press release announcing the veto, the Governor agreed that it was a problem and a study would be the best thing.

Unique among the big four industrial lobbyists, Caven has manpower to aid the cause. The major railroads in Texas—Missouri Pacific, Santa Fe, Southern Pacific and Katy—send down between four and ten lobby-drones during the session to do the dirty-collar work. Each drone is assigned three or four House members a day for lunch. Mr. Caven looks after the Senate.

Caven vehemently disapproves of Price Daniel, Jr. ("I haven't said anything to him except hello since the session started and I don't intend to"), calls lobby reform a false issue, and thinks the present lobby law was adequate and only needed to be enforced.

One of the strongest lobbies in Austin is the Texas Trial Lawyers. The 1100 members are by profession advocates and persuaders; their business is to sell juries. They sell legislators, too. Phil Gauss has been the executive director since 1949 and has had two pieces of legislation on the front burner for a long time. They finally passed this session.

The two long-awaited bills: 1) A bill making comparative negligence part of state tort law, passed last session and vetoed by Gov. Smith. It made it this time and was signed into law on April 9. 2) A bill providing for voluntary first-party insurance. If you choose to pay an additional $25-$35, this add-on insurance will provide up to $2500 in automatic pay offs for injuries and loss—no law suit necessary.

Much of TTLA's strength comes from their political arm, LIFT (Lawyers Involved For Texas). Headed by attorney Wayne Fisher of Houson, LIFT contributes heavily to Texas House and Senate races.

Name any interest you want and it's a safe bet their concerns are represented by an association or lobbyist in Austin. Below is a random sampling of persons and associations which for better or worse hang around the Capitol:

AFL-CIO—The labor movement in Texas has always had the numbers and the money. The increasing urbanization of Texas may give the labor unions the added political muscle they have missed, although union membership is not picking up rapidly. Secretary-Treasurer Harry Hubbard leads a five-man lobby delegation that worked for passage of collective bargaining for public employees (failed) and an upward revision of workmen's compensation payments to injured workers (passed).

Texas Brewers' Institute—Chief legal counsel Dick Cory is the lobby's acknowledged expert on the drafting and constitutionality of legislation. A former House member for 16 years and participant in two previous constitutional revision studies, Cory had an easy session, putting out brush fires and worrying about a future tax bill.

Texas Automobile Dealers Association—An organization of 1450 franchised new car dealers in Texas headed by former Rep. Gene Fondren. On the job for little over a year, Fondren knows the legislature's whims and, along with Cory and attorney Wade Spilman, ranks among the most competent drafters of legislation.

Texas Manufacturers Association—Six thousand members representing 3,000 firms make up this widespread organization headquartered in Houston. Their ability to raise money has declined as has the prestige of the executive director, Jim Yancy.

National Organization for the Reform of Marijuana Laws (NORML)—By taking polls, appearing on TV and radio shows, and by persistent lobbying, state director Steve Simon provided valuable assistance to the already excellent groundwork done by former State Senator Don Kennard's Senate Interim Committee on Drug Abuse. The combined efforts of the Kennard program and the activities of NORML bore fruit on the last day of the session, when the penalty for first possession of marihuana was reduced from a felony to a misdemeanor.

Joe Golman—One of the busiest individual lobbyists in Austin, Golman represents the Dallas Chamber of Commerce, Dallas Community College, and the National Association of Theater Owners. Golman is a popular former House member from Dallas who will commute from Dallas to the Austin office between sessions to keep abreast of legislative business which may affect his clients.

There are many, many more, ranging from the powerful Texas Medical Association to the many other medical-related lobbies; to Allen Commander's efforts to work for the University of Houston in the shadow of Frank Erwin's got-it-down-pat work for UT; to shrimpers and oystermen and every delegation and individual who visits Austin at one time or another.

The lobby is hardly a monolithic body, although its major members share certain basic interests and a certain common folklore. When it comes right down to it, the business of lobbying is the business of petitioning the government: it's trying to right wrongs, achieve a special good, or just to get what you can.

Lobbyists will swear up and down that democratic government could not go on without them, particularly as the world, and governing, become more complex. Most legislators will agree with them. The legislators know how difficult it is to keep informed on issues.

The methods that the lobbyist use are pretty much standard; it is the ends that are different from lobbyist to lobbyist. The danger comes when some lobbyists spend too much time around power, and come to equate the public interest with their own.

In the meantime, Bill Abington of Texas Mid-Continent Oil and Gas is preparing for another session—perhaps a tax session, perhaps the constitutional revision session this spring, perhaps the next regular session. If he could just figure a way to get around Senator McKnight . . . . □

THE HIGHWAY ESTABLISHMENT AND HOW IT GREW.

AND GREW AND GREW

BY GRIFFIN SMITH

Everything happened at once. Texans woke up to discover service stations running out of gasoline all over town. Highway travel was not the quick, easy bet it had been last year. At 55 miles an hour, motorists had the feeling that some giant hand had lifted Dallas and Houston and deposited them a good hundred miles farther apart.

In the midst of it all was Texas, oil-rich Texas, realizing it was an *urban* state—79.7 per cent urban, said the census-takers last time around—with three of the ten biggest cities in the country. An urban state, with some distinctly urban problems—like how to get to work and back, how to get to the store, how to get to school, if the family cars couldn't be counted on to supply cheap transportation as they always had. Not that they couldn't: just that someday soon they *might not*. That was the nagging worry.

In 1974 Texans began to realize that all that advice about public transportation might be more than just doomsday talk from pointy-headed East Coast zealots.

They hadn't been happy, by and large, when congressmen from the urban Northeast successfully "busted" the Federal Highway Trust Fund last year, allowing a portion of federal highway funds to be spent for mass transit systems in the cities. The Southwestern life style depended on the automobile, they told themselves, and roads are God's way of getting around. Texas was lucky

enough to have a first-rate Highway Department—honest, hardworking, smart, and capable of building top-notch highways from a little ol' nickel-a-gallon gasoline tax that was the lowest in the country. Who was worried if all the eggs *were* in one basket? Texas was lucky enough not to need more than one basket.

They forgot the Southwestern lifestyle depended on gasoline too—cheap gasoline, plenty of gasoline, all - night - green - stamps - service - with - a - smile - win - the - contest - pennants - flapping - in - the - wind - free - glasses - *32 - cent gasoline*.

It all happened at once, and the next thing Texans saw was their legislators all decked out as delegates to a Constitutional Convention, rewriting the basic document that a bunch of independent steel-eyed farmers had put together back in 1875 when the state was *eight* per cent urban. Questions about mass transit, highways, and basic transportation policy were suddenly being asked in earnest by those delegates (some of them, anyway) because they had to decide whether to preserve the constitutional provision that guaranteed the Highway Department would have first shot at the money it needed to keep on building roads.

More than any other part of the country, Texas in the spring of 1974 was the place where public officials were forced to stand up and debate about the kind of transportation policy their citi-

zens should have—to argue whether highways ought to have first priority, whether mass transit was feasible, whether the Legislature's hands should be tied by the new document.

As a result the Constitutional Convention has been a grand show. Other states fumed, fussed, and speculated about the problem of getting around. Texans actually had to make some decisions about how they were going to cope with this new topsy-turvy world. At the Big Top in Austin, the Highway Lobby is out in full force, and the spotlight shines on one of the most remarkable bureaucracies in state government.

A Well That Won't Run Dry

The battleground is the so-called "dedicated highway fund," a state constitutional provision that has profoundly shaped transportation planning in Texas since its adoption in 1946. It allocates, or "dedicates," most of the money the state collects from motor vehicle registration fees and taxes on gasoline, diesel fuel, and lubricants "used to propel motor vehicles over public roadways" into a special fund that must be used only for acquiring rights of way and constructing, policing, and maintaining public roadways. The bulk of it goes to the Highway Department. A small portion (less than ten per cent) goes to the Department of

Public Safety; the counties keep a slice of the registration fees, according to a 1929 formula that strongly favors rural counties over urban ones; and one-fourth of the motor fuel taxes are diverted to the public schools.

In a state with nine million gas-gulping cars, trucks, buses, and other motor vehicles, such a scheme provides the Highway Department with a massive chunk of guaranteed tax revenues. None of the other state agencies, from the Air Control Board to the Water Well Drillers Board, enjoys this special luxury. They must each shove and fight every two years for legislative appropriations to run their shop. Only the Highway Department, the public schools, The University of Texas, and Texas A&M University have the benefits of constitutionally-dedicated revenue. The money is there; they know from past experience just about how much of it there will be; and the Legislature merely performs a polite ceremonial gavotte by awarding them biennially what is already theirs.

How massive is this revenue chunk? In Fiscal 1973, the Department drew $454,380,000 from the dedicated fund. That was 64 per cent of its total income; most of the rest, 31 per cent, came from the Federal Highway Administration as matching funds. By way of comparison, the total 1973 appropriation for the Air Control Board was $399 thousand, for the Department of Health $44.9 million, for Parks and Wildlife $39.3 million, and for the Water Quality Board $5.4 million.

By the parsimonious standards of the state budget, Texas has made a lavish commitment to one particular form of transportation. The reason can be traced to the confluence of several currents: a powerful and effective lobby, a bureaucracy that in many ways exhibits the best qualities that government has to offer, and not least the postwar infatuation of Texans themselves with the private automobile—a passion for individual mobility that scarred most forms of "public transportation" with a vulgar social stigma. Each of these currents is a matter of history.

The TGRA: Well-Drillers Extraordinaire

The adoption of the "Good Roads Amendment" by a vote of 231,834 to 58,555 in the general election of 1946 was the climax of parallel and at times consolidated efforts by two different groups. The first of these included business interests having a direct economic stake in expanded, large-scale highway construction. The second included public-spirited citizens who saw in good roads (and the general economic development they might produce) the magic key to the booming, bustling Texas they dreamed of creating. Twenty-eight years later the Amendment remains intact, unaffected by all efforts to divert its dedicated funds to other purposes, and the dual motives that created it are still apparent in the membership rolls of the powerful lobby that midwifed its adoption: the Texas Good Roads Association. The TGRA brought these two groups together in the Thirties and keeps them together today. It is a marvel of symbiosis and stratagem: perhaps the most fascinating lobby in Texas politics.

The combination of "economic" interests and "civic" interests lies at the heart of the TGRA's lasting effectiveness. It has always drawn the bulk of its financial backing from industries that want a transportation system dependent on the use of highways and the construction of more and more of them: the oil companies; petroleum distributors; cement, asphalt, and tire dealers; automobile dealers; bus companies; truckers; and of course the highway contractors themselves. (Highway building is the only industry in Texas that is 100 per cent dependent on government money). Subcontractors also play an important role in highway lobby movements, as do such diverse groups as engineering firms that specialize in roads, and land speculators and developers. They are united by a common desire to preserve, perfect, and expand the highway transportation system. There is no doubt that they have been the muscle behind the TGRA since its inception. In a surprisingly candid article in *Texas Parade*, the Association's Director of Public Relations and longtime President Weldon Hart described its creation 42 years ago:

The Texas Highway Chapter of Associated General Contractors took the lead in getting a committee organized, representing the whole highway industry. [Tyree] Bell represented AGC, Ben Warden the cement industry, Lou Kemp the asphalt industry, Datus Proper the rock asphalt interests, and so on. One of the important moves was to find a president. . . . and the TGRA was in business.

Significantly, the first president was a respected civic leader with no personal ties to the highway industry. His name was William Ogburn Huggins, and he was the editor of the *Houston Chronicle*. His selection symbolized the intention of the TGRA's founders to give their organization the image of a disinterested civic club supporting highways because the state needed them, rather than the image of an economically self-interested industry pleading its case. According to founder Bell, Judge Huggins carried this shrewd decision a step farther by insisting that "for public acceptance, . . . the officers . . . should come from the public generally and not include anyone in the highway industry." His rule remains in force today: all of the officers are, in the TGRA's words, "laymen."

More impressive even than the "laymen" officers, however, are the "laymen" members. Among the Association's 2335 members are 54 local chambers of commerce, 46 cities and counties (some of which pay their annual dues with public funds),* and numerous individuals who are prominent in the social and political affairs of their communities. These are the opinion makers. They are crucial.

Some of them, of course, represent highway-oriented economic interests wearing another hat. Many of the local chamber of commerce officers, for example, have a personal economic interest in some aspect of road-building. Others may have a different sort of self-serving interest: Very few county commissioners have ever been hurt by having a road built in their precincts, and there are still a few who stay in office by tipping off their friends about the paths of new rights-of-way. But most of the laymen are exactly what they seem: well-respected, public-spirited citizens who honestly believe that the welfare of the state depends on a good network of highways built by a Highway Department unblemished by political chicanery. They are not money-seekers, not crackpots; they are the bedrock Establishment of Texas. To an impressive extent, TGRA commands their loyalties.

These laymen are indispensable to TGRA's purposes. Without them the Association is naked, a straightforward phalanx of powerful economic interests. With them, it is something grander than a lobby: it is a movement, a personification of the Texas automobile-highway-mobility ethos. No other lobby in the state has so successfully camouflaged its basic economic motives.

---

* A spokesman for the TGRA says the $25 membership fee paid by cities and counties "doesn't even pay the cost of the material we send out. It amounts to a subscription to our publications for the information they contain. They get a bargain."

If the TGRA loses money on its $25 membership fee for non-profit organizations, it loses even more on the $15 annual fee it collects for ordinary individual memberships. Without the fees for firms ($50) and highway industries ($100), plus additional contributions from its backers, the TGRA could not stay afloat. Its "layman" members are a dead economic loss.

Impressively framed on a reception-room wall in its Austin headquarters is a striking, hand-lettered gubernatorial proclamation issued by John Connally in honor of Highway Week, 1964. The visitor reads:

Highways are derived from vision, and vision is rooted in the people.

The TGRA has actually done much to create the ethos it personifies. Its relationship with the Texas news media is nothing short of amazing. From the day its founders chose an influential editor as the first president, the Association has diligently cultivated good press relations. Journalists have figured prominently in its hierarchies. Among the ablest is Weldon Hart himself, a former aide and confidant to Governor Allan Shivers whom even a political adversary described as "a brilliant writer, a genius." (He also has a sense of humor: one of his recent articles in *Texas Parade* was titled, "The Glory and Splendor That Is Highway Week.") Hart ran the TGRA from 1965 to 1972. Partly as a result of his work, it now counts among its members 23 newspapers and publishing companies, including the *Dallas Times Herald*, the *Dallas Morning News*, the *Houston Chronicle*, the *San Antonio Light*, the Express Publishing Company [*San Antonio Express* and KENS-TV], the *Midland Reporter-Telegram*, the *Lubbock Avalanche-Journal*, and others from Abilene to Longview and Denison to Victoria.

When the dedicated fund is threatened, as it has been in this year's Constitutional Convention, the TGRA can expect prompt and vigorous editorial support for its viewpoint—sometimes by the very next morning in certain member newspapers. But the media can be even more cordial. A set of six TGRA advertisements praising the highway network and defending the dedicated fund was published 150 times last year in Texas newspapers as a "public service announcement," free of charge. Radio and television stations give free air time to its 20- and 60-second "spots." These promote rail, air, water, and pipeline transportation in addition to highways, and the message in some of them bears an intriguing similarity to the paid advertisements of oil companies that help to finance the TGRA. *Texas Parade* Magazine, which was the TGRA house organ for decades, now publishes an article a month prepared in cooperation with the Association "as a valuable contribution to public education."

In the communities, the TGRA promotes the highway ethos in a variety of ways. Part of it is simply good organization work: the Association has area chairmen in 40 cities and a board of directors in each of its 25 districts (the districts themselves coincide precisely with the Texas Highway Department's own districts). The directors constitute a good start toward a "who's who of Texas." For the local, district, and state leaders, there is an endless round of speeches to Lions Clubs, Rotary Clubs, and Chambers of Commerce—a spreading of the gospel to revive the loyalties of fellow laymen and win conversions among unbelievers. The Association has produced a documentary film called "Turning Point," which, according to a TGRA spokesman, "has been used by television stations in most Texas cities—and is in constant use by civic and service clubs each day." Cultivation of lay support never really stops.

But organization, even good organization, has its limits. In the end the special strength of the TGRA comes from the fact that its members participate personally to an unusually high degree in the power structure of Texas. Said one former legislator: "it's not that they contribute so much in campaigns; it's more subtle than that. They belong to the right country clubs, the right power elites."

The Association's public pronouncements exist on two levels. The first is a calm, sober, and straightforward enunciation of the view that highway transportation is intrinsically good for Texas. "This vital transportation resource," says a sample TGRA resolution, ". . . is essential to the State's business, industry and emergency requirements and to the mobility, welfare, and recreational needs of its citizens and visitors." Without the dedicated fund, the argument goes, irresponsible legislators would allow construction to slump into an unpredictable series of peaks and valleys. Highways, "a perishable product," require an average lead-time of eight years from the planning stage to completion, and any skimping on funds one year would have an impact eight years later. The highway industry itself also likes to know the total dollar value of contracts to be awarded in a given year; the security of the dedicated fund relieves them of the anxieties that trouble other industries dependent on the uncertainties of legislative funding. Says the TGRA:

"The contractors who build the state's highways must depend on a 'core of expertise' to get the job done. These are key employees who are permanent, so long as there are contracts to be executed. But if there is a drought of funds . . . then the state's major highway builders must let their key personnel go —and the loser, in the final analysis, is the highway user himself."

The Association's foremost precept is the belief that revenues collected from highway users should be spent only for "costs . . . directly related to highway construction, maintenance ,and improvement." The campaign of "educational publicity" starts from this point.

But there is a second, much more emotional level, in which the dedicated highway fund is viewed as the fountainhead of all good things, and those who would change it as either anti-social knaves or starry-eyed fools. [See "We the People," Texas Monthly, January 1974]. Two years ago, Eugene W. Robbins, then the TGRA vice-president, warned an audience in Gonzales that a "conspiracy is afoot in the United States to stop all highway construction. The plot was hatched in the densely populated Northeastern megapolis but its disciples are spreading throughout the land —including Texas." He described the members of this "conspiracy" as "pseudo environmentalists, rail mass transit zealots, politicians and bureaucrats, and social planners with active support from some news media." Robbins himself, now the president of TGRA, is a mild and personable man, and a visitor to his office who hears him speaking genially and knowledgeably about the state's highway system is likely to wonder just what gets into him (and other TGRA spokesmen) when he stands behind the podium of a small-town meeting hall. Perhaps such rhetorical excess is possible because the Texas highway ethos is so pervasive, leaving the speaker with a sense of freedom to speak his mind because he feels he is among friends who think as he does, far away from the zealots and social planners who inhabit foreign territory. Or perhaps it is something more: a sudden reminder of the fundamental gulf that separates the laymen from the economically self-interested side of the TGRA, a ferocious expression on behalf of those who know that if Texas changes its highway priorities they themselves have a fortune to lose.

The gulf is there. It is too wide to paper over indefinitely, although the TGRA has done a remarkable job of doing so for the past four decades. That is why the Association prefers to speak in glowing generalities that submerge the blunt economics of profit and loss beneath the rhetoric of high public purpose.

How the Well Was Won

The TGRA won adoption of the Good Roads Amendment in 1946 by using many of the same techniques it uses today. If ever there was a broad-based effort to change state policy, the campaign for this amendment was it. Charles Simons, who was executive vice-president of the TGRA at the time, recalls that it had "virtually unanimous support" from political figures. "Governor [Coke] Stevenson was real strong for it. Allan Shivers—he was a senator then—carried it in the Senate, and Neville Colson carried it in the House."

The "layman" members of TGRA were concerned equally with making sure that the highway industry had a steady flow of public funds and with preventing monkeyshines and corruption in the Highway Department. Critics of the dedicated fund today tend to underestimate the extent to which Texans of that era feared political favoritism in the Highway Department. The farmer was still in the mud in those days; inter-city road travel left a lot to be desired; and the prospect that important highway construction would be carried out to suit the needs of some politician's career instead of the logical traffic requirements was abhorrent to many influential citizens. The issue in 1946 was not whether a particular road should be two lanes or four: it was whether that road would be *paved*.

Although the Highway Department in the Thirties and Forties was ably run as a professional, rather than a political, operation, the squalid smell of still-recent history reminded many Texans that unless the Department's planning was insulated from the biennial legislative process, the state might just be living on borrowed time. During the administration of Governor Miriam A. ("Ma") Ferguson in the mid-Twenties, the Department had struggled through a bleak period of chicanery and political patronage. In a single biennium (1925-26) four different men served as Highway Engineer, the Department's top executive position. Ten individuals were named to the three posts of Highway Commissioner. All but one of the division engineers lost his job. Finally the Federal Bureau of Public Roads refused to participate in Texas highway projects because of the deteriorating system. The memory of this experience lingered long after the Department was reorganized in 1927. Not surprisingly, it spurred sentiment for the Good Roads Amendment: the Ferguson fiasco, after all, had occurred less than twenty years before 1946, making it closer in time than the passage of the Amendment itself is to us today.

Securing the Highway Department's finances outside the normal appropriations process was a simple, logical, and therefore attractive panacea to allay these fears. The fact that it would also award virtually permanent protection to a particular special interest's economic needs was seldom discussed.

Most of the resistance to the Amendment came from other interests who had cast their eyes covetously on the same gasoline tax revenues. County authorities, who wanted to convert one-fourth of the tax into a permanent source of county income, had squelched an attempt to get an earlier version of the Amendment on the ballot in 1942. The TGRA's decision to draft their 1946 Amendment to preserve the existing statutory allocation of one-fourth of the gasoline tax to the Available School Fund was a brilliant tactical maneuver that insured the back-up support of the powerful teachers' lobby, both for passage of the Amendment and preservation of the dedicated fund in future years.

Before 1946, Charles Simons recalls, "you had to continually be fighting off the brushfires" that threatened the Highway Department's funds. The voters changed all that. From the adoption of the Amendment, the Department was to grow into the largest, most powerful, and in many ways the most competent of state agencies. Nineteen-forty-six was a milestone, and the years since then are the *Anno Domini* of the Texas Highway Department.

Et in Arcadia Ego: The THD

The modern Texas Highway Department (THD) has far surpassed the most optimistic predictions made for it in 1946. Its reputation is untarnished by any serious hint of scandal. It is among the least secretive of state agencies. It has developed the largest (and many feel the best) system of highways in the United States. Set apart in its own snug —but not little—insular world of engineering excellence, it has an enviable esprit de corps.

The Department's reputation for honesty is especially remarkable in view of the vast sums of public money at its disposal. Scandals of the sort that brought Spiro Agnew low in Maryland are an all-too-common aspect of highway construction elsewhere. They don't happen in Texas. The fact that highway funds are constitutionally protected has of course had something to do with this state of affairs, though not as much as the highway lobbyists and the THD would like the public to believe. Keeping highway building out of legislative politics accomplishes very little unless the department that builds the roads keeps its own hands clean. The special strength of the THD is its conscientious administrative tradition—and that is the result not of some nebulous code of loyalties but of the direct personal influence of specific men in specific positions. The man most frequently credited with developing this high standard of honesty is DeWitt Greer, a quintessential Aggie who served as Chief Highway Engineer (in effect, the Department's executive director) from 1940 through 1967, and is currently one of the three Highway

Commissioners. "The lion's share of the credit goes to Greer," says Garrett Morris, a Highway Commissioner from 1967 to 1971. "Nobody could ever point an accusing finger at him." Although an increasing number of critics question Greer's emphasis on highway transportation, he was primarily responsible for selecting generations of middle-level administrators who have kept the Department out of politics for more than 30 years.

The THD's efficiency and honesty, coupled with Texans' affinity for highway travel, has to some extent made the Department its own best lobbyist. Legislators are reluctant to place themselves at cross-purposes with an agency that is so popular back home. "It's really the fact that they do such a good job, and they're so honest, that's made them into a sacred cow," says one former senator. Then too, voters by and large do not object to things they can *see* as tangible examples of governmental services. "We're really the only state agency that produces a product," says Marc Yancey, one of two assistant highway engineers. "You can't see the welfare product, or even the education product, but you can see ours all over the state. It helps."

The highway system rapidly expanded in the years following 1946. From approximately 28,000 miles in 1947, it grew to 42,000 in 1950 and 62,000 in 1960. It has now passed the 71,000-mile mark. The Department told the Finance Committee of the Constitutional Convention that 21 entire counties and 1716 communities (including 49 county seats) currently are served by no mode of transportation except the highway system. (Supporters of public transportation, of course, consider this a lamentable situation rather than a source of pride). The 1970 census revealed that in 18 Texas counties, the number of registered motor vehicles exceeded the number of human inhabitants.

Highway building is the principal, but far from the only, responsibility of the THD. The Department provides an incredible array of services—some which directly benefit the public and others which reinforce its image as a virtual state-within-a-state. Charged with the duty of promoting tourism, it publishes a semiannual "Calendar of Events" listing everything from the Sweetwater Rattlesnake Roundup to the Houston Livestock Show, along with brochures about historical trails, maps of every county in three different sizes, a monthly road conditions bulletin (the January issue listed 193 construction sites, with detailed information on the location, extent of construction, projected date of completion, and even the type of road surface onto which traffic was being detoured), and the award-winning guidebook, *Texas: Land of Contrast*. Its materials have a well-deserved reputation for thoroughness and polish.

The Department's in-house publications include a slick monthly magazine, *Texas Highways*, a newsletter called "Highway News," and several other newsletters published for specific geographical districts. Various branches produce motion pictures (including a 30-minute sound and color feature on highway beautification), answer telephone calls about emergency road conditions, run computerized data retrieval systems that can locate any magazine article about transportation systems, distribute public service announcements to TV stations (a current "spot" tells how to enter a freeway safely), catalog the archaeological discoveries unearthed in the course of roadbuilding, devise new techniques of highway safety (including breakaway road signs and the ingenious empty-barrel collections called Texas Crash Cushions), and print the tons of manuals, reports, and other documents the Department issues each year. The Public Information office distributes more than 1300 press releases annually (on the average, four or five every working day). So great is the Department's reputation and so deep the lethargy of some weekly newspaper editors that many of these are printed, unchanged, as news stories in small-town papers.

Some idea of the size and complexity of the THD can be gained from a brief glance at its internal structure.

The three commissioners are Reagan Houston (the chairman), DeWitt Greer, and Charles Simons. Houston is a San Antonio lawyer appointed by Governor Dolph Briscoe. Governor Preston Smith had the inspired idea of crowning Greer's career by appointing the retired chief engineer to a commissioner's post; it was like picking Winston Churchill to be king of England. Smith also appointed Simons, a balding, witty gentleman who looks like Sibelius mellowed by a touch of Charles Coburn. These men set the Department's policy, and Chief Highway Engineer B. L. DeBerry carries it out.

DeBerry has separated his giant bureaucracy into two parts and placed an assistant highway engineer over each one. The "operations" side of things is supervised by M. G. Goode, Jr. Its eight sections include Highway Design; Bridges; Maintenance Operations; Secondary Roads; Construction; Right of Way; Materials and Tests; and Planning and Research. Each is directed by an engineer. The administrative side is supervised by Marc Yancey, Jr., a likeable, diplomatic ambassador for the Department who could, in meticulously-chosen language, probably convince the head of a local Sierra Club that a proposed interstate highway through his living room was actually a splendid idea. Yancey's seven sections include Finance;

Motor Vehicles; Travel and Information; Insurance; Equipment & Procurement; Automation; and Personnel.

The day-to-day business of the Department is highly decentralized. Only 400 of its 18,000 employees work in the downtown Austin headquarters. More than 1250 THD buildings are scattered around the state in 25 separate and largely autonomous geographical Districts. Each District is headed by a District Engineer who, in accordance with traditions established by Greer, is expected to handle most of his problems at that level. Interestingly, there is also a "public affairs officer" in each District, a man whose job entails more than answering questions from the public about Highway Department plans. "He keeps apprised of the economic and social conditions in his district," Yancey relates. "He can tell us about the current political climate and things like that."

Because of its solid financial base, the THD has vast resources that other state agencies do not even dare to dream of. Its *Twenty-eighth Biennial Report* covering Fiscal 1971 and 1972 itemizes the 17,989 pieces of "major highway equipment," valued at $19,900,483.50, that the Department owned at the end of August, 1972. In addition to the predictable asphalt distributors, batchers, boilers, core-drills, diggers (posthole), earth-movers, graders, grass-seeding machines, guard rail washing machines (motorized), concrete mixers, power movers (gravely class), nail pickers, paint stripers, pavement breakers, power shovels, road rollers, road rippers, snow plows, mulch spreaders, tractors, trailers, trenchers, trucks, and something called an "unloading machine," the *Report* also lists 868 passenger cars of various sizes (642 of which were equipped with two-way radios) and 3506 pickup trucks. This was a sufficient number of cars and pickups to allow approximately one out of every four departmental employees, including secretaries, janitors, and typists, to be on the road alone at the same instant. When employees of an under-equipped agency like the Park Division of Parks and Wildlife hear this sort of thing, they whimper. Most of them have to use their own cars when they travel on state business.

The Highway Department is, in reality, a separate fiefdom, a veritable fourth branch of government. When asked about its relationship to the Legislature, highway commissioners and the TGRA like to emphasize the constitutional language that makes the dedicated fund "subject to legislative allocation, appropriation, and direction," but this subordination is more symbolic than real. The Department has not been forced to justify a highway expenditure to the Legislature since 1946. While the lawmakers can crack down on the THD

through the appropriations process if they choose (by requiring it to pay the full cost of various expenses like rights-of-way, curbs, and gutters that are now shared with other governments), the dedicated fund revenue *must* be used for highway-related purposes. The Legislature is not free to shift it into mental health or mass transit. Even if the legislators got so mad at the Department that they refused to appropriate any of the dedicated fund for anything, the money would simply pile up and await future legislators, two, twenty, or a hundred years hence, who would eventually have to appropriate it for highways. The Highway Department has the upper hand, and the legislators know it.

Legislators are human and they enjoy the power that comes from being able to insist that an agency justify its appropriations. It is a bit galling, then, to be faced with one that is financially independent enough to get away with saying, politely of course, "We appreciate your suggestions but we don't plan to take them." This bothers the legislator who feels he ought to have the right to balance the relative needs of, say, a hundred mentally retarded children against the need of the city of Taylor to have a four-lane Loop built around its outskirts. But it also bothers the legislator who just feels he ought to have a say in how the state of Texas spends three quarters of a billion dollars every year. The financial independence of the THD has caused more friction than either side is willing to admit.

This resentment rarely flares out into the open because the average legislator is reluctant to oppose a sacred cow like the Department. One occasion when it did, however, was the planned construction of a ten-story, 20-million-dollar THD headquarters building in front of the State Capitol and across the street from the more modest building erected in 1933. San Antonio Representative Jake Johnson, an old foe of the Department, blasted the proposal in the 1971 legislative session, calling it a "monstrosity" that would make the Governor's Mansion directly behind it "look like an outhouse." He asserted that it had been designed to be so tall "in order that DeWitt Greer can look down on the Legislature, rather than the other way around." Johnson nearly blocked the building, but the Legislature eventually settled for suggesting that the Commissioners find some other site. By October, 1971, however, the Department had produced a 25-page, slick-paper pamphlet (at a cost of $1.60 a copy) defending the building's aesthetics, mentioning that the downtown location was convenient to the offices of the contractors who do business with the Department, and suggesting that if the structure was not built, commercial developers might buy the property and erect something even more offensive there. By

March 1972, the Department was contending that even the Legislature could not prevent construction of the building because it would be paid for with dedicated funds over which the Legislature could exercise no control. This struck a nerve. After a personal privilege speech by Representative Frances Farenthold in a June special session, the Legislature ordered the Parks and Wildlife Department to buy the property and convert it into a state park. Governor Smith then vetoed these instructions, leaving the matter more confused than ever. But when the Legislature returned for yet another special session in October, both houses overwhelmingly approved a resolution warning the THD that they were mightily displeased with the whole affair. The lame-duck Governor could not veto a resolution, and the Department, sensing that they had aroused the Legislature's ire, threw in the towel and agreed to build their headquarters somewhere else.

Significantly, however, the Department has never abandoned its claim that it has the legal right to construct buildings out of its "own" funds without legislative approval. And even now, more than a year later, Commissioner Charles Simons gets a wistful, faraway look in his eye when he is asked about the legislative battle. "I really believe that our building, the way we had it planned, would have been a prime asset to that site and to downtown Austin business," he says. "It was a *beautiful* building."

The Commissioners have traditionally had few qualms about putting pressure on the Legislature to accede to the Department's wishes. Most agency heads are rather circumspect about marching out and soliciting public support for their agency's position in a controversial political issue. Not the highway commissioners. In recent months they have become unabashed lobbyists for preservation of the dedicated highway fund. At a luncheon speech to a business men's association called "Fort Worth's Progress, Inc.," last November, all three commissioners thanked Beeman Fisher, a member of the Constitutional Revision Commission (and of the TGRA) for his successful efforts to preserve the fund in the proposed new constitution. They urged the audience to help persuade the Constitutional Convention to keep it there, and, by extension, to keep roads ahead of mass transit as a state priority.

From top to bottom, the people at the Texas Highway Department have a firm faith in the value of what they are doing. But even as they bask in the sunshine of public admiration for their visible accomplishments, they display the faults of people who talk seriously only to others in their own closed circle. The conflicting ideas expressed before the commissioners at public hearings seldom penetrate the bureaucracy itself. If, as some say, the Department exhibits all the advantages of a government run by engineers, it likewise exhibits all the *disadvantages*.

Haunted by the possibility that political meddling could ruin the Department —which of course it could—the postwar leadership and Greer in particular hewed an administrative path as far from politics as possible. To administrative positions he promoted men from within the Department strictly, as he saw it, on the basis of merit. The reasoning was simple: as long as our administrators are men who have served in the Department, as long as they are trained men who have proved their competence and not "outsiders" who might be unqualified or who might rock the boat, we are safe from political interference. Greer was determined to protect the Department by quarantining it. He wanted a bureaucracy composed of engineering professionals, and that is what he got.

Except for the commissioners themselves, who are appointed for six-year terms by the Governor and confirmed by the Senate, virtually all the important administrative positions in the Department are held by engineers who have been promoted through the ranks. "It's kind of like being a doctor: first you have to be an intern," says Marc Yancey. "This is one of the essentials of the type of operation we have." (Starting at the very bottom, however, is not required. Yancey himself left a career in consulting work to join the Department, but he still served six years in the Bridge Division before moving up.) The price for this sort of insulation from politics is bureaucratic inbreeding. Eventually everyone begins to think alike because those who think differently are either not hired, or, if hired, are not promoted to positions of influence. Such a rigid promotional system firmly precludes the possibility that an unorthodox thinker could become Chief Highway Engineer. And only an unorthodox Chief Highway Engineer could choose outsiders with fresh ideas for the middle-echelon administrative positions. It is the kind of unconscious oversight that would come naturally to a trained engineer who began his highway career in 1927 just a few weeks after the Ferguson scandals were ended, as Greer himself did. The formative experiences of this 26-year-old assistant resident engineer in Henderson County were to shape the Department's policies for nearly half a century.

This inbreeding is profoundly reinforced by the fact that the greatest proportion of THD engineers are graduates of either The University of Texas College of Engineering or the Texas A&M College of Engineering. The dominant influences on Texas civil engineers flow from U.T.'s Highway Research Center and A&M's Texas Transportation Institute; the graduates' outlooks are formed there, and, as the Texas Public Interest Research Group (TEXPIRG) has noted, those outlooks are routinely predisposed to favor highway transportation over rail mass transit and other modes.

The current semester at Texas A&M's civil engineering department, for example, includes courses in Highway Engineering; Highway Materials and Pavement Design; Highway Design; Highway Problems Analysis; Structural Design of Rigid Pavements; Roadside Safety Design; and Highway Construction. Only one of the 72 courses deals expressly with urban transportation. Approximately 30 academic civil engineering professors hold joint appointments as research engineers for the Texas Transportation Institute, and they spend, on the average, 60 per cent of their time on TTI research projects. Those projects are heavily weighted in favor of highway problems. At the present time the TTI is conducting 52 separate studies for the Texas Highway Department.

Even before the state's civil engineering graduates have reached the Highway Department, they are intellectually comfortable with its world-view. Perhaps this is because the Highway Department has reached *them* before they reach *it*: both the Highway Research Center and the Texas Transportation Institute are partially supported by Highway Department funds.

All these influences have given Texas an established Highway Department bureaucracy of transportation professionals who think only *roads*. Like other bureaucracies, it exhibits the standard tendency to expand its needs, ambitions, and goals (by 1948, only two years after the Good Roads Amendment was passed, Greer told the Legislature that the Department's needs in the next five years would cost twice as much as the anticipated revenue). What has made the Highway Department different from other state agencies is that it has not been compelled to justify its expenditures against other, non-highway needs. The same things that have helped make it honest and efficient have also made it wealthy, powerful, and inbred. The luxury of its dedicated fund has allowed it the luxury of becoming set in its ways.

These danger signals for the future were fully apparent in 1946, if anyone had stopped to see them. No one did. The Texan's love affair with his automobile continued, raising motor vehicle registrations from 1.9 million in 1946 to 3.1 million in 1950, 4.9 million in 1960, and 8.5 million in 1972. The Department grew with them.

How the Lobby Works

The transportation interests have always been a powerful lobby in Texas. Before the highways, there were the railroads. The modern-day Highway Lobby begins but does not end with the Good Roads Association. True, the Association is the closest thing the highway interests have to a common flag; but the various economic groups that support the TGRA also do some lobbying on their own. Two of the most powerful are the Highway-Heavy Contractor branch of the Association of General Contractors, which represents roadbuilders, and the Texas Motor Transportation Association, which vigorously protects the interests of the truck and bus industries. Opinions differ as to which other groups wield the most power. Former Secretary of State Bob Bullock, one of Governor Preston Smith's closest advisers, insists that no one in the Highway Lobby has more clout than the oil industry. Other observers contend that when hard lobbying is needed, the local chambers of commerce are the most formidable force around. But everyone agrees that the Highway Lobby ultimately draws its strength from its diverse *combination* of interests.

Those who expect to wait around the Capitol and watch the Highway Lobby flex its muscles every two years are, however, in for a disappointment. The mighty highway lobbyists paradoxically do very little "lobbying," at least as that word is ordinarily understood: wining, dining, wenching, and twisting arms of legislators. They don't have to. That is the beauty of the dedicated fund, the glorious legacy of the Good Roads Amendment. So long as Article VIII, Section 7a, of the Texas Constitution remains in the law books, they are safe. And *the only* way that provision can be taken out is by constitutional amendment: a process that requires a two-thirds majority of both houses of the Legislature even to get on the ballot. It is a lobbyist's dream. While the other lobbyists—the doctors, the insurance industry, the brewers, the lawyers, the pot smokers, the land developers, and all the rest—are racing around the Capitol halls trying to get their pet bills enacted or defeated step by tedious step, from subcommittee, to committee, to the floor, to the other house, to conference committee, and to the governor's desk, the highway lobbyists just sit back, act friendly, and smile. All they need is one-third plus one of *either* house of the Legislature on their side, and the dedicated fund will stay safely beyond all danger. Just fifty-one Representatives, say—or better yet, just eleven of the 31 senators. Keep those eleven little sena-

tors, and *nobody* can tamper with the dedicated fund: not the governor, not a majority of both houses of the legislature aroused to high dudgeon, not the voters, not Saint Christopher himself: NO-*body*. The ball, as they say, is in the other court. It is a lovely sort of life.

With such an overwhelming strategic advantage, the Highway Lobby can put out the occasional brushfires without ever bothering to take off its white gloves. Even the brushfires are rare. A 1947 attempt by Senator Grover Morris to create a farm-to-market road program by increasing the gasoline tax was successfully squelched by truck, bus, and oil industry lobbyists, who objected to any "diversion" of gasoline tax revenues (even new ones) away from arterial highways. Two years later these same lobbyists, along with the TGRA, supported the Colson-Briscoe Act financing a farm-to-market road program out of general state revenues. The dedicated fund had been preserved inviolate. By 1968 the TGRA had grown as fond of farm roads as any other kind; it buried a bill by Representative Glenn Purcell that would have, in his words, "put the money where the rubber is" by closing out the farm road program.

One of the liveliest brushfires broke out in 1965 when Bob Bullock, then a lobbyist for municipal bus companies, got a bill introduced that would have given them a rebate on the 75 per cent of their motor fuel tax that went to the Highway Department. Bullock reasoned that city buses operate on city streets, not highways. Most of the companies were on the verge of bankruptcy; and his bill would only have cost the Highway Department two or three million dollars, a drop in the bucket for them. A similar bill had been killed on the House floor in 1963, 80-61, and this time the Highway Lobby was ready. Bullock later recalled: "I had a hard time even finding a sponsor. Finally we got it introduced and had a hearing. Lots of mail started coming in from Good Roads members, editorials started popping up in newspapers saying 'Don't open the door: everybody will ask for rebates.' . . . It went to subcommittee and, man, it never budged at all. They beat the hell out of me."

Bullock described the lobby effort as "a very honorable fight. The oil companies lobbied over a drink. . . . there certainly wasn't any money changing hands, nothing like that. The Good Roads members contribute to campaigns as individuals, and who was I? I represented a lot of broke bus companies, some of them city owned. Face it: a contributor gets the ear of a legislator quicker than a non-contributor. The Good Roads Association is potent. They're political, and they do a damn good job."

Apart from these periodic easy bat-

tles the Highway Lobby has very little to do except to continue nourishing the highway ethos that envelops the legislators when they return home to visit with the constituents. Very little, that is, except for one critically-important function: year-in-year-out, they exert decisive pressure on the selection and confirmation of the highway commissioners who set the policies of the THD. If the commissioners waver, the entire highway building superstructure is endangered. So the TGRA and the other components of the highway lobby pay special attention to gubernatorial politics. Selection of these commissioners is the summit of their lobbying. Their aim is to insure that the state's transportation leadership, like its professionals, thinks only of roads.

A number of exceptional men have served as highway commissioners over the years. Most of them have been chosen in a process dominated by the highway lobby. The TGRA's candidates are not necessarily men with an economic self-interest in roads—just as the TGRA's own officers are "laymen." But they are invariably men having a solid predisposition in favor of the TGRA's roadbuilding aspirations.

Thirteen men have been appointed Highway Commissioner since the Good Roads Amendment was passed. A few, like Garrett Morris and the current Chairman, Reagan Houston, have not been TGRA candidates. Among the others are the following:

* Fred A. Wemple (1947–1953). President of TGRA before serving as commissioner, 1942–43, and again afterwards, 1955–56.
* Robert J. Potts (1949–1955). President of TGRA, 1947–48.
* C. F. Hawn (1957–1963). Member of TGRA Executive Committee before serving as commissioner; president of TGRA, 1968–70.
* Herbert C. Petry (1955–1973). TGRA director before serving as commissioner.
* J. H. Kultgen (1963–1969). TGRA director, 1947–1962; TGRA president, 1951–55. Automobile dealer since 1936. President of Bird-Kultgen, Inc., Ford dealership in Waco.
* Charles Simons (1971–present). Director of TGRA public relations, 1936–1942; Editor, Texas Parade, 1936–1942; TGRA executive vice-president, 1942–1947. Executive vice-president, Texas Mid-Continent Oil and Gas Association, 1947–1971.

The TGRA was unable to say how many of the remaining commissioners had been members of the Association before or after their terms of office. But it is unlikely that they would have protested the appointment of men like De-Witt Greer (1969–present), or Marshall Formby (1953–1959), who ran for governor in 1962 and distributed campaign literature describing himself as "a staunch believer in wide highways" who "helped spend more than a billion dollars for highway maintenance and construction" while serving as commissioner.

During the Constitutional Convention hearings, delegate Jim Vecchio of Dallas brought out the fact that Commissioner Simons had recently applied for a bank charter with, among others, TGRA Board Chairman Russell Perry. Vecchio's questions implied that there might be a conflict of interest if a Highway Commissioner and a top highway lobbyist went into the banking business together. After Simons heatedly responded that, "I don't think his being chairman of the Good Roads Association would influence me for five seconds," the chuckles echoed for days. But the truth of the matter was, Simons was absolutely right. What his critics overlooked was the fact that Simons and Perry *already* thought exactly alike on every important question about the state's transportation needs, and had for years: just as virtually every other highway commissioner and Good Roads official has thought alike for two generations. If the commissioners did not already share the Association's aims, the Association would never have consented to their appointments as commissioners.

The critics mistook an effect for a cause.

Mass Transit in Texas?

The Constitutional Convention fight over the dedicated fund has become a battle over the pros and cons of mass transit. Gasoline shortages have suddenly made the issue very real: how do you get to work if there's no gas for your car? But there is something very one-sided about the now-fashionable assumption around the Capitol that mass transit is needed just because fuel is short. For some people that is reason enough; but for many Texans who don't own a private car and never will, the problem of finding gasoline to propel one is entirely academic. Texas cities with more than about 50,000 residents are so large, geographically, that people who have no private car find it hard to get where they need to go—to work, to the grocery store, to church. For them there is a transportation shortage, not a fuel shortage.

Garrett Morris has seen the problem from both sides, first as a highway commissioner and currently as a member of the State Board of Public Welfare, and the experience has made him a firm believer in mass transit.

"For many people," he says, "the automobile doesn't provide true mobility —the young, the old, the blind, the dis-

abled, the indigent. You've got to make good money to buy a $4000 car and maintain it. Ever since we tore up our streetcar tracks and shipped them to Japan in the Thirties, these people have had a hard time getting around."

Bob Bullock noticed the same thing when he lobbied for rebates to rescue local bus companies in the Sixties. "These transit companies were a losing proposition but a necessary service," he says. "Affluent people don't realize this. I don't understand all about mass transit, but I understand something when I see a bus full of blacks and Mexicans."

This latent class bias is implicit in the attitudes of the middle-class "layman" supporters of the Texas Good Roads Association. TGRA President Eugene Robbins says, "our objection to using gasoline taxes for mass transit is that it places the entire burden on the guy who drives his car—and he may or may not be the one who's using mass transit." The broad front of the Highway Lobby is distinctively white middle class, and such a person, burdened by the already-high costs of running an automobile—or two, or three—sees good sense in Robbins' argument. But others are not so sure. Robert E. Gallamore, Director of Policy Development for Common Cause, recently argued to a Congressional subcommittee that despite the fact that the roads themselves are usually constructed out of highway user taxes, those who use the highways still don't pay the full social costs:

Noise, congestion, and air pollution are shared with others. Large portions of dislocation costs are borne by unfortunate people whose incomes and often whose race do not enable them to move out of the path of new freeways until it is too late to make that choice voluntarily. Gasoline is relatively cheap [this was in 1973] because all tax payers subsidize oil companies through the percentage depletion allowance, intangible drilling cost write-offs, and foreign tax credits. . . . Local jurisdictions pay for traffic police out of general funds. . . .

The auto got us into this mess, say the mass transit advocates, and those of us who are too poor to own an auto now that public transportation has dwindled to almost nothing may reasonably think that there is nothing wrong with taxing the auto to help get us out again.

The Highway Lobby has kept the mass transit advocates off balance by cheerfully agreeing that Texas does need more mass transit—surely does, needs it in the worst way. The problem is, they say, that there's not enough money in the highway budget right now for highways, and besides, nobody has invented any sort of mass transit system that will

work in Texas. They prefer to think of mass transit in terms of large fleets of diesel-powered, rubber-tired buses rolling over . . . roads.

The TGRA has too much political savvy to sit back and allow the increasingly-popular notion of mass transit to be co-opted by the highway critics. Last November TGRA Chairman Russell Perry announced the formation of a 29-member "Urban Mass Transportation Advisory Council" having as its "primary function" the dissemination of information "giving Texas citizens perspective and understanding on urban transportation issues" so that the public will support "reasonable urban transportation programs for Texas cities." At its organizational meeting February 12, the group endorsed the idea of a state mass transportation fund so long as it did not interfere with the dedicated highway fund, and they suggested that the TGRA change its own name to "Texans for Better Transportation" to reflect its "broad concern with the total transportation picture."

The Advisory Council's specific recommendations must await future meetings, but it seems doubtful that its members will discover any "reasonable" programs that require fixed rails or invade gasoline tax revenues. Meanwhile they have the inestimable public relations benefit of being able to disseminate the TGRA position from a letterhead containing the magic words "Urban" and "Mass Transportation."

Despite brave words ("We have the farmer out of the mud. Our challenge now is . . . to get the city dweller out of the traffic jam") the TGRA's position on mass transit boils down to this: do it if you want to, but get your money somewhere else. In a letter to Governor Briscoe in January 1973, the Association listed fifteen "specific actions" they would support. Some of these, like state guarantees for transit authority bonds and passage of legislation to permit establishment of metropolitan transit authorities, were helpful to mass transit without being harmful to the Association's members. Others were a veiled way of saying "leave our money alone" (*e.g.*, "Support of increased Federal and State funding from general funds," "Support the release of funds authorized by Congress . . . but withheld by the Nixon Administration"). The rest were clearly designed to pad out the list: ("Support demonstration projects to prove new systems will work." "Support coordinated planning for all transportation modes," a proposal seemingly indistinguishable from "Support coordination of efforts by state agencies," and, finally, "Support the Texas Highway Department in its desire to help the cities achieve improved public transportation.")

The intensity of the THD's desire to help the cities in this respect is open to question. It does not appear to have grown significantly since DeWitt Greer declared in 1967:

> I do not believe mass transit is the answer in Texas. . . . Texans are oriented to the use of the automobile. It would take a generation to break Texans of the comfortable and convenient habit of riding in the automobile. If we are to please the taxpayers . . . then we must develop more adequate thoroughfares in the urban areas."

To the extent the Department does set its collective mind to considerations of mass transit, it thinks only of buses and roads. Asked about the THD's plans, Commissioner Charles Simons mentioned Houston's heavily-traveled West Loop 610 as evidence that the Department is already "the biggest public transportation system in Texas." Of the auto user, he said that "when it gets to be too inconvenient and too costly to drive downtown, he will use public transportation. When gas is 50 cents a gallon people will go back to buses. We're gonna help them because we have the facilities over which those buses roll."

Today gas is over 50 cents a gallon and there are few buses for Texans to go back to. In the past generation, bus service has been discontinued at the rate of one city per year in Texas, declining from 36 cities in 1955 to 18 cities today. The systems that remain are a pale shadow of comprehensive public transportation.

There are two fundamental problems facing any urban mass transit system in Texas. They figure prominently in every THD and TGRA statement on the subject, and even the advocates of mass transit do not deny them.

One is residential *density*. Texas cities grew fastest in the era after automobiles had become the primary mode of personal transportation. Therefore they sprawl: unlike the closely-packed, high-rise cities of the East Coast, where population densities exceed 20,000 persons per square mile, residential neighborhoods in Texas are spacious, with densities in the vicinity of 3000 persons per square mile. How, ask the mass transit critics, can a bus or fixed rail network serve enough riders within walking distance of each stop to make the whole thing attractive?

The other problem is commercial *decentralization*. Traditional mass transit systems are designed to handle suburb-to-central-business-district movement quite well, but the Shopping Center Society of 1974 spends most of its travel time going places other than the downtown area. Commissioner Simons estimates that only five to seven per

cent of all trips in Dallas County have downtown destinations. How, ask the critics, can a mass transit system take urban Texans where they want to go?

Density and decentralization are the favorite themes at TGRA gatherings where mass transit is discussed. They are treated as insuperable barriers to a mass transit system, at least within the lifetime of the audience, and thus they take on the character of a rhetorical fail-safe system against threats to divert the dedicated fund. If mass transit is impossible, only fools would waste money on it. Especially highway money.

One illustration of this phenomenon occurred at the joint meeting of the TGRA and the Houston Chamber of Commerce last November. The speaker was Dr. R. W. Holder, Associate Research Engineer at the Texas Transportation Institute. He discussed the density and decentralization problems and concluded that

> . . . no rapid transit system in use today appears to be directly applicable to Texas cities. Our urban forms are so different from those of cities in the North and East that we faced a different set of problems.

By this, said Holder, "I do not mean to imply that we cannot solve this problem. . . . We must search for mass transportation system designs that are compatible with our urban forms and" —he added significantly to his highway-minded audience— "[with] our existing urban transportation systems."

One suggestion proposed by Holder was to establish "freeway surveillance and control with priority entry for buses."

As newspaper headlines outside warned of imminent gasoline shortages, Holder concluded by telling his audience:

> Texas is the greatest state in the greatest nation in the world. . . . I see no reason why Texas should adopt an approach of copying urban transportation systems developed for other cities. . . . Let us design our own systems. . . . Let's pioneer the way, and let the rest of the world follow us.

The applause was fervent.

The density and decentralization problems are serious obstacles, to be sure. If the Manhattan subway system could somehow be inserted in the swampy muck that underlies Houston, it still would not fully solve that city's transportation problem. Mass transit advocates merely deny that these obstacles are insuperable. "*No* mass transit system is feasible in Texas," says Buck Wood of Texas Common Cause, "if you start from the premise that everybody has to drive his car to work." Pointing to the rail commuter societies of Long Island and suburban Philadelphia,

where residential density resembles Texas' and people take a bus, drive, or are driven to rail terminals, Garrett Morris remarks, "this density argument sounds good, but I'm not sure it's as valid as people would have you believe. When you've got the necessity for conservation of fuel, density is not the argument it once was. Anyway, the old streetcars worked with lower density that we have today."

Commercial decentralization is not so severe as to prevent the creation of a mass transit system serving major shopping centers as well as the central business district. If our present decentralized shopping patterns grew up in the last 30 years as a direct result of the increased mobility that private automobiles provide, is it not reasonable to expect that with reduced auto use and better mass transit our shopping patterns will swing back toward greater decentralization, giving downtown stores a badly-needed shot in the arm? Is that so bad a prospect?

At the moment, however, mass transit plans in Texas are hamstrung by problems far more elementary than density and decentralization. Though thousands of commuters need to cross municipal boundaries, the cities face difficulties extending their own systems across these lines. The counties lack mass transit authority altogether. An effort to establish a regional transit authority in Houston last fall collapsed in a roar of recriminations. Revenue sources are shaky. The smaller cities cannot (or will not) put together enough revenue to qualify for federal matching funds (Since 1964, Texas has received only $35.6 million in federal aid for improving mass transit, less than one-tenth as much as California, that bastion of the private car, has gotten, and far behind the $260 million for Illinois, the $210 million for Massachusetts, and the $200 million for Pennsylvania. Under the law, Texas *could* have gotten $762.5 million.) Good transit is expensive, like police, fire protection, waste disposal, and other city services. Because it was a profit-making business until very recently, the cities are doggedly reluctant to assume the responsibility of supplying it at a loss.

The Boys on the Bus: The TMTC

The authority that has been charged with helping the cities overcome these problems is the Texas Mass Transportation Commission. In a state where impotent agencies outnumber the eunuchs in a Turkish harem, the TMTC sings its soprano song to an audience of benign neglect. Established by the Legislature in 1969 to "foster . . . the development of public mass transportation, both intracity and intercity, in this state," but without being given funds to do so, the Commission existed for twenty months, after September 1971, with no chairman, no quorum, no employees, no money, and no telephone. In January 1973, it received an appropriation of $80,100, of which $58,000 goes to pay the salaries of Executive Director Russell Cummings and his three employees, "leaving," in his words, "about 22 thousand to do all these great wonders the Legislature requires us to do."

Cummings, a folksy 48-year-old former legislator from Houston's Montrose district, is sensitive to the inconvenience that the present meager public transportation systems impose on racial and economic minorities. He is not, however, a visionary, and he talks a lot about buses. "We're not set in concrete on any particular mode," he says, adding, "—but every rail system in the U.S. lost money last year." He also takes a modest view of his agency's duties: "We are a service organization, not a regulatory authority." Unlike other mass transit advocates, moreover, he takes a hands-off approach to the dedicated highway fund, insisting that "where the Legislature gets the money is their decision. We're not seeking anybody else's funds."

Cummings' caution is understandable in view of the interests of the six appointed commissioners who hired him.

* Chairman Albert Rollins is a member of an engineering firm who previously served as Engineer Assistant for the Texas Highway Department.
* Member Joe P. Cain is president of Lake Truck Lines, Inc.
* Member Robert H. Cutler is Chairman of the Board of ICX Illinois-California Express, Inc., a motor freight carrier. A 32-year veteran of the trucking industry, he has held office in the Texas Motor Transport Association and is past president of the American Trucking Association.
* Member J. W. Porter is Executive Vice-President of Gifford-Hill & Co., Inc., manufacturers of ready-mixed concrete, Portland cement, sand, and gravel. (And, for the record, railroad crossties.)
* Member Clyde Malone is the Manager of the Austin City bus system and a member of the TGRA's Urban Mass Transportation Advisory Council.
* Member James W. Ward was, at the time of his appointment, chairman of the Amarillo Chamber of Commerce traffic committee.

Five of the six (excepting only Porter, a Briscoe man) are the legacy of Governor Preston Smith.

The selection of these particular men to establish policy on the Texas Mass Transportation Commission is compelling evidence that the Highway Lobby has moved as swiftly to neutralize this faint potential threat to highway dominance as they customarily move to influence the selection of the highway commissioners themselves.

So Russell Cummings sits in his tiny office on South Congress Avenue twenty blocks from the Capitol, a distance too far to walk and too humiliating to drive, and types the lead on his latest press release:

1974 is the Year of the Tiger in China, but it may be the Year of the Bus in Texas. . . .

Shootout at the Watering Trough

With these issues, the current Constitutional fight over the dedicated fund is being waged. The Texas Highway Department insists that every penny of its allotted funds, and more, will be needed to finance highway needs for the next 20 years. Even ex-Commissioner Morris agrees with that. The planned reconstruction of 12,000 to 14,000 miles of non-interstate primary highways will, the Commissioners say, require 13 billion dollars. Thirteen hundred bridges are substandard, some of them "damn dangerous," according to Simons. Another 10,000 miles of farm-to-market roads are planned. The suburban loops that were being built five years ago around cities the size of Tyler (pop. 60,000) are now being constructed around Vernon (pop. 12,600), Taylor (pop. 9616), Monahans (pop. 8350), and Perryton (pop. 8100). "Towns that used to threaten to secede if we built loops now ask for us to build them," says Simons. Since the money is available, the loops are built.

The Department's philosophy of loops is interesting. Spokesman Marc Yancey explains:

If you look at history you see that . . . the cities that last longest have a radial design. The center deteriorates, but because it's practical to drive within the radial loop, the center rebuilds itself, like Montrose in Houston is now doing.

Loops have a very good purpose. Rome is a classic example. Athens, Greece, has a radial highway.

Today Athens, tomorrow Dripping Springs.

Maintenance costs are continuing to rise. In the 1973 fiscal year they amounted to $116 million, but Yancey says "costs have gone right through the roof" and the figure will rise to $132 million this year and $150 million in 1975.

Pie graphs distributed to the Convention by the TGRA show the same maintenance figures for Fiscal 1973, $116 million, along with figures for "right of way and construction" totaling $432 million. Apparently the pie graphs were embarrassing. In a season when both the gasoline supply and the dedicated fund are in danger, expenditures for "maintenance" are better public relations than expenditures for construction. The TGRA and the THD quickly began to distribute new charts for Fiscal 1974 containing a "Maintenance and Operation" category that had swollen to $296 million and "right of way and construction" categories that had shriveled to $171 million. Yancey explains that the figures originally described as "maintenance" include only routine things like mowing grass, picking up litter, and filling potholes. He attributes the increase to a simple re-classification of serious maintenance—work designed to prolong the life of a highway by resurfacing, sealcoating, or improving its base. Randall Wood of Common Cause contends that it includes the cost of four-laning existing two-lane highways as "maintenance." There is, in any event, something suspicious about a statement captioned "TEXAS HIGHWAY DEPARTMENT INCOME & EXPENDITURES" that includes $40 million for the Department of Public Safety under the category of "Maintenance & Operation" for the *Highway Department.*

A similar sort of confusion surrounds the impact of the energy crisis on highway revenues and needs in Texas. The Department has based its projections on the assumption that the number of motor vehicles will increase by nearly 50 per cent by the year 2000, and that these vehicles will consume about *twice* as many gallons of gasoline as were sold in Texas last year. Both assumptions now seem dubious, yet the Department has projected that this much traffic will need new roads, that this much traffic will tear up the roads that currently exist. Commissioner Simons says, "we haven't been affected by the energy crisis at all yet."

His confidence is shared by the Department's estimate of its income from the motor fuels tax this year. Even though gasoline stations are closing on every corner, the Department expects to collect $24.7 million dollars *more* from these taxes than it did in 1973. How can this be? The 5¢ tax rate remains unchanged. The prestigious Advisory Commission on Intergovernmental Relations estimates that gasoline tax collections this year will be 17 per cent below those in 1972—a cut of about $39 million dollars for Texas. Does the Department know something the rest of us don't know? Asked about the apparent discrepancy, a THD spokesman said mysteriously that he was confident the estimates were correct and the reason would become apparent "very soon." And laying a finger aside of his nose, and giving a nod, up the chimney he rose.

In the Constitutional Convention the mass transit proponents, led by Common Cause of Texas, have argued first for elimination of the dedicated fund altogether or, as an alternative, for language that would allow some of the money to be used for public education and public transportation systems. The Highway Lobby, as tactically astute as ever, has responded with a proposal of its own: a *different* constitutional provision that would dedicate one-fourth of the present four per cent state sales tax on motor vehicles solely for mass transportation. This plan would provide about $50 million in state funds (matchable with 80 per cent federal funds), while leaving the half-billion dollar highway fund intact. Both sides have claimed popular support for their positions, and each has produced the results of a poll to prove they have it.

A feeble compromise was adopted by the Convention's Finance Committee in February. Delegate Bill Sullivant of Gainesville proposed that the dedicated highway fund be preserved without change, except for a proviso that any *future* increase in the gasoline tax (above 5¢ per gallon) should not go automatically into the dedicated fund. The Legislature that raised the tax would, in Sullivant's plan, have the discretion to give the new revenue to the THD or channel it somewhere else. At press time it seemed likely that this proposal would be adopted by the whole Convention. Certainly it seemed the most that the critics of the dedicated fund were likely to get.

The Highway Lobby has thrown itself energetically into this critical battle. The TGRA provided each delegate with an inch-thick book that is a tangible record of their pervasive ethos-building. It contains newspaper editorials, endorsements of the dedicated fund from dozens of chambers of commerce and county commissioners (many of whom simply filled in the blanks of model resolutions supplied by the TGRA and returned them as-is), and a not-so-subtle reminder that if all the members of all the TGRA member organizations are added together, the Association speaks for 280,500 Texans.

Governor Briscoe has cooperated by issuing a statement declaring the retention of the dedicated fund "is essential if we are going to continue to have an effective highway system." The governor, who campaigned on a platform of aiding urban mass transit, then adds:

Mass transit at some time—and in some form—has to be explored. But mass transportation will not reduce the need for highways. Texans are sort of independent . . . each wants to go in his own car.

Highway building must go on. . . .

The oil industry lobbyists have been conspicuously silent this year (lines at the filling stations prove that they no longer have their old interest in pushing up the demand for petroleum products). By contrast the truckers and bussers (represented by the Texas Motor Transportation Association) have threatened to oppose the entire new Constitution if the Sullivant proposal is adopted.

Despite all the talk about the virtues of the dedicated fund and the need for mass transit, what is really being fought out in the Constitutional Convention is utterly simple. It is whether the people of Texas are going to have the right to change their transportation priorities in the future, through the legislative process, *if they decide to do so.* As long as the dedicated fund remains in the Constitution they cannot do so unless a two-thirds majority of both houses of the Legislature lets them. The votes of as few as eleven Senators can block any change forever — regardless of urban needs, the energy shortage, or the wishes of a majority of the voters themselves. As long as the fund remains where it is, there will *always* be money for highways, and the rest of the public needs will fight it out for what is left. *Can a majority of Texans change the state's priorities?* That is what the battle is all about.

Felton West, the *Houston Post*'s capitol correspondent, put the matter succinctly when he wrote:

Imagine how foolish we'd look today if in 1875 the Constitution's framers had dedicated a 5 per cent tax on the sale of every horse to financing public watering troughs and hitching posts.

But then again, Governor Richard Coke had not told the press:

Texans are sort of independent . . . each wants to ride his own horse.

Cloverleaf Without Exits

Is it endless then, a cloverleaf without exits?

The answer is suggested by the Convention testimony of Commissioner Simons. If the dedicated fund is removed, he told the delegates, the highway system will be "plunged into the heart of politics . . . instead of having highway projects based on traffic *needs*."

"Needs" is the pivotal word. Still influenced by a brief but lurid episode of corruption that flourished and died in less than a thousand days nearly half a century ago, the Department leaders constantly remind themselves of the dangers of political meddling in highway affairs, meddling that substitutes political favoritism for true highway "needs." Even though the Department's reputation is so secure today that it would surely be insulated from legislative logrolling if the dedicated fund were dropped, this fear remains its central organizing Myth, its Homeric legend retold from father to son. In 1925 Troy fell. With his sturdy sailing ship, Aeneas has led his men to Rome.

Singlemindedly intent upon protecting their cherished Department from the indignity of being forced to serve counterfeit *political* needs, the highway leaders never pause to consider whether their own traditional definition of "needs" is losing its validity. To them, transportation needs and "traffic needs" are one and the same thing. Their history, their training, their manner of selection and promotion, indeed their whole experience has led them to identify "traffic needs" with "highways" absolutely. Men whose mode of thinking is bounded by rubber tires and concrete do not speculate on whether traffic needs can become something different in an urban, energy-short era.

If you imply that these external changes in the Seventies have created a situation in which the Highway Department itself has begun to supply transportation that is not based on "needs," the leaders find that statement ultimately incomprehensible. Whether building an interstate or building a loop around Taylor, they are simply doing what they and their predecessors have always done. Interpreting the accusation in the light of their experience they can only think you are suggesting they are corrupt, that *they* build roads as political patronage: for in their injured pride that is the only sort of violation of "needs" they know.

It is not surprising, then, that the Department leaders tend to see the same dangers that the highway builders see— the danger of running out of funds, of not being able to plan ahead. In a real sense the interests of the highway bureaucracy and the highway lobby have become identical. And why should not a commissioner and a lobbyist open a bank together, if there is no longer a point of view to influence "unduly"?

Proposals for mass transit in Texas focus on buses not merely because buses are the only form of public transportation that can be put to work immediately, but also because the idea that transit can be "mass" is an unfamiliar, undigested one. At the very time when lines at the filling stations are demonstrating that transit may have to be "mass," and substantially so, in the very near future, public transportation is still regarded as no more than a means for moving people around whose poverty, disability, or temporarily empty gas tank prevent them from using a private car. Unquestioned is the assumption that we can rely on the automobile . . . forever.

Is there a more sensible way of getting people around than having them propel two tons of steel at eight miles per gallon? Should there be?

Texans may soon be forced to make some hard choices about their transportation policies. At the moment, because of the dedicated fund, those choices are made for them: the Highway Department will go right on building highways until someone tells it to stop or to slow down. They have the money and they define the "needs."

There is no way short of constitutional amendment for the public to redefine those needs or to force their moderation so that more money can be spent on other things. New funds can of course be created for new needs, be they mass transit or anything else. But the highway money will still be spent. And it is as much "misgovernment" to build things the taxpayers do not need, as it is to *fail* to build those things they *do* need. Even if you build them honestly. Even if you build them well. In its studied, proud efforts to avoid making the latter mistake, the Highway Department may now be in danger of making the former.

The reaction of the Department toward suggestions that it be given responsibility for all forms of public transportation, becoming a sort of state Department of Transportation, is a telling commentary on its insularity. All three Commissioners told the Convention that mass transit programs should be handled by some other agency. Commissioner Simons added that putting the two together would "dilute the thrust" of the Highway Department.

Instead of saying, "we are engineering professionals; we are ready to do what the state needs. When you wanted good roads, we built the best in the country. If you want good mass transit, we can build that best too," the Department has fled from the new responsibility.

Through changing times they have remained precisely what the Lobby planned for them to be: a bureaucracy totally committed to roads.

Texans may or may not want a vigorous governmental effort to develop mass transit; different polls yield different results. But if they do, they cannot be optimistic when they see the Highway Department, the Mass Transportation Commission, and the penetrating influence of the Highway Lobby on the selection of the men who set these agencies' policies. They cannot expect the Texas Good Roads Association—even if renamed "Texans for Better Transportation" — to send forth the word to chambers of commerce and local governments that a new day is at hand. Most important of all, they cannot expect their existing transportation bureaucracy to step back and take an impartial look at other types of transportation.

If Texans want this done, they will have to find a way to circumvent the most immovable bureaucracy and the most irresistible lobby in their state. If the people want an exit, they will have to hire their own bulldozer.

PAPER TIGERS

by Mitch Green

Meet the people who don't mind cutting through red tape — as long as they do it lengthwise.

Rolando and Eddie have been cutting hair side by side in their south Austin shop for three years. "We're a team," says Rolando. "A family will come in and Eddie will take the husband and kids and I'll take the wife." But since June something has come between Rolando and Eddie—an eight-foot opaque wall, to be exact. Why? To protect the public, of course. That's what the State Board of Barber Examiners told Rolando and Eddie when the construction crew moved in, and that is the premise on which a good deal of state government's more pointless activity is based. You see, Eddie cuts hair; he's a barber. Roland cuts hair too, but he's a cosmetologist, and to listen to the State Board of Barber Examiners tell it, the commingling of these two acts would be a threat to the health and safety of the public.

The State Board of Barber Examiners is just one of some three dozen state licensing agencies distinguished mostly by their obscurity. As far as the public is concerned, these bureaucratic fiefdoms are like vestigial organs: it's hard to know they exist because they don't seem to do much. But people fortunate enough to be in a regulated profession know better. They understand that mastering the state licensing game is more important than mastering the rules of free market competition and it pays higher rewards.

To each regulated trade, the state licensing agency is many things—all of them good. It is, first and foremost, a guarantee against unwanted competition, a closed shop for professionals sanctioned by the State of Texas. The Texas right-to-work law prohibits unions from having a closed shop, but there is no right-to-work law for prospective plumbers, new car dealers, athletic trainers, lawyers, or morticians. No one can practice any of these professions unless the State of Texas, through one of its licensing agencies, checks him out and gives its approval. The "State," in all cases, really means a board required by law to be filled either largely or totally from the regulated profession itself. Who gets to decide how many car dealers should divide the profits from this year's new car sales? A board dominated by car dealers, of course—and you can bet your monthly car payment that there won't be so many dealers that they have to resort to price wars to get the public's attention.

Theoretically these agencies were created to protect the public from assorted threats to its well-being that unregulated practitioners pose. Judging by a quick glance at some of the regulated occupations, the threat to the public is pervasive. It comes not only from barbers and cosmetologists like Eddie and Rolando, but also from doctors, lawyers, landscape architects, water-well drillers, librarians, social psychotherapists, optometrists, hearing-aid fitters, podiatrists, and many others. With so much danger lurking about, the Legislature has found it necessary to protect us by creating agencies which sell licenses for anywhere from 75 cents to $100. Like McDonald's, the state's name is supposed to guarantee a minimum standard of quality. Unlike McDonald's, if you don't like the state's hamburgers, you can't go around the corner to Burger King. All you can do is move to Oklahoma, and things aren't much different there.

Although their ostensible role is to protect the public, that charge apparently does not include the consumer as you will quickly learn if you call up with a complaint. Licensing agencies have nothing to do with how much a plumber can charge you on Sunday afternoon, with making sure that you get your money's worth for a $15 haircut, or with requiring continuing education for all professionals. Their main role in life is to protect their clients by limiting entry into the field, adopting rules which require the public to use licensees when it's unnecessary or redundant (the State Board of Plumbing Examiners is the champion at this little gimmick), and enforcing restrictions against advertising and competitive bidding (the Justice Department recently filed an antitrust action against the State Board of Public Accountancy over the board's rules against competitive bidding). All in all, it is hard to see how the public is better off than with no regulation at all—or at least that's the view of retiring Dallas State Representative Richard Geiger, who was vice chairman of the House committee responsible for keeping track of the state's dozens of bureaus and commissions and boards.

The essence of the problem is that the licensing agencies exist to serve their profession and no one else. Some are more blatant about it than others. The Motor Vehicle Commission deigns to include two ordinary citizens along with four car dealers, but only funeral home directors are eligible for the State Board of Morticians. The accountancy board isn't even allowed to adopt its own rules and regulations without first submitting them to the members of the profession for approval —this was one of the abuses that attracted the attention of the Justice Department. The bond of the soul between regulators and their clients is perfectly symbolized by a number of Austin lawyers who openly represent both the board and the professional trade association. A conflict of interest? Hardly. Robert Hughes, a respected member of the Austin legal community, has no ethical qualms about his firm representing both the State Board of Morticians and the morticians' trade association. "As far as the regulatory agency is concerned," says Hughes, "the association doesn't have any interests different than the public's. The association hasn't had a disagreement with the board in ten years." Another lobbyist, C. Dean Davis, represents both the pharmacists and the pharmacy board, not to mention the hospital association.

A franchise, then, is a valuable thing, something to be eagerly sought and fiercely protected. It is small wonder, therefore, that the Legislature touched off a minor war when it cut the barber's franchise in half in 1971.

The barbers are no strangers to regulatory battle. As far back as medieval times they were clashing with the butchers, the only other profession with ready access to sharp instruments, for the exclusive right to perform surgery. The barbers triumphed, and the blood-stained sheets which they hung outside after their ministrations evolved into the barber pole.

In more recent times the barbers have been battling not the butchers but the cosmetologists. The barbers were first regulated by the State of Texas in 1929. Dirty towels, lice, and rusty scissors all threatened the public welfare, so barbers were placed under the specially created State Board of Barber Examiners.

As far as the barbers were concerned, things were going along just fine. If anyone, male or female, wanted a haircut the law said only a barber could give it to them. Beauticians and hairdressers, licensed by the State Board of Hairdressers and Cosmetologists, were allowed to cut hair only if it was incidental to their primary service, styling. Then in 1971 the Legislature changed the Board of Hairdressers and Cosmetologists into the Cosmetology Commission and expanded their bailiwick so that cosmetologists could cut women's hair. In 1972 the law was ruled unconstitutional on the grounds that it discriminated on the basis of sex. For the next three years barbers and cosmetologists were free to cut whatever heads they found sitting in front of them. It was during this period that Eddie the barber came to work at Rolando's south Austin shop.

The court's ruling came at an inconvenient time for barbers. Long hair was no longer the exclusive province of hippies and radical students; it was generally fashionable. Yet many barbers weren't adept at the new styles. Men were getting scalped by barbers but couldn't bring themselves to go into a beauty parlor. The natural result was the unisex shop where barbers and cosmetologists worked side by side cutting hair. The public, after all, only wanted haircuts and didn't care what the person wielding the scissors was called. But the barbers did. There are more than 75,000 cosmetologists in Texas and only 18,000 barbers. "If the barbers lose the distinction of being barbers," explains their lobbyist, Austin attorney Charles Babb, "they'll be swallowed up by the beauty chains that are taking over cosmetology. Barbers are really the last small businessmen left, and if they are not kept distinct, they'll be gone."

"Anyone who believes that business is opposed to regulation," Babb adds, "still believes in the tooth fairy."

When the Legislature convened in 1975, both sides were girded for battle. The cosmetologists wanted a law saying they could do virtually everything barbers could. The barbers were prepared to concede that, but they wanted the distinct separation of barbers and cosmetologists working on the same premises. Eddie's troubles began when all parties decided to leave the details of separation up to the respective boards.

State Representative Ben Munson of Denison, the unlucky legislator whose subcommittee was saddled with the task of studying the bill, believed that the agreed-upon version did not require a total separation. That was the interpretation of the Cosmetology Commission, which last November adopted a rule requiring a four-foot partition between barbers and cosmetologists working in the same shop. But keeping barbers separate was a much more vital issue to the barber board. After several fumbling tries and in the face of numerous warnings from Representative Munson, the barber board last June decided to require the erection of an eight-foot opaque wall—plus the display of a barber pole and separate entrances for barber customers. Rolando asked if a glass wall would suffice and the board said no. "That means I'm going to have to put Eddie into a closet," complained Rolando. "How would you like to work in a closet?"

Not only unisex shops were hit by the ruling, but also the mom-and-pop shops in rural areas where barbering and cosmetology are offered under one roof not because it's stylish but because it's convenient. Munson was furious. He threatened the barber board with extinction, but the board turned a deaf ear, its courage no doubt buttressed by the fact that Munson was not a candidate for reelection. Meanwhile Rolando refurbished a storage closet and moved Eddie in.

The barbers-cosmetologists fight is the grudge match of occupational licensing, but the Legislature is besieged by such fights year after year. A committee clerk who keeps track of such things says the Legislature spent more time on haircuts last year than on the public utilities commission bill, and Austin Senator Lloyd Doggett says he got more mail about the barbers last session than anything else. Through the years the Legislature has had to referee fights between hearing-aid dealers and audiologists, individual optometrists and chain optometry stores like Texas State Optical, architects and designers, plumbers and landscape architects, dentists and plastic surgeons, doctors and chiropractors, social psychotherapists and social workers, new car dealers and used car dealers. So desirable is the state's franchise that colleagues within related fields fight over it like urban street gangs vying for territory.

In the early seventies the big brawl was between two rival groups of optometrists. The trick in such cases is to make your side appear to embody good and the other side to embody evil, so the individual optometrists started calling themselves the "ethical optometrists." They don't quite go so far as to label the other side "unethical optometrists," but the Legislature got the idea. "Ethical" optometrists are those in private practice who do not engage in advertising; their opposition generally practices in conjunction with chain stores like TSO or Lee Optical, and, as the ethical optometrists see it, advertise by virtue of their association with the frame dispensers. So far the ethical optometrists appear to have won the battle—the law allots them two-thirds of the seats on the optometry board—but you can be certain that the chain optometrists will continue to apply pressure on the Legislature.

Why should the public care? The head of the ethical optometrists warns that if his group loses control of the board, the quality of visual care will decline; naturally the spokesman for the chain optometrists denies any such thing. (Both sets of optometrists, though they belong to different organizations, have to meet the same standards.) In the end, the whole fight amounts to little more than a bureaucratic spectacle which takes up a lot of the Legislature's time to little purpose. It has also prodded the self-interests of ophthalmologists, who are eye doctors licensed by the State Board of Medical Examiners, and opticians, who don't have a board but would like one.

Some franchises are more valuable than others. Architects feel left out because their licensing law passed in 1936, gives them the right to use the title but doesn't do much else. A designer with no formal training may do anything an architect can. In practice, most large buildings are designed by architects and built under the supervision of licensed engineers. But many smaller structures are handled by designers, many of whom work for contractors. Naturally the architects think the public needs to be protected from this latent danger, and since the public may not be aware of the difference between architects and designers, it is incumbent upon the Legislature to guarantee that only architects can design buildings. So far the Legislature hasn't bought it, but at least a bill to license designers didn't get very far, either.

In recent years the Legislature has become increasingly reluctant to create new licensing boards. That doesn't keep various professions from trying; last session everyone from kennel operators to wrestlers were being considered for a closed shop. But only the social psychotherapists were successful.

What is a social psychotherapist? Texas is the only state that has them; the term was invented by the Legislature to single out the upper crust of the social work profession, the most educated and therefore the fewest in number. They fall just below psychologists and psychiatrists, with whom they were trying to share the franchise for the human mind.

Their argument to the Legislature was that an untrained person could do measureless damage to a person's psyche; therefore the state had a duty to set standards for licensing. But as usual, there was more to the story. Many federal health grants require state certification for social workers seeking federal aid. The whole social work profession was after a slice of the pie, and the psychotherapists successfully used the Legislature to get accredited with Washington—and close the pantry door on everyone else.

The audiologists were less successful. If you have a hearing problem, you go to a hearing-aid dealer, who will test you and, if necessary, fit you with a hearing aid. They perform much the same service as optometrists do for eyes. But the audiologists found this a potential conflict of interest; they argued that they were much more qualified to test and identify hearing problems. The Legislature did not agree, and that guarantees the audiologists will be back this session.

Sometimes conflicting pressures on the Legislature cause it to confuse matters further by granting the same bailiwick to two groups. For years the plumbers had the exclusive franchise for tapping into the public water supply. If you paid a contractor to build a lawn sprinkler, you also had to pay a licensed plumber to connect it. In 1973 the Legislature brought lawn irrigators under the regulation of the State Board of Landscape Architects and gave them the same connection franchise, as long as it was limited to sprinkler systems. The result has been an interagency dispute that not even the attorney general has been able to straighten out. As the law now stands, all the landscape architects who cut into water mains are violating rules of the plumbing board and the plumbers who connect sprinkler systems are violating rules of the landscape architect board.

"It sure seems like a lot of foolishness," says Representative Geiger of the maze of agencies that hide out in little cubbyholes near the State Capitol. "Not one consumer in a thousand cares whether a barber is licensed by a cosmetology board, a barber board, or a health board. These fights make people think the Legislature has nothing better to do."

Despite the apparent folly of the current system, there is only scattered pressure within the Legislature for governmental reorganization. Any legislator worth his salt will rail about an intraprofessional fight he thinks is ridiculous, but chances are he has his own pet agency he'll fight to the death to defend. Even Geiger, apparently a staunch foe of licensing, sponsored the unsuccessful effort by the architects to squeeze designers out of the picture. Still, there are a couple of reform proposals drifting around that may come up for a hearing this session. One is based on the fact that the original reason for licensing occupations was to protect the public health. Licensing agencies should therefore be placed under the Department of Health and Public Resources (or some other superagency). In some respects this would merely give new names to the same old problems, but it would at least have the advantage of putting licensing agencies under a board not dominated by individual professions.

A more creative notion has attracted some attention both in the state and out. It's commonly called sunset legislation, and it has been adopted in Colorado and approved in principle here by the Legislature during the Constitutional Convention. Sunset laws call for the automatic demise of licensing agencies at regular intervals, say, every ten or twelve years. Then, if the agency can convince the Legislature it is necessary, the lawmakers can re-create it. In theory, this makes agencies like the barber board which exist beyond the influence of the Legislature—most don't even need much in the way of appropriations, existing off their license-fee revenue—more responsive. If not, off with their heads.

Sunset legislation will definitely be introduced during the 1977 session. If it is passed, it will be good news for Eddie. Until then, he'll have to stay in his closet. ♥

SQUEAKY WHEELS

*Independent oilmen aren't always the models of self-reliance they used to be;
these days they expect a little grease from the feds.*

In the popular imagination, the independent oilman is the last of the rugged individualists. Not for him a safe, gray life in the bureaucracy of some vast multinational oil company. He makes his own judgments, risks his own money, savors his own victories, and suffers his own defeats. Even critics of the major oil companies point to the independent oilman as an example of free enterprise at its best; in fact, one of the alleged sins of Big Oil is that it has squeezed out many wildcatters.

Unfortunately, rugged individualism seems to be vanishing among independent oilmen too. They have found the contrast between themselves and Big Oil to be of great value in getting preferential treatment in Washington. While tirelessly preaching the virtues of free enterprise, the independents lately have amassed a bouquet of government favors that would make the auto industry green with envy.

The most recent addition to the independents' wish list is an import oil tariff that would not only give them a break from competition but also impose heavy costs on the rest of us. Among the proponents of an import fee is the Texas Independent Producers and Royalty Owners Association (TIPRO). D. K. Davis, its senior vice president, frets about the decline in the average price per barrel of oil—"Every dollar drained away by taxes or lower prices means a reduction in drilling of two thousand wells nationwide"— and warns that our dependence on foreign oil means that "if we get in a shooting war, we'd be in bad trouble." He also complains that the windfall profits tax, because it applies solely to domestic production, unfairly favors foreign producers. Texas railroad commissioner Mack Wallace agrees with Davis.

The proposal may get a sympathetic hearing on Capitol Hill, if only because it would have the side effect of reducing the budget deficit. Congressman Kent Hance of Lubbock told a TIPRO convention in the summer of 1982 that "if a tax has to come, I'd prefer an oil import fee," which would "encourage domestic production and discourage foreign consumption." It's worth noting that the Independent Petroleum Association of America (IPAA), the national trade group, disagrees with

TIPRO on the issue of import fees. At its convention in May, delegates adopted a policy statement that opposes an oil import fee. An IPAA spokesman dismisses the fee as purely a "revenue measure" that would "distort supply and demand."

Trying to shut out foreign oil is not a new idea. The government began enforcing a quota on oil imports in 1959 to protect domestic producers from cheap foreign crude but scrapped the measure when import prices began to climb in 1973. The motive is the same this time around. Falling prices have made the oil business even chancier, forcing many independents out of business. An import fee would raise prices and preserve profits. Independent oilmen, the last of the die-hard competitors, would be spared the obligation of competing with foreign producers.

The U.S. may have been dangerously dependent on foreign oil a few years ago, when it was importing about 45 per cent of its total consumption. Since 1978, however, imports have dropped by nearly half. In light of the transition that American industry has made toward greater fuel efficiency, it isn't likely that imports will rise much even if the economy reaches full strength. An import fee would mean higher energy costs just when supply and demand would naturally keep costs down—not exactly a recipe for economic growth.

The argument that independents suffer unduly from the windfall profits tax is equally flimsy. Using their well-honed image as embattled little guys, the independents lobbied vigorously in 1979 and 1980 for preferential rates, and Congress, as it often has done, gave them what they wanted. The tax laws set up three categories of oil. The first is newly discovered oil, the sale of which is taxed at a rate of 30 per cent above a specified base price. Under this law the majors and the independents are treated alike. But then there are the other categories. On "old" oil (that brought into production before 1979), majors pay taxes of 70 per cent above the base price on their first thousand barrels a day, but independents pay only 50 per cent. The third category is "stripper" oil, from wells that are nearly exhausted. Majors pay 60 per cent on their first thousand barrels a day, but

independents enjoy a rate of only 30 per cent. The windfall profits tax wasn't a great idea, but it's hard to make a case that it's a burden on wildcatters in particular.

And that's not even their biggest tax break. That distinction belongs to the percentage depletion allowance. Repealed for integrated (that is, major) oil companies in 1969 but still in effect for the independents, this favor is worth about $1.6 billion a year, according to Treasury official J. Gregory Ballentine. Instead of having the independents write off the cost of oil rights in the same way that other assets are depreciated—by deducting a percentage of the total investment each year for several years—the depletion allowance lets them deduct a fixed percentage of their gross *sales* right away. This method has two advantages over the conventional one: it provides the deduction sooner, and it increases the value of the deduction. Since the allowance is calculated on gross sales, the oilman may actually get to deduct more than he paid to acquire the rights—one of the few such instances in federal tax law. A producer may pay $1 million to get the rights to the oil under a particular plot of land but get to deduct two or three times that amount if he strikes it rich (although he will still pay taxes on the remainder).

When all their breaks are added up, the wildcatters have about as cozy a deal as anyone could ask for. The Treasury Department says their special tax treatment is worth more than $4.5 billion a year. Jane Gravelle, an economist for the Library of Congress, recently told a House committee that, all in all, independent producers are actually subsidized rather than taxed. "The tax treatment," she said, "is better than having no tax at all."

As if that weren't help enough, TIPRO has also urged the Texas Railroad Commission to reduce the production of natural gas in the state as a boost to prices, which have been stubbornly low. The Railroad Commission used to do that for oil, in the days when cheap foreign crude was driving domestic oilmen out of business. But it's not easy to reconcile the independents' approach with what they were saying a few years ago. "Ours must be the greatest example of free enterprise ever devised, and we must fight for it," wrote the TIPRO president in 1974. Like many businessmen, independents rightly object to the government's habit of trying to outlaw high prices; that's why they lobbied for oil decontrol. But also like many businessmen, they can sometimes see the wisdom of getting the government to keep prices from falling too low.

For Texans accustomed to thinking of the wildcatter as the embodiment of that Texas spirit of self-reliance, this news is nearly as discouraging as it would be to learn that Davy Crockett had behaved less than heroically at the Alamo. If you used to believe the free enterprise rhetoric of the independent oilmen, you're in the same position as the constituents who arrived one day at Louisiana governor Earl Long's office to protest a broken campaign promise. "What'll I tell 'em?" asked the aide assigned to meet with them. Replied the governor, "Tell 'em I lied."✦

Getting the Bugs Out

Can Texas' Boll Weevils fix the Democratic Party?

Once upon a time, the story goes, a backward Southern town was totally dependent for economic subsistence on the cotton fields that stretched for miles in every direction. Then one summer a plague of boll weevils stripped the cotton bare. Businesses went broke and Main Street was deserted and the people of the town cursed the boll weevil for laying waste to the land. To survive, they had to learn new trades and new ways, but after enduring pain and hardship, they built a factory, and another, and another, until one day the town was more prosperous than it had ever been —indeed, more prosperous than neighboring towns that had not suffered the blight. And so the people of the town blessed the boll weevil and erected a monument to the pest they thought had destroyed them but, by forcing them to reexamine the direction of their lives, had saved them instead.

The tale may be apocryphal as it applies to the Old South, but it is a close parallel to the dramatic struggle over the federal budget in the U.S. House of Representatives earlier this summer. A maverick group of 47 Democratic congressmen—eight of whom are Texans, including the leader, Charles Stenholm of Stamford—is officially known as the Conservative Democratic Forum, but everyone in Washington refers to it as the Boll Weevils, the informal designation of a similar alliance of Southern conservatives back in the fifties. The backward but self-satisfied town of the story is the House Democratic leadership under Speaker Tip O'Neill, and by extension the national Democratic party, whose plans for the federal budget were devastated by the Boll Weevils in June. And just as in the story, the Boll Weevils may turn out to be a blessing in disguise that will save the Democratic party from itself—or so say the Boll Weevils.

Not since the days leading up to Richard Nixon's resignation had there been such prolonged tension on Capitol Hill. The budget fight was one of those rare legislative moments when both tactics and policy join in a crescendo, and everyone, from the lowliest aide to the president of the United States, was caught up in it. Even the rhetoric was different; it sounded more like the Iranian Parliament than the U.S. Congress. At stake was nothing less than whether the Democrats can survive as the majority party in the country, and what direction, left or right on the political spectrum, they must take to do so.

These questions, of course, are exactly the sort that have preoccupied Texas Democrats for three decades, which helps explain why Texas has the largest contingent of Boll Weevils of any state as well as the three most prominent (Stenholm; Kent Hance of Lubbock, sponsor of the Reagan Administration's tax bill; and Phil Gramm of College Station, sponsor of the president's budget bill). The rise of the Boll Weevils has helped compensate for the delegation's disastrous loss of influence during the late seventies: six committee chairmen in 1974 reduced to just two in 1978; members with over two hundred years of seniority lost to retirement, including the chairman of the Appropriations Committee (Hance's predecessor George Mahon) and the man who by seniority would now be chairman of the Ways and Means Committee had he stayed on (Stenholm's predecessor Omar Burleson); the brightest young stars burned out (Bob Krueger and Barbara Jordan, both gone).

In one sense it is remarkable that the Boll Weevils have restored the Texas delegation to prominence in just three years. But it is a different kind of prominence, one that is dependent more on individual skill than on the solidarity Texans have been known for in the past. The old Texas delegation did not become the Capitol's most cohesive and powerful by challenging the mainstream of the party. Those congressmen were conservatives, yes, but they were also team players; they adhered to the maxim of their spiritual leader, seventeen-year Speaker of the House Sam Rayburn: to get along, go along. Rayburn's legacy was exemplified by Burleson, who once walked out of a committee rather than cast a decisive vote against the leadership; it survives in older members like Jake Pickle of Austin, who gave up eleven years of seniority on one committee to start at the bottom of the ladder on Ways and Means, just because the state needed another pro-oil voice on that crucial panel. The Boll Weevils are less interested, for the moment, in being team players than in changing the philosophical drift of their party— something the veterans had neither the desire nor, realistically, the opportunity to do.

When he was elected to Congress at the age of forty in 1978, Charles Stenholm seemed to be the type of politician who was destined to disappear quickly into the anonymity of the 435-member House. He had never held elective office before, and his political experience was limited to the periphery: a bit of lobbying for cotton interests, a tour as president of the state electric cooperatives' association, membership on the State Democratic Executive Committee from the Abilene area. His committee assignments in the House were lightweight, and he seemed headed for a career of taking care of constituents and very little else.

What the official biography didn't disclose was that Stenholm's formative political experience had come at the 1972 Democratic National Convention, when he watched Democrats very different from the kind he knew take over the party in Miami Beach. By the time he arrived in Congress, Stenholm had spent the better part of a decade wondering why conservative Democrats, so dominant back home, had so little influence nationally. Toward the end of his first term he used a computer to correlate voting records with committee memberships, and the results confirmed his suspicions: conservatives constituted about a fourth of House Democrats but were almost entirely excluded from the most important committees. Figures in hand, he walked around the House floor collaring like-minded colleagues, and before long they had organized the Conservative Democratic Forum, primarily to promote better committee assignments for members committed to a balanced budget and a stronger defense.

The group got little attention at first, mainly because they didn't follow the usual rules for making a big media splash. They rejected calling themselves a "coalition" or "caucus," which would have signaled outright opposition to the party leadership, and settled instead on "forum," a neuter term. They didn't hire a staff, even though Washington is a town where the number of subordinates is frequently a measure of power and influence, and they had only one officer, with the uninspiring title of coordinator. Indeed, the members had so little faith in their fledgling organization that no one but Stenholm showed any interest in the job, so, still a freshman, he got it by default.

Those who thought about the forum at all expected it to have little, if any, impact. After the post-Watergate Democratic sweep of 1974, there were so few Republicans left that the only role for Democratic conservatives was to help muster the one third of the House necessary to sustain a Gerald Ford veto. But everything changed when the election totals came in last November 4: the Republican strength, down to 143 in 1976, was up to 190, just 27 short of a majority. The Republicans already controlled the White House and the Senate. Suddenly Charles Stenholm and his friends held the balance of power.

Among the beneficiaries of the forum's sudden numerical importance were Gramm and Hance, who both received choice committee assignments earlier this year—Budget for Gramm, Ways and Means for Hance. Within months both were sponsoring Ronald

Reagan's programs in their committees, much to the outrage of Democratic loyalists. That's when the earlier decision to downplay the forum paid off: the group, as Stenholm repeatedly said, took no position and did not presume to speak for any member. So the rest of the conservatives were not immediately enveloped in the fury directed at Gramm and Hance. Meanwhile, the Republicans did not have the comfort of dealing with a formal coalition or caucus that would take a stand binding its members; instead, they had to approach the Boll Weevils individually. The Boll Weevils were in the happy position of being wooed to vote the way they were inclined to vote anyway; their loose organization gave them bargaining power, and before too long there were hints from the White House that Ronald Reagan wouldn't campaign against Democrats who helped out in the budget fight in the 1982 elections.

In the end, the battle over the Reagan budget came down, as often is the case in politics, to a vote on procedure rather than substance. The two budget versions, the Gramm (Republican) plan and the Budget Committee (Democratic) proposal, weren't that far apart, the difference being that the Democrats actually cut more money but left more room for automatic spending increases in the future. The real difference was political: the Democratic leadership, including majority leader Jim Wright of Fort Worth, wanted to divide the president's program into six parts, so that Republicans would have to cast six separate votes against social programs that, for all their shortcomings, have undeniably improved the lot of tens of millions of Americans: Social Security, Medicaid, student loans, federal pensions, food stamps, and on and on. The White House, naturally, wanted a single vote, for or against the whole package, to protect their supporters from the wrath of the special-interest constituencies.

One day before the vote, on the Wednesday before the Fourth of July recess, the House Democratic Steering and Policy Committee escalated the conflict, giving notice that the six-or-one issue would be a party vote—in other words, it would be taken into account when future committee assignments and campaign contributions were handed out. That was dirty pool: in Congress, absolute party loyalty is demanded only on occasional procedural votes, and although the budget question was procedural in form, in effect it was a vote on substance and everyone knew it. The Republicans screamed foul, but they weren't innocent of chicanery themselves: their budget wasn't even written yet; nevertheless, members would have to vote for or against the president without knowing what was in his bill. Wright's comment afterward was direct-

ed at the Republicans, but it could have applied to both parties: "This way of doing business would have been an insult to the Texas Legislature."

On the afternoon of the vote, the halls of the House office buildings, usually crowded with earnest-looking aides on errands, were deserted as staffers clustered around closed-circuit TV sets. After hours of speeches, including a ringing condemnation of Republican tactics by Wright and a relaxed rebuttal by Stenholm, the bells rang to start the fifteen-minute voting period. The TV scoreboard had columns for "yes" and "no" by party; since all 190 Republicans were likely to oppose the procedure backed by Democrats, the magic number was 27—that many Democratic noes would assure a Republican victory (3 of the 435 seats were vacant). The no votes quickly shot up to 20, then hung tantalizingly in the low twenties for more than five minutes before going over the top with only three minutes to go. The final vote was 217-207, with 29 Democrats voting with the Republicans, and as time ran out, the Republicans cheered. Thanks to the Boll Weevils, they had won.

But did the Boll Weevils win? That is the great lingering question of the budget debate. Certainly no one is talking about building any monuments in their honor, except perhaps a political gravestone or two: Mickey Leland of Houston's Fifth Ward called them "traitors to the Democratic party" and wants the House leadership to mete out retribution. The Boll Weevils' disloyalty has made a shambles of the conservative forum's original goal of achieving better committee assignments; Gramm and Hance themselves are in danger of being forcibly ejected from their newly gained seats. (Gramm, who would like to try for the Senate again, almost appears to want martyrdom—and may get his wish—while Hance, who also has Senate ambitions, is more deferential and has the better chance to recover.) Northern Democrats, irate at seeing two members of their own party sponsoring a Republican president's program, may be less inclined to put the next crop of Texans on crucial committees or to support Jim Wright for Speaker.

Loyalists like Leland are incensed not because of the budget cuts, which were inescapable after the Republicans captured the Senate, but because the Boll Weevils spoiled their strategy to keep control of the House in the 1982 elections by making Republicans vote against popular programs and denying them the support of Democrats, so that if the administration's economic approach turns sour, there will be no doubt who is to blame. The trouble with this gambit—aside from the fact that it puts the loyalists in the uncomfortable posture of rooting for inflation—is that

it won't work. The Republicans have their own strategy for 1982, and their plan for wresting away control of the House starts with defeating Democrats who represent conservative districts but don't vote that way. Kent Hance's district, for example, returned a bigger percentage for Ronald Reagan last November than all but two others in the state—the Republican bastions in North Dallas and West Houston. Sentiment in the Boll Weevils' districts was overwhelmingly behind the president on the budget fight, and yet the loyalists insisted on purity when they should have been thinking of survival—their own, for if the Boll Weevils lose, they do too. They're out of power.

The same reasoning argues against a purge of the Boll Weevils. Though the president's party normally loses seats during mid-term elections, the Republicans look like gainers in 1982, particularly since reapportionment will shift sixteen seats from the more liberal Northeast and Midwest to the conservative South and West. If the Democratic edge is less than ten seats, maybe even twenty, the Republicans are certain to offer inducements to get some of the Boll Weevils to switch parties. Any Democrat who wants to spend the next two years doing something besides answering his mail ought to be looking for accommodation rather than revenge. And accommodation shouldn't be hard to find: most of the Boll Weevils will be searching for issues where they can put some distance between themselves and the president.

Sam Rayburn or Lyndon Johnson would have managed the strategy so differently. They would never have thrown down the gauntlet on an issue proposed by a popular president with the backing of public opinion, especially if their side had lost an earlier test of strength on the same subject by 77 votes. Rayburn and Johnson understood the eternal verities of politics: there is always a tomorrow, the pendulum will always swing back. They might have said of Reagan what Johnson, then Senate majority leader, said of Eisenhower: "We have only one president and I'm going to help him," and maybe they would have helped a little more than the president wanted them to. But most of all, they would have gotten the other guy's issue behind them and gone on to more even fights. They certainly would never have alienated the group that held the balance of power. They understood, as Northeastern liberals do not, that conservative Democrats are different from Republicans, even if a lot of the time the only difference is that while both vote against the people, the Democrat feels remorse about it afterward. The budget fight was a time to go along; the Democrats didn't, and sure enough, they're not getting along either.

Politics
by Douglas Harlan

THE PARTY'S OVER

Connally irks Bush. Clements gets Tower's goat. That's the way it is now that Texas Republicans don't have to stick together anymore.

Back during the last presidential campaign, George Bush's national political director, David Keene, could hardly ignore his boss's preoccupation with John Connally. One day he took occasion to kid Bush about it.

"I've finally figured out why you're so obsessed with John Connally," Keene said. "Every time you go to the club to play tennis, Connally has the court reserved."

"You just don't understand us, do you?" Bush replied. "The clubs I'm a member of wouldn't let John Connally in the front door."

George Bush and John Connally don't get along very well. Their relationship is a mixture of personal animosity, different backgrounds, conflicting styles, head-to-head political competition, and a dash of "this town isn't big enough for both of us," even a city the size of Houston. But there's more to it than that. Their discord symbolizes a broader conflict within the ranks of the Texas Republican party, and as the party has grown, that conflict has also grown. Bush and Connally aren't the only Texas Republicans who don't get along; in recent years Governor Bill Clements and Senator Tower have sparred too. Back in the sixties, being a Republican in Texas was like being a

Douglas Harlan, twice a Republican candidate for Congress, is a San Antonio lawyer and political columnist.

Bolshevik in Russia in the days of the czar. There weren't very many of them, and they all had to stick together. But now the party is powerful enough for there to be open struggle within its ranks.

The conflict in the Republican party has to do with party loyalty and with personal style. On the first score, Texans like Bush and Tower who were Republicans during the lean years resent the party-come-latelies like Connally, a Democrat until 1973, and Clements, a lifelong independent except when it has behooved him to be a Republican. On the second, those who joined the party back when Republicans never won elections tend to be more patrician than recent converts. They are old money and the converts are new money, if you will. Bush's pedigree goes back to New England, where his father served as a Republican senator from Connecticut. Tower's nobility is not a birthright—he is a Methodist preacher's son—but a mind-set. He is an unabashed anglophile who studied at the London School of Economics and who has his suits tailor-made on Savile Row. Clements and Connally are both self-made millionaires who have wheeled and dealed themselves into social and political prominence, and they wouldn't have wanted to do it any other way. Both measure a man's success, if not his merit, by the bottom line of his financial statement.

According to his friends, John Connal-

ly thinks George Bush is a weak dilettante, a preppie wimp. Bush's friends say that he, in turn, thinks Connally is a posturing blowhard. Underlying those views is a contrary strain of grudging respect, like that of a professional athlete for his strongest competitor. The origins of the Bush-Connally conflict are unclear, but friends of both date it from at least 1970, when George Bush was the Republican nominee for the U.S. Senate and then-Democrat John Connally was the mastermind behind Bush's opponent and the ultimate victor, Lloyd Bentsen.

For conservatives in both parties, the major task of the 1970 election year was the defeat of Senator Ralph Yarborough, long the leader of liberal Democrats in Texas. Bentsen, under Connally's tutelage, beat Yarborough in the Democratic primary, thereby narrowing Bush's base of support for the general election. But Connally didn't sit back and bask in the glow of Bentsen's primary victory. He worked hard for Bentsen against Bush, appearing in television spots that were highly effective in the closing days of the campaign.

"Connally went beyond the call of duty for Bentsen," a key Bush campaign aide says. "It was almost as if beating Bush was as important as beating Yarborough." Bush can't totally set that 1970 campaign behind him, and he resents what Connally did. But there's more to it than that. Houston has been home to both Bush and Connally for many years now, and state politics is just one area where the two have competed. The civic and social arenas have also been fields of battle. And then there's national politics. Bush, the archetypal team player, was laboring through drudge assignments from President Nixon when, lo and behold, John Connally—still a Democrat—appeared in the spotlight as Secretary of the Treasury. Connally got into Nixon's Cabinet on his own, needing no help from George Bush. As one national political worker says, "Connally can charm the pants off a president."

Most recently, of course, Bush and Connally battled for the 1980 Republican presidential nomination. In the early days of the campaign, polls showed Connally running well, a reasonable prospect for strong competition to Ronald Reagan. In those same polls, Bush's standing was so low as to be represented by an asterisk. David Keene tells of a time when Bush walked into Houston's Petroleum Club and saw Connally seated at a table with a cluster of the city's power brokers. Connally, riding high in the polls, called Bush over to the table.

"George," he said, "I need your help. We're going to have to put a government together," implying, of course, that he had the election sewn up and was willing to let George, the also-ran, have a hand in forming the new government.

"At that time," Keene says, "Bush would have been happy to finish seventh in the primaries if Connally finished eighth."

On the basis of the polls alone, Connally should have been the survivor of the two, with Bush an early casualty, and Connally campaigned that way before the Iowa caucus. According to Mary Leonard, who covered his campaign for the *Detroit News,* Connally never considered Bush's campaign to be a factor and never took Bush himself seriously. "He always belittled Bush and minimized his campaign," she says, "but he never did that to Howard Baker or Ronald Reagan."

Iowa, though, proved the wisdom of George Bush's campaign strategy and gave Connally a clear message: Republican party contacts, longtime allegiances, and strong organization produce results. Bush won Iowa, beating Ronald Reagan as well as John Connally, and his post-victory ecstasy was apparent to all.

Even with Connally long defeated and Bush a strong vice-presidential possibility, Connally still preyed on Bush's mind. In a strategy session to determine what Bush should bargain for if Reagan offered him the vice presidency, David Keene told Bush that he should ask for veto power over appointments from his home state, like LBJ had under Kennedy.

"Is that right?" Bush asked. "Do you mean I could veto the people John Connally wants to push?"

Bill Clements, by his own account, has always supported John Tower for the U.S. Senate. He even suggests that his gubernatorial campaign helped Tower get reelected when they were both on the ballot in 1978, which illustrates the potential for conflict between the two. Tower can just as reasonably argue that *his* campaign put Clements over the top, but he would never say so publicly. And that's an example of their difference in style.

A former key figure in both Clements's and Tower's organizations describes the difference: "Tower puts a polish on reaction, not action. That clearly isn't the Clements way." Clements interprets that response in Tower as being weak and indecisive, qualities the governor in his heart of hearts finds contemptible. And he prefers to think of Tower in those terms rather than try to understand why Tower does things the way he does them. It's easier that way. "Clements *disdains* politicians," a former aide says, "and you can be sure he doesn't think of himself as one."

Before Clements's election as governor, John Tower was the Lone Ranger on the prairie, the only Republican since Reconstruction to have won a statewide race in Texas. He was the de facto head of the party, and the state chairman and the national committeemen and -women held their jobs by virtue of his blessings. Tower prided himself on being involved in the organization and, like people who never miss Sunday school, for many years attended every meeting of the state executive committee. Candidates ran or failed to run at his bidding. Patronage within Texas and in Washington was dispensed through his office alone, and advancement in the party, many thought, was dependent upon genuflecting in his direction.

Bill Clements isn't known for genuflecting in anybody's direction. His fans and detractors alike suggest that his family crest should feature a bulldog with the seat of someone's pants hanging out of its mouth. It is not in Clements's nature to ask anybody's permission, even John Tower's, before setting out to do what he wants to do.

Under the Democrats, the Texas governor—not a senator—has always been head of his party's organization, so it was an open question what would happen when the Republicans finally elected a governor. The party establishment, though, generally assumed Tower would retain his position. Bill Clements assumed no such thing. He figured that the tradition established by Democrats applied to Republicans as well, and he seized the party's mantle without a fight from Tower. That seizure was made easier by the fact that Tower was already a wounded man in his own party. As leader of the Ford forces in Texas in the 1976 presidential

primary, he suffered a humiliating defeat to the Reagan camp—which caused him to lose control of the party organization and to be excluded from the state's delegation to the national convention. Out of that chaos, Clements created order. He did it by appropriating a tradition—albeit a Democratic one.

Tower claims he is happy for Clements to head the party and glad to be free of the responsibilities he once held, since that freedom gives him more time for his Senate duties. That line is transparently phony. Tower may now truly believe that things have worked out for the best, but he ached· while he was making the transition.

Tower's possible appointment as Secretary of Defense in the Reagan Administration and the controversy over deployment of the M-X missile illustrate the problems between the two men. Tower very much wanted to be Secretary of Defense. He paid a call on Clements to discuss the matter, leaving the meeting with what he believed was a commitment of support from the governor. When word that Tower might be appointed was leaked, along with the rumor that Clements would appoint John Connally to fill Tower's Senate seat, Clements told the press, "That's the nuttiest thing I've ever heard."

The Tower people read that to mean that Tower's appointment was the nuttiest thing Clements had ever heard. Clements says that he meant the idea of appointing Connally was nutty. In either case, Clements's bluntness did nothing to advance Tower's chances, and Tower's people believe that the remark was an inexcusable breach of the governor's commitment.

Clements admits that he promised to support Tower for Secretary of Defense but adds, "That's just the first chapter." After the Republicans won control of the Senate and Tower was in line to become chairman of the Senate Armed Services Committee, Clements says, he contacted Tower and withdrew his support, insisting that Tower stay in the Senate to "fulfill his responsibilities to the Reagan Administration, to the party, and to himself." As chairman of the committee he could do much more good. To Clements, that withdrawal relieved him of his earlier commitment. To the Tower camp, that was welching on his promises. In any event, it let Clements off a hook of conscience: he really didn't think Tower was strong enough to be Secretary of Defense.

Whatever his potential as a manager may be, Tower's expertise in defense is generally acknowledged throughout Washington. And for that reason Clements felt that Tower was well equipped to be chairman of the Armed Services Committee. Yet when Tower disagreed with the Reagan Administration's decision to base the M-X missile in reinforced

Minuteman silos rather than shuttle them by train to a variety of possible launching stations, Clements publicly took issue with him.

Clements also volunteered the information that Tower had changed his mind on the issue. That added and unnecessary element in the discussion leads Tower's friends and aides to believe the governor is trying to rub the senator's nose in it, a conclusion that doesn't enhance cordial relations.

With Clements's style it's difficult to decide whether the observation was a deliberate jab at Tower or not. He certainly knows that comments from the governor of Texas can put Tower in an awkward position. Sometimes Clements just speaks and lets the chips fall where they may. Other times he seems to delight in the impact of his remarks, but it's hard to tell for sure which time is which. And in that climate of ambiguity, the Tower camp is left to reach its own conclusions.

In the year since Ronald Reagan's election, rumors have circulated of an informal Clements-Connally alliance against Bush and Tower for power and favor with the president. The conflicts between Bush and Connally and between Clements and Tower give substance to the rumor. The thesis appears even more compelling when the tensions between Bush and Clements are factored in.

The Bush-Clements relationship predates either man's active involvement in politics. Their companies were once involved in a partnership in a drilling operation off Kuwait. Clements claims he recruited Bush to run for the Senate against Ralph Yarborough in 1964, after he himself turned down a request from Republican leaders to enter the race. He paid a price for recruiting Bush, Clements says: he agreed to be Bush's statewide finance chairman.

Despite those long years of association, the 1980 presidential election caused many rough spots in their relationship. The first problem was what Bush perceived as a tilt in Clements's official neutrality during the presidential primaries, with John Connally the beneficiary of the tilt. The early manifestation of that shift occurred during Connally's unsuccessful effort to get a split-primary bill through the Legislature, which would have moved the presidential primary to March while leaving the nominating primaries in May. It was a scheme designed to take full advantage of the early momentum in Connally's campaign.

Clements never said what he would do if the bill came to his desk for approval. That silence, one might argue, kept him true to his pledge of neutrality: support of the bill would have favored Connally, and opposition would have favored Bush. But to the party establishment there was no choice. The bill would have hurt the growth of the Republican party, and Clements should have announced that he would veto it.

Another sore spot between Clements and Bush arose at the Republican National Convention, where Bush partisans perceived Clements to be frantically working to get anybody but Bush selected as vice president. That effort, they believe, was self-serving. Clements is generally acknowledged to harbor national ambitions, which a Texan vice president would seriously hinder. Clements is aware of those Republicans who still have that interpretation of his activities at the convention. "Some people like to swim in their own ignorance," he says.

Clements *was* involved in the effort to persuade former president Gerald Ford to be Reagan's running mate, but he acted, he says, at Reagan's behest, not at Ford's and not on his own initiative. Clements arrived at a meeting with Reagan and a handful of close advisers expecting to be asked for a recommendation for vice president, and he was prepared to push George Bush. "He really had no alternative," a close associate says. But before that matter could be discussed, Reagan stated that he wanted to determine whether a Ford candidacy was conceivable, and he charged the group—including Clements—with the task of investigating that possibility.

After the Ford draft failed and Bush had been selected by Reagan, Clements heard of the Bush camp's resentment of his efforts to get Ford to run. Clements later saw Bush in the lobby of his hotel and, in an attempt to make amends, walked up, put his arm around him, and said, "Congratulations, George. I was all for you." Just then Alan Greenspan, the chairman of the Council of Economic Advisers during the Ford Administration who, with Henry Kissinger, helped quarterback the vice-presidential deal from Ford's perspective, saw Clements, walked over, and said, "Well, Bill, we almost pulled it off!" It was hardly an occasion for Clements to explain the subtleties of his position.

Despite the conflicts among the party's major figures—and the potential for more—the reputed Clements-Connally alliance is vastly overstated. "Occasional working arrangements" might be a more apt description. Connally sometimes gets calls from the White House and was recently appointed to the Foreign Intelligence Advisory Board, but he is really out of the picture at the moment. His political activities have been primarily devoted to paying off his campaign debt, still more than $1 million, according to Julian Reed, longtime Connally confidant.

Clements, in his own way, is working hard to square his relationship with Bush. Jim Baker, Bush's campaign manager and now Reagan's chief of staff, describes that relationship as "healable and healing." And Bush, secure in his victory, has even offered a helping hand to John Connally. Bush sent a letter to his contributors asking them to help Connally retire his debt, which netted Connally about $200,000.

Men who reach the level of political prominence attained by George Bush, Bill Clements, John Connally, and John Tower don't do so without the benefit of healthy egos and strong ambitions. Those egos are bound to bump into each other and their ambitions are certain to clash. Despite being Republican, despite being conservative, despite being Texan, they are natural competitors: for financial contributions, for organizational support, for the spotlight of public attention, and, perhaps, for higher office. If Reagan does not seek a second term and Clements is reelected, it is conceivable that Bush and Clements could be vying for their party's presidential nomination in 1984.

There's another reason conflicts within the Texas Republican party are inevitable. As the party grows and more of its candidates are elected, the opportunities for conflicts are multiplied. And the increased importance of the party amplifies those conflicts when they do occur. In a sense, the success of Texas Republicans has made them more like Texas Democrats, who long ago perfected the art of internal conflict. After all, many of today's Republicans were yesterday's Democrats. ♣

BEHIND THE LINES

by Gregory Curtis

om Sifford is a Democratic precinct chairman in Hurst, a small suburban community between Fort Worth and the Dallas–Fort Worth Airport. Twenty-five years ago, when his youngest daughter entered grade school, he entered college. He promised himself that by the time she graduated from high school he would be ordained as an Episcopal priest, and he did it. All the while, he was helping to raise his family, working as a teletype operator in the communications department of American Airlines, and participating in the local politics of the Transport Workers Union, which in time led to his work in Democratic party politics. He is about fifty years old, tall and lanky, with a closely trimmed beard that runs around the edge of his jaw and the lower part of his chin, a style more typical of the nineteenth century than our own. Estelle Teague, a short redheaded woman of about the same age, is Sifford's Republican counterpart. She has two sets of boy-girl twins, and her husband works for the Federal Aviation Administration. Their rivalry is friendly. Although Teague is a Catholic, Sifford was the first churchman to visit her after a pickup hit her and broke her leg. "Estelle," he said, "I wanted to be sure to get here before the Romans did."

Their precinct, number 172, is one of the few in Tarrant County that have not changed boundaries repeatedly during the last ten years. In 1978 the vote in the governor's race in the precinct was 537 for Clements and 427 for Hill. But this November the Democrats carried it with 646 for White to 609 for Clements. Tarrant County as a whole is something of a swing county for the Democrats. It is not solidly in the camp of either party, but the Democrats have seldom carried Tarrant County and lost statewide. In most elections, and indeed in this last one, the prevailing strategy has been to get out the vote in the strongly Democratic precincts to win there by a maximum margin. Key areas are east Arlington, southeast Fort Worth, and certain parts of White Settlement in the west. Precinct 172, however, is not one of these. It is traditionally Republican, at least at the top of the ticket, having voted for Nixon, for Ford, and mightily for Reagan. It is exactly the sort of middle-class, suburban neighborhood the Republicans are supposed to dominate, particularly here in the Southwest. Clements should have carried the precinct again, but he didn't.

It would be hard to imagine a precinct with less romantically named boundaries. To the east is the Bedford city line, while to the north, west, and south, respectively, are Bedford-Euless, Precinct Line Road, and West Pipeline. And these boundaries look as unromantic as their names. They are lined with Mr. Gatti's, Whataburger, Kentucky Fried Chicken, Long John Silver's, the Hurst Bowl, Dairy Queen, NAPA Auto Parts, Val Oaks Shopping Center, Shady Oaks Shopping Center, and a Texaco on the corner of Precinct and Pipeline offering free L'eggs panty hose with a fill-up. Although newish apartment complexes stand at the southeast and northwest corners, the interior of the precinct consists of modest single-story brick houses with modest yards, built during the early sixties. As a rule, the people who bought these houses when they were new still live in them today. Now those people are forty or older, and as their children have grown, tricycles in the driveway have been replaced by motorboats, Winnebagos, and pickups with campers on the back. The precinct is overwhelmingly white,

although a Mexican American who lives there has won a seat on the Hurst city council. Tom Sifford, the Democrat, guessed that the average household income in the precinct was between $20,000 and $30,000; Estelle Teague, the Republican, put it at $35,000 to $60,000. Whichever guess is more accurate, there is neither visible poverty nor visible wealth. Certain streets are somewhat nicer than others, but as a whole the precinct is as homogeneous as can be.

One might think that Precinct 172's switch was a reaction against Reaganomics, but there's little evidence that that's so. Looking back at local newspapers for election day 1978, one can't help but be struck by how similar the times seem. The weather was the same—mild but cloudy with a chance of rain. Carter was planning stricter controls over the federal budget. Texas Instruments closed at 32⅞ as opposed to this year's election-day closing of 29¾. Round steak was $1.59 a pound then, now it's $1.68 a pound. A lippy owner of the Texas Rangers, Brad Corbett back then, had fouled up a complicated trade with the Yankees. The prime interest rate was 10¾ per cent, while this year's prime, having retreated substantially from its days at 20, was a high but still comfortable 12 per cent.

But there are differences. Some are trivial. The Dallas Cowboys spent the Monday night before election in 1978 losing to Miami 23–16. This year, with the strike in progress, one can't help but wonder whether the boys spent their Monday evening in more or less interesting ways. Other changes are more substantial. In 1978 the *Fort Worth Star-Telegram* carried five pages of job openings in the classified section. This year there were three. And on election day four years ago Harding Lawrence presented to the board of the Dallas–Fort Worth Airport Braniff's plans for a $45 million expansion of their terminal facilities. But even with the slowing of the job market in Texas and the failure of Braniff, the people in Precinct 172 are still living much as they did. No one complained to me because he was out of work, and even reversals in the airline industry like the failure of Braniff or layoffs at nearby Bell Helicopter have had far less effect than one might think. A local real estate salesman said that neither the air controllers' strike nor the bankruptcy of Braniff had had any appreciable effect on the home market; an accountant in the precinct told me that local businesses had shown some declining profits but more, he thought, because of rising labor costs than anything else.

But there were two definite changes between this campaign and the last. One was mundane and tangible; the other was instinctive and vaporous, but all the more pervasive for that. The tangible difference was that a Republican candidate campaigned actively for the Legislature against Charles Evans, a Democrat who has held the seat since 1972. Evans has his detractors—*Texas Monthly* named him one of the ten worst legislators in 1977—but he has his own share of personal appeal and knows how to use it to campaign effectively in his district. In 1980, against a different opponent, Evans had not campaigned at all, even though Ronald Reagan was leading the Republican ticket. He won with 55 per cent of the vote, normally an impressive victory but in his case the lowest winning margin of his career. "After that," he told me, "the Republicans came and tried to get me to switch parties, using those figures to show how the district was getting more and more Republican. But they didn't take into account that I did nuthin'. *Nuthin'.* And I still won with 55 per cent."

This time his opponent, Dr. Steven Weinberg, began campaigning door to door. Evans—who thought, "If he walks, I walk"—had 10,000 leaflets printed. He and his wife began knocking on doors, asking for votes, and leaving a leaflet at each stop until all 10,000 were gone. Evans buried Weinberg at the polls. In Precinct 172 alone, he won 859 to 371. Since the election much has been written about active Republican challengers who awakened the slumbering dinosaur Bill Hobby and angered the aloof aristocrat Lloyd Bentsen into mounting an energetic and unified Democratic campaign that carried White along with it almost as an afterthought. But the results from Precinct 172 make one wonder if local candidates were not at least as effective in getting out the vote. Bentsen won by 80 votes and Hobby by 165, but it was Evans by 488.

The second, less tangible difference lies in the nature of the Republican candidates and campaign. After who knows how many Republican drives to convert the common man, why does a large voter turnout still mean a Democratic victory? In this one precinct, 30 per cent more people voted than in 1978, but three out of four of those additional voters chose White. We telephoned a sampling of people in Precinct 172 to ask why they had voted the way they did. The tedium of making so many phone calls was relieved only by the apparent variety of the answers. One man had voted for White because of utility rates. Another, a teacher, hadn't liked the way Clements treated her profession. One couple "just didn't like the way things were going under Clements." What these replies show is a failure by the Republicans to communicate any consistent message to the people of Texas, except perhaps this one: you're being taken for granted. The Republican slate was full of campaigners so inept that they managed to project only the worst of themselves. George Strake succeeded in making the immensely wealthy Hobby seem to be a down-to-earth country boy with dirt under his fingernails. Jim Collins, by running television commercials asking questions like "Where is Nicaragua, anyway?" made Bentsen appear possessed of the wisdom of Solomon. And what seemed fresh and gutsy in Clements the challenger became arrogant and insensitive in Clements the incumbent.

"The trouble with us Republicans is that we're not talking to the people." This was said to me by a successful businessman in Hurst, active in Republican politics and an effective fundraiser for the party. "I'll tell you something else," he went on. "The people aren't going to listen to us until we change this fat cat image. We can have all these thousand-dollar-a-plate dinners we want, but the people of Texas don't like it. The people of Texas are going to vote for the guy at the barbecue every damn time." 🌶

★POLITICIANS★
LEGISLATORS

THE STAR-CROSSED PALM OF BILLY CLAYTON

Taking a bribe is a crime; taking a campaign contribution is legal. The trouble is that it's hard to tell one from the other.

Billy Clayton should resign. Perhaps it is true, as he insists, that he intended all along to return that $5000 cash contribution handed him by a labor lobbyist. No doubt it is true, as his defenders say, that the FBI's Brilab investigation was a sleazy operation that smacked of entrapment; it is equally true that the quirks of Texas criminal law may provide the beleaguered Speaker of the House with a near-ironclad defense to bribery charges. But none of that helps. Even if Clayton is legally innocent, he is politically guilty. In the policeman's vernacular, he can beat the rap but he can't beat the ride.

Clayton's offense was to break the fundamental law of political fundraising: never take cash in front of someone you don't know. (The someone turned out to be an FBI informant, thereby proving the wisdom of the rule.) Clayton says he took the fateful envelope because he didn't want to embarrass the lobbyist in front of his client, but that explanation won't do. The unpardonable alternative he chose was to allow a total stranger to come away with the impression that the Speaker was for sale. There is something terribly disturbing about a politician who reacts so casually when offered an envelope stuffed with cash. It doesn't matter whether he is corrupt, careless, or just stupid; morally, if not politically, the differences are insignificant. In any case his integrity, his judgment, and his leadership have been compromised beyond recovery.

That is why he has to go. But his demise should not obscure the fact that the Speaker has been more victim than perpetrator. When the FBI came to Austin, they were on a fishing expedition. They didn't even know Clayton's name, and they had no specific politician in mind. Apparently operating on the principle that every man has a price, they picked Clayton and set out to find his. What ultimately doomed the Speaker, though, was neither his own greed nor the FBI's cleverness, but rather a double standard of morality that is pervasive in Texas politics. Bribery is like sex: there's no difference between the legal act and the illegal act except who you do it with.

The following scenario, for example, is not only quite within the law but is so common that in this pre-election season something like it will surely occur dozens of times before the May 3 primary. Senator Truehart has been invited to address the annual dinner of the Texas Widget Association. He is introduced by the chairman of the association's legislative committee, who runs through all the problems his organization needs to have resolved by the next Legislature. Truehart then gets up to speak. "You boys got a great program here," he tells the audience. "I want you to know I'm with you a hundred per cent." Then the script calls for the chairman to say, "You all heard the senator. Now let's show him our appreciation." And they hand him a check for several thousand dollars.

Bribery? Well, the law says that accepting money in exchange for promising a vote is a felony. *Except* (and here's the catch) *when the money is in the form of a campaign contribution*. Under Texas law a campaign contribution, no matter how large and no matter how explicit the quid pro quo, cannot be a bribe. Had Billy Clayton, rather than debating whether to return his windfall, simply put the money in the bank and reported it to the Secretary of State's office, he would have been untouchable. Not until he missed the state campaign law's reporting deadline was he susceptible to accusations of bribery.

Make no mistake about it: both donor and donee know what a large contribution means. Not even the naivest candidate for office believes that the doctors support him because he is a healthy physical specimen or that lawyers back him because they admire his mind. Politics is a game of influence, and every contribution from an interest group is an attempt to buy just that. Only a few of the two-thousand-odd votes a legislator casts every session will involve matters of conscience or issues where his decision is dictated by his constituency. On issues like the long-running war between doctors and lawyers over malpractice insurance, a legislator starts out free to decide what is right. Contributions are intended to see that he doesn't remain that way.

Legislators insist that donations buy access, not promises; they joke about being for rent rather than for sale. But the truth is that in legislative circles one risks virtual excommunication by voting against his contributors. A classic case occurred during the 1977 session, after the highway contractors had prepared the way for a $825 million construction package by handing out contributions of $3000 or more to dozens of legislators. The highway folks still almost lost, in part because of the eloquent opposition of a House member who'd taken the $3000. For weeks afterward he was the object of scorn from lobbyists who weren't even involved in the fray, as well as from some of his colleagues. Other legislators wanted to switch sides and vote against the bill as more information surfaced during debate, but when pressed they would just shake their heads and say something like "Sorry, but I made a commitment."

The real question raised by Billy Clayton's troubles is not what to do about *him*, but what to do about the pervasive influence of money in politics. Bribery is only a tiny part of the problem; far more basic is the fact that, as California state treasurer Jesse Unruh says, money is the mother's milk of politics. Can the system be weaned? Lord knows, the reformers have tried. The Progressives were the first: distressed at the cozy relationship between political machines and business interests, they came up with devices like initiative, referendum, and party primaries to replace nominating conventions—all designed to smash the control of corrupt bosses and restore power to the people. The tide of reform so excited William Allen White that the Kansas muckraker wrote in 1910, "It is safe to say that the decree of divorce between business and politics will be absolute within a few years." Well, seventy years ought to qualify as a few, but here we are, still awaiting so much as a trial separation.

The bosses are gone, to be sure, but the reforms haven't worked as intended. Primaries doubled the cost of running for office—making money even more important than before. They also extended the political season to unbearable lengths, and voters simply got bored. The pivotal 1978 Texas governor's race drew one of the lowest turnouts in recent years. Expanding the vicious circle, candidates have to spend even more money to try to get the attention of an indifferent electorate.

Initiative and referendum work on occasion, but as the spirit of reform drooped and along with it voter interest, both devices were ripe for exploitation by well-financed, well-organized lobby groups. In neighboring Arkansas, for example, the railroads used initiative to pass anti-labor legislation; in California realtors and homebuilders pushed through a prohibition against open-housing laws. In recent years, initiative's most celebrated success was California's tax-cutting Proposition 13, but it too had exactly the opposite purpose from what the Progressives originally envisioned: it clamped the shackles on government, largely to the benefit of the rich.

Undaunted, the reformers keep trying. Four times in the last decade Congress has revised the federal campaign-finance laws. Strict limits have been imposed on individual contributions, disclosure is mandatory, and reports are scrutinized by civil servants with the power to take violators to court. There are so many rules and regulations that the most important operatives in election campaigns these days are not fundraisers and strategists but lawyers and accountants. And despite all the attempts to vaccinate the system against corruption, the disease spreads: more members of Congress are targets of criminal investigations now than at any time since cartoonist Thomas Nast lampooned the Senate dominated by business trusts a century ago.

Reform has fared no better in Texas, despite a tough financial disclosure act adopted by the 1973 Legislature. In that era, at the height of Watergate and just after the Sharpstown scandal, it was widely believed that if candidates had to reveal the true sources of their contributions—instead of, say, listing the anonymous "Committee to Reelect Senator Truehart, $25,000"—an alert press and alerted public would rise up against candidates beholden to big money. So no one paid much attention in 1975 when the Legislature exempted campaign contributions from bribery laws. But something went awry. The public showed scant interest in the long lists of names and dollars, and politicians discovered to their surprise that disclosure did them no harm. So much for one more reform: money continued to purchase influence as before, except that the process had become certifiably legal.

Do not think, however, that the 1973 reform was totally without effect. The emphasis on disclosure scared off individual contributors, the sort of people whose involvement was frequently benign, and encouraged the proliferation of special-interest political action committees (PACs), whose involvement frequently is not. So numerous are the PACs today that a recent booklet detailing little more than their full names sells for $25 and stretches to 71 pages. Their number has multiplied in less than a decade from a few dozen to nearly 1500. The bankers have BALLOT (Bankers Legislative League of Texas); the druggists have PAL (Pharmacists Assist Legislators); the fish processors have, believe it or not, PISCES (Political Involvement of Seafood Concerned Enterprises); and then there's TOT-PAC, which is not a lobby for day care centers but Texas Oil for Texans. Unlike individual contributors, the PACs are highly organized and their influence is statewide. (Doctors, for example, spent upwards of $561,000 in legislative races two years ago, while their nemeses, the trial lawyers, spent more than $334,000.) In short, money, and therefore power, have become centralized within the PACs—exactly what the reformers were trying to prevent.

The effect of all this on the Legislature (and for that matter on the Congress as well) has been nothing short of dreadful. Survival in office frequently depends on whether a legislator placates people with no concern for issues beyond their own self-interest—the single-issue lobbies that have done so much to paralyze the political process. What do the realtors care if teacher accountability isn't debated until minutes before midnight on the last possible night of the session—as was the case in 1979? What do the doctors and lawyers care if no significant energy legislation has reached the floor of either house since 1973, so long as their continuing feud gets its biennial airing?

Why has reform been so singularly unsuccessful? One reason, perhaps, is an investigation like Brilab. It obscures from the public the truth about money and politics. We call one type of gift bribery and the other type a campaign contribution, but in the end there is no difference. Both are designed for the same purpose, to achieve the same result. By pretending that a difference exists, we focus public attention on but a narrow aspect of a broad problem.

We'd be better off, in the long run, simply to abolish the double standard by repealing the bribery laws. Oh, some parts should be retained: a politican ought to go to jail for *soliciting* a bribe (anybody too dumb to come by campaign money legally shouldn't be allowed to hold office anyway). So should nonelected administrators, no matter who originated the bribe. Administrators, after all, are not accountable to the public. But elected politicians are. Billy Clayton's offense was political, not criminal, and the remedy should be political as well.

But there is a broader lesson to be learned from the Clayton case. Laws alone cannot bring about reform. As a people we are obsessed with gadgetry; we believe that a device exists to improve any situation. But what is true in the kitchen is also true in politics: adding new laws and regulations, like so many Cuisinarts and microwave ovens, doesn't necessarily improve public taste. Reform is effective only so long as people care about politics and their politicians; when they stop caring, as they are prone to do, reforms can produce the opposite result. Even disclosure, the most important and valuable of the reforms, is as useful to the lobby—it's nice to know where politicians have their bank loans in case you want to apply a little pressure—as to the public. Yes, money dominates politics, and yes, that is something to worry about. But the more we limit contributions and spending, the more we seem to tilt the system to the benefit of incumbents, rich candidates (who can't be prohibited from contributing to themselves), and the PACs. The reason money dominates politics is simple: interest groups stay involved year after year, and the rest of the people don't. All the efforts of reformers for a hundred years have been devoted to changing this basic law of politics, and they aren't any closer today than when they started.

THE DEAL THAT DIDN'T WORK

by Victoria Loe

As they cut up Texas into legislative districts, the politicians had to please the Justice Department, Bill Clements, blacks, browns, Republicans, and Democrats. And that was the easy part.

Hugo Berlanga is one of the best products of the Corpus Christi Mexican American political machine ever to reach the Texas Legislature. He is bright, tenacious, bursting with voluble charm, and politically shrewd well beyond his 33 years. But in the 181-member Legislature, Berlanga is a man of modest consequence. He is in only his third term. He chairs no committee, has passed almost no legislation, and seldom poses a major threat to other members' bills on the floor. And although senior Mexican American legislators have shown a surprising willingness to follow his lead, Berlanga's influence rarely reaches beyond the Mexican American caucus. His district is equally unassuming: a largely rural swath on the wrong side of Nueces County's tracks whose inhabitants are mostly Mexican American and mostly poor.

Berlanga is not, in short, a man accustomed to deciding the fate of congressmen or shaping the state's political future. This spring, though, he latched onto the session's most important issue: reapportioning Texas' congressional, state Senate, and state House districts. And almost before he knew it, the issue—which could alter the course of both political parties, spell oblivion or survival for white liberals, and determine the lot of minorities across the state—had turned and latched onto him. As the months passed and the strife intensified, events closed in on Berlanga, until on the last day of the session the whole monstrous question sat squarely on his shoulders. Which was by no means as unlikely as it may seem: why it happened is the story of how Texas politics works in 1981.

When the Legislature reapportioned itself ten years ago, someone like Hugo Berlanga probably couldn't have gotten elected at all. In 1971 only 10 Mexican Americans and 2 blacks graced the Texas House. But court-mandated redistricting plans of the past decade have upped that figure dramatically. Today Berlanga is one of 31 minority representatives: 18 Mexican Americans and 13 blacks. Still, the number of minority legislators hardly reflects the number of minorities in the population as a whole; by that yardstick, Mexican Americans alone would be entitled to 32 representatives. In the past, when Mexican Americans were largely locked out of the Legislature, white liberal Democrats had to be relied on to champion their cause. Now times are different. In the view of the United States Congress, the Supreme Court, and most black and brown politicians, only minorities can adequately represent minorities in politics.

A third minority adheres to that premise absolutely: the state's burgeoning Republican party. This year, for the first time since Reconstruction, Republicans held enough seats to make them a force: 38 of 150 in the House, 7 of 31 in the Senate, 5 of 24 in the Texas congressional delegation—plus, for the first time in this century, the governorship. But they thought they deserved more. Today almost half of the Texans who show up at the polls vote Republican in congressional races. The disparity between the number of Republican votes cast and the number of Republicans elected is largely a product of the way districts have been drawn in the past. This session would test whether the fledgling GOP bloc had the muscle to grab a more equitable share.

That question still hangs in the balance; the Legislature failed to draw new congressional districts during its regular session. But the answer is critical to the nation's future. The Republicans need only 27 more U.S. House seats to control Congress in 1982. Texas, with 3 new seats, naturally figures prominently in their designs. Minority legislators like Hugo Berlanga figure prominently too, because creating more minority districts often also means creating more Republican districts adjacent to them. Especially in the cities, population trends make minority gains and Republican gains almost synonymous. History has set the stage for the Democratic party to take a real drubbing; whether it does or not will depend largely on people like Berlanga.

Redistricting is a game most politicians would rather not play at all. Every one of the 181 legislators and 24 congressmen whose political futures were on the line this spring had good reason to be satisfied with his district—it had elected him, after all. True, most incumbents could think of ways to make their districts more politically congenial, but malicious line-drawing by other members could also make all but a handful of districts much, much worse. Faced with that choice, the overwhelming instinct was to settle for the status quo—which would have been fine, too, with most of the citizens who appeared to testify on the matter.

For a good part of this century the if-it-ain't-broke-don't-fix-it mentality actually prevailed. Although each Texas constitution since the Republic has required the Legislature to reapportion itself regularly and the 1876 constitution specified that the redistricting follow the federal census, no new districts were drawn after either the 1930 or the 1940 count. Since the state was becoming more urban, rural legislators weren't eager to put themselves out of work by creating fewer rural and more urban seats. They tried to circumvent that necessity altogether in 1936 by amending the state constitution to limit the number of districts any one county could contain—ensuring that urban areas would be underrepresented—but they still couldn't agree on new districts. (The provision was later declared unconstitutional anyway.) Then in 1948 the Legislature passed a law giving redistricting power to a five-member board—composed of the lieutenant governor, Speaker of the House, attorney general, comptroller, and land commissioner—in the event that the lawmakers failed to reapportion themselves. Not until 1951 did the legislators finally succeed in drawing a new map. They dragged their feet even more when it came to congressional districts, which remained unchanged from 1917 to 1933 and then from 1933 to 1957.

Even into the mid-sixties, some districts contained wildly disproportionate numbers of people. Harris County was allowed only one state Senate district (it now has four and parts of two others) until 1965. The congressman from the most populous district represented four and a half times as many folks as the congressman from the sparsest district. One state senator had eight times as many constituents as another. In this failing Texas was hardly alone: the Tennessee legislature, for instance, had not redistricted itself since 1901, so its districts were even more grossly out of line with population. Besides the shortchanging of urban areas all across the country, legislative districts in the South were almost always drawn so as to make it impossible for black candidates to be elected. In cities with significant black populations, either all candidates were forced to run citywide in multimember districts or the black neighborhoods were divided into little pieces that were then grafted onto larger white areas. In either case, white voters always prevailed. Not a single black served in any state legislature in the South between 1906 and 1966.

The federal courts refused for years to intervene to correct such abuses, but in 1962 the Supreme Court did rule Tennessee's numerically lopsided districts unconstitutional. Then, in a string of related opinions, the Warren Court laid down detailed guidelines to enforce its one-man, one-vote rule (which requires that congressional, state, and local districts contain only minor population deviations) and to ensure that lines were not drawn to diminish the political power of minorities. Congress jumped into the fray in 1965 with the Voting Rights Act, which required Southern states with a history of discriminatory voting practices to submit proposed election law changes, including redistricting plans, to the Justice Department for approval. Texas came under the act in 1975 when it was expanded to include "language" minorities as well as racial minorities. That same year, the Legislature finally outlawed multimember legislative districts, including Corpus Christi's. Hugo Berlanga was elected the following year.

The real impact of the Voting Rights Act, however, was judicial, not legislative. Throughout the late sixties and early seventies, civil rights groups sued state and local governments under the act and quite often won. In the process of deciding those suits, a generation of liberal federal judges appointed by John F. Kennedy and Lyndon Johnson made the Voting Rights Act their own and gave it a scope far beyond Congress' wildest dreams, and that in turn brought forth even more lawsuits. It took a full seven years for all the suits filed in the wake of

Texas' 1971 reapportionment finally to be settled. The weight of all those judicial opinions and the special rules they set forth for redistricting hung heavy over the current Legislature.

The courts have established this general guideline: because blacks and Mexican Americans register less, vote less, and have more children (who aren't voters), a district must be roughly 65 per cent minority to have a realistic chance of electing a minority candidate. But what about areas where minorities have historically participated more or less than average? Are those registration and voting patterns to be taken into account? And what about cities like El Paso, with large numbers of foreign residents? And should blacks and Mexican Americans be counted together in creating the ideal 65 per cent minority district, even where they're polarized and vote for Anglo candidates rather than each other?

Under the rules set by the courts, it's clearly taboo to divide a geographically compact minority community among several Anglo-dominated districts: that's "dilution." But beware of "packing" minorities into one district to diminish their influence in neighboring ones. (If the Voting Rights Act applied to political parties, this prohibition would automatically increase the number of Republicans in office. Texas Democrats have been successfully packing Republicans for years.) Above all, eschew "retrogression," or leaving minorities worse off than when you started.

All these considerations would have created headaches for the line-drawers even if Texas hadn't undergone massive population shifts in the past decade. But it had. The total population increased by 27 per cent, from 11.2 million to 14.2 million. More critically, the way that population was distributed also changed. The inner cities either lost residents or grew more slowly than the state as a whole. The suburbs mushroomed, some by well over 100 per cent. Surprisingly, the regions without major metropolises grew only slightly less vigorously than the statewide average. So redistricting, rather than being the classic urban-rural fight that had been expected, turned out to be the suburbs versus everybody else.

That was bad news for white urban Democrats. A political map of most cities would resemble an archery target, with concentric circles composed of minorities at the center, Anglo Democrats in the next ring, and Republican suburbs encircling all. Minority legislators—who lost population but were protected by law from losing their districts—reached outward to take away the white Democrats' constituents. Since the Democrats were usually short of people to start with, that left them little recourse but to take in suburban constituents. And—poof—their districts turned Republican. In Berlanga's case this process was complete: Nueces County elected two Mexican Americans

and one Republican to the House.

The irony, lost on no one, was that the very politicians who had pushed the Voting Rights Act—the white liberals—were now endangered by their own creation. And regardless of the outcome in Austin, the Reagan Justice Department lurked in the background—an unknown quantity, but it could be expected to look harshly upon any plan that protected white Democrats at the expense of minorities and Republicans.

It all came down to minority legislators like Hugo Berlanga. If they were willing to cede some minority voters to the white Democrats, then quite a few white Democrats would emerge from redistricting unscathed. If, on the other hand, the minority politicians insisted on keeping all the minority voters lumped together, then some white Democrats would be beaten by Republicans. The question facing Berlanga was whether it was an improvement to have a Legislature and a congressional delegation that had more minorities but also more Republicans. Was he a minority politician first, or a Democrat first? It was an agonizing dilemma that he had never before had to face so directly.

Such was the general situation confronting Berlanga and the 67th Legislature. The specifics, it turned out, were even more confusing.

On March 25, 1981, the presiding officers of the Texas House and Senate were each handed a cardboard box. Inside were the final population tallies and ethnic breakdowns for each of Texas' existing 24 congressional, 31 senatorial, and 150 House districts. The data were also broken down by county and by census tract, the basic unit around which most districts are built.

The figures indicated that with 14,228,383 residents, Texas was now entitled to 27 rather than 24 congressmen. One of the new seats, it appeared, would go to the Dallas suburbs; one would go to the Houston suburbs; and one would go to South Texas. Bringing all the districts close to the newly computed ideal size would require some fancy juggling; many, both congressional and legislative, were severely under- or overpopulated.

Houston and the Rio Grande Valley had grown faster than any of the other regions—prompting Berlanga and other Hispanics to call for a new Mexican American congressional district in South Texas. Dallas, Fort Worth, and San Antonio had failed to keep pace, which meant that they would lose representatives. That made them, especially Dallas, the bloodiest battlegrounds of the redistricting war. Dallas's shortfall and Houston's glut also set the stage for a giant tug-of-war, the outcome of which depended on whether the mapmakers started drawing in Harris County and worked north or in Dallas County and worked south. If they began by giving Houston the new districts it deserved, the northern tier of districts in Harris County would push out into the rural areas, starting a chain reaction that would culminate in the division of Dallas County into several little chunks to flesh out rural districts. Conversely, if they started by giving Dallas County the maximum number of complete districts it could justify, the domino effect would work in reverse to reduce the number of districts wholly within Harris County.

Each house of the Legislature had to pass two bills: one for congressional districts and one for its own districts. And the legislators needed to be pretty adept at hairsplitting: congressional districts had to be within a fraction of a percentage point of the perfect size; legislative districts offered a slightly greater margin for error, say 4 or 5 per cent. Of course, a computer can be that precise—and can even theoretically draw districts to conform to all state and federal constitutional mandates and the Voting Rights Act. But in the real world of politics, each bill also had to satisfy enough incumbent legislators to pass: at least 76 in the House and 21 in the Senate (since there a two-thirds vote is necessary to suspend the regular order of business to bring the bill to the floor).

Once each house produced its bills, the other had to concur. In the case of state legislative districts, this was essentially a formality. But it was unlikely that either house would accept the other's congressional plan, so a few members from each house would have to be appointed to a conference committee to resolve the differences. And oh, yes, the Legislature had to do all this in just over two months, before midnight on June 1.

If either house failed to reapportion itself by then—or if the governor *or* the Justice Department *or* the courts rejected the plan—the job would go to the redistricting board. Provided, that is, that no more than 90 days had elapsed since the end of the session. If the plan was thrown out after 91 days, who would draw the next one was anybody's guess: maybe the board, maybe the judge, maybe even the Legislature again in special session. If, on the other hand, congressional redistricting remained undone on June 2, a special session definitely awaited the members; that's why they're back in Austin right now.

Ten years ago, faced with this Herculean task, Lieutenant Governor Ben Barnes and Speaker Gus Mutscher simply drew the state legislative lines themselves, with a fine eye to rewarding friends and punishing enemies. Mutscher's lieutenants remember being called into the Speaker's office to be shown their new districts just hours before the bill reached the floor. In the Senate, Barnes didn't even let a bill get to the floor. He simply threw the issue to the redistricting board, had an aide draw a map on the kitchen table, and rammed the thing past the other four board members. The board ended up drawing a new House

plan as well, because Mutscher had sliced so many county lines to get at his enemies —some of whom found themselves stuck in districts with *two* other incumbents— that his plan was ruled unconstitutional. Eventually, various state and federal courts redrew many of the lines yet again.

This year, though, things were different. What with the departure of the old players and the arrival of new ones— the Republicans, the minorities, and the federal government—the oligarchical days of state politics are, for the moment at least, over. So redistricting was more of a free-for-all. The new districts were largely a product not of ideologies but of personalities: who liked or hated whom; who owed whom; who needed something else from whom; who controlled the flow of information and what price they extracted for it; what would look good, or bad, to the voters back home. Thus, the congressmen who wound up in jeopardy were the ones who, to put it bluntly, had the fewest friends: Democrats Jim Mattox of Dallas and Bill Patman of Ganado (coincidentally, Berlanga's congressman), both of whom made many enemies during their tenures as state legislators, and Republican Ron Paul of Lake Jackson.

The Senate, true to form, went about its redistricting chores with a minimum of unseemly public discord. In short order the more partisan of the two houses turned out a plan for Senate districts that paired freshmen Republicans John Leedom and Dee Travis in Dallas, split Dallas County six ways, and created a new Houston district tailored for Democratic representative Craig Washington. Round one in the Houston-Dallas tug-of-war had gone to Houston, which was not surprising, since both Lieutenant Governor Bill Hobby and redistricting chairman Jack Ogg hail from that fair city. (Round two would go the other way: Bill Clements of Dallas vetoed the plan, preferring to take his chances with the five Democrats on the redistricting board.)

The Senate plan for congressional districts was equally predictable. It, too, was drawn to suit incumbents, particularly House majority leader Jim Wright of Fort Worth (who, except for a near-perfect district for himself, wanted only to keep renegade Democrat Phil Gramm's district out of Tarrant County and to protect Democrat Martin Frost in Dallas). True, a few minor adjustments were needed—like giving back to congressmen Kent Hance and Jack Hightower the counties where their wives' families lived. (When Hance discovered that the counties had wound up in the wrong districts, he telephoned Hobby to suggest a trade, "just so Jack and I won't have to swap wives.") And then there was the matter of which Democrat should be given the best shot at Ron Paul's seat, in southern Harris County. Did it rightfully belong to Senator Chet Brooks or to Mike Andrews, who challenged Paul unsuccessfully in 1980 but remains the favorite of Houston's political

kingmaker Walter Mischer? That little item spawned a complicated series of amendments that persisted right into conference committee.

Jim Mattox ended up with considerably fewer Democrats in his district than the 54 per cent he thought he needed to win. He haunted the halls of the Capitol for weeks (as did Patman's wife, Carrin), working with party functionaries to draft amendments designed to save him. And Democrat Oscar Mauzy of Dallas faithfully offered up each amendment for the record, just as Senator Ike Harris of Dallas sent up amendments for the Republicans. And Ogg relentlessly talked each amendment down to defeat, just as everyone knew he would.

In comparison, the House's approach looked like an exercise in anarchy. It shouldn't have; the nineteen-member redistricting committee, chaired by Democrat Tim Von Dohlen of Goliad, had been compiling exhaustive data on each existing district and conducting hearings for two months. But Speaker Billy Clayton was walking a political tightrope. He was allied much more closely with the Republicans, philosophically and practically, than with the liberal Democrats who had rallied around the man who had earlier challenged him for Speaker, John Bryant of Dallas. Bryant and his supporters had set themselves up as natural targets for elimination, and the demographics were against them, too. The catch was that Clayton wanted to run for land commissioner in 1982. And if he didn't protect enough Democrats in redistricting, Bryant was ready and able to make trouble for him in the Democratic primary. So Von Dohlen, widely feared as a vindictive sneak in 1979, had to preserve the aura of absolute fairness in 1981 in order to protect his mentor's interests.

Looking at the makeup of the House redistricting committee, you wouldn't have given the Republicans a ghost of a chance: seventeen Democrats were lined up against only two Republicans. But the House is not yet, by any reasonable standard, a partisan body. And of the four true heavyweights on the committee (read: inside members of the Clayton team), one was the shrewdest Republican in the Legislature, Bob Davis of Irving, and two were conservatives receptive to the Republican cause, Von Dohlen and Bill Messer of Belton. The sole partisan Democrat who was also truly influential was Craig Washington of Houston, the brilliant black legislator who had hitched his star to Clayton's and risen to be by far the most respected minority member of either house. But Washington had a habit of not showing up at committee meetings.

And then there was Berlanga; it didn't take long for him to come to the fore as a point man for organized Mexican American interests. With Berlanga using his position on the redistricting committee to feed them friendly questions, attorneys for the Mexican American Legal Defense and Educational Fund (MALDEF) deluged Von Dohlen with meticulous computer-generated plans for both House and congressional districts. When they weren't testifying, MALDEF staffers camped out in Berlanga's office, analyzing other proposed plans and mapping strategy.

Others cast their lot differently. Members of the shadowy but vocal Coalition for Minority Representation showed up regularly to tout their plan for a minority congressional district in Dallas comprising most of Frost's and Mattox's black and Hispanic constituents. The coalition's map, it emerged, had been drawn with the aid of the county's Republican chairman. The group hadn't started out overburdened with credibility anyway; many legislators dismissed it as a front for its members' political ambitions. But that didn't diminish the apparent moral force of the minority district concept.

All the time the House redistricting committee was gathering testimony, Davis, Von Dohlen, and Messer privately drew the House's congressional plan, often working deep into the night. Anxiety among the Democrats was running high, but most were too busy worrying about their own districts to interfere effectively. Bob Davis made sure of that. The cagey veteran seemed to be everywhere and to know everything: he rattled more than a few legislators by talking to them about the minute details of their districts. When Von Dohlen at last laid his congressional plan before the committee, it had Davis written all over it.

The plan was even tougher on the besieged Dallas and South Texas congressmen than the Senate's had been. It turned Martin Frost's Dallas district into a minority seat (47 per cent black, 16 per cent Mexican American). It gave Jim Mattox several heavily Republican precincts in North Dallas and Garland. And it gutted Bill Patman by severing the predominantly Hispanic sections of Nueces County and Corpus Christi from his district, running it through hostile Republican territory along the coast all the way to Houston (thereby shoving Republican Ron Paul's old seat into the blue-collar Democratic neighborhoods of Harris County), and removing Patman's actual home from his district.

That put Berlanga in something of a box. No politician in his right mind would openly support a plan to divide his home county, especially when that county has a long history of ethnic polarization. Besides, it's not good form to sit by quietly while one's congressman is getting screwed. That problem soon solved itself, though: Patman showed up to put the final nail in his own coffin. When he chastised Von Dohlen in front of the committee, the chairman humiliated Patman with an unmerciful grilling over his (unfortunately meager) knowledge of the Voting Rights Act. The vehemence of Von Dohlen's response added impetus to the

rumors that he himself planned to seek higher office from that particular corner of Texas and was going after Patman as a favor to local power brokers.

Once the House's congressional redistricting bill was out in the open, howls of protest from a rejuvenated Democratic caucus forced Clayton to abandon his careful neutrality. His staff drafted an amendment to ease Frost's plight, and the committee adopted it 17–2 on a straight partisan vote. Meanwhile, Davis—who still ended up with just about everything he wanted—did a superb imitation of a man suffering a mortal setback. And that was all the Democrats got for their trouble. When they tried to pass a complete Democratic substitute on the floor, they won the Mexican American vote but lost several blacks because their plan siphoned minorities from Frost's district in order to help Mattox. Not even phone calls from Jim Wright, recruited by state party officials to lobby wavering members, could turn the tide. The substitute fell nearly 20 votes shy, and the committee version passed handily, setting the stage for a conference committee clash with the Senate.

As it turned out, the congressional bill was destined to wait on the shelf for well over a week while the House struggled to thrash out its own districts. Senators—and congressmen—eager for a conference committee could only wring their hands and wait. But several things happened during the ten days when the House redistricting bill occupied the House's attention that had a direct bearing on the fate of the congressional plan.

First, Craig Washington appeared on the scene to employ his matchless eloquence and his team status to defend Anglo Democrats and to debunk Republican demands for more minority districts. "When," he demanded of one nonplussed representative, "has the Republican party ever been a leader in advancing minority rights?"

Then there was the case of the missing Hispanics. Berlanga's district was supposed to be 63 per cent Mexican American, but when MALDEF ran the committee plan through its computer, the district came out closer to 55 per cent. Von Dohlen promised to correct the situation, but somehow the corrections kept not quite getting made as the bill progressed from hearings to committee votes to the floor. Berlanga finally got things straightened out, but it took him several nights of staying up all night to do it, and by that time he was a little, well, peeved.

Two other incidents proved crucial in determining the makeup of the congressional redistricting bill's ten-member conference committee. Partisan Democrats wanted one of the five House conferees to be Gerald Hill, a moderate regarded by everyone as *the* reasonable man on Von Dohlen's panel. But they pushed the Speaker too hard, threatening to cause trouble over the House districts unless

Clayton agreed to appoint Hill. And that ensured that Hill was out and Messer—the last person the Democrats wanted in conference—was in.

Finally, there was the Bobby Valles incident. Berlanga and Valles were the sole Mexican Americans on Von Dohlen's committee, which meant that Clayton would appoint one of them as a conferee—appearances demanded it. Valles had more seniority than Berlanga and thus was the natural choice. But he had been seen all session consorting with comptroller Bob Bullock, one of the five members of the redistricting board. Bullock quite obviously couldn't wait to get his hands on redistricting: he had several staffers working full time to lay the groundwork for the board to take over. So when Valles proposed an amendment that turned out to be drawn in a way that would make the whole plan unconstitutional, people immediately suspected Valles of conspiring with Bullock to sabotage the bill. Valles's stock with the Speaker evaporated. And that's how Berlanga ended up on the conference committee.

For everyone but Berlanga, the experience was doomed to be an anticlimax. After the months of holding hearings, after the countless conferences with anxious congressmen, after the scores upon scores of tentative maps, after the midnight strategy sessions, after the days of frantic horse trading and arm twisting, the biggest issue of the session stood an excellent chance of ending in a draw.

The ten conferees represented the leadership of every major faction: two Republicans (Davis and Senator Ike Harris); two Mexican Americans (Berlanga and Senator Tati Santiesteban); one black (Washington); two yellow-dog Democrats (senators Peyton McKnight and Oscar Mauzy); two aggressively conservative Clayton loyalists (Von Dohlen and Messer); and, caught in the middle, wanting badly to pass some kind of bill, Senator Jack Ogg. By the time they convened, only three days remained in the session. But they spent two of those days reiterating their relative positions: Harris and Davis talked up the necessity for a minority district in Dallas, and Mauzy and Washington talked it down. Meanwhile, House and Senate staffers worked to modify each house's bill so that it might get the requisite six votes—three from each set of conferees—needed to make it the official conference committee report.

By the morning of June 1, it was clear that Berlanga and Santiesteban (who had already agreed to follow Berlanga's lead) would be the swing votes. Once again the Republicans would attempt to play a minority legislator off against urban Democrats—only this time the governor got into the act, trying to persuade Berlanga to accept the House version of the plan even though it damaged Frost, Mattox, and Patman.

Clements knew exactly what Berlanga wanted: a new Mexican American congressional district in South Texas. And he knew it was not a purely selfless desire, since if Corpus Christi state senator Carlos Truan ran for Congress, Berlanga had a shot at becoming a state senator. Perhaps if the House version could be drawn to satisfy Berlanga's self-interest, he would give Clements what the governor wanted in Dallas: a minority district to spell finis to Frost and Mattox. Then Santiesteban would fall in line, and the plan would have its three votes on the Senate side: Harris, Ogg, and Santiesteban. (On the House side, Von Dohlen, Davis, and Messer were already solid—which also meant that the Senate's version of the congressional districts, the one drawn to protect incumbent Democrats, was dead in the water.)

Just before the conference committee was to convene that final evening, Clements called Berlanga into his office to show him a new map and discuss possible trade-offs. Berlanga didn't much like what he saw: the plan split three counties, including Nueces, along ethnic lines and created two side-by-side vertical districts in South Texas. Berlanga broached changes, some of which he knew Clayton would resist, and then promised to consider the plan and confer with MALDEF.

At seven the full conference committee met to look at new, modified versions of the original House and Senate bills. The Senate plan contained modifications in Dallas, Fort Worth, and Houston, and—particularly pleasing to Berlanga—created a new Hispanic South Texas district. The House plan was identical to the map Berlanga had seen in Clements's office. Under the baleful stares of Von Dohlen and Davis, Berlanga denounced the Clements-backed version. It would, he predicted dramatically, bring civil war to South Texas. Score one for Berlanga. And back to the drawing board. Berlanga returned to his office to wait for the summons he knew must follow.

The call came at nine-thirty. Already the halls of the statehouse echoed with the laughter of legislators making the rounds of lavish buffets stocked by the lobbies, but for Berlanga the next half-hour would be no party. Tiredly, he picked his way through the drifts of maps and computer printouts that littered his Capitol office.

"A real kitchen cabinet meeting," Berlanga thought wryly as he was ushered into the dining area adjoining the governor's office. The atmosphere in the room was heavy with a curious mixture of urgency and fatigue. Berlanga surveyed the assemblage: Bill Clements, Rita Clements, a couple of aides, Harris, and Von Dohlen, who looked, if possible, even more haggard than Berlanga. They were pulling out the heavy artillery this time for sure. Berlanga braced himself.

Clements took the offensive. "Well?"

he demanded. "Can we cut a deal? What if we throw Val Verde County into the South Texas district?"

Berlanga shot a look at Von Dohlen. Was the chairman really ready to make concessions on the home counties of important friends of Clayton's?

Von Dohlen shrugged. "It's out of my hands. Bigger people than you or me are involved now."

"Well, what's your decision?" Clements pressed. "Will you sign the plan?"

"I don't know," Berlanga stalled. "What else are you willing to give? What about the Hays County split? What about Comal and Goliad?"

The governor jumped up from the table. "I can't go any further without a commitment from you," he said.

Then Berlanga let them have it. "I can't live with your plan—the House plan," he told them. "I can't split Corpus Christi. And I'm not signing on to any plan that guts a bunch of Democrats."

"I'll never accept the Senate plan," Clements warned, "or any plan that doesn't create a minority district in Dallas County."

"Just vote for the House version," Von Dohlen urged. "With only two hours left in the session, Mauzy will probably filibuster it to death anyway. Just help us get *something* out of conference."

"No," Berlanga said flatly.

"Then it's dead," Clements spat, "and you killed it."

And it was. And he had. ♣

The Making Of a Congressman

by Victoria Loe

This month Mike Andrews becomes the first man in Washington from Texas' 25th District. How he got there is a story of the new age of American politics, featuring money, media, and some of the most powerful people in Texas.

The end was as abrupt as the beginning and the middle had been interminable. At 7:11 p.m. on Tuesday, November 2, as the voters of Houston inched their way home on its rain-slick freeways, campaign worker Chuck King listened to the numbers coming over the phone from the Harris County clerk's office downtown. He wrote them down. He hung up the phone. He turned to the mud-splattered, bedraggled group clustered around the tiny black-and-white portable TV on his desk and gave them the news. Andrews: 1816. Faubion: 1557. It took a moment for the truth to sink in; when it did, the little inner circle of Andrews' faithful whooped and shouted, hugged one another and flung high fives. Vic Driscoll, the campaign manager, stood slightly apart, his eyes red-rimmed. His man, Mike Andrews, had won the absentee voting, and Democrats *never* carry the absentees. Now it was almost inconceivable that he could lose. Seventeen minutes later, at 7:28 p.m., Dr. Richard Murray, calling the election for KPRC-TV, declared that the congressman-elect from the newly created 25th District of Texas was indeed Democrat Michael A. Andrews.

The candidate, waiting at home with his family, knew nothing of that. The candidate was in the shower. As he dealt with the accumulated sweat and grime of twelve hours spent shaking hands at the polls, his wife, Ann, took the message from headquarters—including the news that a television camera crew was on its way to the house. The winner would be granted no interval in which to savor that he had at last seized the prize he had been pursuing so doggedly for almost four years. Incredibly, in half an hour, it was all over.

Ten miles away, in a not quite completed Hilton Inn near Hobby Airport, the sense of unreality was even greater. While his supporters nibbled miniature quiches and nursed drinks in the ballroom, Mike Faubion huddled with his wife in a room down the hall. Unlike Andrews, Faubion had seen Murray's pronouncement, but he refused to believe that the race was over. He had proved the prognosticators wrong before.

He had sat in his living room one day in the summer of 1981 and seen a map of the new district in the newspaper, and an idea had begun to grow in his mind. *He* was the right man to represent the district. His house lay right in the middle of it. His law office was inside it. His wife, Tamara, had taught school in it. He was a Republican, and the district had voted for Ronald Reagan. He knew he could win. But the experts had never believed him. They'd said he didn't have enough money to survive the Republican primary; he'd knocked on 10,000 doors and made the runoff. They'd said he couldn't win the runoff; he'd won it. Mike Faubion hadn't come this far just to concede on the basis of 3400 absentee votes. He and Tamara walked down to the ballroom to smile and slap backs and spread the word: we're not giving up, they assured their people, it's too early yet. So the newsmen, impatient for the catharsis of a concession speech, hunkered down to wait, and Mike and Tamara went back to their room, armored in their bright, blank smiles.

An hour or so later, greeting their own supporters at their own party, Mike and Ann Andrews wore smiles that were only a little less dazed. For on that night more still united these two men than separated them. They shared memories of the thousands of miles traveled crossing and re-crossing the district, the anxious poring over of polls, the dawns at factory gates and the midnights plotting strategy. They shared the isolation, the uncertainty, the endless asking, asking, asking—for money, for time, for votes. But now, though neither could quite grasp it, everything had changed. One had won and the other had lost. One would sink back into obscurity, perhaps forever. The other would become one of the most visible, most powerful public men in one of the biggest, richest, most powerful cities in the world.

The Territory

The 300 square miles of real estate that dominated the imaginations of Mike Andrews, Mike Faubion, and some ten other candidates for more than a year is as uninspiring a chunk of coastal prairie as an indifferent Creator ever slapped down upon the face of the earth. It begins on the west at the point where U.S. Highway 90 crosses the line between Harris and Fort Bend counties, and from that undistinguished font rolls eastward across the southern quarter of Harris County, gathering bulk and character as it goes. Gradually the faceless apartment complexes and strip centers of Southwest Houston give way to the aging but respectable brick homes of Willowbend and Westbury, where the long-entrenched middle classes view the world with suspicion from behind thickets of burglar bars and vote Republican. Tucked in beside them is the Jewish enclave of Meyerland, which traditionally casts its ballots in the same direction. Skirting the cities of Bellaire and West University Place, District 25 sidles northward to encompass the blue-chip neighborhoods around Rice University. Then, leaping Main Street, it bursts upward into the imposing high-tech fortresses of the Texas Medical Center.

After meandering to the south, District 25 erupts briefly into the hurdy-gurdy commercialism of Astrodomain before slinking under the South Loop and sliding back into a state of nature. To the east it emerges onto a great swath of black neighborhoods, from middle-class Brentwood to downright poor Sunnyside, both solidly Democratic. It takes in Hobby Airport and the integrated lower-middle- to middle-class subdivisions nearby before crossing the Gulf Freeway into urban-cowboy land—the largely white, largely blue-collar municipalities of Pasadena, Deer Park, and La Porte, which forsook their Democratic ways in 1980 to vote for Ronald Reagan. Running down the coast, it scoops up the bedrock Republican stronghold of Clear Lake City, with its NASA scientists and engineers. Meanwhile, along the Ship Channel, the district's northeastern border, masses the shoulder-to-shoulder phalanx of industrial plants that power Houston's economy: Phillips Petroleum, Exxon, Georgia Pacific, Arco, Goodyear, Tenneco, Shell Chemical, Diamond Shamrock, Boise Cascade, Upjohn, Fluor, B. F. Goodrich.

Of the district's inhabitants (some 524,107 souls by 1980's enumeration), one quarter are black and 14 per cent are Hispanic (although those percentages drop to 20 and 5, respectively, if you count only the registered voters). The district was created by the Legislature in 1981 out of precincts that had previously been divided among one Democrat (Mickey Leland) and three Republicans (Bill Archer, Jack Fields, and Ron Paul). From 1976 to 1980 Republican congressional candidates fared increasingly well in those precincts—garnering 44.7 per cent of the vote in 1976, 47.6 per cent in 1978, and 48.4 per cent in 1980—and Reagan carried the area in the Republican landslide of 1980.

Most of the voters in the district call themselves conservative and most of them vote Democratic, but they are at least one step removed from the mainstream of Texas' historic Democratic conservatism, with its deep rural roots. The district exists because a lot of people left the urban Northeast at the same time that a lot of people were coming to Texas. You might say it simply moved from New York City to Houston. But in the process it changed character. It left as an urban liberal and arrived as an urban conservative, and in that it is emblematic of a shift in American politics that is still under way.

The word most often applied to the district over the course of the campaign was "diverse," but that doesn't fully capture the riot of neighborhoods and interest groups and social classes within its boundaries. It almost seems calculated to make a mockery of the Founding Fathers' idea that a congressional district should constitute a community of interest. Politically, the apt term is "balkanized." Pasadena has always been a hotbed of feuding factions, the unions hold some sway on the east end, and the black community has an indigenous power structure still centered in its churches. But there's nothing even remotely resembling a political boss for the district: asked to name the most powerful person within its boundaries, both Andrews and Faubion drew a blank. In short, the 25th District is just the sort of power vacuum that outside forces inevitably rush to fill.

So the how and why of Mike Andrews' victory is more than a tale of what it took to get elected to Congress in Texas in 1982—although it is that. The process by which the 25th District's seat was filled also revealed the varied interests that care—a lot—who represents southern Harris County in the national legislature, and why they care. What was really at stake in the long campaign was power: for the candidates, the power to become overnight a figure of importance in Texas, with a bright future as a player on a very broad field; for interested parties from the union halls of Pasadena to the boardrooms of Milam Street to the White House, the power that comes from having a voice in Washington and a vote in a tightly divided Congress.

A Bright Young Man

The rap on Mike Andrews is that he's nothing more than a puppet of Houston's downtown business establishment, and while that's not true, his success does illustrate the unsurprising notion that it never hurts to have friends in high places, particularly if those friends need something and you can provide it. In this case the something is a congressman who'll be an insider rather than an outsider, someone suited by inclination and ability and party affiliation to work with the House leadership and, in the process, to look after Houston's interests. In 1980 that person didn't exist; Bob Eckhardt wasn't inclined, Mickey Leland didn't seem able, Bill Archer was of the wrong party, and Ron Paul suffered from all of the above afflictions. Paul—whose 22nd District then took in most of the current 25th as well as Fort Bend and Brazoria counties—is the very antithesis of a team player. Any reasonably bright, reasonably attractive, reasonably personable, reasonably eager candidate who had been willing to challenge him would probably have found favor downtown. And Mike Andrews is more than reasonably bright, much more than reasonably attractive, and extremely personable in an ebullient, self-effacing way that nearly hides the ferocity of his drive to win.

In January 1980, when, at the age of 36, he announced his first congressional campaign, he was also unknown, untried, and very green. Nothing in his background particularly marked him as congressional material. He grew up in modest neighborhoods on the west side of Fort Worth as the son of a watch repairman and a schoolteacher. He went to the University of Texas and then to law school at SMU, clerked for a federal judge, worked for the Harris County district attorney's office, and became a partner at the downtown Houston firm of Baker Brown Sharman Wise & Stephens. He first had the idea of running against Ron Paul on November 7, 1978, the day Paul took—or retook—the 22nd District seat from Democrat Bob Gammage.

On that day he began to lay groundwork, first ascertaining that none of the Democratic machines in the district were strong enough to prevent a party newcomer like himself from running, then assembling the coterie of friends that would form the nucleus of his campaign. Vic Driscoll, whom Andrews had worked with for four years in the D.A.'s office, was a nephew of Ralph Yarborough's; he had cut his political teeth during Yarborough's various runs for the Senate and the governorship. Chuck King, who had been to UT law school and met Andrews

through friends, worked for one of the state's most politically active law firms, Bracewell & Patterson. Dick Trabulsi, a lawyer and liquor retailer who had also graduated from UT, had run Jimmy Carter's 1976 Gulf Coast campaign. But none of them had ever undertaken anything on the scale of a challenge to an incumbent congressman in an urban media market—a feat that would require not only skill, dedication, and luck but also well over half a million dollars.

Andrews announced his candidacy for the Democratic nomination in January. In February Bob Gammage threw his hat into the ring. Andrews' own poll estimated Gammage's name identification at 70 per cent; Andrews' was only 3 per cent. One of Andrews' staff called the hotel of his Austin-based campaign consultant, from the firm of Martin-Rogers Associates, only to be told that the man had checked out the day before. Frantic phone calls to Austin elicited a letter that said in essence: we only work for winners, and you can't win.

Andrews knew his opponents were vulnerable, however. The third Democrat, Joe Pentony, had liberal ties that were hardly calculated to endear him to downtown, and Gammage's performance in Congress had been lackluster in the extreme. So while the world at large wrote off Mike Andrews, he quietly went about winning over not only the voters of the district but the powers that be. Through Trabulsi he cultivated oilman and Carter stalwart Jack Warren, cofounder of Houston's largest privately held corporation, Warren-King Companies, and one of the heaviest hitters in Houston political financing. Andrews' finance chairman, another UT ex named Bob Parker, is a young Turk at the investment counseling firm Fayez Sarofim. Sarofim is a son-in-law of George Brown; Parker's father had been president of Brown & Root. Parker's first act as a fundraiser was to introduce Andrews to Brown over lunch at the Ramada Club. The man who had bankrolled Lyndon Johnson's rise to power was sufficiently impressed with Andrews' discourse on why Paul was beatable—or perhaps with the young candidate's earnest deference—to pledge $1000, the maximum allowed by law.

Next Andrews and Parker approached developer and Allied Bancshares chairman Walter Mischer, reputedly Houston's canniest political kingmaker. "We were so naive," says Andrews, "we thought all we had to do was win over Mischer and the financing would be taken care of." Again their pitch did the trick—sort of. Mischer wrote out a check for $1000. "I looked over at Parker and I could tell he was really pumped up," Andrews recalls. "He turned to Mr. Mischer and said, 'Well, sir, where do we go from here?' And Mischer pulled out the Houston white pages and said, 'This is a pretty good place to start.' After we left his office,

Parker and I just stood on the street corner, looking at each other and wondering what to do."

What they did was start soliciting Andrews' friends, mostly up-and-coming lawyers but also the scions of some of Houston's most prominent men—Corbin Robertson, Jr. (grandson of Hugh Roy Cullen), Lan Bentsen (son of the U.S. senator), Jeff Love (son of the chairman of Texas Commerce Bancshares). Then they sank $25,000 into a series of basic, ten-second, "Hi, I'm Mike Andrews and I'm running for Congress" TV commercials. Suddenly they had a legitimate candidate on their hands; the big donors and political action committees began to take an interest. "We found," says Andrews, "that the way to raise money was with mirrors."

Mirrors like television. Though it has been condemned as too expensive and too superficial, television is practically indispensable for a newcomer going up against an incumbent—especially a newcomer like Mike Andrews. The TV camera plays favorites: it likes some people better than others, and Andrews it likes very much. Through no particular skill or inner virtue, he is compelling on television, a phenomenon that has been pointed out often enough to embarrass him but that he's far too shrewd not to exploit.

In the primary of 1980 Andrews' TV presence, his aptitude for fundraising, and a blitzkrieg get-out-the-vote effort pushed him past Pentony and into a runoff with Gammage. He beat Gammage by outspending him five to one, then prepared for a frontal assault on Ron Paul. He hired veteran Democratic strategist George Christian to pinpoint Paul's weaknesses. Once again the main weapon was TV. Andrews attacked Paul's votes against defense funding and his neglect of local projects in a series of elaborately produced, on-location spots that featured the tag line "Ron Paul is the wrong man in the wrong place at the wrong time." A few days out, Andrews' polls said the race was too close to call. Then, in one of the great, gut-level shifts of American politics, the voters of the 22nd District, like voters nationwide, rose up to repudiate Jimmy Carter and embrace Ronald Reagan, and Mike Andrews lost by a margin of 5500 votes, all of them outside Harris County.

The Battle of Austin

Then the gods of politics gave Mike Andrews a once-in-a-decade opportunity: redistricting. The 1980 census had determined that Texas would get three new congressional seats, one of them either partly or wholly within Harris County. That meant Andrews could run again without taking on Paul or any other incumbent. If, that is, the new district ended up in the right place and had the right boundaries—if Andrews could pull a string or two in Austin.

Of course, he wasn't the only one whose ambitions were at stake. To start with, there were the four Houston incumbents; none of them would want to give up territory to a new district if their own districts became less friendly in the process. Then there were the other Democrats who might want to run; of these the most prominent and frequently mentioned was longtime state senator Chet Brooks of Pasadena. On the Republican side, at least two state representatives, Brad Wright and Don Henderson, had their eyes on the new seat. And complicating things even further was the statewide struggle between the two parties taking place in the Legislature.

Andrews' strong showing in 1980 and his connections to the likes of Mischer and Brown made it unlikely that the Legislature would ignore his interests altogether, but he was hardly assured of getting precisely the district he wanted. That district, he decided, would encompass black neighborhoods from the districts of Leland and Paul, the southwest quadrant of Harris County, and a chunk of Brazoria County, which—1980 to the contrary—generally voted Democratic. He drew up a map, took it to Austin, and showed it to several people, including Lieutenant Governor Bill Hobby. Something very like Andrews' map got incorporated into an early version of the Senate bill, but then Chet Brooks, part of whose power base in Pasadena had been left out of the new district, began to work for changes.

As things turned out, it wasn't hard to strike a compromise that both Andrews and Brooks could live with and that also accommodated the incumbents' desires. In order to create a district that favored a Democrat, the Democratic party sacrificed a chance to make life uncomfortable for Republicans Paul and Fields. The Republican party managed to protect its incumbents, which was as much as it could reasonably hope for, considering its already disproportionate strength in the delegation. Republican senator Mike Richards did mount a last-ditch ploy to remove Andrews' house from the 25th District—a ploy that failed to pass the Senate by one vote, Hobby's tie breaker—but later, when George Brown phoned Andrews to ask if he was happy with the district, he could answer that he was.

The Republicans

The ink on the redistricting map was hardly dry when the pollsters and demographers and political consultants began to descend upon the district. Some worked on behalf of would-be candidates; one, Lance Tarrance, labored in the service of the Republican National Committee (RNC). Politics, it has been said, is the triumph of hope over experience: the 25th District is, by any traditional measure, a Democratic district; nevertheless, the

RNC was willing to spend a great deal of money to procure a statistical analysis the size of the Houston yellow pages that would suggest otherwise. And since the national Republican party consistently outraises, outspends, and outorganizes its Democratic counterpart, the RNC was able not only to finance the study but, as the race wore on, to contribute vast sums of money to its candidate. But the most important thing about Tarrance's poll was that Tarrance did it. Until he miscalled the recent Texas governor's race, Lance Tarrance was one of the hottest Republican pollsters in the country, so hot, in fact, that some people wouldn't give money to a candidate unless Tarrance said he or she could win.

Tarrance told the national committee that the respondents to his poll, taken in November 1981, thought highly of Ronald Reagan and his economic policies and described themselves as conservative. He also told the RNC, among other things, which issues people were most concerned about (crime and inflation), which kinds of radio and TV they tuned in to (easy listening and country; news) what they thought about an anti-abortion constitutional amendment and defense spending cuts (they opposed both), and whether they had made a personal commitment to Christ (56 per cent said they had). Meanwhile, at the University of Houston, Richard Murray, working on behalf of Mike Andrews, looked at the district's demographic profile and its voting history and concluded flatly that a Republican had no chance.

By the March 12 filing deadline for the primaries, the 25th District was sprouting campaign headquarters like mushrooms: seven Republican, three Democratic, one Libertarian, one Citizens party. First out of the blocks for the Republicans was a big, genial, handsome dry cleaning entrepreneur named Larry Carroll. Carroll hired a young woman from the National Republican Congressional Committee (NRCC) as his campaign manager, signed up Lance Tarrance as his honorary chairman, and mailed out a type-heavy, eight-page campaign brochure with a full-color photo of the space shuttle on the cover. All of which was enough to make him look like the front-runner but not enough to bring the big money off the fence when he found himself running against six other candidates rather than one or two. Carroll's major competition was expected to come from J. C. Helms, a Harvard-educated classicist turned developer. Helms got into the race late, but his ties to River Oaks money and his record of party service made him a contender.

Two of the Republican candidates had actually run for office before. Larry Washburn, a civil engineer, had been drubbed in the 8th District's Democratic primary by Bob Eckhardt in 1980, before Eckhardt was drubbed by Jack Fields.

Dick Burns, a lawyer, had nearly won a state district judgeship in 1980. Burns clinched the early-visibility sweepstakes with a rash of billboards and assured everyone that he could win the race without a runoff, but that was about the extent of his campaign.

Two of the three remaining Republicans clearly didn't have a prayer. Everything about computer programmer Pat Angel, from her conspicuous lack of ego to her "Elect an Angel" slogan, screamed noncontender. Joseph Jefferson Burris, a retired city engineer, campaigned on a platform calling for, among other things, an end to the national income tax and the reinstatement of the Republic of Texas.

In the beginning, you would have had to rate Mike Faubion somewhere between Washburn and Burris—that is, between the marginal and the hopeless. Faubion was just 33, he had no political ties to speak of, and although his civil-law practice brought in a comfortable living, he was hardly a wealthy man or an intimate of wealthy men. He didn't have Mike Andrews' entrée, and he didn't have Andrews' talent for asking for money. But a Republican primary in Texas is different from any other kind of election because so few people vote in it. No more than 10,000 Republicans were expected to go to the polls in the 25th District on May 1; if Faubion started early enough, he could knock on 10,000 Republican doors by that date. He raised $10,000 from family and friends and approached Houston consultant Paul Caprio for advice on how to design a push card (so called because it is pushed into the hands of voters) and to order a walk list.

Lists are the sine qua non of every modern political campaign. The kind Faubion began with reflect a person's voting history—which primary elections he or she has participated in. But if a candidate wants a list of people in a certain income bracket or a certain business, or who own homes, or who practice a particular religion or avocation, chances are excellent that that list exists. Every time you deal with a mortgage company, join a professional society or fraternal group or church, subscribe to a magazine, or acquire a credit card, your name is likely to wind up on another list that is for sale.

In December Mike Faubion got his push card and his street-by-street list of Rs (people who had voted in one of the last three Republican primaries), RRs (voted in two), and RRRs (voted in all three) and prepared to announce his candidacy. Paul Caprio came to the event to tell Faubion as a hedge against future campaign expenses, the consultant would have to withdraw. Faubion said there wasn't $25,000 and Caprio said good-bye. On January 4, Mike and Tamara took to the streets as scheduled, knocking on doors from mid-afternoon until nightfall.

But no one, no matter how determined, can run for Congress without a staff. In

January state Republican party director Tom Hockaday mentioned Faubion to a young man named Kevin Burnette, a UT economics graduate who had worked in John Tower's 1978 senatorial and John Connally's 1980 presidential campaigns. He and Faubion met. Then Burnette contacted Denis Calabrese, a senior economics major at Rice, and Lee Woods, a buddy from UT who was in the business of rounding up investors for oil and gas ventures. Woods and Burnette were 25, Calabrese 22. All three were intensely hungry, all three were intensely conservative, and all they knew about Mike Faubion was that he seemed as conservative and as hungry as they were.

They were young but not unschooled in the ways of politics. In addition to pouring money into campaigns, the national Republican party and several conservative organizations have built a cottage industry around educating candidates and staffers; Burnette and Calabrese are among a small army of eager young conservatives who are products of such campaign seminars. Faubion had entered the race planning to sell himself as the hardworking hometown boy; his young aides turned him into the candidate of ideas. By mid-March he was greeting visitors to his office with a rapid-fire stream of policy statements—on a constitutional amendment to balance the budget, six-year terms for federal judges, federal sunset laws, block grants for flood control projects—still coming across as just a trifle callow, perhaps, but gaining conviction with every recitation.

The Democrats

"Callow" is not a word one would apply to state district judge John Ray Harrison. The judge, formerly a Democratic state legislator and mayor of Pasadena, is just about as imposing as a slow-moving, slow-talking good ol' boy who says "thew" for "through" and "wonst" for "once" can be. Harrison announced in December and by March had four-by-eight-foot signs up on what seemed like every street corner east of the Gulf Freeway. His idea was that the east-end cities of Pasadena, Deer Park, and La Porte could at last elect one of their own to Congress. Chet Brooks had decided not to make the race (his Senate seat was safe, Andrews' establishment support was formidable, discretion was the better part of valor), so the obvious choice was John Ray Harrison. The numbers Harrison used to illustrate his contention—that *if* 90 per cent of the voters in Pasadena turned out, and *if* 90 per cent of those voted for him, he would triumph—were a little hard to swallow. But if he was correct, that meant Mike Andrews had failed badly to protect his interests during redistricting. By Andrews' reckoning, the district wasn't supposed to elect a black or an east-end candidate; it was supposed to elect someone *without* a specific constituency, a classic middle-of-the-road candidate like Mike Andrews.

To some degree that description also fit the third Democrat in the race; in his nineteen years in the Legislature and on the Harris County Commissioners' Court, Tom Bass had represented nearly all of the precincts that made up the district. Bass, a wry, spare, somewhat pedantic alumnus of the Legislature's post-Sharpstown reform crowd, figured he couldn't do worse than come in second, even though—in the best liberal grandstanding tradition—he had vowed not to spend more than $50,000 on this primary that was supposed to cost at least $200,000.

That was not Mike Andrews' approach. With redistricting behind him, Andrews moved swiftly to shore up his financial base, beginning in early December with a $1000-a-head reception at the Houston Club whose list of eighty "sponsors" was so loaded with prominent names—including Texas Air chairman Frank Lorenzo, Texas Commerce Bancshares chairman Ben Love, and champion Democratic fundraiser Jess Hay as well as Mischer and Brown—that it prompted one wag to concoct a parlor game called Name the Missing Fat Cat. Harrison and Bass did their best to use Andrews' list of supporters against him, giving copies to reporters and muttering darkly about debts and influence, but to little apparent avail. Then, while his opponents acted as their own managers, Andrews went after the pros: Richard Murray as analyst, former Houston Natural Gas lobbyist George Strong as manager, adman Roy Spence as media consultant, national expert Mary Ellen Miller as phone-bank director, rising Democratic star George Shipley as pollster, and George Christian as all-purpose sounding board and éminence grise. Plus, of course, unofficially, Vic Driscoll, Dick Trabulsi, Chuck King, Bob Parker, and Jack Warren's political money raiser, Bill Wright.

Round One

A primary with this many candidates unfolds with all the finesse of a barroom brawl. Nobody knows quite whom he's fighting, so there are lots of wild punches and unforeseen collisions. Among the Republicans, J. C. Helms came on strong, as expected, with direct mail and radio spots in the last ten days, and on May 1 he walked away with 3441 votes, or 34 per cent. Larry Carroll, whose socko start proved to be his downfall—his campaign overspent itself early and couldn't counter the others' late pushes—took third with 16 per cent. After running virtually no campaign at all, Larry Washburn unleashed four good, solid mailings during the final week and emerged a surprisingly strong fourth. Burns, Angel, and Burris fizzled according to schedule. And Mike Faubion, who had also mailed heavily during the last ten days—one letter bluntly disparaged Helms' chances of beating a Democrat in November—surprised almost everyone outside his own campaign

by waltzing into the runoff with 2494 votes, or 25 per cent.

If there were any surprises in the Democratic primary they were merely of degree—that Andrews did so well and Bass so poorly. The commissioner, who had set out to prove that a congressional race could be run like a local race, spent $45,000 to prove himself wrong. He came in third with 6568 votes (27 per cent). Harrison, who relied heavily on advertising in east-end newspapers to supplement his signs, polled 65 per cent in Pasadena–Deer Park but got buried by Andrews elsewhere, winding up with 30 per cent to Andrews' 43 per cent.

For a quintessential media candidate, Andrews hadn't run much media. There had been an early round of billboards and a slick eight-page brochure that featured the world-class something-for-everyone slogan "He thinks like you do." But he used only one week of sporadic TV, perhaps because the price of a thirty-second spot had jumped 40 per cent since 1980. In fact, the television kid had won with a back-to-basics organizational campaign: key endorsements (by everyone from black politicos Mickey Leland, Craig Washington, and Anthony Hall to the *Houston Chronicle*); day after grinding day of Rotary luncheons, door-to-door campaigning, civic club meetings, and neighborhood coffees; and, above all, sophisticated phone banks to identify and turn out favorable voters.

Accusations

Runoffs breed hysteria. The problem is that people don't vote in runoffs—they've done their duty once and they're just not interested. So the campaigns crank up the volume from strident to shrill to catch the public's flagging attention. J. C. Helms set the pace by running not against Faubion but against Andrews. He challenged the Democrat to a debate and ran ads in the Pasadena and Deer Park papers attacking Andrews' endorsement by Mickey Leland. Meanwhile Faubion sent all his troops into Clear Lake City, where he had been beaten badly in the primary, and hit Republican voters with a last-minute spate of anti-Helms mail. The four mailers, all a forbidding black, attacked Helms for being a bachelor, for having moved into the district to run, and for possessing a Harvard degree, factors Faubion said would drive away the swing voters who were the key to winning in November. Helms' complacency in the face of Faubion's relentless attacks gave Faubion the win on June 5 with 54 per cent of the vote.

On the Democratic side, Harrison and Andrews kept busy heaving accusations of radicalism and racism at each other across the Gulf Freeway. Andrews looked all but impregnable in the western end of the district, where Harrison's tool-of-the-downtown-establishment line was falling flat. The judge's only chance was that the west end would forget the race while the east end stayed stirred up. And his opponent had handed him just the thing with which to stir it. Andrews had run an ad in a black newspaper that showed him embracing Mickey Leland under the headline WE THINK A LOT ALIKE. Harrison issued a press release to the east-end papers, playing on Leland's early radical posturing and painting Andrews as the next-best thing to a Marxist revolutionary. To top it off, Harrison accused Andrews of having dispatched a sound truck into black areas to urge voters to "send the redneck back to Pasadena."

Andrews hurriedly ditched the "We think alike" slogan and denounced Harrison and Helms for attempting "to polarize our district along racial lines." He also called Harrison a puppet of the New Right for having accepted $5000 from the National Conservative Political Action Committee, the infamous NCPAC. The newspapers loved it; day after day the latest barrage from each side landed on the front page of the *Pasadena Citizen*. Harrison's strategy had worked—up to a point. The turnout in Pasadena and Deer Park was higher on June 5 than it had been on May 1, and the judge got 70 per cent of those votes. But all the hoopla had aroused Andrews' voters, too; the final tally was Andrews 11,011, Harrison 8029.

Rich Friends

Summer is a time in campaigns for fence mending and stock taking, for fattening up the treasury and laying out the battle plan for the long ordeal ahead. Scarcely had the last vote been counted than Faubion and Andrews were in the east end, scrambling to win over Harrison's best-known supporters. Both also commissioned polls over the summer, Andrews from Shipley and Faubion from Tarrance. The polls showed that the issues in the election were national and, by extension, that what the national Democrats and the national Republicans said about them, particularly unemployment, was as important as anything Mike Andrews or Mike Faubion said.

In any case, neither candidate seemed likely to galvanize the electorate with his personal vision of the nation's future. Faubion had an agenda, but it differed very little from the standard Reaganite line; oddly, as the president's popularity waned, Faubion seemed to embrace his rhetoric more and more. As late as the final week he was still trying, unsuccessfully, to convince Reagan to campaign for him. Andrews shrewdly stuck to unemployment and social security, playing on the age-old theme of the Democrats as the party of compassion. The ideological difference that communicated itself most forcefully throughout the campaign was in the candidates' attitudes toward government and politicians. Mike Andrews met Gary Hart and John Glenn and came away impressed by their intelligence and integrity. Mike Faubion met George Bush

and Ronald Reagan and had the insight that "they're only men after all."

Without indulging in undue psychologizing, it's fair to say that Andrews is fundamentally an insider in a way that Faubion is not. Andrews had been instinctively readying himself for this race at least since college. In fact one way to define the difference between the two men is to say that Andrews went to the University of Texas and Faubion went to the University of Houston; UT was a common thread that linked Andrews, Parker, Trabulsi, and King to an unmatched statewide web of money and power. Andrews had made the right friends, chosen the right jobs (the D.A.'s office has political overtones, corporate law brings one into contact with the rich and powerful), joined the right breakfast clubs and country clubs (River Oaks), bought the right house (near Rice), showed, in short, that he appreciates how the game is played in Houston. It was vital that he communicate this to the city's establishment because, in the final analysis, this race was a power struggle between Houston's traditional leadership and the national Republican party. Political and business leaders within the district did play a role, but it was largely symbolic. Almost all of the money came from outside.

Basically, there are three sources of political money: rich people, friends of the candidate (or friends of friends of the candidate), and political action committees. The PACs, groups of like-minded individuals who pool their money, can give up to $5000 to a candidate, five times the limit on an individual's gift. There are all sorts of PACs: industry, labor, conservative, environmental, feminist, you name it. But the outcome of the 25th District race hinged on the involvement of the business PACs—which had, for instance, given Jack Fields $270,000 to help him defeat liberal Bob Eckhardt in the neighboring 8th District in 1980.

Faubion was trailing; he needed to raise more money than Andrews just to catch up. PACs are utterly unsentimental, however; they only give to candidates they consider viable. So first Faubion had to convince the business PACs that he could win in spite of the polls, which showed Andrews leading by between 32 and 44 points. On the other hand, donors, and political action committees in particular, don't like to give money to sure winners (why pay to put someone in office if he's going to be there anyway?), so Andrews' fundraising was in jeopardy as well.

The signals had been there as early as the primary, when Andrews' media blitz failed to materialize as expected. In truth, the money just wasn't there, not for him or for anybody; the economy had gotten that bad. And now, with the Houston business community split—Faubion did have a few heavy hitters in his camp, notably homebuilder Bob Perry—many of the big PACs had little choice but to stay on the side-

lines. "The Andrews-Faubion race caused me a lot of grief," says Jack Webb, executive director of HOUPAC, Houston's leading business PAC. "We had a bunch of people on both sides leaning on us, saying, 'You give this boy some money.' We had to say no to some people you don't like to say no to." The grief was merely temporary, however. "The PACs really couldn't lose on this one," says Webb.

In 1980 Mike Andrews had spent $608,000 running against Gammage, Pentony, and Paul. Paul had spent $640,000. Now, in the late summer of 1982, Andrews confided that he might have no more than $120,000 with which to wage his fall campaign. Faubion by mid-October had received nearly $57,000 from the NRCC, the RNC, and other Republican and conservative groups. But other than those infusions and a limited amount from business PACs, the Republican wasn't faring much better than the Democrat and was, in fact, digging deeply into his own pockets.

A dearth of money wasn't the only way 1982 was different from 1980. Running against Paul, Andrews had been the underdog, always on the attack. Now he was the certified front-runner, the target for a candidate who had demonstrated a relish for hardball. Since any misstatement or seeming contradiction was sure to be seized on as proof of insincerity, it was best for him to say as little as possible. Short of money, knowing that the attack would come but not knowing precisely what it would be, Andrews was forced to play defense—being careful, of course, not to appear defensive. George Strong, whose strengths are media and strategy, stepped out of the manager's role; Vic Driscoll, a steady, methodical organizer, stepped in. The campaign brochure was scaled down to four pages. Plans for TV were put on hold. Even some of his own supporters began to wonder aloud why Mike Andrews wasn't waging a more aggressive campaign.

Worrying

Faubion wasn't likely to win the race, but Andrews could still lose it. So far he'd escaped from blunders like the Leland– "We think alike" ad remarkably unscathed. But if Faubion could scrape up enough money to get on TV and could play effectively on the class issue Harrison had exploited, and if Andrews ran out of money and made any major errors, the complexion of the campaign could change in a hurry. Most of all, said Kevin Burnette, "I just don't want to wake up on November third knowing there was something I could have done that I didn't do." So as their campaigns went public again in September, both candidates were running hard and, to some degree, running scared.

Nine months of campaigning had battered all traces of callowness out of Mike Faubion. As he sat in his rather shabby storefront offices near the Medical Center in early October, smoking and letting his mind play over the shape of the campaign, he still exuded the impatience of the true believer but no longer the impatience of youth. Weariness had burnished the edges of his personality into even more prominence. Let others say his cause was hopeless; with satisfaction he examined the bulwark of stratagems that insulated him from their nonbelief.

He had gone to an NRCC candidate school in Washington. He had run TV—in August, no less, long before the herd of candidates had come bawling into Texans' living rooms. The NRCC had paid $18,000 for seventeen airings of a commercial, filmed in a machine shop, in which a man told voters that Mike Andrews was a slick opportunist and Mike Faubion was a straight guy. He had gone to Israel, demonstrating to the Jews in the district that not only Democrats cared; that might even win him the endorsement of the *Jewish Herald Voice*. His staff had divided the precincts in the district into four categories—Jack Fields' old precincts, Republican precincts, Pasadena, and Democratic precincts—and targeted the first three for as many as six pieces of direct mail. His phone banks were busy every night, and they showed that far from trailing Andrews, he held the lead. True, the phoners were using what are known as advocacy calls, making a direct pitch ("Mike Faubion has been endorsed by Ron Paul and Jack Fields, while his opponent is supported by Mickey Leland Can I tell Mike Faubion that he can count on your support on November second?") rather than simply asking whom the citizen planned to vote for. But how misleading could the results be?

Andrews didn't know about Faubion's phone results, and he believed he was still ahead; but he never relaxed. In early October, taping a local Issues and Answers program with Faubion, he worried about what to say in his opening remarks. He fidgeted on camera as Faubion accused him of fuzziness. (Vic Driscoll, watching on a monitor and buoyed perhaps by the sight of his candidate on TV, was characteristically calm. "Look at Faubion sneer," he said. "He thinks he's really put Mike in a box.") Later, taping his first radio commercial, a nice soft spot about social security that stressed his compassion, the candidate fretted that his delivery wasn't exactly right. Driscoll liked take seven. "Let me do it again," Andrews insisted. Take twelve sounded fine. "No, let's do another one." And another, and another, up to take twenty—which really was better than the rest.

By mid-October the Faubion onslaught was in full swing. There were ads in the *Pasadena Citizen* denouncing Andrews' supposed inconsistencies (which in private Kevin Burnette cheerfully admitted were negligible) and branding him a big-spending liberal. For Republicans, there was a pro-Faubion letter from George

Bush and a mailer that proclaimed, "The race between Mike Andrews and Mike Faubion . . . is really a fight between Tip O'Neill and Ronald Reagan." In Jack Fields' old precincts the mailer stressed Fields' endorsement of Faubion. Pasadena got a special version of a crime piece that went elsewhere and two pieces that exploited the issues of class and race that Harrison had harped on, contrasting Faubion's working-class roots with Andrews' posh address and country-club membership and resurrecting the Mickey Leland endorsement. "I'm more like you," Mike Faubion assured the voters of Pasadena. And he was right.

Faubion's strategy had been laid out for months, but now a new urgency fed his attacks. At the suggestion of the RNC and NRCC, Kevin Burnette had stopped making advocacy calls and begun actually polling. The numbers looked far, far worse. He had known Faubion wasn't really ahead, but the new numbers showed him barely holding his own even in some of the Republican precincts. And Pasadena, so vital to their plans, was a huge, worrisome cipher—almost 50 per cent undecided.

Andrews' phone bank had been making advocacy calls, too, but it was run by a company whose founder, Mary Ellen Miller, had *invented* phone banks—under the auspices of the RNC, no less. While Faubion's staff laboriously tabulated each night's results by hand, Andrews' numbers were fed to a computer in New Orleans. Miller had also developed complex methods for estimating how many of the respondents were telling the truth (rather than saying yes or no to get the pollster off the phone) and which way the undecideds would break and who would actually vote. So Andrews knew he was holding his own. But still he worried: when would Faubion's real attack come and what would it be? Andrews favored delaying the next round of tax cuts; would Faubion hit that? Andrews had defended one of the Houston policemen accused of drowning a Mexican American prisoner in the mid-seventies; would that be it? Thus far he had not reacted to Faubion's needling, and that had been the smart course. But sometimes, when the accusations got serious enough, you had to strike back, if only to make your own people feel better.

Kevin Burnette worried too. Faubion had mail hitting throughout the district; Faubion was all over the radio dial with spots denouncing Andrews as a country-club swell and spots featuring Eddie "I'm Mad" Chiles, spots introduced by Reagan and spots saying Andrews was going to take away the people's tax cuts. And the numbers just weren't moving.

Burnette perked up momentarily when he went to the printer on October 25, just eight days out, to inspect the final round of mail pieces—he was particularly proud of the ones aimed at Mexican Americans and blacks, which began with the ques-

tions "Are you about to vote for the man who defended the killer of José Campos Torres?" and "Will Mike Andrews protect your civil rights in Congress?" But back at headquarters, as the evening wore on, he grew quieter and quieter. Finally he sat, his elbows on his knees, staring at the floor. "I just don't know how to beat this guy," he said at last. "We've done *every-thing*. I don't know what's happening, but the Pasadena precincts tell me it's not moving as it should." He nodded to the next room, where Tamara Faubion's mother and father were stuffing envelopes. "Look at those people in there. They got into this because I told them they could win."

The Last Minute

On Tuesday, one week before election day, Faubion gathered the press on the steps of Andrews' Pasadena headquarters and challenged the Democrat to produce a written endorsement from John Ray Harrison. Thus far, Harrison's conspicuous absence from the race had been only a minor irritation to Andrews; Faubion was trying to make it a substantial embarrassment. The judge had told Faubion's people, or they thought he had, that he would not restate the cursory endorsement he had given Andrews after the runoff.

The following afternoon, Wednesday, Faubion greeted a throng of steelworkers as the shifts changed at ARMCO's huge Pasadena plant. These were the very people who Lance Tarrance and the RNC had been assuring the world could be won over to the Republican party, but across the street, the sign on the union hall marquee read: "Remember Reaganomics—Vote Democratic." Most of the workers were friendly as Faubion grabbed their hands—unless, that is, they thought to ask which party he represented. "Go to hell," they told him then, or "Who's your opponent? He's my man," or "I made that mistake the last time around," or "Ugh, now I have to go wash my hand."

On his way out Faubion made a call back to headquarters. All was not well. "What's happened?" he asked. "*He did?*" That morning, at a press conference in Pasadena, John Ray Harrison had endorsed Mike Andrews. The challenge to Andrews had blown up in Faubion's face. The candidate began to laugh thinly as he headed for his car. Twenty minutes later he and his aides were closeted in an office with Republican state representative Randy Pennington, who had been acting as an unofficial advisor to the campaign. Faubion looked on morosely as his fundraiser, Lee Woods, called an acquaintance at the *Chronicle* to find out how the news of the endorsement would be handled. Then Pennington called Bob Perry, who had supported Harrison before becoming Faubion's chief financial backer, and asked him to call the judge. Tell Harrison to phone the *Pasadena Citizen*, Pennington urged Perry. Tell him to say nice things about Faubion and ask that the endorsement be downplayed.

If Harrison did make the call to the paper, it didn't work. The *Citizen* put the story exactly where it had put the news of Faubion's challenge, right in the middle of the front page. So the next day, Thursday, began well for Mike Andrews. He breezed into Bill Wright's office in the mood to raise a lot of money. They reviewed the list of people who had promised to contribute but had not yet sent checks. Then they went to work on the phones, sounding for all the world like two backslapping good ol' boys expertly working a crowd.

"Hi, podner! How you been?" Wright bellowed good-naturedly at one of the laggards. "Mike Andrews needs money."

"That's right," Andrews confirmed on his extension. "I'm at Wright's office. Bring sacks of money."

Wright chuckled. "One check will do—one with three zeroes on it."

Back at Andrews' headquarters the morning quickly went sour. The candidate sat down heavily and stared at the mailer on his desk. "Are you about to vote for the man who defended the killer of José Campos Torres?" it demanded. He read it slowly, carefully, then wearily turned it over and studied each page again. "I don't think it will hurt," he said softly. "I'll kill him in the black community. I'll get 95 per cent. If he were smart he'd run black radio too." He paused, then began to examine the piece again. "I just don't know how to judge. I'm so tired."

Thursday afternoon, while Andrews' staff wrestled with what to do about the Torres mail, Mike Faubion went into the studio to cut a spot for black radio. Fundraiser Lee Woods had nixed the idea for lack of money earlier, but after the Harrison endorsement fiasco he had relented. Faubion's script pulled no punches. Mike Andrews "is a fake and a hypocrite," he intoned with relish.

"We'll outkick Andrews," Kevin Burnette gloated. "We've got Eddie Chiles doing some really rabid antiliberal spots against Andrews to run in Pasadena. And rednecks don't mind negative campaigning, I don't care what you say."

That same evening, Mike Andrews' steering committee met to review election-day strategy and receive Richard Murray's projections. The candidate looked utterly tired but utterly determined. He and a black staffer had just made a radio spot to rebut the Torres mail. The discussion turned to whether 75 phones were absolutely necessary on election day; the campaign could save $2400 by having only 40. Andrews was adamant: there would be 75 phones.

Murray saw no way Andrews could lose. "Faubion's attacks have no predicate," he assured the group. "He needed at least three weeks of TV to establish his name ID. People are saying, 'Who is this Faubion guy?' What he's doing would have been great in eighty, but he's two years too late."

Black Sunday

Now, with only four days left, the campaigns hit an odd sort of dead space. The die was cast—the mail was out, the radio spots were running, the debates and speeches were over. There wasn't much to do but phone and walk and try to stay upright. On Halloween morning, with two days to go, Andrews and his wife did what he had often done during the past several months: they made the rounds of black churches in the district. At the Brentwood Baptist Church the candidate sat very still as the words of the sermon rolled over him in great sonorous waves: "Every problem is an opportunity. The walls *will* come down. The rivers *will* divide. The giant *will* fall."

They visited three other churches, and at each one he was permitted to address the congregation. At the Mount Hebron Baptist Church, moved by the soaring harmonies of the gospel choir, he gave perhaps the best speech of his campaign, rocking toward his audience with every phrase.

"I'm a Democrat," he told them. "I'm proud to be a Democrat. The Republicans will tell you things are about as good as they are going to get. I don't believe that." He told them then how he had been scolded when he was ten years old for drinking from a water fountain marked "Colored." "How far we have come," he said. "How far we have to go." And then he quoted Theodore H. White quoting John Kennedy in 1960, who was quoting from a letter written by Abraham Lincoln. "I know there is a God, and I know He hates injustice. I see the storm coming, and I know His hand is in it. But if He has a place and a part for me, I believe that I am ready." A soft chorus of Amens told him they were with him now, and he closed while he had them. "Tuesday is election day," he said. "I need your vote. *We* need your vote. Go vote. Go. Vote."

The Verdict

Vote they did. In the muggy early morning of November 2 the polls of Southwest Houston hummed, but that was to be expected. The Republican suburbs always vote and vote early. As one drove eastward across the district, however, the surprise began to mount. There were people at the polls in the black precincts, lots of people. Pasadena was turning out too, and an exit poll by the *Pasadena Citizen* showed a remarkable number of straight-ticket Democratic votes. By early afternoon a wall of slate-gray clouds was advancing from the northwest. At Andrews headquarters Chuck King was playing ringmaster, sending out two-person teams to walk precincts and get out the vote. In

the lulls he took calls from staffers at the polls; all reported turnouts running twenty, thirty, fifty bodies ahead of Richard Murray's predictions. At 1:30 the storm broke in the east and the calls changed: it was flooding in La Porte (groans); Clear Lake City was underwater (cheers). Murray called at 2:45 to report that his exit polls showed Andrews with 59 per cent.

By 3:30 it was raining hard all over the district. At Faubion headquarters the word from Southwest Houston was very bad. Burnette had planned to send block walkers out late to catch people after work, but the rain had intervened. Only seven precincts had been walked. Burnette stood staring angrily out a window. He wheeled with a fierce shrug of disgust and spat, "This rain is killing us." But it wasn't the rain, and he knew it. It was the turnout. For as evening fell with the rain, the polls were still crowded. And that, finally, did kill the Republicans, including Mike Faubion.

On Wednesday, the day after, Faubion was stoic, Tamara sweet and dazed. People were already asking him to run again in '84, the candidate said, but it was too early to contemplate that. "We have to rebuild our empire first," Tamara said, thinking perhaps of the nearly $50,000 the campaign owed the candidate—$50,000 he might well never see. Upstairs, Burnette emptied wastebaskets overflowing with soft-drink cans and fast-food wrappers. His man had lost 38 per cent to 60 per cent (the Libertarian and the Citizens party candidate had split the other 2 per cent), but he had no regrets. "I wouldn't do anything differently," he said. "I would only do more." It was really Governor Clements' fault, he said. Reagan had alienated the workingman, and Clements had only made things worse. He'd taken all the money, he'd let his organization run roughshod over lesser candidates, but most of all he'd driven away the white working classes. 'Pasadena was having none of Mike Faubion," Burnette said. "We just couldn't get through."

The Next Step

Basking in the rare glow of a genuine Houston autumn afternoon, Mike Andrews let his mind roam forward. How would he choose a staff, he wondered. Which committee assignments should he seek—Energy and Commerce? Appropriations? Public Works? Where could he best establish himself within the party, yet not be put to too stern a test of loyalty? How would the men who had helped put him in office deal with him now? In short, how did one go about this business of being a congressman?

He of all people had contemplated the potential influence of the position he had won, what it could mean to be not just a congressman from Houston but *the* congressman from Houston. He and his friends hoped that, believed that they were witnessing a great transfer of power in the city, and that they were among the inheritors of that power. The mantle had skipped a generation, they said; now the Bob Parkers and the Bill Wrights and the Vic Driscolls and the Dick Trabulsis would assume it as the Browns and the Mischers let it fall. And Andrews knew without their telling him that they were capable of dreaming far beyond anything they had yet accomplished.

He was still adjusting to the idea of being a congressman and already his tailor was addressing him jokingly as "Mr. President." A few days after the election he visited the office of his former law firm, and as a crowd of young lawyers gathered round to congratulate him, one burst through good-naturedly with, "Okay, when are we going to run for the Senate? When are we going to run for president?" The congressman-elect laughed along with everyone else, but he shied away from the questioner. It would be political suicide, and he knows it, to entertain such speculation openly. Let those around him entertain it if they must—after all, it was the aura of possibility that hung so richly over his campaign that was his true achievement. And if in the dead of night the demon ambition comes to whisper in his ear, "What if? What if?" and sometimes he allows himself to listen, who can blame him? For this is the last, sweet, hidden secret of politics: that sometimes, most times, the triumph of hope over experience is an illusion . . . but not always. ❧

A MONUMENTAL MAN

by Paul Burka

Robert Caro's evocative biography of Lyndon Johnson hits the mark on a forgotten Texas but misses the real LBJ.

Lyndon Johnson did not make life easy for his biographers. He laid false trails and destroyed true ones—even going to the extreme of arranging the removal of unflattering pages from college yearbooks—and surrounded himself with people so loyal that to this day they will not talk to interviewers without the blessing of his widow. Most of all, though, Johnson has defied definition simply by overpowering researchers with a presence that, in the words of his latest chronicler, Robert Caro, "seemed at times to brood, big-eared, big-nosed, huge, over the entire American political landscape." The shelves are full of Johnson biographies—everything from J. Evetts Haley's polemical *A Texan Looks at Lyndon* to the recent efforts by Merle Miller, George Reedy, and Ronnie Dugger—but not until Caro's long-awaited first of three volumes, *The Years of Lyndon Johnson: The Path to Power*, does Texas' first president come alive on the page and the mystery of what made him both a mighty force and a controversial symbol through four decades of American politics begin to be solved.

Ordinarily that would be high praise. But *The Path to Power* was meant to be more. Seven years in the making, the work of a Pulitzer prize–winning biographer, 882 pages long, exhaustively researched, excerpted at length in the *Atlantic* to nationwide publicity, this book was conceived by its author as the definitive work on Lyndon Johnson, the book that would not just begin to solve the mysteries but would solve all of them for all time. In that it falls short, and not by a little. Robert Caro has produced a great *book*—full of unforgettable scenes, tense drama, piquant details, and original history—but in the end it must be judged as *biography*, and as biography it rates no more than fair. Nobody tells a story better than Caro, but biography is more than storytelling; it is also analysis. And Caro's analysis suffers from two serious infirmities. One is a deep-seated hostility toward the complicated world of Texas politics that bred Lyndon Johnson, whom Caro regards as the instrument of "the robber barons of this century [who] have drained the earth of the Southwest of its riches and have used those riches to bend government to their ends." The other problem is Caro's excessive reliance upon the theme laid out in the opening scene of the introduction.

It is, admittedly, a wonderful scene. Told to Caro by Brown & Root's George Brown, who was there, it has then-congressman Johnson, poor but desperate not to be, turning down a proffered share in some oil wells because, he says, it would kill him politically. For what office, Brown wonders to himself, would having oil properties kill a Texas politician? And then he realizes there is only one: the presidency. Time after time Caro returns to the major and minor premises of the anecdote: (1) Johnson always knew he wanted to be president, and (2) everything he did was designed to propel him toward that one goal. Consequently Caro's Johnson is a man "unencumbered by philosophy or ideology," a man hungry "for power in its most naked form, for power not to improve the lives of others, but to manipulate and dominate them," a man so determined to realize his ambition that "no consideration of morality or ethics, no cost to himself—or anyone else—could stand before it."

Not even Robert Caro's immense writing skills can restrain Lyndon Johnson within this narrow framework. Time after time Johnson surfaces—almost despite Caro rather than because of him—as a more complex and even more decent person than the words themselves admit. In the end Caro is ensnared in his own superstructure: too often he stretches his proof or warps his analysis in order to pull Johnson back inside the confines of that one anecdote. Even as Caro dwells on the dark side of Lyndon Johnson—his blatant defiance of his father as a boy, his manipulation of campus politics in college, his shameless flattering of those over him and his equally shameless exploitation of those under him, to name a few—the feeling grows that there is more to this man than Caro is letting on.

The Johnson of *The Path to Power* is rarely likable, frequently malevolent, occasionally sympathetic, but always competent, astonishingly competent. We see him at seventeen, studying law in California under the tutelage of a cousin, somehow managing to keep the office functioning while his mentor is away on a two-month drinking spree—a runaway who had never been outside the Hill Country nonetheless able to advise clients to their satisfaction. We see him teaching at a Mexican school in Cotulla, and he is the best teacher that ever taught there. We see him coaching high school debate in Houston, and he is the best debate coach that Texas has ever seen. We see him as a congressional aide, so skilled at obtaining patronage that his boss—a representative lacking influence, seniority, or much interest in his work—ends up dispensing more New Deal jobs than any other congressman; he was the best there, too. We see him at 25, still a lowly aide, beating the vice president of the United States in a skirmish over patronage. We see him as a New Deal administrator, the state director of the best National Youth Administration program in the country. We see him as the most successful political fundraiser since Mark Hanna half a century before. And we see him as a congressman—as Caro writes, quoting veteran New Deal political operative Tommy Corcoran, "the best congressman for a district there ever was."

Caro is the first biographer to make clear just how able the young Lyndon Johnson really was, even if his acknowledgment remains unspoken at times and grudging at others. But the reader is left to wonder how this Lyndon Johnson jibes with the Johnson of the book's central thesis. Was it ambition alone that made him the first debate coach to tour the state in search of opponents? Was it ambition alone that made him go from town to town buttonholing farmers, trying to convince them that they must somehow find the $5 necessary for an electrical hookup? The Johnson of those stories has a passion and a commitment that belie Caro's main argument.

When the first part of the book, the Texas part, isn't trying to hammer home the lessons of the opening anecdote, Robert Caro is at his best. Using obscure but firsthand sources (he even found the man who cut Johnson's hair in San Marcos) and little details that give the presentation the ring of authority (he describes the way Johnson ducked into doorways to comb his hair whenever an influential person approached—and the color of the comb), Caro has, in the best sense of the phrase, rewritten history. The Lyndon Johnson of earlier books, who admired his Populist father, who followed his mother's teachings, who was a popular campus figure in San Marcos, is altogether different in *The Path to Power*. Because Caro will probably be the last biographer to interview Johnson's now-aging contemporaries, his view will be the

one that survives. And that view is not only of Johnson but also of the other main character in the book, Texas itself—the Texas of the teens and twenties and thirties. This is the rural Texas of Pa Ferguson and kneepads for picking cotton and wood stoves that had to be fed all day, even in the searing summer heat; the Texas that was an economic and psychological colony of the Northeast; the Texas before electricity, the Texas before oil.

Read Caro's chapter on Southwest Texas State Teachers College and you will understand the depth of feeling in rural Texas even today about education as a political issue, and why Texas is still at the bottom nationally for college tuition. Caro takes us back to enrollment day, 1927, when students from nonaccredited high schools came to San Marcos to beg admission, knowing as Lyndon Johnson knew that this was their one chance to escape a life of physical toil. Read the chapter on Lyndon Johnson's first campaign and you will understand something of the mystique of highways in Texas, for Caro writes of the terrible isolation of the Hill Country when Johnson searched out voters farm by farm, turning off the main highway onto roads that were unpaved and ungraded and then cutting off onto other roads that were mere paths into the hills, looking for someone to take his message to.

All of these influences helped shape Lyndon Johnson, but by far the greatest was the Hill Country itself, the land that during his presidency would become known for its idyllic beauty. But the reality of the Hill Country for young Lyndon was altogether different, for Caro shows how it broke not only the finances but also the spirits of men, including Johnson's father. "The fire in which he had been shaped—that terrible youth in the Hill Country" forged Johnson for all time: the iron will, the driving energy and ambition of a man "fleeing from something dreadful," the need to dominate others and bend them to his will.

Unfortunately, the book does not consistently reach the same heights in dealing with Johnson's life as an elected politician. There are still wonderful passages, even wonderful chapters—most notably, the haunting story of bringing electricity to the Hill Country. But while Caro has learned some aspects of Texas very well —its land, its people—he has been less adept at learning its politics. The second half of the book, the political part, is most successful when it is *not* about Lyndon Johnson.

Caro is particularly unconvincing in making three charges against Johnson stick: that he was a poor congressman, that he was treacherous to his friends, and that he lacked any political philosophy. The chapter evaluating Johnson's performance as a congressman uses standards straight out of a high school civics text—"a legis-

lator is a maker of laws"—leading Caro to condemn Johnson for not introducing more bills of national significance and, believe it or not, for failing to insert remarks into the *Congressional Record*. Caro compares Johnson unfavorably to Maury Maverick, his San Antonio colleague and friend, who headed a group of young congressmen that met every week to discuss strategy "for confounding the House's conservative leadership."

But there are other ways to play the game. As a freshman Lyndon Johnson gained entrée to an after-hours drinking group composed of then-majority leader Sam Rayburn and Rayburn's peers in power. Which was more important—to meet with Maverick's dissidents or with the power structure no freshman had ever been so close to? As a result of his relationship with Rayburn, Johnson was also invaluable to young New Dealers in the White House, among whom he had a reputation as "a great counter" in predicting votes. Which was more important— to introduce bills or to help the president's bills pass? Because of his contacts, he succeeded in getting for his district a dam that was in desperate political and legal trouble and, subsequently, rural electrification aid for which the district was not technically eligible. Which was more important—to have speeches in the *Congressional Record* or to be "the best congressman for a district there ever was"?

Caro, of course, attributes Johnson's unwillingness to be a highly visible, ideologically committed congressman to his ever-present ambition. ("The House seat was only a staging area; it was not the destination at the end of that road. . . . No matter how safe a particular stand might seem now, no matter how politically wise, that stand might come back to haunt him someday.") But there is another, simpler explanation. The kind of congressman Robert Caro admires would have been an outsider with no access to the leadership, no intimacy with Rayburn, no alliance with the White House, no dam, no electricity, and no political future—not just for the presidency or a Senate race but even in the House. Sure, Lyndon Johnson was consumed with ambition. But ambition was not the only fuel that powered the engine. He was an insider not only because of ambition but also because he understood the game. To write of Johnson that "colleagues committed to causes began to regard him with something akin to scorn" is to miss the essence of Lyndon Johnson, which is that he returned the favor.

The book's view of Johnson as a backstabber lies behind one of its most sensational—and dubious—chapters. Caro tries to show that the young congressman turned on Rayburn, his political godfather, in order to advance himself politically. Although Caro's mini-biography of Rayburn earlier in the book is a masterpiece, this account of the 1940 presidential campaign—when Rayburn found himself obligated to his old Texas friend, Vice President Jack Garner, who was challenging Roosevelt's renomination—fails to deliver the goods. Caro charges that Johnson, acting through allies running the Roosevelt campaign in Texas, exploited Rayburn's dilemma by trying to discredit him in Roosevelt's eyes; the object, Caro says, was for Johnson to emerge as the president's man in Texas, especially in the awarding of federal defense contracts.

As Caro concedes, however, Rayburn was never interested in political spoils like contracts or patronage and thus was not a rival for the role Johnson coveted. Nor does Caro demonstrate that Johnson's Texas allies were acting at his direction and for his benefit. In fact, they were powerful and ambitious men with an agenda of their own in a fight that was for high stakes quite apart from Lyndon Johnson's future—their own influence and control over the state Democratic party for years to come. The whole notion of a plot against Rayburn is based on Caro's interpretation of telegrams sent by Johnson's allies—subtle inferences that would be worthy of a State Department diplomat poring over the latest communiqué from the Kremlin. But Caro only sees the absence of a smoking gun as further evidence of Johnson's deep cunning. The entire chapter is the work of an author reasoning backward from his own thesis: everything Johnson did was designed to advance himself toward the presidency; therefore, if he advanced, he must have planned it that way.

Finally, and most seriously, Caro fails to shed light on what is the central question about this most elusive public figure of our time: did Johnson really believe in anything other than expediency? Caro's answer, of course, is an unequivocal no. Johnson's ambition, he writes, was "unencumbered by even the slightest excess weight of ideology, of philosophy, of principles, of beliefs."

But the rhetoric outweighs the proof. Amazingly, considering the magnitude of Caro's research, he cites only one vote in the entire book: Johnson's aye in 1943 to continue funding for the House Un-American Activities Committee. That, Caro says, was a sign that Johnson's abandonment of New Deal principles and programs had begun, and his onetime liberal allies recognized it as such. Maybe they did, but the vote shouldn't have come as any surprise—Johnson had voted the same way in 1940 and 1941, while he was running for the Senate as a New Dealer. But you won't find those votes in the book. Nor will you find a mention of Johnson's crucial vote in 1938 for the first minimum wage bill, which was highly unpopular in Texas. Anything that doesn't support Caro's thesis is omitted.

Caro never explores the vast middle ground between believing in nothing and being a committed ideologue; just as with Johnson's personality, he sacrifices nuance for dramatic effect. To Caro it is "symbolic proof" of Johnson's lack of principle that in one summer he could work simultaneously as a congressional aide to Richard Kleberg, one of the most conservative members of Congress, and as campaign adviser to liberal Maury Maverick. To seasoned politicians, this is symbolic proof only that Caro doesn't understand politics. Alliances like that one occur all the time, especially when the principals, like Kleberg and Maverick, are friends. The game transcends ideology.

The Path to Power never does. If only Robert Caro had been able to overcome his good-guys-and-bad-guys view of politics, he could have seen that Lyndon Johnson, while certainly not an ideologue, nevertheless was of a piece, a logically consistent political figure. But Caro can't forgive him for taking money from oilmen and Brown & Root, "the robber barons of the Southwest"; he can't forgive him for allowing the big economic interests to be a part of his political universe instead of fighting them the way his father and Sam Rayburn once did.

Had Caro understood the politics of Texas as well as he understood its history, he would have seen that Johnson's relationship with those interests provided the clue to his philosophy. Lyndon Johnson was a New Deal liberal only in the sense that he believed in a strong central government that helped people. He never shared the liberalism of those New Dealers who viewed politics as an extension of a class struggle: he was not for labor against capital or for a wholesale redistribution of income for its own sake. Those threads were consistent throughout his entire life. Lyndon Johnson can only be understood as a *Texas* politician; while his ambitions were national, his philosophy was thoroughly Texan. He was the only politician to survive the transition of Texas from a rural to an urban state; he survived it because he saw it coming—and welcomed it. Johnson came to power in an era when Texas was still a province. He was friendly with Dr. Bob Montgomery, the UT economics professor who hated the big Northeast corporations and told everyone who would listen that Texas was the largest colony owned by Manhattan. Another Johnson mentor, Austin power broker Alvin Wirtz, shared the same viewpoint; he regarded the 1940 fight for Roosevelt against Garner as a war against the Wall Street bankers. Johnson likewise regarded the Northeast as the enemy, whether it was Wall Street or the Kennedy liberals; and it follows that the big Texas interests, insofar as they were countervailing forces, were in Johnson's cosmology on the side of the angels. To Lyndon Johnson, the "robber barons of the Southwest" were not robber barons at all; they were liberators of colonial Texas.➔

THE TEN BEST AND THE TEN WORST LEGISLATORS

It began with the Capitol almost burning down. It ended with Governor Mark White burning up over teacher salaries. But in between, the 68th Legislature was anything but fiery.

The predominant emotion during the 1983 session was anxiety—something new to Texas politics. In recent years the Legislature has had lots of money to spend, low turnover, and little pressure from the public. Suddenly the rules changed. The good old days of multibillion-dollar surpluses were replaced by a budget crunch. Almost a third of the House and Senate was new, the most radical turnover since Sharpstown. And as is always the case when times are hard, people wanted government to *do* something.

The budget crunch seemed to take the fun out of the Legislature; there wasn't even any room to logroll. The session plodded along dispiritedly. Mark White couldn't decide whether he wanted a tax increase. Then he couldn't decide what kind of increase he wanted if he wanted one. Early on, the Senate bogged down in a battle over Bill Clements' holdover appointments and couldn't get unstuck; the House bogged down while Speaker Gib Lewis tried to undo the damage of his failure to disclose his financial holdings. Nothing happened. Then, when the big issues—trucking deregulation, utility reform, interest rates—finally reached the floor, they all fizzled out into deals with no clear winner. April turned into May and the governor still hadn't phoned in from Mars to say what he wanted. Horse racing died. The son of son of son of water package died. Teacher salaries died. The tax bill was murdered.

A bad session? Not at all. In fact, while the headline-grabbing issues were running into trouble, the budget crunch was having a completely unforeseeable effect on the session: it was turning out to be a blessing in disguise. After a decade on the crest of the oil boom, the state bureaucracy was cushioned in blubber. The budget crunch forced the Legislature to hunt for all the fat that had accumulated over the years. It found plenty—especially in higher education, which underwent its first close inspection since the huge expansion of the sixties and early seventies.

Almost all the Legislature's accom-

plishments can be traced back to the money crunch. Without it, prison reform would have been impossible; the state would have gone on building maximum-security prisons ad infinitum. The crunch eased the way for PUC reform and lower interest rates too.

It was, in sum, a pretty good record. To make it better, this was one of those rare sessions when the good was not canceled out by the bad. The Legislature passed only one bill that should shame the collective conscience: the one that made it next to impossible for cities to get rid of existing billboards—and Mark White saved the day by vetoing it. In fact, the only group that didn't fare well this session was teachers, who didn't get their 24 per cent pay raise.

That defeat did not augur well for White, who had made education and teacher pay his number one priority. But then, little did. By remaining aloof from the tough negotiating sessions on PUC reform in the House and Senate, he blew his chance to earn legislators' respect, choosing instead to stick with the one issue, an elected commission, that he couldn't and shouldn't have won. His tax bill follies were pathetic, as he successively embraced and dismissed highway bonds, gasoline taxes, severance taxes, and sin taxes. His treatment of legislators, including stumping against several in their home districts, made Bill Clements look like Emily Post. Without question he was the big loser of the session.

Lieutenant Governor Bill Hobby, suzerain of the Senate, was the big winner. If he were eligible for the Ten Best list, he would be at the top. During his tenure, Hobby has reshaped the Senate in his image, changing it from a brawling House of Commons to a restrained House of Lords. The best senators are Hobby's alter egos on the floor: never provincial, always pragmatic, only interested in sound public policy.

Then there's Gib. His ethics problems were foolish (and illegal; he paid an $800 fine in May), and his limited understanding of substance was deplorable. Yet he was never in any serious danger of a palace coup, even when he was at his nadir. Why not? It was partly because Lewis is not a threat to the House. While his predecessor Billy Clayton was a strong prince with weak

barons, Lewis is a weak prince with strong barons; in this session the committee chairmen had most of the skill and most of the power. But it's also because Lewis did some things right this session. He was right to oppose the tax bill (even if there was a lot of self-interest in that decision); a tax bill would have destroyed the discipline needed to cut the fat out of the budget. And his rule change to choose the members of the appropriations conference committee exclusively from among chairmen of the substantive budget and oversight subcommittees—that is, from experts—was a stroke of genius. It was a built-in brake on logrolling. This year there are more major committee chairmen on our Ten Best list and fewer on our Ten Worst list than ever before; Lewis deserves some credit for that.

Our criteria for Best and Worst rest on personality rather than ideology, because that is how legislators judge their colleagues. They don't want to know whether a member is conservative or liberal; they want to know whether he is smart or dumb, honest or venal, industrious or lazy, open-minded or closed-minded, straightforward or backstabbing. Apart from openly partisan battles like redistricting, an accurate assessment of personality is far more useful to a legislator than the knowledge that someone is a Republican or a Democrat.

A legislator on the Ten Best list uses his good qualities to the fullest. He wants to be at the center of action, and his colleagues want him there. He inspires respect rather than fear. To succeed he must be a student of the process—the rules, the rhythms, the reins of power—and the better student he is, the more he will succeed.

Negative qualities are not enough to land a legislator on the Ten Worst list; it is the aggressive use of such qualities that is fatal. The old adage "Lead, follow, or get out of the way" is peculiarly applicable to the intensity of the brief session. In life the sin may be not trying to lead; in the Legislature it is trying when one is unable.

Of last session's Good Guys, only three repeated: Ray Farabee, Bob McFarland (who moved from the House to the Senate), and Bill Messer. As for the Bad Guys, let us all breathe a collective sigh of relief: eight of them aren't here to kick around anymore. Two returned to try again. Senator John Leedom was still good for a few laughs, but he'd lost his shock value. As for Senator Carlos Truan, he confined his bumbling to issues so minor that he too escaped.

THE TEN BEST

KENT CAPERTON
Democrat, Bryan

Sophomore Caperton came into his own this term as a brilliant forger of coalitions, the archetypal New Senator: the young moderate who can—and will—deal on anything. Hardly the kind of guy you'd peg as an Aggie; small and unprepossessing, with thinning hair and a prominent forehead, he's more brain than brawn. Unlike some of his other bright colleagues, uses his intelligence as a tool rather than a weapon: doesn't put anyone down, doesn't make enemies. Attacked a huge work load with energy, discipline, and organization; full of enthusiasm for the job of being a senator.

Classic Caperton scene: late at night, in some conference room, extracting commitments from factions warring over utilities regulation or gas credit cards or venue legislation—the kind of major, complex issues that can make a senator's reputation. Negotiating endlessly with crack lobbyists on such hotly contested issues is even less fun than being locked in a room full of two-year-olds who haven't had their naps. But Caperton's blend of patience, humor, and toughness invariably carried the day.

Knew how to play good cop–bad cop despite his deceptively mild appearance; seemed to have a sixth sense about where the pressure points were, where each side could and couldn't give. Since 1963 one legislator after another has attempted to revamp Texas' cumbersome venue law, which governs where lawsuits can be tried; not one could get antagonistic trial lawyers and defense counsel into line. Caperton did. With negotiations falling apart, he shrewdly recruited Supreme Court chief justice

Jack Pope, in whose soothing presence both sides turned reasonable and gave up points they held dear.

Not loath to take on the big guys. During negotiations over the credit card processing fee that oil companies charge gas station operators, took on Exxon's world vice president for marketing—and prevailed. Never too full of himself to attend to the small stuff: testified for his compromise gas credit card bill in front of a House committee, something few senators deign to do.

Keeps the pressures at bay by relying on a top-notch staff. As a new member of the important Finance Committee, hired an LBJ School of Public Affairs graduate specifically to follow financial issues. Some fault him for overreliance on aides during PUC negotiations, but as legislative issues grow more complicated, Caperton's efficient use of staff may be the wave of the future.

Senate-watchers occasionally gripe that Caperton has a finger too often to the wind and is too eager to deal rather than fight. They point to the PUC legislation, where, they say, he didn't wrest enough consumer concessions. In fact, he was far better for consumers on the PUC than was Lloyd Doggett, who

FLOP OF THE YEAR
Special Award

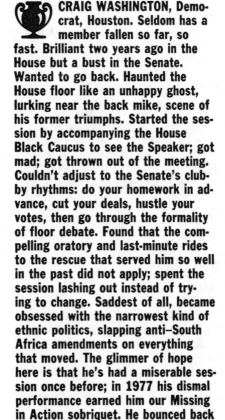

CRAIG WASHINGTON, Democrat, Houston. Seldom has a member fallen so far, so fast. Brilliant two years ago in the House but a bust in the Senate. Wanted to go back. Haunted the House floor like an unhappy ghost, lurking near the back mike, scene of his former triumphs. Started the session by accompanying the House Black Caucus to see the Speaker; got mad; got thrown out of the meeting. Couldn't adjust to the Senate's clubby rhythms: do your homework in advance, cut your deals, hustle your votes, then go through the formality of floor debate. Found that the compelling oratory and last-minute rides to the rescue that served him so well in the past did not apply; spent the session lashing out instead of trying to change. Saddest of all, became obsessed with the narrowest kind of ethnic politics, slapping anti–South Africa amendments on everything that moved. The glimmer of hope here is that he's had a miserable session once before; in 1977 his dismal performance earned him our Missing in Action sobriquet. He bounced back then; Washington rooters hope he can do it again.

bothered to attend precious few of thirty-plus negotiating sessions. And whenever Caperton appeared on the scene, things just worked better. It once seemed almost too much to hope that mossback Bill Moore would be replaced by someone who would undo some of the mischief his district has been responsible for over the years. But it's happening.

BILL COODY
Democrat, Weatherford

What's this? Bill Coody (rhymes with "grody," which before this session accurately described his reputation) on the Ten *Best* list? Did the printer get mixed up? No, and neither did we. True, Coody is a rogue who reeks of old-style politics. But it just so happens that Bill Coody, of all people, did more good for the people of Texas than any other member of the Legislature, and if that doesn't qualify someone for the Ten Best, what does?

Like an old tree that had done nothing for years, Coody finally burst into bloom. The cause of this totally unexpected flowering was his escape from the seedy Liquor Regulation Committee. Switched to the chairmanship of the Financial Institutions Committee and proceeded to astonish colleagues, lobbyists, and perhaps even himself by declaring war on banks. The result: Visa and MasterCard interest rates that will be among the lowest in the country, saving Texans millions of dollars.

Brilliantly irascible, profoundly profane. Called bankers "greedy bastards" and "loan sharks with college degrees and three-piece suits." In a private meeting with three bankers, interrupted their explanation of graphs showing that banks were losing money on credit cards

BEST SINGLE PERFORMANCE
Special Award

CHET BROOKS, Democrat, Pasadena. Singlehandedly pulled Houston out of the recession with his raids on the state treasury during final budget negotiations. Argued with passion and skill for the small (but, thanks to Brooks, increasing) number of urban programs in the appropriations bill. Knew from long years of experience where his forays would be most effective; every time Brooks said, "One more little item, Mr. Chairman," you could pack up another million dollars and ship it to Houston. So why isn't he on the Ten Best list? As usual, he's too close to folks you ought not to be too close to—as when he gutted a bill requiring nursing homes to install sprinklers. Guess what lobby contributed $5650 to Brooks last year?

by turning to a colleague and saying, "They actually think I care about their problems." When the bankers tried to repeat their case for public consumption, Coody broke in with "I could hardly sleep last night thinking you had lost that money."

This is not exactly material for the how-the-legislature-works pamphlets that tour guides hand out to Capitol visitors. But there are rare times when such tactics are exactly what's called for—and this was one of them. The banks, used to getting their way, needed to have it drummed into them that the Legislature wasn't going to roll over and play dead for them this time; Coody's very orneriness made the point better than a more conciliatory approach would have. His antics drew press coverage that put interest rates on the front pages all across Texas and drove the haughty banks to the conference table. The Legislature might have voted for lower interest rates anyway, but not without a bloody floor fight that would have forced members to choose between consumers and an awesomely powerful lobby. Coody spared his colleagues that agony; by the time his bill reached the floor, it was a done deal.

One of the best in floor debate; has the cunning of an old boar that knows every path and hiding place in the thicket. Rooted out one of the sneakiest ploys of the session: after a six-hour debate over trucking deregulation, caught Charlie Evans of Hurst trying to slip a controversial amendment past a weary House. Evans said it was innocuous; Coody knew it wasn't. A master of more moods than a house cat; knows when to be belligerent and when to be shamelessly charming. Adopted the latter tactic to accomplish the near-impossible feat of killing a state agency by stripping it of its budget in floor debate (the victim was an energy advisory council that, said Coody, "couldn't find a quart of oil in an Exxon station")—and used the money to fund a pork-barrel amendment to the appropriations bill. Rather than boring the House with long-winded justifications, Coody simply said, "Members, we don't need this agency, but I need the million bucks." It was outrageous but effective—an epitaph for Coody's entire session.

RAY FARABEE

Democrat, Wichita Falls

The refutation of former U.S. Speaker Thomas Reed's observation that a statesman is a politician who is dead. The most respected member of the Legislature: carries the best bills, runs the most important committee, and has the longest vision, though the competition in this category is limited. Not a technician to equal Bob McFarland or a master compromiser to equal Kent Caperton, but has a higher role—to define, by example, what a

senator is supposed to be.

A case in point: his handling of a bill that, depending on your point of view, either protected struggling offshore oil operations from annexation by greedy coastal cities or protected greedy offshore oil operations from annexation by struggling coastal cities. Senate regulars, whose frequent pastime is the inspection of Farabee's feet for evidence of clay, hinted that he had sold out to Big Oil in furtherance of his suspected ambition to seek statewide office. Some sellout. By the time his bill reached the floor, Farabee had already cast the tie-breaking vote in his State Affairs Committee to keep alive an unrelated bill Big Oil was sworn to kill. Then he agreed to a compromise on the annexation bill despite having the votes to run over the opposition. "If I were in a fight to the death at the Alamo, I wouldn't want Farabee as my second in command," griped one observer. "He'd be out cutting deals with Santa Anna." But the Senate got the message: consensus over confrontation.

Involved in everything, though not always visibly. One of the few senators who will work just as hard for a bill that doesn't bear his name as for one that does. Farabee's own achievements bore the same low-profile but high-import stamp: the first major revision of the mental health code in 25 years, three prison reform bills, and a constitutional amendment to allow garnishment of wages for child support. Once again the Senate got the message: substance over show.

Reached his peak—as usual, without advance fanfare or ensuing glory—in the final negotiations over the state budget. Sat aloof from the usual haggling, hoarding his chips for a raise in Texas' paltry welfare spending (forty-ninth in the nation). Up against tradition, which dictated putting off welfare until the very last—when, not coincidentally, there is never any money left; also up against unsympathetic colleagues eager to claim dwindling dollars for their own purposes. Farabee pounced at exactly the right time in exactly the right way, slipping welfare into a package that incorporated all the loose ends, including the solution to an impasse over state employee raises. This time the whole Legislature got the message.

JAY GIBSON

Democrat, Odessa

The closest thing to a hero the 68th Legislature produced. Did the best job on the most thankless task against the longest odds and the strongest opposition—and not only won but won for the best reasons: he worked hard, he fought clean, and he was right.

As chairman of a budget subcommittee, Gibson tackled the session's Mission Impossible: cut the higher education

budget enough to avoid a tax bill, without doing harm to the state's colleges and universities. Among the obstacles were (1) his immediate superior, House Appropriations czar Bill Presnal of Bryan, whose primary mission in life is to claim in the name of Texas A&M every loose penny in the state treasury; (2) the Senate, which was determined to protect politically potent UT and A&M from the knife at the expense of smaller—and less influential—schools; and (3) the University of Texas, which adamantly refused to accept any cuts and vowed to defy Gibson to the death. It didn't look like a fair fight, especially since in two

---

FURNITURE

Special Award

 The term "furniture" first came into use around the Legislature to describe members who, by virtue of their indifference or ineffectiveness, were indistinguishable from their desks, chairs, and spittoons. It is now used, casually and more generally, to identify the most inconsequential members. Our furniture list for the 68th Legislature:

NEW FURNITURE

> **Billy Clemons, Pollok**
> **Joe Gamez, San Antonio**
> **Noel Grisham, Round Rock**
> **Dudley Harrison, Sanderson**
> **L. B. Kubiak, Rockdale**

USED FURNITURE

> **Erwin Barton, Pasadena**
> **Reby Cary, Fort Worth**
> **Tony Garcia, Pharr**
> **Jim Horn, Lewisville**
> **Kae Patrick, San Antonio**
> **Senfronia Thompson, Houston**

ANTIQUE FURNITURE

> **Charles Finnell, Holliday**
> **Leroy Wieting, Portland**

---

previous terms Gibson, by his own admission, had done little more than have a good time. But the job made the man.

Came up with a novel way of minimizing the pain, telling schools how much to cut and letting them decide for themselves what to sacrifice—a hands-off approach that was anathema to senior budget writers, who have been known to dictate details as small as the color of car paint. Went eyeball to eyeball in conference committee against grizzled Senate veterans who resisted his upstart notions with the ferocity of Pharaoh resisting Moses.

Not understanding his approach, the Senate at first accused him of overspending; he immediately produced a handout proving that his budget spent less than theirs. Then they argued that the two budgets were irreconcilable; he disarmed them with country-boy explanations like "I just said, 'assuming you have to die, where do you want to be shot?' " Never lost his temper or his sense of when to fight and when to yield. Slowly but relentlessly, like grass pushing up through concrete, broke through the Senate's resistance.

With each imperiled small-college program snatched from the Senate guillotine, it became apparent that the smaller schools were getting a fair shake for the first time in years—and that oil-rich UT and A&M would have to shoulder their share of the cuts. A&M surrendered gracefully, but UT began dropping nukes, sending the chairman of the Board of Regents to Odessa to get influential alums to encourage Gibson to see the light. It didn't work. On the climactic day, Gibson and the Senate had a stare-down over his insistence that the UT medical schools ante up millions from their dubiously accumulated discretionary funds, and the Senate blinked. The final package was a total victory for Gibson, including a fledgling desert-study program at Sul Ross State that he had been battling to save since day one; when it was salvaged, the crowded room erupted in cheers.

Within a week Gibson won the budget battle, solved an acrimonious dispute between Odessa and Midland, and received, in the Legislature's closing hours, a humanitarian award from the Black Caucus. On the final night of the session, while revelry was going on all around him, Gibson stood quietly off to one side, tie loosened, subdued and reflective, with the air of someone who had proved himself to himself. A playboy no more, he was a player now.

GERALD HILL
Democrat, Austin

In baseball, when a pitcher's fastball is swifter than it looks, he is called sneaky fast. In the Legislature, when a player is swifter than he looks, he's called Gerald Hill.

A mild-mannered, low-profile kind of guy who speaks softly and carries a small stick—or so it seems. "He's not really a bill passer," said a House committee chairman, but when the House totted up the scorecard, lo, Gerald Hill's name led all the rest. Had more bills set on the regular calendar than any other member; passed legislation taking on political heavies like the Gabler textbook fanatics (Hill's bill gives textbook supporters a chance to answer their critics) and South Texas nabob Clint Manges (Hill limited the size of campaign contributions in judicial races after Manges contributed $340,000 to one supreme court candidate last year).

Sometimes the best measure of a member's effectiveness is what *doesn't* happen. Consider the case of the Local and Consent Calendars Committee, which oversees those all-important local bills that endear reps to the home folks. When Hill was named chairman, there were a few groans because he was in position to pile up bargaining chips for a future Speaker's race. But when the session was over, for the first time in memory the committee had not drawn a single protest.

Plays the legislative game almost as though he wants to be underestimated. A Mr. Nice Guy in committee; as former chairman of Elections, became the rock of his panel without ever upstaging this year's successor. "You can go to him with the dumbest scheme, and he'll tactfully tell you what's wrong with it and how to fix it," says a committee colleague, who didn't find out secondhand. Never attacks, but digs in to defend his own positions with the tenacity of a tick. The only member of the Legislature who said he was for a tax bill and would vote for a tax bill, and then *did* vote for a tax bill even as members of the Ways and Means Committee shrank from Mark White's tax package as from the Green Slime. Refused to give up on a state employee pay raise despite an empty treasury; added a rare floor amendment to the appropriations bill, ensuring state workers a pay hike—and did it with a shrewd parliamentary trick that saved rather than cost money.

Put a stop to the worst power play of the session after discovering that the Speaker's lieutenants, in a rage over Agriculture Commissioner Jim Hightower's intervention in the truck deregulation fight, had vowed to shred his agency's budget. Didn't rail about right and wrong but gave exactly the right advice: you can't win a press release battle with Jim Hightower. The best thing about Gerald Hill is that the House isn't likely to turn into a snake pit as long as he's around.

LEE JACKSON
Republican, Dallas

The case for Lee Jackson was succinctly stated by a colleague on the Ten Best list: "He's so far ahead of the rest of us it's not even a race." Why this kind of tribute for someone who is not quite in the top rank as an orator, a power broker, or a bill passer? Because Jackson is to the Legislature what Greenwich is to time—the standard reference point for what is right. Approaches every issue and every vote by considering not whether it will affect his buddies or his reelection but whether it is good public policy.

Inspires more tributes to fairness than the rose in English verse. When a bill abhorrent to his civilian employer was sent to his Business and Commerce Committee, Jackson had an opportunity to curry favor with the boss by burying the bill in a hostile subcommittee. Instead, he warned company lobbyists that if he got so much as one phone call from corporate executives about the bill, he'd make certain that it passed. Cast the decisive vote in subcommittee to keep alive a controversial bill benefiting service station owners, even though he found it philosophically objectionable, because of what he believed was a larger principle: major bills shouldn't be killed without giving the full committee a chance to express its will. Because of Jackson's clemency, the bill survived to become law, leading a lobbyist to say, "He's so fair that sometimes you'd rather he was on the other side."

One of the most recognizable figures on the House floor: walks with his head sticking forward, in a pose reminiscent of a figurehead on the prow of a ship. One of the most active figures as well. A ringleader in the floor fight against a spendthrift college-construction plan; then followed through in a House-Senate conference committee by insisting on, and getting, strict controls on bonding authority. Opposed a dumb bill creating native-Texan license plates by appealing to the members' sense of dignity. Rising to the compliment, the House discovered same and killed the bill.

His own legislative program, like his demeanor in debate, is clean and scrubbed: a strong ethics bill (most of which was incorporated in the law that finally passed) and a variety of good-government ideas (most of which, sad to say, died in the Senate after Jackson had shepherded them through the House).

Jackson is not and will never be a member of the House inner circle. It is not a place for the urban or the urbane. But even his exclusion by the good ol' boys is a sign of respect, an acknowledgment that he has the same shortcoming that Disraeli observed in Gladstone: "He has not a single redeeming defect."

RAY KELLER
Republican, Duncanville

The right man in the right place at the right time. Untied the Gordian knot of prison reform, but unlike Alexander of Macedon, did it with common sense rather than the sword.

Could have pouted away the session on the back benches after getting stiffed by Speaker Lewis in committee assignments (though made a chairman, Keller received neither the committee he asked for nor the seat on the power-brokering Calendars Committee he was promised as a consolation prize); instead, used his minor committee to play a major role. As Law Enforcement chairman, refused to follow the traditional legislative script: give prison officials all the money they want and tell the folks back home that you're for law and order. When a rock-ribbed, tough-on-crime conservative like Keller decided that the business-as-usual approach cost far too much money and showed far too little success, he made prison reform respectable.

Jaws hit the floor the day Keller began talking in committee about a no-growth policy, sounding like an environmentalist who'd wandered into the wrong meeting by mistake. Not only would there

be no new prisons but he also wanted to take $200 million from the prison system and spend it on halfway houses and better parole supervision. In the beginning even his own committee was against him. In the end—after Keller shrewdly arranged for the poor fellow burdened with defending the state prison system in federal court to show up during budget deliberations—heresy became doctrine. The House passed the entire reform package without a single hostile question in floor debate and without a dissenting vote on six of the seven prison reform bills.

A team player in the best sense of the term. When other lieutenants were besieging the Speaker with self-serving advice that plunged Lewis into hot water with the Senate, Keller established himself as a loyal voice of reason. In the heated battle over trucking deregulation, when most team insiders were all for running over the pro-deregulation forces, Keller made sure that Lewis didn't give his imprimatur to a phony compromise. Used teamwork on his own program as well. Drew on colleagues for his ideas on prisons (Jim Rudd of Brownfield), but he was no mere coach getting the credit for his players' touchdowns. Says a fellow member of the Ten Best list: "Only Ray Keller could have made it happen."

BOB McFARLAND
Republican, Arlington

Got a problem with a bill? Call McFarland, the Senate's handyman who can fix anything. The opposite of a cockroach—the legislative term for someone like Al Edwards, who falls into things and messes them up. Messy things fall into McFarland's hands and he cleans them up.

Rode to more rescues than the U.S. Cavalry. Speaking of which, the horse-racing bill would have been stillborn but for McFarland. Looking for a way he could support it, came up with an amendment calling for a statewide referendum that pried it loose from a Senate committee. Helped save the antitrust bill proposed by attorney general Jim Mat-

tox after proponents had written him off as a negative vote; they paid him a courtesy call that turned into a six-hour line-by-line marathon through a 65-page bill. When McFarland finished, the bill was palatable to conservatives, and Mattox, the most partisan Democrat this side of Tip O'Neill, was tossing bouquets to a Republican.

Also restored to working order the ethics reform package after state Democratic chairman Bob Slagle claimed that outlawing the conversion of campaign contributions to personal use discriminated against impoverished minority legislators. Some Republicans were all for letting this embarrassing defense of sleaze get the blame for killing the bill; McFarland rejected partisanship in favor of patching up. His remedy: an advisory commission to determine when conversion is okay. Slagle agreed and promptly joined the swelling ranks of Democrats moaning because McFarland is a Republican.

Everybody wanted McFarland on his dance card. In the closing days of the session, served on a Guinness-record fifteen conference committees to settle differences between House and Senate bills. Passed major bills on prison reform, the state's debt-ridden unemployment fund, nepotism, and the re-creation of state agencies under the Sunset process; also found time to negotiate agreements on interest rates and venue reform. Came close to pulling off the coup of the session, proposing a compromise to the notorious billboard bill that would have made it cheaper for cities to get rid of the signs, but changed only nine votes when he needed ten.

As upright in posture as in principle. Stands, chin pointing heavenward, as though he were posing for an old daguerreotype. Traces his ideological independence to his work as an FBI agent in the South during the racial unrest of the sixties, when he helped track Martin Luther King's assassin; prides himself on not having knee-jerk reactions to social legislation. The most noteworthy aspect of McFarland's performance, however, is that it took place during his first session in the Senate, where freshmen are supposed to learn rather than teach. With a little experience, he may amount to something.

BILL MESSER
Democrat, Belton

Everybody puts him on their Ten Best list—except, that is, those who put him on their Ten Worst list. The case for Messer as Best: he manipulates the levers of power in the House better than anyone since Ben Barnes. The case for Messer as Worst: he manipulates the levers of power in the House better than anyone since Ben Barnes.

Confused? So is everybody else. Messer is the most dominant, formid-

BEST ONE-LINER
Special Award

🏆 Shortly before the House voted on horse racing, Joe Gamez of San Antonio approached HUGO BERLANGA of Corpus Christi, the sponsor of the bill. Said Berlanga to Gamez, who earlier in the session had been arrested for DWI and at the same time was found to have been driving for years without a license: "Don't flake on me, Gamez. It may be your only means of transportation."

able, elusive, and ultimately fascinating character in the Legislature. Let's dispense with the items everyone agrees on. First, has no peer in passing major legislation: carried a huge load, from the Railroad Commission Sunset bill to the revision of the antitrust laws, and knew every line of every bill. Second, he's smart as hell: made the session's most reprehensible bill—protection for billboards against tough local ordinances—sound like it was devised by Solomon himself. Foes were stunned when Messer, answering their claim that the industry was welshing on a deal cut in 1973, cited ten-year-old transcripts from memory to show that there had been no meeting of the minds. Third, he was the most prominent member of the House this session, by virtue of his position as chairman of the absolutist Calendars Committee—a maze with dozens of blind alleys through which a bill must travel before it can reach the floor. Fourth, he's part of the business lobby family (literally, in one case, since chemical industry advocate Harry Whitworth is his father-in-law). Fifth, he is utterly fearless, as befits someone whose name in German means "knife." Sixth, there is more to his cherubic face and rosy cheeks than meets the eye.

For the anti-Messer camp, composed mostly of lobbyists on the losing side of Messer bills and some wary legislators, it will be the blackest day in Texas since the Alamo if Messer ever realizes his ambition to be Speaker. They grimly forecast the return of the days before 1973 when the business lobby called all the shots and legislators were either on the team or total outcasts.

What's wrong with this picture? Everything. Unlike, say, a Bob Vale, who always has one eye on his contributions list, when Messer sides with the lobby it is out of informed conviction. The proof lies in the independent way he handles his bills (he accepted an amendment to the trucking compromise against the wishes of the industry) and in his successful sponsorship of some of this session's best public-interest bills—antitrust, a new civil code, a major change in the civil service law that allows local police and fire chiefs to choose their top assistants.

As for power, sure, Messer uses it. He used Calendars to delay bills he didn't like and hurry along bills he did, as has every Calendars chairman before him. Unlike most of his predecessors, though, he based his decisions solely on substance and philosophy; he didn't use his power to reward his friends or hurt his enemies or further his Speaker ambitions (which, if anything, were slightly diminished after he became controversial). The problem in the House this year was not that Messer was too powerful but that almost everyone else was too docile. Instead of fighting back, they just grumbled. Messer didn't have to run

over anyone; he dominated by default. What the House could use is more people with his ability and appreciation of power. He needs the competition.

STEVE WOLENS
Democrat, Dallas

Talented, independent, and fearless—a combination as hard to find this session as a ground swell to declare quiche the state dish. Craves a good fight for its own sake; the kind of legislator who would rather hurdle a high fence than walk through an open gate. More often than not, landed on his feet rather than his derriere.

A carnivore who tore into the meat of the House rather than its plenteous vegetables. Invariably, when Wolens got up to speak both the subject and the opposition were weighty.

Revels in taking on complicated issues; his mind stores facts like a camel stores water—they're there when he needs them. Within one week, handled controversial bills on three of the most difficult issues of the session—securities, antitrust, and credit insurance.

Mounted the session's only successful challenge to House titan Bill Messer, amputating a gangrenous section of an otherwise worthy Messer bill—over the loud objections of the victim. Took on a close ally of the Speaker's in a battle over securities regulation, something no one except the two of them understood, and came within seven votes of winning—an amazing achievement, considering the herdlike proclivity of the House to follow the team blindly when faced with a soporific subject. In the best debate of the session, a duel in the Appropriations Committee with Jim Turner of Crockett, destroyed a team scheme to let members vote for a teacher pay raise without actually setting aside any money. Even the Speaker was not immune: Wolens induced committee colleagues to submerge their sense of self-preservation and strike $14 million for a new osteopathic library in Fort Worth that was coveted by Lewis.

At his best in debate; not even Messer is his peer. In their one confrontation, left his adversary no room to maneuver, offering to withdraw his amendment if Messer could find a single precedent "in Texas law, in federal law, in the law of any state or country" for the provision Wolens found objectionable. Messer couldn't. Won his appropriations duel over teacher salaries with a crisp attack on the team plan—"I have three objections. One is procedural, one is technical, one is substantive"—that even the most obtuse member could follow.

He was the House's consummate lawyer: his arguments were sharp and even brilliant, his analysis keen, his research first-rate. But as with any good lawyer, you sometimes felt that Wolens would have argued just as brilliantly for the other side had the mood so struck him.

He simultaneously led fights *against* regulation of securities and *for* regulation of air conditioning contractors.

For all Wolens' unquestioned skills, the nagging question that won't go away is this: to what end? To reach the very top rank, a legislator must have a consistency of philosophy and purpose to give meaning to all those skills. Otherwise he is a mere air plant, nice to look at but never rooted. In Wolens' case, the roots are still lacking.

THE TEN WORST

AL EDWARDS
Democrat, Houston

So unseemly was Edwards' performance during the past session that it is destined to become the stuff of legend. In an ordinary year, Edwards is a legislative nonentity who cleaves unto his pet issues: trains and Juneteenth. But his role in this year's horse-racing battle left colleagues longing for those days—and left Edwards the pariah of the decade.

Found himself the swing vote on the committee empowered to strike horse racing dead or send it to the House floor for a vote; proceeded to milk the situation for far, far more than it was worth. Unlike Lubbock senator John Montford, who used a similar position to win concessions for his district, Edwards never made it clear what he was looking for in exchange for his crucial vote—and therein lay the problem. To be blunt, there was no evidence that Al Edwards was trying to solicit a bribe, but if he was not trying to solicit a bribe, he acted exactly like a man who was.

Coy as the town strumpet, hinted at God-knew-what to the press, sometimes shifting position three times in a single interview. "Right now my vote is no, but I've got some things working" was one enticingly vague quote. Members and lobbyists, aware that Edwards was contemplating an expensive race for Harris County commissioner, grew nervous about the implications.

What was clear was that Edwards was reveling in the attention: the constant temperature-taking by the press, the hand-holding by bill sponsor Hugo Berlanga, the audiences with heavies like Speaker Lewis. Ultimately—and too late, as it turned out—voted to send the bill to the floor, but not without lots of posturing about his convictions as a Christian that sent eyeballs rolling heavenward.

Indifferent to the important stuff; anything but indifferent to his own self-interest. Proposed a preposterous $1 million interim study of bullet trains (normal budget for such a study is $50,000), which left Edwards-watchers wondering how much time he wanted to spend studying where to locate tracks in that commissioner's precinct he covets.

Got himself appointed to the subcommittee considering a county roads bill introduced by El Franco Lee, his prospective opponent in the commissioner's race, then took a walk to prevent a vote on his rival's bill.

The extent to which Edwards had been ostracized was demonstrated the last weekend of the session. He wandered into the Quorum Club, which was packed with legislators, all· of whom were letting bygones be bygones and downing a few with people they had fought with all session. From table to table drifted Edwards, a Flying Dutchman looking for safe harbor. But none would have him. Finally he gave up and vanished into the night, alone.

Brotherhood Awards
Special Award

First prize: RANDY PENNINGTON, Clear Lake. While slashing funds for a migrant workers' program, declared, "I understand migrants. I eat tomatoes." Second prize: Senator JOHN LEEDOM, Dallas. His response to Craig Washington's description of what it's like to be black in South Africa: "Speaking of minorities, you should have been a Republican twenty years ago."

Frank Eikenburg
Republican, Plano

Natural furniture whose explosive temper catapulted him out of that neutral category—right onto the Worst list. At his best, a harmless rich kid who careens around the House like a wobbling top, blissfully unaware of what's what. At his worst, a snit-throwing disturber of the legislative peace, possessed of a bush-league mean streak that makes it impossible for him to deal effectively with other members, even when he has it under control.

Burst into prominence as a freshman last session by telling Craig Washington, who was opposing draconian drug penalties, that he hoped Washington's children grew up to be drug dealers. Has subsequently proved that the venomous attack was no fluke. Exhibit A: during his 1982 campaign for reelection, called rape "a victimless crime." Exhibit B: fuming about the Plano Planning Commission's tabling of his wife's zoning request, Eikenburg threatened a lobbyist for Texas cities that he'd better "take care of business"—then ranted and raved to other members about the situation. Exhibit C: when a woman lobbyist forgot to deliver a legal memorandum to Eikenburg on the appointed day, he threatened to condemn her to other House members as the worst lobbyist in Austin, and he chewed her out savagely in public until another member felt obliged to come to her

rescue. "His mind," says one Capitol veteran, "is not sufficiently connected to his tongue."

Some might dispute that his mind is connected to anything at all. Nowhere was Eikenburg's inability to think straight more apparent than on a classic bit of news film masterminded by Capitol reporter Carole Kneeland, who caught the Eik (pronounced as though you'd just seen a mouse) voting repeatedly for the absent Randy Pennington—violating a House rule often honored in the breach—and asked him why he'd done it. With camera rolling, Eikenburg stared goggle-eyed at Kneeland for a full minute and nineteen seconds and then, like a kid with his hand in the cookie jar, mumbled, "Excuse me. I have to go back to a committee meeting," and ignominiously fled. Almost any other member could have finessed the moment by explaining that everybody does it, by claiming he had permission, *something.* Not Eikenburg.

Innocent of skills, Eikenburg was nevertheless quick to blame others for his misfortunes. Accused Kneeland of having been put up to that embarrassing news film by the horse-racing lobby. Accused trial lawyers of killing one of his four paltry bills; they hadn't even known it was on the calendar. Had the temerity to complain to colleagues about how hard it was to be rich.

Wants to be a state senator. But perhaps his true calling was apprehended by the lobbyist who, seeing Eikenburg leaning over the rotunda railing and pointing domeward, said, "That's what he's suited for! A tour guide!"

Bill Hollowell
Democrat, Grand Saline

The most misunderstood member of the Legislature—and that is not a compliment. Yes, he accepts no campaign contributions and always speaks and votes his mind. Unfortunately, that is the locus of all the trouble. Blustery, parochial, obstreperous, and uninformed; a reincarnation of the worst qualities of William Jennings Bryan, of whom Woodrow Wilson said, in words that apply equally well to Hollowell, "He is absolutely sincere. That is what makes him so dangerous."

At his worst on the powerful appropriations conference committee, where he was one of ten legislators with the final say on the state budget. This should have been his hour to shine: the treasury is short of money, the conferees have to cut the budget to the bone, and Hollowell postures as a guardian of the public purse. The committee rose to the occasion, all right, but Hollowell was a Lilliputian among Gullivers.

A know-nothing and proud of it; made no effort to see beyond his multitudinous prejudices and repeatedly had to be set

straight by senators and staff. Griped that too much of the state's money went to Houston; fought urban appropriations without regard to merit. His resistance to a vocational education program caused a rural senator to make a speech—something that never happens in conference committees—directed at Hollowell, on the importance of vocational education in general and the high success rate of the program in particular.

A total stranger to rational argument. When Jay Gibson tried to preserve a Chihuahuan Desert study at Sul Ross State because the low-enrollment college needed special programs to attract students, Hollowell retorted, "Let them study something worthwhile. That desert will be there awhile."

Ignored the significant for the trivial. Reserved his greatest wrath for an obscure segment of the educational bureaucracy known as regional service centers; carried around a file folder stuffed with audit reports documenting misuse of state funds at one center. Threatened to unleash the General Investigating Committee, which he chairs, to hound the centers. It was vintage Hollowell: uninformed (the offending employee was fired as soon as his indiscretions were uncovered) and misdirected (the committee ignored indiscretions much closer to home, namely, the exorbitant expense reports filed last year by Houston legislator Ron Wilson).

Hollowell did leave one legacy for the session: a proposal that if adopted by the voters will become the silliest amendment ever added to the Texas constitution. In the case of nuclear attack, the Legislature would be authorized to fill sudden vacancies from the ranks of former members. Poor Texas. It is not enough to bear the tragedy of nuclear war; we must then suffer the indignity of entrusting our survival to the likes of Bill Heatly and Bill Moore. Thanks, Mr. Hollowell, but it was hard enough the first time.

Sam Hudson
Democrat, Dallas

Stop. Consider this a warning. What follows is not for the skeptical. They will never believe a word of it. But we're not making it up.

Poor Sam Hudson doesn't have any more idea of what is happening on the floor than the schoolchildren who file into the gallery, sit for five minutes, and leave. It took him—no kidding—two sessions to figure out that the phone on his desk on the House floor was a direct line to his office. One day this year he saluted colleague Tom DeLay with "Hi there, Ron," which might be dismissed under the heading of "accidents can happen" if the incident had not occurred (a) during the last week of the session after

Special Award

 There was a lot of competition this year for the final slots on the Ten Worst list. It hardly seems fair to the losers to let their efforts go unnoticed.

It's time for Senator OSCAR MAUZY (Democrat, Dallas) to head for the barn and hang up the old saddle. Once a great senator, he no longer has any fire except for partisan fights like appointments. Perhaps there's another stall in that barn for nitpicker MILTON FOX (Republican, Houston), who delights in killing otherwise uncontested bills that he discovers cost one penny more than the paper they're printed on. BILL CEVERHA's (Republican, Richardson) sodomy bill tried to outlaw such wanton acts as foreplay, but Ceverha was less concerned with the activities of consenting legislators—he crusaded against stronger ethics laws all session. Finally, let's not forget JIMMY MANKINS (Democrat, Kilgore). Losing to infamous self-shooter Mike Martin in 1980 was bad enough; then he came back with a bill to give prisoners $100 and a one-way ticket to Washington, D.C.

♦

(b) DeLay and Hudson had shared an office suite for four months.

Still not convinced? Try this one. Hudson introduced a bill calling for the reorganization of the Texas Indian Commission. At a committee hearing on the bill, he called, with great flourish and fanfare, his first and only supporting witness—who proceeded to tear his bill apart.

More? No problem. Hudson actually got a bill up for debate this year without going on a hunger strike, no small feat considering that in 1977 he had to resort to a 68-day fast. The current bill was aimed at preventing voter intimidation by banning all signs at polling places except those prescribed by the Secretary of State's office; not a bad idea, only—oops—the bill read, "*pro*scribed." House members had hardly stopped yukking over that one when here came another Hudson bill, this one making it a felony to wear masks at Ku Klux Klan rallies. Oops again: it also made felons out of kids on Halloween.

Despite five terms in the House, remains oblivious to basics. Even the teenage pages know the procedure for debate—bills are voted on twice, but the second time is usually a formality and amendments then are discouraged both by rule and by custom—but not Sam. Dormant while the House gave preliminary approval to a dogfighting bill, then erupted with ten amendments during the ritual of final passage. Mercifully, Speaker Lewis shut him off after four had failed by overwhelming margins, less in the interest of saving time than of quieting the dozens of members who had seized the opportunity to practice yelping and howling.

None of these shenanigans came as any shock to Hudson's colleagues; what did shock them, however, was Lewis' decision to reward Hudson with a committee chairmanship. Lewis tried to minimize the damage by giving him a committee with jurisdiction over ceremonial resolutions, but even that turned to disaster. Like a wayward blade of grass on a putting green, it introduced a fatal eccentricity into the rolling course of events. On the day the horse-racing bill finally came up for debate, 75 members voted to kill the bill, 74 wanted to keep it alive . . . and Sam was missing. Supporters scoured the Capitol and nearby eateries while tension filled the chamber and metallic voices boomed out: "Is Mr. Hudson on the floor of the House? Is Mr. Hudson on the floor of the House?" It was no use. Sam was presenting one of his resolutions to a political friend—back in Dallas.

GLENN KOTHMANN

Democrat, San Antonio

Hilariously inept. Enjoyed, if that is the word for it, what everyone agrees was his best session, yet it wasn't close to keeping him off the Ten Worst list.

Kothmann's problem: hubris. He actually tried to be a player this session. The Valero bill pretty much sums up the results. Valero, a gas pipeline company headquartered in Kothmann's district, needed a Senate sponsor for a bill to solve a local problem. But the company had a problem of its own. Kothmann, you see, is not very good at passing bills. So the company bypassed him, choosing instead John Traeger of neighboring Seguin. The slight infuriated Kothmann, and he vowed to kill the bill. As fate would have it, his was the swing vote in committee. Only he voted *for* the bill by mistake.

May be the only senator in Texas history to climb as high as fourth in seniority without being named a committee chairman. Thank God. Doesn't have the foggiest understanding of substance; during the hearing on the intricate issue of trucking deregulation, resorted in desperation to letting lobbyists in the gallery signal him how to vote. Doesn't have the foggiest understanding of procedure, either. Momentarily took over the gavel in State Affairs one day, only to be baffled by a routine motion (to substitute a House bill for a Senate bill) that is used dozens of times each session to speed bills through the process.

Only person to assess Kothmann's performance as outstanding was Kothmann himself, in response to a question from a local reporter. At Kothmann's insistence, both the question and the answer were in writing; verbal interviews are just too tricky. But the reporter didn't mind; "even when he's talking to you, he's inaccessible," says she.

Gets no sympathy for his bumbling, unlike most sad sack legislators, because, in the words of one lobbyist, "I've never met a man in politics who's so petty." Won his last primary by only 99 votes, a calamity for San Antonio on the scale of the great flood of 1921; spent this session poring over his opponent's contribution list and swearing vengeance against anyone whose name appeared.

Seeks the spotlight as often as water runs uphill. Even has other senators introduce guests from his district and explain his bills in committee. Couldn't avoid taking the floor to debate his bill requiring voter registrants to reveal felony convictions; it was a fiasco. Had to be coached through procedural motions by the chair, then looked pleadingly around the floor for help when other senators started asking questions that couldn't be answered by "yes" or "no." Silence reigned until someone took pity and spoon-fed him the answers. Senators mercifully called a halt after a series of pointed questions (later described by a colleague as "target practice on a whale tied to a tree") ended with, "I think you have a bad bill, Senator." Kothmann responded, "Thank you, Senator."

JAN McKENNA

Republican, Arlington

Every legislator has his element: Jan McKenna's first session proved hers was hot water. A world-class waffler, developed an abiding fondness for the little white "present" light that lets members off the hook from voting yes or no. "I'll vote 'present' unless you need me," she assured one lobbyist sincerely. Flaked early on the horse-racing issue, first telling lobbyists she'd vote for it, then changing her mind on the nonsensical grounds that it was local option.

Bounced through the session like a legislative accident looking for places to happen. She found them. Stunned the Criminal Jurisprudence Committee by proposing bills that were already law. Acted the playground brat: when a fellow Republican asked to be recognized in committee and was ignored, McKenna turned to him and, like a three-year-old in a sandbox, said, "Nyah-nyah-nyah." He responded in expletive-deleted terms—and people drank toasts to him all weekend.

In Urban Affairs, allied herself with mischief-maker extraordinaire Randy Pennington to form the 68th session's Fun Couple. With Pennington egging her on, moved to appeal a parliamentary ruling by chairman George Pierce, a serious breach of legislative etiquette not to be undertaken lightly. After a stern lecture by committee vice chairman Al Luna, sensed the disapproval of her peers and timidly voted "present" on her own motion.

McKenna tried to play with the big kids, then flip-flopped like a demented acrobat when she saw her routines weren't going over. Reached the depths with her mercifully unsuccessful efforts to resuscitate the defunct Ben Barnes bill, one of the sorriest special-interest measures of all time (named for former lieutenant governor—and law school dropout—Ben Barnes, it allows legislators to become lawyers without attending law school). Unable to win support for her own bill and dearly wanting to be a lawyer herself, McKenna trotted hither and yon searching for a host bill onto which she could tack the odious Barnes parasite. At the eleventh hour, latched on to an Oscar Mauzy bill, assuming it was vital to the senator; she was wrong. When pressed about her shenanigans, denied responsibility and pointed the finger at other members. Typically, ended up voting to reconsider her own amendment.

McKenna herself explains her antics as the errors of a freshman. But she perversely chose to ignore advice from the most-respected strategists and rules pros in the House, who counseled her not to appeal a chairman's ruling and to go about her Barnes work in a straightforward rather than a sneaky way. That's not enough to get you onto the Ten Worst list, and neither is picking Randy Pennington as your mentor—although that's debatable. What made McKenna a Worst was her uselessness in the most fundamental legislative sense: she was incapable of making the decisions her constituents sent her to make.

RANDY PENNINGTON
Republican, Houston

With his sepulchral eyes and narrow gaze, Pennington may be the only member who unfailingly looks as if he's up to no good. It's no illusion. A professional troublemaker, he abhors nothing so much as a dead calm. Some legislators come to Austin concerned about issues; Pennington comes hoping to bring the full powers of his office to bear against his enemies.

And who might these enemies be? For starters there's everyone who has ever run against him. A sore winner, regularly sues his beaten opponents. Took a sudden interest in housing authority reform this session; by golly if his latest

opponent, Bob Graham, wasn't an investor in a subsidized housing project. Tries to stick it to law firms that have supported his opponents too; killed one of Jimmy Mankins' bills because attorneys involved in Mankins' water

authority bill had contributed to vanquished Pennington foe Bill Carraway.

Another pet Pennington hate: the bad ol' City of Houston, which annexed his Clear Lake homeland some years back. Threw the House into a turmoil when a Dallas hotel-motel tax bill came up for debate; tried to graft on an amendment to hobble Houston's convention center plans. Played the spoiler in Urban Affairs, where his chief role was to mess up the committee process by offering endless points of order and plotting untoward parliamentary ploys. Ignoring four months of committee negotiations over Houston civil service reform, staged such a parliamentary song and dance that even Urban Affairs chairman George Pierce—who received $2000 worth of millionaire Pennington's campaign largess—got fed up. Glaring icily, Pierce slammed down his gavel and interrupted, "Mr. Pennington moves the meeting stand adjourned."

Showed as little regard for legislative codes as for his colleagues. Sneaked through a controversial resolution demanding a Metropolitan Transit Authority audit (take *that,* Houston!), in violation of the universally held principle that the resolutions should be kept noncontroversial. Declined to answer questions about what the resolution did; then the instant it passed, scurried to the press table with an explanatory news release.

Some actually defended Pennington, saying that he was better this session than last. Poppycock. It was all on the surface. He has learned more about the game and has discovered how to mask his vindictiveness. But Pennington's newly acquired veneer of civilization only makes him more dangerous.

CARLYLE SMITH
Democrat, Grand Prairie

Like Hester Prynne, wore a scarlet *A* around his neck—but his stood for "albatross." The one member of the Legislature whose support for any cause was instantly fatal.

Spent the session launching assaults on embattled Speaker Gib Lewis; they turned out to be kamikaze missions. So inept at guerrilla tactics that he actually ended up creating sympathy for Lewis. Worse, he scared away others who might have tried, had Smith not preceded them; he gave dissent and independence a bad name.

Had every reason to know better. In three previous sessions he'd watched John Bryant and Ron Coleman (both now in Congress, to Lewis' everlasting good fortune) put on a clinic on how to fight a Speaker. Alas, Carlyle wasn't taking notes. Otherwise he would have known to:

Pick the right issues. Bryant and Coleman chose water, agricultural tax breaks, and school finance, where they could use the complexity of the subject and their superior knowledge to tack on clever amendments, sway uninformed members, hint that skulduggery was afoot, and earn the grudging respect of the opposition. But Smith concentrated on horse racing and banning open containers in cars—emotional issues where there was little chance of changing votes or winning anyone's respect.

Never get personal. Bryant and Coleman played hardball, but always on the issues, trying to goad the Speaker into pettiness first. But when Smith asked the

HONORABLE MENTION
Special Award

🏆 It would be nice to report that the competition for the Ten Best was as spirited as for the Ten Worst; alas, such was not the case. But here are the best of the rest: Senator ED HOWARD (Democrat, Texarkana) is a refreshing presence. He won't barter away his vote, won't logroll on the budget, won't carry special-interest bills, and manages to be very conservative without being beholden to the business lobby. BOB SIMPSON (Democrat, Amarillo) is so trusted as chairman of the Insurance Committee that the rest of the House just goes along with what he decides. WAYNE PEVETO (Democrat, Orange), who turned a nightmarish DWI bill into a workable law, may not appear in these pages again. If he's really hanging up his gavel, as is rumored, he can look back and know that he left the state in better shape than he found it. GEORGE PIERCE (Republican, San Antonio) doesn't want to look back at all. His Urban Affairs Committee included four of the Ten Worst— Edwards, Eikenburg, McKenna, and Pennington. He deserves an honorable mention just for surviving.

House to exhume the open-container bill from a committee graveyard, he made the error of trying to cast Lewis in the role of undertaker. The House disagreed —by more than a hundred votes.

Don't waste your ammunition. The biggest danger for insurgents is that they try to fight too many battles. Eventually no one listens anymore. For Smith, eventually came early. He and an ally proposed an amendment to elect the PUC, with commissioners taking office on January 1, 1985. He lost. Then he proposed an amendment to elect the PUC, with commissioners taking office on January 2, 1985. He lost again. Then, yes, January 3, 1985.

Timing is everything. After they lost a battle, Bryant and Coleman let someone else fight the next one while their wounds—and credibility—healed. But Smith, after getting drubbed on the open-container vote, marched straight into the billboards floor fight—and got drubbed again.

By the time the session entered its last month, Smith carried such a stigma that members begged him not to speak for their bills or amendments. Ignoring pleas to stay away from the microphone, he mortally wounded his comrades' attack on the worst bill of the session, a scheme to override local billboard ordinances. Lobbyists actually incorporated Smith into their strategies, searching for ways to prod him into opposing their bills. Said one: "There is not another member or lobbyist who wouldn't love to have Carlyle on the other side. It's worth an instant sixty votes."

MARK STILES
Democrat, Beaumont

A good ol' boy gone berserk. First day of the session, freshman Stiles went around hugging Speaker Gib Lewis and slapping the parliamentarian on the back. Clenching a fat cigar between his teeth, he swaggered into a crowded elevator and bossed the House sergeants around. In short order he found himself on State Affairs and Ways and Means, two plum committee assignments usually denied freshmen. "Gee," thought observers, "this guy must be going somewhere." He was—straight downhill.

Promptly made a fawning declaration of non-independence to the press in which he all but vowed to kiss the hem of Gib's garment daily. Appointed himself apologist for Gib's failure-to-disclose woes: mere "zip code errors," pronounced Stiles. "If the Speaker stopped

suddenly, Stiles' nose would be broken," snapped one disgusted freshman.

Took to calling everyone Bubba. Made sure little cartoon figures labeled "Bubba Likes It" appeared on members' desk video screens when certain bills came up; actually thought it helped his cause. Failed to combine his Bubbaship with any real legislative skills, assuming that the Speaker's blessing was all he needed to get his program through.

Charged into the legislative china shop with the horns of a bull but the hide of a rabbit. Bullied witnesses, yet couldn't deal with adversity himself: made an art form of the hissy fit, huffing agitatedly back to his desk when thwarted at the mike. Stormed out in mid-hearing when committee chairman Fred Agnich held up his hunting bill. Unwisely called Agnich Daddy Warbucks in private; was then stunned when Agnich, with obvious relish, rose later in the session to smite another Stiles bill with deadly points of order.

Brought a new word into the legislative lexicon—"nimby," as in "not in *my* back yard." Had the most parochial legislative package imaginable, including an ill-fated nimby bill that would have repealed the statewide property tax appraisal system in order to solve some Jefferson County problems and another that would have outlawed hazardous waste disposal sites in Liberty County. When colleagues advised him that someone would surely raise points of order about the narrow scope of this bill, Stiles—feeling his sworn fealty exempted him from the rules—blithely assured them the Speaker would rule his way. He was wrong.

By session's end, the floor had turned openly hostile, hissing and catcalling when Stiles took the mike. He had even veteran lobbyists mixing their metaphors wildly ("A time bomb heading for a banana peel," goggled one). But Stiles represented something more than an overweening freshman or a bad joke. He was the bad old days come back to life— a man with no beliefs save in his own advancement, a legislator who shamelessly declared he'd do anything to curry favor, including bargain away his independence for a mess of Speaker's pottage. "He's poisoned his reputation," mused one thoughtful freshman. "And what else does a member have up here?"

BOB VALE
Democrat, San Antonio

The kind of politician who confirms your most cynical fears about politics. Combines an in-

finitesimal sense of public responsibility with a spectrum of values that begins with money and ends with money. If money is the mother's milk of politics, as former California House Speaker Jess Unruh once postulated, then Bob Vale has yet to be weaned.

Not a crook—Vale is too smart to deal in quid pro quos, which is where tawdriness gives way to crime—but rather a parasite on the body politic. Says one lobbyist: "He has all kinds of fundraisers, needs, officeholder expenses he's always telling you about, or he'll ask you to 'throw some business my way.' " (Vale, a lawyer, has used his office to drum up business before: he was reprimanded by the State Bar in 1972 because he represented clients for the sole purpose of obtaining a legislative continuance—the mandatory postponement of a criminal trial as long as the Legislature is in session.) "I don't deal with him. I won't deal with him," says another lobbyist.

Here's what happened this session to one who did. The lobbyist was explaining his side of one of the session's major issues when Vale interrupted. "How much did you contribute to my last campaign?" he wanted to know. The lobbyist wasn't sure, but he remembered making a contribution. "Well, it can't have been too much because I don't remember it," said Vale.

On the rare occasions when he chooses to employ his talents, as in his battle to save Bill Clements' appointment of Sam Barshop to the UT Board of Regents, he is a shrewd and tenacious adversary. Up against the governor, the Democratic party, and a dozen senators, Vale called in every chit and nearly pulled it off, thus demonstrating that he can play senator when he wants to. For the most part, though, he doesn't want to. Acts like he's allergic to major legislation; turned down an offer to be lead sponsor of the water package. A member of the conference committee on college construction, an issue vital to UT–San Antonio; appeared to doze through the first meeting and never contributed anything. Serves, sort of, on the powerful Senate Finance Committee, where a colleague evaluated his work as "useless."

How bad is Bob Vale? During one lunch break, Kothmann was eating with several others in a local lunchroom when up walked Vale. As Vale sat down, Kothmann got up and fled, abandoning a half-consumed sandwich. When Glenn Kothmann runs away from someone, folks, that's as bad as bad can get.🌿

★POLITICIANS★
EXECUTIVES

THE GOVERNOR'S NEW CLOTHES

by Stephen Harrigan

Rip away Bill Clements's gruff, uncomplicated, free-enterprising public image, and you'll find . . . a gruff, uncomplicated, free-enterprising kind of guy.

"I'm a nuts and bolts guy," said Bill Clements. "I'm a fire by friction man. I'm not long on self-indulgence. I'm a why and a wherefore guy."

The governor tapped me emphatically on the knee and then sat back in his airplane seat, fixing me with a wily, self-satisfied stare.

"You know," he went on, "when you're raised during the Depression, there is indelibly imprinted upon your being your impressions of that period. I don't know of anybody that went through that so-called quote-unquote Great Depression that was not tattooed in the process. But irrespective of the circumstances of the times, you have to maintain a sense of humor and perspective."

Clements leaned forward again. "Nothing," he said, "is ever so bad that it can't be worse. Or better. Think about that."

He stared at me once more, as if in that way he could verify that I was indeed thinking about the maxim he had just put forward. I stared back, since the governor of Texas is a man in whose presence one takes pains not to appear as a sissy.

His eyes were a flat, institutional gray, and they did not reveal where, or in what manner, he had been "tattooed." The rest of his appearance was, as the clothing label puts it, "exclusive of ornamentation." He wore a colorless sport coat not much enlivened by a lapel pin depicting the Texas flag, and his face had the in-

flexible features of a bird of prey.

Lately I had found myself musing about Bill Clements. In moments of downtime brain activity, as my mind hovered at the lip of sleep, I would see an image of the governor of Texas. This suggested to me that in some fashion the man was using the primal circuits. It was not just his spectacular orneriness that had lodged him in my imagination, but the persistent impression that he was real, that he belonged to that tiny group of human beings who are never in disguise.

That, of course, is an unlikely quality for a politician. It was obvious to me from my initial meeting with him that Clements was wary and ambitious, but what I found appealing about him was the way he had not bothered to construct a facade to hide these traits. I wanted to watch him at work, to see if he could pass through the dull, unctuous moments of a governor's daily rounds without losing his raw edge. It was apparent to me that the only way to understand Bill Clements was to watch him in action.

What you notice about Bill Clements, and what he wants you to notice, is that he is a businessman. For him the world revolves smoothly around the principles of free enterprise, and he stands plumb to the axis. From that vantage, things can be grasped, understood, made to work.

The main thing that Clements has made work is Sedco, one of the world's largest drilling equipment companies, which he founded in 1947 and whose management he has passed down to his son Gil. From Sedco Clements is extravagantly wealthy, and there is no question that this wealth suits him. You cannot encounter his ferocious confidence without realizing that he is a self-made man who thoroughly approves of his creation.

We were sitting in a cluster of swivel seats at the rear of the Grumman propjet that the citizens of Texas have made available for the governor's use. Clements and his wife, Rita, were flying to Corpus Christi to preside over a black-tie dinner at the Town Club, one of a series of such events meant to raise money for the restoration of the Governor's Mansion. After the election, they had found the mansion uninhabitable, full of cracks and peeling wallpaper, furnished with random mail-order antiques, and equipped with no fewer than nine useless fireplaces.

It was Rita Clements who was spearheading the drive to restore the mansion. The governor made note of this fact and then delivered himself of a long sales pitch on the project, declaring that "that old mansion up on the hill is a great reservoir of what Texas is all about." While he talked, his wife looked out the window into the night sky. She wore a mink jacket and a large, unwieldy necklace. The governor's blustery manner threw her natural reserve into conspicuous relief, so that she appeared serene.

"When we move in," Clements was saying, "God willing in June or July this summer, that Governor's Mansion will have gone through a three-million-dollar renovation. It'll have 1850s furniture, pine floors, and working fireplaces, and be a place that all Texans can take pride in."

"Dear," said his wife, "don't you need to change?"

The governor excused himself and went into the rear compartment of the airplane, emerging a short while later in a tuxedo. He did not appear transformed.

"You gotta help me, dear," he said, handing his wife a bow tie with a big elastic loop. "The one thing I can't do," he explained, as he obligingly turned this way and that at his wife's direction, "is put my tie on."

When Clements sat down again I asked him about his library, which I had heard was one of the most extensive private collections of books on Texas history.

"I guess I first developed an interest in history at my mother's breast," he said. "Some of the first money I made working on the drilling rigs in South Texas went into those books. Those were some of Dobie's early books. I believe he was writing that *Yaqui Gold* book back then. I have a very comprehensive set of books on Sam Houston. There may well have been seventy-five or eighty books written on Houston."

Clements's speech was clipped and emphatic, and not particularly fluent. He had a front-line system of responses, ready to be launched at a second's notice, but otherwise it seemed that each individual word was hauled up, like a heavy piece of machinery, from some great storage bay deep inside his brain. As he waited on the next shipment of words, he would sometimes hold his hands at chest level and make a gesture with them like a boxer's feint.

"Houston is my favorite character," Clements went on, "as far as Texas is concerned. He is a very sophisticated, complex person. It's no accident that Kennedy included Sam Houston in that *Profiles in Courage*. Houston set the precedent for us. He ran for governor and was elected for one reason: to preserve the Union. He never believed in secession per se. States' rights, yes. Secession, no."

"What was it that he tore up and threw in the fireplace?" his wife asked.

"Oh, I've forgotten, Rita. But it was some document. Some document he tore up and threw in the fireplace."

The governor's plane landed at the Corpus Christi airport a stately half-hour or so behind schedule. The night was appallingly cold, but since there were two DPS cars parked within ten yards of the ramp, our experience of it was brief.

> "Clements is extravagantly wealthy, and his wealth suits him. You cannot encounter his ferocious confidence without realizing that he is a self-made man who thoroughly approves of his creation."

"The Town Club," Clements mused when his car was under way. "Is that not the successor to the old Dragon Grill?"

"Yessir," said the Texas Ranger behind the wheel. "Sure is."

"How about that. The old Dragon Grill, Rita, was the R&R spot on North Beach in the late thirties. They had super food. Then they moved closer into town and established this place called the Town Club. Boy, you could get the best broiled flounder you could ever put in your mouth. I guarantee you that to come in from that brush country and get a broiled flounder like that was something else."

Clements was sentimental about this country; it had been the landscape of his young manhood. He told me he had come to South Texas from his home in Dallas in 1934, just after he graduated from high school. He was seventeen. He had been offered several football scholarships, but at that time his family was desperate for income. During Clements's boyhood the financial reversals of his father, who was in the farming and ranching business, had been chronic, and now, in the midst of the Depression, the crisis was severe. Clements worked as a roughneck in the oil fields for fifteen months, spending half his salary on living expenses and sending the rest home. When his father found a job managing a ranch outside of Dallas, Clements went back home and spent two and a half years studying engineering at SMU before he got "itchy" and returned full time to the oil fields without graduating.

"Back then," he explained, "you could make more money working on a rig than you could as a lawyer or a graduate engineer. Rita, do you know what a graduate engineer got back then?"

"I don't know. Two hundred a month?"

"Baloney! It was a hundred and ten. But you could go out in the oil fields and work on the derrick floor and make three

---

hundred a month. So where do you think I went?"

"To the oil fields."

"I went to the oil fields. I lived in Sinton, Robstown, Bishop, Inez. I lived in every part of this country. Just a youngster out of high school. I went where the rigs went. I lived at the bakery for a dollar a day, room and board. I ate 'em out of house and home. They'd fix you a lunch with two sandwiches, a raw onion, and an apple, and then you'd come in at night and you'd have chicken-fried steak."

The governor paused for a moment, then went on in a low, distracted voice. "And I never felt lonesome," he said, "and I never worried about nothin'."

At the Town Club the mood was warm and indulgent. There were a few reporters in the lobby, and they asked Clements about an important senatorial race in the Valley and about the effects on the poor of the president's proposed budget cuts. The governor said that he thought his candidate would win and that Reagan had a solid feel for the underprivileged.

"Now, you all are not supposed to interview the governor," a woman scolded. "He's supposed to be in a reception line."

By and by the governor shook off the reporters and ascended by elevator to a room where a combo was playing "Yellow Bird" and red-jacketed waiters stood about impassively, holding trays of cheese puffs. The reception line was more or less a formality, since the governor knew many of these people well. They were his sort of people, and they were not without funds.

"Hi, Richard," he would say, "good to see you. Hi, Alice, good to see *you*."

Meeting strangers, the governor was cautious, even suspicious. He had a way of turning a casual introduction into a subtle duel of eye contact. He would hold a handshake a beat or two longer than necessary as he gave his opponent a sly, appraising look. But there was also the slightest play of mirth on Clements's face, a hint that you were being drawn into his confidence at the same time as you were being sized up like a piece of merchandise. It was an old managerial technique, a kind of shorthand hypnosis. The governor's initial impression was so intense and ambiguous that the average flustered citizen could not help feeling somewhat under his power.

It was fascinating to watch this continuous dominance. It was not a dominance based on grace or natural presence. It was a battle that had to be won, a position that had to be defended, every moment. "I am not a Republican governor," he said, poking a man repeatedly in the chest, "I am a governor for *all of Texas*!" He was always on the attack, moving forward, cocking his head upward to compensate for his lack of height, **keeping his** feet firmly planted.

But most of these people were not strangers, and the governor was noticeably at ease with them. It was no accident, I felt, that his personal history should be entwined with those of the people in this room, and that his politics should speak to their needs. Clements was a supremely pragmatic man, and money was the single most pragmatic and visible standard. He knew how to read people who had money. The rich were observable, but the poor were ineffable and vague.

Standing with his wife in the reception line, Clements projected none of the suave apartness of a conventional politician. He was an unlikely governor, not just because he was the first Republican to hold that office since Reconstruction, but because it was so plain that he was a man used to simply doing business, a man who you would not think could abide the diluted powers and incessant scrutiny of public office.

Clements had long been a heavy financial contributor to national Republican politics. In 1968 and again in 1970 he had been approached to run for governor of Texas as a Republican, but the idea did not catch up to him until much later, after he had served presidents Nixon and Ford as Deputy Secretary of Defense. It was essentially an office management position, involving running the Pentagon on a day-to-day basis, but it gave Clements such a thorough, top-secret grounding in national defense that he could not help being horrified by the policies of Jimmy Carter. Clements became convinced that a Republican quest for the governorship was "not a mission impossible. It was a mission *possible*." He asked John Connally, George Bush, Anne Armstrong. Nobody wanted to take the mission. Then one evening in the fall of 1977, after an intense discussion with his wife, he decided to do it himself.

Clements spent the better part of an hour mingling with the guests at the Town Club, and then seats were taken and the Lord was invoked. "Grant," it was requested, "that we may be grateful stewards of Your great gifts."

After dinner the governor and his wife were introduced, and they each spoke for a few minutes about the importance of the restoration project. In one corner of the room a display on the mansion had been set up, and there was an elegant little booklet at each place setting that included a stamped envelope in which guests were to insert their pledges, but the sales pitch itself was very low-key and chatty.

"After we spent seven million dollars getting him elected," Rita Clements said, "and we walked into the mansion and the walls were cracked and paint was peeling off, I said, 'My God, am I going to leave my house in Dallas for this?' "

There was no way to predict what the pledge cards would finally read, but the

> "During his campaign Clements was caught in a traffic jam on the Gulf Freeway in Houston. He walked around and tapped on car windows, saying, 'Hi, I'm Bill Clements. I'm running for governor.' "

evening was clearly a success. "Well," Bill Clements said in the car on the way back to the airport, "there were lots of nice people there tonight. It's fun to have those roots go back almost as far as you can remember. If you really want to find out something about me you ought to talk to those kinds of people. You ought to go back to them and ask, 'What kind of a nut is this guy?'

"There's no crucible," the governor reflected, "that cooks so well as time. Those people are still there and that relationship still exists. That's what counts. Don't you agree?" he asked his wife, rubbing her knee with his hand. She looked at him sleepily, not answering.

"I know you do," he said.

The Clements entourage flew on to Houston that night and put up in the Guest Quarters, an exclusive hotel where all the rooms were suites and all the phones had rows of blinking extension lights. On the way into central Houston on the Gulf Freeway, Clements reminisced about the time in his campaign when he had been caught in a traffic jam on this stretch of road and had simply gotten out of his car and walked up and down the freeway, tapping on windows and saying, "Hi, I'm Bill Clements. I'm running for governor."

He moved easily from that kind of reverie into a discussion of the traffic problem in Houston. There was always a formal pitch to his voice, but it was interesting how often he lapsed into the cadence of public speech.

"It's not so much one person, Rita," he said now, in reference to solving traffic congestion. "What you have to do is marshal the talents and visions and dreams of a whole lot of people."

The stately, measured tone of his conversation discouraged me from asking questions. I could not enter his mood. His mind seemed to move ahead on its own track, as unswervable as a road grader. He was neither a public man nor a private man. He was a businessman.

The hotel where Governor and Mrs. Clements stayed was across the road from the Galleria. The governor entertained the notion of driving over there in the morning and buying a pair of shoes, but the prospect did not excite him. "Buying a pair of shoes and getting a haircut are the two damnedest things you have to do," he said. "They're tough."

Fortunately the demands of his office provided Clements a convenient excuse to put off his shopping trip. He elected to stay in his hotel room that morning, going over a speech on his anticrime package that he was to make to an Exchange Club luncheon that afternoon. Rita Clements, however, was going shopping, and I joined the little security entourage that went with her to the Galleria. She was shadowed with the utmost discretion by a Texas Ranger and a DPS security officer; they walked along with her, scanning with their eyes the tiers of the mall, monitoring their watches to make sure she was on schedule.

The first lady was a very handsome woman of precise appearance. She moved through the Galleria with great assurance and polish, slowing down as she approached every door, confident that it would be opened by someone. Her retinue of two security officers and a reporter did not seem to bother her in the least, and she chatted amiably about all the time that she and her husband had spent in the Galleria during the campaign and about the stationary bicycle the doctor had prescribed for the governor after he had injured his hip playing handball. For all of this, she came across as a very subtle woman who played the game of politics several layers deeper than her husband.

"Name?" asked the receptionist in the optical shop where she went to have her sunglasses repaired.

"Clements."

"Cleemons?"

"No. C-l-e-m-e-n-t-s."

She strolled down to an art gallery dominated by a stuffed polar bear and filled with cowboy paintings, sea chests, model derricks, wooden Indians, and big cat skins. "You certainly have an attractive shop here," she told the owner.

"I'm looking for an anniversary gift for Bill," she said to me. "Something that would look good in his office.

"Hmmm." She paused to look at a ghastly statuette of a football player with a buzzard perched on his shoulder. "That's the first time I've ever seen a bronze done of a football player. And here's another one. My gosh, what has he got on his shoulder?

"This is nice," she said, indicating a clear glass dome under which were displayed two stuffed quail. "Bill really enjoys hunting. Both quail and duck. He keeps telling me he'll teach me how, but it's a little late in life for that."

Mrs. Clements asked the owner for his card and left the shop still considering the purchase of the stuffed quail. She met the governor in the lobby of the hotel, and they were driven downtown to be guests of honor at the Sixteenth Annual Crime Prevention Luncheon.

"Lord," intoned a chaplain from the Harris County Sheriff's Department, "we thank Ya for the Exchange Clubs of Greater Houston." Mayor Jim McConn welcomed "Governor Clements and your lovely wife, Rita, Mr. Secretary of State and your lovely wife, Annette," and several other dignitaries and lovely wives. He proclaimed it Crime Prevention Week in Houston. Colt pistols in walnut boxes were awarded to the two men named policemen of the year.

Weldon Smith, an old friend and business associate of Clements's, introduced the governor. "I was one of the few people," Smith said, "who, when Bill Clements announced he was running for governor, was convinced he could win."

That was not much of an exaggeration. Clements's candidacy had been taken no more seriously than that of any other Republican contender, which is to say it had been all but ignored. The defeat of the Republican gubernatorial candidate in Texas was thought to be merely a formality, part of the ritual by which the anointed Democrat coasted into power. Clements disrupted this ritual, first by spending an astonishing amount of money and then by managing to project his blunt, cranky personality to an electorate that had not yet begun to grasp the full extent of its impatience with wavering, apologetic statesmen like Jimmy Carter. On television Clements came across as unsophisticated and abrasive, but the Democrats who misread these traits as stupidity were not quite plugged in. John Hill, Clements's opponent, was quiet and sophisticated. He spoke with a courtly lisp. Deep in some primitive lobe of the voters' brains there was no contest. Nobody really wanted a gentleman as governor of Texas when it was possible to have a roughneck. On election day the world as Texas had known it for a hundred years came to an end. All of a sudden here was Bill Clements, a Republican, literally governing in his shirt sleeves.

When Clements came to the podium he thanked Smith for his gracious introduction, made a few casual remarks, and then segued into his prepared remarks, which detailed the ten major points of his crime package. Some of these proposals —notably the one calling for wiretapping —were provocative and controversial, but in form the speech was classically dull. Even an audience that was packed with law enforcement officers had trouble rising to the applause lines.

"Boy, I tell ya," I overheard someone saying in the men's room afterward, "if he'd had eleven points to that thing I woulda never made it."

"He's a great governor, though," said the man standing next to him.

"Sure is, isn't he?"

"He doesn't pussyfoot around. He means what he says."

Clements was running late. He had just managed to extricate himself from a media knot and was visibly preoccupied when another reporter, a young woman, approached him in the hallway. "I understand," she said, "that you want to do something about the overcrowding of prisons."

"I don't want to," he snapped. "I plan to." The governor's manner flustered the young reporter. She muttered something about having phrased the question that way in order to save time.

"Well, if you're in such a big hurry," Clements said, suddenly seized with anger, "you oughta go ahead and leave."

The woman was shocked. She somehow recovered herself, asked another question, and received a calm, civil reply. But it was a nasty, lingering moment. There did not seem to be anything personal in this exchange. The reporter had simply run afoul of Clements's momentum; she had interfered with the process of government.

As a governor, Clements was unusually accessible to members of the press, but he was also unusually annoyed by them. He seemed to understand the function of the press but not its motivation. Everything to him was already clear, already explicable. Reporters operated in a world of ignorance and supposition. The people he had the most use for were those who did not just *want* to know things but who knew them already.

Clements's next order of business in Houston was a tour of M. D. Anderson Hospital and Tumor Institute, the cornerstone of the gargantuan cancer center operated by the University of Texas. The tour was not entirely ceremonial. Although the governor of Texas inhabits a constitutionally weak office, he does have a certain negative authority in that he can veto budget items from the Legislature. Therefore it was in the best interest of various state agencies to justify their existence to him.

When Clements arrived at M. D. Anderson, the hospital staff was assembled in the lobby, applauding and cheering. Out of this crowd came three or four men in lab coats who began guiding the governor and his wife at a brisk pace through the halls of the hospital, talking about bone marrow transplants.

"You take what out of 'em?" Clements was asking as the doctors bustled along with their hands behind their backs. "Marra?"

"Marrow," they said, putting him into an elevator. "Bone marrow."

The elevator doors opened on another team of doctors. "Dr. Udagama here," one of these doctors said, "is our resident artist, and we thought we'd show you his work."

All eyes turned to Dr. Udagama, who in turn gestured toward an old man who stood supported by his wife in a corner of the reception room. It was pointed out to Clements that the man had an artificial nose.

"Isn't that marvelous," the governor said. "You know, I just came back from a couple of weeks in the mountains and I had a nosebleed. Will that nose of yours bleed?"

"Well, sir," the man said, laughing and tottering on his feet, "I hope not."

"Well," Clements said again. "Isn't that marvelous."

"Yessir," the man answered, "it sure is."

The tour continued through corridors and wards filled with patients who looked up at the passage of the governor with little more than mute acknowledgment of the diversion he presented. In one of the hallways he walked into a nest of reporters. "I don't want to answer questions," he said. "That's not my purpose in being here at all."

The reporters, unperturbed, joined the procession as it made its chaotic sweep through the hospital. Clements was paraded past picture windows through which he could observe patients being treated; he was escorted into the rooms of sleeping children.

"That's amazing," he said, tight-lipped, as he was fed information about the treatment of these cases. He was sensitive enough to know that the powers of intrusion of even a governor were limited.

The tour ended in a punch-and-cookies reception, and after that the governor was taken to a lecture room where Dr. Charles LeMaistre, the president of the University of Texas System Cancer Center, gave a suave little talk and slide show about the goals and needs of the hospital.

"Now, wait a minute," Clements said at the end of this talk, referring to a chart that demonstrated a rise in the incidence of cancer in Texas. "These are absolute numbers there on the chart, and here you're talking about *rate*. There's a difference. All the demographics show that from 1980 to 2000 our population in Texas is going to increase fifty per cent. So on a population basis per hundred thousand you're actually having a decrease."

I lost track of the distinction the governor was making, but his argument seemed to perk him up. He had been clearly uncomfortable in his tour of the hospital, a practical man recoiling not just from the suffering he saw around him but from the random, amorphous nature of that suffering. Now, away from that chaos, he was taking comfort in charts.

"Well, Mickey," he said to LeMaistre after these demographic matters had been discussed, "it's been a very, very fine presentation."

LeMaistre presented the governor and his wife with two T-shirts to be worn during their "relaxation time." The shirts read: "Fighting Cancer—Now That's a Job."

The routines of statecraft brought Clements back to the Capitol. In the Governor's Reception Room, which contained a model of the Liberty Bell, a saddle, a display of silver serving platters, and other such forbidding knickknacks, he held one of his weekly press conferences.

"It seems to be the mode of operation these days in Washington," he said, "to announce ground rules for press conferences. We'll continue to observe the same rules as before, and that is that whoever yells the loudest gets the question."

They asked him about his $35 million emergency appropriations bill to relieve overcrowding in Texas prisons, about wiretapping and bilingual education. Some of these questions he answered in a straightforward manner, but overall he was impatient and suspicious.

"If you were a Vietnamese fisherman in Seabrook—"

"Fortunately, I'm not. I happen to be governor. That's a better job."

"Do you have any objections to Mr. Estelle's ideas on work release?"

"I'm not going to discuss it anymore until I see what his plan is. I have no comment to make. Why should I make a comment?"

"Wouldn't it have been better to build this facility two years ago?"

"You know, your hindsight is remarkable."

And so it went. It seemed obvious that Clements did not hold weekly press conferences to indulge a fondness for passing on information to the electorate. It was a lion-taming session, a chance to face down the beast, smell its breath, and escape unharmed and exhilarated.

The next day he was on another tour, inspecting the fusion reactor at the University of Texas, then shuttling across campus to be guided through the scholarly artifacts stored in the Humanities Research Center. On display in the HRC was one of the original Gutenberg Bibles.

"This," said a small, intense man with an eccentric haircut, "is one of the most remarkable monuments of Western civilization. It reveals the birth of the greatest art form of our time. We live by it, our souls are structured by it." The man was teetering on the verge of rhapsody. Clements brought him back to earth by

asking how much it had cost.

"Two million dollars," he said proudly.

"Cheap, huh?"

The governor was then shown a playbill from 1753, a group of mannequins dressed in foppish costumes from the Ballet Russe, and Vivien Leigh's dress form from *Gone With the Wind*. What he responded to most were two sketches by President Eisenhower that hung in a replica of John Foster Dulles's study.

"You know it's remarkable the talent Eisenhower had," he said.

Clements seemed to harbor a mild appreciation of the Humanities Research Center, but I doubted if all these scholarly oddments hit him where he lived. "Hmmm," he kept saying. "That's a great asset for the University. *Very* interesting."

"I never think about a so-called public self," the governor said the next day in his office, slouching on a sofa and sipping hot tea. He had spent most of the morning posing with the representatives of every Boy Scout council in Texas and had just now come from the House Chamber, where he had given the scouts a speech and signed a proclamation declaring it Boy Scout Week. As he left he received a standing ovation, and the applause was like a wave that deposited him at the door of the House Chamber and then immediately receded. It was astonishing to see how quickly and thoroughly that sort of adulation could disappear.

"For instance," he went on, "I'm not gonna change my way of dress to create an image. I'm not gonna cut my hair short or grow it long. When you start thinking in terms of how this looks to the public, then you lose your character, whatever that character is. That's sheer dishonesty, in my opinion.

"You don't have to tell me a lot of politicians do that. When I first started campaigning these professional people came in. They were telling me that there's a school you can go to in New York City, this so-called charm school, where they teach you how to dress, how to move your hands, how to speak. Baloney. I have a very strong feeling that under no circumstances do I want to be anything but me."

I remembered a man who had walked up to him at a public function and held out a hand. The governor had shaken it, asked where the man was from, and said, "Good. Good to see ya." But the man just stood there, wanting something, wanting *nothing*. Here he was, standing next to the governor of Texas, and he did not want the moment to pass. I don't believe Clements understood this, the helpless rapture of the average citizen. Had the man wanted to ask for a pardon for his brother on death row, had he wanted to protest a budget cut or invite

the governor to a bake sale, he would have made sense, he would have fit into the equation. But Clements could not imagine this man—being this man—any more than he could imagine being a Vietnamese fisherman instead of governor. His intelligence was a powerful, fixed instrument like a headlight.

I had that man in mind when I asked the governor if it was ever frustrating to him, having to hobnob with the rich and powerful all day rather than with the average citizen.

"I'm not sure there is any such thing as an average citizen," he said. "As I circulate around you'd be amazed at how much work is being done. Whether it's something like going to that Exchange Club lunch—I saw people I had to say things to that were involved in state business. I went to a private dinner last night and what we ended up talking about ninety per cent of the time was state business. Bum Bright [the Dallas trucking magnate who is one of the richest men in Texas] was there, and he wants to talk about A&M. There were three bankers there who couldn't have a meeting of the minds about what could be done with usury laws in the state. What is this ordinary citizen we're talking about? Is it bankers? They're ordinary. Bankers or ordinary former students of A&M? Bum may be the chairman of the board of regents, but he's an ordinary Aggie."

The next time I saw Bill Clements he was at the National Governor's Conference in Washington, D.C., striding purposefully through the Hyatt Regency hotel with a stack of briefing books under his arm.

I followed him around for a few days, watching him vote gleefully against a modest position statement meant to express the governors' concern about acid rain. In the same vein, he proposed an amendment to another statement to prevent the Environmental Protection Agency from "diddlin' with our groundwater." It was put about that he had presented Ronald Reagan with a cowboy hat made from the pelt of an albino beaver.

Clements was prominent at this conference, especially so in meetings dealing with international trade and foreign relations. He came across in these gatherings as well informed, fair-minded, deferential. Here, among his peers and the representatives of favored nations, he displayed none of his renowned surliness. He was almost gracious.

On one memorable occasion Bill Clements and Jerry Brown met in their capacities as members of the Southwest Border Regional Commission.

"And that reconsideration, Jerry," Clements was saying in regard to some esoteric point involving the funding of the commission, "would be along the lines of some sort of state match with a federal match. The percentage is unknown. I think our recommendation would have a strong influence on what finally happens."

Brown did not respond. He just sat there, cradling his forehead in his left hand while he mechanically forked up the white, glutinous object on his plate—fish, perhaps—with his right.

"How does all that sound to you?" Clements pursued.

"I want to think about it."

"Can you think and eat at the same time?"

"I always do."

Clements sat hunched over his place setting with his soup spoon poised in midair. He was staring at the governor of California as if he were a creature on exhibit. There was a wary, bemused rapport between the two governors, and in some odd way they seemed allied against the other participants in the conference. Not politically allied, of course, since Clements was a soup-to-nuts laissez-faire Republican and Brown seemed to be on some ambiguous spiritual errand. But one noticed them; they both had a certain compelling charmlessness.

The meeting halls of the Hyatt Regency were filled that week with young, vigorous, even-spoken governors, the sort of men who might take a seat next to yours on a shuttle flight and, in the space of thirty minutes, convince you afresh of the fundamental reasonableness of the democratic enterprise. Gathered together in one place, these governors canceled one another out. They looked forlorn, milling about in the lobby, adjusting their hornrims, wearing name tags with a little yellow ribbon that read "Governor."

Bill Clements stood on the back portico of his Highland Park home, looking out over the manicured acreage sloping down to Turtle Creek. "Here comes one right over us," he said, indicating a wild duck. *"Quonnnck! Quonnnck!"*

The duck called back.

"Hear 'im?" Clements said. "Hear 'im answer me? I never use a duck call. I always do it with my mouth. *Quonnnck! Quonnnck!* We've got coons back here, too. And we've got the ducks and the geese and the swans. And we've got a few quail on the place. Some owls, and squirrels, of course. So it's a fun place. This is what keeps me invigorated."

Clements had grown up within a mile of this house. He was born in 1917 in a house that his parents had built on Maplewood. When his father's financial troubles began the family moved to a two-bedroom cottage on Normandy Street, where Clements achieved the distinction of growing up poor in Highland Park. He used to fish for crawdads in a creek on the SMU campus and hang out at the World War I barracks at Love Field where the Boy Scouts met. He loved Sunday school. His father

pitched on the church hardball team, and some of Clements's fondest memories are of those games and the picnics that took place afterward. He had an "absolutely marvelous, wonderful boyhood."

His first realization that his family didn't have money came when he was nine or ten years old and began to notice that all of his friends were going to camp. The camp tuition was $250 for six weeks, and to earn the money the young Clements went to work selling produce from a neighbor's garden. He also cleaned out his mother's chicken house, which he remembers as a "terrible chore." He became a Boy Scout and achieved Eagle rank. He went to high school and made all-state on the football team and edited the annual. He described both scouting and high school as "absolutely marvelous, wonderful experiences."

We went back inside. It was a large house, a mansion, filled with Mrs. Clements's graceful antique furniture and the governor's manly bric-a-brac.

"I'm interested," said the governor, "among other things you need to know, in art."

He pointed to a painting by a famous Western artist. "This was really in his best period," he said. "It was painted in 1911. I've got some others that were earlier. Before about '05 his work was really primitive. It didn't have the flow to it. Most people don't know it, but around 1900 he went to Paris and studied with the post-impressionists. Oh, sure. See, you get back here a little bit and the sage takes shape. But up close it has no shape at all. Amazing, isn't it?"

The governor showed me a painting by a man he termed "the best duck painter in America."

"That's called *Morning Mist,*" he said. "You can see the mist coming out of the water. I had him paint me a companion one called *Evenmoon.* Ever hear that word? It's a good word. That's when the sun is comin' up in the east and the moon is goin' down in the west and they're both level with each other. I was out huntin' ducks one day, and the sun was right at my back and shinin' on the ducks, and sure enough, there was the damn evenmoon up ahead. So I had this artist go down there to East Texas and paint those ducks for me."

There was a piano, with the sheet music to "The Impossible Dream" resting on the stand. A small downstairs library was filled with leatherbound books from the Franklin Library, a subscription book service that had sent the governor of Texas such volumes as *The Unmade Bed* by Françoise Sagan and *Jailbird* by Kurt Vonnegut.

The governor showed me his upstairs study, filled with Defense Department mementos, model airplanes, medallions, and framed portraits of famous Americans. After that we went down to the dining room, where a maid named Bessie served us breakfast.

During breakfast the governor talked about Sam Houston again. "He never recovered from Texas' seceding from the Union. It broke his heart. You hear about that, but in this case it really happened. He fought for independence in San Jacinto in '36, and what we're talkin' about is an act of secession in '61, so for twenty-five years here's a man who had only one thing on his mind, and that was Texas."

I wondered what it was about Sam Houston that intrigued Clements. Compared to the rest of the hardheaded free-enterprisers who had seized Texas from Mexico, Houston had been almost mystic. But Clements had fashioned Houston in his own mind as a clear, appraisable figure, a man you could do business with. Houston had invented Texas; Bill Clements, through sound management, would make it work.

Clements was scheduled to fly to Laredo that day, to address a conference on border industrialization and to meet the newly elected governor of the Mexican state of Tamaulipas. He had agreed to take me along and to stop by his Sedco office on the way to the airport so that I could see his library of Texana.

The governor got behind the wheel, and the Ranger who had meant to drive sat in the back seat.

"Boy," he said, inclining his head toward Turtle Creek, "as a kid I fished ever' hole on that whole watershed. Occasionally I'd catch a small bass. Mostly it was sun perch. You know those lakes there up at the country club? We'd dive in those lakes at night for golf balls. That caddymaster over there knew we were doin' it. Seldon McMillin and I would go down and feel for 'em in the mud. You get one of those Spalding balls that some guy had hit just once, you could sell it for fifty cents."

The Sedco offices were located in an old school building that Clements bought at auction in 1969 and then had restored. "The walls are solid brick," he said as we entered the building, which was staunch and lovely. "They're called bearing walls. The building is a structure in which the walls bear all the load."

Clements indicated a row of plaques on the wall. "Lo and behold, we won every architecture award in the country, even the national awards. We didn't have anything in mind of that nature—just doin' our thing, so to speak."

Clements's own office was in the southwest corner of the building. It was a paneled room neither too large nor too small, dominated by a mounted kudu head.

"It's really an antelope, is what it is," Clements said. "It's said by those who know to be the most prized trophy because of its horn configuration. That's why when people are given an honorary degree it's called a kudu."

On his desk was a piece of scrimshaw, a whale's tooth etched with the design of a

Trident submarine. "Just imagine," he said, "a thirty-billion-dollar weapons system. I fought like a tiger for it and it carried in the Senate by one vote. And I was the one who prevailed on that senator to cast that vote."

The library branched out from his office, rows and rows of ten-foot-high shelves filled with books about Texas. *Bigfoot Wallace, A Dynasty of Western Outlaws, Cow by the Tail.* The books were arranged by author and cataloged on file cards, and new titles were secured for Clements by a book dealer. The governor was a very rich man now, and it was evident that he bought his culture in bulk. But it was not difficult to imagine him 45 years ago, a young man in from the oil fields, chancing upon a book by J. Frank Dobie, turning it over and over in his hands to get an idea of its heft, and finally thinking something like "Hell, I'll just buy this thing." But perhaps it was not that idle a decision. After all, what would better motivate a young man to accumulate a library of Texas history than an unconscious desire to someday be a part of it?

The luncheon meeting of the industrialization conference took place in a utilitarian auditorium in the Laredo Convention Center. At each place setting there was a pile of little packets of salt, salad dressing, and Coffee-mate, which were brushed aside by waitresses in clear plastic gloves in order to make room for plates containing big, tough steaks.

The governor of Tamaulipas gave a boring speech, and then Clements gave a boring speech in which he said he favored the expansion and construction of international bridges and railheads. Then the two governors disappeared into a conference room for a few hours.

"I enjoy those fellas," Clements said after he emerged. "I'm really impressed with those Mexican governors."

The bluebonnets were out along the runways of the Laredo airport, and Clements admired them as he took his seat. The plane took off with such immediacy that I barely noticed when we left the ground.

We had a rambling discussion on the way back to the Capitol. The governor said his first memory dated from the age of three, when he put in an appearance stark naked at a party his mother was having in the back yard. He said he has no recurring dreams. He never thinks about reincarnation. He believes his high energy level has something to do with his ability to drop off to sleep within a matter of minutes. He is an implementer. He likes conversation with meat on it.

There was a lull. The governor glanced at a newspaper that was lying on the seat in front of him, then looked up and reestablished eye contact.

"Well," he said, rubbing his hands together, "ask me anything you want."♣

James A. Baker III, Esq. Politician

by Taylor Branch

In old-money Houston, they told James Baker to rise above politics. He listened well. Now he's running the White House.

During the fall of 1981, as the Baker family nervously prepared to take the president of the United States turkey hunting under the South Texas skies, everyone wondered whether Whispering Jack Garrett could be trusted to behave himself. A rice farmer rich enough to swap prize cattle with the leading families of South America, Garrett is also down-home enough to sport a salt-and-paprika beard and colorful opinions about nearly everything, including the "screw-ups" of the Reagan administration. "Daddy, don't you *dare* say anything to the president!" warned his daughter Susan, who is married to President Reagan's chief of staff, James A. Baker III, the leader of the hunting trip.

They couldn't watch him all the time, of course. As they lay in the sun waiting for the birds to come in, Garrett managed to snatch a little time alone with President Reagan. "I couldn't help it," Garrett recalls. "I talked to him just like anybody else. I said, 'Mr. Reagan, a great wrong has been done to some friends of mine down on Matagorda Island.'" He told the president that his friends had owned the island until the Air Force appropriated it for target practice during World War II and that the federal gov-

ernment had managed to find one excuse after another to hold on to the land. Garrett declared that the return of this chunk of land to its rightful owners would prove that Reagan meant what he said about getting the government off the backs of the people. Then he handed Reagan a little note laying out the facts and figures of the outrage.

A few days later, in the Oval Office, President Reagan asked his Big Three advisers if there were any further items on that morning's agenda. Michael Deaver, Ed Meese, and James Baker said no. The president reached into his pocket. "Well, I've got something," he said. "Jack Garrett told me about a problem with Matagorda Island down in Texas. He gave me this note. I want you fellows to look into it."

James Baker was already on his feet in a panic. He feared that his boss and his colleagues would think he was making deals and trading favors just like any other politician. "Mr. President, I swear I didn't know a damn thing about this!" he exclaimed, turning red.

President Reagan and his two longtime aides deadpanned as long as they could, savoring the moment. Something had finally bothered the amiable machine known as the

Miracle Man and the Velvet Hammer, demonstrating that nothing can mortify James Baker so quickly as the implication that he has allowed family or friend to take advantage of his official position. Baker's integrity is his exposed nerve. It is the only thing about which he can't take ribbing, because it is at the core of his vision of himself. He reacted as though a hundred years of Baker family tradition had been impeached.

Which it had—though only as a joke. President Reagan broke the tension by laughing heartily, as did Meese and Deaver. "My father-in-law is a real character," said Baker, trying to recover.

Appropriately, Whispering Jack Garrett's note went into Ed Meese's briefcase, not to be heard from again for months. Around the White House, that briefcase is compared to the Black Hole of Calcutta, in tribute to Meese's penchant for losing track of important documents. Meese is not known for being organized or for accomplishing complex tasks, and, for that matter, neither is Deaver. Those skills belong to Baker, the outsider, the man who runs the White House.

Baker is a new breed in several respects. Unlike his father-in-law, Jack Garrett, he is not a Texan of the old school. Instead, he appears colorless even to some of his closest friends. At the White House, Baker wears boots under his suit pants on Saturdays, but the only other cowboy leather on him is invisible, worn on his character. He is deceptively tough, even ruthless.

Baker is also a new kind of politician. He embodies the modern trend toward greater influence on the part of political staff aides, who seem to run the government while the elected officials tend to their images. Numerous insiders assert that Baker is the most important functionary in the Reagan White House, running it on his common sense and managerial skill. When a crisis must be managed, a major bill passed, a political alliance formed, Baker is the one in charge of making it happen. At the same time, however, Baker has the appearance of a political novice. He has never cared for political ideas, and he blushes over Whispering Jack's antics with President Reagan. He seems to be a prude, the spiritual descendant of the dollar-a-year patricians who once volunteered their services to the government.

The contradiction between the novice and the pro, the tough guy and the prude, results from the fact that there are really two Bakers. One comes from a hundred years of Houston tradition in a family that has always looked down on politics as a messy business. This Baker is trained to be dutiful, honest, and self-sufficient. He works hard and dabbles in hobbies. He is a proud, self-contained man who is neither awed by powerful politicians nor subject to the hunger that drives them. The other, newer Baker is consumed by politics. He views it as a game, and he plays to win, using all the patrician skills and self-confidence he developed in Houston.

The Houston Baker resisted politics until he was 40 (he's 52 today), and then he entered the field strictly as a tourist. As a review of his life will show, it took the death of two Bakers, the death of one political stranger, and the terminal illness of another politician to facilitate Baker's spectacular rise to the White House. Still, the two sides of him are often at war. The Houston Baker demands integrity; the political Baker demands a life without boredom. James Baker in the flesh tries to have it both ways.

Thirteen years ago, as Lyndon Johnson was retreating to the Pedernales at the head of a long line of Lone Star license plates, only a fool would have predicted that men like James Baker and George Bush, who were not even very popular in their home state, would restore Texas to prominence in national politics. Not only were they not popular, they were Republicans. In Johnson's time the Texas Republican party was a small, forgettable mixture of right-wingers and two-party-system do-gooders. Its few election victories—most notably John Tower's in the 1961 U.S. Senate race—were regarded as flukes.

Back then Ronald Reagan was considered a fluke, too—a divorced, nostalgic movie actor who could succeed only in a state like California. Ronald Reagan and Texas Republicans have become respectable together in the last decade, as the conservative West and Southwest have become more important in the political life of the nation. Even so, one would expect the new breed of Texas Republicans to come from the mold of John Connally, who, for all his flaws, is unmistakably a Texan, fully in the booming, extroverted tradition of Lyndon Johnson. That's why nobody in Houston paid much attention when George Bush and his campaign manager, James Baker, announced that they would challenge Connally for the 1980 presidential nomination. "People came up to me on the street in Houston and said, 'What the hell are you doing?'" Baker recalls. "They didn't give George a chance. It's hard to remember now, but back then Connally cast a big shadow in Texas."

Bush didn't. He didn't seem right for Texas, with his small bones, thin features, and clothes that fit. Bush was a Yankee transplant from Connecticut, an Ivy Leaguer, and even worse, he was the quintessential gray flannel man, with a small, reedy voice like Dick Cavett's that was always saying nonfolksy things. Not even a Madison Avenue magician could put George Bush convincingly on a horse. He was a fraternity house politician; he excelled at the delicate art of blending in.

Now Bush is vice president of the United States, of course, and Connally is back in his old law practice. And James Baker is chief of staff in the White House. Of these transitions, Baker's is the most remarkable. Ronald Reagan picked George Bush to be his running mate only because he had to. At the 1980 Republican convention in Detroit, candidate Reagan labored to avoid running with Bush, whom he regarded as a wimp unsuited for either the presidency or Nancy Reagan's company. By contrast, Reagan picked Baker because he wanted him. In a purely voluntary act, Reagan reached out to the wimp's campaign manager—to a man who had worked for Reagan's major opponents in 1976 and 1980, who had never really supported Reagan, and who evinced no particular interest in Reaganomics or any other political doctrine.

By all accounts, the selection of Baker was one of the shrewdest moves thus far in the Reagan presidency. The reasons, like Baker's talents, are hidden. The chief of staff is even less flamboyant than George Bush, if that is possible, and he has none of the earmarks of a born politician. Baker did not grow up living and breathing politics, like his predecessor under Lyndon Johnson, Marvin Watson. He was not tortured by issues of political morality, like Bill Moyers. He did not grow up wanting to run for office, like his friend George Bush, who has always gone after office the way a hound chases fur. Until he was forty, Baker confesses, he had been known to skip the voting booth to go

hunting on election day. He liked to lie in the sun, watch the backs of his eyelids, and let the world of big-time Houston law practice seep out of his mind. He did not read books about politics. In fact, he hardly read books at all. He took no interest in Houston affairs, and he cannot remember ever reacting to national or global political events. He has no political memories to speak of. No conversations or opinions stand out. The Berlin Wall draws a blank. So do Sputnik, the Cuban missile crisis, and even the John F. Kennedy assassination. "I was completely apolitical," he says. "Those things were outside my life."

One may wonder how such a drab, apolitical man—with such a volatile sense of integrity—could flourish in the Reagan White House. The conventional wisdom, not to be entirely disbelieved, is that Baker is a consummate "technician" of politics. His friends and enemies alike say he's a master of detail, a "lawyer's lawyer." Adjectives are piled on him: "efficient," "low-key," "competent," "professional," and so on. Baker reaches into his own ample store of clichés to allow that he "keeps the train running on time" and that he is "good at keeping a lot of balls in the air at once." He always has "plenty of work on my plate" and he never "lollygags" like the Reagan Californians. In short, Baker is an efficient workaholic.

Baker's vociferous critics on the far right allow all this and add that he is a stalking-horse for George Bush, who in turn is the representative of the corporate, Rockefeller wing of the Republican party. As such, Baker is the tool of the status quo, seeking to sabotage the electoral mandate of the "rock-hard Reaganites." In other words, Baker is a closet liberal among Republicans, and he succeeds because he has the clandestine support of the establishment. So say the New Right, the Moral Majority, and such conservative journalists as columnists Evans and Novak.

It is true that Baker is a pragmatist, and that he often opposes the Reagan ideologues. But he is no squishy liberal, and he is certainly not the pawn of George Bush, as one inside glimpse of Baker at work will show.

In May 1980 Ronald Reagan had the Republican nomination all but won. His remaining opponent, George Bush, stayed doggedly in the race, against the advice of his campaign manager, James Baker, who argued that Bush was crossing the line of decency. Baker said that Bush was about to acquire the stigma of a stubborn spoiler who persisted in the race only to torment the obvious nominee and thereby to divide the party. Bush countered that he was determined not to be a quitter.

While Bush was barnstorming through New Jersey, Baker held a small meeting at the Washington headquarters of the Bush campaign. "Jimmy made the decision to knock George out of the campaign without telling him," says one of Bush's campaign aides of that meeting. "He knew that the only way to do it was to hit George across the forehead with a two-by-four. It had to be done. Jimmy Baker had to cut his best friend off at the knees, and he did it."

At a press conference Baker announced that Bush was withdrawing from the California primary for lack of funds. This move effectively eliminated Bush from the race. In New Jersey, the candidate learned of Baker's statement from reporters who had seen the news flashes. Aides say Bush went into shock and flew back to Houston for an emergency council. He *still* did not want to quit. Some Bush family members vowed never to speak to Baker again. They said he was cold, arrogant, traitorous. How could he not have told Bush in advance?

"Well, that's not easy to say," said Baker, sitting next to a warm fireplace in his office at the White House. "But the truth of the matter is that he wouldn't have paid any attention and he might have reacted just the other way. He might have said something to make it harder to get out. Look, when you're a candidate, you're like a duck. You wake up in a different place every morning and you don't know where you are."

And how can Baker justify having gone against the candidate's wishes, knowing Bush wanted to stay in the race? "By the results," he said. "If he'd gone into the California primary, he wouldn't have that office in there." Baker pointed through an oil painting of a cavalryman shooting at an Indian, which hangs above the fireplace, toward the White House office of the vice president. "He wouldn't be vice president. At that point, we'd done everything we could do. We'd established political strength. All the other candidates had self-destructed. George Bush was the logical running mate, but he was not particularly popular with Governor Reagan. Even as it was, Governor Reagan looked everywhere he could not to pick Bush. If George had further alienated him back then by entering a primary in Governor Reagan's home state as a pure spoiler, there's no way he'd be where he is."

Baker looked briefly at the fire. He was smiling amiably, as usual, but he had been speaking quietly and slowly. "When we started that campaign, George Bush barely showed up in the polls," he added. "Now he's vice president of the United States. And he's only fifty-seven years old. I'd say that's pretty good."

Baker rested his case. With these few words, he had shown more personality than he likes to show the world. Baker is a man who wears everything easily—his millions, his pedigree, his country club tennis championships, his political accomplishments. In Houston, even the people he has climbed over seem genuinely devoted to him. They can't remember any bad stories about Baker. Then again, they can't think of many good ones, either, because Baker tends to do the right thing in a way that leaves no smudges on the memory.

His mother, Bonner Means Baker, an 87-year-old grande dame who sits in her parlor with a radiant smile on her face and a little bell in her hand, which she tinkles to call one of the maids, says that Baker has

every good quality there is. "I have always been proud of him," she says. "He's never done anything to make me feel otherwise."

Asked what memories of her son's life stand out for her, she trips over the thought briefly and then begins to laugh. "Goodness," she says. "I can't really think of any." After a few moments she recalls that Jimmy ran away from home when he was six or seven—but only for a few hours to go to the circus. (Still, she had called the police, fearing a Lindbergh-type kidnapping.)

Mrs. Baker has lived in the same house in Houston for the past 55 years. The last four digits of her telephone number have been the same since 1937. She remembers when the City of Houston changed her address to Bissonnet Avenue. "It used to be Poor Farm Road," she says. "I wish they'd kept that name."

Later, when talking about how generations of Baker men have been trained to work smoothly in the background, she asks a maid to bring in the article about Captain Baker, James Baker's grandfather and most famous ancestor. The maid returns with the yellowed front page of a newspaper, mounted in a frame. There is an ancient photograph of the stern, old-fashioned Captain Baker below a headline setting forth his advice to aspiring lawyers: WORK HARD, STUDY, AND KEEP OUT OF POLITICS.

"I'm going to send that to Jimmy up in Washington," says Mrs. Baker. She adds that she is only half serious when she complains about her son's descent into politics. (She roots openly for his opponents, hoping he'll lose and come home.) But she says the other Baker men, in their day, were deadly serious. To the Bakers, politics was surer to corrupt an upright man than a lifetime of whorehouses and booze. "If his father were living, I doubt he would have let Jimmy go to Washington."

The chief of staff turns this tradition into an advantage. He sees it as a kind of vaccine that partially immunizes him against the lures of power. His strength is his objectivity, his ability to remain himself. Being a Baker, he does not allow his world to be distorted by the politician's craving for office, and neither is he a "creature" of his boss, as Hamilton Jordan was for Carter, and Bob Haldeman for Nixon. He can hit George Bush with the two-by-four, and if it becomes necessary, he might do the same to Ronald Reagan.

That is the idea, anyway. Baker admits that he has become "hooked" on politics, but he and his friends say his character has not changed. The warning system of the old Houston Bakers still runs in his blood.

All the first sons have been named James Addison Baker. Friends call the chief of staff Jimmy. His son is Jamie. His father was Jim. His grandfather was called Captain Baker even by intimates. His great-grandfather was Judge Baker. Mrs. Baker, Jim's widow and Jimmy's mother, believes there was yet another James Addison before

Judge Baker. That would have been back before the Alamo. "We never talk about him, though," she says. "In any family, you can go back far enough to find something unpleasant, I guess."

Judge Baker returned from Confederate service during the Civil War to find that he had been elected a local judge in one of the counties near Houston. It seems that he was too busy seeking his fortune to spend much time on the bench, but he kept the title for honorific purposes, as was common in those days. In 1872 Judge Baker added his name to the Houston law firm of Gray & Botts, which had been formed six years earlier. Today Baker & Botts is one of the twenty largest law firms in the country. In Houston, it is synonymous with legal royalty, conservatism, and clout.

Part of the antipolitical tradition of Baker & Botts can be traced to the original partners' firsthand experience with the horrors of the Civil War. A new impetus came along in the 1880s and 1890s, when the federal and state governments began a protracted war against the great bronco capitalists: the railroads, the banks, the trusts, and the titans of interstate commerce. Baker & Botts represented the companies, to whom the politicians and the voters were the enemy. According to the official history of Baker & Botts, the partners fought valiantly for "the safe conduct of the great properties committed to the guidance of the firm in that period of popular unrest and radical legislation."

Most of the great properties were owned by Jay Gould, the firm's principal client in those years. Gould was one of the most energetic and least scrupulous of the robber barons, a man who made and stole millions in the railroad business while living in luxury. Naturally, he hired the best lawyers he could find to defend the "Gould System" of railroads and his other sprawling interests. From the standpoint of the lawyers at Baker & Botts, their association with Gould was as challenging as it was lucrative. In addition to voluminous commercial work, they had to fight off claims that Gould was a fraud, a cheat, and a monopolist. To do so, they had to portray the politicians who were trying to regulate him as ignorant, corrupt opportunists, and they had to show Gould by contrast as a vital, responsible engine of progress. The latter part of this task was made difficult by the fact that Gould himself was always watering stock and bribing legislatures. And to make matters worse, Gould liked to brag of these exploits in public, usually with a girlfriend or two hanging on his arm.

To compensate for the behavior of clients like Gould, the lawyers at Baker & Botts climbed to the heights of decorum. They were rigorously proper, starchy, and controlled. They stamped out all sentiment or extravagance that might lead to scandal. They lived well, but always in the background. In a standoff between rascals, the firm's own dignity might tip the scales in favor of the great properties.

Rising to the desired posture, the lawyers

at Baker & Botts abstained from all legal work that acknowledged any connection to human nature. (To this day, the firm abhors criminal cases, divorce proceedings, and personal damage suits.) The goal was to elevate law to its driest, most intellectual plane. The firm grew rapidly, adding E. H. Harriman and other wealthy Yankee businessmen to its list of commercial clients in Texas. Judge Baker's son, Captain Baker, was in charge by the turn of the century.

Ironically, Captain Baker made his name and secured his family's fortunes with his performance in a spectacular murder case. He represented William Marsh Rice, a multimillionaire investor and cotton trader who divided his time between Houston and New York. When Rice died in 1900 in New York, a prominent New York attorney surfaced with a brand-new will—supplanting an old will drafted by Captain Baker—for the newly deceased Mr. Rice. Captain Baker hopped on his private railroad car and sped to New York.

Arsenic and mercury were detected in Rice's body, and there was evidence that he had been suffocated with chloroform. Under interrogation by Captain Baker himself, Rice's humble manservant confessed that he, in cahoots with the New York attorney, had murdered the old man. The servant later recanted and then reconfessed. The attorney's murder trial was a prolonged media feast—similar in many respects to the Harry Thaw murder trial of that same period (as recounted in *Ragtime*)—with Captain Baker featured almost daily in the *Times*. The defense argued that Captain Baker had .rumped up the murder charges because he was a beneficiary of the original Rice will. But the jury believed otherwise. The prominent New York attorney was sentenced to the electric chair, whereupon a great cry of protest was raised in influential circles of New York society. New York's governor granted a commutation and, years later, a full pardon.

Captain Baker returned triumphantly to Houston with Rice's fortune, which became the foundation of Rice University. Baker served as the university's board chairman until his death in 1941, and Baker College at Rice was named for him. He was also the first president and a major stockholder of the South Texas Commercial National Bank (now Texas Commerce Bancshares), a perpetual member of many corporate boards, and a leading (but strictly private) city father of Houston. When the first ship steamed up the new Houston Ship Channel to the Turning Basin on November 8, 1909, it was Captain Baker who presided over the celebrations as King Nottoc. That's "cotton" spelled backward, after Houston's most valuable export in the early days.

Captain Baker brought back from his trips to New York a conviction that a stiff Northern education was essential for any Baker offspring. He believed that the Yankee schools would not only add a touch of class to a rough-cut Texas youth but would also parch out of him the kind of mustang fever

that could prove ruinous to Baker & Botts. Accordingly, the captain's son, Jim Baker, prepped at the Hill School and graduated from Princeton before entering law school at the University of Texas. Then he went off to World War I. In a courageous, though foolhardy, deed, young Baker once ran impetuously across no-man's-land and jumped into the German trenches, capturing a handful of enemy soldiers. He returned to Baker & Botts as a war hero, an Army captain.

In Houston, the soldier became plain Jim Baker again, because the family had room for only one Captain Baker. Although the hero of the Rice trial had never served in the military and had acquired his title from an elite men's social club called the Houston Light Guards, the rank had become an integral part of his name and persona. His reputation overshadowed his son, who always did the proper thing without attracting attention. Jim courted and married a Houston woman named Bonner Means, who as a young girl had been fond of riding her Shetland pony through the heart of the city, across meadows that in her lifetime would be stacked to the sky with concrete, steel, and money. She was a Bonner, from one of the original landowners in the Humble oil field. She was also a Means. "My great-great-uncle [John Hugh Means] was governor of South Carolina when the first shot was fired at Fort Sumter," she says proudly. In 1930 Bonner Means Baker gave birth to her first son, Jimmy, who would become Ronald Reagan's chief of staff.

During the Depression, the Baker extended family took supper together around an enormous table. The maids always served three separate meals—one for the patriarch, Captain Baker, who was a diabetic; one for an uncle who refused to eat vegetables; and another for everyone else. Absolute silence was demanded of the children until the table was cleared, at which time Captain Baker presided over his own kind of catechism. He asked each of his numerous grandchildren to stand and recite something interesting he or she had learned that day, promising a dime to the one whose recital pleased him most. Competition was fierce for both the money and the honor. Sometimes, as a test of nerve, Captain Baker would offer a dime to the grandchild who could walk through a pitch-black drawing room without stumbling or crying out in fear, and sometimes he held out a dime to the one who could eat the most vegetables at dinner.

Jimmy's father, Jim Baker, then in his prime, would be fully dressed for duty at Baker & Botts when he walked into his son's bedroom each morning at the same time to announce the hour. If the heavily sleeping boy did not promptly plant his feet on the floor, his father would waste no time in pouring a pitcher of cold water on his head, drenching pillow, bedclothes, and son. Jimmy's mother considered the practice cruel, but she acknowledged that it was an effective form of discipline.

Actually, Jim Baker took a slightly less authoritarian approach than his own father

had, though the difference was no doubt lost on the young ones. When Jim had announced his intention to specialize in trial work at Baker & Botts, Captain Baker had peremptorily vetoed the idea, on the grounds that the Rice trial was all the family could stand. (Trials, Captain Baker believed, were public spectacles filled with passionate arguments and other things dangerous to lawyers.) Thirty years later, Jimmy Baker took up the practice of law with the same intention, and his father raised no objection. By Baker standards, this acquiescence signaled a breeze of liberalism.

"I wanted to be a trial lawyer, and I tried it for a while," Jimmy Baker recalls. "But not for long. I didn't like the way people lied all the time. That's what they did. The witnesses lied in the courtroom, and there was nothing I could do about it. It was very, very frustrating. So I quit." Jimmy Baker would practice corporate law the way his forebears had: hidden from public view.

This aversion to lying, like most of Baker's characteristics, would seem to rule out a life in politics. But he has been able to turn it to his advantage. In the White House he has at times advanced himself as the resident stickler for the truth. A few hours after the assassination attempt against President Reagan last March, there were rumors that Secretary of State Alexander Haig and Secretary of Defense Caspar Weinberger were quarreling childishly over who was the ranking government official during the crisis. The Department of State and the Pentagon each denied the rumors, but chief of staff Baker publicly told reporters that they were true. Yes, Haig and Weinberger had disagreed rather strongly, he said, but the problem had been cleared up. This statement settled the matter.

The incident might be taken as a demonstration of Baker's impetuous honesty, but it was something altogether different. Of all the many misstatements by Haig and Weinberger, Baker chose to contradict only this one, and he did so because a number of factors converged in support of the move. First, there was duty. The president had been shot and was then in surgery, and during the national crisis it was not healthy to let the press keep jumping on Haig and Weinberger for lying about their quarrel. Second, the facts were known to many witnesses, so Baker ran little risk of being challenged by either official. Third, Haig and Weinberger had told the same lie at the same time. This rare concurrence allowed Baker to rebuke each one without giving political advantage to the other. Even before the assassination attempt, Haig and Weinberger had been jockeying rather brazenly to expand their influence at the White House, and Baker took advantage of an opportunity to check them both at once. He made the point forcefully that the White House was in charge. His move was honest, but it was also very calculated. That is his style.

Baker retains his phobia about lying, but he takes full advantage of the verbal maneuvering that the rules of politics allow. He hints. He qualifies. He says nothing, if necessary. Above all, he leaks things to the press. Many regular correspondents are agreed that Baker is the most adroit leaker in the White House.

Late last summer Baker spent a few days with the president's entourage in California. There was ominous talk of huge budget deficits in the future, and there were rumors that the president might cut the defense budget substantially in order to avoid the deficits. One evening an unusual mood settled over the traveling press corps. The reporters seemed smug, close-mouthed, evasive. They did not try out tomorrow's stories on each other, which meant that somebody was hoarding a scoop. As the last deadlines passed and it became safe for the reporters to boast about their stories, they discovered to their astonishment that nearly a dozen of them were running the same exclusive: that President Reagan had almost certainly decided to cut a whopping $35 billion from the Pentagon budget. Baker had leaked the story to every one of them.

As it turned out, Reagan rejected the Pentagon cut. Similarly, he rejected the idea of proposing tax increases in his 1982 State of the Union address, in spite of a prolonged pro-tax-increase leaking campaign by Baker and his allies. In both of these cases, the chief of staff no doubt reasoned that the leaks allowed Reagan to find out in advance how the public might react to a certain course. There seems to be an accepted code of leaking. Classified information is out. It is all right to leak on one side or another of a pending policy decision, but it is never all right to leak criticism of the decision after it is made. In fact, it is never proper to leak criticism of the president, but it is acceptable and even desirable to leak criticism of aides whose mistakes hurt the president, so that they can take the heat instead of him.

After the White House admitted that President Reagan had been allowed to sleep all night while Libyan jets attacked U.S. fighters over the Mediterranean, White House leaks soon appeared stating that Ed Meese was on duty and should have waked the president. There have also been stories suggesting that Meese too often leaves the command center to make trivial political speeches and that he mishandled the administration's policy on tax exemptions for segregated private schools. Baker had complicity in all these leaks, but they came from Michael Deaver as well. This is a crucial point. Baker is still the newcomer to the Reagan camp, while Meese and Deaver have each been there fifteen years. On leaks that affect the delicate arrangement among the Big Three advisers, Baker hesitates to move alone. Fortunately for him, Deaver shares his vigilant concern about Reagan's image. The two of them believe that a large part of politics is about how things look to the public. Meese cares more about substance and tends toward sloppiness, so he is vulnerable.

White House reporters estimate that Baker sees twice as many news people as Meese and Deaver put together. He cultivates them. As soon as he knew that he would hold a post in the Reagan administration, he called many of the reporters he had known in the 1976 and 1980 campaigns to invite them to call on him in the White House. He would be available.

Baker knows that press relations is a game of give and take. Reporters print stories that serve his interests, but they also criticize him occasionally. He learns little bits of useful gossip from reporters, but he knows that he must make news for them. Baker is especially wise on this last point. He always makes sure that White House reporters come away from a Baker interview with "something to write," even if it's not earthshaking. Meese, on the other hand, tries to be accommodating and yet fears that the reporters' gain is his loss. He instinctively deflects questions with his vague answers, and reporters complain that they come away with a notebook full of garble.

Nearly all reporters like Baker personally. So do congressmen and other politicians. Everyone says he is extremely competent in the White House, and even his enemies say he is a nice guy. "He's really amiable, for a Republican," says one liberal reporter. His heritage might lead one to anticipate a snob, a stuffed shirt, but this particular Baker has developed a warm streak. He seems especially likable because he clearly enjoys what he is doing in the White House. He enjoys it because he is less desperate about his job than most politicians, who become slaves to their importance and their fame. Baker's secret weapon is that he is in politics largely for the fun of it.

After fifty years and a stretch in a criminal asylum, the humble man-servant who had confessed to the Rice murder decided to shoot himself in the head. His suicide was the subject of an obscure news item out of Baytown in 1954. That same year, Captain Jimmy Baker received his discharge from the Marine Corps and went back to Texas with his wife, Mary Stuart, and their infant son, James A. Baker IV. Like his father, Jimmy was a graduate of the Hill School and Princeton University, and he continued in the Baker mold by enrolling at the University of Texas law school. He also submitted when instructed to join Phi Delta Theta, his father's fraternity in Austin.

This was a major test of his obedience, for fraternity membership brought many special hardships to Baker. Everyone else in his pledge class was fresh out of high school, eager to drink beer and chase girls. Baker was the only non-undergraduate. He was seven years older than his pledge brothers. And more important, he was a married man. At the end of the day's classes, Baker would rush home to wave quickly at his wife and son. Then he would rush back to the frat house so that the Phi Delt brothers could throw raw eggs down his throat all night. The ritual hazing was severe in those days.

During Hell Week, one of Baker's Phi Delt brothers recalls having to wear a necklace of a dozen dead shrimp for seven full days—to classes, to the fraternity house, everywhere. Another contemporary says that Baker had to spend the week with a dead fish tied to his penis. Baker says he remembers the fish but not how it was attached. He says the entire fraternity experience was an ordeal for his wife. He, being an ex-Marine, took it more or less in stride.

"I did that for my father," says Baker. "He wanted me to do it because he had done it. He believed it was the smart thing to do. If you're going to practice law in Texas, you go to the law school in Austin and make all the contacts you can. They'll pay off later."

The dutiful son resented his father's narrow road more at the time than he does now. With hindsight, he says it was all good for him—the cold water, the fish, the spartan rules. "My old man was tough with me," he says, adding that he has appreciated his father's regimen since watching so many of his own contemporaries fall prey to alcoholism and mental instability, the time-honored sinkholes for rich kids. Baker kept his drive. He worked hard and gloried in testing himself against the elements, as did Teddy Roosevelt. Even today, he is proud that he has never allowed a single piece of shelter to be constructed on his 1800-acre hunting spread in Pearsall. There are a few oil wells, but otherwise there is nothing more than a loose tent on the bare ground. Every few years, when the tent gets nasty, Baker simply burns it and sets up another one somewhere else.

After law school, Baker was obliged to depart from 85 years of family tradition. Baker & Botts would not allow him to join the family firm; a strict anti-nepotism rule had been instituted there in the early thirties. So Baker found a job with Andrews & Kurth, another well-established Houston firm. While not quite as large or powerful as Baker & Botts, it was even more conservative. Andrews & Kurth was a throwback to the nineteenth century, with a reputation for such tight-lipped professional discretion that it could satisfy even the mania for secrecy of its most famous and demanding client, billionaire recluse Howard Hughes.

Judge Melvin Kurth's idea of law practice involved a lot of stiff parchment, old books, and candlelight. He resisted all modern conveniences, and his frugality obliged the younger partners to introduce changes by careful conspiracy. Baker learned this strategy the hard way. At a staff meeting when the firm was preparing to move from the Gulf Building to the Exxon Building, he stood up and inquired about the proposed new Xerox machine.

Baker knew instantly that he had made a mistake. Everyone in the room except Judge Kurth froze in terror. The old tyrant scowled, sniffed, and swelled up like a blowfish. *"What,"* he thundered, "is a Xerox machine?" Baker's indiscretion delayed the arrival of the Xerox by several months.

He worked long, tedious hours, gaining a reputation as "Mr. Memo" because he could reduce complicated legal questions to concise notes for his mentor, Harry Jones. Baker's contemporaries at Andrews & Kurth say he was known for his technical skill and his lack of pomposity. They found the latter trait somewhat surprising in a Baker. Some of the lawyers went so far as to say that Baker concealed a mischievous streak behind his professional demeanor. One partner, Robert Weatherall, recalls that he returned from lunch one day with a large group of stuffy banker clients, all of whom were shocked to find "Mr. Toad" painted on Weatherall's door in official-looking letters. The humorless bankers demanded to know the meaning of it, declaring that they did not retain Andrews & Kurth for such frivolity. "I know that son of a bitch Baker was behind it," laughs Weatherall now. "But he wouldn't admit it, even when I threatened to go to Judge Kurth."

Throughout the sixties, Baker threw himself into commercial law. He performed his duller duties with aplomb—merging companies, drawing contracts, making deals. After a time, he spiced up his practice by investing his own money in some of the ventures. He became president of a realty company and was instrumental in organizing a Houston brokerage house. As a lawyer and investor, he helped incorporate a successful well-servicing business called Welltech, which he and the other investors later sold to the Bechtel Corporation and the Hanna Mining Company at a healthy profit. By the end of the decade, Baker had earned his own small fortune to supplement the substantial inheritance that would be due him on the death of his father. (Baker estimates that his immediate family—his mother, his sister, and himself— is worth $5 million.)

Jimmy Baker's life changed permanently in late 1968, when doctors diagnosed a virulent, incurable cancer in his wife, Mary Stuart Baker. Her health deteriorated rapidly over the next several months, and Baker faced not only the grief of her death but also the prospect of raising their four young sons by himself. "The toughest thing I ever had to do was to tell those boys what was happening to their mother," he says.

It took sixteen months for her to die. Near the end, Baker would often shuttle between the hospital and the office several times a day. His partners at Andrews & Kurth are still struck by the memory of Baker returning from the hospital, time after time, always silent. "Sometimes he'd pour himself a drink," says one. "On days when it must have been especially rough. But he never said anything. He never complained."

When it was over, Baker tried to take stock of himself. He says he realized that he had been a less-than-perfect father and husband. He had worked too much, by habit and by inclination. Now he needed to establish a life with his sons, but grief drove him to work more, or to hunt. He also realized that he had conquered most of what there was to

conquer in Houston law practice. What lay ahead was more money and more work, both of which had lost some of their appeal.

Baker moped a lot, which for him meant that he disengaged his afterburners and worked like a normal person. Two things interrupted his moping. One was the fresh chaos of being the only parent to four sons whose ages stretched from Little League to first growth of beard. The other was Houston congressman George Bush, who persistently urged Baker to get into politics. Bush had already run once for the Senate and was planning to do so again. He wanted Baker to go after his seat in the House. Baker refused. Then Bush pressed Baker to help in his Senate campaign. He said Mary Stuart, a native of Ohio and a staunch Republican, would have liked it. As a pioneer precinct chairman in Houston in the fifties, she had often found herself alone at Republican meetings.

In the end, Baker agreed to work as a volunteer as long as he did not have to travel outside Houston, away from the boys. The candidate was delighted, but Baker says he knew that his friend had pulled him into the campaign mostly as a form of therapy. That fall, Bush lost the Senate race to Lloyd Bentsen. Baker claims that he didn't do much to help. He also recalls, however, that Bush carried Houston by exactly the margin they had thought was required to win the state.

Years passed at Andrews & Kurth, and Baker did some minor work as a Nixon fundraiser. In 1973, shortly after his father died, Baker married Whispering Jack Garrett's daughter Susan, who had three children by her own first marriage. Susan had been one of Mary Stuart's best friends. The Bakers spent the remainder of that year trying to blend their seven children into a new family. They once had three in the seventh grade at the same time. In 1977 they had a daughter of their own, Mary Bonner.

Meanwhile, George Bush served as ambassador to the United Nations and then as semi-ambassador to China. When Secretary of Commerce Rogers Morton visited Bush in Peking, Bush urged him to lure Baker to Washington somehow, to help nurse the Republican party back to health after Watergate. Morton's entreaties soon threw the Baker household into strong disagreement. This is when, Jimmy's mother says, her husband would have scotched the idea of a trip to Washington—if he had been alive. Susan Baker was reluctant to go because she had achieved a tentative peace among her seven kids and had settled them in various Houston schools; but she did like big-time politics. Her husband didn't particularly like politics, but he was intrigued by the thought of a tour in Washington. A high post there would be a respectable diversion.

Inevitably, the move was complicated. Some kids went to the capital and some stayed in Houston when Baker went to Washington in August 1975 to become Under Secretary of Commerce. The job involved low-key promotional work with businessmen, which suited Baker perfectly,

and by all accounts he proved himself a gifted administrator. Public controversy touched him only once, when Baker, the devout Texan, kept boasting in speeches about how the Ford administration had tripled American trade with Arab countries. B'nai B'rith spokesmen roundly attacked him for not doing enough to stop those same Arab countries from blacklisting American companies that tried to do business with Israel. Baker was still clarifying his remarks on this subject when his first Washington boss, Rogers Morton, tried to recruit him for the Ford reelection campaign.

At the time, President Ford's campaign was hitting a banana peel at every stride. Challenger Ronald Reagan had defeated the president in six straight primaries. Rogers Morton had been pressed into service as Ford's campaign chairman after Bo Callaway was implicated in a ski lodge scandal. President Ford misspoke himself every time he tried to refute Reagan's charges of incompetence. His campaign staff was disorganized; its chief delegate hunter had just been killed in an automobile accident.

Late in April 1976, President Ford invited Baker to accompany him on a campaign trip to Houston. Returning on *Air Force One,* Ford asked Baker to take over as chief delegate hunter. "That ended it," says Baker. "I couldn't say no to the president of the United States." Thus Baker began his career as the reluctant campaign operative. This is a modern role. It used to be the candidates themselves who had to be coaxed and drafted.

Baker moved in quickly, picking up aides wherever he could find them. He avoided grand strategy and political gab to concentrate on the realities as he saw them. Primarily, he saw that Reagan and Ford were running nearly even toward what might be the first wide-open convention in decades. Baker reasoned that the game would turn on about a hundred uncommitted delegates, plus a few "soft" ones on either side. Setting about to identify them, he told his regional and state directors to find and report on the marginals. He wanted to know everything about them—their worries, their birthdays, their neighbors' names, their heroes, their favorite colors, everything. "We got to know those people," says a Baker delegate hunter. "Sometimes we'd get all excited in the headquarters if delegate Fred in Iowa told us something we could use. Jimmy always wanted to know what the delegates needed to hear to commit to Ford. Then we'd try to let them hear it. If you had a tough one right on the edge, Jimmy would talk to the guy himself. He was always soft-sell, but he was trying to figure out what they wanted."

The system was humming by the end of May. Baker secured an hour of President Ford's time each day for "campaign calls." Early every morning the nominees' names would filter up from the phone callers to the state and regional directors and finally to Baker himself, who wanted fifteen to twenty words on why President Ford should call delegate X that day. Then Baker had to weed out the extras, deciding whether it was more important to congratulate the Minnesota delegate on her daughter's college graduation or to tell the Louisiana delegate that President Ford shared his concern about levee repairs on the Mississippi River. His rule of thumb came to be that most delegates wanted little things and that they could be swayed by the majesty of the White House. "It's very difficult to look the president of the United States in the eye and tell him you're not with him," he says.

His only strategic recommendation about the campaign was that President Ford should say less in public and do more with the delegates in private. Baker helped shift Ford into a presidential mode, accenting the positive. Whenever Baker announced new Ford delegates, he released their names and telephone numbers to the press so that reporters could verify his claims. Gradually, this policy put pressure on John Sears, Baker's counterpart in the Reagan campaign, who was always claiming newly converted Reagan delegates but withholding their names. Reporters came to doubt Sears when he announced that Reagan had enough votes to win. "We probably would have beaten them if Baker hadn't brought order to the Ford campaign," Sears comments. "He was the only new guy over there, and suddenly they quit making mistakes."

Later, at the Kansas City Republican convention, President Ford and his chief of staff, Richard Cheney, made a tough decision: they decided to replace Rogers Morton as chairman of the fall campaign against Jimmy Carter. Morton was dying of cancer. Moreover, his fondness for alcohol was leading to major gaffes. Asked what he planned to do about the fact that Ford trailed Jimmy Carter by thirty points in the polls, Morton had said he sure didn't plan to rearrange the deck chairs on the Titanic. Such blunders would never do.

They gave the job to Baker, although he had never run even a statewide campaign before. His rise in politics had been one of breathtaking speed. Only one year after leaving Houston, he was in charge of the incumbent president's campaign.

Ford reduced Carter's lead steadily through September and October. Baker generally kept the campaign on the high road, but in the last week, when it appeared that Ford would fall short, the campaign resorted to a dirty trick. A black Republican minister sought entry to services at Jimmy Carter's church in Plains, Georgia, and he had no sooner been turned away than four hundred telegrams went out over Baker's signature, asking black ministers across the country how Carter could hope to end racism in the whole nation if he was helpless in his own church. The incident made national news, but reporters expressed suspicion of the telegrams because of the timing.

"It was rigged," says Baker today, painfully. "Our special voters' group sent somebody down there to set it up. But I didn't know a thing about it. Neither did [political director] Stu Spencer. And it was a terrible mistake. It backfired. I think it really hurt us."

By the end of election day, Carter had won and Baker was forever hooked on politics. He still talks about how a swing of 17,000 votes in Ohio and Hawaii would have reelected Ford. In retrospect, he says that the preconvention delegate work was "demeaning" because he had to minister to so much pettiness, but the general election was "exciting." Since then Baker has told friends that he could never go back to the full-time practice of law. It would be too dull. He speaks of politics as the only game in which "the whole world can turn upside down overnight . . . Everything goes for one day." Baker became a political junkie in the fall of 1976, three years after his father died.

Immediately after Ford's defeat, sober Republicans spoke of their party's possible extinction. An incumbent president had narrowly missed losing his party's nomination for the first time since Chester Arthur, and he had been the first since Herbert Hoover to lose the bid for reelection. The party was bitterly divided between the center and the right; Ford and Reagan thought of each other as losers. People said the party stood for nothing except Watergate. In this sour atmosphere, insiders began fighting over control of the party almost before the polls had closed.

Baker's telephone was now in the conspiratorial grid, and his name was on the wires. Curiously, each Republican camp, conservative and liberal, thought of Baker as a secret ally. When Senator Jesse Helms announced that he wanted to restructure the Republican National Committee along rigidly conservative ideological lines, Michigan governor William Milliken put out the word to party liberals that they should thwart Helms by making Baker party chairman. John Anderson campaigned quietly in support of Baker. Simultaneously, the Reagan forces out west began maneuvering against the candidacy of former senator William Brock, whom they viewed as a squishy, semiliberal has-been. They quietly approached Baker, whom they saw as a closet conservative among the Ford people.

For several months Baker thought the two wings of the party might try to parry each other by picking him. He considered his position a tricky one. He might become the consensus choice for party chairman, but it was also possible that each side would wind up feeling deceived. Suddenly, ugly rumors started circulating about Baker's "million-dollar surplus." He had been so tightfisted at the end of the Ford campaign that he left a large surplus that, had it been spent, might have kept Gerald Ford in the White House. Baker, they said, had too much of an "accountant's mentality." They blamed him for losing the election.

"It was the Brock people," says Baker. "They surfaced that stuff to destroy any possibility that I might become national chairman." He is still sensitive about the charge, citing all kinds of reasons for the surplus and precautions he took in later campaigns to prevent a recurrence. At the time, the attack was enough to make him withdraw his name from consideration. He says he did

not want to become a battleground for the two wings of the party.

The next year, 1977, was when the partners at Andrews & Kurth say Baker started just putting in time at the office. His mind was on politics, which was too bad, because the firm was fighting a titanic legal battle over the estate of Howard Hughes. There were dozens of phony wills and hundreds of sharp-eyed lawyers in the thick of a fight that should have warmed the heart of Captain Baker's grandson, but Jimmy Baker was trying to decide whether to run—yes, *run*—for governor or attorney general of Texas.

Baker formally announced his candidacy for attorney general in February 1978. He had rejected George Bush's advice that he run for governor, reasoning that he couldn't raise the money required and that a Republican in Texas would have a tough time defeating a conservative Democrat like Dolph Briscoe. In the attorney general's race, Baker thought he would be running against Price Daniel, Jr., a liberal who was expected to win the Democratic nomination over conservative Mark White.

As always, Baker was organized. On the day of the Democratic primary, he had letters already written and addressed to all of Mark White's $50-and-up contributors, urging them to support Baker instead of the pinkish Price Daniel now that White was out of the running. Unfortunately, Baker had to burn all the letters: White upset Daniel in the primary.

"The same thing happened to me that happened to George Bush in 1970," says Baker almost wistfully. "He filed to run against [liberal] Ralph Yarborough and wound up running against [moderate] Lloyd Bentsen. I planned to run against Daniel and wound up against White. We both were aiming for liberals, because in Texas a Republican still has a hard time against a conservative Democrat—unless you're Bill Clements and you throw in four and a half million dollars of your own money."

He pushed on gamely with the campaign, though he and White had many mutual friends in Houston and agreed on practically every issue. As a result, they spent most of their time trying to out-law-and-order each other, buying television ads showing cell doors slamming shut on criminals, blissfully ignoring the fact that the Texas attorney general has very little to do with criminal prosecution. The issue provided something to discuss, anyway. Otherwise, the election turned on party identification, name recognition, and the effectiveness of the respective campaigns in selling a personality. Baker churned his way through dinners and fundraisers in the big cities, showing up as often as possible with his new baby daughter in his arms. He doted openly on Mary Bonner Baker and still does. "I'm one of the few politicians who brings his own baby to kiss," he told audiences all over Texas.

Trying to combat White's advantage as a Democrat in Texas, Baker enlisted the aid of every big-name Republican he could find. Republicans who liked him or wanted him to owe them a favor, or both, paraded through

Texas. Ronald Reagan and Gerald Ford made appearances for Baker. So did John Connally, William Simon, Congressman Jack Kemp, Senator Robert Dole, and, of course, George Bush, one of Mary Bonner's godfathers.

At the time, at least half of these men planned to run for president in 1980. Consequently, Baker took care with his diplomacy, abiding by a strict, almost chivalrous code of loyalty that had served many Bakers well. At the beginning he considered his allegiance to lie with former president Ford. He reminded Ford of this and told him he would support a Ford presidential candidacy in 1980. In the event that Ford decided not to run, however, Baker said he would feel bound to help his friend George Bush. At this, Ford gave his thanks and released Baker to work for Bush.

When John Connally offered to give a fundraiser for Baker, he learned that Baker was eager for his help but wanted Connally to understand in advance that he was committed to Bush in 1980 if Bush decided to run. Connally said he understood and would help anyway. Baker delivered the same message to Lyn Nofziger, a Reagan aide who came to Houston looking to enlist Baker in the 1980 Reagan campaign.

These courtesies are important to Baker. Four years later, he still recites the successive steps in order, like a Renaissance prince tracking the path of honor through the tangled plots at the king's court. He wants to be straightforward, to say no in advance if he must say no, and to increase the value of his word. His mind seems to be heavily engaged in resolving conflicts among past, present, and future commitments, as though politics were only a matter of working out the calculus of duty in a changing world. It would never occur to him to spend time analyzing the differences of opinion among the candidates on the issues of the day. "I'm more interested in the contest than in the philosophy," he says.

He lost to Mark White in the 1978 election, polling 46 per cent of the vote. For such a competitive person, he seemed remarkably good-natured about his defeat. He kept saying he was happy to have gone through a race as a candidate, "to see what it's like on the other side." He and Susan were seen playing tennis in "Mark White for Attorney General" T-shirts. It was as though Baker had gone through a rite of passage but was well aware of the advantages of having lost. As a politician, he took a tennis player's approach, working up a clean, competitive sweat and then retiring, win or lose, to share a drink with his opponent. His gentleman's view also extended to his meager campaign debt, which he regarded as a black mark against his credit and his name. Without delay, he sent out appeals for donations to meet his obligations. The donations exceeded the debt, and Baker promptly sent partial refunds to each contributor. "When those checks went out, it was one of Jimmy's proudest moments in politics," Susan Baker recalls. "I've never seen anything make him happier."

The refunds would have pleased Jimmy's father, and they demonstrated that a politician could be honest. The Houston Jimmy Baker was still there, but the political side was growing. Baker aimed to get back on the faster track in politics, outside Texas.

After the election, the Bakers and Mary Bonner went to Florida for a week's vacation. George Bush called almost as soon as they arrived, already itching to get going on his presidential campaign. The Iowa caucuses were only fourteen months away. Bush, for one, was not overly morose about Baker's loss. Now he had the only campaign manager in the field who had gone through a presidential race at the top. Even better, Baker insisted on working for nothing.

Baker's first act as manager of the Bush campaign was to draw up detailed budget projections. He finished them in January 1979. A year later, after Bush had stunned the political world by beating all the other Republican candidates in the Iowa caucuses, Baker brought out his original figures and showed them proudly to aides. His fundraising projections had fallen within 0.7 per cent of the actual first-year revenue, and spending was off by only 9 per cent. The accountant was still going strong.

So was George Bush. Flushed with the victory in Iowa, he steamed into New Hampshire with brash announcements that he now had momentum ("the Big Mo") on his side and would knock Ronald Reagan out of the race with one more victory. This was characteristic of Bush. It was also characteristic of Baker and other Bush aides that they winced out loud to reporters whenever Bush set himself up for a fall with glib remarks. "We'll have to do something about that," Baker would say wearily.

John Sears also arrived in New Hampshire in a good mood. As in 1976, he was Reagan's campaign manager, and he was confident, even though Reagan had not done well in Iowa. Sears is an archconservative, but he is also a political professional of considerable pride. He thought about political strategies day and night. As a pro, he resented the parochial concerns of the Californians attached to Reagan by friendship and long service. It was his consuming desire to replace these aides with seasoned professionals whenever he could, and he had been highly successful in recent months. He had knocked Lyn Nofziger out of the campaign, and then he had gone after Michael Deaver in a showdown at the Reagan home. "Governor," Sears told Reagan, "it's not going to work unless I have control of the posture of the campaign. Mike and I can't share that, so you'll have to choose between us."

Whereupon, as Sears had hoped, Deaver fell loyally on his sword, saying, "Governor, I won't allow you to make that choice."

In New Hampshire without Deaver, Sears sprang a brilliant trap on Bush and Baker by manipulating the arrangements for a Bush-Reagan debate in such a way that it became a Reagan-versus-everybody-else debate,

with Bush sitting sullenly on the sidelines, refusing to let the other guys play. Most experts agree that Bush's chances of being elected president in 1980 ended that night. For John Sears, it was a moment to savor. Walter Cronkite called the next day and asked if he might drop by. He congratulated him for "putting the wood to old George." No one was congratulating Baker.

A few days later, in one of the surprise moves that argue for a steady detachment in politics, Ronald Reagan fired John Sears and his professionals. Reagan didn't care about Sears's brilliance or even about what Walter Cronkite was saying. He and Mrs. Reagan missed Mike Deaver and were determined to make sure that Sears did not go after Ed Meese. "I'm well aware of the Sears lesson," says Baker, who has gone on to the White House while Sears has retired to do lawyer-lobby work in Washington. The lesson, of course, is that you don't push Reagan into a corner in matters of sentiment. He may give ground, but he will snap back.

More generally, the episode illustrates Baker's durability. He has become a political pro, but the reserve and the stature he inherited keep him from becoming a "hired gun" like Sears. Baker tends to focus on the long haul and keep his battles in perspective, whereas Sears pressed every small advantage to the limit. Political ambition inevitably becomes a weakness in those who don't learn how to control it. The Houston side of Baker remains his protection on this score, as he has been able to say convincingly that he can always go back home if things don't work out in Washington.

After New Hampshire, the task for Bush was not to collapse, as Connally and the other candidates were doing. It was the primaries Bush won after Iowa that effectively demonstrated his resilience and strength, preparing him for national office. Bush ducked his head, gritted his teeth into a smile, and butted his way through the grueling primary schedule. His endurance, at least, proved equal to his lifelong ambition to win a major elective office like his father had done.

Baker was not so sure about his judgment. He and other Bush aides were quoted regularly in the press about how Bush "failed to put an issue base under his momentum." Bush was always saying the wrong thing, charging off on one tangent or another, a puppet of his own optimism. His aides were always rolling their eyes and telling reporters they'd have to repair the damage.

To some extent, this phenomenon of the sage adviser and the bumbling candidate is a natural product of the nominating system. The candidate is always on the run, without much time to think, and the press waits to ambush *his* errors, not the aides'. Moreover, the aides spend more time with reporters. While the candidate is smiling on the podium, regurgitating the standard speech, his aides are often huddled in the corridor with reporters, giving them the lowdown. Political advisers, as a class, are men and women with tapeworm egos—the kind who will fight each other desperately for a campaign post even if it is scheduled to end in two or three weeks. Not surprisingly, these people often speak to reporters about their bosses as though *they,* not the boss, should be running. Of course, they are more likely to do so when they are not quoted by name.

In most cases, a reader would do well to recognize these superior remarks for what they are—part of the advisers' fantasy life, transmitted through symbiotic journalists. With Baker, however, the critical remarks conveyed more of the truth of his political relationship with Bush. Unlike most advisers, Baker was at least Bush's peer in age, wealth, and station in life. Baker had already finished a successful career in law, and he seemed content with himself. Bush seemed to be chasing his oxygen supply in politics. If he lost, it would be a taste of death for him, as it is for many politicians. Baker, on the other hand, would probably just put on a "John Connally for President" baseball hat and go hunting. (He did exactly that after the campaign.) He was happy to be in the game; his future was not wrapped up in Bush's prospects.

One thing that vexed Baker in 1980 was Bush's stubborn devotion to his private secretary, Jennifer Fitzgerald, a middle-aged woman who is to Bush what Rose Mary Woods was to Nixon. By all accounts, Fitzgerald combines her native England's proclivities toward haughtiness with the fire of her Irish name. Although technically only Bush's secretary and appointments aide, she reportedly dominates Bush and his other advisers, determining who gets to see him about what issues. Bush aides have called her a Rasputin and a bureaucratic terrorist who flies into a rage if matters pertaining to Bush are not cleared through her.

Naturally, Baker clashed with Fitzgerald over a thousand issues, many of them having to do with her informal control over Bush's schedule. Fitzgerald is a woman of determination and refinement; she went to Madeira, the school that produced the explosive Jean Harris (a fact that still inspires jokes within Bush's staff). She enjoyed having candidate Bush meet with corporate executives, garden clubs, and art associations. Baker, as campaign manager, was trying to combat Bush's image as a rich preppie by scheduling him with groups of factory workers, policewomen, and public school teachers—to show Bush as a man of the people. Time after time, he would hear that Bush had canceled a blue-collar campaign stop to attend another elegant luncheon. And invariably the switch could be traced to Fitzgerald.

Baker finally made a very un-Bakerish move: he threatened to quit if Bush didn't fire Fitzgerald. Bush protested, saying that he was entitled to at least one aide who was utterly devoted to him and what *he* wanted. Baker persisted, arguing that Fitzgerald's wretched judgment was a threat to Bush's career and that her fiery temperament made it impossible for the campaign organization

to function smoothly. Bush asked for time to think it over. He finally agreed to transfer Fitzgerald from Houston to his New York campaign office. He would yield no further.

During the 1980 campaign, one of Bush's first acts as vice-presidential candidate was to rehire Fitzgerald. After the inauguration, she was made Bush's assistant for appointments and scheduling. By the beginning of this year, three Bush aides had resigned amid reports that they could not work with Fitzgerald. Rich Bond, who left Bush's staff in December to become deputy chairman of the Republican National Committee, went so far as to say on record that Fitzgerald is "an immensely difficult person to work with."

To this day, Baker refuses to say anything about Fitzgerald except that she remains a "severe management problem" for the vice president. And he never says anything personally critical of Bush, even off the record. But the record and the comments of his assistants in the chief of staff's office make it clear that Baker believes he has outgrown Bush in politics—and he is probably correct. He has certainly behaved that way. After administering the two-by-four to Bush in May, Baker went back to Houston and waited. After Reagan finally called Bush to offer him a spot on the Republican ticket (Baker answered the phone), Baker remarked to his aides that he wanted to work on the Reagan side of the general election campaign against Carter, not the Bush side. This was precisely what the Reagan people had in mind. So Baker asked Bush's permission to work out of Reagan's office, and, permission granted, he considered his loyalty transferred to Reagan. All these changes were accomplished before the Republican delegates left the convention in Detroit.

In the fall of 1980, Baker used an office on the fourth floor of the Reagan headquarters outside Washington. It was known as Honcho Hall because Ed Meese and Michael Deaver also had their offices there. As the newcomer, Baker moved gingerly, offering opinions only when asked. His first contributions to the campaign rode on the strength of his old accounting skills. "We found that you need a guy like Baker to run a campaign under the new reporting laws," says an aide who had gone through several campaigns with Reagan. Baker became the manager and detail man, freeing Meese and Deaver to do what they wanted. As always, Meese wanted to be a sounding board for Reagan, and Deaver wanted to make sure the Reagans were given their due in all things, from press coverage to maid service.

Baker's only front-line assignment was to negotiate with the Carter people over the conditions of a presidential debate and to help coach Reagan for his performance. In these roles Baker worked efficiently, and he also boosted Reagan's confidence. "Look, I had run two candidates [Ford and Bush] who debated Reagan, and I'd seen how good he is from the other side," says Baker. "I thought he'd beat Carter."

His contributions made a strong impres-

sion on Michael Deaver, who knew that neither he nor Meese had the management skills to run an intricate operation like the White House. Deaver had never pretended to have them; he had always been content to be a personal aide and confidential adviser to Reagan. But Meese considered himself a management expert, and no one wanted to tell him otherwise. Meese clearly expected to get the top job in the Reagan White House—chief of staff.

Deaver took his worries to Nancy Reagan, who agreed that a delicate sidestep was needed to get Meese out of administrative responsibilities without hurting his feelings. She also agreed that Baker was a shrewd man with valuable organizational gifts. She could sense his loyalty even though she did not know him well. Moreover, say old Reagan aides, Baker was "her kind of man": rich, well spoken, honorable, decisive, and self-possessed.

Almost immediately after the election, Deaver and Nancy Reagan went to the president-elect with their plan: Baker should be chief of staff and Meese should be counselor to the president in charge of all policy formulation. They reasoned that Meese would buy this because he would be deciding what to do, with Baker merely implementing the decisions. The two of them plus Deaver would constitute the Big Three. There would be a strict rule that they agree unanimously on all major personnel decisions. That way, newcomer Baker would never be able to subvert Reagan's wishes. Both Meese and Deaver would have to approve every big move he made. The proposed arrangement had a constitutional ring to it—three branches of advisers, checks and balances.

As expected, Meese balked at first. To him, the plan smacked of a rebuke, no matter how much sugar Reagan sprinkled on it. But he finally agreed.

Baker himself was reluctant, as usual. This time he had a special worry: his own hide. He knew from rumor and observation that the Californians around Reagan were a cliquish group given to infighting. He had seen them destroy John Sears and other outsiders. He had also seen even longtime Reagan intimates like Lyn Nofziger getting tossed overboard and later being retrieved. He knew full well that the chief of staff is a natural target of criticism. "That's part of the job," says Baker. "I knew that. You're supposed to protect the president by taking the shots for him."

Baker flew to Washington for prolonged negotiations with Meese, who was still feeling slightly wounded by the drift of things. They began their talks somewhat wary of each other. Meese feared that Baker would supersede him as Reagan's principal adviser; Baker feared that he would have the responsibility for making things run smoothly without the requisite authority. Gradually, they reassured each other with a long exchange of commitments about their respective prerogatives. Then Baker, ever the lawyer, retired to put the highlights of their understanding on paper.

The resulting document has become known in the White House and around Washington as the contract between Baker and Meese (it is reproduced on page 152). Actually, it is far simpler than people might expect. Looking at the divided functions, a student of bureaucracy would gather that Meese's chief purpose was to guarantee his place on the highest committees in government: the National Security Council, the Domestic Policy Staff, the Cabinet, and the ill-fated Reagan "Super Cabinet." He seemed to care about stature, whereas Baker focused on mechanics. A Baker partisan would say that Baker had cheerfully given Meese every position he wanted in return for one function: control of all the people and paper flowing to President Reagan. This secured Baker's position; in a bureaucracy like the White House, paper flow, which sounds mundane, is power, because it determines what the president knows about and therefore what he does.

A subtler Baker ploy is the provision about his office location. He realized that most turf battles in the White House have to do with access to the president and that access is determined by physical proximity and by status, as reflected uncannily by the size and location of offices. Experts on the minutiae of White House power games always point to the workmen who swarm continuously over the building, partitioning some offices and expanding others in accordance with the changing influence of the occupants. Baker knew that it was important to freeze his choice of office in writing, trivial as it may seem to outsiders. Furthermore, Baker knew enough about the White House to reserve for himself the "old Haldeman office." Meese took the one with the nice view of the Pennsylvania Avenue lawn. Baker's has a poor view, but it is the only office large enough for big meetings. As a result, he can host whatever conclaves he wants. Everyone else has to wait for an available conference room—or come to Baker. By specifying his office location in such a general document, Baker revealed the degree to which he has become a political animal.

The bargain was struck, which meant that Meese's last administrative chore was serving as director of the Reagan transition, before the inauguration. His performance in that job must have made Deaver and Nancy Reagan glad that they had recruited Baker, because Meese's transition quickly became an object of public ridicule. Three or four people often claimed to have the same job. The offices swarmed with ardent job seekers, since Meese found it difficult to say no to anyone who swore fealty to Reagan. In an embarrassing omen for the fiscal promises of the Reagan conservatives, the Meese transition suffered a sizable cost overrun.

Baker assumed the White House management duties on Inauguration Day. Depending on one's point of view, Meese was then either yanked out of management or elevated to the higher world of policy, or both. Early on, Meese appeared in the news almost every day, speaking officially for the ad-ministration on everything from school lunches to nuclear missile targeting. In general, Deaver looked after Reagan's body; Meese, his mind; and Baker, his political interests. They were functioning smoothly by the time of their first major crisis: the day Reagan was shot.

As always, Deaver had been at the president's side and had rushed to the hospital with the Secret Service. He stayed with Reagan while the doctors worked over him, and he greeted Nancy Reagan when she arrived. Baker and Meese came from the White House. The Big Three listened to Reagan's jokes as he was wheeled to the operating room. They conferred briefly with the doctors. Then they retired to a broom closet to decide whether to invoke the 25th Amendment and make George Bush the acting president. They agreed not to; the president's prospects were good, so why advertise a constitutional crisis to the world? Then Baker set the plan of action: Deaver would stay with Nancy Reagan at the hospital; Meese would go to the airport and meet Bush; Baker would go back to the White House. Tight-lipped, Meese rode off to the airport.

One might have expected that Meese, the "assistant president," would go to the White House and Baker would go meet his friend Bush. "That's just the point," says Baker. "It was a great crisis. Everything was confused. We thought Brady was dead, and we didn't know how serious the president's wounds would be. In that situation, I did not want to go meet Bush because I didn't want anybody to start rumors that I was out there plotting with my best friend of twenty years to take over the government by proclamation. It could have happened."

Baker thinks of things like that. His aides say that he also wanted to be at the White House because he anticipated trouble with Haig and Weinberger. Both of those officials were notorious for trying to talk Meese into their schemes for a Super Cabinet in which they and a few others would be elevated above their fellow Cabinet officers. (The heart of the plan was that the Super Cabinet members would get offices at the White House.) Baker's aides say that Baker felt he would be able to handle Haig and Weinberger more firmly than Meese could.

Baker's first skirmish against the extreme right wing of Reagan's constituency took place in February and March 1981, mostly out of public sight. Although the issue at stake was nothing less than the Reagan administration's fundamental philosophy of government, the stake at issue was the control of a suite of offices at the Executive Office Building, next door to the White House.

These offices were occupied by members of Reagan's "kitchen cabinet," the group of wealthy men who had long been friends and political advisers to the president. At Reagan's invitation, they came to Washington to help select the members of the Cabinet, but then, unexpectedly, they de-cided to stay on—to party and to participate in the selection of subcabinet officers and other officials.

The kitchen cabinet was made up of two self-proclaimed conservative "bomb-throwers"—Bill Wilson and Joseph Coors—and half a dozen millionaire socialites, including Justin Dart, Alfred Bloomingdale, Charles Wick, and Holmes Tuttle. These men, particularly Wilson and Coors, took up the cudgels for the disgruntled conservative job seekers, publicly criticizing the administration for appointing "moderate" Republicans to key jobs. That's when the trouble began. The kitchen cabinet mounted such an effective guerrilla campaign that White House personnel manager E. Pendleton James once flew home to California in a huff. (James, Ed Meese's old Yale roommate, came back after some soothing talk from Meese.) James, Meese, and Baker soon decided that the kitchen cabinet had overstayed its welcome. Deaver agreed with them for his own reason: these men were embarrassing the president, therefore they must go. What upset Deaver was that the members of the kitchen cabinet and their wives were too eager to talk with reporters about how they were having raspberries and flowers flown up from Chile, chefs flown in from California, and hairdressers and clothes designers flown in from everywhere—all for their parties. Deaver thought they were giving the administration too much of a Marie Antoinette image.

Making the decision was easy. But these men had been with Ronald Reagan much longer than Meese or Deaver, not to mention Baker—some of them since the old *General Electric Theater* days—and getting rid of them was a delicate matter. At first the Big Three tried standard bureaucratic discouragement. The kitchen cabinet members, not being regular government employees, found that they could not get permanent passes to their offices at the Executive Office Building. Nor could they obtain parking spaces, which meant that they had to park far away or take a limousine to work, and they also had to wait every day to be cleared through the security gate. This became tedious. Moreover, they could not clear visitors into the building, since technically they were visitors themselves. And finally, the kitchen cabinet members couldn't get fancy White House staff ID badges.

The battle escalated when President Reagan flew off to Ottawa for meetings with Pierre Trudeau. While he was gone, workers showed up at the kitchen cabinet offices to disconnect the phones. They said the space had been commandeered by political affairs chief Lyn Nofziger, who controlled the adjoining offices.

Alarms went out. Nofziger, fetched to contradict the workers, said he had given no such orders. (Nofziger, in fact, was one of the few who openly sided with the kitchen cabinet members in their efforts to cram Reaganites into the government.) The telephone workers said orders were orders, but Wilson and Coors fought them to a standoff in the halls. By now the situation was getting serious. Paranoia and tension built to the point that kitchen cabinet supporters say they spent several entire nights guarding the offices to make sure no one changed the locks or yanked the phones.

But soon the phone workers were back. This time their orders were traced to a legal opinion by White House counsel Fred Fielding that the kitchen cabinet members could not occupy government space and have access to government documents without going through hiring procedures. Coors and company were outraged. What had happened to the volunteer spirit, or frugality in government? They beat back the Fielding move, only to have another objection advanced by Ed Meese himself.

"Under the laws of the executive branch, they could not stay in those offices without making certain financial disclosures that they were not prepared to deal with," says Meese. "It's complicated, having to do with the Advisory Committees Act and other laws. But basically their work was done by the inauguration anyway."

Coors and Wilson gave in by the middle of March and were soon followed out of the White House by a number of other conservative ideologues. The high-roller parties stopped hitting the papers, which made Deaver happy, but the conservative attacks only grew stronger. Publications like *Conservative Digest* and the right-wing weekly *Human Events* began to break with their political hero, Ronald Reagan, over the treatment of the kitchen cabinet. They attributed the administration's behavior to the insidious influence of James Baker. In defense, Baker said the decisions had been approved by Meese and Deaver also.

Nevertheless, the conservatives began to single Baker out as the primary cause of the administration's "softening." Baker's straightforward manner facilitated their attack on him, because he did many things they could point to as evidence. It was Baker, for instance, who told former congressman Donald "Buz" Lukens that he couldn't be Reagan's White House director of congressional relations.

"He told me face to face," says Lukens, who had supported Reagan for president continuously since 1968. "He told me I was too much of a conservative ideologue for that job. But I've won more elections than Mr. Baker ever won." Lukens responded to Baker's rejection by publicly blasting the Reagan administration, which even his supporters admit was a mistake that made him almost impossible to hire thereafter. Still, the conservatives found it galling to hear that a loyal Reagan man like Lukens had been rejected on the grounds of his political philosophy by a Ford-Bush man like Baker.

"That's ridiculous," says Baker. "I informed him of the decision because that's my job. But the decision up here was unanimous, like all the rest of them. They know that. Not only that, it was the *right* decision. For that job in particular, you need a mechanic. You want somebody ideologically neutral, because you're going after the

marginal votes in Congress."

To support his contention, Baker speaks fondly of the Reagan administration's "seven great legislative coups in a row" during its first year. He names them one by one, from the budget-cutting resolutions and the tax cut bill to the Senate resolution on the sale of AWACS planes to Saudi Arabia. Baker says he jumped in to work on all these fights personally, alongside his congressional relations staff. He revved up his old delegate-hunting system. He called for daily reports on who the soft votes were and what might be likely to push them Reagan's way. The contests summoned up his adrenaline. He stayed at the office even later than his usual nine o'clock at night, making congressional calls, and he used "the big weapon," President Reagan himself, in ways he thought most effective.

All the landmark battles in the Congress were like little election campaigns, which is precisely why Baker liked them. "There's less bureaucracy when there's a vote coming up," he says. "And you get more done in less time. Decisions get made faster because it's a faster track. To me, that's exciting." Even inside the government, what hooks Baker about politics is the part that translates into victories and defeats as determined by numbers on tally sheets. Only that focused excitement makes it worthwhile to put up with the rest of the aggravation.

Baker arranged to have the sound system from the Senate floor piped into his office at the White House. On the night of the AWACS vote—"That's the one everybody expected us to lose," he says—he and President Reagan sat there together, marking a big tally sheet as they listened to the vote. The names rang out one by one, and the votes were cast exactly as Baker had assured the president they would be. When it was over, President Reagan drew a happy little face on the bottom of the tally sheet and signed his name. Baker had it framed as a memento of his finest moment as chief of staff.

Unfortunately for Baker, there haven't been any stirring legislative victories since the economy sagged and the huge deficit projections arrived late last year. The administration seems to have lost a great deal of its charmed hold over Congress and the voters. Conservative spokesmen have renewed their attacks on Baker, arguing that his liberal influence has brought hard times to Reagan. "To implement the Reagan revolution with pragmatists like Baker is like trying to play the piano with boxing gloves on," says M. Stanton Evans, a conservative columnist. *Conservative Digest* devoted an entire issue early in 1982 to attacking "the Bush network" within the Reagan administration, with Baker serving as the chief liberal villain.

Baker is clearly nettled by his conservative attackers. He says they are "very hypocritical in their approach." Some of them, he points out, claim to speak for Reagan even though they supported other

Republicans early in 1980, just as Baker did. "They're just trying to keep their mailing lists up-to-date," he says. "To do that, they've got to stay to the right of this White House." Most cutting of all, Baker intimates that the right-wingers just want jobs in the government or little niches in Washington—no less so than the clinging New Deal do-gooders whose habits they say have ruined the country.

What really separates Baker from the conservative ideologues is temperament. The latter feel a gripping sense of urgency about the corruption of the world. They talk about blood and revolution in politics, whereas Baker talks of a game of gentlemen. "I have always believed that you can be political adversaries without being political enemies," he says.

"Let's be honest about it," says John Lofton, Jr., editor of *Conservative Digest*. "To guys like Jim Baker, we're a little *vulgar*. When they're out on the verandah of the country club, they don't want to talk about abortion. Abortion means dead babies! They don't want to talk about revolution."

Baker is in an odd position. He is in charge of implementing what is called the great Reagan revolution, but he does not believe in some of its more revolutionary concepts, such as supply-side economics. As one of his aides puts it, he is "a conservative who never bothered to memorize the theology." He is for business and the Pentagon ("I'm as big a hawk as you can be," he says. "I'm a Marine, for Christ's sake!"), against busing and abortion. A close Texas friend remembers one discussion on a long night drive to a hunting trip; Baker, acting out of pure conservative instinct, took Anita Bryant's side in an argument about whether homosexual teachers would "prey upon" students in classrooms. But he stops short of the newfangled supply-side belief that the rich, spared of burden from taxation, will work miracles to revitalize the economy. Ever the pragmatist, Baker would like to be shown. In the meantime, he is worried about deficits.

He has recommended cutting taxes only insofar as the government succeeds in cutting spending. If that were done, and if the economy were to recover, only then would Baker spend the new government revenues to build up the Pentagon. This is an old-fashioned conservative approach based on horse sense. By focusing relentlessly on the size of the federal deficit and on reducing Washington's presence in American life, Baker would satisfy himself with the monumental—though by Reagan's own standards insufficient—feat of changing the overall direction of government. He is skeptical of President Reagan's decision to assume the success of supply-side economics in advance and to spend its bounty on the Pentagon ahead of time.

Baker expresses his doubts but then swallows them to work for the program. He says that Reagan is the best possible president and that Reagan is far more gifted than he as a political seer. "I'm not a man of vision," he says. "I don't pretend to be. But you don't need one here. Not in my job. You need a man of vision in the Oval Office, and we've got one."

The conservatives aren't the only ones after Baker. "You make enemies in this job," he says. "That's the nature of it, because you're saying no ninety per cent of the time. I understand that, but I'm still not used to it."

He admits to being a little tired of his job. In addition to his enemies, there's the bureaucracy and the work load. For the first time in his life, Baker seems to find work a burden—even there in the exciting White House, surrounded by limousine drivers and helicopters. He no longer bothers to camouflage clear differences of opinion with his colleagues. He disagrees most often with Meese.

When the administration announced in January a reversal of tax policy toward segregated schools and then engaged in an embarrassing minuet of backstepping, sidestepping, and denial, Deaver outdid Baker in leaking to the press his criticism of Meese for shepherding the original change through the Treasury Department. Meese leaked his version of events in rebuttal, and then Deaver and Baker struck again with more pointed detail. Still, months later, Meese asserted blandly in an interview that there had never been any differences among the Big Three over the policy. "We all agreed that I had very little to do with the change," he said. "Those decisions were made entirely over in the departments."

"That's just not true," retorts Baker with a sigh. "Our communication system here broke down because of Ed's failure to tell us what was going on." Asked why he did not act to thwart the policy change when he learned of it two days before the original announcement, Baker seems exasperated. "To stop it at that point I'd have had to go against everybody at once," he says.

Baker's partisans come close to self-pity as they lament his doing the work and also un-

doing the mistakes. As for Meese, it is almost fair to say that he is a roving mistake in search of a title. By unanimous agreement, he was originally placed in a policy role because of his deficiencies as a manager. Since then, his numerous misstatements as a policy spokesman have caused the White House to invent a new term for him: now Meese is a "synthesizer." Nevertheless, Meese himself still insists that he'd rather stay in the executive branch than go to, say, the Supreme Court, because he'd like to use "my primary expertise, which is management." Such remarks from Meese make Baker roll his eyes.

Baker speaks wistfully of the great legislative battles of 1981, as though he doesn't expect to see such glory again. At this juncture, the latest Reagan budget is meeting serious resistance in Congress because its proposed deficits are too high, and it seems the president will have to back down some if he wants another big win on Capitol Hill. Meanwhile, rumors are flying that Reagan has privately decided not to seek a second term. That would presumably leave the way clear for another George Bush presidential campaign, but Baker, it seems plain, has had enough of being second in command to Bush.

Baker isn't saying exactly what his plans are, and he almost certainly doesn't know himself. He now openly entertains the idea of not moving back to Houston, because he thinks the quality of life has deteriorated there. But he scoffs at the notion that he might stay on in Washington to become a fixture in the permanent political establishment. Susan Baker adds that she can't imagine living in Washington without the White House job, because life in the capital is so narrow and confining. Republicans in Texas had polls taken this year on his chances of defeating Senator Lloyd Bentsen. The results were mildly promising, but Baker ruled out any race because of his commitment to Reagan. He has lately begun to look past that commitment. He has even had to spend some time denying that he is plan-

ning to run for president himself. His prospects as a candidate depend on one's assessment of our political ills—whether we need officials of integrity and competence or whether the national emergency is so great that we need leaders of extraordinary vision. The last three presidents have been hounded out of office because the public lost faith in their integrity or their competence. That would bode well for Baker. On the other hand, the last big Texan in the White House went home sad because he hadn't seen what was happening in Viet Nam. Ominously, Baker might possess even less foresight than Lyndon Johnson. The old master was capable, at least, of having political dreams; he conceived of his Great Society and made it a reality, however flawed. Baker has never demonstrated the slightest capacity for political inspiration. He and his family have worked *for* the men of vision, from Jay Gould to Ronald Reagan, not among them. Baker would have to transcend his past to become an original politician of hope.

As to his character, the question about Baker is not so much exactly what he will do as how he will resolve the almost perfect tension between his Houston side and his Washington side. So far he has been able to draw the maximum political advantage from his family's antipolitical tradition. He has been in control of the conflict between what he was raised to do and what he is doing now, but it would seem that he cannot forever avoid a dilemma: the longer he remains in politics, the more the patrician Houston Baker fades and the Washington Baker takes over. And since it was his Houston qualities that originally made him so special, even in politics, he runs an increasing risk of turning into an ordinary politician whose entire life is wrapped up in the next election—the kind of person old Captain Baker would have called a hack. That would be a terrible fate to befall Jimmy Baker. He is still a Baker, after all, and he likes being one. All he wants is a little more than his inherited share of the action. ♣

MARK WHITE'S COMING-OUT PARTY

In his first hundred days in the governor's mansion, the man we thought was a bland conservative has played the fiery populist, to rave reviews. Can it last?

They're talking about raising oil taxes in Austin these days, which is a sure sign that something different is going on in Texas politics. The conservatives want to empty the prisons instead of stuff them with every miscreant in sight. The hardy perennial dream of raiding the Mississippi River to make West Texas bloom has finally been abandoned. The highway department even agreed to spend money on a rail line the other day. About the only thing that hasn't changed is that the new Speaker of the House suffers from the same amnesia about his personal finances that afflicted his predecessor: just as Billy Clayton forgot about $5000 in cash in his desk drawer, so Gib Lewis couldn't remember that he and some buddies in the liquor business own a bank.

Nowhere is the evidence of change more visible than in the Capitol quarters of the governor and his staff; even a visitor who had spent the last six months in hibernation would know instantly that power had changed hands. Under Bill Clements the office had a corporate feel: women in tailored dresses, young men in three-piece suits and blow-dried hairstyles, clean air and clean ashtrays, and an aura of discipline and confidence. Under White women wear skirts and blouses, many men are in shirtsleeves, and the atmosphere comes close to the chaos of a political boiler room. Tobin Armstrong, the blueblooded rancher who handled Clements' political patronage, occupied a

BY PAUL BURKA

spacious office overlooking the Capitol's south lawn. Dwayne Holman, the political pro who does the same job for White, has a windowless cell barely large enough for a desk and one visitor's chair. The air is dense with stale smoke; at two o'clock one afternoon I counted 31 cigarette butts in his ashtray.

Not many people expected White to occupy these offices at all, much less to charge them with nervous energy. Despite ten previous years in office, first as Dolph Briscoe's Secretary of State and then as attorney general, he had never made a single imprint on public policy. White just seemed so, well, ordinary. His life history tracks the demographics of modern Texas so perfectly that it could have been formulated by a computer. He is young—at 43 a generation behind Clements. He was born in a small town (Henderson, in East Texas), but his family soon moved to the big city (Houston). He is a Baptist. His father is in business for himself, but White, a lawyer, is of the post-entrepreneurial generation. He has a two-income marriage; throughout his term as attorney general, his wife, Linda Gale, sold real estate. Now, as the hundredth day of his administration approaches—the traditional end for political honeymoons and the first occasion for evaluating chief executives—White has established himself as the most substantive, most politically sophisticated governor of Texas since John Connally twenty years ago.

It is not only the fact of Mark White's success that has utterly surprised people who have watched him for years; it is also the particular form that success has taken. Who would have thought that the man once touted as the conservative Democrats' great White hope would be soberly described as a populist by the *New York Times*? Or that the man who went to Washington in 1974 to oppose the Voting Rights Act would receive 86 per cent of the Mexican American vote in 1982? Or that the man who ran his first statewide race as the darling of the business lobby would run his second as the scourge of the utility companies? While we're at it, who would have thought that unemployment in Houston would approach 10 per cent or that the oil boom would end as quickly as it began? All of the unforeseeables are related. They indicate that Texas politics is entering a period of volatility without precedent in the state's modern era.

Consider the situation that confronted White as he took office in January. The succession was abnormal: White was replacing a Republican governor, the first time anyone had done so in a century. The demands were abnormal: newly powerful partisan constituencies—blacks, Mexican Americans, teachers—were insisting that he set himself apart not only from Bill Clements but also from caretaker Democratic governors like Dolph Briscoe and Preston Smith. The Democratic party was abnormal: the conservative wing that had spawned White was no longer dominant;

the four other new state officials who were sworn in in January (attorney general Jim Mattox, land commissioner Garry Mauro, treasurer Ann Richards, and agriculture commissioner Jim Hightower), potential critics all, were to the left of center. And the state of the state was abnormal: the treasury was running dry, the victim of an economic slump that had Texas on the verge of its first real fiscal crisis in nearly a quarter of a century. But White had run for governor promising big spending increases for education and welfare: where would the money come from? To make matters worse, the question of how much money the state could legally spend under its pay-as-you-go rules would be answered by state comptroller Bob Bullock, who had already announced for White's job in 1986. White could solve his fiscal dilemma by proposing a tax increase, but only at the cost of creating a political dilemma: Briscoe and Clements, White's two predecessors, ran for ten years on the ever-popular slogan No new taxes.

Of all White's problems going in, the most serious was his own reputation. When he ran for attorney general in 1978, he was regarded as merely dull, a protégé of the even duller Dolph Briscoe; by the time he'd served one term, as Bill Clements kept pointing out during the 1982 campaign, White had added incompetence to his repertoire. This was one time when campaign rhetoric was close to the truth. White was a mediocre attorney general, especially when judged against John Hill, the man he succeeded. Hill, using his considerable reputation as a trial lawyer to lure talent from the state's top firms, assembled a first-rate law office. White promptly dismantled it. Some of Hill's best people fled; others got the boot, causing more to flee. Lacking Hill's professional credentials, White couldn't recruit equivalent replacements. Nor was he an administrator: on more than one occasion his lawyers failed to show up for trials, resulting in cases lost by default.

In big cases White won about as often as the Houston Rockets. He sued Montana over its rapacious 30 per cent coal severance tax, which is passed along to Texas customers. He lost. He defended the state bilingual education plan. He lost. He defended the state prison system, and again he lost.

He did beat Bill Clements, but even that did not immediately enhance White's stature in the eyes of his political peers. They knew White hadn't won on his own: his 53 per cent of the vote trailed the rest of the Democratic ticket by at least 7 percentage points. Most significant, White captured only 45 per cent of the Anglo vote, barely topping the 44 per cent Hill got while losing to Clements in 1978. The pros looked at the numbers and saw that White had ridden into office on the coattails of a get-out-the-minority-vote drive funded by and designed for Lloyd Bentsen and Bill Hobby.

There is an old saying about luck: the first time is chance, the second time is coincidence, the third time is design. White wasn't supposed to beat Price Daniel, Jr., in the 1978 Democratic primary for attorney general. Then he had to face Republican James Baker in the general election. Last year's governor's race against Clements, a lavishly financed incumbent, carried the longest odds of all. Considering that White has defeated (1) one of the best-known names in Texas political history, (2) the current acting president of the United States, and (3) Texas' first Republican governor in a century, it ought not to come as a complete surprise that he has more on the ball than was commonly supposed.

His first act as governor was to fulfill a campaign promise to take the lock off the governor's mansion. Never mind that the chain White snipped off with the largest bolt cutters he could find was placed there by his own aides or that security guards replaced the lock a few days later. White had served notice that he understood political theater, a legitimate tool of governing that Texas governors have neglected for too long.

The bolt-cutting episode set the tone for the first hundred days. Lamenting the plight of the poor, White mentioned that there were shanties within walking distance of the Capitol; when challenged by a reporter, he took the press on a walking tour to prove his point. He returned to the black churches where he had campaigned to say thank you—an obvious ploy, perhaps, but followed by the less obvious one of getting the word out through black ministers that no one had ever done it before. (That wasn't quite so, by the way: Ben Barnes had, for one.) He went to the Rio Grande Valley, where business was ailing because of the disappearing value of the Mexican peso, and likened conditions there to the aftermath of a hurricane—and then he went to Washington to petition the Reagan administration for federal disaster aid. He bought television time in major markets from Houston to El Paso to plead for public support in his drive to make the Public Utility Commission an elected body. (In El Paso seven thousand people signed petitions supporting White and sent them to their state representative—a Republican.) When two of the three PUC commissioners resigned without notice one day at noon (the third quit a few weeks later), White turned a possible embarrassment into an asset by filling the positions before sundown. Before his hundred days were half over, White's theatrics had cast him as the hero in a drama that had a little of everything: a dragon (the PUC), a Greek chorus (the Legislature), a tragic theme (the fiscal crisis), even a lean and hungry Cassius (Bob Bullock).

By the beginning of March, six weeks

into the new administration, a curious thing started to happen in Austin. In Capitol corridors and at political watering holes, Mark White began to be discussed with the mixture of obsessive interest, admiration, and jealousy that befits a star. Two lobbyists debated into the small hours one night over drinks whether White had really known where the shanties were all along or had sent his staff out hunting for them. Politicians searched their memories for fragments of conversations that might provide insight into White's developing character; the right nugget conferred instant status. After the visit to the black churches, an Austin lawyer confided to a friend, "Hey, I knew this was coming all along. Ol' Spence [Roy Spence, an Austin advertising executive and a political consultant] told me last summer that Mark would be the most liberal governor in Texas history." It didn't take long for White's aides to pick up on the trend and exploit it. They began to leak stories of White's Lincolnesque greatness to friends, and then they let the political rumor mill do its work. I have heard four different versions of how White discovered the shanties—my favorite is the one that has the governor so determined to do good that he prowls the streets alone at night looking for poverty to redress. According to another tale currently circulating, White likes to stop at highway rest areas to ask people about their utility bills.

"You aren't getting sucked in by that Saint Francis of Assisi stuff, are you?" one of the state's leading pollsters and media consultants asked me. He leaned back in his chair and laughed. "He's not Saint Mark of Austin. All those stories are coming straight out of his staff." But even he was not completely immune. "I'll say this for him. Some mornings he walks over to his barbershop just to visit with the guys. All by himself."

But White's first hundred days have been more than show. What impressed the political fraternity as much as his theatrics was his adroit handling of the job of governor. In three areas—staff, appointments, and politics—he has managed to reverse the mistakes of his years as attorney general.

He certainly had enough warning. First there was Clements, graceless to the end, cheerfully delivering as his parting shot a forecast of disaster for his successor. Even White's close advisers told him that he had to get his act together. The first indication that the new administration might exceed expectations came when White enticed his friend Pike Powers away from a lucrative Austin lobbying job with the Fulbright & Jaworski law firm to serve as chief of staff. Powers' arrival assured that

White would not make the fatal error of surrounding himself with the shopworn Briscoe crowd that had given him his start in politics and now wanted back in. With the addition of former state senator Max Sherman (who, after the legislative session, will become dean of UT's Lyndon B. Johnson School of Public Affairs) and former House member Susan McBee, the new staff struck exactly the chord White was aiming at: experienced, respected, shrewd rather than cunning, conservative but in no way ideological, of unquestioned integrity, without an enemy in the world.

White's handling of appointments followed the same pattern. He touched the necessary bases for a Democrat—blacks, Mexican Americans, women—but in a way that was politically astute and noncontroversial. That is not as easy as you might think. A governor in a state as large as Texas uses his appointments to ingratiate himself to all sorts of groups with which he is less than intimate, and unless he knows what he is doing and gets good advice, he can easily end up with a political hack who can quickly become an embarrassment. *Vide* Anne Gorsuch. Or, closer to home, the Houston Sanitation Department under Mayor Jim McConn. His appointees couldn't get the garbage picked up, and thus McConn became a former mayor.

This difficult job was made more difficult by the extravagant promises White made during the campaign. Cynics said White could never fulfill his promise to appoint a real housewife to the PUC—too risky, they said, predicting he'd name a lady pol instead—but White turned up Peggy Rosson, a sure-nuff housewife who, as a member of the El Paso utility board, knew more about the subject than just the size of her latest electric bill. White accomplished the near-impossible when he named Mario Yzaguirre of Brownsville as a UT regent without generating a murmur of protest from normally fratricidal Mexican American politicians. He maneuvered expertly out of a corner after the labor establishment united behind former AFL-CIO president Hank Brown as their candidate for commissioner of labor and standards. Trouble was, Brown dated from the sixties and the bitter intraparty split among Democrats; to appoint him would have been waving a red flag before old-line conservatives. Instead White chose Allen Parker, a young black union official from Houston who had supported him in the Democratic primary—and quietly reminded state labor leaders that *they* had sided with Buddy Temple.

White also had to rebuild the old Democratic coalition that had disintegrated under Briscoe when urban conservatives defected not because of policy differences but because of repeated personal snubs. White courted the big-city tycoons in clever ways that neither risked the wrath of liberals nor tied his hands

politically. Elvis Mason, chairman of InterFirst, the state's biggest bank holding company, got an appointment—but instead of heading a major agency, Mason is chairing a task force on unemployment whose recommendations White can accept or bury. One day before his budget address, White invited the chief executive officers of the major bank holding companies to the governor's mansion for lunch and an advance sales pitch for his proposals. But there was one old-line Democrat whom White had no hope of coaxing into his camp. That person was state comptroller Bob Bullock.

Except for the absence of uniforms, a visitor to the fourth floor of the state's finance building might think he was in the Pentagon. "Secure Area, Badge Required," warns a sign on the wall. "No One Allowed Beyond This Door Without an R Badge." To gain entry one must produce an unmarked blue card and hold it up to a small, dark screen set in the wall. If all goes well, this sensor will tell the door that the bearer of the card is allowed to pass, and the lock will disengage. Then and only then can one gain admittance to Bob Bullock's computer room, where dozens of high-tech machines and thousands of computer files contain everything a tax collector—or a political candidate—might need to know about Texas: the entire federal census, the sales tax records of every business, production figures for oil companies, even redistricting information in the form of precinct election returns.

This room says everything you need to know about Bullock. He is very good at what he does, and he is more than a little eccentric. Here are produced the numbers that form the basis of Bullock's state revenue estimate—the ceiling on state spending that is the main weapon in his political arsenal. Bullock's power over the state budget poses two problems for Mark White. First, with a stroke of his pen Bullock can declare that the Legislature has overspent his limit and annihilate the entire appropriations bill, all in the name of fiscal responsibility. The resulting turmoil would be to the advantage of the comptroller and to the disadvantage of the governor—which is exactly why Bullock might do it. Second, Bob Bullock is not someone you want for an enemy, and Bullock does not like Mark White.

White's adversary is the most complex, contradictory figure in Texas politics. Bullock's personal excesses are legendary: drinking (he completed a California rehabilitation program in 1981), chain-smoking (which led to lung surgery and throat lesions), depression (more medical treatment), and a fondness for acquiring airplanes and other luxuries for his agency (which provoked a grand jury investigation in 1979 that turned up nothing illegal). But professionally he has been first-rate. In 1975 he inherited a musty bureaucracy notorious for its minimal audit and collection practices; big companies with political muscle had been allowed to hold on to their sales tax receipts for months before forwarding them to the state. Bullock beefed up the auditing staff and put a stop to the hoarding of sales taxes with some well-publicized raids. He was the first statewide official to hit big business where it counts—in the pocketbook—and he never suffered a scratch.

Yet Bullock's competence always seems to be overshadowed by his personality. No matter that his office has some of the best talent in state government and one of the lowest employee turnover rates: he is better known for hiring old cronies like retired legislator Bill Heatly and for his impulsive firings of top aides. Bullock's disregard of convention, however, is so brazen that it has become an essential part of his power. The revenue estimate is a case in point. It is widely believed in the Capitol that in past years Bullock kept the estimate artificially low until the Legislature gave in to his budget requests, at which point he suddenly discovered extra money for the lawmakers to spend. It hardly matters whether Bullock fudged the estimate or not; what matters is that the Legislature thought him capable of it.

The typical politician abhors making enemies and wants most of all for everyone to love him. Not Bullock. He craves respect rather than love and relishes having enemies. Like most of Bullock's likes and dislikes, his antipathy for White has a long history—back to 1973, when White replaced Bullock as Secretary of State. Officeholders are seldom fond of their successors, and it did not help matters that White got rid of some of Bullock's old employees. But even had their paths not crossed, Bullock and White were not destined for closeness. As politicians they are of different generations. Bullock is the last survivor of the cutthroat days—he was a legislator in the fifties, a lobbyist in the sixties, a backroom operator for Preston Smith in the early seventies. He keeps score, and his scoreboard never shuts down. White is a creature of the post-Sharpstown era. He is a true media politician, the first Texas governor who is better on TV than one to one. White's passions are always under control; Bullock's seldom are. Both are good political tacticians, but their styles are opposites: White is best at subtle machinations, Bullock at hardball and keeping on the pressure. He recently turned up the heat on White by hiring six former Clements staffers and campaign aides.

Any hope of détente vanished during White's tenure as attorney general. Bullock asked White to rule that the comptroller had broad powers to audit state agencies and generally act as a fiscal czar with more search-and-destroy power than the governor. White, with admirable foresight, disagreed; Bullock called White dumb. The administrative mess under

White only fortified Bullock's bile. Now he can get even, for until the day the state budget is safely signed into law, Mark White's future is Bob Bullock's hostage.

In one sense Mark White's first hundred days are a triumph. The new governor has accomplished one of the most difficult tasks in politics: he has changed his image. People take Mark White seriously now, and not only in Texas. He has been to Washington twice and has two more trips scheduled; he was the first governor invited to address the Democratic National Committee; he has been discovered by the *Washington Post*; he is mentioned as a possible vice-presidential candidate. But all those achievements have the effect of raising the ante for White. Theatrics aren't enough for him anymore; he needs a record. He is no closer to solving the two substantive issues of the legislative session—how to balance the budget and whether to elect the PUC—than he was a hundred days ago. Out of 181 legislators, there are few that he can count on as devoutly loyal. His victory in the one major battle he waged during the first hundred days—persuading the Senate to nullify Clements' holdover appointments—owed as much to partisanship as to his personal strength. For White, the second hundred days will be much, much tougher than the first.

In trying to figure out how he'll handle them, it is crucial to understand that White isn't as transformed as the conventional wisdom would have it. The main difference between White as governor and White as attorney general is not a new personality but a new job. The AG's office is not a bully pulpit. As Jim Mattox recently learned, you can't just jump on a soapbox and attack the Public Utility Commission—it is your *client*. The attorney general is more administrator than politician—but White is more politician than administrator. The governor's office is far more suited to his talents.

As for his conversion to populism, that too can be ascribed to something other than revelation. White is simply traveling a course he has been over before: he always pays his debts to the people who put him in office. It is his creditors who have changed, not White. Dolph Briscoe made him his Secretary of State, and White dutifully did anything Briscoe wanted. When Briscoe feared the rise of Raza Unida, White took up the fight against extending the Voting Rights Act to Texas, even though it endangered his own political future. Automobile lobbyist Gene Fondren and Houston power broker Walter Mischer bankrolled White's race for attorney general, and White returned the favor by throttling back his consumer protection division, even at the cost of the one issue an attorney general can easily exploit. The last governor's race was decided by Democratic regulars, especially

minorities, and White has already started retiring those obligations—through appointments, through partisan rhetoric seldom heard from a Democratic governor of Texas, and through touching base with people like San Antonio mayor Henry Cisneros. This time he can retire the debt without hurting himself politically.

There is, however, one way in which White has changed. He has won an election in which many of his old supporters deserted him and his opponent spent an unprecedented $13 million, and the experience convinced him that something is going on out there. The question is, What? The two decisions he must make—whether to support a tax increase and whether to go to the mat for an elected utility commission—depend on his figuring out the answer. He needs to decide where he thinks Texas is headed, in particular, whether there's still a place here for a non-ideological, noncontroversial, right-of-center Democrat like, for instance, the old Mark White.

On his issues, the choices are quite neat. The budget comes down to basic questions about what state government should be. Will Texas continue to be characterized by a lack of faith in government as a way of solving social problems—a tradition that has its roots in the frontier, in Reconstruction, and in the peasant villages of Mexico? Or is Texas now a modern industrial state, ready to endure the burden of higher taxes in exchange for raising the abysmal level of state services—forty-ninth in welfare payments, thirty-first in teacher salaries.

The utility battle presents another fork in the road. Forget for a moment that White has personal reasons for wanting an elected commission: the public won't be able to blame the governor when the bad news arrives in the mail. (And bad news will be arriving soon, since the nationwide breakup of AT&T may cause local phone rates to double.) That aside, the larger question at stake is whether the state's all-out commitment to economic growth, a public policy heretofore immune to assault, should be subject to compromise like everything else. An elected PUC would face intense pressure to hold rates down—especially electric rates—and it would find that the only sure way is to cut down on the construction of power plants. But that would imperil the economic future of the state. Without sufficient power reserves, there would be no new industry, no growth. Is that most sacred of Texas political cows, the good business climate, no longer so holy?

Sometime in the second hundred days Mark White will have to make up his mind. In the meantime he is like the nineteenth-century French statesman Alexandre Ledru-Rollin. "There go my people," he said. "I must find out where they are going so I can lead them." ❧

GEORGE BUSH, PLUCKY LAD

Like the hero of a boys' novel, George Bush moved from the East to the wild and woolly West. He wanted to prove himself, by golly, to Yale, Procter & Gamble, and the old man.

BY HARRY HURT III

On the afternoon of March 30, 1981, Vice President George Bush was flying high over Texas. He had just finished making a speech at a cattle raisers' convention in Fort Worth and was en route to Austin to address a joint session of the Texas Legislature. At about 2:40 p.m., his press secretary telephoned him aboard *Air Force Two* to report that President Reagan had been shot at outside a Washington hotel but not injured. Half an hour later Bush got a second call: Reagan *had* been wounded but had walked into the hospital under his own power.

The old line about the vice president's being a heartbeat away from the presidency was, with Reagan in surgery, uncomfortably apt, but what was noteworthy about Bush's behavior was the absence of any hint of eagerness about assuming the job every vice president wants so badly. House majority leader Jim Wright of Fort Worth, who was traveling with the vice-presidential party, remembers that Bush reacted with complete disbelief that anyone could "could work up a feeling of sufficient malice for President Reagan to want him dead." In keeping with standard national security procedure, a military aide aboard Bush's plane carried a plastic American Tourister briefcase—the "football"—that contained a duplicate set of the secret codes essential to U.S. defense. Bush saw no need to open the football—effectively taking over as America's commander in chief, until he had been able to determine the true extent of President Reagan's injuries.

By the time *Air Force Two* touched down in Washington, Bush had already rejected the advice of Secret Service agents that he helicopter directly to the White House lawn. Instead, he ordered the chopper pilot to fly him to the vice president's residence at the Naval Observatory, and he traveled the remaining distance to the White House by motorcade. He was accompanied in the motorcade not

by White House chief of staff James A. Baker III, an old friend of his (that would have started talk of a power grab), but by presidential counselor Edwin Meese III, Baker's archrival. Later that evening, when it became clear that President Reagan would indeed survive, Bush issued a succinct but reassuring statement; "The president is still in charge. There has been no mechanism put in place to transfer authority."

For the next twelve days Ronald Reagan remained in the hospital, and George Bush ran the country—very modestly. He presided over Cabinet meetings in Reagan's absence, but he refused to sit in the president's chair. He greeted foreign dignitaries, met with congressional leaders, and supervised the White House staff. But he did not sign any treaties, initiate any legislation, or order any change in personnel. The thrust of his every action was to keep the president informed of what was happening, not to assume the powers or prerogatives of the presidency. As one Reagan loyalist told a reporter afterward, "He had the perfect touch. In the moments after the shooting, you know the situation was not exactly harmonious among some of the rest of the people in the administration. But Bush came through like a star."

George Bush has had few opportunities for stardom in the two years since the assassination attempt. Under the Constitution, the vice president's one and only official duty is to preside over the Senate. As president of the Senate, he supposedly serves as a counterpart to the Speaker of the House of Representatives. But unlike the Speaker, who not only has full voting powers but also determines the House legislative agenda, the vice president does not usually participate in the daily operation of the Senate and can vote only on the rare occasions when there is a tie. Bush has been called to the Senate chamber in anticipation of such deadlocks fewer than twenty times, and not one of them ever

materialized. In his two and a half years in office, Vice President Bush has yet to cast a single vote.

The vice president's constitutionally limited ability to affect government and the legislative process has led many of Bush's predecessors—and most of the general public—to perceive the office as an inconsequential sinecure. John Nance Garner, the ornery and clever infighter from Uvalde, said being vice president wasn't worth "a warm bucket of spit." Lyndon Johnson called it "the worst job in government." Spiro Agnew said he often felt he might just as well have stayed in Baltimore. Nelson Rockefeller claimed that the only change he made in his life after becoming vice president was to read the obituary page first thing every morning to see if it contained the name of his boss. But George Bush doesn't complain.

In a recent interview aboard *Air Force Two*, after declaring that President Reagan would seek reelection, Bush said he no longer harbored the burning ambition for the Oval Office that had propelled his dogged presidential campaign in 1980. "I'm not one of those who felt from the day he was born he was going to be president," Bush said. "I also feel less of a churning, less of a restlessness about it all. I mean, *che sarà, sarà*. Do your best. If you're interested politically, do the right things politically, or don't do things that could be bad politically. But don't be uptight about it. In this job, the best politics is no politics. That doesn't mean you don't have private thoughts. But I don't consider it of first importance. You could add an 'I don't care,' but I guess I do. I don't know."

As vice president—and during all of his political career—George Bush has had an image problem. Yes, he's loyal; yes, he's a good soldier; yes, he's a man of character. But is he tough enough to be president of the United States? The answer is almost always no. Bush has been described as a wimp, a preppie, a cloistered Ivy Leaguer, and a walking watercress sandwich. Although his performance as vice president has won high praise even from his critics on the right, he is still widely regarded as the perfect—and perpetual—number two man. Democratic pollster Peter Hart says Bush has the soul of a vice president.

But George Bush can't be dismissed so simply. No vice president can. Of the fifteen presidents in this century, six were previously vice presidents. And for Bush the standard vice-presidential odds would seem to be considerably increased: nobody has been vice president to a 72-year-old president before. As Bush himself puts it, "I'd say I have a lot better shot than some in this country of two hundred fifty million people."

Besides all that, wimps don't keep coming back for more the way Bush has. After twice losing U.S. Senate races in Texas, in 1964 and 1970, Bush appeared to be finished in elective politics. He then spent more than five years toiling at various thankless jobs—ambassador to the United Nations, head of the Republican party during Watergate, special envoy to China, chief of the Central Intelligence Agency. Despite warnings from family and friends not to take those posts, Bush accepted each one—and always managed to land on his feet, not only unscathed but politically rejuvenated. In the 1980 presidential primaries, he came out of nowhere to win the Iowa caucuses and establish himself as the most serious challenger to Reagan.

What motivates this man who undoubtedly has the best actuarial chances of anyone in the country to be the next president? A close look at George Bush reveals that the key to his character is an old-fashioned, almost adolescent concept of heroism.

In Bush's youth, teenage boys of his social class in the East often read Owen Johnson's Dink Stover books, a series of boys' readers that were roughly equivalent to the Hardy Boys books, which came later. Written in the second decade of the century and reprinted right through the forties, the Dink Stover books celebrate the moral crises of a young scholar-athlete as he makes his way through prep school at Lawrenceville and college at Yale. In *Stover at Yale,* the hero jeopardizes his chances of being tapped for one of the elite senior secret societies by decrying the undemocratic bylaws of the sophomore secret societies. But when Tap Day finally arrives at the end of Stover's junior year, he is tapped by the most prestigious secret society of all—Skull and Bones—because of the respect he has won for "doing the right thing," and he winds up a hero. This two-step process—Doing the Right Thing, followed, after appropriate suffering, by Heroic Acclaim—is the basis of George Bush's vision of the world. It has informed both his career and his beliefs about politics and government.

Bush came by his view of the world through inheritance—that is, through his father, Prescott S. Bush, Sr. Most men approaching their sixtieth year have arrived at a considered view of the strengths and weaknesses of their once-almighty fathers. Not George Bush. The vice president still considers the patriarch of the Bush clan—a Dink Stover-style Yalie who was tapped for Skull and Bones and later for the U.S. Senate—to be a hero of the highest order. Prescott Bush was the man who did everything and did it honorably and well. George Bush's life has been a struggle to live up to his father's example without destroying—or even questioning—the great man's myth.

When George Herbert Walker Bush drove his battered red Studebaker into Odessa in the summer of 1948, the town's population, though constantly increasing with newly arrived oil-field hands, was still under 30,000. There were only two local radio stations, no TV, and not much that could pass for culture besides the Odessa Chuck Wagon Gang's occasional barbecues and an assortment of bars with names like the Tumbleweed, the Silver Saddle, and the Oasis.

George Bush, then 24, had graduated from Yale just a week before he showed up in Odessa to learn the oil business. He was a lean and lanky six feet two, with crystal-blue eyes, neatly combed brown hair, and the kind of clean-cut, delicately handsome features that seemed to sing out "I'm a Yankee Doodle Dandy." He was the son of a wealthy and social Eastern establishment family and also accomplished in his own right: a World War II pilot decorated for heroism, a Phi Beta Kappa student, the captain of a championship college baseball team. He was married to the daughter of a prominent family from Rye, New York, and he was the father of a two-year-old son.

By the time his wife and son arrived from the East, Bush had established the family's first Texas residence in a frame duplex on East Seventh Street, a few blocks from the oil-field equipment warehouse where he was going to work. The Bushes had the only car and icebox in their neighborhood, and the only bathroom on the street. They had to share their toilet with the other tenants of the duplex, "two ladies," as Barbara Bush says, "of interesting occupations and one child."

What drove George Bush to this ghetto for West Texas oil-field trash was not the allure of instant riches, which was Odessa's great temptation to most people; it was his father. At six four and 220 pounds, Prescott Bush was charming, dark-haired, and extraordinarily handsome, with a presence often compared to that of Gary Cooper. Born to a middle-class Ohio family, he had graduated from Yale in 1917. He played the piano, sang with the Whiffenpoofs, and lettered in golf and baseball. He went on to become an accomplished tennis player, a partner in the Wall street firm of Brown Brothers Harriman, and the moderator (the equivalent of an unpaid mayor) of Greenwich, Connecticut, town metings. "My father was very strong," George Bush recalls. "He was so strong and so big and kind of overpowering—loving but overpowering."

Aware of his advantages and those his children would inherit, Pres Bush taught his offspring the importance of public service, the desire—indeed, the duty—to "put something back in." But he did not do his teaching in loving lectures in his study or at the dinner table. He was too busy for that. Instead he taught by example, by doing. "I just watched him with admiration," George remembers. "When everybody else was going off to have two martinis before dinner, he'd be down there as chairman of the town meeting."

George's mother, Dorothy Walker Bush, was an equally impressive person. She came from a St. Louis investment banking family that had established the Walker Cup prize for amateur golf, but she had made her own name as a tennis champion. She was an old-fashioned lady who wore white gloves, referred to her shoes as slippers, and worshiped in the Episcopal church. But she could beat younger women, like her daughter-in-law, at paddleball, playing either right-handed or left-handed. Like her husband, Dorothy Bush was both highly principled and very, very competitive.

George caught the family's competitive spirit and zest for achievement at an early age. Born in Milton, Massachusetts, on June 12, 1924, he was the second-oldest male child in the family, but he quickly became the undisputed star. Whereas his older brother, Prescott Junior, suffered from weak eyesight and gimpy knees, George seemed to have inherited all his father's natural gifts save the ability to sing and play the piano. After the family moved to Connecticut, George attended the Greenwich Country Day School and the Phillips Academy in Andover, Massachusetts, where he excelled in both sports and studies. What he now describes as a privileged life included being chauffeured to school, attending cotillions for the suburban scions of Rye and Greenwich, and vacationing in Maine. But upon graduating from Andover in 1942, he postponed college to enlist, and at eighteen he became the Navy's youngest ensign.

In a 1944 attack on the Bonin Islands that earned him the Distinguished Flying Cross his plane was hit by enemy fire at the start of a bombing run. Instead of retreating, Bush completed the run, then bailed out over open water and was picked up by an American submarine. He returned stateside for more flight training and was preparing to go back into combat when the atomic bomb ended the war.

Bush got married in January 1945 during what he expected to be only a brief furlough. He and his bride, Barbara Pierce, a student at Smith College and the daughter of the president of the McCall Corporation, had met at a Rye-Greenwich dance a few years before the war. George had seen her dancing with a friend of his and, as Barbara recalls, "very nicely went up to someone and asked him to introduce us." Although Barbara attended George's prep school graduation, she did not see much of her husband-to-be until after he came back to the States. "We were very young," she says. "I was only nineteen, and he was twenty. He just looked like a little baby. But it was wartime. A lot of other couples were getting married at a young age. The war just did that."

Bush got his discharge as a lieutenant (junior grade) in the fall of 1945 and immediately entered Yale. The couple's first child, George Walker Bush, was born the following summer. The proud father's college classmates nicknamed him Poppy, which had been his maternal grandfather's nickname at Yale. Bush went on to become a Phi Beta Kappa economics major, and like Dink Stover and Pres Bush, he was tapped for Skull and Bones. But he was proudest of his accomplishments as a jock. In addition to playing varsity soccer, he was captain of the varsity baseball team his senior year, and as a weak-hitting but sharp-fielding first baseman, he helped Yale win two NCAA Eastern Division championships.

The turning point in George Bush's life came in the spring of his senior year. He could have pursued a conventionally attractive career in the East. His father's partners even had Brown Brothers Harriman's nepotism rule waived so that George could join the firm. But, says Barbara Bush, George wanted to "do something he could touch." The couple briefly considered going into farming, and George weighed several job offers from the big corporations that routinely interviewed Yale seniors, but the comopany that made the best impression, Procter & Gamble, turned him down. "I'll never forget it," Bush recalls, "I've had an I'll-show-these-guys attitude ever since."

Then Pres Bush, who served on the board of Dresser Industries, introduced his son to Dresser's president, Neil Mallon of Dallas. Mallon offered George a job in West Texas at the company's oil-field-equipment subsidiary, and he accepted. "If I were a psychoanalyzer, I might conclude that I was trying to, not compete with my father, but do something on my own," Bush says today. "My stay in Texas was no Horatio Alger thing, but moving from New Haven to Odessa just about the day I graduated was quite a shift in lifestyle."

Granted, George Bush's move to Texas was unorthodox, but it was also consistent with the Dink Stover ethic. It was a break with tradition, a departure from the preordained path through life, and it carried the risks of failure and social ostracism and also the possibility of triumph. Although going into the oil business instead of investment banking did not connote oedipal violence, leaving the East was a sign of leaving the nest, of an escape from the shadow of his father. But it wasn't a breaking off of relations. After all, his father had gotten him the job.

Uncle Herbie

George spent his first few months in Odessa as a sales trainee. In addition to peddling drilling equipment in the oil patch, he painted pipe and swept out the warehouse. Dresser then transferred him to California, where he covered the oil fields around Bakersfield, Ventura, Compton, and Richard Nixon's hometown of Whittier. He and Barbara also had a second child, a girl whom they named Robin.

In 1949 the Bushes moved back to Texas and bought a house in a GI-bill subdivision of Midland known as Easter Egg Row. The neighborhood got its name from its tiny, box-shaped houses, which were painted in a rainbow of bright colors in an effort to give them individual identities. Although owning a home on Easter Egg Row beat sharing a toilet with other tenants, the Bushes' new neighborhood certainly wasn't Greenwich. Sand piled up against the houses like snow, in drifts two and three feet high, and blew in through the windows, the doorjambs, and the cracks in the siding. "People were always having to scrape sand off their chairs and dinner tables," recalls a former resident.

The Bushes quickly discovered that they shared the difficulties of West Texas desert life with a whole generation of young newcomers very much like themselves. Part of this crowd consisted of Southerners and Midwesterners, people from Oklahoma, Kansas, Missouri, and other, more populous regions of Texas. But a surprising number came from back East and were known generically as Yalies. "The people from the East and the people from Texas or Oklahoma all seemed to have two things in common," recalls Bush's Texas-born former neighbor and partner John Overbey. "They all had a chance to be stockbrokers or investment bankers. And they all wanted to learn the oil business instead."

No one was more representative of the newcomers than the Liedtke brothers, Hugh and Bill, who had come down from Tulsa. Their father was legal counsel for Gulf Oil in Tulsa. Both brothers were graduates of Amherst College, with law degrees from the University of Texas. Hugh, the older of the two, also had an M.B.A. from Harvard. The Liedtkes opened a law firm shortly after arriving in Midland, but they devoted most of their time to forming oil partnerships.

The Bushes and the Liedtkes quickly became friends, partly because, as Hugh puts it, "there wasn't a damn thing to do out there except be friends." In a town whose second-rate movie house was the foremost cultural institution, entertainment consisted mostly of going over to friends' houses to cook steaks in the sandstorm, have a few drinks, and talk about the oil business or their infant children. They played touch football games on Sundays and exercised together in the local gym before work in the morning.

Gradually they shed at least the outer trappings of the East. Barbara Bush recalls' that one morning shortly after moving to Midland George decided to go for a jog down the highway in a pair of Bermuda shorts. He returned to the house blushing and embarrassed after having been whistled at and catcalled off the road by passing West Texas truck drivers. He put away his Bermudas, along with his pin-striped suits, and began wearing the khaki pants and open-collared shirts favored by local businessmen.

After Bush had finished a two-and-a-half-year apprenticeship with Dresser, he and John Overbey, an oil and gas lease broker, decided to go into business for themselves. In 1951 they formed the Bush-Overbey Oil Development Company. Their idea was to buy the mineral rights to land next to or near properties that were about to be drilled on. If a well were to come in on one of those properties, their own leases would skyrocket in value. The money for the venture came from Bush's maternal uncle George Herbert Walker, Jr. Uncle Herbie, as George called him, was the head of the investment banking firm of G. H. Walker & Company, and while he did not have the physical stature or the awesome talents of Pres Bush, young George regarded him as a surrogate father. Uncle Herbie attended his nephew's college baseball games, played golf with him, and even vacationed with George and Barbara every year for the first twenty years of their marriage. The $300,000 capital he provided came from the designated high-risk portion of assets he invested for a group of large British trust funds.

One of the few embellishments Bush has allowed in his life story is the notion that he built himself a business from scratch. In fact, he did it with family money—including money from his father. John Overbey says Prescott Bush put about $50,000 into Bush-Overbey. But it is significant that most of Bush's start-up funds came not from his father but from his mother's side of the family, which must have made it seem to him like starting from scratch.

Bush-Overbey proved to be a moderately successful enterprise—it earned a profit from the first year on—but both partners decided they could do much better by joining forces with the Liedtke brothers. Bush-Overbey represented the foreign and Eastern clients of Uncle Herbie's investment banking firm, and the Liedtke brothers had raised their money from friends back in Tulsa. In 1953 each group contributed $500,000 to the formation of the Zapata Petroleum Corporation, named for the Mexican revolutionary Emiliano Zapata. They spent all of their start-up money on a single oil field, which ultimately produced 130 successful wells. Bush and Overbey soon had the means to move from Easter Egg Row to better Midland neighborhoods.

With the biggest oil drilling boom in American history going on all around them, three of the four Zapata founders concluded that the next logical step was the formation of a drilling company. The fourth, John Overbey, politely dropped out. Bush and the Liedtkes purchased seven onshore drilling rigs and then decided to take an even greater plunge, into the new and much riskier business of offshore drilling. In 1955 the Zapata Off-Shore Company offered $1.5 million worth of its stock to the public. It had built three rigs when, thanks to some big oil finds in the Middle East, the Texas boom suddenly went bust.

George Bush began spending most of his time scurrying around the country "stretching paper"—making new financing arrangements—with the pension funds and endowments that were Zapata Off-Shore's lenders. In almost every instance, these financial institutions wanted part of the company's equity in exchange for extending repayment schedules. But Bush held firm. When the dust cleared, he had managed a refinancing plan without giving up a single share of stock to the company's creditors. Back in Texas, he demonstrated equal firmness in attending to the unpleasant task of cutting back Zapata Off-Shore's staff. "When you talk about being tough-minded in business," says Hugh Liedtke, "the examples are a little harder to illustrate than in a political situation where you can declare war or not declare war. I've seen Bush let people go, terminate them, even though they were his personal friends. But he did it because it had to be done. And the remarkable thing was, he did it in such a way that he was still friends with them later."

Bush had also had to cope with family tragedy. His four-year-old daughter, Robin, died of leukemia in 1953. Already active in the YMCA, the Episcopal church, and the chamber of commerce, Bush became chairman of the Midland Cancer Crusade and increased his involvement in community affairs.

By early 1959, with U.S. drilling activity only partially recovered from the bust, an East-West split developed within the Zapata ranks. The Liedtke brothers and their Oklahoma investors wanted to concentrate on exploring for oil and gas, but

Bush believed that there was still a great future in contracting out offshore rigs. Sources close to the principals say that a personality conflict between Uncle Herbie, who had provided the investors for Bush's half of the original partnership, and Hugh Liedtke, who even then had his sights set on running a major oil company, widened the rift.

So Bush and the Liedtkes negotiated a complex but amicable parting. A series of stock swaps left the Liedtkes in control of the original Zapata Petroleum Corporation, whose annual revenues had grown to about $1 million. Bush and Uncle Herbie's clients wound up with controlling interest in the $4.5-million-a-year Zapata Off-Shore Company. At a market value of about $10 per share, Bush's personal holdings in Zapata Off-Shore were worth about $600,000. He wasn't yet a full-fledged self-made millionaire, but for a 35-year-old Yalie who had learned the oil business from scratch, he was doing very well. He decided he could do even better if he moved his company and his family to the city where the offshore action was: Houston.

"It's the Right Thing to Do"

George Bush seemed destined to run for something almost from the moment he arrived in Houston. His father had run for the U.S. Senate from Connecticut in 1950, lost, been elected in 1952, and then reelected in 1956. When Pres Bush set an example, it was never lost on his son. But Bush quickly learned that the local Republican party was split. On one side were the forebears of the New Right, the conservatives, and on the other were the moderates, who were often internationalists and were associated with the northeastern, Rockefeller wing of the party. Since Bush, despite his ten years in Texas, naturally fell into the second category, the conservatives were not kindly disposed toward him.

The Republicans of Harris County had their big shoot-out over the 1962 county chairman race. The conservatives were led by State Senator Walter Mengden, and the moderates rallied behind James A. Bertron, who was the incumbent county chairman. The conservatives accused the moderates of being too liberal. However, Bertron and his moderates eventually won out. The following year Bertron resigned to move to Florida and was succeeded by George Bush.

Bush entered Texas politics like a reluctant debutante. He had not been especially active in the 1960 presidential campaign, the 1962 midterm elections, or the 1962 county chairman fight. This apparent lack

of interest concerned both his father and his Houston friends. In 1961, shortly after John Tower won a special election to the U.S. Senate, Senator Prescott Bush pulled James Bertron aside at a Washington fundraiser and asked him, "Jimmy, when are you going to get George involved?"

"Senator, I'm trying," Bertron replied. "We're all trying."

When first offered the Harris County party chairman's job, Bush politely begged off. But Bertron and other local party leaders insisted. While Bush's ingrained sense of public duty was probably what finally prevailed upon him to accept the job, the timing was also significant. In 1962 Senator Prescott Bush completed his second term and chose not to run for reelection because of poor health. George Bush took over as Harris County party chairman in 1963.

Before Bush had served a full year, he decided to resign to run for the U.S. Senate against liberal Democrat Ralph Yarborough. He first had to beat former gubernatorial candidate Jack Cox in the Republican primary. After winning that race (which was more a popularity contest than an ideological slugfest) Bush entered the general election with an indisputably conservative (though not extremist) platform that opposed the Civil Rights Act, the Nuclear Test Ban Treaty, and admitting Red China to the UN. Even so, Bush's position did not effectively appease the dissident conservatives in the party.

Yarborough won the 1964 race, but he got only 56 per cent of the vote, trailing Johnson's presidential coattails by 7 per cent. Bush won 1,134,337 votes statewide, which made him the biggest Republican vote-getter in Texas history. He decided to make politics a full-time job. Houston's growth had prompted the creation of a new congressional district on the affluent West Side that appeared to be brimming with potential Republican voters. In 1966 Bush, then 41, resigned from Zapata Off-Shore, sold all his Zapata stock, and announced his candidacy for the new 7th District's congressional seat in the 1966 election. The sale netted Bush $1.1 million. But within eighteen months Zapata Off-Shore's stock zoomed from about $20 a share to $87 a share. By selling out, Bush had, in effect, left at least $3.5 million lying on the table.

Bush says now that what happened to Zapata Off-Shore after he sold out was "kind of ironic" but adds that he has no regrets. "By then I was pretty sure I wanted to be in politics," he says. "I didn't have as a goal a stacking-up of money. If you're going to build something or add to productivity or something like that, I could make a very stimulating case that would be worth doing. But the idea of just going out and making money for the sake of it doesn't interest me. If I didn't have any capital at all, I might be viewing that quite differently." That's hardly the way the Liedtke brothers or most other Texas oil men think; the ethic of the oil business is that money is a worthwhile goal, if only because it's how you keep score. What Bush had wanted from the business was something entirely different—the opportunity to prove himself on his own terms, like all his boyhood heroes.

In the 1966 congressional election, the voters of West Houston gave George Bush the kind of landslide victory that Texas Republicans had previously only dreamed about. He beat district attorney Frank Briscoe, a conservative Democrat, with 57 per cent of the vote. Upon arriving in Washington, Congressman Bush became one of the few freshmen ever to gain a seat on the Ways and Means Committee. His knowledge of oil and gas and general economic matters impressed committee chairman Wilbur Mills. So did his support for family planning, which prompted Mills to nickname him Rubbers. But what many still regard as Bush's toughest and truest test of character was the vote on the open housing provision of the Civil Rights Act.

When the generally quite conservative Bush announced that he intended to vote in favor of the open housing provision, his Houston constituents reacted with a vengeance. His office was deluged with hate mail and anonymous phone calls issuing death threats. The Houston establishment threatened to marshal all its funds to ensure his defeat if he sought reelection in 1968. Bush agonized over the decision for weeks but didn't change his mind. Bill Liedtke, who had moved to Houston to help his brother launch the giant takeover bid that created Pennzoil, recalls his old friend's grace under all this pressure with a revealing anecdote. One afternoon in the midst of the open housing controversy, Bush went to Liedtke's new home in the affluent Memorial area to take a much-needed break. As the two men sat around the swimming pool, Bush summarized his position in a single sentence that could have come right out of Dink Stover: "It's just the right thing to do."

After open housing passed in Congress, Bush returned to Houston to meet with an angry group of oilmen and other businessmen at the Ramada Club. According to one friend, the young congressman told his critics, "I did what I thought was right. We agree on most issues. This one we don't agree on. I hope I still have your support. But if I don't have your support, I hope I still have your friendship. If I don't have your friendship, I'm sorry, but I have to vote with my conscience." In 1968 Bush was reelected to a second term in Congress without opposition.

Immediately upon returning to Washington, he determined to challenge Ralph Yarborough again in the 1970 Senate race. Nixon had almost carried Texas in the 1968 presidential campaign, and Yarborough opposed the war in Viet Nam, which Bush believed most Texas voters supported. Wouldn't Texas prefer a second Republican senator to Yarborough?

Even the undisputed patriarch of the Texas Democratic party, former president Lyndon Johnson, sent Bush an encouraging signal. Bush slipped away from Nixon's inaugural festivities to say goodbye to Johnson as LBJ made his final flight back to Texas aboard *Air Force One*. Johnson felt so touched by Bush's gesture that he grabbed the congressman by the lapels and told him, "You come see me down at the ranch."

Bush took Johnson up on the invitation a few weeks later and, well aware of LBJ's open hostility toward Yarborough, mentioned that he was thinking of giving up his House seat to run for the Senate. "Boy," said Johnson, "the difference between the House and the Senate is the difference between chickenshit and chicken salad."

But the logic of Bush's campaign was instantly destroyed when a wealthy, little-known conservative Houston businessman named Lloyd Bentsen upset Yarborough in the Democratic primary. In the fall campaign the media portrayed the race as a contest between Tweedledum and Tweedledee. The final tally showed Bentsen with 53.4 per cent and Bush with 46.6 per cent. (A few years later it was reported that during the campaign Bush had accepted a $106,000 cash contribution from a $1.5 million secret account called the Townhouse operation, filled with donations from big Nixon backers like Chicago insurance magnate W. Clement Stone. Bush didn't report the donation, but he has never been charged with violating campaign finance laws.)

"Boy, You Can't Turn a President Down"

In 1970, at the age of 46, George Bush suddenly found himself with nothing to do. His oil company was out of his hands. His congressional seat had been passed on to another Republican, Bill Archer. The next Senate race in Texas belonged to the Republican incumbent, John Tower. A bid for the governor's mansion would have meant taking on another conservative Democrat and so was out of the question. Bush was being labeled a has-been, a loser. Then Richard Nixon came to his rescue. In early 1971 Bush was appointed ambassador to the United Nations.

It was Bush's first big-time appointive office, and while he assiduously Did the Right Thing, it didn't seem to produce results, perhaps because he was working for Henry Kissinger. In October, as Kissinger was making his second trip to Peking, a coalition of Third World countries succeeded in bringing to a vote a resolution to admit the People's Republic of China to the UN and expel Taiwan. Bush, who had been kept completely in the dark about Kissinger's dealings with China, voted against the resolution on America's behalf, but it carried anyway, prompting many of its supporters to start dancing in the aisles. Bush returned from the proceedings looking more distraught than his staff had ever seen him. He seemed to take the vote as a personal defeat. He declared it "a day of infamy."

Being at the UN gave Bush the chance to see his father more often. Whenever Pres Bush dropped by, George would kiss and hug him like a little boy. "I never saw a man show so much affection for his father," says one member of Bush's staff. On October 8, 1972, Pres Bush died of cancer. His death came suddenly and almost unexpectedly. Worse, the patriarch of the Bush clan spent his last days at the Sloan-Kettering Cancer Center in New York, the same hospital where George's young daughter, Robin, had died nineteen years earlier.

In January 1973 President Nixon called his UN ambassador to the White House to discuss a new post. Barbara Bush begged George to take anything Nixon might offer *except* the chairmanship of the Republican National Committee. Although Nixon had just trounced George McGovern in the 1972 presidential election and Kissinger had declared that peace in Viet Nam was at hand, the Watergate scandal was gathering momentum. Taking charge of the Republican party at that moment looked like a no-win situation.

That was precisely why Nixon asked George Bush, with his squeaky-clean public image and his devotion to team play, to run the RNC. And Bush, a deep believer in the fundamental goodness of the Republican party and in the institution of the presidency, said yes. Taking the RNC job was the Right Thing to Do, even if it was bound to hurt Bush's career. When Bush told Barbara what had happened, he explained his decision with the words "Boy, you can't turn a president down."

On the job, Bush publicly defended Nixon with a vigor so complete that it later came back to haunt him. But friends say that Bush agonized behind the scenes throughout the Watergate saga. One veteran RNC staffer recalls, "The White House staff called him on more than one occasion at the RNC office and said they wanted something done in support of the president but that they wanted it to appear that it had been done at the initiative of the RNC. Bush would say it wasn't going to be done by the RNC, and he got mad at them for raising the issue. These were matters he took care of himself when he was being criticized in the press for not being tough enough on Nixon. The only reason I knew about it was that I could hear the screaming coming out the door."

Early in the long series of Watergate investigations, Texas congressman Wright Patman's House Banking Committee revealed that Bill Liedtke and Robert Mosbacher, another longtime political and oil business friend, had contributed to a $700,000 fund to help finance Nixon's 1972 reelection campaign. The money was collected before the April 1972 start date of a new campaign-financing law, so it did not have to be—and was not—publicly reported. Instead, the money was flown to Washington in Pennzoil's private plane and deposited at the offices of the Republican party finance committee. Later about $100,000 of it was transferred through Mexico to the bank account of Watergate burglar Bernard Barker. Although neither Liedtke nor Mosbacher nor any of the other contributors ostensibly knew their money would be used to finance the Watergate break-in, the mere connection tarnished both their reputations and Bush's.

On August 6, 1974, presidential counselor Dean Burch showed Bush the famous "smoking gun": a transcript of the June 23, 1972, White House conversation in which Nixon personally ordered the cover-up of the circumstances surrounding the Watergate break-in. The Right Thing to Do had changed, and the once-supportive Bush pressured Nixon to resign.

When newly sworn-in president Gerald Ford ranked potential vice-presidential candidates, Bush scored highest. But Ford ultimately decided on the older and more experienced Nelson Rockefeller, and he appointed Bush as the nation's first special envoy to the People's Republic of China. It wasn't the world's most demanding job, but it gave Bush a welcome opportunity to read, to travel, and to resume writing the notes and letters to friends and political acquaintances that won him a reputation as a master of the personal touch.

A year into the job, Ford asked Bush to take another post that nobody else seemed to want: heading the CIA. Wisconsin representative William Steiger cabled Bush in China: "Please do not do this." But once again Bush found it impossible to say no to the president, even though, as part of the terms of his confirmation, he had to agree to stay out of politics until after the 1976 election. He spent the next year at what he later described as his best job of the decade. He could finally call the shots, and it so happened that his preoccupation with integrity was just what the agency needed. Bush helped write an executive order protecting U.S. citizens from CIA spying, and he worked to restore morale at the agency by improving its public image and protecting its bureaucratic interests.

After Jimmy Carter won the 1976 election, he got a thorough briefing from Bush that, according to some press reports, was followed by Bush's request to stay on at the agency. Bush denies this. "I told him

that I thought it would be best if he got somebody else," he maintains. "Whether I would have done it if he had asked me to, I don't know."

Bush was 52 and once again without a job or an apparent political future. He had never won election to anything bigger than a seat in Congress, and he had been no more than mildly successful at the Washington appointments game. He returned to Houston to accept an executive position with First International Bancshares, joined the lecture circuit, and took a visiting professorship at Rice University. Then he began planning his comeback.

Running for President

In October 1977, Bush made his first trip to China as a private citizen, accompanied by a group that included *Washington Post* political correspondent David Broder, James Baker, Dean Burch, Hugh Liedtke, and Texas state representative Chase Untermeyer of Houston. On the way back home, Burch recalls, they "stopped in Guam to refuel at about three or four o'clock in the morning. George got out and wrote postcards to all the RNC people in Guam. It was then that I realized he intended to run for president."

It was not until late fall of 1978 that Bush started mentioning the idea himself. At the time, the Democrats were posting overall gains in the midterm elections, and the Carter administration was not yet in disarray. "I think, looking at the political situation, you would think you didn't have a chance," he says today. "But by then I was wholly immersed in the public light, and I had a wealth of experience and I perhaps immodestly felt I could do it. I remember [columnist] Rowland Evans coming down to Houston saying we had no chance at all. Absolutely none. But having thought it out and talked to friends, feeling it wouldn't be easy but that there was certainly a chance, I just decided we'd do it. Go try."

One of the first and closest friends Bush discussed his presidential race with was James A. Baker III, the scion of a Houston legal dynasty. In 1970, after the death of Baker's first wife, Bush had asked him to run the Houston branch of the Bush for Senate campaign to get his mind off the tragedy, and Baker had been involved in politics ever since. In 1975 Bush got Baker the job of Under Secretary of Commerce. In 1976 Baker became Gerald Ford's chief delegate hunter and campaign manager, and he returned to Texas to run for attorney general in 1978. He was still licking the wounds from his defeat by Mark White when he agreed to manage Bush's presidential campaign.

Bush announced his candidacy at a Houston press conference on May 1, 1979, and promptly disappeared, or so it seemed. Most stories on the upcoming

campaign focused on Ted Kennedy's potential threat to Jimmy Carter and on the activities of a roster of Republican contenders that included Ronald Reagan, John Connally, Howard Baker, Robert Dole, John Anderson, and even Gerald Ford. But while his competitors played wholesale politics in the mass media, Bush quietly played retail politics in the small states with the earliest primaries, especially Iowa and New Hampshire, whose caucuses kicked off the election year. In so doing, Bush was playing to his strengths: his charm and good looks, his youthful energy, his astonishing memory for names, his mastery of the personal touch. He and his family went to almost every city and town in the state. Bush called hundreds of Iowans on the phone, wrote letters to volunteers and supporters, jotted thank-you notes to reporters who wrote about him.

A similar person-to-person network fueled the Bush fundraising effort. Most of the campaign's fundraisers were Bush family members and longtime friends: brothers, sisters, cousins, old business acquaintances, former school chums, former associates from career stops like the RNC and the CIA. Bush eventually collected $22 million, more than any other presidential candidate except Ronald Reagan. And on caucus day in Iowa the results were 31.5 per cent for George Bush, 29.4 per cent for Ronald Reagan, and 15.7 per cent for Howard Baker. John Connally got only 9.3 per cent of the vote.

Bush suddenly jumped from obscurity to the cover of *Newsweek*. He had trailed Reagan 45 per cent to 6 per cent in polls taken at the beginning of 1980. The week after the Iowa caucuses, the polls showed that the gap had narrowed to only 6 percentage points, 33 to 27. Unfortunately, when the campaign moved on to New Hampshire, the Bush people found that Reagan's team had done a more thorough job of retail politics than they had—and on top of that, Bush walked right into a Reagan trap.

It happened the night of a TV debate in Nashua, New Hampshire. The local newspaper sponsoring the event had invited only Reagan and Bush. Since Bush now hoped to narrow the Republican campaign to a two-man race, the exclusion of Baker, Dole, Anderson, and the other contenders suited him fine. But after Baker and Dole protested to the Federal Election Commission, the FEC ruled that the candidates—not the newspaper—had to pay for the debate because it constituted an illegal campaign contribution rather than an open forum. Given that Bush had already spent his authorized limit on the New Hampshire primary, the Reagan people had to bear the full cost of the program—and as long as they were paying, they decided to invite everyone.

When Bush entered the gymnasium where the debate was to take place, he was surprised to see Howard Baker, Robert Dole, John Anderson, and Philip Crane waiting in the wings. All four took the stage along with Reagan and Bush. Reagan opened the program by saying he wanted to make a statement, but the moderator cut off his microphone. Reagan, playing the aggrieved good guy with consummate skill, said he had paid for the microphone and should therefore be allowed to speak over it, but the moderator insisted that the other candidates leave the stage. Instead of leaping to his feet and inviting the others to join in, Bush reacted exactly as the Reagan team had expected him to: he just sat there, implicitly taking on the role of the heavy. Baker, Dole, Anderson, and Crane proceeded to steal the show by holding a rump press conference in an adjoining room, during which they accused Bush of unfairly shutting them out and of being afraid to meet them head-on. Bush, of course, wasn't really afraid. He was just abiding by the rules, but he lacked the wit to see instantly how he would look.

The beginning of the end for Bush came in May. Jim Baker had sent Rich Bond and several other staffers to California with orders to run a low-budget "diversionary" campaign in hopes of tying up Reagan's assets while Bush struggled to erode Reagan's growing strength in the East. Then, on Friday, May 23, while Bush was campaigning in New Jersey, Baker apparently caught his own candidate by surprise with the announcement that Bush was withdrawing from the California primary for lack of funds. Bush immediately flew home to Houston to huddle with his family and campaign staff.

When Bush met with Baker, finance chairman Robert Mosbacher, and other staffers the next day, he and his family wanted to stay in the race. But Mosbacher produced figures showing that the Bush campaign was already $1 million in the red, and he expressed little hope of attracting much more money in the face of Reagan's primary victories. Baker added that Reagan had already amassed nearly enough delegates to assure a first-ballot victory at the Republican convention in Detroit. Even if Bush managed to make inroads in California, Baker argued, he could go to the convention only as a spoiler, which would probably ruin his chances for the vice-presidential nomination. Playing spoiler could also touch off a bitter internecine battle at the convention that would be televised across the nation.

It wasn't until that last point that Bush began to give in. Finances are not a problem, he argued; we can get the money somewhere if that will secure victory. Bush also dismissed the idea that staying in the race might harm his vice-presidential prospects; he wasn't running for the number two spot. But when he assessed Reagan's overwhelming delegate lead, he had to admit that his chances of catching

up looked slim at best. The Republicans didn't need a divisive and ultimately self-defeating fight at the convention. Viewed in that light, withdrawing was another Right Thing to Do. He would make the announcement on Monday.

Exhausted, Bush and his advisers decided to go out for Mexican food. Although Bush had spent nearly two decades in politics and government, he rarely provoked any reaction in public—indeed, he was often not even recognized. But when he walked into the Mexican restaurant that night, the other diners broke into applause. Bush's chest seemed to swell up like Superman's. As soon as the applause subsided, Bush told Baker and Mosbacher that he had reconsidered. He was a competitor, not a quitter. He would stay in the race until the end. He had Done the Right Thing by staying in, he had suffered defeats, and now, just like in the script, he was a hero.

Baker and Mosbacher had to spend the rest of the night reconvincing Bush of the case they had argued all day long. Finally he promised that he would not change his mind again. On Monday, May 26, 1980, he called a press conference in Houston to announce his formal withdrawal from the presidential race and his full support for the candidacy of Ronald Reagan.

Politics is at once a romantic pursuit and a practical one. By the time Bush got to the Detroit convention, he was running hard for vice president—never mind what he had been saying a few weeks earlier. Now his biggest problem was that a movement was afoot to pick Gerald Ford as Reagan's running mate.

Members of the Bush inner circle describe their leader's reaction to the Ford rumors as a mixture of shock, disbelief, anger, and despair. When he returned to his hotel room after addressing the convention, a mob of reporters was waiting to quiz him about the movement to draft Ford. "Oh, shit," he muttered uncharacteristically to his small entourage. "Let's go have a beer. I think I can stop all this political-figure stuff now."

The Bush party went to the hotel bar and ordered a round of beers, but the reporters followed right behind. Someone offered to pick up a few six-packs around the corner instead, and the group reconvened in the privacy of Bush's suite. It looked like this was the end of the line: more than a year and a half of hard work down the drain without even a consolation prize. Before long most of his supporters had drifted off to their rooms, and Bush was alone with Barbara, Jim Baker, Dean Burch, and their mutual disappointment. Then the telephone rang. It was Ronald Reagan, calling to ask Bush to be his vice-presidential nominee.

The Perfect Vice President

George Bush began his first term as vice president of the United States by cutting a deal with his boss. He borrowed the particulars from his Democratic predecessor, Walter F. Mondale. In essence, it was a blueprint for the perfect vice presidency: not too strong, not too weak, never on center stage but never out in the boondocks. The three main points were complete access to the president at all times, complete access to all presidential information, and the freedom to take on special assignments of an important but not all-consuming nature. It seems to be working.

Bush has carte blanche to enter the Oval Office unannounced at any time, day or night, though he often abides by a self-imposed check of the president's schedule before barging in. Like Mondale, Bush enjoys the privilege of an office in the West Wing of the White House—the true corridor of power—in addition to the traditional vice-presidential offices in the old Executive Office Building and on Capitol Hill. Besides attending all Cabinet meetings, Bush has a private luncheon with the president every Thursday. And like Reagan, Bush receives a regular early-morning briefing on national security matters from the CIA.

In addition to putting Bush in charge of presidential task forces on regulatory relief, the Atlanta child murders, and drug smuggling, Reagan named him head of a new top-level Special Situation Group with specific authority to handle threats to national security—a job that then Secretary of State Alexander Haig wanted badly. At the same time, Bush was able to reject assignments he didn't want, like playing point man and chief publicist for the ill-fated New Federalism program.

What Bush really spends his time on, though, is representing the administration and the party on the road. In the first two and a half years of his term he has logged 344,364 air miles and visited 48 states, 33 foreign countries, and 3 U.S. possessions. In 1981 he visited British prime minister Margaret Thatcher, French president François Mitterrand, and Philippines president Ferdinand Marcos, and he undertook a swing through Latin America. Last year Bush interrupted a tour of Africa to attend the funeral of Soviet president Leonid Brezhnev and, along with Secretary of State George Shultz, he met the newly installed Soviet general secretary, Yuri Andropov. This year he toured Europe again to sell to our allies Reagan's "zero option" plan for bilateral nuclear disarmament in Europe. Within the United States last year he made 155 appearances on behalf of 120 candidates in state and local elections. In the last two years, according to his staff, Bush has raised $16 million from personal appearances before candidate and party groups and $12 million from a special vice-presidential direct-mail effort. All this is classic vice-presidential stuff, but Bush works especially hard at it, and every trip builds up the stack of chips he can cash in later.

Bush is one of the few people in the administration whose general advice to the president will always be listened to and sometimes followed. As chief of the Special Situation Group, he recommended sanctions against the Soviet Union and Poland after the crackdown on the Solidarity movement. When the administration's proposal for selling AWACS planes to Saudi Arabia ran into unexpectedly staunch opposition, Bush convinced the president of the need to lobby the Senate in person, and he himself also lobbied. After returning from his meeting with Andropov, Bush urged the president to press for approval of the M-X missile program at once. He failed in his attempts to persuade Reagan to support a simple extension of the Voting Rights Act instead of backing a weakened House version. But he successfully persuaded the president to reverse his previous decision to award tax exemptions to schools practicing racial discrimination. In the fall of 1981, after budget director David Stockman's embarrassingly candid interview with the *Atlantic,* Bush opposed several White House aides who wanted Stockman's head to roll. He presented the president with a detailed analysis of the article, then advised Reagan to act fairly and leniently if he felt Stockman could be trusted to carry out the administration's program despite the reservations he expressed in print.

Out of the same motive—the desire to preserve his reputation and Reagan's trust—Bush is an ardent anti-leaker, Presidents hate leaks more than anything. White House sources say Bush rarely speaks up in Cabinet meetings, whose substance often filters out to the media. He prefers to offer his views in the privacy of his weekly luncheons with Reagan, and he is extremely proud that there have been no leaks from these luncheon discussions in the 28 months since the inauguration.

Bush has made some mistakes. One of the clumsiest was his 1981 toast praising Philippine president Ferdinand Marcos as a champion of democracy. But the most widely publicized was last year's denial of ever having called his boss's views "voodoo economics." When NBC found a videotape of Bush saying the fateful words during the 1980 Pennsylvania primary, the vice president had to eat crow. Bush blamed the foul-up on press secretary Peter Teeley, now on leave of absence, who wrote the phrase during the campaign and then told Bush that he had

never actually used it in a speech.

By the time Reagan delivered his second State of the Union message in January, the Democrats had again dredged up voodoo economics as a rallying cry in their attack on the president. When Bush arrived at the House chamber for the speech, House Speaker Tip O'Neill couldn't resist needling him: "You really believe it is voodoo economics, don't you, Mr. Vice President?" Bush could only laugh and reply, "The guy who wrote that's been fired."

A more serious problem for Bush has been the turmoil and morale problems on his staff. By the second anniversary of Reagan's inauguration, 15 upper-level aides on the vice president's 69-member staff had either moved on to other jobs or announced their intention of doing so. Among those who have stayed are Chief of Staff Daniel J. Murphy, a 61-year-old retired admiral who served under Bush at the CIA, and Jennifer Fitzgerald, a 51-year-old British-born woman who has been with Bush since CIA days and was recently elevated from appointments secretary to executive assistant.

Former Bush staffers describe the highly disciplined Murphy as a good guy, but Fitzgerald gets vituperative reviews. She has been accused of bungling in the 1980 presidential campaign by canceling Bush appearances at factory sites in favor of luncheon club speeches. Critics of her performance say she misrepresents staff scheduling requests and blocks access to her boss. Fitzgerald and current staff members contend that she has been unfairly blamed. Press secretary Shirley Green maintains that the vice president has complete confidence in Fitzgerald and points out that unflattering remarks about her may result from her role as the person who says no to people on her boss's behalf. Green also points out that the people who have left the vice president's staff have all gone on to better jobs. A number of the vice president's close friends worry that "the Jennifer problem"—or the appearance of one—may inhibit Bush's future political career. "There's just something about her that makes him feel good," says one trusted Bush confidant. "I don't think it's sexual. I don't know what it is. But if Bush ever runs for president again, I think he's going to have to make a change on that score."

Barbara Bush has also won praise for her performance as second lady. Although members of the vice president's staff say she can be snappish and judgmental at times, they add that she often retracts such comments upon realizing how they sounded. Known to her husband and friends as Bar, she has a remarkable gift not only for names and faces but also for researching and remembering associated personal facts like the birthdays, family triumphs, and family tragedies of people she has met only once or twice. Her one constant frustration is her gray hair, which makes

her look much older than her husband even though she is really a year younger. Irreverent family members refer to her as the Silver Fox. Strangers often come up after one of her husband's public appearances and tell her how much they enjoyed her son's speech. It annoys her that she appears to be aging more quickly than her husband. "I hate it," she says simply.

George Bush, by contrast, seems to have almost no complaints. He even compares his job favorably with running the CIA. "The CIA had ingredients this job doesn't have—more decision-making as head of a big agency—but this job is closer to the heartbeat of running the country," Bush says. "I kind of give Mondale and Carter credit for a quantum leap forward in making the vice president a useful person. But I now see Mondale running for president and kind of jumping away from Carter. I couldn't do that. It's just not the way one conducts one's life. There's no honor in it, no integrity. It's too selfish. That's why I have a relaxed view about doing my job. I could no more try to position myself to look good on some issue that might be popular at the moment for future political gain, and in the process turn my back on the president. I just couldn't do it."

The Next President?

Could George Bush be president? Lately there have been some positive signs. A Gallup poll of 358 Republicans, released in February, showed Bush to be their leading choice for the 1984 nomination, should Reagan choose not to run. A *Newsweek* survey by Gallup released in March showed that 57 per cent of all adult voters sampled—Republicans, Democrats, and independents—would not like to see Ronald Reagan seek reelection; those sampled would be more likely to vote for Bush than for Reagan by a margin of 48 to 41.

Bush continues to have what one Republican party official calls "an incurable New Right problem." Almost the entire leadership of the conservative movement has declared its continuing philosophical opposition to Bush. "George Bush is an establishment, big-business, moderate politician who will go where the pressure is," says Richard Viguerie. "And the pressure in this country is strongly to the left. If the president gives it to him, if he announces he won't run with one arm around Bush and one arm around Paul Laxalt, there's no way to compete with that. But if the race is wide open, Bush couldn't do it. There are far too many conservative candidates who could compete with him."

The people to whom Viguerie alludes are men like Congressman Jack Kemp, Senator Jesse Helms, and Senator Paul Laxalt. The more moderate senators

Howard Baker and Robert Dole might run too, and Baker, in particular, could tap the frustration of Republican moderates with Bush over his enthusiastic embrace of Reaganism.

After twenty years in politics, Bush is still far easier to place by his class than by his beliefs. He firmly maintains that he could give it all up if the breaks don't go his way. "As far as I know now, if I don't stay on this current path, I will get out of politics and stay out of politics," he says. "Just as I've shifted gears in my life before, I'll shift them again. I don't want to leave the impression that I'm lacking interest in what I'm doing. But I just don't want always to be plotting a political future."

As Bush predicted, those close to him, including his son the former congressional candidate, say the gentleman doth protest too much. "I think that when the bell rings and the field is wide open, and it's not a question of President Reagan but of who can best run the country, the competitive juices will start flowing again," says the younger George Bush.

"I believe George Bush will run for president again," agrees his old friend and former campaign finance chairman Robert Mosbacher. "He has the fire in his belly."

The fire in Bush's belly is fueled by his father's legacy. Even as vice president, Bush is still occasionally visited by little old ladies who want to see if the son is as handsome as the father was, and invariably their conclusion is "not quite." Although Bush now holds the second-highest office in the land, he has yet to win a statewide election (other than a primary) on his own. Prescott Bush won two campaigns for the U.S. Senate from Connecticut. George Bush never could beat his father at golf, even when the old man was in his seventies. As yet, George Bush has not beat his father in politics either.

Vice President Bush naturally holds to the line that the Republican nominee for president in 1984 will be Ronald Reagan. So do the latest Washington rumors. Both the president and his wife are said to have taken a liking to life in the nation's capital and are now reportedly determined to remain in the White House for another four years. Reagan is said to feel a passion about completing his conservative revolution and to think that only he is both conservative enough to do the job and popular enough to be elected.

But when Bush was asked if he thought he'd make it to the Oval Office himself before the year 2000, he gave a revealing reply. "It'll have to be before then," he laughed, "or I might not be ambulatory."

Some quick age and election-year computations suggest that the vice president may be underestimating himself. If Reagan is reelected in 1984, he will be nearly 74 years old on Inauguration Day. On Inauguration Day of the year 2000, Bush will be 75. Between now and then he will have at least three more chances at the presidency—four if Reagan does not run for reelection in 1984. He has been so virtuous as vice president, not to mention previously, that he must believe with every fiber of his being that the job *ought* to be his—that the nation will tap him and he will march into the White House to general applause, with the ghost of Pres Bush smiling approvingly from on high. That, after all, would be the Right Thing for America to Do.✦

Jim Hightower promised to help Texas farmers get a fair shake. He's not doing so badly for himself either.

COSMIC PLOWBOY

by Peter Elkind

n the rainy evening of November 2, 1982, Jim Hightower drove from his disheveled campaign headquarters in Austin to the swank Bradford Hotel to claim victory in the race for Texas agriculture commissioner. Six hundred giddy supporters greeted him, ready to celebrate the election of Texas' most liberal statewide officeholder in a decade. "It's a referendum on Reaganomics, nothing else," Hightower told the cheering crowd. "It's a case of growling stomachs. Farmers are hurting." Hightower had won election as a populist in a campaign that had agricultural conglomerates as its main target. He had traveled the state, sledgehammering the "big boys" for screwing the little folk, blasting the corporate middlemen for cheating the family farmer out of a living wage and gouging the consumer, lambasting the system that has filled our food with chemicals and drained it of taste. Time after time he had repeated his pledge to "chase the hogs out of the creek."

A few weeks after the election Hightower drove to the Austin Club—a den of lobbyists, lawyers, political hacks, and corporate barons—to feed with some of the biggest hogs wallowing in the water. Jim Hightower had lunch with Harry Whitworth and his cronies from the Texas Chemical Council. Whitworth, a portly 62-year-old former state representative, is the president of the group. He also represents the Texas Agricultural Chemicals Association and the Texas Agricultural Aviation Association. He is one of Austin's most powerful lobbyists, known for the dove-hunting junkets he sponsors for chosen legislators and, jokes Whitworth himself, for being "more conservative than Attila the Hun."

The forty-year-old Hightower had made a career of attacking everything that Harry Whitworth represents, and the lobbyist—like just about everyone connected with large agricultural businesses—worked and spent in vain to keep Hightower out of office. But that was *before* the election. Now Hightower and Whitworth's group had business to conduct. "Look, I want to get along with you," Hightower said. "I want agriculture in Texas to be improved, and I realize you fellas have a big stake in it. You don't need to worry about me doing anything crazy." Whitworth left the meeting wary but reassured. "I don't see him as carried away with liberalism," he said later. "He wants to do a good job. I don't think he'd let beliefs get in the way."

To liberal purists, such meetings (Hightower has held many since taking office) are cause for alarm—grounds for the fear that their Great Hope has begun to sell out. But to those more pragmatically inclined, Hightower's fence-mending means that he is far more than a hope. For Jim Hightower's first year in office has been a stunning surprise: the candidate who beat up on the big boys has become an officeholder who realizes that to get anything done he must do business with them. "My opponents have assumed I'm ideological," says Hightower. "I'm not. I came to play. This is not a kamikaze liberal thing. It's not going to be 'four years and we're going to be rid of this schmuck.'"

Hightower has recently worked hard at playing the pragmatist. He knows that ideologues do not go far in Texas politics—certainly not as far as he wants to go. In place of ideology and traditional labels, Hightower has offered a vaguely defined populist philosophy focused on the premise that big is bad. "The central fact of economic and political life in Texas," he once wrote, "is that too few people control all the money and power, leaving the rest of us with very little."

Attacking those in power is most easily done from the outside, and Hightower has spent most of his adult life there. It has been an unusual route to political office. In past years, Hightower wore a beard and a ponytail and marched on the Pentagon to protest the Viet Nam War; while other ambitious young men went to law school, Hightower dropped out of it; while others declared for local office, planning to work their way up, Hightower ran the *Texas Observer*. Even now he remains unwilling to bring his personal life in line with political convention. Divorced from his college sweetheart, he has lived with Susan DeMarco since 1976. They have declined to marry; moreover, Hightower has appointed her (at $1 a year) to a key position in his department.

Five years ago Hightower had campaigned for no higher office than that of student body president at North Texas State University. In 1980, despite being outspent two to one, he won 48 per cent of the vote in a race for a seat on the Texas Railroad Commission. And last November he swept into the agriculture job, winning all but seventeen counties.

Today he is Texas' hottest political commodity. In a second-level state office, he attracts as much attention as Mark White does from the governor's mansion. Hightower's name is tossed about when prospects to head the Agriculture Department in a Democratic administration are discussed. His pronouncements are closely monitored by the national press, and Washington's *City Paper* has named him one of "ten Americans who should be president." Although Hightower has never raised one tenth of the money Mark White spent to become governor, already he is eyeing that job. "As much good as I could do as agriculture commissioner, I could do more good as governor," he says. He probably will not challenge White in 1986 if the governor seeks another term, but "if Mark White were to take a hike," says Hightower, "I'd take a run."

The national press has seized on Hightower's election—and that of fellow liberals Ann Richards, Jim Mattox, and Garry Mauro—to proclaim a leftward shift in the state's politics. Hightower, similarly, is eager to portray his rise as the product of social forces. "I happen to be, through no genius of my own, a person who is right for this time in Texas," he says. "I think I am quintessentially a 1980's Texan."

Don't believe it. Texans don't share Hightower's populist orientation any more than the average politician shares his background. A poll taken for his 1982 campaign showed that, far from identifying with any populist movement, Texans disliked the label. For every voter who said he would be more likely to vote for a candidate who called himself a populist, *sixteen* said they would be less likely to do so. Rather than reflecting a welling up of populist-progressive sentiment, Hightower's election was the result of his own political talents. He won by campaigning as a farm-bred good ol' boy—although he actually grew up in a small town and spent most of his adult life in Washington. He won by blaming incumbent Reagan Brown for rising food prices and the demise of the family farm—although the Texas agriculture commissioner had almost no power to affect either.

During his first year in office, Hightower has made many mistakes. But he has also displayed an ability to make the most of his position—including an unexpected gift for turning bitter enemies into dispassionate opponents and converting fence sitters into friends. "To tell you the truth," said Harry Whitworth, leaning over a table at the Austin Club one day, "he's a likable fella. There are a lot of horse's asses in politics. He's just not one of them."

Hightower's desire to succeed has prompted him to recant past writings, cozy up to legislators he once ridiculed, and grub for contributions from lobbyists. He is not selling out, but he is clearly learning to play the game. His path—first as unconventional outsider, then as maverick candidate, and finally as officeholder—is a study of what happens when a skilled critic of the system becomes a skilled practitioner within it. The education of Jim Hightower is a lesson in itself.

The Longhair

"I don't want to give you a big ol' long speech," said Jim Hightower. The 250 priests, nuns, and farmers attending the National Catholic Rural Life Conference in Des Moines, Iowa, were relieved. The proceedings were taking place outdoors, on a hillside that sloped down to a makeshift stage, and October 4, 1983 —cold, misty, and gray—was no day for marathon oratory. Hightower, standing behind a small podium, wore a brown suit, a white shirt, a red tie, and brown cowboy boots. He removed his glasses and jiggled his big white hat behind his back. There was a nervous edge to his voice as he began to speak; he is an impatient, restless man who writes standing up and drives with one foot on the accelerator and the other on the brake.

"What's happening in agriculture today is not a pretty sight," Hightower said. "It's uglier than my face." The priests and nuns laughed; here was a live one. "We're talking about three squares a day and where it's going to come from. . . . You can make a small fortune in agriculture; the trouble is, you've got to start with a large fortune." The crowd laughed again. Hightower was starting to hit his stride. "While farm income has been going down, you don't see anything going down at the supermarket, do you? Something funny's going on there. Somebody gets the money." Hightower paused, letting the implicit question sink in. "It's the *monopolies*," he announced. "The *oligopolies*. The whole thing's out of whack. They're taking too much, and they're leaving too little for the rest of us. . . . Government is not on the side of the farmer. Government is on the side of the big boys. . . . We've got to raise less corn and more hell!" he declared. "And that's what I'm going to do." The priests and nuns and farmers jumped to their feet.

"I was never so impressed with anybody in my life," says Mabel Schweers. A 65-year-old woman who has raised eleven children, she and her husband are losing the family farm in Iowa, where they have lived for forty years, to a foreclosure proceeding. They believe

Jim Hightower speaks for them. "He understands us," Mrs. Schweers says. "I had no doubt that he knew exactly how things were."

When James Allen Hightower ran for Texas agriculture commissioner in 1982, his opponents challenged his qualifications to speak for the beleaguered small farmer. Hightower responded by telling newspaper reporters he had grown up on a family farm in Fannin County. It is not true. W. F. and Lillie Mabel Hightower raised their three sons in a comfortable middle-class household not far from downtown Denison, an old working-class railroad town in northeastern Texas. Hightower's childhood farming was limited to summer visits to his aunt Eula and uncle Ernest's two-hundred-acre farm north of Ector, about twenty miles away. The Hightowers were in the publications business, distributing magazines wholesale around the Sherman-Denison area and selling them in a downtown shop.

Lillie Mabel Hightower is a pleasant, quiet woman with a strong-willed streak that she has passed on to her middle son. She expects Jim to run for governor someday and believes he would like to be president "if he could help the country." W. F. Hightower, a waggish seventy-year-old man known to local folks as High, sold off the family wholesale business ten years ago but still runs the retail store, called the Main Street News.

High is a delightful bundle of nervous energy, down-home philosophy, and cornbread wit—sort of Jim Hightower's Miss Lillian. Now semiretired, he spends his mornings at the store, yakking with his cronies; he keeps a stool and a folding chair for them near the front magazine rack. He greeted me with a handshake and a few gentle ribs, happy to talk about Jim. "He was always smart and kind of precocious," said High, recalling the time his five-year-old son memorized " 'Twas the night before Christmas" in one pass. "He just had a photographic mind."

As he talked, High unpacked a stack of *Iron Man* magazines; a muscleman, his bulging, knotty body covered only by a pair of tiny briefs and a coat of oil, graced the cover. When two teenage girls stepped up to the counter to pay for sodas, High snatched the top copy of *Iron Man* and thrust it in front of their faces: "Have y'all seen this latest picture of me?" The girls giggled, left their money, and walked out. "If it keeps going like this, we're going to be like India," High continued. "We're going to have a caste system—the very, very poor and the very, very rich." He confessed having voted for two Republicans, Ronald Reagan and Richard Nixon —"two of the biggest mistakes I ever made." Two more customers walked into the store and shouted their greetings.

High waved and turned back to me. "I told Jim before he went to college, 'Don't ever be scared of anybody, no matter who it is. They all put their pants on the same. Don't ever let them bull you.' I think that kind of stayed with him."

At Denison High School, Jim was only five feet eight and 110 pounds, but he still started at linebacker for the varsity Yellow Jackets. "He was a little bitty boy," recalls Herman Bailey, then the head football coach. "He wasn't as big as a bar of soap, but he was a tough little toot. He was very aggressive." Classmates liked Jim's friendly manner; they elected him president of the 1961 senior class and voted him Most Pleasing Personality. A good student who always got high marks without studying much, he decided to attend North Texas State University in Denton.

In college Hightower jumped into campus politics, becoming the chairman of freshman class beanie sales. He joined the Sigma Phi Epsilon fraternity—Greeks invariably won the top student offices—and was elected vice president of the student body as a junior. During a successful race for student body president, he displayed an early awareness of the value of good press; part of his five-point platform was the creation of a student government public relations agency.

But Jim Hightower was no hell-raiser in college. There were no attacks on the university establishment, no sign of the folksy populism, the ten-gallon hat, or the cowboy boots that have become his trademarks. Twenty years ago Hightower was a neat, polite young man who wore his hair close-cropped and his ties narrow. He helped pay his college expenses by working part time at the Denton Chamber of Commerce, where he fit in well.

In May 1964, during his junior year, Hightower went on a blind date with Cynthia Hamra, a tiny, dark-haired woman of Lebanese descent who was majoring in music at NTSU. A month later, they began dating regularly. "I thought he was a lot of fun," says Cynthia, who now lives in Alexandria, Virginia. "I could tell right away that he was on the move, and that was very attractive to me." Three months later, on September 9, Jim and Cynthia— without telling either set of parents—were married. He was 21. She was 20.

Like many other ambitious young men, Hightower saw Washington and law school as routes to power. When he graduated from North Texas State in 1965, he packed up his green '55 Chevy and headed off to George Washington University law school. Finding the study of legal cases boring, he quit after a week. When Cynthia joined him in Washington in October, he had taken a job with the Library of Congress legislative reference service, doing research and writing speeches for congressmen. After a year, the Hightowers packed up again, this time so Jim could enroll in a master's program in international affairs at Co-

lumbia University in New York. There, too, he pulled up short and quit the two-year program halfway through. The moves put a strain on the couple. Money was tight; Cynthia didn't like New York; and Jim, smoking a pack or two of Marlboros a day, still weighed about 110 pounds and suffered from pneumothorax —a painful condition in which lung tissue collapses.

In June 1967 they moved back to Washington. Cynthia found a teaching job in a suburban Maryland school system, and Jim returned to the Library of Congress. In September he signed on with Texas senator Ralph Yarborough as a legislative aide. An unabashed liberal and a leading Southern progressive, Yarborough made a deep impression on Hightower. He had won election by stumping small towns and county courthouses, running as a populist and serving up folksy oratory in a heavy East Texas drawl—a campaign style Hightower would later emulate.

Two steady incomes brightened life a bit for the couple. In early 1968 they bought a townhouse on Capitol Hill. Jim had quit smoking in New York and was putting on weight, and his health was improving. A month later he got his draft notice. He reported to the draft board but was ruled 4-F because of his lung condition.

Living in Washington during the murders of Robert F. Kennedy and Martin Luther King and the protests against the Viet Nam War, Jim and Cynthia, like many politically active people in their twenties, moved slowly to the left. Hightower left Yarborough's office in February 1969 to work with the Rural Housing Alliance, a public-interest group that introduced him to César Chávez and the plight of the rural poor. He let his hair grow below his shoulders—when he drove in a convertible he tied it back in a ponytail—and sprouted a beard. He began rethinking his plans to run for office someday, voicing doubts about the justice of the political system. He and Cynthia marched against the war. "We were probably on the border of being radical liberals," says Cynthia. "Many of us were disillusioned."

Yarborough's fate contributed to that feeling. In the May 1970 Democratic primary, Lloyd Bentsen, using advertisements linking Yarborough to the riots at the Democratic National Convention in 1968, knocked the senator out of office. Hightower had left his Senate staff job by then, but he was bitter about Bentsen's lowball tactics. "That was cheap shit," he says.

In late 1970 Hightower obtained a $65,000 foundation grant to create his own public-interest group, the Agribusiness Accountability Project (AAP), headquartered in a converted Georgetown warehouse. The group's premise was that giant corporations, like General Mills and Del Monte, were taking over the food business, squeezing out the family farmer, pushing up prices for the consumer, and lowering the quality of what we eat. Such themes have been Hightower's message ever since. Then, as now, he presented them not from a radical or liberal perspective but as a populist call for action. "He always wanted to disassociate himself from liberals," says Susan Sechler, who was an AAP staff member. "He thought of liberals as being tough on questions of human rights but too soft on economic democracy issues. Populism was a way he could talk about distribution of income without sounding like a socialist. It was an American way to talk about economics and the distribution of income."

As a nonprofit group, the AAP was barred from lobbying; it delivered its message instead through a series of muckraking investigative reports. Hightower's first book, *Hard Tomatoes, Hard Times,* was researched by an AAP staff member from New Jersey named Susan DeMarco, and it made Hightower's reputation in Washington. A scathing attack on agriculture's sacred cows—the land-grant college system, agricultural extension services, and 4-H clubs—the 1972 report charged the universities (Texas A&M among them) with using public funds to do research benefiting giant food conglomerates while neglecting small farmers, farm workers, consumers, and the rural poor. *Hard Tomatoes* would later cause Hightower political problems, but at the time it was a sensation, as well as a lesson in what the media could help him accomplish. Widely discussed in the press, the book prompted a round of congressional hearings and debate and established Hightower's group as a foil to the federal agricultural policies of Richard Nixon and Earl Butz. Washington reporters covering federal agricultural policies often relied on the group's research for alternative views.

Hightower traveled the country making speeches for the AAP. The task made him extremely nervous—he took too many notes and spoke too formally—but it gave him experience that gradually sharpened his speaking skills. In 1975, his last year with the AAP, Hightower published his second book, *Eat Your Heart Out: Food Profiteering in America.* The book, which was well received, describes the growing corporate domination of the food industry.

Hightower's domestic life, however, had suffered during the AAP days. Jim and Cynthia separated in April 1972. In 1975, they were divorced. Not one to talk about his personal problems, Hightower told a friend simply that the marriage had "run aground."

His political life continued to pick up speed. Through the agribusiness project, Hightower had become close friends with Fred Harris. The former Oklahoma senator had run a six-week populist campaign for the 1972 presidential nomination under the informal slogan "No more

bullshit." Hightower's 1982 campaign would use a more demure version: "No more bull." Harris was gearing up for the 1976 race, and in 1975 Hightower signed on, at no salary, as campaign manager. This time the theme was "The issue is privilege," and the platform was a radical one: break up the giant corporations, soak the rich, develop massive public-employment programs.

Harris' strategy followed a 1974 memo that Harris, his wife, LaDonna, and Hightower had drafted for running a "people's campaign." Like Yarborough's, this campaign would serve as a model for Hightower's own races in 1980 and 1982. Harris rode around the countryside in a camper and stayed in the homes of supporters. A fiery, entertaining speaker, he gave speeches while holding up a loaf of Wonder Bread, pointing out that it was produced by the giant ITT conglomerate and noting how much its price had jumped in just a few years. Harris and Hightower put together a capable, energetic political organization, but Harris couldn't attract many votes. He dropped out of the race on April 8, three months before the Democratic National Convention.

Jim Hightower came back to Texas after being away for eleven years. The immediate reason for his return was the editorship of the *Texas Observer;* the long-term plan, according to Hightower's parents and friends, was to run for office. Hightower and Susan DeMarco had become involved while working together in Washington, and in the fall of 1976 they moved into a 76-year-old frame house in South Austin.

Hightower, who would remain at the *Observer* for three years, wasted no time in making changes. The small liberal biweekly became a populist sheet that attacked everything big—big bank holding companies, big food and chemical conglomerates, big newspaper and restaurant chains. Lively and satirical under his predecessors Molly Ivins and Kaye Northcott, the *Observer* became sober and weighty, filled with charts and graphs and statistics. Hightower ran it like a politician. He recruited teams of volunteers to conduct exhaustive research and organized fundraising parties. The money allowed the journal to run color regularly for the first time and to increase the number of pages in each issue. It also introduced Hightower to a network of liberal political activists and moneymen who would help him when he announced for office.

In early 1979, while planning his campaign for a seat on the Texas Railroad Commission, Hightower continued writing critical stories about the regulatory agency. Publisher Ronnie Dugger, wary of suggestions that Hightower was using the *Observer* for his own political purposes, sat down with his editor. "It had simply come to the point where he was too close to being a candidate and an editor at

the same time," says Dugger, who announced Hightower's resignation in the June 22, 1979, issue. In a July 27 farewell column, Hightower discussed his plans to run for office, offering an explanation that has been much quoted since: "There comes a time when writing about the bastards isn't enough."

Hayseeds and Hee Haw

A month after Ronald Reagan swept Texas in the 1980 presidential race, Jim Hightower told a reporter he was wrong to think that Texas was a conservative state. "Texans are mavericks; they're anti-establishment," Hightower said. "Asked whether they're liberal or conservative, they'd say they're conservative. But ask 'em if they hate the utility companies—hell, yes."

It was on this premise that Hightower based his determined two-campaign drive for state office. It was a pitch that enabled him to reach beyond the state's small liberal constituency and to piece together a winning coalition of traditionally antagonistic forces: farmers and farm workers, minorities and rural poor, urban liberals and small-town rednecks. Hightower was able to appeal, as he puts it, "to the bean-sprout eaters and to the snuff-dippers" by positioning himself on the side of the little folk.

"The big boys are making a killing off people like you and me, tossing us pigs' feet and pork rinds," Hightower told campaign crowds. "I want some ham for a change. Huey Long used to say, 'If you want some ham, you've got to go into the smokehouse and get it.' Well, by God, we're gonna get it. And I don't just want the ham, I want the whole hog."

In his 1980 race for railroad commissioner against incumbent Jim Nugent, Hightower called himself "the candidate of Texans who don't own an oil well." In 1982 he shrewdly drew urban consumers into the agriculture race, which they had usually ignored, by telling them: "If you eat, you're involved with agriculture. And if we eat, it's time for all of us to get involved in food politics, because we're all getting ripped off."

As a candidate, Hightower has all the right equipment. He is the best political orator in the state and a master of humorous one-liners. "President Reagan's idea of a good farm program," he said recently, "is *Hee Haw.*" Hightower also has incredible energy. He runs a frenetic campaign, rushing from rural county courthouses to big-city meetings and urging his staff to give him a tighter schedule. He starts early and campaigns until 10 p.m.

Most important, Hightower is a genius at attracting free media coverage—absolutely crucial for an underfunded liberal taking on big-money conservative opponents. He does it by being colorful, quotable, and accommodating. This year a *Time* magazine photographer, interested in shots of Hightower in a farm setting, accompanied him on a small-plane hop to a meeting in Crowell. When bad weather made landing there impossible, Hightower instructed the pilot to land in Waco. Once on the ground, Hightower piled into a taxicab and ordered: "Take me to a plowed field." They arrived at the desired setting, and Hightower posed amid the wheat stalks, holding up a handful of dirt. The photographer snapped his shots, the group drove back to the airport, and the plane returned to Austin.

As he crisscrossed the state during his campaign, Hightower visited small-town newspaper offices, posing for pictures with the editors and leaving press releases that were often published verbatim. To big-city media, his down-home rhetoric, underdog image, and clever use of props made great copy and good film. When Hightower announced for agriculture commissioner, he did it from the bed of a pickup filled with bales of hay; when he paid his campaign filing fee, he did it with a basket of 1500 one-dollar bills. But Hightower himself is the best prop of all. How many candidates wear a three-piece suit, boots, and a white ten-gallon hat?

His position as a media darling allowed him to give Jim Nugent a stiff fight in the 1980 Railroad Commission race. Hightower staked out a clear position: he would oppose all utility rate increases unless someone could convince him to vote for one. He had the big boys so upset that they held meetings at the Houston Petroleum Club to figure out how to keep him out of office. Their money made the difference, and Nugent won by 53,000 votes.

After the defeat, Hightower's forces regrouped and identified their mistakes: not raising enough money to buy television ads (Hightower had collected $177,000, well short of the $250,000 he'd thought necessary to run a winning campaign) and taking a constituency for granted. While Hightower had done remarkably well in the cities—winning Houston, Fort Worth, and the usually conservative Dallas—a last-minute round of Spanish advertisements won Nugent the Mexican American vote in the Valley.

Looking to capitalize on campaign publicity, Hightower's team shopped around for another office that he could seek. "You can't hold on to name ID forever," says Kristy Ozmun, Hightower's 1982 campaign manager. "We looked at what was up in two years." There was to be a seat on the Railroad Commission up for grabs, but that was not the campaign of choice. Says Ozmun: "There was a feeling that you get to have a loser image if you lose the same thing twice."

Instead, Hightower lowered his sights and took aim at agriculture commissioner Reagan Brown. "I took what people considered a reasonable step, picking a winnable office. It had a winning issue: farmers' going broke. It had a tired

agency." In addition, says Hightower, "the prize was worth it. There's a lot of flexibility in these statewide executive offices. There's a constituency as big as the governor's."

The job looked winnable because of its incumbent. Reagan Brown was a buffoonish, lackluster Dolph Briscoe appointee who had demonstrated how little the Texas Department of Agriculture truly had to do. In a state with annual agricultural receipts of about $10 billion—the third largest in the nation—one would expect the job of agriculture commissioner to be an important one. But it isn't, because all key farm policy decisions are made at the federal level. The agency's legal responsibilities are limited mainly to marketing (promoting the sale of Texas agricultural products) and regulating (inspecting and licensing a hodgepodge of items such as seeds, pesticides, grain elevators, gasoline pumps, chicken eggs, bread bakers' scales, and flower nurseries). Brown's marketing program consisted basically of distributing posters of fruits and vegetables, and his regulatory staff supervised itself. That left the commissioner free to pursue his stated goal of breaking the world record for most speeches made in a lifetime.

Hightower offered a dramatically different vision of the job. He stumped the state with a sack of groceries, talking about all the bad things that had happened in agriculture during Brown's term in office: how many farmers had gone broke, how much farm income had fallen, how much the price of white bread had risen. Brown protested meekly that he had no authority to do anything about that, that the TDA is a regulatory agency, not a policy-making one. Never mind, said Hightower; all of those things had happened without Reagan Brown's raising so much as a peep of complaint. Brown, Hightower declared, was sitting idly by while the huge conglomerates were paying the farmer less and charging the consumer more. Said Hightower, "There's a hell of a lot more to being agriculture commissioner than sticking a straw in your mouth and humming 'Thank God I'm a Country Boy.' "

As commissioner, Hightower pledged, he would find ways to bypass the middleman. He first promised to establish a statewide network of farmers' markets. Though the overall impact of such markets would be negligible, it was a brilliant idea symbolically. It would allow the farmer to sell his produce directly to the consumer for more than he could get from Safeway. The consumer, in turn, would get a fresher product at a lower price than he would pay at the supermarket. Hightower also promised to arrange the direct sale of more Texas goods in the U.S. and abroad. Most of all, he pledged to use his job as a bully pulpit—to go to Washington to fight for a decent national farm policy, to serve as an advocate for farmers.

Brown struck his best blow by digging up a copy of Hightower's *Hard Tomatoes* and handing out press releases with excerpts of the challenger's 1972 attack on the powerful agriculture establishment. In his book Hightower labeled the land-grant system "incestuous" and "a failure"; he said agricultural extension "largely is irrelevant in today's rural America" and "not much good to anybody, except maybe 15,000 extension agents who otherwise would have to look for work"; and he called 4-H clubs "a frivolous diversion of 72 million tax dollars."

Hightower responded to Brown's attack by selectively quoting some of the few flattering things the book has to say about the land-grant establishment and accusing Reagan Brown of circulating "lies" and "a smear sheet." Hightower completed the flip-flop by telling reporters that agricultural research was being given inadequate funds and that "you won't find a stronger advocate of 4-H clubs." He promised, "I'm going to be the best friend A&M ever had."

Now, with the election over, Hightower is more open about backing off the report he wrote eleven years ago. He says *Hard Tomatoes* used "too broad a brush" by employing a limited number of examples to attack the whole land-grant system. "We used those few examples to generalize from that to indict the whole system." As for the remarks about 4-H: "We treated it too lightly." Hightower says he would be less critical of the land-grant colleges today. "I'm not changing my tune," he added. "Writing a book is different from running for political office, which is different from holding political office." Which is to say, where you stand depends on where you sit. Which is to say, he's changing his tune.

But in a campaign dominated by image and mudslinging rather than by substance, that issue and most others got lost. It was far more entertaining to watch Reagan Brown self-destruct. First, to show a television reporter that fire ants were a problem, he stuck his arm in a mound of them and—surprise—got 32 bites. Then, with the primary only four days away, he referred to Booker T. Washington as "that great black nigger"—with television cameras rolling. He then blamed the remark on food poisoning from a bad turkey sandwich. Finally, in a speech at North Texas State, Brown lamented that Texas clothing had become so popular that at a recent meeting "you couldn't tell the Jews and the Texans apart." Hightower cleaned up in the primary, winning 60 per cent of the vote. The Republicans, who had fielded a token candidate in the primary, drafted a replacement: Fred Thornberry, a politically obscure expert on chicken farming from Texas A&M. With industry money, Thornberry spent $500,000 in the general election, but even at that, he was outmatched. Labeling the Democrat a radical with "a hippie philosophy," Thornberry stirred up a name-calling fight—clearly a losing proposition. Hightower dismissed the Republican as "the professor of chickenology" and rolled up 63 per cent of the vote. Hightower the candidate was a hit.

The Commissioner's Education

A short time after his election, Jim Hightower arranged a meeting with Dr. Perry Adkisson, a deputy chancellor at Texas A&M who oversees the agricultural experiment station and the land-grant college's extension service. "We had lunch right after he was elected," Adkisson told me. "He said, 'I would like to come over there sometime and talk to all the county agents and assure them I'm supportive of them, that I'm not a bad guy.' He made a point to indicate that he's not anti-extension service, that he's not anti–land-grant college, that he's a pragmatic person who understands the realities of the world. He's been very cordial, very cooperative." When I asked him about all those nasty remarks that Hightower had made in *Hard Tomatoes*, there was a pause. "You sometimes say things in one situation," Adkisson explained, "that you may later regret in another."

In the weeks following his election, Hightower met with representatives of the chemical companies, the large commodity groups, the cattlemen's association, even the supermarket chains—the reviled middlemen whom he had drubbed en route to victory. To the supermarket people Hightower made a plea that their buyers purchase more Texas produce; if they did so, he explained, he'd be happy to help promote their supermarkets.

Everywhere he went, Hightower promised that even those who had worked against him would get to participate in policy discussions, that no one would be shut out and that there would be no surprises. His lack of vindictiveness helped when it came time to retire his campaign debt. In 1980 he had refused to accept contributions from interests he would regulate; now, in the fashion of more conventional officeholders, he held fundraisers to collect the lobbyists' cash. "They created the goddam debt," he says. "They can pay for it."

But it was Hightower's appointments that did the most to calm agribusiness moguls who feared that he would fill the department with Trotskyites. Says Hightower, "They believed I was going to roll in Jane Fonda and put her in charge of the agriculture department, that I was going to have a whole bunch of lawyers and be a regulatory pain in the ass." A pair of surprising but shrewd high-level staff appointments helped to alleviate those concerns. To fill the job of deputy commissioner, the agency's second-

ranking position, Hightower persuaded 67-year-old Walter Richter, a former state senator who had voted for Reagan Brown, to come out of retirement. Richter, the chairman of the Travis County Democratic party, is a well-known, well-liked man, a low-key liberal whom lobbyists can count on not to do anything crazy. Hightower's choice for the department's number three job, that of associate commissioner, was an outright stunner: Crockett Camp, an Alcoholic Beverage Commission staff member who had worked for rural conservatives Billy Clayton and Jim Nugent. It was a smart choice. Hightower's team of outsiders didn't know how to fill out a requisition form, much less how to get a budget passed. Camp, a nonideological hired gun, can trip the levers of power blindfolded. Hightower's selection of Richter and Camp—not the top choices of his liberal backers—showed that he recognizes that in Texas politics last week's enemies may become this week's friends. "I think Hightower would break down and hire a Republican if that's what it took to get something done," says Camp.

Another Hightower appointment was more controversial: that of his housemate, Susan DeMarco, as assistant commissioner for marketing and agricultural development. She is responsible for turning his most important campaign promises into reality. "There are certain things he wanted to do that were going to be difficult," says DeMarco. "If he were going to do it, he'd have to have somebody he could trust to make it happen."

It is a rare Texas politician who would choose to risk votes rather than formalize a long-term intimate relationship. It is an even rarer politician who would dare to appoint the woman he lives with to work for him. That Hightower has done both makes clear the importance of Susan DeMarco in his thinking. "She knows more about agriculture than anybody in the department," says Hightower. "I'm willing to take the heat because it will be a better department."

DeMarco, who has worked as a consultant for the U.S. Department of Agriculture, helped reorganize Hightower's department and helped decide which Reagan Brown holdovers should be fired. She is not pleased about working for $1 a year—the post normally pays about $49,000, and she has no doubt that she deserves it—but she says people would misunderstand if she were paid.

Some legislators, noting that nepotism laws would bar DeMarco from working for the TDA if she and Hightower were married, are none too happy about it anyway. Several of them tried to interest the Capitol press corps in doing a story on the arrangement. Many reporters checked into it but decided against doing articles after learning that DeMarco was unpaid. No one wrote anything until early October, when a story by Harte-Hanks Austin

bureau reporter Jay Rosser appeared in some of the chain's papers. Quoting unhappy former TDA employees, the article said there was controversy because DeMarco had presided over the firings, and it identified her as Hightower's "live-in companion." Hightower shrugs off the criticism: "How much regular folks think it's an outrage I don't know. I don't think it'll be fatal. During the campaign there was a rumor that I was homosexual. This is better than that."

Hightower's appointments have set a sharply different tone for the Agriculture Department. Under Reagan Brown, the TDA was a white-shirt-and-tie kind of place. Hightower has filled his office with bright, energetic folk—many of them young, several of them from the campaign—who at first knew more about getting things done than they knew about agriculture. He has made a point of hiring minority administrators; his executive meetings look like sessions of the United Nations. The atmosphere is informal. Jeans and short sleeves are common attire. A giant Linda Ronstadt poster hangs on the wall outside Hightower's office, and when administrative meetings drag on past 5 p.m., as they often do, Hightower breaks out the beer and Texas peanuts. "You get the feeling there is a lot of activity," says one legislator. "It traditionally has been a lackluster department. You'd go in at two minutes to five, and the agency was empty." Even the agency's library has changed; Hightower has added such magazines as *Mother Jones, Small Farm Advocate,* the *Progressive,* and the *Nation,* to the subscription list.

One day in 1981, while spending the year between his two campaigns as president of the Texas Consumer Association, Jim Hightower drove into Johnson County, the legislative district of State Representative Bruce Gibson. Gibson had backed an interest-rate bill in the Legislature that the consumer group opposed, and Hightower was eager to talk about it. Having Bruce Gibson as your representative, Hightower told the lawmaker's constituents, is "like getting bit by your pet dog." In 1983 Hightower took office only to find that Gibson was a member of the House Agriculture and Livestock Committee—the body with life-and-death power over his budget. The new commissioner's sharp tongue, an enormous asset in his dealings with public and press, proved a considerable liability in dealing with the Texas Legislature.

Lobbyists representing regulated industries are paid to get along with whoever holds the reins of power; in the Agriculture Department, that means Hightower. But in the relationship between the TDA and the legislative branch, it is the boys in the Capitol who call the shots and the young commissioner who plays the supplicant. For Hightower, that has not been an easy role. "I'm used to defining the agenda," he says. "I don't like people getting in my way. I don't like people telling me no. I don't like going through a whole lot of process getting approval to do something. My instinct was, 'Here's my program, and of course you agree with it.'" Of course they didn't. Many legislators saw Hightower as an ambitious far-left demagogue, more interested in moving up than in dealing with agricultural problems. Several, like Gibson, had been the targets of Hightower's pointed remarks.

When the new commissioner submitted his budget request, he immediately ran into trouble. In a year when money was tight, Hightower asked for a 44 per cent increase over the TDA's 1983 budget, including a staggering total of 135 new positions (a jump of 25 per cent). As the legislators looked at the request more closely, they discovered other surprises. The day he took office, Hightower awarded a $9500 contract to a Washington consultant named Jim Rosapepe; the budget included $159,000 more to hire Rosapepe's firm on a long-term basis. Rosapepe, it turned out, was an old buddy of Hightower's from the Fred Harris campaign. The Rosapepe contracts were for the job of representing Hightower in Washington—a role the governor's office of state-federal relations is supposed to play; the first that Mark White's staff knew of the consulting contract, which would have required White's approval, was when a notice appeared in the *Texas Register*. With one stroke, Hightower had handed legislators an excuse to accuse him of both cronyism and empire building and had given Mark White and his staff cause to wonder whether he was pulling an end around.

Hightower acknowledges that on its face the arrangement looked unseemly. But he says he needed the contract to keep informed about federal agricultural policies. "The [governor's] Washington office was not set up. I couldn't wait for everybody to get appointed up there." He says Rosapepe was appointed, despite his inexperience with agricultural issues, because of his good Washington contacts and his ability. Rosapepe's background as a Hightower crony was a plus, the commissioner says. But for legislators looking to smack the new commissioner around a bit, Hightower had delivered a convenient excuse. "To spend forty-three hundred dollars a month on somebody who doesn't know anything about agriculture . . . is a crime against the people of Texas," railed Representative Bill Hollowell. "We don't need any cronyism." Hollowell drafted an amendment to the budget bill specifically barring Hightower from hiring a Washington representative. Hightower retreated. "Anything I do in Washington, I want to do through [the governor's] office," he said.

Legislators also discovered that Hightower, who had criticized Reagan Brown for his devotion to his department's airplane, wanted aircraft funding doubled so he could purchase a bigger, faster plane. They chopped his aircraft allocation by 60 per cent. The commissioner got a different plane—older than the one he'd had in the first place.

While Hightower's budget was being carved up, the new commissioner blundered over legislative issues. Hightower's biggest faux pas came during the hot debate on trucking deregulation. After weeks of intense lobbying on both sides, Speaker Gib Lewis, in a rare display of leadership, moved to work out a compromise. At the last minute, Hightower sent a sharp letter to the floor taking a strong position in favor of deregulation. The move was perceived as a clumsy attempt to bust up the deal, and the Speaker took it personally. Buddy Jones, Lewis' top aide, called Crockett Camp, demanding to know what the hell Hightower was doing. "The leadership of the House was thoroughly pissed," says one legislator. "He almost got his budget gutted over it." In fact, the move had revealed poor staff coordination rather than arrogance. Hightower and Camp rushed over to the Capitol to smooth the ruffled feathers.

Another embarrassment came during the gasohol debate. Comptroller Bob Bullock had suggested repealing the tax break given to gasohol producers as a quick way to ease the budget crunch. When Representative Stan Schlueter, carrying the ball for Bullock, brought a repeal bill to the House floor, Hightower jumped in with a strong statement opposing it. The repeal would kill the nascent gasohol business in the state, a potential boon to grain producers. Schlueter, furious, took the microphone to attack the rookie commissioner as a phony, now siding with the big boys he had publicly kicked. "'Whole Hog' Hightower, you all know him," Schlueter sneered. "He's the guy who bought a big cowboy hat and a pair of boots and called himself a farmer and rancher and got himself elected ag commissioner." The legislators hooted and clapped.

"When Hightower came here in January, the only contact he'd had with the Legislature was as an outsider," says Camp. "When there was something he wanted, he did it just the way he campaigned for office: he did it with press releases. That is not the way you deal with the Legislature. Jim has basically had to muzzle himself." After getting cuffed around a good bit, Hightower started to get the message. He began working less through public statements and more through Camp. He used his press skills to pat legislators on the back instead of to stab them, and he worked with the senators and representatives one-on-one. Says Hightower, "I had to back away personally and say, 'I've got to get these people on board with me, got to be a lot more accommodating of their needs, of their whims, of their biases.' It's important to go through the game. If you're in the legislative process, you have to deal."

The restraint paid off. Hightower ended up with a $2 million increase for his 1984 budget. It was about a quarter of the boost he wanted, but 10 per cent more than the department's 1982 funding. Not bad for a tight budget year. "That's a lot better than some folks did," says Representative Pete Laney, a farmer from Hale Center. "If he hadn't changed his attitude, he wouldn't have gotten anything. Politically, Jim grew up real fast."

Going Whole Hog

Hightower had proved himself a quick study in the arcane but important science of dealing with the Texas Legislature. That's necessary to get the money and the laws to do what you want. But then you have to *do* it—you have to deliver the goods. Hightower won office by making a lot of promises, some specific, some vague, but he made one big promise above all: to do something concrete to help the farmer.

For the past year Hightower has had his chance. He has demonstrated what a smart man can do with a small job. He has opened four farmers' markets. He has cleverly promoted the nascent Texas wine industry with wine tastings all over the state. The press, naturally, was invited to attend and drink up, and the grapes got plenty of publicity. He pushed a bill through the Legislature to make tax-exempt bonds available to Texas farmers who want to begin processing their own agricultural products—to get into the business, for example, of turning their onions into onion rings. Farmers today get only 28 cents out of the food dollar, and the agricultural development bonds will help some Texas farmers pocket a bigger share. Hightower has also brought sanity to the war against the fire ant. Instead of trying to drown the state in toxic chemicals with aerial spraying—Reagan Brown had asked for $18 million to do that—he set up a pilot program to test a nonpoisonous substance that kills off the ants. In the meantime, he has helped local officials arrange discounts on volume purchases of insecticides for topical use.

Most of all, Hightower has gone to bat publicly for the farmer in matters that Reagan Brown would have considered none of the agriculture commissioner's business. When the U.S. Department of Energy pushed plans to put a nuclear waste dump in Panhandle farm country, Hightower flew to Hereford and vowed to fight the scheme. When three utility companies proposed running a 400,000-volt, 150-mile power line through prime farmland, Hightower asked the Public Utility Commission to force them to reroute it.

A man who had already shown himself a master at using a bully pulpit, Hightower in April started speaking from an even bigger platform. With the help of his friend Rosapepe, he arranged to be appointed chairman of the Democratic National Committee Agriculture Council, a job that makes Hightower the Democratic answer to Reagan administration farm policies. Hightower's public relations talents have brought national attention to the cause—as well as to his own. He is now included in the national committee's strategy sessions and mentioned as Walter Mondale's choice for U.S. Secretary of Agriculture.

From this position Hightower has skillfully flayed the Reagan administration for its convoluted farm policies. When U.S. Agriculture Secretary John Block refused to release deteriorating grain stored in a Plainview warehouse for livestock starving from the West Texas drought—saying it was still marketable for human consumption—Hightower used state authority to send in grain inspectors. They found that most of the corn was already unfit for human consumption and was rapidly turning into worthless powder that not even livestock could eat. Hightower's incessant criticism of Block on the drought issue may have seemed to some like making political hay out of the ranchers' misfortune. But in late October, clearly in response to an assortment of such political pressures, Block told a Texas congressman that he wouldn't fight federal legislation forcing discounted sale of the corn to ranchers. Hightower has also taken action on his own, arranging for farmers in East Texas to sell hay that is worth little in their part of the state at below-market rates to West Texas ranchers. Even the conservative Texas Farm Bureau liked the idea. Hightower's performance in office has won grudging respect even from those predisposed against him—Representative Bruce Gibson, for example. "He's trying a lot of new stuff," says Gibson. "Eighty per cent of it might not work. But at least it's an effort."

Reagan Brown had criticized Hightower for promising far more than he could deliver, for suggesting that he could make a real difference in the price of groceries and the plight of the family farm. That criticism is correct. A hundred farmers' markets won't budge the statistics on average farm income or consumer food prices. Texas grapes aren't about to put California vineyards out of business. And agriculture development bonds won't save the imperiled family farm. Its demise is already a sad foregone conclusion. Hightower's program, rather than helping those in dire straits, will involve only farmers strong enough to incur more debt. But that doesn't mean that Hightower's efforts are meaningless. What he is doing will make a difference to some people. It may be only a few, but that doesn't seem like too small a task. What Hightower is offering may be viewed as a series of demonstration projects, examples of what an alternative approach, energy, and imagination can produce. Perhaps most of all, it is another kind of demonstration project—a display of what Jim Hightower can produce.

How far can he go? Maybe no further. There are plenty of folks who can tolerate—perhaps even vote for—Hightower as agriculture commissioner but who would fight like hell to keep him from becoming governor. Texans are a pretty conservative bunch when it comes to deciding who should live in the big white mansion in Austin. Hightower's biggest victory, remember, came against Reagan Brown; Garry Mauro or Buddy Temple would provide far stiffer competition. Running for governor would force Hightower to take positions that might fracture his delicate coalition. It's much tougher to keep everyone happy when you're after a job that requires hard choices. And then there's the money problem. To run a winning campaign, Hightower would need millions more than he has ever raised.

But he's sure he can do it. "The kind of issues I ran on in the last election, I would run on for governor," he says. "When you run for governor, you get so much coverage. They can't keep me off the TV sets. They can't keep me out of the newspapers. They know that. My assumption is there's a whole constituency out there that agrees with me. There's a whole world out there that wants someone like me."

★POLITICIANS★
JURISTS

The Real Governor of Texas

by Paul Burka

No one cast a single vote for him, but everyone in Texas lives beneath the power of a solitary judge in Tyler.

Mary Jane Blakley could hardly believe what she was hearing. She had driven into Bay City that late summer day in 1972 to handle the routine transfer of her son Mark from the Van Vleck school system to Bay City High. It was something she had done for the last two years without encountering the slightest problem. After all, Mark wanted to study pre-med in college, and Van Vleck's tiny high school just didn't offer the advanced science and math courses that were available in Bay City. It was routine, just routine, something Mark's older brothers had done on their way to becoming nuclear engineers, something people did all the time. This time, however, a clerk was telling her that there would be no more transfers, that what she wanted was impossible. No, the school board hadn't changed the rules. Bay City, and in fact the whole state, had been ordered not to accept such transfers by a federal judge sitting more than 250 miles away in Tyler, a judge with, Mrs. Blakley thought, the unlikely name of Justice, whose name she'd never heard before and who undoubtedly had never heard of her. What in the world was he doing in her life?

Judge William Wayne Justice of the Eastern District of Texas has entered the lives of a lot of people in his ten years on the bench: parents, politicians, police, school administrators, timber barons, hardened criminals, youths gone astray, environmentalists, illegal aliens, and just about everybody who lives in and around Tyler. He has been called a dictator and a tyrant by some, a hero and a godsend by others. The State House of Representatives, in a show of support for a legislator enraged by one of the judge's rulings, passed a bill to establish a halfway house for wayward juveniles next to the judge's tree-shaded home. He is the most active, and consequently the most powerful, of the 22 men who serve as federal district judges in Texas—a group of men who are appointed for life and who must answer to no one except other federal judges.

In many ways these men, with Judge Justice foremost among them, are the real governors of Texas. They make far more decisions that touch people's lives and influence the course of events than Dolph Briscoe, John Hill, or a score of legislators. They decide where and with whom your children go to school, who you can vote for and how much weight your vote will have, and many less cosmic but nevertheless vital public issues, such as whether commuter airlines can use Dallas' close-in Love Field or San Antonio

can build an expressway through a public park. Nationally, federal judges have laid low a president of the United States, caused IBM stockholders to lose more than $5 billion in a week, enjoined drilling for oil and gas off the East Coast in the face of a national energy emergency, restructured professional sports by striking down contracts binding players to their teams, and, of course, done more to change the course of relations between the races in the South than the might of the Union Army.

Despite their immense power, federal judges are largely anonymous and, if they can stay away from controversy, are likely to remain so. Chances are that no layman and only one Texas lawyer in a thousand could recite the roster of federal judges sitting in Texas. Hundreds of thousands of Houstonians knew that Joe Campos Torres had drowned in Buffalo Bayou after being beaten by police, but Ross Sterling was virtually unknown outside the legal community until he set off a series of demonstrations by handing down a benign one-year sentence to policemen convicted of violating Torres' civil rights.

Wayne Justice is undoubtedly better known than any of his Texas colleagues (especially now that Sarah Hughes, who administered the oath of office to President Lyndon B. Johnson, is in semiretirement), but he is hardly a public figure. His impact on the state in the seventies, particularly in school desegregation, has been greater than any other public official's, yet his name, face, and deeds remain unknown to most Texans. Except in the relatively few school districts where desegregation suits have been filed in local federal courts, he oversees all school integration in Texas to this day. The Texas Education Agency has had to create a special division just to administer his orders. Judge Justice has ordered school districts to consolidate, ruled that Mexican Americans must be considered a separate racial group, appointed entire school boards, and banned transfers between school districts that affect racial balance. (It was this last provision that ensnared the Blakleys of Van Vleck.) His decisions have been front-page news locally from Tyler to Del Rio.

He has also had a profound effect on local politics. He forced reapportionment of a number of East Texas city councils and commissioners courts and cast the decisive vote on a three-judge panel that threw out multimember legislative districts for more than four million Texans in Dallas, San Antonio, Fort Worth, Galveston, Corpus Christi, and other metropolitan areas. Only recently he hit

> **"'I'm a conservative judge,' Wayne Justice insists. 'I've followed the Supreme Court in every instance. If they change, you'll see my decisions change. I'm a professional.'"**

The story of William Wayne Justice is in many ways the story of the revolutionary developments that have taken place in American politics in the quarter-century since *Brown* v. *Board*. The balance of power among the three branches of government has shifted: the executive branch has been wounded by Viet Nam and Watergate, Congress has been floundering for years, only the judiciary has flourished. Wayne Justice has been in the forefront of this judicial revolution. But the story of Wayne Justice is more than just the story of another activist judge. It is the story of how the law works, for the judge himself contends steadfastly that "in every one [of his controversial decisions] the law was clear—I had no choice." It is a political story, for Wayne Justice is one of the last of his generation, the Ralph Yarborough liberals, still in power. And it is above all a personal story: a story of the bitter conflict between an old Southern town committed to a set of values and a way of life, and a judge no less committed to different values and a different way of life; a story of how lives of ordinary people like Mary Jane Blakley are touched by the law.

It is hard to imagine a less likely spot for an activist federal judge than Tyler, a picturesque town of 63,000 located just outside the giant East Texas oil field and just inside the Piney Woods. Proximity to trees and money can do a lot for the appearance of a town, and Tyler has made the most of both. It is best known as a rose-growing center, but if statistics were kept on such things, it might also be famous as the Texas city with the most $100,000 homes per capita.

The south side is the wealthy half of the city, with subdivisions like Oakleigh Woods, where oil millionaires have built homes that resemble Ramada Inns in size and, alas, architecture. The central city, memorable for its red-brick streets, is economically dormant, the better retail stores having abandoned the area for shopping centers south of town. The square has been left to the banks and the Smith County Courthouse, but the spiritual center of town is a short walk away, an intersection where two of Tyler's most influential institutions occupy adjacent corners: the First Baptist Church and the federal courthouse, facing each other like fortresses across the Rhine.

Wayne Justice grew up only 35 miles to the west, in neighboring Athens, but he is still considered an outsider, and for good reason: Athens is a universe away, with a different geography and a different political tradition. Athens is outside the Piney Woods, in the Post Oak Belt; in the judge's youth, it was farming country and not such good farming country at that. Athens is in Henderson County, the home of longtime liberal leader Ralph Yarborough and

the timber industry right in the pocketbook with a decision that has halted clear-cutting (a harvesting technique that means just what it implies: indiscriminate leveling) in national forests. In another long-running case he ruled that the way the State of Texas treats juveniles in its custody amounts to cruel and unusual punishment; many suspect he is about to say the same thing about the state's prison system in a case currently before him. The juvenile decision forced sweeping changes in the Texas Youth Council, and a ruling against the Department of Corrections (regarded as the best prison system in the nation by some authorities and as one of the most provincial by others, but undeniably the most economically efficient) could cost the state millions of dollars. Another decision with possible consequences for the state treasury was his recent ruling that Tyler schools may not charge tuition for children of illegal aliens—an order that could still be extended to the rest of the state.

A single federal judge exercising this much power over the affairs of a state would have been inconceivable a generation ago. Until recently, business in the federal courts was pretty much limited to suits between citizens of different states, federal criminal cases (automobile theft, mail fraud, and the like) and matters of federal law, like bankruptcy, antitrust, and labor relations. Civil rights cases were rare, and most of those were summarily dismissed. Any school child, for example, who complained in federal court that the principal made him cut his hair would have been laughed out of court and his lawyer summoned into chambers for a tongue-lashing about wasting the court's time. Structurally nothing has changed: the district courts, where Wayne Justice does his work, are still the bottom rung of a three-tier system, the level where cases are actually tried. Above them are ten circuit courts (Texas is in the Fifth Circuit), which consider appeals from the district court and either affirm (uphold) or reverse (overturn) the trial judge's decision. At the apex of the triangle, of course, is the Supreme Court. But the rather placid life district judges enjoyed a quarter-century ago has been swept up in the turmoil that followed the Supreme Court's fateful *Brown* v. *Board of Education* decision on school desegregation in 1954. Southern resistance to desegregation pushed judges into using unprecedented powers to obey the Supreme Court's mandate to eliminate segregation "root and branch." It is not a long step from ordering school boards to adopt busing plans to telling states how to run prison systems. Inevitably, the declaration in *Brown* that separate but equal is "inherently unequal" meant the recognition of other civil rights, leading to an explosion of litigation: in 1960 around 200 civil rights cases were filed in the entire country; by 1977 the number had ballooned to 17,000.

> **"One case quickly took on a larger significance. The issue was who ran the schools—the students or the administration. The answer, of course, was Judge Justice."**

one of the cradles of Texas populism. It is also yellow-dog Democrat territory; George McGovern was the only Democratic presidential nominee in a hundred years who failed to carry Henderson County. On the other hand, populism and its instinctive support for the underdog never touched Tyler. Tyler was a city of influence: it produced three governors and a United States senator before World War I, and its businessmen and bankers were statewide political kingmakers in the days when Texas was still primarily agricultural. The Depression changed nothing, for it arrived about the same time as the East Texas oil boom. While farmers were going broke around Athens, new oil millionaires flocked to Tyler to escape the rigs and roughnecks and were assimilated into the local gentry. The city continues to be dominated by the same oil and mercantile families who have run things as long as anyone can remember. Tyler is one of the few cities where hustlers and hucksters are on the outside: real estate developers, ambitious young lawyers, car dealers, promoters have little political impact. The business oligarchy has stuck to a deep philosophical conservatism of the old school that asks little from government; they are people who are used to having things their own way and they look upon outsiders like Wayne Justice with suspicion. Tyler regularly votes Republican in presidential elections; the last Democrat to carry Smith County was Harry Truman in 1948.

Even though both towns were soul South—Athens was totally segregated as late as 1964—race relations followed the same pattern as politics. "There's no meanness in Henderson County," says a lawyer who's tried cases for twenty years all over East Texas. "Blacks get more than justice. There's a feeling that whites shouldn't be allowed to overreach or take advantage of blacks. It's paternalism, but it's better than Tyler, where you've got the oil mentality of whatever happens to you is your own hard luck. There's no sympathy for the underdog. But even Tyler is better than Longview or Marshall. Over there, if you're black, you're wrong."

Wayne Justice was raised in the Henderson County populist tradition. His father, Will Justice, ran unsuccessfully for Congress in the thirties, but he was best known as a country lawyer of near legendary stature. He won so many improbable cases, civil and criminal, that a joke began to circulate that "there is no justice in East Texas but Will Justice." Those who remember him say he was a mesmerizing orator, a seat-of-the-pants lawyer with an intuitive feel for people, especially potential jurors.

Will Justice lived for a time with Charles and Nannie Yarborough in nearby Chandler; their young son Ralph would run for state attorney general in 1938. Wayne was

only sixteen that year, but he campaigned for his father's friend; eventually, of course, Yarborough ran three losing races for governor and became the central figure in Texas politics of the fifties—years when Democratic Governor Allan Shivers endorsed a Republican presidential candidate, years of walkouts and rump conventions and fights between liberals and conservatives that got so rough liberals were once locked out of a state convention by armed state troopers. Wayne Justice was a loyal member of a group who called themselves the coon hunters—all liberals, mostly lawyers, and Yarborough's closest political friends.

Justice went to UT law school in the early forties, where he was, in his words, an undistinguished student who was more interested in politics than law. The *Texas Law Review*, where hotshot students publish their legal research, contains no mention of his name. As a lawyer he turned out to be very different from his father: he had less instinct for people and little rhetorical ability, but he was a careful worker who probably knew more about the law. The difference between father and son carried over into politics. When Wayne Justice learned his law partner (and wife's brother), Mike Rowan, was supporting the hated Shivers for governor over Yarborough, he demanded to know how Rowan could be for "that Republican son of a bitch." Will Justice, though, would pick up the newspaper and needle Rowan gently about Shivers' latest statements. Rowan soon left the firm; he lives in Tyler now, but the political animosities linger.

Wayne Justice's closeness to Ralph Yarborough and his loyal service to the liberal cause paid off after the Democrats recaptured the White House in 1960. Yarborough was United States senator by this time, and he used his patronage to get Justice appointed U.S. attorney for the Eastern District of Texas. The job was situated in Tyler, but Justice chose, significantly, to live in Athens and commute. His record as U.S. attorney gave little indication of what lay ahead after he stepped up to the bench. He was not known as a crusader against either racial discrimination or political corruption, though there was plenty of both in East Texas. His biggest impact came when he successfully prosecuted slant-hole oil well drillers in a very complex and difficult case. The trial was highly publicized in the area and Justice won it, but to no avail. The judge made it clear from the beginning he didn't think much of the whole proceeding. His light sentence was a slap on the wrist for the defendants and a slap in the face to the prosecution; above all it was a clear demonstration of the power of a federal judge. Several years later the judge died, and after some infighting between Yarborough and LBJ, Justice got his seat. It was just in time. Wayne Justice was in the last batch of Lyndon Johnson's judges to be confirmed by the Senate in the spring of 1968.

Soon after Justice took the oath of office, lawyers in the Dallas civil rights division of the Justice Department speculated about what kind of judge he would be. Those fresh out of law school doubted that he would be particularly friendly to the government, since his record as U.S. attorney didn't point in that direction. But the head of the office felt otherwise. "I know this man," the veteran lawyer told his staff, "and I have a feeling that if we give him the right case on school integration, he'll go with us in a big way." The thesis wasn't long in being tested. Desegregation had been proceeding pretty well in East Texas in the late sixties. In most instances no court action was necessary: HEW simply negotiated contracts with local districts on how to desegregate. But Richard Nixon's election gave hope to recalcitrants. Perhaps desegregation wouldn't be necessary after all. In September 1969 the Tatum Independent School District fifty miles east of Tyler decided to ignore its contract and substitute a freedom-of-choice plan: students could go to whatever school the wanted, but the local board would take no affirmative action.

Seldom have the wheels of justice turned so fast. The Justice Department learned on a Thursday that Tatum had reneged. By the following Wednesday they were in Tyler asking for a restraining order. Two days later there was a hearing where Judge Justice made clear he would hold the school board in contempt of court. On Monday school opened on an integrated basis.

The Tatum decision had no impact in Tyler, but it was a harbinger of things to come, in both result and residual ill will. Although they had no legal leg to stand on, some community leaders in Tatum felt they had been bludgeoned into compliance. Judge Justice's first clash with Tyler came when he presided over the local desegregation suit in late 1969. Though integration was inevitable, the school board was sullen and uncooperative. The litigation did nothing to improve the judge's standing with his new south Tyler neighbors. (The Justice family at last moved from Athens when he was named to the bench.) But the real fire storm began in 1970. In the space of little more than a year, Tyler was racked with all the same kinds of controversies that were popping up all over the country: disputes over long hair, school discipline, racial discrimination.

It all started when a professor barred a twenty-year-old student at Tyler Junior College from taking a final exam in a government class because his hair was too long. Soon afterward three students were not permitted to register at the college because their hair did not comply with the college's dress code. In the spring of 1971 racial trouble flared up at northside John Tyler High School over a cheerleader election; more than two hundred blacks

were suspended for taking part in a demonstration on school grounds. Meanwhile, in another lawsuit that would turn out to have important ramifications for Tyler, Judge Justice effectively took control of school desegregation for the entire state; his order against transfers affecting racial balance was aimed at the substantial number of rural whites who regularly sent their children out of predominantly black rural schools into larger, whiter urban schools. The final blow came late in 1971 when the Texas Education Agency, acting under orders from Judge Justice, forced southside Robert E. Lee High to abandon its confederate theme: no rebel flag, rebel mascot, or "Dixie" as the school song. It looked for a while as if the rebel cannon had to go too, but when research uncovered the fact that it was actually a U.S. Army artillery cannon of Mexican War vintage, use of the cannon was declared proper. (It is not recorded whether Mexican American students protested the decision.)

Each of the controversies quickly ended up in Judge Justice's lap. These were not just ordinary lawsuits; larger issues were at stake and everyone knew it. Emotions ran high; school board meetings drew standing-room-only crowds, and letters crowds, and letters from readers swelled the newspaper. Many people said the issue was discipline, but the fight was really over something far more fundamental: the community's sense of virtue and propriety. The things they'd seen on television—riots, demonstrations, drugs, all the traumas of the sixties—were at last on their doorstep, and they were determined to keep them out. In their minds the only thing that could thwart their will was a single federal judge.

The junior college hair dispute was weighted with this symbolic importance. Tyler Junior College was the pride of the community. It was one of the oldest junior colleges in the state, and the administration, which ran it, in the words of one former student, "like a military operation," seemed to mirror community mores. At the hearing, college officials contended the hair regulation was essential for maintaining discipline and a proper educational environment. On the last day, Judge Justice appeared on the bench with a number of open lawbooks. These proved to be cases supporting his yet unannounced decision, which he handed down promptly without apparent deliberation—against the college. Community leaders were dismayed at the ruling ("This will destroy the college," one of the city's leading lawyers glumly predicted), but they were infuriated by the judge's failure to contemplate, to give the appearance of taking their arguments seriously. Technically Judge Justice was blameless: he had had plenty of time for research, there

was ample precedent to support his conclusion (including a decision by a Houston federal judge involving San Jacinto Junior College), and the college had presented more emotion than evidence. But for someone who had spent so much of his adult life in politics, Wayne Justice displayed an astonishing lack of political finesse.

It was a characteristic that would surface again and again; even his staunchest admirers lament the fact that he has never attempted outside the courtroom to make his peace either with the citizenry or the local bar. Shortly after the controversies at the junior college and the local high schools, a local politician saw him having coffee alone at the old Blackstone Hotel. The politician sat down at the table, a rare gesture in itself, and said, "How's my friendly neighborhood school administrator?" William Wayne Justice was not amused. If someone devised a litmus test for good old boys, Wayne Justice would flunk it. He never fraternizes, seldom speaks to Tylerites on the street unless spoken to first, and remains to this day a shy, courtly, formal man. He is a member of the Tyler Petroleum Club (dating back to when he was U.S. attorney) but when he lunches there, he might as well be invisible. No one speaks to him and he speaks to no one, while handshakes and greetings swirl around him in the room.

If the junior college hair case drew the battle lines between judge and community, the two high school imbroglios ended all possibility of rapprochement. The black protest at John Tyler erupted when the school administration distributed cheerleader ballots identifying candidates by race and stipulating that students vote for four whites and two blacks. (The white-black ratio at the school was 62-38.) A black walkout quickly led to a demonstration, suspension of all participants, stringent readmission rules, and a lawsuit. Once again the case took on larger significance. The issue was discipline—who ran the schools, the students or the administration? The answer, of course, was Judge Justice. He barred the school district from suspending the demonstrators; that alone was enough to irk many people, but he really seemed to cross the line separating adjudication from administration when he ordered the school to choose two more cheerleaders, one black, one white, more accurately reflecting the racial ratio.

The politically well-connected minister of the First Baptist Church still regards this decision as devastating to the moral fabric of the community. He holds Judge Justice primarily responsible for the breakdown of discipline in the schools, and to prove his point he told me sadly, "Little girls are afraid to go to the bathroom." Of course that same fear can be found in Dallas and Houston, among other places, but the judge's antagonists cannot believe that it would have happened here regardless. "You see, this man's a socialist," the minister added. "He wants to tear down what we have and replace it with something else."

Oddly, the dispute that sealed the isolation of Judge Justice from the community never even reached the lawsuit stage. When the Texas Education Agency ordered the school board to abandon the Southern theme at Robert E. Lee High or face the loss of accreditation and $800,000 in state funds, many Tylerites saw the threat as going after a fly with a sledgehammer. Since Judge Justice had ordered the TEA, in the statewide school integration case, to investigate complaints about school symbols that threatened racial harmony, he naturally got the blame.

"There's a difference between being proud of your Southern heritage and being racist," says Bill Clark, a local lawyer and state legislator. From the school cases of 1970–1971 forward, Wayne Justice has always been viewed by much of Tyler as an outsider bent on destroying everything they hold dear. The judge got unsigned hate mail (". . . if you want some more black school districts to integrate, why don't you move to Africa . . ."), obscene phone calls in the middle of the night, a few personal threats, and the silent treatment from people on the streets. He raised the insurance on his home and increased security at the courthouse. For a time the stairway to his courtroom was sealed off. Phrases like "undeterred by community hostility" began to appear in his written opinions. Tyler's leading beauticians refused to do Mrs. Justice's hair, and a repairman walked off the job when he realized whose home he was working on. In lighter moments the anti-Justice crowd joked that the court clerk ought to amend the daily incantation of "God save the United States and this honorable court" by substituting *from*. Local cars displayed "Will Rogers never met Judge Justice" bumper stickers. High school students went door to door collecting signatures on recall petitions, though you can no more recall a federal judge than you can reverse the flow of the Mississippi River. Inevitably, one unsuspecting volunteer rang the judge's doorbell and asked Mrs. Justice for her signature. A not-so-distant cousin wrote a letter to the Tyler paper professing shame at being related to the judge.

Much of the open enmity of the early seventies has been calmed by the passage of time. The petitions disappeared and the obscene phone calls have stopped. Sue Justice no longer has to have her hair done in Athens. Tyler Junior College wasn't destroyed after all, and the Lee Red Raiders are no less beloved than were the Lee Rebels. But the underlying social antipathy in this very social town continues unabated. Wayne Justice is such an avid follower of UT football that Darrell Royal once had him sit on the bench during a game, yet when Tyler honored hometown Heisman Trophy winner Earl Campbell last winter, the judge was not invited to the festivities. The usual plaques, certificates, and photographs that clutter the offices of most public figures are missing from his chambers; the sole memento is a football autographed by the 1972 Longhorns.

The judge's admirers—his former law clerks, old friends from Athens, the Ralph Yarborough coon hunters—have a simple explanation for the venom directed at him: he broke the stranglehold of an entrenched conservative gentry on a closed town, and they couldn't abide it. Undoubtedly that was a contributing factor, but it doesn't explain the depth of the anti-Justice feeling. I talked to secretaries and schoolteachers who shared the sentiments of oilmen and establishment lawyers. These are people who ordinarily couldn't care less who runs Tyler, but there is something about a judicially ordered transfer of power that people find upsetting and disorienting, because it is beyond their reach. "People in Tyler," says Smith County Judge Billy Williamson, "like to think that a judge is supposed to guarantee fair play, not be a player himself." The law is so pervasive, so powerful, so much at the heart of how society is organized, that people instinctively want it to be permanent and predictable—and the judge who determines it to be neutral. As usual, myth is not reality: the law is not static and justice is not blind. But no one really likes to be reminded just how arbitrary the process is—how easily precedent and language can be shaped to arrive at almost any conclusion. One eminent jurist has estimated that nine-tenths of the cases that have been decided in the highest court of England could have gone the other way with no violence to the common law. Wayne Justice's real problem with the people of Tyler is that he wasn't politic enough to shield them from the sad truth that the law is as arbitrary and human as the rest of society.

What happened in Tyler reveals a lot about Wayne Justice as a person—sensitive to injustice but sometimes insensitive to people; courageous in the face of hostility but with a footnote, for he was unburdened by any fondness for the community or any desire to be accepted by it—but, more important, it helps explain why Wayne Justice is in the forefront of the judicial revolution. A number of judges might have struck down the Tyler School District's peculiar readmission procedures for suspended black students, but it is hard to imagine anyone other than Wayne Justice ordering the election of two new cheerleaders. What makes Wayne Justice different from most other judges is his willingness to go all the way with a remedy once he's decided an injustice exists.

In case after case, Wayne Justice has issued orders of a scope unknown and undreamed of as recently as fifteen years ago. In school desegregation cases, he insists on "true integration as opposed to mere desegregation." After ruling that juveniles in state custody have a constitutional right to treatment, he went on to specify exactly what that meant, including which IQ test the state must use and what kinds of psychological and psychiatric services must be available. In discrimination cases, Judge Justice repeatedly has not only found for the plaintiff, but also awarded substantial attorney's fees.

His penchant for sweeping remedies is no secret, of course, and lawyers know how to maneuver cases into his court by a time-honored practice known as forum shopping. (Judge Justice is hardly oblivious to this ploy: he jokes that the case load in Tyler has seen a remarkable increase since he came on the scene.) It works like this: Texas is divided into four judicial districts, one for each compass direction; Wayne Justice is one of three judges in the Eastern District. In theory, jurisdiction follows geography—an equal opportunity suit against, say, a Lubbock contractor couldn't be tried in Tyler—but in some cases that limitation has little significance, particularly in major cases involving the state. In the juveniles' suit against the Texas Youth Council, for example, the presence of one institution in the Eastern District (the rest were in the Western District) was sufficient to get the case before Judge Justice.

When liberals decided to challenge the legislative redistricting law of 1971 for not measuring up to the one-man, one-vote standard, they ignored flagrant abuses in places like Dallas and San Antonio, and instead pored over figures and maps for days trying to find something wrong in Judge Justice's segment of the Eastern District (Justice holds court in Sherman, Paris, and, of course, Tyler). "The whole outcome turned on forum shopping," chortles an attorney for the liberals. "We couldn't be sure he'd rule for us, but we knew if he did, he wouldn't let an election take place under an unconstitutional law. Other judges might have found for us, but they'd have said, 'Yes, it's unconstitutional, but we're not going to interfere until the next Legislature has a chance to correct the problem.'"

That is why Wayne Justice is a judicial revolutionary. He is no Brandeis or Cardozo, authoring brilliant, incisive legal principles that will live for ages. Instead he is one of a handful of judges —the best known is Frank Johnson of Alabama, whose health prevented him from becoming head of the FBI—who have grasped the lesson of *Brown* v. *Board*: ultimately the remedy is more important than the substantive decision. Judges have always been part of the power equation of American politics— few powers are more potent than the ability to strike down laws as unconstitutional—but until recently their power has been mostly abstract. No longer: judges run school districts, prison systems, mental hospitals, and state property tax administrations.

Perhaps the best illustration of this judicial revolution, and Wayne Justice's place in it, is the legal battle that grew out of a squabble between two school districts 400 miles from Tyler in Del Rio. No one in that border city could have suspected that a lawsuit brought by the U.S. Justice Department in 1970 to eliminate nine all-black school districts in East Texas would end up setting off a legal donnybrook in their remote corner of Southwest Texas. When the East Texas case began, it appeared to be nothing more than an effort to force consolidation between the black districts and their white counterparts. Many of the white districts didn't even contest the suit; several didn't bother to hire lawyers. It had all the earmarks of a minor case whose outcome was preordained. True, the Texas Education Agency was also a defendant in the case—by supplying the black districts with state funds they had contributed (and, said the feds, consented) to the dual districts—but lawyers for the state regarded that as merely a formality.

That illusion didn't last long. Once Judge Justice had jurisdiction over the TEA, he ordered it to be responsible for eliminating segregation in the entire state—a responsibility that, needless to say, the Texas Legislature had never assigned it. (The idea actually originated with the Justice Department, but the judge embraced it with enthusiasm.) Suddenly a minor regional case

had statewide ramifications.

Part of the judge's order was the ban on transfers that impede integration— the provision that thwarted the Blakleys of Van Vleck. In Del Rio the controversy soon involved the whole town. The area had two school districts, Del Rio and a small one on the edge of town known as San Felipe, encompassing mostly Mexican American neighborhoods. But San Felipe also took in Laughlin Air Force Base, and that's where the trouble began. For years the air base had bussed children of military families into Del Rio to avoid the overcrowded, understaffed, and educationally weak San Felipe schools. When the base learned, in the spring of 1971, that Del Rio would not accept any more transfers, a number of Anglo officers exploded with rage. A lawyer then with the state attorney general's office recalls that a high-ranking official vowed he'd close the base before he'd send his daughter to San Felipe. The bluster was sufficient to cause civic leaders to worry that Del Rio might actually lose the base or, at the very least, some government funds handed out to areas with large federal installations.

No doubt Del Rio Anglos would have been happy to perpetuate the dual school districts, but the conflict cast things in a different light. Del Rio wanted that air base and its payroll at all costs. So the school district decided the best way out of the controversy was to absorb San Felipe. But San Felipe wouldn't cooperate. They didn't want to consolidate; their schools might not be good, but at least they were *theirs*. A larger, wealthier Del Rio would obviously control the merged district. So if Del Rio wanted consolidation, it would have to go to court to compel it, and that meant going before the judge who had jurisdiction over the Texas Education Agency and thus over school integration for the whole state. No one in Del Rio knew anything about this man named William Wayne Justice.

A school board lawyer asked the state attorney general's office for advice (Crawford Martin was still AG) and was told, "*Don't* go to Tyler. Whatever you do, stay out of Tyler." They had seen Judge Justice manipulate one school case; there was no telling what he'd do with this one.

Undeterred, Del Rio asked Judge Justice to consolidate the districts. San Felipe fought back, even hiring skilled Odessa trial lawyer Warren Burnett, but to no avail. Burnett presented one of his classic jury summations, but there was no jury, only Judge Justice; no sooner had Burnett concluded his analysis of why the court couldn't consolidate the districts than the judge announced that he could and would. That was the good news for Del Rio. The bad news was that the district had to submit an equal educational opportunity plan for the court's approval, including extensive bilingual and bicultural programs. The old Del Rio board (the judge had also named a new consolidated school board) howled that this was far too costly and unworkable besides: there weren't enough bilingual instructors in the whole state, they claimed, to meet the judge's standards. So the new board worked out a compromise with the federal government, but that was torpedoed when San Felipe representatives, still smarting over the loss of their schools, claimed they'd been excluded from secret negotiations. The situation degenerated rapidly and Judge Justice lost his patience. It is never advisable to test the patience of a federal judge regardless of his ideological bent, and Wayne Justice is no exception. He charged the Del Rio people with acting in bad faith (a claim Del Rio lawyers vehemently denied) and handed down what an assistant state attorney general of that era still calls "the goddamndest cradle-to-grave order in legal history." It was a complete program for running the Del Rio schools, dealing with everything from preschool programs for three-year-olds to curriculum for every grade to parental involvement. So comprehensive was the bilingual plan that it even called for Anglo children to learn Spanish.

Ironically, little of this ever came to pass. The districts consolidated, all right (and the air base continued to pump millions into Del Rio's economy) but the rest of the order was never enforced. Perhaps its scope was too much for the appellate judges on the Fifth Circuit Court of Appeals: although they did not reverse Judge Justice outright, they shifted administration over the order closer to Del Rio, where it wound up in the San Antonio court of Judge John Wood, probably Texas' most conservative federal judge. The Department of Health, Education, and Welfare, which had actually drawn the order, failed to follow it up, and Wood dismissed the whole proceeding. But that does not vitiate the importance of the case for students of judicial activism. A federal judge had handed down a ruling that neither of the original combatants, San Felipe or Del Rio, had wanted; the outcome was one of the most sweeping, comprehensive, detailed orders any judge had ever issued—and it had been affirmed by an appellate court. No one understood what that meant any better than William Wayne Justice.

William Wayne Justice turns out to be an unlikely revolutionary. Unlike many Texas liberals of his generation, he is neither naturally gregarious nor gone to seed. He dresses conservatively ("my protective coloration," he once told an aide)—dark suits, white shirts, plain ties, often a hat—and lives a spartan existence: seven days a week at the office, jogging four miles at least five times a week, and a diet consisting mostly of yogurt and salad without dressing. The social ostracism leaves him unaffected—it's conceivable he prefers it that way—though his wife has been deeply hurt by it. There is virtually nothing about the man to suggest he is one of the leading judicial activists in the nation—except, of course, his decisions.

Indeed, even when he talks about the highlights of his years on the bench, Wayne Justice doesn't dwell on his rulings. His greatest source of pride is an obscure statistic: he went almost ten years before the Fifth Circuit overturned one of his rulings in a criminal case. He has a professional's pride in his work, prefers research to running a trial, and loves to talk about procedural innovations he's developed to make a case run more smoothly. His father, Will Justice, was an expert at what his son calls the "pitfall theory of justice"—digging traps for the unwary opposition, objecting to evidence, springing surprise witnesses—but such tactics have no place in Wayne Justice's courtroom. The judge utilizes an elaborate pre-trial order that all but eliminates the surprise factor; his courtroom is a place for professionals, and most lawyers—there are exceptions—appreciate it.

If he is biased (and most lawyers would agree that all judges are; the only question is to what degree) then sensitivity to abuse of power is no doubt at the heart of Wayne Justice's judicial philosophy. The politics of the fifties continue to have their impact on him, for he spent the decade as an Out; the state and its apparatus were the province of the enemy, and he was never a part of the world that accepts the necessity and value of bureaucratic convenience. He is passionately strict about proper procedure, the formal dance of justice. His own criminal trials are a model of correctness: he goes through the entire litany with defendants—"Do you know you are entitled to a lawyer? Are you aware you do not have to make a statement?"—and expects no less of state judges and administrators. To Wayne Justice, there are few offenses more serious than failing to play by the rules. In reaching his decisions, for example, he is more care-

ful than many judges to touch the obligatory bases of evidence and precedent. His opinions are buttressed with excerpts from trial testimony, and his most controversial actions—the Tyler Junior College hair case, the confederate symbols at Lee High, even his ruling that juveniles in the custody of the state have a constitutional right to proper treatment—followed squarely in the footsteps of other judges.

But ruling on the law is only one of the functions of a judge, and in civil rights cases, at least, it is probably the least important one. Most civil rights suits eventually turn on how the judge interprets the evidence (usually the province of the jury, but partly because Congress didn't trust Southern juries, there is no jury in civil rights cases). The stratagem hasn't always worked the way it was supposed to, because many Southern judges excel at a charade Wayne Justice calls "playing the game." Faced with, say, a massive school bussing suit, a judge will blandly declare it has no merit and throw it out of court, knowing he'll be reversed by a higher court. (The Dallas school integration case has bounced back and forth to the Fifth Circuit so many times it sometimes appears they're playing catch.) In the meantime, the judge can continue to enjoy golf at the country club, and when the appellate courts at last make him crack down, he can say his hand was forced. Judges appointed for life may be insulated from political pressures, but few are as oblivious to social pressures as Wayne Justice.

No one can accuse Wayne Justice of ducking the tough ones. If anything, he goes to the opposite extreme. After a routine hearing in the early seventies, a young lawyer from the Justice Department was part of a group talking shop with the judge when the conversation turned to the future course of constitutional law. Wayne Justice said he felt juveniles and mental patients incarcerated by the state had a right to proper treatment; in fact, he added, if the case were before him, that's how he would rule.

A couple of years later, the Texas Youth Council refused to let some youths meet with their attorneys, the lawyers responded with a suit for access, and the case ended up in Judge Justice's court. But it soon took on greater significance, as cases in that court have a tendency to do. This time, though, the way it happened was a little unusual. Judge Justice called the Justice Department lawyer and told him, "Remember that discussion we had on right to treatment? I think I've got a case for you." He followed that with a letter, the Justice Depart-

ment eventually contacted the kids' lawyers, the lawyers agreeably broadened their lawsuit and asked the Justice Department to intervene. Sure enough, the judge ruled that juveniles had a right to proper treatment.

Some would say that in molding the shape of cases in his court, the judge exceeded the bounds of propriety; others would defend it as no less than his duty. Regardless, it is something not all judges would condone and still less would do: another example of how Wayne Justice uses the full extent of his powers. But the real issues raised by this kind of judicial involvement transcend Wayne Justice. Where does it all end, and, ultimately, is it a good thing?

There are some signs the judicial revolution has already reached its peak. The Supreme Court has been cutting back on federal court interference with state criminal prosecutions, and it has also found more and more excuses to defer to states in other areas of the law. Indeed, most judicial activism today is pretty much limited to the civil rights arena, but that's still a huge area.

Closer to home, the Fifth Circuit has begun to look long and close at Wayne Justice's decisions. He has such an unflagging reputation as an activist that conservative appeals judges (and the Fifth Circuit splits close to even in philosophy) make a habit of sending their clerks to inspect his rulings. Last fall in reviewing the TYC case the appellate court didn't exactly reverse him on the right-to-treatment issue, but they sent the case back to him for reconsideration, an unusual procedure. And that wasn't all. They sent along a warning that the judge's order was "excessively detailed" and reminded him that there is more than one constitutional way to run a rehabilitation program. The significance of the opinion did not escape Wayne Justice. "I'm a conservative judge," he insists. "I've followed the Supreme Court and the Fifth Circuit in every instance," he says. "Yes, I've been in full sympathy with the decisions I've cited. But if they change, you'll see my decisions change. I'm a professional and I don't like to be reversed."

Does this herald the end of an era in Texas jurisprudence, the decline of Wayne Justice's influence over the state? Probably not. Federal judges are too much a part of the political process of modern America. The way Americans look at their government has changed radically in the last half-century; they have come to see the government as provider rather than policeman. The law has adapted to the change: judges used to direct the government *not* to do things; today judicial activists are telling government what *to* do. Nothing the Fifth Circuit says can turn back the clock or reverse the relationship between people and government. The Fifth Circuit's message to Wayne Justice was to slow down, not change direction.

Perhaps the clear-cutting case sheds some light on what may be expected of a somewhat tempered Wayne Justice. He could have handed down one of his sweeping rulings, finding that clear-cutting was so harmful that it must be banned forever. Or he could have barred clear-cutting on the grounds that it endangered the survival of a rara avis. Instead, he based his decision on narrow procedural grounds; the ruling simply requires a delay for a proper environmental study. That may not be very dramatic, but it was sufficient to stop the cutting and more likely to be upheld on appeal.*

Whatever the future of judicial activism, its past should be seen in perspective. Wayne Justice has opposite-minded counterparts on the other end of the judicial spectrum. If he is inclined to be sympathetic to civil rights complaints, there are other judges—John Wood in San Antonio, for example—who are likely to dismiss them unheard. And there is always the specter of the late Judge T. Whitfield Davidson of Dallas, who once threw the Dallas school integration suit out of court with the comment that "the *real* law of the land is the same as it was on May 16, 1954"—just before the Supreme Court's decision in *Brown* v. *Board*.

Nor should the kind of wide-ranging orders typical of Judge Justice be dismissed solely as power plays. Judges learned the lesson of desegregation the hard way: when courts spoke in general language like "with all deliberate speed," there was no way to enforce an order. The more hostile the state authorities are—and every state agency Judge Justice has had in court was initially hostile—the more detailed and specific orders have to be if a judge has any hope of their being obeyed, or of making a contempt citation stick.

Undoubtedly judicial activism can take credit for most of the political advances of the last twenty years. Judges broke the legal stranglehold of segregation on the South. They made legislative bodies more representative; they brought the vote to the disenfranchised; they protected the rights of people whom state authorities had trampled on unchecked for years. But it was not without cost. Tinkering with machinery may solve one problem but create hidden stress elsewhere; in the case of the political mechanism, the vulnerable spot has proved to be the legislative branch. Politicians like to scream about judicial interference with their territory, but the truth is that many have discovered political advantages in letting judges take the heat for tough decisions. In Alabama, for example, the Legislature was so delighted a federal court had finally forced revision of the property tax system—an issue they had wrestled with for years—that the state didn't even appeal the decision. What happens to a democracy when the creativity of its legislative branch is stifled? Defenders of judicial activism would respond that, yes, it would be preferable for the legislatures to act, but since the legislatures have defaulted on their duties, then the courts must fill the gap. It's an argument Judge Justice himself has used. But it begs the question. The real issue is, Did the legislatures have a duty in the first place? (And how do we find out? Why, the judges will tell us.)

Ultimately, though, the real problem with judicial activism is not its effect on the system, but its impact on individuals who are left without recourse. The legal system can resolve narrow controversies between individuals, or general conflicts between interest groups, but it can't seem to do both at once. There is no way to prove the valid exception to a judicial ruling without a long, tedious, and expensive process: hearings, briefs, arguments, research, and that's only one case. What if, as in the case of Judge Justice's order banning transfers, hundreds of people want exemption? Of course, a court can always delegate some decision-making power to a state agency like the TEA, but inevitably a bureaucracy under the watchful eye of a federal judge armed with contempt power will not have flexibility uppermost in its mind. People like Mark Blakley always get caught in the net.

Oh yes. Mark Blakley never did become a doctor. He never did even finish college. He dropped out after a year and works for a soft drink company. Somehow, he says, he never felt the same about school after a federal judge entered his life. ◆

---

*It wasn't, though. Just before press time, the Fifth Circuit reversed the decision.

Long Row to Hoe

Panhandle farmers don't cotton to changing their ways.

Just about everybody around Hereford feels misunderstood these days. The problem, as the local merchants, ranchers, and farmers who gather at Dickie's restaurant will tell you, is lawyers, Harvard-educated government lawyers with no knowledge of, or sympathy for, Panhandle ways. These lawyers, they say, are stirring up Mexican American farmworkers and misrepresenting the decent, hardworking folk here as heartless, cold-blooded exploiters of the poor.

But walk from Dickie's across the four lanes of U.S. 60 that bisect the town and into the storefront offices of Texas Rural Legal Aid (TRLA), and you enter a different world. Families of migrant workers sit patiently in folding chairs in the cinder-block foyer, waiting to seek redress for wrongs they think their employers have committed. It is a measure of the cultural barriers that divide not only Hereford but the entire fourteen-county area served by TRLA that while anybody who has the inclination can walk from one side of the highway to the other as I did, nobody does.

Ever since lawyers Bill Beardall, Ed Tuddenham, Inez Flores, and Jennifer Harbury opened TRLA's doors in October 1978, they have found themselves at the center of controversy, accused of everything unholy from fomenting revolution to neglecting to bathe. The summer after her first year at Harvard, Harbury interned in the Valley, at the TRLA office in Weslaco, and it was her enthusiasm for TRLA that persuaded her friends to come to Hereford.

TRLA is supported by grants from the congressionally funded Legal Services Corporation (LSC), which was formed by the Office of Economic Opportunity in 1974. Supported by such establishment-oriented groups as the American and Texas bar associations, the Legal Services Corporation is set up to provide equal representation in the courts for people who cannot afford to pay private attorneys. Although long accepted in much of the country (the U.S. Senate recently voted 55–14 to finance LSC for 1981–82), the idea strikes many Panhandle residents as unadulterated socialism. The opening of legal aid offices in rural areas of Texas has prompted angry resolutions from the bar associations of Erath, Eastland, and Palo Pinto counties and from the West Texas County Judges' and Commissioners' Association. "Their perception," says Clinton Cross, coordinator of the Texas Legal Services Center in Austin, "is that we're funding a side. Mine is that we're funding a process."

But Cross is being a bit disingenuous, as is Hereford TRLA office director Bill Beardall when he says, "We couldn't effect widespread social change here even if we wanted to." A native of Memphis, Beardall spent a fair amount of time at Harvard explaining to curious and sometimes antagonistic classmates that day-to-day Southern life was considerably more complex than what they saw on the evening news or in the movies. He sees the same oversimplification happening in the Panhandle, and his work has been made more difficult by news stories out of Hereford that have pitted the bad guys against the good guys. "They amount to a loosely fictionalized version of the real situation," he say

Beardall and his young associates—all four are under thirty—are not the only ones concerned about misrepresentation. Hereford has changed from an agricultural village of 2500 into a prosperous town of 18,000 in the last forty years. The growth, according to chamber of commerce president Mike Carr, is largely because of Mexican Americans who came up from the Rio Grande Valley to pick crops and stayed to work year-round in feedlots, meat-packing plants, and feed mills or to found their own small businesses. Carr fears that the image of ethnic polarization resulting from TRLA activities will make it difficult to attract new industry. Like all the Anglos I talked with in Hereford other than those in the TRLA office, he spoke of the many fine Mexican Americans in the community in a manner that echoed the "good Negro" talk in small towns across the Deep South. He was desperately sincere but uneasy nevertheless.

On the surface, life in Hereford appears unchanged, but the kinds of class action lawsuits TRLA has filed on behalf of its clients do represent a significant threat to the Panhandle way of doing things. Although Congress made migrant farmworkers and their employers subject to the federal minimum wage in 1974, few ranchers or growers in the area paid any attention to the law. Themselves at the mercy of a fluctuating commodities market and the vagaries of the weather, growers here have gone about their business in the traditional way, hiring temporary labor to sack onions, hoe cotton, pick lettuce, and perform other agricultural chores at the going rate, which is now about $1.85 an hour. (The federal minimum wage is $3.10.) Some growers prefer to pay for piecework, reasoning that the fast adult workers can do quite well—and some can—and that the rest, children and older workers, make what they are worth.

From the employer's point of view, then, the traditional way is a classic free market, which requires neither explanation nor defense. Most seem to believe that the migrants would be satisfied with the situation too, were it not for the meddling of outsiders like TRLA. The presence of the lawyers at a recent strike in the onion fields near Hereford illustrates the point. Local growers are convinced that they were there to stir up unrest among the workers; the lawyers maintain they were merely doing their job. Although TRLA is forbidden by law to help organize farmworkers' unions, they can represent union workers, a distinction that their adversaries think is too subtle.

Deaf Smith County sheriff Travis McPherson, an unlikely-looking rural Texas peace officer in his business suit and necktie, has vowed to use every legal and political means to put TRLA out of business. "When you go on a man's land and stir up trouble among his hired help," McPherson says, "to me that's in bad taste."

To a man, the growers I talked with agreed with McPherson. Corn, sunflower, wheat, and cattle raiser Joe Andrews recalls a time a few years back when bad migrant housing conditions drew publicity on national television, bringing a group of airmen from a nearby Air Force base with a truckload of canned food and children's toys. "What they didn't realize," he told me and a tableful of nodding companions, "is that those poor migrants made more money than they did. There wasn't a family out there bringing in less than a thousand dollars a month." Food stamps, he alleges, could increase that income to $20,000 a year, which leads him and others to believe that if migrant workers dwell in hovels, that is how they prefer to live.

The view is, of course, quite different from the other side of the fence. I accompanied three paralegals from the TRLA office to the Lamb County hamlet of Earth on a routine visit to clients. There two women, permanent residents of the area who depend upon seasonal farmwork for much of their income, told us of being blackballed from employment after they signed a complaint alleging that they were not being paid minimum wage. Sitting in their starkly furnished frame home, I heard stories of employers who expected workers to kneel clipping and sacking onions for several hours at a time in 100-degree heat, who did not provide drinking water or toilet facilities, and who routinely docked pay, even at the $1.85-an-hour rate, for such infractions as pausing to sharpen tools. The employers answered all complaints by threatening to hire illegal immigrants for even less.

"In such a climate," Bill Beardall says, "it is a real act of political courage for one of our clients to say, 'I've had enough,' and sign his name to a complaint." Fully 90 per cent of TRLA's caseload consists of routine agricultural employment complaints, most involving the minimum wage. The standard procedure is to send the employer a letter informing him of the complaint and offering to meet and resolve the situation. Most of the time, the lawyers say, landowners either ignore the letters or respond with angry defiance.

The TRLA lawyers have come to respect their opponents more than they would have anticipated. "You don't have to spend a lot of time fooling around behind legal smoke screens to find out what's at issue," says Beardall. "People here will stand up and go to the wall with you on a matter of principle, even when they don't expect to win. That makes my job much more difficult, but I can't help but admire it."

S. T. Rendón—in his coveralls and straw hat the oddest and most engaging professional consultant I have ever met by a considerable distance—also warned me not to go away with the wrong impression. Rendón, a former migrant worker who says he grew up in the back of a truck, is working up a congressionally mandated study of farmworker housing. He claims that before TRLA came to the Panhandle, no local lawyer would have dreamed of taking a case involving migrant tenant rights. It wouldn't pay and it would scare away other business. "But I don't want you to think these growers are all racists and fools," he said. "This kind of change can't come without friction."

Even the other 10 per cent of TRLA's cases would be considered routine in much of the rest of the country, which is one reason the young attorneys have lost few of the lawsuits they have brought to trial. It required no sophisticated legal expertise for TRLA to halt the Castro County Housing Authority's practice of arbitrarily evicting migrant workers—some tenants told stories of being kicked out at gunpoint because they changed from one employer to another and of having their belongings hosed down because they preferred not to work for certain employers. In another pending case TRLA alleges that Plains Memorial Hospital in Dimmitt violated the Hill-Burton Act—which specifies that hospitals that accept federal funds cannot turn away indigent patients—when it refused to admit a sick child whose Mexican American parents could not come up with a $225 deposit. The child died.

One reason Sheriff McPherson may have such a grudge against TRLA is a suit they have brought on behalf of Pedro Cervantes, who was stopped by DPS officers who suspected he was an illegal immigrant. He was kept three days in the Deaf Smith County jail without being charged because he could not produce a birth certificate on the spot. Once the Border Patrol finally arrived, Cervantes was released. The mere fact of brown skin should not require that a person carry identification papers that an Anglo does not have to have.

When cases like those come walking in the door, it is difficult to sustain the illusion of a happy, robust peasantry that was doing fine until the outside agitators arrived, and just as hard for the agitators to leave, even for the rather large financial rewards a Harvard law degree can command. Maybe the best way for the local authorities to get rid of TRLA, or at least to quiet the lawyers down, would be to clean up their own act.

The Strong Arm of the Law

San Antonio DA Sam Millsap is battling criminals, judges, and everybody else.

It's 10:55 a.m. one August day in San Antonio, and Sam D. Millsap, Jr., Bexar County's tough-talking rookie district attorney, is huddled in his wood-paneled office with one of his assistants. The two men, dressed in prosecutorial dark suits, are plotting strategy against a local judge who has been defying Millsap's well-publicized campaign to throw drunk drivers in the slammer. Millsap took office in January pledging jail sentences for even first-time DWI offenders, but the judge has continued to let them walk away with probation. "The judge knows absolutely nothing about the law," says the assistant DA, pleading for transfer to another courtroom. "What he knows about the law he has learned from defense attorneys." The assistant casts harsher aspersions on the judge's good name before Millsap decides on a plan of action. Millsap instructs the assistant prosecutor to begin combing the judge's rulings for legal errors that are serious enough to allow Millsap to seek embarrassing reprimands from a higher court or perhaps even a judicial misconduct charge. "I took [the judge] on in private, and I took him on in the press," says Millsap. If the assistant can come up with the goods on the judge, says Millsap, "we'll go to the mat with him." The assistant DA is pleased with his boss's support. "I've understood since you first took office what it is to be in a truly political atmosphere," he says. "Obviously, you know what you're doing in the political arena. We should all take notes."

Meet Sam Millsap, at 36 the youngest, brashest big-city DA in the nation. In nine months Millsap has warred with judges, juries, state legislators, the local sheriff, county commissioners, the county hospital district—and, oh, yes, assorted criminals. Millsap's blustery rhetoric and confrontational style, combined with a handful of dramatic cases, have made him the Texas criminal justice system's hottest item. Political gossip even has him on the list of potential successors to embattled Texas attorney general Jim Mattox, should he resign (though a private feud between

Millsap and Governor Mark White makes such an appointment unlikely). Not bad for a man who has never tried a criminal case. Says Millsap: "The excitement in August of 1983 as far as district attorneys are concerned is in San Antonio."

Excitement there is. In a city where politicians thrive on controversy, Millsap has remained popular by generating plenty of it. But will the system of justice in Bexar County pay a price? Even some of Millsap's political allies are wondering. "I'm concerned about some of the rabble-rousing," says criminal lawyer Gerry Goldstein, a member of Millsap's campaign steering committee and general counsel for the Texas Civil Liberties Union. "Pounding on judges and juries serves no end but making a fair trial in our community a difficult thing."

A local magazine profile of Sam Millsap used the word "mean" thirteen times, but it is not a word that comes to mind when one meets him. Blond-haired, with a boyish face and a toothy smile, he looks more like an overgrown Eagle Scout than the sort to inspire fear. Millsap, who grew up in San Antonio and went to the University of Texas law school, says he has known since childhood that he would run for office. Years later, bored with private civil practice in San Antonio, he decided that the job of district attorney was the one he had been "born and bred for."

His May 1982 Democratic primary defeat of incumbent Bill White was nothing short of a political mugging. Millsap, knowing White was more accustomed to argument in the courtroom than in the media, shrewdly went on the attack. He produced statistics suggesting that White was letting violent criminals and drunk drivers off easy, and he pledged to cut back sharply on plea bargaining. In 1978, when one of White's deputies discovered a few kids tearing down one of his campaign posters, White issued an order authorizing law enforcement officers to gun down anyone committing such a dastardly crime; in 1982 Millsap used the incident

to dub him "Shoot-to-Kill Bill." "My goal was to keep jabbing at him to the point that he would take a swing at me in public," says Millsap. That didn't happen, but White did stage a last-minute round of massage-parlor raids that made him look foolish and desperate. Millsap, attracting a peculiar coalition of reformers and hard-line conservatives, took 61 per cent of the primary vote and faced no Republican general-election opposition.

Unwilling to let White remain in power any longer than necessary, Millsap threatened to throw the incumbent out the window if he found him in the DA's courthouse office after midnight on New Year's Eve. Millsap and his chief deputies were sworn in at 12:01 a.m. That morning, boxer Tony Ayala, Jr., a San Antonio native, was arrested in New Jersey on sexual assault charges. Millsap wasted no time in blaming White for the attack, noting that Ayala had been allowed to remain free on probation despite two similar brushes with the law in Bexar County. "If I had been DA, Tony Ayala would never have committed the crime . . . because he would have been jailed back in 1980," Millsap told reporters. A month later, an investigation into mysterious baby deaths at Medical Center Hospital (see "The Death Shift," TM, August 1983) put Millsap on front pages across the country. And when he learned that Bexar County sheriff Joe Neaves allowed off-duty volunteer reserve officers to carry weapons, Millsap vowed to stop the practice, complaining that the officers were "armed to the teeth."

Unlike most DAs, who limit their public comment to cases before their office, Millsap views his position as a sort of bully pulpit—a platform to create issues by speaking his mind. "I like for things to go my way," he explains. "I want to be one of the people defining the debate."

To do that requires a mastery of public relations rather than of the law, and Millsap, who sets aside an hour every day for reporters, has learned to orchestrate the randy San Antonio papers like a maestro. In fact, the day I spent with him offered a continuous display of local media politics, beginning with his strategy session against the judge, running through an extended press conference (even though nothing of great importance was going on), and culminating in a meeting with Houston H. Harte, the chairman of Harte-Hanks Communications. The highlight seemed to be a midafternoon phone chat with acerbic local columnist Paul Thompson of the *San Antonio News*.

Thompson wanted to talk to Millsap about the judge who has been putting DWI offenders on probation. "It's obvious to me that the people of Bexar County want to see drunk drivers off the roads," said Millsap. "The interesting thing is, we just don't seem to be able to get his attention. That's the thing that's really disturbing." Millsap listened briefly, then began talking again. "The only other rational explanation—and I wouldn't want this attributed to me—" he told Thompson, "is that [the judge] is as dumb as a brick." Millsap gave me a wink. "He's as dumb as a *brick*." After hanging up the phone, Millsap summoned the assistant prosecutor who works in the judge's courtroom. "Paul Thompson just called," Millsap told him. "He is on the [judge] deal. I wish you would call Thompson. Be comfortable with him. Tell him I suggested you call. Answer his questions." Finished, Millsap waved his assistant out of the room: "Go talk to him right now, because he's writing."

Criminal attorneys in San Antonio, astonished by Millsap's freewheeling attacks on judges and juries that don't rule his way, say the DA should devote more energy to winning cases and less to chasing headlines. "He tries a lot of things in the media, and he has a comment for everything," says Alan Brown, Tony Ayala's San Antonio lawyer. "He must like to see his picture in the paper and hear his name. I call it demagoguery." Lawyers view plea bargaining as the grease that keeps the creaky wheels of justice moving; many predicted that Millsap's pledge to reduce it would result in clogged court calendars and jury acquittals of many defendants who would have served at least some jail time had prosecutors been willing to cut a deal. Millsap acknowledges that the acquittal rate for the DA's office has risen—from 27 to 34 per cent—during his first six months on the job. But his statistics also show that his office has cut plea bargaining dramatically and that average sentences have soared.

You'll hear no soft-headed talk about rehabilitation from Sam Millsap; he doesn't believe it works. Millsap wants to lock criminals up and throw away the key. "I want the average sentences to be longer in Bexar County than they are in other metropolitan areas," he says. "People who commit crimes of violence and people who commit economic crimes and are repeat offenders need to be sentenced to long periods of time in the penitentiary. Period." As for nonviolent criminals: "The typical burglar or auto thief is a bum; the overwhelming majority are strung out on some kind of dope."

Millsap's friends believe that his combative style will mellow over time. "He's just feeling his oats," Goldstein says. "I think Sam will calm down and become a prosecutor rather than a political proselytizer." Millsap realizes that he needs to moderate his "tendency to seek conflict as a tool." He adds, "You don't have to pick a fight on the street every time there's been a disagreement. There are many times when that's unnecessary and many times when it's counterproductive. I don't think I've learned enough about how to distinguish between those situations." At the same time, even Millsap's critics recognize his intelligence and give him credit for cleaning house in the DA's office (more than half of White's staff has been replaced) and for raising salaries enough to attract talented prosecutors.

"There are a lot of people who believed I would fail—and fail early—as DA, that I was just a shooting star with crazy ideas that would fade out," he says. "People are beginning to accept that I'm not a shooting star. It doesn't mean they like me; they don't in a lot of cases. But I think they recognize they're going to have to deal with me."

The Last Patrón

McAllen's mayor is used to getting his own way.

Othal Brand, the strapping 61-year-old mayor of McAllen, walked swiftly from the Senate Chamber after making his final plea and headed for the water fountain. His face red, he wiped tears from his eyes and accepted the embrace of a Mexican American friend who had testified on his behalf. During the three-day hearing, Brand had emphatically denied that he had for years condoned police brutality against Mexican American prisoners in his Rio Grande Valley city. The tears were uncharacteristic of Brand, a cantankerous fellow who is inured to—indeed, who frequently invites—adversity. But he saw the handwriting on the wall: Senator Hector Uribe was going to invoke his senator's privilege of veto power over state appointees in his district to block Brand's nomination to the board of the state Department of Corrections.

Only a few weeks earlier, Brand had just barely managed to win reelection, fending off a highly organized campaign to dump him. The nationwide press coverage of videotapes of the police brutality added fuel to the already volatile race, in which each camp accused the other of racist tactics.

Made public only as a result of a string of police brutality suits filed by American Civil Liberties Union lawyer James Harrington, the tapes showed officers punching, slapping, and kicking prisoners. Most of the abuse was dealt out by the department's tough night shift, a group of officers who, when off duty, wore T-shirts emblazoned with the legend "C-Shift Animals." The police officers were caught on film by a camera posted above the booking desk, placed there in 1973 to protect officers from unfounded charges of police brutality. During a federal court hearing that began on March 24, Harrington entered as evidence tapes showing eleven incidences of brutality. A few days later, local television stations aired some of the shocking footage, and hordes of journalists descended on McAllen.

Almost as shocking was testimony in the same trial that Mayor Othal Brand had known about the police brutality for years. Brand denied it, but that didn't take the political heat off. The election was less than two weeks away and his opponent was exploiting the issue to the hilt.

This was not the first time Othal Brand has been entangled in controversy, and it won't be the last. Long before the infamous tapes made headlines, Brand's controversial political style itself—his penchant for confrontation, for twisting arms, for name-calling—was the issue. Even his political allies are uncomfortable with his long history of embarrassing imbroglios.

Othal Brand could have stepped out of the pages of a Horatio Alger novel. He built a multimillion-dollar agricultural empire from scratch, starting out as a teenager in his native Georgia, where he bought up produce from farmers and hauled it to market, where he sold it at a profit. Then he cast his eye westward, toward Texas' tropical Rio Grande Valley, the "Magic Valley" where crops flourish year-round. He scoured the countryside, buying up dozens of acres here and there. In 1953, after more than ten years of shuttling back and forth between Georgia and the Valley, Brand moved to Texas permanently and built an agricultural empire that now spans the globe. He owns 40,000 acres in Texas, Colorado, Idaho, and California. No matter the time of year, the conveyor belts at Brand's huge McAllen packing plant are laden with onions, cabbage, cantaloupes, bell peppers, or strawberries.

In 1960 Brand won the first of his three terms on the McAllen school board. His tenure was marked by temper tantrums when members didn't go along with him. In fact, once Brand became so angry at a board member who voted against a pet project that he struck the man.

He won a seat on the city commission in 1973, and in 1977 he beat the establishment candidate and became mayor. Brand is a take-charge mayor. He continually interferes in the affairs of his department heads and calls them on the carpet at public meetings for not following his instructions. He questions engineers' figures and lawyers' advice. During his reelection campaign, he bragged at a Rotary Club gathering about stifling a recent round of police promotions initiated by police chief Roy Eckhardt. He has always believed city hall should be run like a business, and as mayor, he acts as its chief executive officer.

Brand's other public skirmishes have been fought in his fields, where farmworkers have worked feverishly to organize a union. During the 1975 wildcat strike by melon workers, a television crew filmed Brand as he jumped out of his pickup truck waving a pistol at strikers on his land. Throughout the years, there has been a lot of bad blood—and lawsuits—between Brand and the farmworker organizers. He is perhaps their most formidable obstacle. When the Texas Farm Workers struck the fields of Charles Wetegrove, the largest onion grower in Raymondville, in 1979, Brand marched in with his own workers and harvested his part of the crop, crippling the strike.

But it wasn't until last year that Brand's political hegemony was seriously challenged. Brand and the McAllen city commission tried to sell the aging municipal hospital to the private Hospital Corporation of America, and that turned out to be his big mistake. When doctors Ramiro Casso and Lauro Guerra discovered the plan, they rushed to court to stop it because, they argued, a profit-making corporation wouldn't be interested in caring for the area's large indigent population. The commission countered by calling a referendum. It was a smart move—in the history of McAllen city politics, the Anglos had never lost an election. Though the city is 70 per cent Mexican American, many Mexican Americans don't vote. But this time they were effectively organized, and Brand's hospital referendum failed by 118 votes. Casso and his fledgling minority coalition saw the vote as a chance for them to end Anglo domination of city hall once and for all; Casso decided to run for mayor. Many major cities in the Valley have elected Mexican American mayors, but McAllen's Anglo north side has consistently voted against anyone with a Spanish surname—even when the candidate has been anointed by their own.

Casso's people knew what they were up against; they launched a massive voter registration drive on the Mexican American south side. By election day, April 4, the numbers were clearly in their favor—60 per cent of the voters on the rolls were theirs. Brand and Casso quickly disposed of a third mayoral candidate, Commissioner Mike Frost. Casso got 5793 votes to Brand's 4924. Because of Frost's 2017 votes, there would have to be a runoff.

By then, the videotapes of the police officers had been broadcast nationwide. On Spanish-language radio, Casso called Brand a dictator and a barbarian who permitted "beatings of our sons." Brand fended off the accusations, claiming he had rushed to a grand jury upon learning of the brutality in 1980. But in federal court hearings in March, a police officer testified that he and six other officers had complained to Brand about the brutality long before that. Furthermore, police captain Jim Bormann, keeper of the tapes, testified that orders had filtered down from Brand's office to destroy the tapes. Brand says Bormann is wrong.

Brand tried to focus attention on his accomplishments as mayor. He had pushed through a massive public works project to clean up the poverty-stricken *colonias* on the south side; he was plunging ahead on airport expansion and a new international bridge; McAllen had a clean bill of financial health as the Valley's retailing center. He also called in all his political chips—over the years he has spread his money far and wide, donating thousands of dollars for scholarships for poor Mexican American students, financing construction of a Boys' Club on the south side, kicking in money to church and civic group coffers. In the classic *patrón* tradition, Brand can be quite generous to people who are loyal to him. And the indebted were called upon to support him publicly. The Reverend Carlos Cajina of the south side Mexican Christian Church Disciples of Christ posed for Brand's political ads and even posted a Brand billboard on church property.

But the Brand campaign had its nasty side, too. Just days before the runoff, he took out a full-page ad with the headline "Who Is Really Mayor Brand's Opponent?" Pictured at the top of the ad was Dr. Casso at a rally with Cesar Chavez, head of the United Farm Workers. At the meeting, the UFW had thrown its support to Casso's campaign, and Brand's ad warned that "outside" forces were going to take over the city. The north side came out in droves, with a turnout of 83 per cent. And though the south side also went to the polls in unprecedented numbers—61 per cent—Brand defeated Casso by nearly nine hundred votes.

Governor Bill Clements had earlier nominated Brand for the board of the state Department of Corrections, but he withdrew the nomination at Brand's request when the police scandal broke. After the election, though, Clements nominated Brand a second time, feeling that his friend's victory had vindicated him. But Senator Hector Uribe disagreed. As Brand's hometown representative, Uribe had been urged by Mexican Americans to invoke senatorial courtesy to block the appointment. The Senate Nominations Subcommittee set a hearing for May 20, and Brand, not one to back off from a fight, flew to Austin with two planeloads of supporters to defend himself. The hearing was pure theater; the tall, white-haired Brand vehemently denied any wrongdoing. "I'd have to be a fool to allow that to go on," he told the Senate panel, "and I'm no fool." In objecting to Brand's appointment, Uribe concluded, "The crux of this matter is not what Mayor Brand knew, but what he should have known," and he prevailed upon the Senate to deny the appointment.

Brand is already spoiling for more fights. He has fed McAllen's voter registration rolls into computers in an attempt to identify voters he says are registered in four or five precincts, as well as dead people he says were drafted by the Casso camp. Brand says he has already turned over his evidence to a grand jury investigating allegations of voter registration irregularities. His hope, of course, is to disqualify voters who rallied to the Casso cause. If he is successful, it will be bad news for the senator who busted him, Hector Uribe, who must face an election next year. Othal Brand gets mad—and he also gets even.

Mr. Rogers, Tough Guy

El Paso's mayor plays by his own rules. He also gets results.

Some people think the quintessential story about Jonathan Rogers's first year as El Paso's mayor is the time he took off his belt and swatted an elementary school student who was visiting his tenth-floor office. Others think it's an exchange that took place at a public meeting between Rogers and John Guerrero, the head of the policemen's union. After Rogers cut him off with a curt "I speak when I want to speak," Guerrero protested that Rogers wasn't following *Robert's Rules of Order.* "I follow Rogers's Rules," the mayor replied briskly.

If Rogers sounds a little obnoxious, that's probably because he is. Even his best friends agree on that. We're talking about a man who makes Bill Clements look mellow. But for the most part he's getting high marks for the job he's done as the mayor of Texas' fourth-largest city, the often forgotten mountain kingdom of El Paso. "He's so abrasive it just shakes you up sometimes," says Jack Morris, the executive director of the El Paso Chamber of Commerce. "But politicians so often make their every move according to what they think people will like, and that's not always for the best. On the administration of the city's affairs, he's been a superior mayor. There's no question about it."

Most Texans know of Houston's Kathy Whitmire, Dallas's Jack Evans, and San Antonio's Henry Cisneros, all heralded as part of a wave of hardheaded, business-oriented municipal leaders of the eighties. But the purest and perhaps the most successful example of the breed is Rogers, a 54-year-old millionaire mortgage banker who had never run for office before taking on and defeating political veteran Ray Pearson last year.

Rogers's immediate predecessor, former FBI agent Tom Westfall, was generally regarded as even more obnoxious than Rogers, though not nearly as successful. In fact, from the beginning El Paso's mayors have been a little strange. The first, Ben Dowell, elected in 1873, coincidentally or not was also the owner of El Paso's first saloon. Prematurely white-haired, he looked as though he was peering out from a snowy forest of beard and hair. When he lost his bid for reelection by a healthy 33–13 margin, he established a tradition: incumbent mayors have gotten booted out of office regularly ever since. One great moment in El Paso's mayoral history was the time Mayor C. E. "Uncle Henry" Kelly, who served from 1910 to 1915, confronted Pancho Villa in the Sheldon Hotel. Villa had his heart set on shooting Giuseppe Garibaldi, grandson of the Italian liberator and leader of a Mexican revo-lutionary group, but Kelly managed to talk him out of it and has been heralded for that feat ever since.

Rogers's achievements haven't been quite as colorful, but they may be as impressive. He inherited a projected budget deficit of about $1 million and in four months turned it into a $689,000 surplus. He published the names of delinquent taxpayers, including some of the biggest businesses in town, which helped bring in $700,000 in unexpected revenues. He hacked off a lot of people along the way, but the consensus is that his fiscal triumphs have outweighed his public relations blunders.

Rogers's most prominent feature is a set of fierce, bristling eyebrows that sweep upward, giving him the look of a cossack in businessman's garb. But what's most memorable about him is his voice. He speaks in a low, breathy murmur, his words coming out in short, compact bursts that sound as though they could be coming from the mouth of a recent Republican president who neither starred in movies nor regularly knocked his head against the doorways of airplanes.

"I'm not a politician. I'm a businessman," Rogers says in vintage Nixonian tones. "You've heard it said there's some controversy about the way I do the job. I want it done today. I don't want it done next week. Or next month." He leans back in his chair and assumes a characteristic pose, his left index finger affixed to the left side of the bridge of his nose. "I'm told I'm too abrupt and abrasive. Is that a criticism? Or is it a compliment? Because things are getting done."

Rogers grew up in Connecticut, graduated from Yale, and settled in El Paso when he married a local girl—Pat Murchison, one of *the* Murchisons—after a stint in the military. Since 1964 he has been either president or board chairman of Mortgage Investment Company. He got into last year's mayor's race late, but hefty spending and hard campaigning based on the idea that El Paso needed a tough businessman as mayor helped him to overcome Pearson's early lead.

El Paso is not the world's easiest city to run. It faces the same kinds of demands on services that afflict any rapidly growing city, exacerbated because it has grown faster than almost anyone realizes, from about 300,000 people in 1970 to about 450,000 now. Actually, even those figures are deceptive, because with approximately 1 million people just across the border in Juárez, El Paso is part of a metropolitan area of almost 1.5 million people.

Nor does the political climate make the mayor's job any easier. The term lasts for only two years, but no one has managed to win two consecutive terms since Judson Williams served from 1963 to 1969. (It's hard to figure out why he was so big on keeping the job—his second year in office was highlighted by having loads of manure dumped on his porch and in front of the mayor's office as a protest against a proposal to regulate horses and cows within the city limits.) Westfall went out in a blaze of acrimony, more or less as he had come in. His predecessor, Ray Salazar, has a $4 million slander and libel suit pending against Westfall and the *El Paso Times* as a result of the 1979 campaign. Despite his lack of tact, Rogers hasn't started any feuds of that magnitude, although he may have made an enemy for life when he vetoed the city council's approval of a heliport for flamboyant detective Jay J. Armes. "He's a man who reacts by impulse, and you mark my word, he's a one-term mayor," Armes fumes. "We've got another Hitler down there."

Rogers, to his credit, seems totally uninterested in the extracurricular scheming and feuding of political life. He appears genuinely intent on running the city with the same monomaniacal attention he gave to his mortgage banking business. He's even less the politician and more the manager than Evans, Whitmire, or Cisneros—even more prone to drone on about managerial innovations like computerizing city hall, cutting staff, or instituting creative financing through certificates of obligation. And in this era of diminished resources for local governments, perhaps he's right when he says, "I think cities are going to business-oriented people because a city is a business. Last year we had a ninety-one-million-dollar budget. You better get a professional to take care of that kind of money."

Still, even Rogers can enjoy a political lark now and again. At the end of an hour-long interview, he got a mischievous look on his face and began talking about one other triumph of his administration. "We took a tour of Edwards Air Force Base in California and pretty well convinced the papers that we were taking a tour of Hawaii—at taxpayers' expense," he said, suddenly unable to get a huge smile off his face. "It was very simple. We left Hawaiian folders on a secretary's desk and let it go at that. The stories didn't run, but they came very, very close. The papers told us they did, anyway. So what if the reporters say no one was fooled?" By that point Rogers was so delighted he couldn't talk, and he finally gave in to a thirty-second fit of the giggles.

"You've gotta have some fun," he concluded, returning to his Nixon voice. "You've gotta keep them on their toes."

Whitmired

How do you make Houston work with no money in the till?

The events of this past spring must have been the most unpleasant of surprises to Houston mayor Kathy Whitmire, who was supposed to usher in a new era of low-key, professional management at city hall. On the theatrical level, there was her headline-grabbing feud with city controller Lance Lalor, during which the mayor asked the city council to sue Lalor to get him to implement a revised budget for the city. On the political level, there was an unexpected challenge from her former fundraiser and backer Bill Wright, who has already raised half a million dollars and lined up such heavies as developer Walter Mischer to back his mayoral bid. And on the fiscal level, there was the rather dismaying realization that Houston, of all places, is facing budget problems usually associated with the Detroits and Newarks of the world.

At the heart of Whitmire's difficulties is a simple irony. She was elected to improve city services and efficiency at city hall. But her term in office has coincided with the steepest economic downturn Houston has seen since the Great Depression. How she handles that problem should go a long way toward determining whether she'll be more than a one-term mayor.

There wasn't any big secret behind Kathy Whitmire's appeal to Houston voters. When she was elected Houston's forty-seventh mayor, in November 1981, it wasn't because she was an inspiring speaker or a charismatic politician or an overfunded creature of the downtown business interests. Rather, she was a hardworking, sober-thinking CPA who pledged to make Houston work, and people had begun to notice that it didn't. In many ways Kathy Whitmire was cut from the same cloth as Jimmy Carter, and her underlying campaign theme—a Carter-like insistence that she was a professional who would do a professional job as mayor—held great sway with Houstonians; she looked mighty appealing next to her good-ol'-boy opponents, incumbent Jim McConn and Sheriff Jack Heard.

During the seventies Houston clearly grew faster than its ability to provide services, but it hit an economic stone wall because of the oil glut—at just about the time Whitmire took office. Whitmire, essentially playing out her campaign promises, began presiding over an ambitious expansion of city government. Even as Houston's economy was deteriorating, in 1982 city hall hired 4052 new employees. This increased the city's work force by nearly 925 people, most of them policemen and fire fighters, and nearly doubled the increase of 1981. The result of these intersecting curves—economic downturn and bureaucratic upswing—was a series of fiscal revisions that saw the city's annual budget drop from $671 million to $636 million and made city hall a battleground for much of the year. "The administration was new and very anxious to deliver on promises of better-managed city services, and as a result I think they had blinders on," says Lalor, a likely mayoral candidate in the future. "They saw the world through rose-colored glasses because they were focusing exclusively on the internal needs of the city and didn't look outside to see what was happening. It's been a very disruptive year. No one has known what they were doing."

Whitmire can point to some real successes: a 15 per cent increase in the number of police on the street, a continuation of the large-scale street resurfacing begun under McConn, three new libraries, and a doubling of park area when the Army Corps of Engineers let the city take over the 10,500-acre Cullen Park, on the west side. And Whitmire says she has instituted management changes that should allow the city to operate more efficiently in the years to come. "We've been putting into effect the kind of budget and planning processes I think will be effective over the long term," she says. "At the very least, we're far better prepared to deal with the management of the city than we were two years ago."

But talking about progress and getting people to believe it are two different things. Whitmire says that since 1981 the on-time ratio for the Metropolitan Transit Authority's buses has jumped from 47 per cent to 90 per cent. But judging from the Letters to the Editor columns in the newspapers and the shaky status of the proposed rail plan, it hardly seems as if there's a sudden perception of the MTA as a paragon of mass-transit. Similarly, the city may be resurfacing 430 miles of streets a year, but its people are probably more aware of a recent Channel 11 series showing city employees working four-day weeks, snoozing on the job, and driving aimlessly around town in city vehicles.

With no immediate upturn in the oil business in sight, Houston will face at least another year of extremely tight budgets. Most program cuts were reduced this year by deferring equipment purchases and maintenance and by using federal revenue-sharing funds for general operating expenses. But the purchases can't be put off indefinitely, and the federal government is scheduled to cut out revenue sharing in September. Congress could still decide to restore it; if not, that's $24 million the city can ill afford to lose. The long-term outlook is equally troubling. Houston ranks second only to New York in public debt per capita. That means 18 per cent of the city's expenditures must go to debt retirement, which is not the most desirable use of city funds in tough times.

Only months ago a serious mayoral challenge to Whitmire seemed unlikely, but Wright's campaign has picked up a lot of momentum. It's being taken seriously, if only because of the size of the war chest Wright has been able to accumulate in the early days of his campaign. Wright's challenge is a reminder of how evanescent politics can be. Whitmire's 1981 posture of the low-key CPA bringing order to the runaway locomotive of Houston development seems already dated. And besides blasting her for her handling of the city budget, Wright is faulting her for lacking an overall vision of the city and for not being interested in a Henry Cisneros–like recruiting effort to lure high-tech firms to Houston. She says that's the job of the chamber of commerce.

Still, Whitmire hasn't given her opponents a great number of issues to hound her with. The budget chaos has been one, and some of her stands—like supporting disannexation of Clear Lake, an almost blasphemous step back from Houston's manifest destiny of growth—have worried some of her business supporters. But her biggest problem is one of personality. Whitmire likes to deal with her small, closely knit group of aides but doesn't seem comfortable with many others, and she has alienated some supporters by being inaccessible. "She doesn't listen to people," says Wright. "She has an arrogant way of running the city. If you ask around, almost everyone will tell you the same thing."

The appearance of being inaccessible and closed-minded is indeed an obstacle, especially for someone who came in with as tenuous a political base as Whitmire's. But if Wright has been able to take a few good shots at her, it will still take some doing to show why Houston should boot Whitmire out of office when she's had only two years to deal with issues that developed over decades. Except for Mischer and a few others, the business leadership is behind her. She may not be the world's most colorful mayor, but no one seems to doubt that she's an honest and hardworking one, not to mention a welcome change from the good ol' boys of the past. Despite her shortcomings, most political watchers expect her to win a second term.

Houston's biggest worry, though, remains the delivery of city services. Some departments, notably parks, are nervous about the possibility of layoffs next year. The maintenance and delayed purchases can be deferred only so long. And departments that in recent years have budgeted for anticipated growth will be in for a shock if the city's revenue picture stays tight for longer than one more year. To cite one small example, Houston has a new library set to open and three others on the way. The library department will be hard put to open them on a budget about the size of or smaller than last year's. That's a typical dilemma. Whitmire's brave talk notwithstanding, it takes a magician rather than a manager to do more with less.

MAYOR *of the* UNFINISHED CITY

Can Dallas keep booming forever? Yes, but now there's a price to pay — and Starke Taylor has to decide if it's worth it.
by Jim Atkinson

"THIS THING'LL ALMOST JUMP OUT FROM UNDER YOU," says Mayor A. Starke Taylor, Jr., of his BMW 745i Turbo. "Watch this." The mayor jams down on the accelerator, and the car leaps ahead of the rest of the traffic on crowded Belt Line Road. "See what I mean?" I nod nervously. Dallas mayors have always made me uneasy for a variety of reasons, but I never thought I'd be white-knuckling it down Belt Line because of Hizzoner's hot-rodding. ¶ Outwardly, A. Starke Taylor, Jr., looks like what you would get if you called central casting and asked for a Dallas mayor. He is silver-haired, tennis-court tanned, and trim; a self-made millionaire; a free-enterprise, good-for-Dallas kind of guy. ¶ But the new mayor is full of surprises. Despite ties to the city's wealthiest developers, he ran his campaign this past spring on the platform of planned growth, a phrase that usually makes developers do a Danny Thomas with their martinis. He claimed he didn't really want the job but then spent almost a million dollars acquiring it. He lives in far North Dallas, that enclave of new wealth, yet he based much of his campaign on revitalizing southern Dallas County. He's the shy, retiring type, but barely a few weeks into his tenure he silenced a bickering fellow council member sternly: "I *am* the mayor, and I *am* running this council. Do you understand?" Besides all that, he once prayed the night before a Dallas Park and Recreation Board meeting that his fellow board members would make the right decision. ¶ Those and other matters are why I am headed for the Oak Cliff Country Club to lunch on Salisbury steak and watch the new mayor stump for the upcoming rapid transit referendum. I am curious about what other surprises the mayor may have in store. Lately Dallas has had more than its share of them—mostly bad ones. ¶ I'll let you in on a dirty little secret: Dallas likes to think of itself as the City That Works, but it hasn't been working very well lately, and no one seems to want to admit it. The chamber of commerce still peddles the fiction that Dallas, the Time-of-Your-Life City, has largely escaped urban malaise, but one has only to drive the length of the city to see that urban malaise is exactly what is plaguing Dallas. Major freeways and roads are choked; the major effort to remedy the situation has been the completion of the Woodall Rodgers Freeway, which state highway experts and local police officers immediately criticized as being inadequate and hazardous. Lax zoning and blind development have created an office glut downtown, more traffic problems in far North Dallas, and commercial encroachment into the city's older residential neighborhoods. Inadequate solid-waste treatment facilities are polluting seven of the city's nine sources of water. Even after months of laborious examination of cable television services, the franchise awarded Warner Amex has become an embarrassment; at last report, installations and repairs were behind schedule, and the company had extended service to only 20 per cent of the potential users. Although numerous and expensive attempts have been made to enliven the inner city, downtown Dallas still rolls up its sidewalks at 6 p.m. sharp. Over the past decade, crime has increased, but the police force remains understaffed. Parts of Dallas are in abject poverty. The city's high schools are still troubled by below-average test scores. West Dallas is threatened by hazardous levels of lead pollution in the air. And the city staff recently announced glumly that despite huge jumps in the appraised values of commercial and residential property, Dallas will probably face its third consecutive tax rate increase next year. The list goes on and on.

In the face of all this, Starke Taylor is certainly saying the right things. As we speed down the Dallas North Tollway, the conversation shifts from fast cars to the future of the city. Taylor says he is for planned growth and stricter zoning laws; he is for revitalizing the simmering ghettos in South Dallas and West Dallas; he is for mass transit to unclog the freeways; he is for making Dallas not only more prosperous but also more livable.

What Taylor intends to *do* is another matter. Just as Dallas' problems have changed, so has the nature of the city. Unlike any other Dallas mayor, Starke Taylor has not been presented a nice, tidy, homogeneous city whose people have common goals and a willingness to be governed by a quiet and nonpolitical board. He presides instead over a city that is split between inner-city and outer-city interests and, more than that, between residents who want a stable, predictable city and those who prefer to live in a perpetual boom town. Taylor is an important figure in the passage from a downtown power center to a northern-suburb power center, from leadership by bankers to leadership by developers, and from a white-collar mentality to an open-collar mentality. But more than anything else, Starke Taylor sits on the cusp of Dallas' transformation from a simple, easily governed place to a complex, political city. That means that he has to be not only a leader but a politician—whether he likes it or not.

Later in the day, as the mayor finishes a lackluster speech on the transit referendum, he hints at the answer. "There's a writer following me around today," the mayor informs the

"Taylor is an important figure in the passage from a downtown power center to a northern-suburb power center, from leadership by bankers to leadership by developers, and from a white-collar mentality to an open-collar mentality. He sits on the cusp of Dallas' transformation from a simple, easily governed place to a complex, political city."

crowd. "And I'll tell you the same thing I told him. I'm going to do what's right, and I'm not going to be political. If people don't like what I do, then they can get rid of me and get another mayor. That's really the way I feel about it."

"STARKE TAYLOR IS EITHER THE most devious or the most naive politician I've ever seen," a well-wired North Dallas Republican told me one day. "He's a complete mystery." It's true. When Taylor ascended the podium at the Hyatt Regency on election night, a decided winner over former mayor Wes Wise, the scene had the aura of an encounter with an alien. Who *was* this guy and who sent him to us?

The bewilderment was understandable. Taylor was a businessman, all right, but he was a new and different sort of businessman, from a new and different business power base. He had made his money in cotton, not banking or insurance, and unlike the mayors produced by the old downtown business establishment, he hadn't "run the chairs" of civic service before ascending to the city's highest post. The United Fund, the Civic Opera, the Fair Park Board—the traditional steps on the ladder to the mayoralty—are not to be found on Taylor's résumé. Except for a stint as president of the Park and Recreation Board from 1979 to 1982, he was an outsider to the infrastructure of civic power. Most significant, he came from far North Dallas, from that awesome new city that has grown up north of the LBJ Freeway during the past ten years. The endless rows of glittering glass office towers, the fancy highrise hotels, the huge, garish mansions of Bent Tree in this new Dallas, are ominous and foreign turf to the rest of the city. And the establishment that built them, that profits from them, is not that of Highland Park. Starke Taylor hadn't merely won out over an opponent who was much better known; he had cemented the first real shift of power in Dallas since the Dallas Citizens Council took control of city hall in the late thirties.

Rumblings of that shift began seven years ago with the candidacy of developer Robert Folsom, also from far North Dallas. The downtown establishment—the heads of the major banks, insurance companies, and utilities—was in disarray following the five-year tenure of Wes Wise, the former sportscaster who had wrested the mayoralty away from the downtown crowd in 1971. Half a decade of Wise's finger-to-the-wind polemics and, more to the point, his flaunting of the old ways had left the old boys desperate to recapture city hall.

Though Wise's tenure represented more a symbolic loss of establishment power than an actual one, the old boys felt left out and cut off. Wise had never done anything overtly to hurt their interests, but he hadn't really done anything to help them either. They felt that the city was stagnating, that the boom might end if the business community didn't put a forceful representative back in the mayor's chair.

For the first time in the establishment's history, however, there was a split in the ranks. Many of the older downtown businessmen wanted R. L. Thornton, Jr., son of the city's most famous establishment mayor, to run. A younger group

—in particular, Republicans John Leedom and L. E. Guilliot—thought Thornton would lose because of his obvious ties to old power. Leedom and Guilliot suggested as an alternative candidate Bob Folsom, a former school board president and wealthy far North Dallas developer. Like Taylor, Folsom wore few of the traditional civic badges; indeed, he seemed to have spent most of his adult life at the simple business of making money. But he was young and vigorous and available. The old boys relented, some with great reluctance, and a transfer of power took place.

One of Folsom's aides in the campaign—his campaign manager, in fact—was Starke Taylor, his tennis buddy and real estate partner. The ensuing campaign against Garry Weber, a populist in the Wes Wise mold, was the longest and bloodiest in Dallas mayoral history. Eschewing the low-key, almost invisible approach of previous business-backed candidates, Folsom and Taylor got down in the trenches. Eyebrows were raised and fingers pointed —mainly at Taylor—after fliers asserting that a Weber victory would hand the city over to the black community turned up at North Dallas doorsteps during the final weeks of the campaign.

Though both Taylor and Folsom have denied that they had anything to do with the flier, they cannot deny that it was North Dallas that eventually gave Folsom a scant thousand-vote margin of victory. Although Weber had managed to patch together an admirable coalition of minority and other inner-city voting blocs, the Folsom election firmly established the preeminence of populous, heavily Republican North Dallas. That wasn't lost on developer John Stemmons and the rest of the older downtown bunch, for not only had civic power generally been controlled by downtown corporate executives but those corporate executives had also usually been Democrats—conservative Texas Democrats, but still Democrats. Now they had a businessman back in the mayor's seat, but he was a developer and a Republican.

No one could miss the difference in style. Downtown boys R. L. Thornton, mayor from 1953 to 1961, and Erik Jonsson, mayor from 1964 to 1971, had been genteel and aristocratic. They were seldom seen or heard from, and they rarely deigned to dirty their hands with anything smacking of politics. Thornton was a banker, so he worked to establish the city as a white-collar commercial center on the plains. Jonsson, a founder of Texas Instruments, was a technocrat, and he busied himself with projects like the DFW Regional Airport. If there was a shared charge among the old boys, it was to keep Dallas a safe place for business, a city unaffected by the racial and economic problems that were changing other cities.

But those men were board chairmen, men used to leading in the abstract. As a developer, Robert Folsom brought a rougher, more direct, and more urgent style to the mayor's office. Folsom had made millions spotting openings, seizing opportunities, and beating the other guy to the punch, and he ran the city in much the same way. When he wanted a downtown sports arena, he didn't want to bother with long-

"The aggressiveness of the developers during the Folsom years spawned an organized, middle-class, white opposition to the policies of city hall. In older neighborhoods like East Dallas and Oak Lawn, young couples who had sought stable neighborhoods began to organize. The neighborhood groups were not to be politely ignored."

term studies and public referenda; he railroaded it through. His predecessors' vision of the city had been limited, but it had been a vision of a finished place. Bob Folsom never entertained any notion that Dallas would—or should —one day be a finished place. He governed by the developers' credo that he could always do just one more deal. The dirt literally began to fly. During Folsom's tenure about 47 million square feet of office space, $214 million worth of hotel space, and $178 million worth of retail space were slapped up in the city, and countless other buildings were planned, zoned, and approved.

Most of that growth was in the far North Dallas area, Folsom's home turf. Far North Dallas is a mass of land mostly north of the LBJ Freeway, about ten miles from the city's central business district. The area includes the tiny incorporation of Addison and parts of somewhat larger suburban cities, such as Farmers Branch, Carrollton, and Plano, and it even spills over county boundaries. In 1971 the area was bleak, idle farmland, acres and acres of North Texas black dirt waiting for developers to discover it. They did. That year there were a pitiful 1.4 million square feet of office space in far North Dallas; by 1980, the year before Folsom left office, the square footage was 7 million, and more important, city projections showed that by the year 2000 there would be twice that, a full 16 per cent of the office space in Dallas. It was also predicted that the central business district's share of office space would meanwhile decline substantially. Shopping centers cropped up like dandelions in far North Dallas. Retail growth is still so rapid there that even conservative city planners estimate that by the year 2000 the area will contain 43 per cent as much retail space as existed in the entire city in 1980.

Far North Dallas was too rapidly becoming a commercial center, a new downtown with a sense of itself wholly different from that of its predecessor to the south. The sensibility that prevailed there was one that valued shiny office towers and new tract homes, freeways and wide boulevards, and constant reminders of change and growth.

The aggressiveness of developers during the Folsom years spawned an organized, middle-class, white opposition to the policies of city hall. In older neighborhoods like East Dallas and Oak Lawn, young couples who had sought stable neighborhoods began to organize groups that opposed the pro-developer bias at city hall. These Dallasites preferred peaceful tree-lined streets and refurbished turn-of-the-century cottages, and they wanted to live in a diverse but settled place. They wanted things to stay the way they were.

The neighborhood groups were not to be politely ignored, as the occasional eccentric demagogue at the weekly city council meeting had been ignored when he took his three minutes at the mike. These folks knew how to fight. Even in their fledgling days, neighborhood groups were able single-handedly to defeat proposals such as a transit line along the Katy right-of-way and the double-decking of Central Expressway. That may sound like small potatoes to people accustomed to organized opposition and special-interest groups, but even as late as the seventies Dallas had few such political organisms with any power.

The neighborhood movement changed the political topography of the city. As other cities fractured along racial and economic lines, Dallas split between old-city and boom-town camps. The tension between the two groups has always been subtle, but it is growing stronger. Bob Folsom left the office in 1981 somewhat weary of its controversies. He'd governed the city in the best way, the only way, he knew how: by building. It was difficult for him to understand that his notion of progress was viewed by others as not only unprogressive but also destructive. His decision not to run again was more a resignation than a retirement.

WITH FOLSOM'S CAMPAIGN CHAIRMANSHIP and his stint on the Park and Recreation Board under his belt, Starke Taylor was approached to run as Folsom's successor. He rejected the offer. He had recently sold his cotton firm and was looking forward to semi-retirement in the more relaxed role of an investor. Personal tragedy had savaged his family during the previous year; his daughter had committed suicide, and his stepson had died in an auto accident.

Starke Taylor insists he didn't have the political bug anyway. Though his father had been mayor of Highland Park and a founder of the Dallas Country Club, Taylor was satisfied with having transformed his father's small cotton firm into one of the largest firms on the Dallas exchange. He'd joined his father in the business in 1946, after college at Rice and service in the Navy. At the time, they ran a four-man operation that dealt exclusively in the domestic cotton market. Capital was tight, and Taylor Senior, in his late fifties, was not inclined to expand.

Despite the size of the firm, Taylor's dad had been one of the better-known traders on the small exchange. He was an outspoken, stubborn, hot-tempered character, known for asking strangers to leave the floor if they didn't look right to him. He is remembered to this day for his relentless campaign to keep another firm, H. Molsen & Company, off the exchange because he feared that the German immigrant Molsen was a Nazi sympathizer.

Taylor Junior inherited most of the firm's traveling responsibilities when he joined it. He reestablished ties with textile mills in the Southeast United States and explored new export possibilities in Europe, where trade was just beginning to reopen. It was during the sessions with textile-mill managers and cotton farmers that he developed his easy and affable manner that distinguishes him from most previous Dallas mayors. Unlike the businesses that shaped those leaders, the cotton business is informal, performed via handshakes and hurried phone calls. Even today the cotton exchange building where

Starke Taylor cut his teeth as a businessman has a rural, short-sleeved sort of atmosphere, and strangers still say "hidy" in the hall.

When his father retired in 1962, Taylor Junior began an extensive expansion program. He spread the firm's name more widely throughout Europe and the rapidly growing Asiatic markets. The firm's capital and line of credit grew as it continued buying, warehousing, and then selling all its own cotton. In the early seventies it really took off. Taylor had long felt that cotton prices would shoot up as a result of inflation and the oil embargo (which would make synthetic fibers more expensive). He had been steadily stockpiling cotton and when the markets shot up, he was sitting on a gold mine. The firm became one of the largest in the Southwest.

By the late seventies, though, Taylor had wearied of the business. The magic of futures speculation had worn off, he was tired of the travel, and neither of his sons wanted to take over. Because of its tremendous success in the early seventies, the firm was an attractive acquisition to the huge conglomerates that were beginning to dominate the business. In 1980 Taylor sold the business to the Swiss firm Volkart Brothers.

He moved on to investing in real estate —mostly with his old friend Bob Folsom —but he still keeps up with cotton futures, and that rough-and-tumble, loose-and-easy cotton business continues to influence his personality. Not long after his election, Taylor was dubbed His Bubbaship by a *Dallas Times Herald* columnist. The nickname fits like a glove. He's free with slaps on the back and slouches comfortably in his chair when being interviewed. He is almost self-consciously inarticulate in that charming, self-effacing country-boy way and is given to interrupting a sober exchange with questions like, "Do you like your work?" But he never lets you forget he's in command.

There is another side to him too. Starke Taylor doesn't like to look back. If there is a consistent thread in his views of business, of life, of government, it is that you take your best shot and see if it works; if you go bust, tomorrow's another day. It's an attitude that made him a millionaire several times over, and it will be interesting to see how it manifests itself in politics. Good leadership requires guts and a willingness to take risks. But if a politician's view is "if they don't like what I do, they can go and get another mayor," it's clear that communicating with the citizenry is low on his priority list.

AFTER TAYLOR TURNED THEM DOWN IN 1981, the new boys looked to Jack Evans, head of Cullum Companies, which owns Tom Thumb/Page, the grocery and drugstore chain. Evans, another far North Dallas resident, was a shy, almost bookish sort who had earned his way into the inner circle as chief executive officer of the

company owned by longtime Dallas civic powers Robert and Charles Cullum. Evans hardly had the vitality and commitment of a Folsom, but as a custodian of the new boys' interests he would do just fine. He too was reluctant to take the candidacy. A few years earlier, he had been the victim of a corporate kidnapping, and as late as 1979 he'd told friends he would never accept a public post for fear of endangering himself and his family again. But after considerable persuasion by Folsom and the rest of the boys, he finally gave in.

Evans' style as mayor was the opposite of Folsom's, and that came to grate on a number of the new boys. Evans saw his mission as one of ameliorating festering conflicts between special interests, of mediating—or at least glossing over—the growing animosity between folks who lived in the inner city and those in the outer city. His philosophy was simple: be nice. The effect, though, was only to make the neighborhood groups and other special interests that much more aggressive. Sensing weakness at city hall, they became more vocal at zoning hearings and city council meetings. When Evans announced in late 1982 that he would not run again—like Folsom, he had grown tired of the job—most of his former supporters were surprised, but more than a few of them admitted privately that they were relieved.

This new business establishment realized that it would lose control if it didn't come up with a more forceful personality at city hall. Besides that, the dreaded Wes Wise was once again nipping at their heels. They considered him to be a politician of more flash than substance, a big talker who rarely followed up, a man who seemed to be interested in only the ceremonial aspects of the office. After losing a run for Congress in 1976, Wise had lain low for a few years, then run for and captured an at-large council seat in 1981. Wes Wise, the curse of the business community, the uppity independent who had so badly embarrassed the old boys in 1971, was planning to do the same thing to the new boys a decade later. And this time the stakes were much higher.

It was Jack Evans who first approached Starke Taylor again. A week later, Folsom had dinner with Taylor. It was Folsom, the most powerful personality in the city during the past decade, who persuaded Taylor to accept the mantle: It's no fun, he said, but thinking back on it, I'm not sorry a bit I did it. Besides, there's no one else. We need you.

That was the kind of pitch Taylor had trouble turning down. He decided to run for mayor, as he would somewhat self-consciously joke later, to "one-up my dad." The transfer of power was complete. The old boys hadn't even been consulted on this one.

THE OFFICES OF JOHN WEEKLEY AND ENID Gray are a modest little affair on Mc-

Kinney Avenue in Oak Lawn, the sort of place where one might expect to find an artisan's studio. It certainly doesn't look like the center of political power in Dallas. But the political consulting firm that eventually won Starke Taylor the mayoralty is just that. Weekley and Gray were longtime Republicans; Gray had come out of the steel-trap North Dallas Republican organizations. The two had recently been involved in Clements' first campaign for the governor's office and had directed the successful runs of Sheriff Don Byrd, Congressman Steve Bartlett, and a host of other Republican candidates for lesser offices.

Media consultant Judy Bonner Amps, who teamed up with Weekley and Gray in Taylor's campaign, had worked the other side of the fence but with no less success. Beginning with Democratic state senator Oscar Mauzy, Amps had nurtured and managed the political campaigns and, to some extent, the careers of a number of prominent Democrats, including Congressman Martin Frost, former city councilman and county judge Garry Weber, and former county chairman Ron Kessler in his unsuccessful 1980 state Senate race. It was Amps who had helped to devise Weber's close 1976 campaign against Folsom.

In 1979 Weekley, Gray, and Amps had joined forces and since then had run and won every major bond campaign for the city. Combined, they knew more buttons to push, more chits to collect, more mistakes not to make, than all of the elected officials in the county put together. If you wanted something done politically in Dallas, there was only one place to go, and that's right where Taylor went, check in hand.

It was clear from the outset that the 1983 mayoral election would be an extremely tough race for the establishment to win. Taylor was the best available candidate, but an early survey taken in October 1982 showed that though 91 per cent of those polled knew of Wise and most recalled that he'd done a reasonably good job as mayor, almost no one knew who Starke Taylor was. The consultants had another, more difficult problem, which they came to call the Folsom Problem: Taylor would be tied to Folsom, and if Wise capitalized on that connection, it could block crucial neighborhood-group support before Taylor even had a chance to articulate a platform.

As it turned out, Wise helped them solve that problem. In January superdeveloper Trammell Crow, who seems to enjoy surprising his colleagues, sent out a bombshell of a letter endorsing Wise and asking selected friends to contribute to Wise's campaign. Once the consultants had caught their breath, they realized that the Crow letter could help them more than hurt them. If Starke Taylor was castigated by Wise for his association with a big-time developer, then Taylor could do the same to Wise.

They decided to build Taylor's platform largely on the amorphous phrase "planned growth." He would be for planning, which would mollify neighborhood groups, but he would still be for growth, which would reassure the developers who were already filling his campaign coffers. The key was to discuss planned growth only in the abstract.

With their issue chosen, the consultants went to work on the candidate himself. Taylor's one-on-one abilities were fine, but he was a disaster in front of groups. When Wise confronted him with the Folsom Problem, Taylor ducked it and appeared defensive. He lectured rather than spoke, tried to make too many points too quickly, and in general came across as confused and unsure of himself. Wise, meanwhile, was the same confident, polished candidate who had taken the city by storm in 1971. Though Taylor's campaign fundraising was surpassing Wise's ten to one, Wise was still the front-runner through the fall and winter, into March 1983. "I was banging my head against the wall, trying to get him to be tougher," says Amps, "but we needed to make him an entity. The only way was mass media."

Over the course of several strategy sessions, a plan was hatched. An additional $300,000, which Folsom agreed to get, would be needed for a media blitz of both print and electronic spots. "We wanted to emphasize that he was a successful businessman and all of the other qualities that voters have always liked," says Amps. "That and the planning issue were to convince people to trust him."

At the same time, Dallas media consultant Lisa LeMaster and Chicago-based consultant Bob Moomey began to work on Taylor's public style. No more prepared texts; no more dull lectures. If asked a troublesome question, Taylor was to say that he wasn't going to respond until he had all the facts. The image that emerged was just what the consultants wanted: a strong independent businessman who understood the city's problems, a developer who was for planning, a rich guy you could trust.

Meanwhile, Weekley and Gray began plying North Dallas Republican phone banks, the same kind of banks that had helped carry Bill Clements to the governorship. The strategy was to cut potential losses in the inner city and build wide margins in the northern, Republican areas. City fathers still like to lean on the myth that Dallas city politics is nonpartisan, but the truth is that in every bond and council election since the mid-seventies, North Dallas Republicans have delivered the crucial votes. The area is so populous and so well organized that a candidate or an issue can carry the entire city by winning the two North Dallas council districts by a wide enough margin.

That is precisely what Starke Taylor did. He whipped Wise with 54 per cent of the vote, but he did so by carrying those two districts. Taylor's election signaled a lot of things. It proved that if you take an unknown and spend $952,000 on him, you can get him elected against almost anyone, even someone with nearly 100 per cent name identification. It ushered in big-bucks professional campaigning in Dallas elections. Starke Taylor is the first business-backed candidate to be shaped to the specific desires of the voting public. His victory also solidified the Republican party's dominance over city politics. And it fomented the first real political dialectic in the city's history: outer city versus inner city, new city versus old city. When those assembled at Taylor's victory party began singing his campaign song, "Taylor Stands Tall for Dallas," the question was, which Dallas would he stand tall for?

STARKE TAYLOR DOESN'T LIKE TO TALK politics. He's uncomfortable with the philosophical. Taylor won't concede that North Dallas is split off from the inner city or that he will have to side with one faction or the other. But he is aware of the tensions he must attempt to mediate over the next two years.

His first major moves upon taking office were designed to assuage inner-city worries. The West Dallas and South Oak Cliff ghettos had long lived under a cloud of poison from two lead smelters nearby. Taylor appointed a blue-ribbon task force to study the problem and report to the council. People there also lived under a darker cloud—poverty. Taylor appointed a 115-member task force to look at revitalizing the economy in those areas. Setting up the task forces was a relatively bold move. No Dallas mayor I can recall has ever recognized the black population and its problems in such a direct way. On the other hand, task forces aren't elected and aren't accountable to voters. They work for the man who appointed them, not for the public they are presumed to be serving. They are really something of a cop-out.

Taylor says his philosophy is to "use the wealth of talent in the private sector" for "the public good." That impressive thought sounds like it came out of the typewriter of Judy Bonner Amps, who, incidentally, still works for the mayor as a political consultant. Too often task forces merely create the illusion that something has been done about a pressing problem. Taylor's seven-member task force on lead pollution was headed by the Sanger Harris CEO, Jack Miller, and coordinated through the Dallas Alliance, a group of younger business leaders. It studied all the available literature on the ten-year-old lead-pollution problem, interviewed residents of the neighborhoods, and then presented the city council with a thickly worded document confirming that there was a problem—which everyone from the city attorney's office to the Environmental Protection Agency already knew.

Taylor then took action on an issue that perfectly captured the conflict between the inner city and the outer city. Since the late seventies, support for widening thoroughfares to make commuting easier has come primarily from Northeast Dallas and contiguous suburbs, such as Garland. The East Dallas communities through which the roads would be widened have naturally been dead set against it. The issue had been kicked around, studied and restudied, put off, and cycled and recycled through public hearings and committee meetings for years. Unfortunately for Starke Taylor, the problem was plopped in his lap soon after he took office last May. Political observers, particularly those from the inner city, considered it the first real test of what Taylor had meant when he talked about planned growth during his campaign.

As is so often the case in politics, however, the matter was resolved by a behind-the-scenes compromise. This time Taylor chose to be political. He and the rest of the city's political leadership had staked an awful lot on an upcoming referendum to fund the Dallas Area Rapid Transit (DART) system, which would provide light rail and expanded bus service in the city. Well aware that opposition from the East Dallas neighborhood groups could defeat DART, Taylor decided on a quid pro quo: you can keep your streets, but just make sure you get your people out in support of the proposed one per cent sales tax to fund DART over the next fifty years. About a month before the city council was to vote on the proposal to widen some East Dallas thoroughfares, a dozen or so neighborhood leaders from that area met with Taylor at a home on stately old Swiss Avenue. The mayor's assurances that he would back their position against the wider streets left some of them a bit skeptical, but after Taylor's influence killed the proposal, all but one of them began organizing their neighbors in support of DART. Starke Taylor had thus assuaged their worries that he would be an outer-city mayor. But did he do it for the right reasons?

Discussions about extra parking downtown, measures to improve Central Expressway, and various ideas for a master land-use plan had been cast into limbo for the past two years in the hope that voters would accept a mass-transit system as the answer to all their problems. On August 13, when the DART proposition passed with 58 per cent of the vote, you could almost hear a collective sigh of relief from the city's business community. Taylor and other supporters claim that the mere existence of the 160 miles of light rail projected for DART will create a land-use plan for the city. Rail service will allow a badly needed increase of density in certain sparsely populated corridors, providing a web that will hold the sprawling city together. It will eliminate the need to renovate Central Expressway and other major arteries and will solve the city's in-creasing parking problems. It will make the city better for both the North Dallas businessman and the South Dallas construction worker.

Like most mass-transit plans, DART looks terrific on paper but is based on optimistic guesses and prayers. After asking Dallas citizens for billions of dollars to throw at the problem, DART proponents admit that the system will displace only about 5 per cent of all trips taken in the city on any given day. On major thoroughfares, the impact will not be dramatic. Even with DART trains and buses, the average daily load on North Central Expressway will continue to increase. Moreover, the DART rail plan relies primarily on existing rights-of-way owned by railroads that have not yet made any commitment to sell or lease those rights-of-way to the transit authority. The crucial rail link—running north to south along Central Expressway—will require state approval, which has not yet been granted.

DART officials admit that the rail service, with average speeds of 30 to 35 miles per hour, will often be more time-consuming than a trip by auto. And of course, the DART board can't guarantee that the system will be finished on time and within its budget. They haven't even selected what sort of vehicles DART will use. When voters committed $8.75 billion to mass transit, they may have thought they were voting for a service or at least a plan, but what they got was only a notion.

One thing that can be said about DART is that its existence on paper will benefit the city's development community. Money follows transportation, and if anyone has doubts about who was behind the transit plan, he need only peruse the list of donors to its $1 million war chest. DART was sold as the ultimate public service, but there wasn't much money from the general public on that list. Rather, there were $5000 and $10,000 donations from developers like Jim Williams and Bob Folsom and the Canadian firm Cadillac Fairview—and a $25,000 contribution from the Watson & Taylor Companies, a realty firm. Taylor is the mayor's son.

Even as the last vote was being tallied, land values in and around the proposed terminal sites and along the proposed rail routes began to shoot upward. The success of the system rests on something that is music to any developer's ears: "high density." Because Dallas' growth has been typical Sunbelt sprawl, many of the areas along proposed rail arteries are too lightly populated to meet minimal ridership needs. Solution? Increase density. That means more apartments, office towers, and hotels. DART may end up solving Dallas' transportation problems, but from another view it seems to be just one more way to keep the party going and the dirt flying, to keep Dallas an unfinished place, to refuel the myth of the perpetual boom town.

DART WILL DOUBTLESS PROVIDE STARKE Taylor and the rest of the city's leadership with an easy out on many of the other issues facing the city. One issue that Taylor probably won't be able to avoid, however, is the upcoming showdown on the city's lax zoning policies. Last spring city manager Charles Anderson issued the most important public document in the city's contemporary history: an extensive white paper that attacked the heart of the boom-town ethic. In general the paper urged the city to exert more influence over the nature, extent, and location of development by tying proposed developments to existing density, controlling the height of office buildings in certain areas, and, most important, radically revising the city's controversial cumulative zoning law.

Dallas has long looked down its nose at Houston's helter-skelter development, which has resulted from Houston's lack of zoning laws. But Dallas zoning laws are no better. For example, a light-commercial designation does not restrict the developer to building dry cleaners and dress shops; it includes many other land uses, such as office towers. By far the most controversial designations are the three industrial ones, which allow a developer to build just about anything he wants to—from a factory to an office complex to a shopping center. He doesn't even have to tell the city what he's going to build, and he has practically an eternity to keep changing his mind.

To understand the destructive effects of such permissive zoning, drive down the North Dallas Parkway to its intersection with—or more properly, its collision with—the LBJ Freeway. On the northeast corner sits Houston developer Gerald Hines' glittering, geodesic Galleria shopping complex. A good example of the build-it-and-see-what-happens thinking that has prevailed in the city since the Folsom years, it has created traffic problems that may never be solved. The land it sits on was zoned industrial in the late sixties, and for many years city planners based projected traffic flow and parking needs there on a factory's being built on the site. But its industrial zoning designation allowed the developer to build a shopping center, and when the Galleria opened its doors in 1982, city officials had little to say, except to report that the retail use would generate about sixteen times the traffic that existing roads could handle.

When the complicated verbiage of Dallas zoning law is peeled away, the remaining question is whether Starke Taylor—and, under his leadership, the city planning commission and the city council—will be able to say no to such reckless development in the future. The city staff's proposals are farsighted, but the staff can only recommend. It's up to the mayor to get proposals enacted. Only time will tell how many of them fit Starke Taylor's definition of planned growth—if he has one.

Thus far the signs have not been encouraging. Taylor backed off from his August 15 deadline for considering city manager Anderson's proposals in earnest, and some of the wording in Anderson's white paper has been softened in response to developers' reaction to the idea of increased city control over development. Taylor pledged during the campaign that he would vote against any zoning proposal that would increase traffic in a given area, but now committees working on the proposed changes have replaced that notion with a toothless provision that encourages development where city facilities are adequate. And to the dismay of neighborhood activists who are measuring the mayor's commitment to their cause by the number of changes on the North Dallas–dominated city planning commission, Taylor has pressed for the reappointment of incumbent chairman John Evans over Mary Ellen Degnan, who was considered more sympathetic to neighborhoods. Planned growth was easy to talk about, but so far Taylor's actions have not convinced many people of his sincerity.

Starke Taylor doesn't like to admit it—indeed, he acts as if he's not even aware of it—but he has collided with the most complex and troubled political times in the city's history. A hundred years of boom-town philosophy have resulted in benign neglect of the city's basic functions and services and have raised the question of whether the City That Works is really just getting by. The most difficult task for Starke Taylor will be to make livability catch up with prosperity. In recent months homeowners in North Dallas have begun to organize, and they sound very much like the East Dallas neighborhood groups. They are asking for a moratorium on rezoning in North Dallas until traffic is unsnarled and sensible zoning laws are put in place. Can it be that the new Dallasites have become frustrated with living in an unfinished city?

Bridging the gap between two white, middle-class constituencies will require political decisions made by a politician. Taylor is enough of a politician to get himself elected and to shunt problems away from his desk, but his willingness to solve problems politically is still in doubt. "You get in a business situation and you're used to making decisions and seeing things happen, and you see something that can be done today and you do it," he told me one morning. "You come down to city hall and you see things can't be done that way. You have to go through the bureaucratic process. You might even have to have a public hearing. It's not the way I like to do business, but it's the way you have to operate."

The reluctance in his tone is more than a little troubling. A series of task forces and a mass-transit plan that reads like escapist fiction may carry him through. But I get the feeling that before it's over, Starke Taylor will have to make a tough political choice, say no when it would be much easier to say nothing. Will he?

ONE DAY, AFTER A VISIT WITH THE MAYOR, I drove around in far North Dallas, past the offices and hotels and apartments of that new mecca. I cruised through the prestigious Bent Tree development, past mansions that all looked like huge park pavilions, past phalanxes of shiny Cadillacs. I came upon the mansion that belongs to Starke Taylor. It is an impressive contemporary affair, one of the loveliest homes on the block. Or at least it looks like it will be, when it is finished.◆

★CITIES★
EPISODES

Cable Madness

Houston succumbed. Now, can Dallas escape?

It all began a year ago with the charge that a former city councilman was trying to bribe the Dallas City Council on behalf of a cable TV company. It ended, for the time being, in late October amid a frenzy of vindictive rumors, veiled threats of lawsuits, and much slinging of mud. In between, there were grand debates over sexual morality, dark innuendos about the motives of Dallas's upper-crust cable investors, the indictment of two men for allegedly trying to sell phony trade secrets to one of the competitors, a loyalty oath à la Joe McCarthy, the sudden revelation of a businessman's will à la Howard Hughes, and a series of desperate "leaks."

It was, everyone agrees, the cleanest franchising process ever conducted by the cable TV industry in a major city.

It's no longer any great secret that the wiring of America for cable television has turned the city halls of Texas into seething Turkish bazaars filled with the kind of sophisticated business hucksters who make aluminum siding salesmen look like the angelic host (see "Invasion of the Cable Snatchers," TM, March 1980). The players were no different in Dallas, but all the rules had changed. The city fathers were adamant about it: no matter what has happened elsewhere, it won't happen here.

There were three principal reasons for this display of moral rectitude, and two were bad. The first was that the Dallas public utilities department had been studying cable TV for several years, beginning with a special task force in 1972 that set out the guidelines for a first-class system and advised the council to wait for the technology to mature. Hence Dallas avoided the mistakes of cities like Austin, which granted a franchise in the sixties and is now going through much pain and expense to bring it into the twentieth century, and San Antonio, which granted a franchise three years ago after a cursory review and minimal competition.

The second reason was that in October 1979 Councilman L. A. Murr and council candidate Larry Davis accused an ex-councilman named Jesse Price of offering them either partnerships or subcontracts in the event that Sammons Communications—Price's employer—received the franchise. Price denied the charges, the police investigated and dropped the case for lack of evidence. Nevertheless, the mere suggestion of bribery strengthened the council's ethical fervor.

Finally, the city had before it the example of Houston, where the art of franchise trading was elevated to new heights, resulting in a grand jury in-

vestigation and hints by members of a new city council that some franchises might be revoked. The Dallas papers, unlike those in Houston, subjected the franchising process to such intense scrutiny that it was virtually impossible to work out any closed-door deals.

Six of the nation's largest cable companies eventually applied for the franchise, expected to generate tens of millions in profits over the next fifteen years. But some of them never seemed to grasp the fact that Dallas was different. Cox Cable of Atlanta launched a long-running controversy in February when it went out of its way to announce the names of its local partners. In any other city, this practice—in which prominent local citizens lend their support in exchange for a percentage of the profits—would be standard operating procedure. In Dallas, it caused such an avalanche of adverse publicity (the papers called it "Rent-A-Citizen") that local partners in Cox, Vista Cablevision (owned by Time, Inc.), and United Cable Television of Denver resigned in embarrassment.

The Rent-A-Citizen brouhaha eventually led to an ordinance forbidding all employees of cable companies to talk to the council or the city staff. City manager George Schrader went even farther by drawing up a loyalty oath: council and staff members were asked to pledge in writing that they wouldn't go to work for a cable company for two years after the franchise was granted. Councilman Fred Blair was the only holdout; he said it was "ridiculous." In the nervous atmosphere of the moment, everyone thought *he* was ridiculous.

After the whole franchising process had been thoroughly sterilized, the game began in earnest. But it was more like six games, with everyone playing by a different set of rules. Some believed that the council, when all was said and done, would still be swayed by the local powers—like socialite Annette Strauss (who threw her support to Cox), home-builder Dave Fox and former Republican party leader Ray Hutchison (Vista), Earth Resources founder Dan Krausse (United), or State Representative Lee Jackson (Warner Amex). Storer Cable of Miami Beach relied on its paperwork; it had no local partners and was rarely visible. Sammons Communications of Dallas didn't try very hard to prove technological superiority or political clout. It invited the council to presume that all the contenders would provide equally good service and relied on its status as the hometown kid, even bringing 82-year-old company founder Charles Sammons to a council presentation. There Sammons revealed that he

had willed 51 per cent of Sammons Enterprises to five Dallas charities; a vote for Sammons, he implied, was a vote for hometown philanthropy.

The oracle of the campaign was a man named Harold Horn, of the Cable Television Information Center, who was paid $70,000 by the city to evaluate the six proposals. As Horn worked through the long, hot summer the cable companies looked for a forum—*any* forum—that would get their message to the quarantined council. Sammons opted for $150,000 worth of newspaper advertising, invoking the names of the five local charities, while Cox threw an expensive cocktail party for representatives of the city's performing arts groups. The Black Chamber of Commerce charged the companies $650 each to present dog-and-pony shows at its Juneteenth celebration, and Vista started a not-so-subtle letter-writing campaign to encourage citizens to lobby the council. In one of the most bizarre episodes, project director Anne Hall of Warner Amex cooperated with the police in a sting operation that resulted in the arrest of two men who had allegedly solicited $250,000 from her in return for secret city hall documents that would "guarantee" the franchise. (The information turned out to be neither secret nor damaging.)

The final report by the consultant, rendered in mid-October, was remarkable mainly for the clear-cut certainty of its conclusion. Horn said, in essence, that Warner Amex was the best of the six companies. Sammons, he added, deserved "serious consideration" because it appeared to be a little cheaper. And the other four simply didn't measure up.

The devil himself couldn't have designed a conclusion more calculated to haunt the council. Warner Amex had no local partners, but it had been declared the clear technological winner. Sammons was perceived by many as a close second, and it was a hometown company. Moreover, three other companies had shareholders who had staked their reputations on success, including Vista, notable for its minority partners.

It is some measure of how airtight the process was that on the day before the final vote, I talked to three different people who told me the fix was in—either Sammons or Warner or Vista would win it on the first ballot. Meanwhile Councilman Don Hicks was spreading a rumor about dirty deeds in Warner's past; when I asked him to produce his evidence, he said, "I can't recall *where* I heard that."

On the night before the vote, Anne

Hall of Warner had a nightmare. She was locked in a closet at city hall and was yelling for someone to get her out. As she heard approaching footsteps, she panicked. "What if it's a councilman?" she thought. "I can't talk to him." Then Councilman Rolan Tucker opened the door, and she knew all was lost. She woke up, scared to death.

By the end of the first ballot Hall had begun to cry. The pressure, which had been building for over a year, was too much for her. All her worst fears were being confirmed. Despite Horn's report, Warner got only three and one-sixth votes—from Steve Bartlett, Sid Stahl, Elsie Faye Heggins, and Max Goldblatt (who split his vote among all six firms). On the second ballot she picked up one more—from Joe Haggar, who switched from Storer. And on the third, she got the deciding vote from Ricardo Medrano. Only three councilmen— Mayor Robert Folsom, Hicks, and Tucker—held firm for Sammons.

The city staff breathed a sigh of relief. The best company had won. It will be several years before other Texas cities realize just how great a coup Dallas has achieved. In Houston, for example, the most daring feature the council required was a movie channel. In Dallas, Warner Amex will be offering not one but four similar channels, and a good deal else. Whereas Houston required companies to provide only 35 channels, Dallas will have 152, including 30 channels for community access alone. That includes 8 for the use of Dallas schools and colleges, 4 for professional education, 2 for city government, and 1 each for Hispanic groups, the elderly, blacks, religious organizations, women, and the public at large. Warner will supply 33 people to help citizens use the equipment; most of the Houston companies will supply one. Other offerings will include ten production studios, ten mobile vans for remote broadcasts, a "narrowcasting" channel for restricted audiences, and, perhaps most important, 52 channels to be used by institutions (such as libraries and hospitals) for data retrieval or teleconferencing. As one observer said after the vote, "Houston got an entertainment system. Dallas got a *communications* system."

Postscript: At press time, a Sammons supporter named Cherre Felton filed a petition to force a referendum on the awarding of the franchise. It's the same kind of petition that delayed cable TV franchising in Houston for six years. If Warner Amex is defeated at the polls, Dallas will set another record—for time wasted trying to be honest.

BAD WATER

Austin's Barton Springs, the best place to swim in Texas, is now dangerous to your health.

Early in the morning, Barton Springs pool is the placid blue of an aquamarine. A swimmer can plunge in and, if he narrows his line of vision just slightly, forget that he is in the heart of Austin. He can pretend he is the only person in the world. That is something no one in any other Texas city can do. Of course, most people go to Barton's in the peak of summer (330,000 went last year), when the place becomes Texas' little Côte d'Azur. But whether people in Austin take to the waters alone or with gaggles of others or not at all, they share an intense pride in Barton Springs. It's their jewel, and they know that everyone else in Texas is envious.

But something has gone wrong at Barton Springs. On a chilly day in early February the pool had to be closed because the water contained too much fecal coliform and fecal streptococci—organisms that come from the excrement of humans and animals. These organisms themselves are not dangerous, but all sorts of unhealthy viruses and bacteria can be present with them. You don't want to swallow even a teaspoon of water contaminated with fecal coliform or strep, nor do you want to get it in your eyes.

If you live in Austin, you have heard the oracles for many years: Barton Springs, they said, is headed for ruination. Most people didn't listen, or listened and nodded. But this time Barton's is clearly in trouble. In the last two decades a lot of changes have taken place around Barton Creek and the creeks near it—and more are planned. With a little sustained observation of man's impact on nature, one can't help but draw conclusions. The two most recent and visible changes have been the opening of Barton Creek Square Mall, which sits on a bald man-made mesa about half a mile from Barton Creek, and a new extension of the MoPac expressway, which also skirts the creek. The city is thinking about extending MoPac further, this time across Barton Creek itself; in April, Austin voters will decide if they want that to happen. Maybe the contaminated water at the springs and the opening of the new mall and expressway are just a coincidence—or maybe growth is catching up with Barton's.

The U.S. Geological Survey began a limited series of water-quality tests on Barton Springs in 1978, but in July 1981, because of concern over the contaminants that were turning up, the USGS started doing various tests once a week and after significant rains. Following downpours in August and October, fecal coliform and fecal strep

soared beyond all bounds of health safety. The organisms disappeared after a couple of days, but because the pattern kept repeating itself, the city decided to close the pool for a few days after each rain of an inch or more. Then the pattern was broken by the weekly USGS test on the very dry day of February 16: the fecal coliform was higher than ever.

Bacterial contamination is not all that has shown up. After an October rain, the USGS test showed the presence of diethyl phthalate, which is used in making plastics and is high on the EPA's list of pollutants. The fecal coliform has made people more angry, but the diethyl phthalate is of greater concern. Fecal organisms die, but plastics don't.

With summer approaching, the city is trying to find out what's awry. But pinpointing the source or sources of any contamination could be difficult because the springs are linked in a subterranean labyrinth not just with Barton Creek but with five other creeks in southwestern Austin. Rainwater flows down those creeks until it reaches a hundred-square-mile area called the Barton Springs recharge zone. There the water filters into the ground or plunges into cracks and faults and begins its underground journey through the limestone aquifer to the springs; because of the way the land tilts, about 80 per cent of the water that passes through the aquifer will someday flow out at Barton Springs. Since the springs are fed by rain, runoff from anywhere in the six-creek system can carry contaminants into Barton Springs. The best guess is that the fecal organisms are coming from somewhere in or near Barton Creek. The high concentration at first seemed correlated to rainfall, so the USGS hydrologists figured that the contamination was related to storm runoff, which is very dirty these days, especially along the most developed two miles of the creek above the pool.

But after February 16, the city realized that the contamination could be coming from other sources as well. It could be pervasive contamination from too many septic tanks in the area; it could be a broken sewer line in or near Barton Creek. Last fall the city started running TV cameras in the oldest sewer lines in the Barton's area to look for cracks. In early March it located one line that appeared to have some cracks in it. The USGS has also given the city colored dye to throw down several manholes when it rains to see if traces show up in the springs. If sewer leaks are found and fixed, well and

good. But what about the runoff?

Roads and parking lots can be described in two words: filthy and impenetrable. Consider this statement from a text entitled *Urban Stormwater Management:* "Street runoff is composed of many of the pollutants found in sanitary sewage, with comparable concentrations." The authors, John Mason and Edward Rhomberg, go on to mention other pollutants found on city streets, like animal wastes, zinc, copper, nickel, chromium, cadmium, and pesticides, not to mention a lot of trash. Rain runs off asphalt and concrete in sheets, taking with it whatever is on the pavement until it can find open ground or a crack in the limestone to seep into. If the runoff percolates through soil, it is cleansed, but if it falls into a crack, it goes into the underground water system as is—dirty.

To varying degrees, all six of the sister creeks in the Barton recharge zone are crisscrossed with streets, covered with subdivisions, and blotched with parking lots. Two of the biggest expanses of asphalt, which are most awesome seen from the air, are the 65 acres of the Toney Burger activity center (a public school recreational center and bus depot) and the 110 acres of Barton Creek Square. The parking lot at Toney Burger is designed to pool rainwater, which is then slowly released into Williamson Creek; this arrangement prevents floods, but unfortunately the water is not filtered. Barton Creek Square has installed three ponds to filter the water that runs off its parking lots; they should be adequate for most rains that hit the Austin area.

It is almost masochistic to look back on things that can't be undone. But—assuming there is a correlation between what's happening at Barton's and what has happened all around it—the major development in the area painfully demonstrates the damage of slow, incremental change wrought by a relative few and unheeded by most (see "Up the Creek," TM, September 1979). First and foremost, Barton Creek has become a bed for sewer lines. From an environmental standpoint, leakage is the least of the problems with sewer lines; the biggest is the irrevocable way in which they multiply and spread from office complex, to residential neighborhood, to shopping center. The city laid the first sewer line in Barton Creek above the pool in 1966. Another section went in without proper permits, and more equipment, which doubled the sewer's capacity, was installed without city council approval. Roads, of course, are the other arteries that encourage development. The biggest in the Barton Creek area is MoPac. The bigger the road, the more convenience stores, fast-food franchises, and strip shopping centers it attracts. Whether these businesses are eyesores or boons to the local economy is really beside the point; what matters is that they all have asphalt or concrete parking lots.

In 1979, too late to do much good, a band of people loosely clustered around two organizations called the Zilker Park Posse and the Save Barton Creek Association got the city to pass a moratorium on new subdivisions and water-wastewater connections in the Barton Creek area. It was a token move at best, since it did not apply to developers whose projects had already been accepted by the city's Planning Department. The moratorium pretty well epitomizes the history of development around Barton's. It is essentially a game between three factions—bureaucrats and politicians who claim to want to save Barton's; a citizenry that in a clumsy, amorphous way loves the springs but can't rally the money or expertise or time to keep up with the city or with the developers; and the developers themselves, who are a good five to ten years ahead of everyone in their plans for the land west of Austin. The developers always win. One reason they do, of course, is because—the future of Barton Springs notwithstanding—they are selling what a lot of people want: homes and apartments and offices overlooking lovely creeks.

The one result of the moratorium that offered some hope of controlling development was a series of three ordinances designed in theory to control growth along the creeks where Austin has jurisdiction. The Barton Creek Ordinance is the strongest of the three, but it is not without its problems. For one thing, it applies only to land that must be approved for subdivision. It can't restrict building on single sites that don't have to be subdivided—that is, the kind of large tracts that shopping malls are usually put up on. Sometime this spring or summer, the city council is supposed to consider adding that section, but how strict it will be no one knows. Under the ordinance it is also possible, for instance, to trade some parkland here for more asphalt there or to get simple waivers approved. Since its passage, ten variances have been requested by landowners and developers—and ten have been granted. Some were totally benign requests dealing with small plots of land, but one case, which concerns the only large piece of commercial property to be considered under the ordinance, is an interesting test of the ordinance's strength. It involves the Brodie tract, 164 acres on Barton Creek. Local developer Porter Young owned an option on the property, but he sold it to New Orleans businessman Fred Gottesman, whose son, Sandy, lives in Austin and will develop the property. The three variances Porter Young requested and was granted and the trade-offs he got seem to violate in critical ways the spirit of the ordinance: two allow dense

development near the creek, and the third permits a 15 per cent increase in pavement on one portion of the property. Young gave 84 acres to the city for a park, the designs for the property include the construction of storm-water detention ponds, and Sandy Gottesman gives every indication of being a concerned developer. But in the end, because of the inherent flexibility of the ordinance, several hundred thousand square feet of offices and six hundred condominiums will someday be built very near Barton Creek.

Even if the city were absolutely ironfisted with developers, its legal authority stops about five miles outside the city limits. The city can do little except acknowledge whether at some point in the future it will provide developers with the water and wastewater services to open up their land. In the last few years, the city—that is, the citizens—has said no to several water and wastewater items in bond elections. On top of that, the city's philosophy lately has been to deny or limit service in environmentally sensitive areas, the logic being that if it did so, no one would build there—a naive assumption, of course. Developers have gotten the message from both the voters and the city. They have simply gone elsewhere for services, as their recent maneuvers with the Lower Colorado River Authority (LCRA) have shown. Within the last year, seven developers who own about seven thousand acres along or near Barton and its sister creeks have contracted with the LCRA to purchase water from the Colorado River.

The lesson to be learned is that if Austin is going to protect resources like Barton's, it has to have control over how those resources are used or abused. It doesn't have much control when it sends developers somewhere else for services. One recent example is Canadian-based C.G.S. Development, which asked the Texas Department of Water Resources if it could dump treated sewage (an average of 300,000 gallons a day) into Williamson Creek, one of the creeks in the recharge zone. That waste would slip into the ground like water through a colander, and while it is technically not dangerous, it is, as one hydrologist puts it, of "substantially less quality" than the water Mother Nature provides us. The request has yet to be heard.

In early March the city council voted to extend regular water-quality tests at the springs and also to test storm-water runoff at Barton Creek Square. At the very mention of the springs, Mayor Carole McClellan ripples with zeal: "We will commit as many dollars as necessary to find the source of the problem." The question is, is it too little too late? Barton Springs in many ways is the most visible symbol of an acute problem that Austin faces. It is a city caught between a wealthy and aggressive group of developers, who liberally fund the campaigns of mayors and members of the city council and a not so wealthy but vocal group of no-growthers, who pull at those same elected officials' sleeves and heartstrings. The result is that

Austin is stymied, and not just on the future of Barton's. But can the city, which professes to care, do anything to save Barton's? Can the state? Can the man on the street? Yes, all of them can, and here's how:

•The city should honor the Barton Creek Ordinance like one of the Ten Commandments; it should pass the overdue section that regulates the density of development on single tracts of land. It should be tight with trade-offs and variances, especially with commercial developers.

•It should expand protection of all six creeks in the Barton Springs recharge zone, first by going back and strengthening the other two ordinances. Another way to restrict growth in this area would be to allow developers to expand their projects in less critical parts of the city in exchange for restricting development on their landholdings in southwestern Austin.

•It should buy up land around Barton Springs whenever and wherever it can.

•The state should become more active in protecting Texas' natural wonders—local government has neither enough money nor enough clout. The Department of Water Resources should be very stingy in granting permits to dump sanitary sewage in the creeks west of Austin.

•More important, the Parks and Wildlife Department should search for land in the Barton Springs recharge zone. It maintains that there are already enough parks in that area for the local population, but it needs to expand its thinking: parks are not just for people, they're for land and water preservation as well.

•Austin's no-growthers should realize that their closed-door attitude will do more harm than good for Barton's. Austin's population will almost double by the year 2000. It is far better, in terms of the city's tax base and its environmental quality, for Austin to have control over the services it provides those people than to have them form satellite communities outside the city's purview.

•The residents of Austin should vote no on the southern extension of MoPac on April 3. If the construction phase wouldn't wreak havoc, if the effects of runoff were clearly understood, if the Barton Creek Ordinance were tighter, if the expressway could be made a parkway with no frontage roads, then the extension might be okay. As it is, there are too many unknowns and variables.

The fate of the springs is larger than a local issue. Barton's is an exquisite jewel in a state with few. And it isn't hundreds of miles out of the way; it's in the heart of a city in the heart of Texas. Already the future looks grim. Should you go swimming there? Should you take your kids? Is the contaminated water the result of all the development? Will the city have to start chlorinating the pool? Will the situation get better, or is a holding pattern the best we can hope for?

Singular works of nature like Barton Springs are in the same category as great works of art—but they are infinitely harder to protect. We can't put them in museums or bank vaults, and that has always been the dilemma in the attempt to save natural places in Texas and across the U.S. People generally recognize the beauty of mountains, forests, rivers, and springs, but the history of growth and expansion tells us it is a whole lot easier to ruin those places than to save them. That doesn't mean we shouldn't try.♣

FANTASY ISLAND

Some of the old downtown crowd want to put an island in the middle of Houston's Buffalo Bayou. But wait, guys, you didn't clear it with Mayor Whitmire, and she has a whole new set of rules.

Just past the northernmost edge of downtown Houston—past the rows of skyscrapers, past the cutesy redevelopments, past the old, decrepit buildings sitting along the banks of Buffalo Bayou, past even the bayou itself—there lies a small, weedy, 34-acre peninsula that has been created by an oxbow in the bayou. From Main Street, where the oxbow begins, it is difficult to make out the peninsula; it is hidden by bridges and concrete embankments and railroad tracks. These acts of man long ago obscured the act of God.

The peninsula is an industrial ghetto, full of old plants and older warehouses. Some of the rotting buildings are abandoned, and those still in use don't look much better. The streets, full of potholes and weeds, are really just long driveways that dead-end behind the warehouses. The baked brown grass is littered with dirt and gravel

BY JOSEPH NOCERA

and broken beer bottles. At the water's edge the grass is taller and greener, growing wildly amid a tangle of trees and shrubs that gets thicker and more impassable with every step. The bayou is brown and murky, full of muck—and prone to flooding. From almost any point on the peninsula the Houston skyline is easily visible, yet you can't shake the feeling that you are utterly cut off from the city.

As it happens, a number of people have been looking rather intently at that peninsula during the past few years, and they don't see the murky water or the decaying warehouses. They see something else entirely—an area magically transformed. Where there are 34 acres of peninsula, for instance, they envision 34 acres of . . . *island*. Fantasy Island, if you will. The island has been created by cutting a channel from one side of the oxbow to the other. The water level is low and steady: no flooding on Fantasy Island. The men eyeing this pathetic patch along Buffalo Bayou don't see weed-ridden lots either. They see chic hotels and glorious, plentiful retail space, with high-priced shops and fancy glass-paneled shopping malls. They see high-rise condominiums. They see half a dozen office buildings, one or two as high as fifty stories. Down by the waterfront they see a touch of San Antonio—a lovely riverwalk paved with quaint brick and lined with sidewalk cafes and boat docks from which tourists can take little boat rides up and down Buffalo Bayou. And—who knows?—on those days when the imagination really runs wild, they might even see an MTA subway station on the island.

Who are these men who want to turn a peninsula into an island? Most of them are members in good standing of the Houston establishment—people like real estate developer Walter Mischer, former city attorney Jonathan Day, and architect S. I. Morris, head of the most politically well-connected architecture firm in Houston. During the administration of Mayor Jim McConn, they were "the golden boys" at city hall, to use Morris' phrase. They knew the right strings to pull. They knew how to get things done. Once men like these had made the Houston Intercontinental Airport a reality and the Astrodome too. And in the process of bringing to life these civic amenities, they had made a little money too. They did good for Houston and so did good for themselves. Now they were going to try again.

For a while it looked as if Fantasy Island, a huge and complex development project involving both public and private money, had a fair shot at becoming a reality. But in November 1981 Houston elected former city controller Kathryn J. Whitmire to be its mayor, and all of a sudden McConn's insiders could no longer find the right strings to pull, at least so far

as city hall was concerned. Today, to their great disappointment, Fantasy Island remains a fantasy.

But does that mean that Kathy Whitmire is opposed to the creation of Fantasy Island? Well, no, it doesn't. Even though not one demonstrable step has been taken toward the completion of the project since she became mayor, Whitmire takes a back seat to no one when it comes to proclaiming her unstinting devotion to the project. "I am convinced we can do it," she says. But for Whitmire, up for reelection this month, Fantasy Island is a whole mayoralty in microcosm. Before she took office, the golden boys could pretty much have their way with city hall. Since then, she has seen to it that there are no more golden boys in Houston. Does that mean there won't be any Fantasy Islands either?

COCKTAILS AT THE CLUB

It is October 1, 1981, less than two months before Whitmire's election. Two dozen or so men and women are sipping cocktails and munching shrimp at the Plaza Club, high atop the One Shell Plaza building in downtown Houston. The Plaza Club often seems like the fraternity house of the Houston establishment; at this late-afternoon reception, the establishment has gathered to get a firsthand look at plans to beautify a lengthy stretch of Buffalo Bayou, all the way from River Oaks to Houston's Fourth Ward. It surely needs beautifying. Houston has never been much for creating urban amenities—although it is the fourth-largest city in the country, it ranked number 140 in park space at the last official count—and its historic neglect of the bayous that run through the city is an urban crime. This is particularly true of Buffalo Bayou, the longest and most important of Houston's eight bayous. Buffalo Bayou runs through the heart of the city, it offers a little geographic variety, and it has historic significance—the Allen brothers founded Houston along its banks in 1836. Yet it is a potential resource that the city has perversely buried over the years.

Before the Plaza Club reception is over, the guests will be asked to contribute to bayou beautification. Even without seeing plans or hearing presentations, they know that this is something they are likely to do, an inclination caused by a complicated mix of noble and selfish instincts. Everyone in the room realizes what an asset Buffalo Bayou could be, and everyone would genuinely like to see it become that asset. But they also realize that if Fantasy Island is the centerpiece of a bayou

beautification plan, then almost everybody attending this affair will in some way profit from the project.

On the island there will be land to buy and sell, buildings to develop, and roads to build. But even those without a piece of the island will be able to profit from its development. Buffalo Bayou has always been the northernmost boundary of Houston's downtown, a line of demarcation beyond which fifty-story high rises would never sprout. Fantasy Island, however, would turn the "wrong" side of the bayou into the right side. A fancy island development north of downtown would be a powerful magnet; inevitably, it would pull downtown toward it. In the process all that land in the northern part of downtown, now largely the preserve of derelicts and restorationists, would become infinitely more valuable. That point is lost on no one in the room.

There is another reason that the reception guests are likely to throw a little money at bayou beautification. Walter Mischer is behind it. Along with James Elkins, Jr., the chairman of First City Bancorporation, and S. I. Morris, the benevolent dictator of Morris*Aubry Architects, Mischer has helped organize this reception. They are McConn's golden boys.

Mischer, Elkins, and Morris never do make it to the reception themselves. As their emissaries, they send Barry Goodman, the former head of the MTA, now a private consultant, and former city attorney Jonathan Day, who also has a reputation for knowing his way around the corridors of power. Since getting into the consulting business, Goodman has had as one of his chief clients something called the Buffalo Bayou Transformation Corporation (S. I. Morris, chairman) a nonprofit entity created in the summer of 1980. At the reception it is Goodman who outlines the plans of the Buffalo Bayou Transformation Corporation. What he unveils is pretty vague, but the drawings look nice. The island has been clearly delineated. Buffalo Bayou looks like an amenity. The people at the Plaza Club nod their approval.

Now it is Jonathan Day's turn to speak; it has fallen to him, as the attorney for the Buffalo Bayou Transformation Corporation, to make the pitch for money. He explains that funds are needed for a campaign to ratify an amendment to the Texas constitution that was approved by the Legislature in the last session. Like all constitutional amendments, this one must be passed by the state's voters in a referendum, and it is on the November ballot. Proposition One, it is called.

What the amendment will do, Day says, is allow Texas cities to establish a complicated taxing mechanism called a tax increment district. If the referendum passes, the Houston City Council could create such a district in the area surrounding Buffalo Bayou. That would permit the Buffalo Bayou Transformation Corporation to capture enough tax money to begin fulfilling its self-appointed task. No one in the room doubts that the people behind this plan have the clout to win approval from the city council. They ante up, mostly in chunks of $1000 to $3000. Mischer, Morris, and Elkins borrow $25,000 from Elkins' bank and lend it to the effort. In all, more than $75,000 is raised.

The Plaza Club reception was supposed to be the starting point for the island's development; instead it turned out to be the high point. A month after the fundraiser, Proposition One did pass; on the same day, Mayor James McConn lost his bid for reelection. Seven weeks after that, and ten days before Kathy Whitmire took over as mayor, the city council unanimously agreed to set up a tax increment district around Buffalo Bayou. The deal seemed greased. And then . . . nothing. Since then—since Kathy Whitmire has been in office—the tax increment district hasn't collected a penny in taxes, and the Buffalo Bayou Transformation Corporation has had so little to do that in effect it exists on paper only.

PARKS GOOD, ISLAND BETTER

The story of Fantasy Island begins in the late sixties, with a young landscape architect named Charles Tapley. Being a landscape architect, Tapley naturally looked around Houston at places that could use some landscaping, and there was Buffalo Bayou. Tapley was not the first person to notice how badly the city had treated Buffalo Bayou, but he was the most persistent, and by the early seventies the city was occasionally giving him contracts that allowed him to put his ideas on paper. They were "received with a yawn," says Tapley.

His big break came in 1979, when the Wortham Foundation, the philanthropic arm of an old-line Houston family, gave the chamber of commerce about $500,000 as seed money to begin doing something about the bayou. The chamber hired Tapley to work up a master plan for four miles of the bayou (from Shepherd Drive to downtown, and later extending east to Hirsch Road). Tapley's sketches emphasized parks, landscaping, and flood control improvements, not commercial development. But his plans also included the riverwalk and the island, ideas he had come up with in 1976 while teaching a course on the bayou at the Rice School of Architecture.

In the summer of 1980 Tapley presented his plan to the city council, which approved it unanimously. The council also allocated $1 million for construction of a demonstration park project on a small stretch of the bayou between Allen Parkway and Memorial Drive. The Wortham Foundation kicked in another $500,000 for the project. At the same time, the council approved Tapley's recommendation "that a single purpose non-profit corporation be formed to guide the development" of his master plan. Thus was born the Buffalo Bayou Transformation Corporation, S. I. Morris, chairman.

S. I. Morris likes to say he was the logical choice to be chairman of the Buffalo Bayou Transformation Corporation, and there's some truth to that. He is the vice chairman of the Houston Parks Board, a nine-member group that advises—and raises private money for—the city parks department. But Morris, a small, thin, courtly man of 69 who is known to everyone as Si, is also one of those Houstonians whose business interests are inextricably bound up in his civic activities. Being on this board or that commission brings Morris into contact with other influential people, some of whom are in a position to decide such things as, say, which architect should design their company's new building.

Tapley's plan had official city council approval, but Morris, the new bayou czar, had no intention of carrying it out exactly as it had been written. "It was not what I had in mind," he says now. Instead, he latched on to the island as the way to make the deal work. And why not? Tapley's plans had always stressed parks over development, and a decade later, all he had to show for it was a puny little demonstration project. If you were going to make the thing move, you had to get other players involved, and to do that you had to show them something besides trees and fountains. The island was the key partly because building the channel cut was necessary to control flooding. (As one Harris County expert put it, without a substantial flood control program, "the only thing you'll be selling on the riverwalk is scuba gear.") But more important, an island meant big-time development, and development was what tended to capture the imagination of the players Morris wanted to involve. A parks plan might be good for Houston; a parks plan and an island would be *really* good.

Morris soon began sending out signals that he was moving the project in that direction. He hired as his consultant not Tapley, the outsider, but Barry Goodman, an insider. Tapley was slowly being pushed to the sidelines. ("He was always butting his nose in," says Morris.) Goodman, having just left the MTA, had a Rolodex full of the same names as Morris' Rolodex; in Morris' view, those connections meant that Goodman was a man who could make things happen. Another move Morris made was to ask Jonathan Day, who had strong connections at city hall, to handle the transformation corporation's legal needs. Along with his new sidekick, Goodman, he began consulting regularly with Walter Mischer and James Elkins to get their blessing. (As Morris explained, Mischer and Elkins were members of an "executive subcommittee" that he had put together to get "private sector input.") The emphasis began to shift from Tapley's vision to Morris' vision. People stopped thinking of the project as a bayou beautification project and started calling it a bayou *development* project.

Within months, Goodman had discovered that the island had very few owners, chief among them the Southern Pacific Railroad, which held about 40 per cent of the land, and Walter and Robert Hecht, the co-chairmen of the board of the Oak Forest Bank, who owned another 25 per cent. That meant that two big deals would capture most of the island acreage—much cleaner and simpler than having to make a thousand little deals with small landowners. And wasn't it convenient that Walter Hecht was a close friend of Walter Mischer's and that the Allied Bank, where Mischer served as chairman of the board, held some of the Hechts' notes for the property? Goodman sent letters to the principal owners to find out whether, further down the road, they would be willing to sell their land. Letters came back: they would be, under the right circumstances.

Things started heating up. Clayton Stone, executive vice president of Gerald D. Hines Interests, one of the biggest developers in town, expressed an interest in Buffalo Bayou and the island. Joe E. Russo, a developer whose new 26-story Lyric Office Centre is the high-rise office building closest to the bayou, called Morris and Goodman and told them that he wanted to be a player. Mayor Jim McConn made it clear to Morris that he was on the team. Morris and Goodman began receiving letters from people like Don Rogers, executive director of the Downtown Houston Association ("I want dubs on the paddleboat concession"); and William Sharman, a small developer who has done some nice renovation work at the north end of downtown ("I had an excellent meeting later that morning with Mr. Mischer and found a most sympathetic ear"), and groups like Hope Development, a black consortium ("Hope wants maximum involvement in the bayou project"). The University of Houston Downtown, whose one-building campus sits on Main Street directly across from the island, signed on. It had an ambitious expansion plan that it hoped to have incorporated into Goodman's plans.

With the help of the chamber of commerce, Goodman and Morris raised some money to cover the burgeoning expenses of the Buffalo Bayou Transformation Corporation. Gerald Hines agreed to contribute $20,000. Shell Oil gave $10,000. About $100,000 of the original Wortham Foundation grant was turned over to the transformation corporation. In all, Morris and Goodman raised nearly $300,000 in

1981, of which $129,000 went to Goodman for his services. Tapley, meanwhile, received about $30,000 that year from the transformation corporation and never quite realized how far things had shifted from his original plan.

THE MAXIMUM-DEVELOPMENT SCHEME

What would be done with the island once it was built was a subject of much discussion in those heady days. Goodman brought potential island developers together to kick around ideas. During one such meeting someone suggested that the entire city government be moved, lock, stock, and barrel, to the island. As later stated in a memo, "This would allow the city to sell the land it currently has City Hall on, which would be extremely valuable property, to an office developer." Well, that was one idea that would never get past the kicking-around stage. Goodman, however, had come up with three development schemes—minimum, medium, and maximum—for the island. The minimum and medium plans would convert warehouses—"(where possible)"—into office buildings, and in so doing would raise the value of the property from between $6 and $15 a square foot to between $25 and $45 a square foot. In addition, the medium plan called for some low-rise condominium development. But Goodman's heart really lay with the maximum-development scheme. As he put it in a March 1981 memo to Morris, "This development scheme would likely be founded upon a major high-rise hotel or hotels . . . [and] high-rise residential housing. . . . The office buildings would likely be in the ten to thirty story range with a fifty story or larger a possibility." He went on: "An average property value would be $90 per square foot." Here was Fantasy Island.

Who was going to pay for all this? Goodman and Morris had originally assumed that the island would be privately owned; as Morris told the city council, "It's not something we would call on the city to participate in." But it seemed unlikely that it could be privately financed. Just to create the island—digging the channel cut, making the necessary flood control adjustments, relocating Southern Pacific's railroad tracks—was going to cost somewhere in the range of $40 million to $50 million. Throw in the riverwalk and the boat docks and landscaping—and streets and other necessities without which development was impossible—and you were up in the $60 million to $70 million range. And that didn't even include the actual sale of land to developers, or the building of buildings, or all the rest of it. Seventy million dollars just to get the land ready!

Morris and Goodman knew full well that there was no one in Houston willing to put up that kind of money. The payoff to developers was too far down the road—perhaps years away. So instead, they promoted Fantasy Island as a "public-private partnership." As they conceived it, the public partner would construct the channel cut, handle the relocation of Southern Pacific's tracks, pay for the flood control program, and make the necessary improvements on the land—in other words, make the island developable. With that taken care of, the private partners would be happy to take over.

The main problem, then, was getting money from the public partner. To construct the channel cut, there was an obvious source of public financing: a Harris County flood control bond. The channel, as originally conceived by Tapley, was primarily a flood control device. Now the golden boys seized on that rationale. In a December 1981 meeting, county commissioners were "briefed on specifics of flood control improvement with emphasis on the diversion channel," as Goodman later described it in a memo to Morris. ("It was my recommendation," Goodman added, "that we confine our presentation largely to flood control considerations.") County judge Jon Lindsay and the other Harris County commissioners eventually agreed that it was a worthy project; they added $13 million for the channel cut to a county bond referendum. In May 1982 the referendum passed.

Morris and Goodman thought they might have similar good luck at the federal level. Goodman talked to a number of federal agencies that hand out money for development projects. Tapley was even trotted out to give the dog-and-pony show to some federal bureaucrats who had come to Houston. He tried to take the officials—about fifteen in all—for a scenic ride down the bayou, but their boats promptly got mired in midstream. The lead boat, trying to get unstuck, showered the second one with gallons of muddy water. Alas, it was not a successful outing. Alas, too, not long after the formation of the Buffalo Bayou Transformation Corporation, the Reagan administration came to power in Washington, and federal money became harder to get.

THE GOLDEN BOYS TRIUMPH

By the middle of 1981 Goodman and Morris had shifted their attention to another potential source of public money: tax increment financing, which allows a certain small section of a city—the tax increment district—to make municipal improvements now and pay for them with tax revenues generated later. The money comes from the higher taxes generated by the improvements. (The improvements lead to development, you see, which leads to higher property values, which means higher tax revenues.)

Tax increment districts are becoming increasingly popular across the country. They have been used to build a subway station in San Francisco and to improve utilities in Los Angeles, and in 1981 they came to Texas, in the form of a constitutional amendment pushed through the Legislature by Senator Ray Farabee of Wichita Falls. It wasn't long before other people, in other Texas cities—including S. I. Morris and Barry Goodman—got interested in what looked like a promising new financing idea. Morris and Goodman realized that if Harris County could build the channel cut, tax increment funds could do the rest. With the money, they could build sewer lines and streets, and they could relocate the railroad tracks and create the riverwalk. Tax increment financing could build Fantasy Island.

To them, tax increment financing seemed to be the perfect solution. They would have to get the city council to designate the area surrounding Buffalo Bayou a tax increment district, but they didn't think that would be much of a problem. And as long as Jim McConn was mayor, it was a pretty safe bet that he would appoint to the tax increment board the people who were behind the Buffalo Bayou Transformation Corporation—the way tax increment financing works, voters have no say in who the members are or what they do with their funds. S. I. Morris stood a good chance of being the person most responsible for allocating the tax increment money, a significant bit of power.

And finally, most alluring of all, was the possibility that if Morris and Goodman moved quickly enough, they would be able to capture more than just future tax revenue. They would also be able to get their hands on some *immediate* tax money—money they could spend pretty much as they saw fit.

The reason for this was complicated. Under the 1981 amendment, once a tax increment district was created, the amount of tax money received by the city, the county, and the school board from the properties within the district's boundaries would be frozen at that year's level. For the life of the tax increment district, no taxing jurisdiction would get more revenue from those properties, no matter how much the property taxes increased. In theory, it was assumed that whatever tax increases occurred would be a result of the improvements made by the district.

In Houston, however, there was an extenuating circumstance, never anticipated by the 1981 constitutional amendment, that worked to the advantage of the Buffalo Bayou Transformation Corporation: a long-awaited, long-needed tax revaluation of all the city's properties was scheduled for 1982. Everyone in Houston knew that this revaluation would significantly raise property taxes, and indeed it did. The city alone gained about $17 million in 1982. A tax increment district set up before the end of 1981 would be entitled to all the extra money generated within its boundaries by the revaluation—which turned out to be a sweet $4 million a year, every year.

What ensued was a concerted push to set up the tax increment district before the end of 1981. The first hurdle was getting Proposition One—Farabee's constitutional amendment allowing tax increment districts in Texas—approved by the voters in November. To that end, Day and Goodman set up a political action committee, called the Committee for Improved Communities and backed by Morris, Mischer, and Elkins. In October the Plaza Club fundraiser was held, and soon thereafter the committee was sponsoring ads extolling the virtues of Proposition One. In November the amendment passed, 473,000–339,000.

Then, with less than two months to go, what remained was to get the city council to agree to the creation of a district. There were two potential obstacles: Harris County judge Jon Lindsay and school superintendent Billy Reagan. If they opposed the tax increment district—and why wouldn't they? it took money away from them—city council passage would become difficult.

The solution was simply to make sure there was something in the district for both Reagan and Lindsay. For Reagan it was a vocational school, to be built near the bayou with tax increment district money. Reagan agreed to support the district. For Lindsay (according to Goodman and Morris) it was a huge parking garage that would be built within a block of the county's main office building, which is located on the banks of the bayou. Lindsay says that if such a plan was ever devised he never heard about it, but, for whatever reason, he made no move to stop the creation of the district. On December 22, 1981, Jonathan Day and S. I. Morris were able to go before the Houston City Council and tell the council members that neither Reagan nor Lindsay opposed the idea. The council unanimously legislated the tax increment district into being—with ten days to spare.

Day had another suggestion for the council. He recommended that as an interim measure the board of directors for the new tax increment district be composed of the members of the board of the Buffalo Bayou Transformation Corporation. That, too, was approved unanimously. S. I. Morris was crowned chairman of the tax increment district. Fantasy Island was what they call "wired." But it wasn't to be.

BRAVE NEW RULES

Not long after the tax increment district was created the problems began. First, Judge Lindsay, who hadn't said a word in opposition up to that point, started grumbling about the district. He decided that he didn't like the city's skimming off potential county revenue. Then the school board weighed in. It quickly realized that, because the district had been established in 1981, the schools were in a position to lose nearly $2 million in revenue. Then it learned that other cities within the school district's jurisdiction—Bellaire, for instance—were also planning to set up tax increment districts, thereby making the potential revenue loss much more painful. Eventually the school board passed a resolution asking the city to abolish the tax increment district.

But most important of all, ten days after the passage of the tax increment district, Kathy Whitmire replaced Jim McConn as mayor. During her campaign Whitmire had come to represent, as much as anything else, a repudiation of the old ways of doing things. Mischer had lined up against her, as had a good number of the golden boys, but their opposition actually worked in her favor. They were McConn's cronies; Whitmire had no cronies. Their mayor was a bumbler; she would be competent. Their mayor was a home builder, an amateur; she was an accountant, a professional.

Like Jimmy Carter, she was elected not so much because of what she was for, but because of what she was against. She was against the way city government had always operated in Houston—the same people pulling the strings, the same companies getting the contracts, the same small group of people profiting.

In the aftermath of her election, however, the people backing Fantasy Island had high hopes that she would line up behind the Buffalo Bayou Transformation Corporation. Jonathan Day went to see one of the mayor's aides to talk about the tax increment district. As the aide recalls the conversation, Day asked some questions about Whitmire's attitude toward the bayou project (she was for it, he was told), but he spent most of his time talking about the composition of the board. Were there people Whitmire wanted on the board, he asked. Did she want Si Morris to resign, for instance?

It was the wrong approach. Offering the winner a piece of the action was playing by the old rules. The new mayor was studiously uninterested in who served on the board. And it eventually dawned on Morris and Goodman, as their work ground to a halt, that she had no immediate plans to use the mechanism they had so painstakingly set up to make the project move—the tax increment district. They couldn't understand why not.

To hear Whitmire and her aides explain it, the tax increment concept had a multitude of flaws that had to be overcome before it could be used in Houston. A court challenge to a tax increment district in El Paso put the whole idea of tax increment financing in legal limbo. How could Whitmire collect money for a tax increment district if there was a chance that it might be declared illegal? If a tax increment district did issue bonds, they would probably cost more in interest than general revenue bonds. What kind of sense did that make? A new mayor needed to be on good terms with the county judge and the school board, and collecting money for the tax increment district would be sure to damage relations. After the oil boom ended and Whitmire had to lay off city employees to keep Houston in the black, it became impolitic for her to set aside money for a big development scheme. And through it all, the new mayor was bothered by the way the district had been rushed through in order to capture the revaluation money. It offended her. In her view, that was not the intent of the constitutional amendment, and even if it didn't violate the letter of the law (and it didn't), it just struck her as *wrong*.

To Morris and Goodman, all of these flaws, except the political problem caused by the city's money crunch, were quibbles, merely excuses for not moving ahead. When the new city attorney, Hank Coleman, sent Jonathan Day's law firm a list of narrow legal questions about the district in mid-1982, the backers of Fantasy Island had a hard time taking them seriously. The mayor was stalling, they thought. When they heard about her objection to their plan to capture the revaluation money, they became even more agitated. How could she be worried about the intent of Proposition One? What they had done was perfectly legal and, to them, perfectly sensible. They had used the law to their advantage. If you were going to make things happen, that was precisely the sort of thing you did.

Morris and Goodman tried to get in to see the mayor, to talk to her about tax increment financing. In the fall of 1982 they drew up a proposed agenda for a meeting and then sent it to Whitmire's aides. They got nowhere. "These guys didn't even have a plan," says one aide now. "She would have had a million questions that they didn't have answers for. It just didn't make any sense to have a meeting."

They were frustrated at every turn. In April 1982, Goodman thought that the bayou project would soon be on its way and hired an associate to work on it full time. Seven months later he took her off the project; there wasn't anything for her to do. Morris began answering queries about the progress of the bayou project with notes like this one to a member of Gerald Hines' staff: "Our problem is that we haven't been able to get the mayor going." He no longer had access to city hall; he didn't even know most of the people over there.

In March 1983 he received a letter from a former classmate of his at Rice, Knox Banner, now a Washington consultant.

Banner had recently met with some of Whitmire's staff, and he wanted to pass on to Morris what he had learned. "Mayor Whitmire has at least two Rice graduates who are key members of her staff," Banner wrote, "John Chase, Assistant Director; and Jerry Wood, Director of Research. If you didn't know them before, you now have three possible points of beginning [the other being Joanne Adams, the mayor's assistant for cultural affairs, and another Rice graduate], but [proceed] *very* carefully, I suggest. . . . You may wish to seek more information on all three from the Rice Alumni Office before you strategize your gentle approach." Even a Washington consultant had more access to Houston's city hall than Morris did.

Still, where did that leave Fantasy Island? To McConn's insiders it seemed dead in the water, and there was little doubt in their minds as to where the blame lay. Kathy Whitmire had killed Fantasy Island with her legalistic and picayune complaints. They tended to take this rather personally—they weren't accustomed to losing—and it wasn't long before a theory developed according to which the real reason Whitmire had shut down the tax increment district was because it was part of the baggage from the previous administration. Any project backed by Jim McConn and run by S. I. Morris, the theory went, was something Whitmire was going to be against, no matter what its merits.

There was a grain of truth to that theory. Morris "probably feels that way because he doesn't have his personal plaything anymore," Whitmire said bitingly when I talked to her. But she insists that Fantasy Island is not dead, and that in her own way, she has been working as hard to see it completed as he ever did. It's just that Whitmire's conception of working on it is a good bit different from that of Morris and Goodman.

For instance, she sees her hiring of a new planning director eight months ago as an action that is pushing the project along. The new man, Efraim Garcia, came from San Antonio's city development agency; he says that when he took the job, Whitmire told him that the bayou project was to be one of his top priorities. (His familiarity with the San Antonio riverwalk is one reason he was selected.) So far, though, it is hard to see how that rather vague mandate is going to

metamorphose into Fantasy Island. What Garcia has done for the bayou is what he used to do for San Antonio—play the game of federal grantsmanship. But to go that route is to resign oneself to the project's being done only in the bits and pieces that fall comfortably within federal guidelines.

In fact, from Whitmire's perspective, everything she has done so far—much of which has had the effect of stalling the project—has actually helped it. The legal queries—well, they had to be cleared up, didn't they? The refusal to go along with the tax increment district—well, it did have an awful lot of problems, didn't it? The shutting out of S. I. Morris—well, he did represent the bad old days of Houston politics, didn't he? To her, this is not quibbling, it is good government.

If Whitmire ever does build a Fantasy Island, it will be on her terms, which means it will be the cleanest, most antiseptic, most apolitical deal you ever saw. And therein lies the trouble. Can you be completely clean, completely antiseptic, completely apolitical, and still build something of the magnitude of the island development? If you look at the great projects of Houston—for instance, the Ship Channel, which opened in 1914 and helped make Houston; the Astrodome, which first opened its doors in 1965; the airport, which opened in 1969—they were all deals from which insiders profited, to one degree or another. In retrospect, it seems pretty small-minded to begrudge them that, since such projects have obviously been boons to Houston.

But somehow, in more recent times, the delicate balance between noble instincts and selfish ones, which had always informed civic achievement in Houston, was tipped. The selfish—in the form of greed—has begun to outweigh the noble—the desire to get something good done for the city. Instead of doing good for themselves while doing good for the city, the civic achievers were doing good for themselves at the *expense* of the city.

When cable television came to Houston in 1980, it appeared that Walter Mischer and a few of his friends used the city's power to grant cable television franchises mainly as a way to make money. The idea of bringing a first-class cable system to Houston never seemed to be a big part of the equation. After the dust had settled,

they had made millions of dollars and the city was saddled with plenty of cable TV problems. The proposed MTA line also had all the earmarks of a deal that helped the few at the expense of the many. People in Houston have sensed this shift and have acted accordingly. They bounced McConn out of office and elected Whitmire. They trounced the MTA plan too. Both times, it seems clear that the electorate did the right thing.

And yet you're still left wondering about Whitmire's ability to get things done herself. Yes, she says she can make Fantasy Island a reality, but how? A mayor of a city as large and as messy as Houston is forever going to be handling the emergencies of the moment, while Fantasy Island goes to the back burner. A mayor with Whitmire's mind-set is always going to be able to find legitimate nits to pick, while Fantasy Island gets put on hold.

Most important, a mayor with Whitmire's background is always going to rank cronyism just after the bubonic plague on her list of evils. Whitmire's vision of government makes no distinctions between what was good about the old way of doing things and what was bad. To her, it was all bad. But it wasn't. It was bad when the city was the tool of the cronies; it's not bad at all when the cronies are the tool of the city. That's just good politics.

If Kathy Whitmire doesn't want Fantasy Island to be S. I. Morris' plaything—fine. There is no reason it should be, especially since Morris (and Mischer) are now supporting Bill Wright, her opponent in this month's mayoral election. But it does have to be *somebody's* plaything. In such a situation, she and the city would have the final say, but she could also leave the day-to-day negotiating to, well, to cronies. If she doesn't want Morris, she should find one of her own supporters—someone like James L. Ketelsen, the head of Tenneco—and tell him: it's your plaything. Give him—or someone—the authority to broker between the various interests and cut deals with the county and the school board. (And if that someone should happen to make some money in the process, that's all right too.) If she wanted Fantasy Island badly enough, she would do that. She would put aside her distaste for cronyism—for the messy business of politics—to help make Fantasy Island a reality. If she did that, she would be doing good for Houston. And good for herself. ❧

Dog Day in Dogwood City

Incorporating a small town in East Texas incorporated a passel of problems.

The Smith County courthouse. Tuesday, September 20, 1983. Not since the epochal wet-dry election in Noonday at the beginning of the year has this distinguished old building been such a caldron of controversy, a veritable arena of angst. There—that would be Bill Frizzell, the attorney for the plaintiffs, the blond, rakishly handsome one. And there, there's the attorney for the defense, Buddy Rogers. And in the limelight, of course, is Elcie Mae Perkins, the East Texas earth mama, the indomitable one. Eat your heart out, Racehorse. Cullen Davis' sinuous shenanigans may have played well in the Panhandle, but in Smith County these days, the true ticket to titillation is Elcie Mae Perkins and the Battle of Dogwood City.

Well, no, Howard Cosell wasn't really there, but he should have been. Two staples of Texas life are the small-town feud and the political squabbling that flares up at even the hint of a wet-dry election. Both are coming into play in the furious battle over whether Dogwood City, a 230-person hamlet on Lake Palestine in East Texas, will continue to exist.

The beginning of the Battle of Dogwood City dates from mid-1982, before the town was incorporated and Elcie Mae Perkins was elected its first mayor. It was also before Danny and Larry Busby's convenience store burned nearly to the ground because the town didn't have a fire department and had to depend on the volunteer force from nearby Noonday. Back in the summer of '82, Perkins, who sells shoes in Tyler and also owns a campground in Dogwood City with her husband, Buddie, decided that the town needed police and fire protection and the other basic services of a real city: dopers had invaded some nearby campgrounds, and the number of serious auto accidents on Texas Highway 155, which runs right through the middle of town, was up to ten per year. Unlit back streets were beginning to encourage muggings and rapes.

Perkins began knocking on doors and was surprised to find that most everyone she talked to agreed with her, except for some of the people in the more affluent Malibu Bay and Lakeway Harbor subdivisions. So she and Buddie and Larry Busby hired a surveyor to draw up some proposed city lines that included all the residents of the tiny peninsula except the two subdivisions. The Smith County judge approved the application to incorporate and the plat, and a referendum was set for January 15, 1983. That was when things started to get a little nasty.

Smith is a dry county, which means liquor can be sold only in cities that vote to allow it. As an unincorporated area, Dogwood City had no choice but to stay dry. Once it was incorporated, it could approve liquor sales. Now, in Texas there's a long tradition of setting up tiny towns that exist for no purpose other than to sell booze. Perkins says liquor sales were the last thing on her mind when she began to push for incorporation, but the liquor issue nonetheless immediately became the focus of the incorporation election. Bizarre anti-incorporation literature began to turn up in Dogwood City mailboxes. One hand-printed piece said, "Vote no! Incorporation for the sale of liquor! Whiskey will bring profiteers, blacks, drunks, rapists, thieves and armed robbers!" You get the general idea. There were also charges and countercharges of harassment and various sorts of skulduggery, such as mysterious cars that followed campaigners at night.

Perkins sees various villains in this drama, including J. D. Snowden, a cantankerous septuagenarian who spearheaded the local opposition. But she directs most of her ire toward the big-money liquor interests in neighboring counties (like Henderson and Gregg), which stand to lose a lot of business if liquor is ever sold in Dogwood City. Her chief suspect is Reginald Ormsby, who runs Foot's Liquor Store in Coffee City, just over the Henderson County line. Ormsby appeared two days before the election to stir up opposition in the two disenfranchised neighborhoods, where many residents felt they had been arbitrarily cut out of the vote. And Perkins was convinced that Ormsby's money was financing the anti-incorporation campaign.

Ormsby says that Perkins' accusations are a crock. "I had nothing to do with any of it," he says. "I went down there before the election and told them they had to fight, because I thought there were some folks getting flat run over. I won't deny that if they went wet and some store jumped in front of me [closer to Tyler] it would get most of my business. If they'd run a legal election, I'd have nothing to say in it. But they didn't, and that was my concern." Ormsby further alleges that one of Elcie Mae Perkins' main abettors in the incorporation campaign, Jim Acker, is a liquor store owner himself and just wanted to get his foot in the door in Dogwood City.

Whatever the case, the incorporation narrowly passed, 47–40. But the next day, J. D. Snowden and Frizzell began working up a suit against the new city, alleging that Malibu Bay and Lakeway Harbor had been arbitrarily excluded from the original plat. A couple of months later, the attorney general's office agreed to join the suit. After a summer of threats and counterthreats, and a remarkable amount of East Texas media attention, the case was finally heard in late September.

The plaintiff's case was simple. "The only legal issue was that those people lived in a natural part of the community and they were arbitrarily denied their due process to vote in the election," says attorney Frizzell. "The law says you can't do that." The city's defense was that the aggrieved parties were seeking the wrong kind of relief, and too late at that. "They could have petitioned to be added to the plat before or after the election," says Dogwood City attorney Buddy Rogers, "and they could have filed an election contest within thirty days after the election. They could still file to be annexed, and we'd take them. Why didn't they do any of that?"

After two days of somniferous and confusing testimony, the jury retired for thirty minutes and returned a verdict in favor of the plaintiff, rendering Dogwood City null and void. Dogwood City residents were so exercised that a few of them scuffled with Ormsby in the hallway. Elcie Mae Perkins was furious and made vague charges of hazy miscarriages of justice. She vows that the city will appeal the case and will stay in business pending the appeals. "If that higher court says we got nothing," she says, "I guess we'll just go have another election including those people."

If that should happen, the Battle of Dogwood City could end with no Dogwood City to battle in. According to Frizzell, the majority of the residents of Malibu Bay and Lakeway Harbor would probably vote against incorporation. "They just wanted to stay the way they were. That's what this case is all about," says Frizzell. Oh.

★ISSUES★

BEHIND THE LINES

This December, four of the largest school districts in Texas were deeply involved in desegregation decisions that would shape their destiny in the eighties. Fort Worth was putting the finishing touches on an agreement to cut back busing and restore neighborhood schools. Houston was also on the verge of ending its long stay in court, without busing and with its neighborhood schools intact. Dallas and Austin, however, faced court decisions that, particularly in Austin's case, seemed likely to require the most ambitious busing plan yet seen in Texas. The natural question, of course, is "Why?" Why are students in one Texas city to be bused and those in another Texas city not to be? Why are children in one school district assigned to neighborhood schools without regard to their race and those in another city assigned to distant schools *because of their race*?

No wonder the ordinary citizen is confused. Dr. Martin Luther King, the saint of the great movement to desegregate American life, expressed the goal so well: "I have a dream that my children will live in a nation where they will not be judged by the color of their skin but by the content of their character." In Austin and Dallas today, in the name of desegregation, his children would be judged by the color of their skin. More confusion surrounds the fact that a national commitment to eliminate segregation in schools has ended up with the courts' ruling that suburban districts—whose all-white schools are havens for white flight—are in compliance with the Constitution (basically because they had no blacks to segregate) and that their neighboring urban school districts—with almost no schools that are all white—are not. And year in, year out, those urban schools become more and more segregated.

These contradictions have sapped our national will to end segregation, and the sad thing is they are not inevitable. A desegregation plan that serves the best interests of its community should accomplish several major goals: it should eliminate any vestiges of the dual school systems that assigned black and white students to separate schools because of their race; it should improve educational opportunities for all children; and it should foster understanding and cooperation among races and ethnic groups. To meet these goals, a mandatory busing plan is the least desirable approach. It assigns students to schools by race, just as the dual system did. It disrupts education by taking children out of their neighborhoods against their will. And it increases racial tension by placing the onus for that disruption on minority children. Better solutions are possible, and school boards and minority leaders with vision have worked to find them.

Houston's desegregation plan emphasizes neighborhood schools and voluntary integration. Thousands of Houston students do ride buses to schools outside their neighborhoods, but they are bused *because they want to be,* because they and their parents think it is better for their education. The student and his parents are, after all, the real parties in these desegregation suits. A plan that gives them the freedom to improve integration by improving their education is destined to be more successful and more stable than a mandatory busing plan that relies on coercion. The Houston experience has shown that such a voluntary plan can produce integrated neighborhood schools whose students consistently surpass their supposedly superior suburban counterpar[t] [stan]dardized tests. It can produce, in short, better e[ducation] which is what all parents—black, Mexican A[merican] and white—want for their children.

Minority parents don't like mandatory busing much more than white parents do, but they are placated by their attorneys, who explain that they insist on busing because it is "the law of the land." That's simply not true. When it comes to desegregation plans for specific cities, there is no such thing as a clear and consistent law of the land. The desegregation plan of a given urban school district is nominally a response to the Constitution of the United States, but it is even more the result of the school administration's diplomacy, the attitudes and personality of the minority plaintiffs, and occasionally what the U.S. district judge had for breakfast. The final character of a school district's plan (provided the U.S. Justice Department or national civil rights organizations stay on the sidelines) is largely the product of how much vision the minority plaintiffs' attorneys and the school board have, and how well they get along.

Plaintiffs in Houston and Fort Worth, for example, have been willing to accept desegregation plans that are considerably less stringent than the courts might require. Weldon Berry, the NAACP attorney in the Houston case for more than twenty years ("too damn long," he says), gives that district good marks. "There is little overt racism here," he says. "The school board is making a sincere effort. Nobody in Houston wants busing. Blacks don't like it any more than whites, since blacks are usually the ones that end up being bused. What we need to do here," he continues, "is get more whites back in the district. We need to revitalize inner-city neighborhoods and build housing young couples can afford." Berry is philosophical about the future: "I'm no longer asking them to do the impossible. Everybody is more realistic now."

That same sort of positive, cooperative spirit has evolved, after years of enmity, in Fort Worth, where the NAACP and the school board have found a common interest in preserving a strong neighborhood school system. (In the process they finally laid to rest the old myth that to be in favor of neighborhood schools was to be against effective desegregation. Precisely the opposite is true today.) But in Dallas and Austin the minority plaintiffs and the school board seem to be always at each other's throats. The plaintiffs' attorneys, for their part, seem determined to get their pound of flesh now that they have the upper hand at last. "In a lawsuit that's in such an adversary situation," one plaintiffs' attorney told me, "you start wanting to win. And then you start wanting not just to win, but to beat your opponent, and beat him good." At the moment of such victory, as in Austin, the plaintiffs' attorneys can lose sight of their community's best interests and, with a snap of their fingers, demand that thousands of schoolchildren be bused; or they can work for a voluntary solution. The choice is entirely theirs. Seldom do private individuals, accountable to no one, hold such power. The best plaintiffs' attorneys exercise it wisely and without vindictiveness. Others, human nature being what it is, do not.

Minority plaintiffs, however, are not alone in polarizing the issue. In desegregation, as in dancing, it takes two to tango. Some school boards have fought every desegregation order and made few efforts to enhance the educaional opportunities of minority children. In contrast, the Houston School Board decided in 1971 that they would accept the court-ordered desegregation plan without further appeal and simply take the heat for the decision. The heat was so intense that those school board members were virtually driven from public life (although one, Eleanor Tinsley, was recently elected to the Houston City Council). But by their statesmanship they gave Houston almost a decade's lead over other Texas districts that kept their cases tied up in court. In 1975 their successors implemented, without waiting for a court order, a comprehensive plan of magnet schools (specializing in a wide range of programs, from engineering to performing arts) that were designed to improve desegregated education in 54 schools. One plaintiffs' attorney involved in several cities' suits described that move as a "positive, voluntary step that showed a sincere commitment to desegregation." That same attorney, however, had no good words for the school boards in Dallas and Austin, and therein lies much of the reason for the harsher desegregation plans those cities now face.

Practically speaking, the relative number of white students in a district also has a great deal to do with how comprehensive the desegregation plan will be. Big-city districts like Dallas, Houston, and San Antonio have been steadily losing white students, but to attribute that loss entirely to white flight is a mistake. School districts in these cities' best-known suburbs—Highland Park, Spring Branch, and Alamo Heights—have also lost students; in the past six years, for example, Spring Branch's enrollment has declined by 20 per cent, partly because its population is aging, partly because white birth rates are down, and partly because young parents can't afford houses that close to the central city. As a result of similar factors, both Houston and Dallas have around 30 per cent white students, down from more than 50 per cent in both districts a decade ago. There isn't a great deal of desegregation that can be accomplished with so few whites. Even if whites were distributed evenly among the district's schools, it is hard to maintain the legal fiction that a black child in a 90 per cent minority school is segregated while one in a 75 per cent minority

school is not.

Austin, on the other hand, is one of the few urban districts that still has a white majority. But as a plaintiffs' attorney in another district said about Austin, "It's tempting for the plaintiffs not to worry about whites fleeing the system when you've got a white majority. When you get down to thirty per cent or so, however, you start worrying about keeping the whites in." Although a few minority activists want whites to flee the city schools so they themselves can have more power, the simple truth is that when whites retreat to private schools to avoid busing, they tend to become foes of the public schools. They begin voting down bond issues and taxing authority, and, in no time at all, a healthy public school system can be destroyed. "The time for moderation," the plaintiffs' attorney continued, "is when you still have the whites, not after you've lost them."

Too often overlooked in this confusion over desegregation is the true central question: what kind of education are these schools providing? For the past 25 years parents have been influenced by two powerful but contradictory myths about integrated education. Whites have regarded integrated education as inferior, while blacks have seen it as superior. As a result, whites have fled from integrated education just as determinedly as blacks have pursued it. There is, however, absolutely nothing that destines predominantly black schools to be inferior, and a growing number of blacks have come to consider racist and insulting the myth that their children can learn only if they are in school with whites. They believe that, given good teachers and sufficient resources, their children can learn as well on their own. Even more important, more and more black parents are insisting on strong schools in their neighborhoods to hold their communities together. Mexican Americans have similar concerns, intensified, if anything, by their strong neighborhood identifications and their desire for bilingual education programs. The statistical evidence is fairly neutral: in some schools minorities do better in integrated classes, in others they do not.

But the myth that integrated schools are inferior to all-white schools is easier to puncture. The tenacity of that myth, spread by

suburban educators and realtors, has led young parents who want the best education for their children to suburban districts. Those districts, however, do not necessarily have better schools. Recent test results show that children in the 33 Houston elementary schools most like those in the highly touted Spring Branch suburban district scored a full *seven months* ahead of the suburban children, and *four* months ahead of students from Cypress Fairbanks, Humble, and Alief. All but two of those Houston schools have enrollments that are between 10 and 75 per cent minority children, yet test scores for these schools were significantly higher than those of all-white schools in the suburbs. A rational parent, black or white, choosing the best school for his child would have to pick one in Houston. The same clear superiority of the Houston schools is evident when their students are compared to those in other urban districts, to other students in gifted and talented programs, and even to other students in disadvantaged schools. Across the board, Houston students score as well as or better than comparable students anywhere.

The lesson in these test results, and in the many innovative programs that a large district like Houston can support, is that middle-class parents who sincerely want the best education for their children should send them back to urban schools. To choose private or suburban schools may be to shortchange their children, not simply in terms of the somewhat abstract benefits of a multiracial experience, but also in terms of the concrete advantages of superior education. Until Houston stopped worrying about desegregation and started worrying about excellence in education, about all the district could do to defend desegregation was to tell parents it was good for the nation for their children to go to Houston schools. Now they can say it is good for the children. Most cities have not expended as much effort to improve integrated education as Houston has, but with good leadership, parental support, and cooperation from their desegregation plaintiffs, they could. The fact that integrated schools can be superior, as they are in Houston, is a sign that urban education can work. There are few greater signs of hope in America today.♦

William Broyles, Jr.

Double-Talk

In the bilingual education bout, maybe the kids know best

The Mexican American boy pounded his bat on home plate. "¡Despacio!" he called out to the pitcher. She lobbed him a slower ball and he let it go by. "¡Despacio!" he insisted. The infielders set up a derisive chatter in Spanish and English as a warm south wind blew in clouds of dust from Mexico. "That wasn't too fast," the pitcher said. The boy repeated himself and she shouted, "Voy a matarte"—"I'm going to kill you"—and showed him what a fast pitch looked like. He popped it up to second base.

It was just another playground softball game in Rio Grande City on a gusty spring day. I had come to the border town, whose schools are housed in the buildings of Fort Ringgold, a nineteenth-century U.S. Cavalry post, because kids like these are at the center of a growing dispute among grown-ups over bilingual education. Federal judge William Wayne Justice is currently considering a charge by the Mexican American Legal Defense and Education Fund (MALDEF) that Texas is not meeting the needs of Hispanic schoolchildren. The outcome of the case could have enormous impact on Texas' future: at stake are not only thousands of jobs and millions of dollars but also the question of whether a generation of children will be encouraged to think of themselves as American citizens or ethnic tribesmen.

Speaking Spanish in Texas classrooms was frowned upon for decades, and teachers often spanked children who did so. That treatment helped spur a heritage of bitterness among Mexican Americans as well as a reaction in the opposite direction that could be almost as hurtful as paddling a child for speaking his native language. Texas education commissioner Alton Bowen discovered how deep feelings run when he addressed a meeting of school administrators last October. In his speech Bowen applied the melting pot metaphor of American society to the issue of bilingual education. "Race and language are extremely important elements of any group's heritage and should be maintained," he said, "but the responsibility for such language and cultural maintenance is with the home, the family, the community, and not with the school." Bowen's opinion, which most Americans of all ethnic persuasions would describe as common sense, was denounced by State Senator Carlos Truan of Corpus Christi, Ruben Bonilla of the League of United Latin American Citizens (LULAC), and Juan D. Solís of the National Association for Bilingual Education.

Under current Texas law, schools with at least twenty students in the same grade who speak a foreign language must pro-vide bilingual instruction in all classes from kindergarten through third grade (and through fifth grade if local authorities think it is necessary). Older students who have not acquired adequate English skills must receive an hour a day of English instruction. The idea—which educators call the transitional method—is to teach children English without letting them fall behind in their basic subject matter.

According to MALDEF, that's not going far enough. The San Francisco–based organization has asked Judge Justice to rule that Texas must fund a bilingual education program from kindergarten through high school and in all subjects from physics to wood shop. They say that the very high proportion (30 per cent) of school dropouts among Mexican Americans constitutes proof that more bilingual instruction is needed.

Other bilingual advocates want more than that. Dr. Josué González, appointed by President Carter to head the Education Department's Office of Bilingual Education, says that the melting pot idea is outdated. González, who is a native of Rio Grande City and a former professor of education at SMU, advocates biculturalism, a radical departure from the original goals of bilingual education. He thinks public schools have a constitutional mandate not only to teach Mexican American children to speak English but also to nurture their cultural identity and self-esteem. One wonders what America would be like today if González's ideas had been in vogue a hundred years ago.

MALDEF's request for a judicial opinion is based on Lau v. Nichols, in which the U.S. Supreme Court ruled that San Francisco had to do something—the court didn't specify what—for Chinese students who spoke no English. For the past six years the Office of Civil Rights has been trying to use Lau v. Nichols as a precedent for cutting off funds to school districts deemed not in compliance with bilingual requirements. The trouble is that the feds have never spelled out the remedies.

The result in Texas has been chaos. Districts like Austin—which pioneered in the area of bilingual education and which recruits teachers from the Valley—have been charged with noncompliance for not hiring enough bilingual teachers. In fact, the teachers do not exist. The state has a serious shortage of qualified bilingual teachers already, and bilingual specialization is very unpopular among education students. Last year, for example, Texas teacher training schools graduated only 349 bilingual education teachers.

Having lost an attempt to cut funding to a school district in Alaska last year because the Lau remedies were yet un-written, the government is now trying to come up with guidelines. It must decide how students are to be chosen for the program and whether parents are to be consulted, along with a host of other tricky questions that, taken together, come down to one: is the goal to teach English or to preserve Hispanic and other minority cultures? If what I saw in Rio Grande City can serve as a guide, the answer seems to be to teach kids English.

About 98 per cent of Rio Grande City's inhabitants are Mexican American. Many were born—and almost all have relatives—south of the border. They earn their living primarily as government workers, school employees, shop clerks, merchants, ranchers, and seasonal vegetable pickers; a notorious few are drug traffickers. Starr County, of which Rio Grande City is the seat, is one of the poorest counties in the United States. Unemployment chronically runs at 31 per cent. But poor as it is, Starr County is more prosperous than the neighboring Mexican state of Tamaulipas. For all the fascinating mix of languages and culture in the border area, the river is the great clarifier. Nobody of Mexican origin wants to go back, and everyone knows that work above the level of stoop labor is not available to non-English speakers and never will be.

School superintendent A. E. García told me that nearly all students in Rio Grande City are enrolled in bilingual classes from first through sixth grades (fourth, fifth, and sixth are supported with federal funds). Dr. García is happy to play grantsman because the federal dollars provide higher salaries and nicer classrooms than he could otherwise afford. And he is happy that no one gets spanked anymore for speaking Spanish. But practically speaking, his schools are doing pretty much what they have done for years: teaching English. I went to bright classrooms full of button-eyed first-graders who understood my English and giggled at my Spanish. García did not worry when his own children almost forgot Spanish while he was studying at the University of Texas at Austin, because he knew they would pick it up as soon as they went back to Rio Grande City. They did.

At Rio Grande City's spacious new high school, principal Ruben Sáenz boasted that 189 of 220 graduates last year went on to some kind of post-secondary education. Like everyone I talked to in Rio Grande City, Sáenz was disarmingly honest. He says he doesn't know whether the current bilingual program works better than other teaching methods, but he rejects the argument that Texas should provide Spanish-language instruction in all subjects at all grade levels. "It is not simply impractical but impossible," he said. Sáenz told me he has visited allegedly "bilingual" classes north of San Antonio taught by non-native speakers whose incompetence he found shocking.

Bilingual education came into being in 1968 as one method among many to help poor children learn English. It has metamorphosed since, with the aid of MALDEF and its philosophical allies in the federal bureaucracy, into a constitutional right. Yet there is still no conclusive evidence that it works better than other methods; some studies say it actually provides a haven that hinders children from learning English. As generations of immigrants in this country have proved, children can learn languages with astonishing rapidity when they have to.

Those who are making the big push for more bilingual education often do so because they feel they have lost part of their own cultural identity in assimilating the majority culture. And they have. But they have gained a lot too—a rich mix of culture and opportunity made up of the contributions of countless nationalities and yet uniquely American. First-graders in Rio Grande City know that. The grown-ups will catch on sooner or later.

BEHIND THE LINES

Not too long ago I drove to Paint Rock, out near San Angelo, hoping to spend some time with Mrs. Ellen Sims, who had been a neighbor of my great grandfather's when he was the editor of the *Concho Herald* in the twenties. Mrs. Sims was not at home, but presently a big Chevrolet pulled into the driveway and out she stepped. I asked where she had been. "Well," she replied, "I heard from a neighbor that there'd been some rain out toward Veribest, so I went to see for myself."

By her fascination with rain Mrs. Sims proved she is a Westerner. And by my surprise and amusement at that fascination, I revealed myself for what, in spite of my attraction to the West, I am—an Easterner. My family has been in Texas for generations, but growing up in East Texas is like growing up rich. The rich can afford not to be preoccupied with money, and Easterners can afford not to be preoccupied with water—they have plenty of it.

When Billy Clayton, the Speaker of the Texas House of Representatives, proposed in December that the state's oil and gas revenues be set aside to establish a fund for water projects, he was speaking as a Westerner. Clayton is a Panhandle farmer. The Panhandle's prosperity since World War II has been based on underground water, and the water is running out. Clayton is not the only one concerned. The High Plains–Ogallala Council, a confederation of six Great Plains states (including Texas), is drawing up a plan—the latest in a long line—to carry water from the Mississippi River system to the Texas Panhandle, possibly via a five-hundred-mile canal from the great river's tributaries in Arkansas. Like Clayton, the council invokes the specter of a new Dust Bowl if the High Plains states don't get water to replace their dwindling underground reservoirs. But East Texans have a hard time believing they should spend billions of dollars, jeopardize the environment, and rip up hundreds of miles of good farmland in order to help grow corn in an arid region that perhaps is better suited, in the long run, to grazing cattle and sheep.

Underlying these political differences is a deeper truth: we are shaped more by geography than we care to admit, as anyone who travels by air from Houston to El Paso can plainly see. Our nation may have been divided between North and South by history, but by climate and geography it is split between East and West. From Houston the pine forest stretches east to the horizon, forming a vast carpet that extends to the Atlantic. To the west the land changes gradually from shades of green to shades of gray and brown, from forest to desert. Beyond El Paso are alkaline flats spotted with creosote bush, a desolate landscape that continues west hundreds of miles to the Pacific. The two cities might be on different planets.

East of a line drawn from Laredo through Abilene and on up along the eastern edge of the Panhandle (more or less along the 100th meridian) are the state's largest cities and the great majority of its population. West of that line is almost half of Texas, but only a fraction of its people. In East Texas enough rain falls to permit the kind of agriculture and society that developed in America from the time of the Pilgrims. In West Texas that agriculture and society are impossible. On that fact turns much of the history of America in the past century. During America's first two hundred years the pioneers moved west from the Atlantic through the great Eastern forests. Between the 100th meridian and the Coast Range, however, Americans confronted an arid, treeless landscape that covered a full 40 per cent of the original 48 states but was impervious to the tools, the habits of life, and the culture that had developed between the Atlantic and the Mississippi Valley. Both the pioneer family and its log cabin culture were stopped dead by those plains, which for years bore on maps the legend "The Great American Desert."

But even if the West was a desert, it did not lack for riches. Sadly, those riches have not been husbanded. They have been plundered. The plundering did take great measures of sweat, courage, technology, and hope. If only we had added vision and foresight we could have used the West as a source of prosperity for generations. But in less than twenty years we slaughtered the beaver, then the buffalo. Next we overgrazed the rich prairie grasses, turning thousands of square miles of the West into desert as barren as Afghanistan. And then we plowed up the prairie itself, pulverizing its soil so the winds could blow it away. With each new plundering came a short-lived boom, always followed by bust. The latest boom, the irrigated farming of the Panhandle, seems destined to meet the same unhappy end. Panhandle farmers, however, come from tough, resilient stock. They suffered through decades of austerity on the plains, and they don't want to give up their newfound prosperity without a fight.

A century ago the Panhandle was the last refuge for the southern buffalo herds. Huge ranches like the XIT, the Matador, and Charles Goodnight's JA replaced the buffalo. But because of overgrazing, bad winters, and economic depressions most of these big ranches were carved up into smaller ranches and farms around the turn of the century. For a generation the farmers were blessed with abundant rainfall. From Texas to the Dakotas they pushed out onto the plains, building sod huts, plowing up the prairie grass, and perhaps planting some flowers around their doors to bring color to the bleached-out landscape. But drouth came in the twenties and thirties, breaking the hearts and backs of thousands of farm families, parching their fields, and withering their flowers. Dust storms carried huge clouds of dirt all the way across the continent and out into the Atlantic, the final resting place for some of the best topsoil on earth.

But even in the worst years of the Dust Bowl some farmers had begun to tap the plains' greatest resource. Beneath the swirling dust, from Midland to South Dakota, lay a vast underground lake of fossil water millions of years old, trapped in sand and porous rock, a reservoir called the Ogallala Aquifer. Beginning in the fifties, High Plains farmers pumped from it such riches of water that they converted six million acres into fabulously productive cropland.

There is only one problem with the Ogallala: it's running dry. Unlike the Edwards Aquifer, which underlies Austin and San Antonio, the Ogallala is not replenished by rainfall. After only a generation of intensive use it is more than a third gone. There may be thirty years' worth of water left in some areas, but in others—around Lubbock, for example—barely a decade's worth remains. Wells have to be dug deeper and deeper, and the average well now waters about half the acreage it covered in the fifties. More and more of the wells are beginning to gasp and croak, their pumps lifting up not water but air. The aquifer is the mother lode of Panhandle farming, and like a gold mine it is being mined out.

For 25 years Panhandle farmers have been lobbying for an elaborate system of aqueducts to replace the Ogallala with water from the Mississippi River system. Texans outside the Panhandle have been less than loyal to these plans, and on two occasions the voters of Texas have defeated referenda for funding them. The people of the High Plains are understandably frustrated that the rest of the nation, not to mention the rest of their own state, fails to appreciate the miracles they have wrought or the fundamental need to do whatever is necessary to continue working those miracles.

The East, however, has always misunderstood the West, and vice versa. Few Westerners have much curiosity about, or sympathy for, the decaying cities of the East. The Northeast, which controlled capital and power in America, thought it natural for the West to provide the raw materials for Eastern prosperity while also serving as a dumping ground for the immigrants pouring into Eastern cities. Horace Greeley wrote, "Go west, young man," but he did not move west himself. The laws supposedly designed to promote the settlement of the West were hopelessly at odds with its reality. The Homestead Act generously assumed that 160 acres would support a family, but in the West few families could survive on such a plot.

Time and again the simple facts of nature drove homesteaders off the plains. The soil was rich in nutrients and could support certain crops that were raised by dryland techniques designed to conserve the little rain that fell by thwarting its natural evaporation through crusty soil. But no matter how skilled the farmer, dryland farming has always been a marginal proposition. Towns were built around farms and abandoned and built again, each new cycle the triumph of hope over experience.

Then irrigation farming changed all that and the desert bloomed. The Panhandle has become some of the world's richest and most productive farmland, testimony to our indomitable determination to transform nature into opportunity, no matter how often nature refused to cooperate. To sustain that determination now requires that we decide whether to replace the water of the Ogallala with the distant waters of the Mississippi River.

It is true that the High Plains farmers, like the buffalo hunters and ranchers before them, abused the wealth nature gave them. They used the Ogallala as if there would be no tomorrow. They planted crops that require tremendous amounts of water, such as corn, then flooded their furrows with many times the water the crops needed. They refused to adopt cooperative approaches to water conservation and fought any attempt to impose conservation upon them. They showed a great lack of interest in farming techniques that would have saved water, techniques that allow farmers in arid regions like Israel to obtain bountiful yields with a fraction of the water used by the Panhandle farmers. If the Israelis had been blessed with the Ogallala, they would have made it last for centuries. As always in the West, the Panhandle farmers took nature for granted.

But we should resist the temptation to transform the plight of the Panhandle into a morality play. Those of us in the East—particularly East Texas—can't afford to watch smugly as the hard-won prosperity of the High Plains deteriorates into a new agricultural depression and a new Dust Bowl. Agriculture is too important to our economy not to give the Mississippi River plan a fair hearing. Will its potential benefits make up for its stupendous cost and potential environmental damage? And equally to the point, will the farmers be able to pay for the water once it gets to the Panhandle, given that the cost of pumping the Ogallala water, in a new era of high energy prices, is proving to be more expensive than many farmers can afford? Billy Clayton's water resource program also merits serious attention. It's quite possible, however, that calm and rational analysis of our state's water needs and agricultural potential may show that investing vast sums of money in bringing water to the arid Panhandle would be far less productive than improving farming in *East* Texas.

One of the great ironies of the Panhandle agricultural miracle is that irrigation has transformed natural grazing land into such efficient farmland—temporarily, at least—that much of the natural farmland of East Texas has been converted into grazing land or taken out of production entirely. These Eastern blackland prairies and coastal plains get plenty of rain and are suited by nature for the annual production of crops. Through proper management they might yield an agricultural bonanza equivalent to the bonus production that unregulated irrigation has brought to the High Plains. At the same time we could protect the High Plains' prosperity by investing in new agricultural technology to improve yields while using less water.

Any solution to the inevitable playing out of the Ogallala Aquifer is going to be emotional and divisive, as the problems of the West have always been. But when we face the West, when we face ourselves, we must first question whether perhaps—just perhaps—we have overstepped ourselves, whether we are trying to make a land carry more civilization than, in the long run, it can. And that is a very un-Western idea.

William Broyles, Jr.

Case Closed

Harris County shuts down its abortion clinic.

Joseph Graham gets depressed when he thinks about Texas Right-to-Life's failure to pass any anti-abortion bills during the 1981 legislative session. Graham, a professor of philosophy at the University of St. Thomas in Houston, is also the Texas representative to the National Right-to-Life Committee, so he spent a lot of frustrating hours at the Capitol, watching the group's bills die in hostile Senate committees.

For victories, he should have stuck closer to home: in May pro-lifers shut down the abortion clinic at Houston's Jefferson Davis Hospital, the only publicly funded abortion facility in Harris County. It was a coup such as they have been able to manage in only three other counties in the United States.

Jeff Davis has operated its Voluntary Termination of Pregnancy clinic since 1973, opening it just six months after the Supreme Court handed down its famous decision legalizing abortion. From the beginning, the hospital board had to overcome opposition from anti-abortion groups and the county commissioners' court. The commissioners actually tried to strike the clinic from the hospital's budget, but their attorney advised against it. The court, he said, did not have the authority to veto a line item; it must either accept or reject the entire budget. So the commissioners restored the money, and apparently gave the clinic little thought over the next eight years. During that time, the hospital terminated over four thousand pregnancies, eight hundred of them last year.

But the mood of the country has changed since 1973, and this spring Houston Right-to-Life sensed that the time was ripe for another all-out assault. Weeks before the commissioners' May 14 budget hearing, right-to-lifers were out pounding the pavement with petitions in hand. The Sunday before the meeting, they stood outside area churches and collected 10,000 signatures. Some of the movement's leaders called the commissioners personally to urge them to strike the abortion clinic's $127,000 allotment from the budget. The National Abortion Rights Action League and other pro-abortion organizations soon got wind of the move and started alerting their members.

The seven members of the hospital's budget board, who had no inkling of what was afoot, put the final touches to their $129.4 million budget in early May. The only trouble they expected from the commissioners was over a tax increase to fund the purchase of a geriatrics center. But two days before the hearing, board chairman Quentin Mease met with Commissioner Tom Bass, who surprised him with the news that the court might turn down the hospital's budget because of the abortion clinic.

The pro-lifers had approached Bass, a Roman Catholic with ten children, to act on their behalf. At first he rejected the idea. But his callers persisted, reminding him that the Supreme Court ruled last year that governments aren't obliged to use tax money to support abortions. The tax angle appealed to Bass. He is no stereotypical opponent of abortion. He is a liberal—one of the Dirty Thirty state legislators who pushed for liberal reforms in the late sixties—and he considers himself a feminist. "But this is one issue I can't agree with them on," he says. "I feel the fetus is a human being."

That sentiment aside, the commissioners were acting totally out of character in raising the issue. Abortion is a classic no-win vote, one that politicians normally shun like leprosy. That's why the right-to-lifers bombed at the Legislature: Lieutenant Governor Bill Hobby sent their bills into oblivion to protect legislators from having to cast politically damaging votes. And in Houston the commissioners had an easy out—they weren't allowed to veto specific expenditures.

Nevertheless, Bass decided to force the issue. Politically, he may have had nothing to lose; he has already put out the word that he expects redistricting to ruin his district and that he may not run again in 1984. The way to get around the line item veto question, he figured, was simply to reject the whole budget—and keep on rejecting it until the hospital board deleted the funds itself.

On the night of the hearing, more than one hundred people squeezed into the commissioners' meeting room. They squirmed in anticipation as the hospital board presented its budget, and then fourteen speakers assailed the clinic's funding, using familiar arguments against "baby killing" and likening the clinic to Auschwitz. On the other side,

three speakers urged the commissioners to keep the clinic, stressing "a woman's right to privacy—and choice." Then Bass made a short speech announcing his opposition to using public funds to pay for abortions and recommended that the commissioners vote the budget down and kick it back to the hospital board to cut out the clinic.

Going into the meeting, no one had had a clear idea of how the votes would break down. Graham felt the pro-lifers could count only on Bass and county judge Jon Lindsay, who had spoken against abortion in the past. The votes of commissioners Bob Eckels, Jim Fonteno, and E. A. "Squatty" Lyons were up in the air. But the suspense didn't last long. When Fonteno, one of the swing votes, seconded Bass's motion, the anti-abortionists looked like winners. Eckels offered that he "wasn't that opposed to abortions" and voted with Lyons to approve the budget and keep the funds intact. Lindsay voted against the clinic, just as Graham thought he would.

The right-to-lifers left the meeting flushed with triumph. But the members of the hospital board were furious. At their next meeting, they decided to bounce the budget right back to the commissioners without touching the clinic funds. So the commissioners requested once again—this time after 85 people aired their views before the court —that the hospital delete the abortion funds. Finally the board members decided, as one of them put it, "to face up to political realities." The third-round budget did not fund an abortion clinic.

Pro-abortion activists were appalled. "Taking abortion rights away from the poor is the first step," warned Pat Lane, president of the Texas Abortion Rights Action League. "Their ultimate goal is to pass a human life bill and take it away from everyone." The clinic's closing has lit a fire under organizations like Lane's, and they are lobbying against a bill already before Congress that would define life as beginning at conception. It has also fueled the anti-abortion movement in Texas. In San Antonio pro-lifers have already collected 30,000 signatures protesting Bexar County Hospital's abortion unit. And they plan to use them. *Susan Duffy*

GOD'S HAPPY HOUR

by Dick J. Reavis

In most of the country prohibition is long forgotten, but in rural Texas the Lord's people haven't given up the battle against the bottle.

The people who live north of Silsbee and in the northern part of Hardin County, about twenty miles west of Louisiana and twenty miles north of Beaumont, lined up in single file, like the pines along their thoroughfare, Highway 92. The line began at the front door of the Jack and Jill day care center, went all the way around the side, and stretched onto the little parking lot in back. The women, who were dressed mainly in polyesters and denims, had umbrellas with them, for there was rain in the air; tropical storm Chris had passed during the night. The men, most of them in jeans, Western shirts, and gimme caps, smoked cigarettes or stood with their arms crossed at waist level, eyes turned down toward their boots. They were all neighbors, but there was no banter because the event that had brought them together that day, though it might cause guffaws elsewhere, was taken seriously in Hardin County. By the process of direct democracy, those voters were about to decide a controversy not merely of politics but of human nature. That September Saturday, they would mark their ballots either for sin or against it. They would vote Hardin's Precinct 2 wet, or dry.

The Hardin vote is of interest not so much for its outcome as for the old legal and moral tempests resurrected by it. In American and Texan politics, prohibitionism is a venerable, though in most areas disappearing, issue. America's founders were foes of whiskey: the Continental Congress, for example, called on legislatures to put "an immediate stop to the pernicious practice of distilling grain." Drys claim Abraham Lincoln and Jefferson Davis as spokesmen, and the reformed drunk Sam Houston is counted too. Despite his support, the prohibition movement was weak in Texas until after the Civil War, in part because abolition and women's suffrage—both unpopular in Texas—were its sibling causes.

But when it took hold here, prohibition stuck; in many places it is still with us. Texas drys first made themselves felt in 1875, when provisions urged by Colonel E. L. Dohoney, founder of the state's Prohibition party, were written into our constitution. By its terms, counties, justice precincts, and incorporated cities may vote to prohibit or restrict the sale of alcoholic beverages. Thanks to the efforts of the Women's Christian Temperance Union and the Band of Hope, the union's youth corps, four fifths of the counties in Texas had already voted themselves dry by 1918, when the Legislature enacted a state prohibition law eighteen months before national prohibition took effect. Prohibition was popular enough that the state statute was not repealed until 1935, two years after the nation went wet again.

Repeal hardly laid the issue to rest. In the ensuing decades, conservatives, because they were *socially* conservative, argued for government regulation of liquor and liberals argued against it. The wet-dry issue was so hotly debated that the earmark of graying liberals in Texas is that at an early age, before they were versed in other issues, most of them took a wet stand on liquor. "I was just a kid when Wichita Falls voted wet," says Jim "Lopez" Smitham, part owner of two of Austin's leading liberal hangouts, the Raw Deal restaurants. "That was the first election I paid attention to. I was for the wets, if only because my dad was a Roosevelt Democrat."

The trend in a thousand post-Prohibition local option elections was from dry to wet, but the change was stubborn, slow, and incomplete. At the end of World War II, two thirds of the counties in Texas were wholly dry, and it would be nearly thirty years before liquor gained the upper hand. The dry cause was dealt its death blow in 1970, when the state's voters approved a constitutional amendment that for the first time authorized liquor to be sold by the drink. Today, in Houston, Dallas, Fort Worth, San Antonio, and Austin, liquor-by-the-drink profits underwrite a whole world of evening restaurants, and the cafe society that revolves around them has given new blood to nightlife districts. Still, a third of Texas is dry by law, and two weeks out of three, or about 35 times a year, a liquor election is held somewhere in the state. A profession has arisen consisting of election coaches whose sole occupation is giving campaign advice to wets or drys. Most local option elections are called by wets and won by drys: only two elections out of five open new territory to booze.

Maps of wet and dry areas have for a century divided the state roughly along a line from El Paso to Orange. Above that line, anti-alcohol sentiment finds a home, though drys must fight to hold sway. Below that line, the friends of liquor—Catholics, blacks, people of Mexican, German, and Czech descent—prevail and always have. White Anglo Protestants have traditionally been dry, and the prohibition controversy has been fought on their North Texas turf. The big cities are alcohol oases: except for the period of statewide prohibition, booze has almost always been welcome in Houston and San Antonio and tolerated in Dallas, but not until the last decade did restrictions fall back in Lubbock and Abilene, and to this day you can't buy a six-pack in Tyler. In towns and rural communities where the frontier ethic survives, in places like Altoga, Corinth, Ferris, Lone Grove, Sweeny, and Tow, full-fledged prohibitionism lives on. And last year it became a force to contend with in Hardin County's Silsbee and Caneyhead, communities barely above the El Paso–Orange liquor line.

The Gentlemen's Agreement

Hardin's Precinct 2 is a 15-by-24-mile stretch of the Big Thicket whose western corner takes in part of Kountze and whose eastern edge is the Neches River. In between, on street after street, are homes owned mainly by men who work at the refineries in Beaumont, Port Arthur, and Orange. Silsbee, the chief trade center for Precinct 2, is a town of almost eight thousand people wedded to rural living. Most homes in Silsbee's environs sit on acre-and-a-half lots, surrounded by tall trees. Stump removal is an important service, and small merchants and tradesmen set up shop in their homes rather than move their businesses to town ("Welders Caps Made Here," reads a sign along Highway 92). In Precinct 2, Baptists are the religious moderates; it is the Pentecostals who are respected for keeping "strong religion" alive. In bygone days, northern Hardin was moonshine territory, and the county's people have not entirely cast off their old ways. Like jealous twins, hard drinking and hardshell religion share North Hardin's affection.

Prohibition had a bitter taste in Hardin. Wets did not like it because, by all reports, moonshine was poor whiskey. Drys did not like it because moonshining's child was corruption in local government. The county emerged from the Prohibition era determined to legalize liquor, but with limits. It developed a core of politicians, preachers, and liquor retailers who were dedicated to moderation and compromise, the guardian angels of legal liquor.

Second-generation liquor dealer Harvey Cunningham is one of them. A tall, solidly built, big-voiced man of 53, he has a personality consistent with East Texas tradition. As East Texas men are supposed to do, he has mastered the Dixie graces. Harvey likes to tell jokes, but he won't tell most of them in mixed company. Cunningham is the name everybody gives to the community where he resides, but Harvey won't call it that because he

knows what modesty means. At home with his wife, he plays the Southern gentleman, talking proudly of his lineage and mentioning, by the way, his financial contributions to the good work of the North Hardin Baptist Church. At work, he lets himself be a more Western rascal of a man, usually dressing in jeans, boots, and a cowboy hat with a big feather hatband, always gibing himself or his associates. Harvey Cunningham is the sort of man with whom you'd like to go pig hunting in the Neches River bottoms, not because you could be sure of a kill but because you could count on conversation that was nearly ribald.

When Harvey was a boy he earned pocket change—and sometimes more—by picking up discarded whiskey bottles and reselling them to North Hardin moonshiners for a nickel apiece. One of his customers was his grandfather Jeff Cunningham, a man who tinted his moonshine amber with red oak chips. Albert Cunningham, Harvey's father, bootlegged Jeff's product to lumber camps nearby, and as Harvey remembers it, "Daddy never saw any money until he started selling whiskey." Albert started selling legal whiskey in 1935, a few months after Texas repeal, when he opened one of the liquor stores Harvey operates today in Precinct 2, just south of the Tyler County line.

An oval portrait of Grandfather Jeff, uncharacteristically clad in a Sunday suit, hangs on a wall of Harvey Cunningham's house. The portrait is an altered enlargement of the only photo Harvey could find of his grandfather. The original, made at Huntsville, shows Jeff wearing a striped prison suit. Harvey begged me not to bring this up, for the past weighs heavy in East Texas, but Jeff was sent to prison for the murder of S. L. "Curly" Drake, a North Hardin neighbor. Curly was the father of F. C. Drake, who at 73 is still a formidable figure in North Hardin liquor circles. F. C. Drake is the dean of North Hardin's modern prohibition movement.

F. C. Drake grew up in a clearing called Drake's Settlement, just south of Cunningham. In his youth he went hoboing on trains, drank hard, and saved little. One Friday in the late twenties, drunk, hungry, and so darkened by smoke that only his sister recognized him as kin, F.C. straggled home from the tracks and lay down on the porch of the family home, where he passed out from drink or exhaustion. When he had rested, he went on a moonshine binge again, only this time he did not get so drunk as to lose his reason. On Sunday morning, still tipsy, he walked into a wooden-frame makeshift church in time for a sermon. F.C. was overcome by the Lord that morning and began setting his life right. He studied for the ministry, preached at backwoods churches, founded a church himself in the early forties, and in 1954 opened the Evergreen Assembly of God church on Highway 92, about two miles north of

Silsbee. It is there that he made a name for himself in liquor politics.

The Evergreen church is a one-story, pink brick building with a peaked roof, located across Highway 92 from a big convenience store that, thanks to Drake's efforts, has never sold beer. The congregation at Evergreen is smaller now than in years past, but even if only two dozen believers show up on a Sunday, Reverend Drake struts his finest skills for them. Though he is balding and nearly deaf in one ear, Drake is a pulpit stormer. White-templed and pink-faced, he stomps, gesticulates, and shouts out in glossolalia to make points, lacing his sermons with expressions like "this dark, evil, God-hating world" and exclamations like "Hallelujah! Amen! Great God!" When Reverend Drake reaches his preaching stride, his faithful are put on edge not only because the oratory is impressive but also because they know he has a weak heart and are afraid he'll drop dead in mid-sermon. In private conversation Drake comes across as clever more than sincere, as crafty more than straightforward. When I asked if he hadn't dropped out of high school, Drake's response was, "I don't know if I should tell you that. It might not make me look good."

By law, cities and justice of the peace precincts—there are four to eight in every Texas county—are the smallest jurisdictions that can be declared wet or dry. Silsbee and Precinct 2, the northern quarter of Hardin County, were wet when Drake opened the Evergreen church, and there was little reason to hope for change. But he saw a way to win a partial victory. Most of the residents of Precinct 2 lived on the south end of Highway 92, just outside Silsbee's city limits and near his church. Drake first strengthened his hand by organizing a civic association dedicated to prohibitionist ends, then went to the precinct's liquor retailers with a proposal: if they would keep their liquor stores on the north end of Highway 92, the people who lived on the south end—including Drake's faithful—would make no move to vote the precinct dry.

Perhaps because he wished to avoid controversy for business reasons, or perhaps because he could not deny a request made by the man his father had orphaned, Albert Cunningham agreed. So did other liquor men. Under Drake's persuasion, so did a series of county judges. Starting in the early fifties, when the deal was struck, whenever anyone applied to a county judge for a permit to sell beer anywhere within a five-mile strip on the south end of Highway 92, Drake and his supporters would show up to protest. The permits were always turned down. The south end of Highway 92 was dried up by a gentlemen's agreement, though not by law.

The Liquor Store

Cecil C. "Bosco" Phillips, 29, a propane jobber, and Tommy Bohler, 35, an electrician, are picaresque characters whose lives seem to be taken from country and western music's Moe and Joe duets. They are the sort of men who put stock in beer, overweight gold jewelry, pickup trucks with glass-pack mufflers and custom paint jobs—and money. They were mere children in Hardin when the Drake-Cunningham agreement was reached, and they don't think they gained much by it. Late in 1981 they decided that they could profit by opening a business at a spot where there would be no competition, inside the five dry miles of Highway 92. They called their projected enterprise the Liquor Store.

The liquor industry in Texas is regulated by the state Alcoholic Beverage Commission, a bureaucracy of seven hundred people known for both its power and its obscurantism. The law requires the ABC to submit applications for beer licenses to the discretion of county judges, but for some reason licenses to sell hard liquor are the ABC's to grant. If they could get a liquor license from the ABC, Phillips and Bohler reasoned, Hardin County judge Ray Martin could have none but punitive reasons for afterward denying them a beer permit. By going to the ABC in Austin before coming into county court, Phillips and Bohler hoped to sidestep Drake and his supporters.

Their scheme was shared by another man their age, Johnny Westbrook, a tall, affable highway patrolman with the flattopped look of a fifties rock 'n' roller. Westbrook wanted a share of the new liquor store but could not act on his own, since highway patrolmen in Texas are forbidden to own businesses that dispense alcoholic beverages. So Linda Westbrook, Johnny's short, outspoken wife, signed the Liquor Store's partnership documents.

The ABC requires liquor license applicants to have suitable buildings for their businesses. Early last year Phillips and Bohler, along with Westbrook, hired a construction firm to erect a building on the property they had selected. One afternoon midway into the project, a man in work clothes knocked on the door of Drake's home. The workman, who was employed on the construction site, told Drake that the structure he was raising was to be a liquor store. Drake's pink face flashed red. Not only was the building within the dry sector, it was also at the entrance to the Silsbee Little League Park. At that location, Drake told the workman, the liquor store was bound to attract the notice of children, who would grow up thinking that drinking was a normal and respectable part of adult life. Reverend Drake wanted to shield children from the sight of liquor business, and he knew other preachers would agree.

A dozen ministers from the precinct held a meeting to decide what to do. They had no reason to believe that far-off ABC officials would honor the old, extralegal Drake-Cunningham agreement. The only sure way to prevent the Liquor Store from opening, they decided, was to do what, for moral reasons, most of them believed should have been done long before—vote Precinct 2 dry. Drake is not the sort of man who welcomes an open, knock-down-drag-out electoral fight, and he was aging and in poor health besides. The preacher most willing to lead was newcomer Larry Blackmon, pastor of the Good Shepherd Baptist Church, located three miles north of Silsbee in the middle of the dry strip.

The Good Shepherd Church is a red brick building with a big parking lot. Most of its seven hundred members are from refinery-worker families, and most of them live nearby. In doctrine, ritual, and membership, Good Shepherd is as simple, straightforward, and utilitarian as its common brick exterior. There are no hand-clapping spirituals sung in Sunday morning services there, as there are in Drake's church, just standard hymns sung by a choir from the *Baptist Hymnal*. At Good Shepherd there is no tongue-talking in the pews, nor are there any fainting and convulsing believers in the aisles, as at North Hardin's more fervent congregations. Cool rationality is the trait that Baptists share with denominations on the moderate end of the Christian militance scale—with Methodists and Presbyterians, for example. A strict doctrine banning drinking, dancing, and petting is what Baptists share with the more excitable fundamentalists.

The short, muscled, brown-haired Blackmon is a Protestant conquistador, a crusader in a baby-blue suit. He is the sort of Baptist who goes looking for battles. ("If I do not declare iniquity to the world," he tells his congregation, "then those people that live and dwell in sin will be held accountable, and I will be accountable for them dying and spending an eternity in hell itself.") Though he speaks with a high-pitched voice and is no spellbinder in the pulpit, he warms to personal contact and is fired with the spirit of organization. Blackmon is experienced in liquor skirmishes, too; two years ago, while pastoring a church in rural Arkansas, he joined a successful countywide prohibition campaign. Blackmon is a persistent and zealous man, but not even he realized how big a task he was taking on: it had been six years since any jurisdiction in Texas had changed from wet to dry.

The Troubleshooter

Before a local option election can be set, it must be requested by petitions signed by a number of the precinct's voters equal to 35 per cent of those who cast ballots in the last gubernatorial election. County officials told Blackmon and his allies that in Hardin's Precinct 2 the formula required 562 signatures. Some three weeks after church volunteers began collecting signatures, they turned the completed petitions in to the county clerk's office, and the move was reported by the local newspapers. A clipping service routed the stories to the Austin office of the Wholesale Beer Distributors of Texas, where Jim Hay read them. Hay is a 65-year-old, graying veteran of Rainbow Division infantry duty in World War II now employed as a local option troubleshooter. He promptly set out for Hardin, where he found that the county's two dozen liquor vendors were apprehensive, unversed in the law, and unorganized. Hardin's stand-in county clerk—the elected clerk was serving out a mail fraud sentence—had already counted the signatures on Blackmon's petitions and okayed them. The community believed that an election was at hand, until Hay, with his expertise in technicalities, noted a flaw. Though the instructions on voter petitions are printed in both English and Spanish, no one in Hardin had added a Spanish explanation that the purpose of those particular petitions was to call a wet-dry election. Though nobody knew anyone in the county who could read Spanish but not English, Hay's protest stopped the petitions cold. The interval gave him time to call together the 27 liquor retailers in Precinct 2.

Hay naturally had to begin with Walter Santos of Silsbee. Santos is a good man to get to know, but it takes leaden ears to do it. Though he is no taller than a Toyota, Santos can outboast, outbully, and probably outcurse any man in Hardin County. A self-made man of the first order, he says that he grew up in Louisiana so poor that he quit school and went to work at the end of the sixth grade. By the age of eighteen, as he tells it, he was a labor contractor in the timber camps. He came to Hardin to work for Kirby Industries and bought beer joints as a sideline. In nearly thirty years as a proprietor, his operations have never been halted for even a day by an ABC suspension order, because—and he is the first to let you know this—he doesn't tolerate looseness or trouble in his places. Short, squeaky-voiced Walter Santos, who weighs about 150 pounds, is very much like the old cherry bombs: little, loud, and potentially dangerous.

It is likely that someone from the rough lumber camps or watering holes in the region would have killed Walter a long time ago had he not been married to his tall, hefty, smiling wife, Bettye. Walter fulminates, Bettye calculates. A former barmaid in one of Walter's clubs, Bettye is now owner of the Triple S Lounge, Hardin's leading beer joint. The Triple S, located on the eastern edge of Precinct 2, is an L-shaped place, with carpeted floors and a ceiling festooned with gimme caps. It's the sort of place where a young workingman can take his wife for a polite billiards game. Because Bettye and Walter are old-timers in Hardin liquor circles, it was likely that one of them, along with Harvey Cunningham, would be chosen to head the liquor defense campaign. Because she is competent and pleasant, Bettye took the honor.

The liquor retailers held their first meeting with Jim Hay in April in an upstairs room at the Bluebonnet Cafe in Silsbee. The group eventually decided to name itself Citizens for Common Sense, to hire an attorney, and to assess its members for the cost. Hay explained to the group the complexities of local option law and told how to manipulate the law's restrictions to their advantage.

Wets and Drys

By what they claim was coincidence, Bosco Phillips and Tommy Bohler were drinking coffee downstairs at the Bluebonnet when the retailers filed upstairs for their meeting. The established liquor crowd invited the two would-be vendors to attend the upstairs meeting, and they did, but they chose not to participate in the committee's work. Phillips and Bohler say that the retailers did not sincerely welcome them; members of the group say that Phillips and Bohler did not really want to help. The reason for the cool relations is that only a belief that liquor is actually good—a belief that does not exist in Hardin—could have united the established liquor retailers with the upstarts. As it was, Phillips and Bohler were viewed by their brethren in the liquor trade simply as competitors.

Yet all Baptists and Assembly of God believers and Church of Christers and Pentecostals and Mormons—all the drys, in other words—even though they compete for supporters, presume themselves to be brothers in the cause of biblical living. The ideals to which their churches subscribe include a notion that everybody in Hardin holds, one that perhaps everybody in the world holds. It says that clear-headed rationality is an exemplar of the finest in human nature, a condition to be guarded, respected, and cultivated with all the resources at our disposal. Church people believe that we can live up to our ideals and that even if we can't, it is worthwhile to try. Without ideals, they point out, we would probably revert to barbarism in short order.

The real—commerce is real—not the ideal, is the touchstone of the wets. No one in Hardin's wet camp believes in liquor the way drys believe in Christ. Nobody stood up in the retailers' meetings to declare in an evangelical voice that liquor is good and that the world would be a better place if we all had a drink. In Hardin, hardly anybody will vouch for liquor. In Texas cities, there are thousands of people who believe that liquor is a wonderful social lubricant, that it eases worries and calms fears, that liquor, like good food, is both a necessity and a pleasure. But in Hardin, where the fundamentalist

tradition runs deep, as it does in most of rural Texas, very few people regard liquor as one of the blessings of life. Both Harvey Cunningham and Tommy Bohler told me that if the world were as it should be, everyone would practice Holiness living, including abstention. Another retailer told me that he didn't drink and never had. "I don't feel the need to," he said, adding that if people bought his wares, human weakness was responsible. In Hardin County, where as many as a third of the men and half of the women are teetotalers, the view is that sobriety is a virtue and any diminution of sobriety is a sin. If drinking and the abuse of alcohol are inevitable, it is because, as Hardin's wets and drys both believe, human nature is flawed.

Because human nature is dualistic—we cannot be entirely what our strengths call on us to be or entirely what our weaknesses would make us—perhaps we need the counsel of both wets and drys. But the electoral process does not allow us to vote for both sides of the question, and the choice is hard. Either we vote dry, in affirmation of hope for ourselves, or we vote wet, in recognition of the uncomfortable fact of our frailty. Drys have an advantage in any election because the more cheerful ideological terrain is theirs. Since the case for liquor in places like Hardin County is entirely practical and is generally bound to commerce, wets have difficulty uniting people whose interests are practically—commercially—in contradiction. The interests of the applicants for the Liquor Store's license were, to a Harvey Cunningham, those of business rivals at best, those of spoilers at worst. After the Bluebonnet Cafe meeting, the Liquor Store's backers dropped out of the sight, if not out of the mind, of the established crowd and made no attempt to influence the election that would determine their common future in Hardin.

Playing Hardball

The dry forces did not give up when their first set of petitions was voided. They went back to the courthouse, got new petitions, and began seeking signers again. This time the month-long task was shortened because the drys took advantage of the May 1 Democratic primary.

Small-town and county politicians win or lose elections not because of their platforms and programs—most don't have any—but because the voters believe or don't believe that they are upright, reasonable, and intelligent. Professionals in local politics have always tried to steer away from liquor disputes because a wet candidate is seen as less than upright and a dry as less than reasonable. But politicians can't always keep themselves above the fray. Hardin's incumbent county judge, Ray Martin, was assailed as wet because he had approved beer permits for stores bordering the dry strip. Emmett

Lack, a former county judge and Martin's most likely opponent in the May 1 Democratic primary, was reviled as a dry because his wife had signed a liquor vote petition, even though her name was later scratched out. All the candidates for county judge denied loyalty to both the wet and the dry causes, but suspicions generated by the liquor campaign probably took a handful of votes from the front-runners and gave them to Pete McKinney, the dark horse in the race, who wound up winning in the runoff. Larry Blackmon and the drys, though they stopped short of endorsing Lack and turning out voters, did show up outside the polls to seek signatures for their petitions. The tactic worked. On May 4, three days after they had begun, the drys brought their second set of petitions back to the courthouse. They had gathered 709 signatures.

A liquor petition must be signed more carefully than a check. The signer must be a registered voter in the jurisdiction involved, must write his name as it is shown on voter records, must list his address in the same way, and must copy down his registration number correctly. Jim Hay had taught all this to the wets, who were on the lookout for errors in the dry petitions. Through their attorney, at a county commissioners' meeting held the week of June 14, they challenged signatures on the new petitions. Until the early hours of morning, with both wets and drys looking on, the commissioners scrutinized signatures. The signature of Mrs. Leo H. Scott was cast out because she failed to sign her name "Mattie R. Scott," and that of Ella Kelley was voided because she did not sign "Mrs. Riley B. Kelley." Richard W. Ellis was not counted as a signer, even though his registration number identified him, because he signed his name "Dick." Carolyn Daves was not counted because she omitted the initial "S." in her signature. Robert M. Stephenson was disallowed because he signed "R.M.," and William David Wiggins was nixed because his name was signed "Wiggins, William D." Several couples had their signatures negated because the names or registration numbers of both appeared in the same hand. By the time the commissioners had finished picking over the petitions, 576 good signatures remained. The drys had come to the meeting thinking 562 was their magic number, but the commissioners decided that absentee votes in the 1978 gubernatorial election should be factored into the formula, and that yielded a new requirement: 620 signatures. A few minutes before dawn, the drys learned that they had failed.

The drys went back to the courthouse for new petitions early the following month, and July became a time when activists at Good Shepherd devoted Thursday nights, usually reserved for courting sinners, to door-to-door signature seeking. Liquor sermons were preached, too. Most of Blackmon's remarks were of a calculatedly eclectic nature. Though he did not neglect the Scriptures, Blackmon built his arguments in a bigger field. Using statistics supplied by Texas Alcohol-Narcotics Education, a nonprofit local option data house in Dallas, the pastor talked about the problems of traffic congestion, drunk driving, and the public cost of policing alcohol use. By bringing in issues like safety and taxes—issues of concern even to drinking men—he hoped to broaden the base of his crusade. "Do you as a parent, or grandparent want your children faced with a potentially dangerous Liquor Store on their path for physical activity?" he wrote in a mailing to voters. "Would you want them walking by when someone who's had too much decides to drive in and get some more? or when someone driving by hurries in to get some? I for one do not want to have to preach the funeral of any of our children!"

The summer was a season when not only sermons but bad news pushed the people of Good News forward: despite objections raised in Austin by several laymen, accompanied, to be sure, by Reverend Blackmon, the ABC approved the Liquor Store's application for a license. And a pair of convenience stores in the dry strip, both owned by out-of-town interests, applied for licenses to sell beer. Blackmon and Drake complained that one of the stores was located just 330 feet from the front door of Drake's Evergreen church. But the Texas statute on liquor outlet locations requires a distance of only 300 feet between a retailer and a church, so the convenience store was within the law. Judge Martin, even more wary of the liquor issue than he had been before his defeat in the May primary, announced that he would reserve judgment on the beer applications for as long as the law would allow: sixty days. His object was to sidestep the need to rule. Martin figured the drys would succeed in getting an election called before his September 13 deadline, in which case he would not have to reveal his feeling about liquor with a yea or a nay. When the drys' new petitions were presented August 9, only a few names were scratched, largely because this time around the petitioners had carried a voter registration printout with them. On August 13 the commissioners set the liquor vote for September 11, two days before Judge Martin's deadline.

The Price of Liberty

All day Saturday, September 11, the people of Precinct 2 lined up to cast ballots at the Jack and Jill day care center and four other polling places. About seven o'clock a throng gathered outside the county clerk's office at the courthouse to await the results. Blackmon and a handful of his co-workers were there. A liquor retailer was on hand, and the three Liquor Store licensees—who had not yet opened their business, pending the outcome of

the day's vote—were also standing by. A drunk sailor wandered into the crowd and intermittently argued with Blackmon about the Bible's lessons on liquor. People fidgeted and waited and held their breath each time a voting station's count was announced. By eight all the polling stations but one had reported, and the count was 841 wet, 843 dry, too close for comfort. The box at the Wiley Mae Pentecostal Church would decide the election. About eight-thirty, its results were posted: 156 wet, 161 dry, enough to give the drys a 7-vote margin in an election of 2001 votes.

Though a victory celebration was called off, the house was full at the Triple S Lounge that night, and for the first time since the contest had begun, Bettye Santos kept shop in a foul mood, for she knew that in her own place of business were more than seven nonvoters who could have turned the election around. Her fears had come true. "I've warned my people to register and vote," she had told me several nights earlier, "and they say, yes, they'll do it. But they just sit here, sipping their suds. Friday night will come, and they'll sit here, sipping, and on Saturday they'll get up late, or forget, or go to the lake. Then they'll come in here on Saturday night, and they'll say, 'Uh-oh, what happened? You mean they voted us dry today?'" In a way, the outcome of the election was deserved at the Triple S, and even Bettye Santos felt that way. The price of liberty is . . . well, you've heard it before.

The New Order

After the debacle, the Citizens for Common Sense regrouped. Though the retailers in Precinct 2 now had only thirty days in which to clear their shelves of booze, they decided to continue their fight. Harvey Cunningham, who estimated that 80 per cent of the sales at his liquor store were owed to beer, agreed with Bettye that the best recourse was to move for another election instead of demanding a recount. There are eight gradations of wet and dry in Texas, and the category that promised to salvage the most of Precinct 2's liquor trade was the one that would legalize beer and wine while outlawing other beverages. The proposal would preserve business-as-usual for 23 of 27 outlets, mostly convenience stores, and, since it would keep the door shut on the Liquor Store, would not thoroughly offend most of those people who had voted dry. In a second election, drinkers would have an incentive to vote, too: for more than a month before any new election could be held, the precinct would be wholly dry.

The Citizens went through the steps they had watched the drys take six months earlier. Petitions were taken out, voters were registered, signatures were checked. The work went smoothly and quickly: in less than a week the petitioning was all

done. A vote was called for Saturday, November 6, and the wets prepared as perhaps only East Texans can. Hardin County is the sort of place where, several years ago, one officeholder taped Boys Town photos of another officeholder to a courthouse wall—with a group of spectators and the victim's wife looking on. With the rough-and-tumble of East Texas politics in mind, Bettye Santos in an October newspaper ad chided her community for "allowing an outsider"—Blackmon—"to come in and put down, degrade, and insult, people who have raised good outstanding young people in our community; now I ask," the ad closed, "is that fair or really leading a truly Christian life?"

Even minors got into the act. In early October Silsbee High School's *Tiger Rag* published front-page stories in which the editor and the features writer, both students, indicated support for the drys. The *Rag* also ran a sixteen-inch modern version of the Pledge, in the form of a parent-teacher contract. By its terms, parents would bind themselves to provide transportation or taxi fare to inebriated teenagers. The parents would also bind themselves to get alternative transportation when drunk.

In an election-eve advertisement captioned BE NOT DECEIVED, Blackmon quoted a biblical injunction against liquor and charged that "certain retailers are only concerned about making money." But Bettye Santos and the Citizens for Common Sense, in their last advertisement before the vote, struck back by blaming the Hardin liquor controversy on an unnamed individual identified four times as an outsider. "If he didn't like our county as it was, why did he decide to settle and live here? After all the damages have been done will our outsider still be here?" the ad asked.

A few days before the vote, Reverend Drake hedged his bets by opening the Evergreen Christian Center Outreach Chapel. The new building was a twelve-by-twenty-foot affair built of wood, with imitation stained glass windows. It sat on concrete blocks in the front yard of the Evergreen church, and its front door opened onto the public easement of Highway 92. The distance from the chapel's front door to that of the convenience store that had applied for a beer license last summer was well under the 300-foot minimum. "They may beat me some of the time," Drake told me, "but you know, they won't beat me always."

Though television weathermen predicted a chilling norther, election Saturday dawned with picture-perfect autumn weather. The wind was strong enough to bring orange leaves down from the hardwoods along Highway 92, but only light clouds crossed the sky and the temperature was in the upper sixties. At a truck repair shop just off Highway 92, behind the Jack and Jill where the voters had gone for the last election, they lined up again to make their choice. They gathered in twos and threes at the Wiley Mae Church, at the city hall in Kountze, and at two other polling places. All day long the citizenry filed in and out, this time in short-sleeved blouses or T-shirts, summer wear. This time, too, the mood was different: people talked and joked as they waited in line.

At the truck garage—located, ironically, between the building erected for the Liquor Store and the Silsbee Little League Park—blue-jeaned Bettye Santos stood beside her black 1976 Cadillac, waving at voters as they entered. Walter Santos did the same from behind his pickup just outside the entrance to the Kountze city hall. Other liquor supporters stood near other polling places, and a pickup loaded with a portable marquee and a public address system cruised the streets between the voting boxes, urging a wet vote in Precinct 2. Pairs of election workers beat the backwoods for the wets, and women dialed the phones, getting out the vote. This time the wets had done their homework.

Darkness came about six o'clock, but still Bettye and her aides did not leave their posts. They were on hand about ten minutes before seven, closing time for the polls, when four pickup trucks roared up to the garage, one behind the other. The seven men they carried were welders from GF Fabricators, men who only an hour earlier had been repairing an offshore oil rig at a dock in Sabine Pass, nearly fifty miles away. Portly, bearded 25-year-old Randy Eddins was still spotted with grime and still wearing his welding cap when he marked the last ballot cast at the big box in the garage. He was tired of driving into Silsbee to buy the beer he had been able to purchase nearer to home before the September election, he said, and he cast his ballot for the wets.

When ballots were tallied that night, all five voting places, plus the absentee box, yielded wet majorities. The count was 1647 for the sale of beer and wine, 1123 against. What had happened in this second round of the liquor contest was that more than 700 additional citizens had gone to the polls and more than 600 of them had voted wet.

Even before the ballots were counted, the liquor retailers and their election troops were celebrating with beer, barbecue, and dancing at a party barn in Precinct 1. When the tally was reported by radio, James "Peewee" Flanakin, a short, red-faced, boisterous convenience store owner, stood atop a table and, waving his Halliburton cap in the air, hollered, "We won! We won! Waxahachie! Waxahachie!" Just why Flanakin cheered "Waxahachie" was a mystery to some of the revelers, especially the ladies, who were not familiar with the shaggy dog story about Waxahachie that the men had been telling, but it didn't matter: everybody was too high-spirited to be curious. Harvey Cunningham, in his feathered cowboy hat, took a few swigs from a bottle and decided to carry off what might ordinarily be regarded as an impolitic act. With a comrade, he changed the wording on the marquee of the sound truck. "We Won," the new message read. Harvey parked the truck on the southern boundary of Precinct 2, where passing churchmen could see it.

As Harvey was making that change, Reverend Larry Blackmon, in his gray blazer, was climbing atop an aluminum A-frame ladder in the front yard of the Good Shepherd Baptist Church. He took down the letters from the church's marquee, which had urged passersby to vote against the liquor proposition. In their place he posted a new greeting: "All Outsiders Welcome."✤

BEHIND THE LINES

by Gregory Curtis

I can recall, dimly, when there were no Dallas Cowboys or Houston Oilers. I can remember when there *were* Dallas Texans, who later became the Kansas City Chiefs. But I cannot remember, in all the fanfare and high expectations that accompanied the arrival of professional football in Texas in 1960, any public debate over one grim, criminal, and certain result: that it would cause people in Texas to gamble more. Of course there was gambling in football before 1960, but it was limited to college games and professional games in distant cities. With the Cowboys, the Oilers, and the Texans, the bookies would have three professional teams whose existence would bring about more games to wager on and a passionate local interest that would prompt betting by those who would never have considered risking a penny on the outcome of Cleveland against Baltimore. Betting on professional football is now so pervasive that there are very few of us who could not, if pressed, find a friend who has a friend and get a bet down. But no one to my knowledge has ever proposed that we save our society from this pervasive criminal activity by banning the Cowboys and the Oilers.

At present there is a bill before the Legislature to allow pari-mutuel betting on horse races in Texas. Like football, horse racing is a major spectator sport. In fact, more people attend horse races than football, baseball, or basketball games or any other sport. Legalized betting on horse races produces a local cottage industry that breeds and stables horses and the various jobs that are needed to maintain and service a major sports stadium. Furthermore, the state gets a portion of every dollar that is bet. All kinds of figures are being tossed around by both sides to prove how much or how little economic impact horse racing would have in Texas, but it's certainly fair to say that it would be a significant plus. In California, the state most similar to Texas where racing is well established, the state's share of the wagers was $120 million in 1981. But the amount of tax revenue and the extent of the economic impact are not the true reasons for favoring or opposing the bill. The real question is whether we should legalize this form of gambling.

I was quite surprised, therefore, to find that gambling itself was not the main complaint of the bill's opponents. At least it wasn't their stated complaint. Through five long hours of testimony before the House Urban Affairs Committee, to which the bill had been referred, gambling was addressed as a moral issue only twice, and then in such an oblique fashion that any legislator whose attention had momentarily wandered might have missed those references entirely. The hearings were so tedious that it was only afterward, as I walked away, that I realized the tedium was the most important thing of all, that it meant victory for betting on horses in Texas—if not in this Legislature then soon enough.

Twenty years ago hearings over horse-race betting drew blood as two soulful Texas traditions met head on. From one side came the tradition of the horse and horseman, the ranch and rancher, the wildcatter and high roller, the boot stomper and the open range; from the other side came the Bible and the preacher, the farm and the farmer, thrift and propriety, the stern lawman and fenced pastures. Under the Capitol dome they faced off against one another, the men who wanted to bet on the horses and the men who believed with every fiber that it was *wrong*. Once, horse racing's most fervent proponent, the redoubtable Red Berry, state senator from San Antonio, listened to a minister rail in a committee meeting about the sin of gambling and the evil men who would bring it to Texas. Berry listened, and when the oration was over, he stood up and said, "F— ya, preacher." Of course, with friends like that, horse racing lost.

This time there was no such passion. Governor John Y. Brown, Jr., of Kentucky testified that horse racing was the pride of Kentucky, that Texas could be a great boon to racing, and that in its hundred-year history in Kentucky racing had not attracted organized crime or unseemly people and behavior. Hugo Berlanga of Corpus Christi, who is carrying the bill in the House, stressed that it meant jobs and tax revenues and that "most importantly, horse racing is as Texan as the longneck beer and the rodeo." Tim Curry, the district attorney in Tarrant County, testified that the bill presented no particular problems of law enforcement. Several horsemen spoke, but the message by now was repetitive: horse racing and pari-mutuel gambling would increase state revenues and encourage the growth of an industry without increasing crime or attracting organized crime.

The opposition was led by Allan Maley, Jr., of Dallas, a pleasant, silver-haired gentleman who is executive director of the Anti-Crime Council of Texas. Despite its title, there is some question about just what this organization is. Although Maley claims that his council is a widespread organization concerned about all types of crime, he could not, just two days before the hearings, give me the names of any members other than himself. He also claimed that the Anti-Crime Council had been involved in lobbying efforts in the Legislature since 1968. When I asked what issues other than horse racing the council had taken a stand on, Maley said, "Well, I can't remember." Then he added, "A lot of what they do about crime in the Legislature doesn't have much sex appeal."

Maley's argument was that pari-mutuel gambling will not generate as much revenue as its backers claim and that it will attract organized crime, not so much at the track as through the proliferation of bookies handling bets off the tracks. His evidence for this was rather slight, consisting of snatches of testimony at government hearings concerned more with casino gambling than horse racing and of a witness from Delaware who claimed to be a reformed compulsive gambler and was notable mostly for his self-absorption ("I fit exactly the psychological profile of a compulsive gambler—male, highly intelligent . . ."). Even Weston Ware, testifying for the Baptist Christian Life Commission, kept his moral fervor in check and insisted that this was simply a practical issue. "Our state has a work ethic," he said, "and keeping gambling out of Texas is good public policy." Only one witness, an elderly man named John Selcraig who had come on his own behalf to testify, really insisted on what was at stake. "Horse racing is legal in Texas," he said. "It's gambling that's illegal. Isn't that what's happening here?"

But that was as close as the hearing ever came to passion, to confronting morality. The days when strong religious feeling played a visible part in Texas' public life are, for better or worse, quickly fading.

I know that gambling has its terrible side. My friend Ross, twelve years ago a suicide, began his downward spiral when he left his job to follow the ponies. There are those who can't control their gambling and there are those who gamble away money that should go for food or rent. These things happen, and they are not to be taken lightly. Liquor, cigarettes, automobiles, and a host of other pastimes and possessions also have the potential to cause pain and suffering. Our goal as a society should be to allow pastimes and possessions for the many while giving aid and comfort to the few who are their victims, even knowing that those people are often victims because of their own freedom of choice. Consequently, I am not convinced that such tragedies alone make gambling on horses wrong any more than I am convinced that even $1 billion in taxes would make it right.

Let's consider for a moment what parimutuel wagering really is. Every bet made goes into a pool; after the race those who have bet on the winning horse get all the money in the pool divided up among them—after 15 per cent is deducted. In Texas 5 per cent would go to the track, 5 per cent to purses, and 5 per cent to Aid to Families With Dependent Children. Thus neither the track nor the state has any stake in the outcome of the race. Each will receive the same share of the pool no matter which horse wins. All that is really happening is that the people at the track are betting among themselves. It is precisely the same, technically and morally, as one friend's saying to another, "I'll bet you ten dollars the Aggies beat the 'Horns." This isn't the least bit immoral, but rather it is one of life's agreeable pleasures.

In casino gambling, by contrast, the player bets against the house, and for him to win, the house must lose. That's a powerful incentive for the house to cheat. This fact, combined with the huge amounts of untraceable cash, is what invites corruption in casinos and is why the mob controls Las Vegas. But organized crime is not a force at the tracks, according to the California attorney general's office. Think of the names of the first families of racing—Whitney, Vanderbilt, and, in Texas, Kleberg. These people just aren't mobsters.

Texas is now completely surrounded by states that allow betting on horses, and at least half of the patrons of those tracks are Texans. Texas, not other states, should be the one to benefit from their wagering. And Texas should be able to enjoy the one sport in which people from all classes rub shoulder to shoulder and conversation is as easy as "Who do you like in this race?" Spending long, bright afternoons watching glorious animals round the curves of a white fence and head for home is a fine contrast to life's normal humdrum. Horses stand at the center of Texas history and are part of the image of its soul. And so, finally, is freedom. Why can't we, at no one's expense but our own, put $2 on the nose?

The Beaten Path

"There are two reasons for the shoddy condition of Texas' roads: big trucks and small cars."

Driving I-10 these days is an undulating experience. Close your eyes and you'd swear you were in a speedboat slapping across another boat's wake. Along a lot of stretches—between Columbus and Houston, for example—the road looks like it is in the care of the Antiquities Committee, not the Highway Department. The shoulder has separated from the pavement and grass is growing in the fissures. Cracks squiggle across the highway, potholes yawn like moon craters, and every sixty feet or so a black hump of asphalt bisects the highway where broken joints in the pavement have been repaired. I-10 is falling apart, and it's not an isolated case.

Texas' interstates, state highways, and farm-to-market roads just aren't what they used to be. Not long ago, Texans could brag—and did, ad nauseam—about their highways. Doubters needed only to cross the state line to Louisiana, Oklahoma, or Arkansas to realize just how good Texas' highways were. But the days of supremacy are gone. We are now in a pothole with our neighbors.

Dr. Frank McCullough, head of the Center for Transportation Research at the University of Texas, wrote a pamphlet this year called (keep those eyelids open, folks) "Pavement Structure Wearout, A Crisis in Transportation Systems." The title may not exactly soar, but the tract is one of those unsung academic documents wherein an engineer makes himself clear to the common man. He explains the history of road building in Texas, how our roads have fallen into disrepair, and why we should fix them now rather than later. He doesn't threaten us with death on the highways (although a lot of our crumbling roads are unsafe). Instead he talks money. "Our highways can get rougher, and it won't be a catastrophe," he explained to me. "But if we don't do something soon, it will cost a lot more. It's like a leaky roof. If you fix it right off, there's very little damage. After it's gotten worse, the damage is tremendous, and so are the repair costs."

The Highway Department claims, however, that it is running out of money to make those repairs, a declaration that's apt to furrow the brow of the average driver, who is already paying 15 cents in taxes on every gallon of gasoline he pumps. This year the department will spend about $1.5 billion ($700 million comes from gasoline taxes, $400 million from the state treasury, and $400 million from the feds). The department asked for a whole lot more in the last legislative session—about $2.7 billion.

Instead, it got $1.9 billion.

I am as leery as the next person of a colossal bureaucracy that gobbles billions of dollars, especially when all we have to go on is past performance. Granted, the department gave us great highways, but some of them are *too* great. Back when the highway commission was run by rural West Texans there was a building spree out in their part of the state comparable to the pharaohs' building the great pyramids. That's why we have a four-lane divided highway, Texas 302, between Odessa and Notrees but a two-lane chills-and-thrills ride on Texas 71 between Houston and Austin. Now at least the commission is weighted with members who live in the part of the state that has people and traffic, and a lot of what the department says actually jibes with what you can see for yourself on the highway.

There are two reasons for the shoddy condition of Texas' roads: big trucks and small cars. The state's relatively prosperous economy in the eighties has brought not only more people to the state but also more trucks carrying things like beer and breakfast cereal to those people. Few people have anything against trucks, but the truth is, they chew up highways, and no Texas highway planner was expecting so many and such big ones. Major highways were designed for trucks that weigh considerably less than today's legal limit of 80,000 pounds, and some truckers carry overloads that bring their total weight to as much as 100,000 pounds.

Truckers call small, economical cars "roller skates," and more people in Texas are driving them now. They may not wear out concrete, but they do damage the highway budget. Since Texas registration fees are based on weight, the fees on small cars are low. And given the good mileage such cars get, their drivers also pay less in gasoline taxes. In terms of taxation they are almost getting a free ride.

Overall, Texas has been kind to the driving taxpayer. The state gasoline tax, which is 5 cents on the gallon, is the lowest in the U.S., and it hasn't gone up a penny since 1955. Vehicle registration fees are also the lowest. These taxes are put in a sacrosanct piggy bank called the Dedicated Highway Fund, set up in 1946 (one quarter of the gasoline tax goes to public schools; about the same percentage of vehicle registration funds goes to county roads). The Dedicated Highway Fund has had various critics over the years, but nonetheless it financed those roads we used to brag about.

The system began to fall apart in the mid-seventies with the Arab oil embargo, the gas shortages, and 90-miles-per-hour inflation—all of which, remember, brought on the brigade of roller skates. And indeed in 1977 the Highway Department had to come begging to the Legislature. Rather than raise our taxes then, however, the lawmakers came up with a way to siphon money from the state treasury with a complicated formula, called the highway cost index, which was designed to keep pace with inflation. But an unexpected thing happened: inflation more or less leveled off in Texas, which kept the highway cost index from generating as much money as was expected. At the same time, all those people—and all those trucks—started flocking to the state. Our highways have deteriorated much faster in the last few years than anyone ever dreamed they would—while the highway cost index has been stuck in second gear.

The Highway Department hasn't exactly panicked, but it is certainly getting edgy. The 5-cent-per-gallon federal tax increase, which began in April, has given the department a little relief, but because state funds aren't going up concurrently, the relief will be short-term. Federal money is matched with state money, but the bulk of that match goes for interstate and U.S. highways, not for the 100,000 miles of farm-to-market roads. Naturally, the Highway Department is going to put its money on federal projects, where it will go the farthest. This year there has been just enough money to break even, but the Highway Department makes the following predictions: In 1984 there will be enough money to match federal money, with none left over for state and farm-to-market roads. In 1985 the department will be $124 million short of matching federal funds, again with none for state projects.

Theoretically, then, a lot of the problems like the ones I described on I-10 will be taken care of, but what about the state and farm-to-market roads? At this point the issue becomes more than just driver comfort and wear and tear on vehicles. It becomes an issue of safety as well. Many of the roads that are maintained only by state money are two-lanes and undivided, yet they have been engulfed by cities (like FM 1093, which is known to most people in Houston as Westheimer) or swamped by heavy truck traffic (FM 154, FM 2237, and FM 2762 near La Grange broke down under the load of oil field trucks during the Austin chalk oil boom). These roads have become escape routes from the cities, just the reverse of their farm-to-market designation. Ranch Road 620, near Lake Travis, for instance, is winding, narrow, and poorly surfaced, and it has no shoulders. Yet for years it has been heavily traveled by University of Texas students, Austinites, and second-home dwellers from Houston, Dallas, and San Antonio—many of them driving while drunk. The Highway Department wants to widen and divide 620, but that project is number thirteen on its district list of farm-to-market priorities, a list that vies for attention with 5033 other state and federal projects.

Last spring Governor White said he would not support increased highway funding, and legislators shot down a proposal—it never even made it to the bill stage—to double auto registration fees. They also killed in committee a bill to increase the state gasoline tax (it would have changed the 5-cents-a-gallon tax to a 5 per cent tax based on the wholesale cost of gas, but right now

wouldn't be costing taxpayers any more than the flat fee, since the wholesale price is around $1).

Mark White's current crisis is teachers' pay and with a characteristic display of either-or reasoning he seems to think we can have good roads or good teachers but not both. If a special session is called after the Select Committee on Public Education releases its study, there are rumors that the highway lobby may try to convince the governor to consider a bill to increase the state gasoline tax. If he goes for it, it will be not so much because of any highway crisis but because one quarter of that tax goes to public schools.

This past year journalists writing in *Fortune* and *Inquiry* and as close to home as the *Texas Observer* were highly skeptical about the need to repair our public works, but their complaints were really criticism of what the twentieth century hath wrought—the passenger car, huge bureaucracies (the Highway

Department employs 14,000 people), and a society that relies on trucks to deliver its breakfast cereal.

I am very sympathetic to those complaints, especially those concerning trucks (nothing would be better for Texas highways than if all trucked merchandise could be carried by rail). But all those grievances become irrelevant when there is no train or plane from Austin to Muldoon, and I have to go there on roads that are uncomfortable or unsafe. Everything should be done to spare us from another nibbling tax—truck weight limits should be strictly enforced and the Highway Department shouldn't spend our money building highways to nowhere—but if the time comes when we have to raise a state gasoline tax that hasn't gone up since 1955, we'll just have to live with it. If I am ever flattened by a semi on a two-lane undivided highway, I would like my tombstone to read: "She would rather have paid 5 cents more on the gallon."

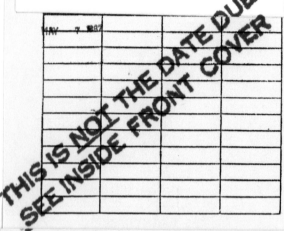

THIS IS NOT THE DATE DUE
SEE INSIDE FRONT COVER

© ACC, 1977